The Little, Brown Handbook

THE LITTLE, BROWN HANDBOOK

SECOND CANADIAN EDITION

H. Ramsey Fowler *University of Memphis*
Jane E. Aaron *New York University*
Murray McArthur *University of Waterloo*

with

Deane E. D. Downey *Trinity Western University*
Barabara H. Pell *Trinity Western University*

Addison Wesley

An imprint of Addison Wesley Longman Ltd.

Don Mills, Ontario • Reading, Massachusetts • Harlow, England
Melbourne, Australia • Amsterdam, The Netherlands • Bonn, Germany

Publisher: Brian Henderson
Managing Editor: Linda Scott
Editor: Elynor Kagan
Cover Design/Page Layout: Anthony Leung
Production Coordinator: Linda Allison
Manufacturing Coordinator: Sharon Latta Paterson
Printing and Binding: Transcontinental Printing Inc.

The publishers will glady receive information enabling them to rectify any errors in references or credits.

Canadian Cataloguing in Publication Data

Fowler, H. Ramsey (Henry Ramsey)
The Little, Brown handbook

2nd Canadian ed.
Includes index.
ISBN 0-673-52538-4

1. English language—Grammar—Handbooks, manuals, etc. 2. English language—Rhetoric—Handbooks, manuals, etc. I. Aaron, Jane E. II. McArthur, Murray Gilchrist, 1953– . III. Title.

PE1112.F685 1998 808'.042 C97-932704-0

ISBN 0-673-52538-4

Printed and bound in Canada.

A B C D E -Trans- 02 01 00 99 98

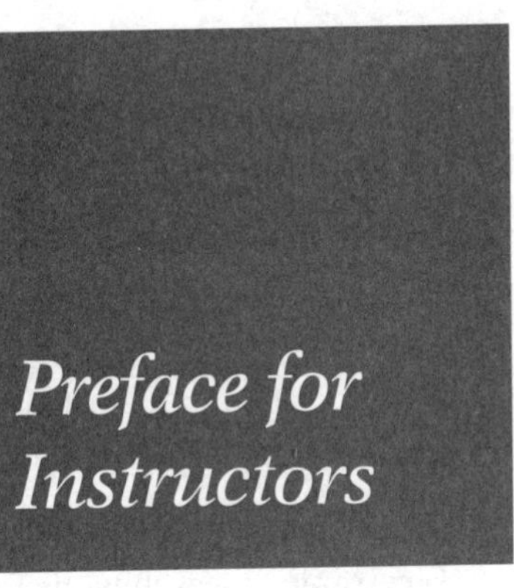

Preface for Instructors

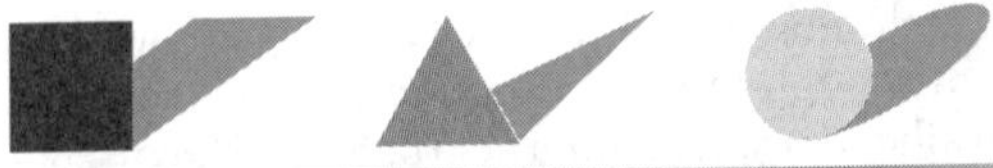

The second Canadian edition of *The Little, Brown Handbook* is an extensive revision of the seventh American edition (published 1997). It incorporates most of the improvements to the latest incarnation of this very successful textbook, especially major additions to the sections on computing, online research, and the use of the World Wide Web. This edition also draws on the first Canadian edition of *The Little, Brown Handbook* by Deane E. D. Downey and Barbara H. Pell (published 1991). Like the first Canadian edition, this text sets the highly successful features of the American edition within a Canadian context. We have adapted the American text to reflect Canadian culture, geography, politics, history, academic practices, weights and measures, customs, and folkways. We have also tried to recreate or mirror the complexities of Canadian realities, and these complexities include the reality of North American life. Therefore, we have retained some of the American references that would be familiar to most Canadians. Above all, we have tried to reflect the complexity of our students' concerns and enthusiasms and to represent those issues in the broadest possible regional and multicultural context.

The second Canadian edition of *The Little, Brown Handbook* appears amid a sea change in writing instruction caused by computers. Electronic media are transforming classrooms, research methods, forms of presentation, even the writing process itself. Revising *The Little, Brown Handbook,* we faced a dual challenge: to revamp the book so that it serves computer-using students and teachers and yet to retain the handbook's strengths as a comprehensive, clear, and accessible reference guide and classroom text.

The list of changes in the second Canadian edition could run even more pages than it does. Here we hit the highlights.

Computers in writing and research

We have woven computers into the cloth of the handbook:

- **Tips for computer use** appear throughout the chapters on thinking, writing, and research writing. Signalled in the margin by the computer image shown here, these tips range from journal keeping to revising on a word processor to downloading sources. (See pp. 512, 519, and 683 for examples.)
- **Electronic research** is the focus of the book's most substantial additions. We provide guidance on conducting electronic searches (p. 512), including guidelines for selecting key words. We also provide a thorough introduction to electronic sources, especially those available over the Internet (p. 519). The discussion ranges from electronic addresses to Web search engines to synchronous communication.
- A new section on **evaluating electronic sources** gives students concrete, usable advice for separating the worthy from the worthless (p. 544).
- **Documenting electronic sources** receives special attention with each documentation style covered: MLA (p. 593), Chicago (p. 686), APA (p. 702), and CBE (p. 720). We supplement the MLA models with those endorsed by the Alliance for Computers and Writing (pp. 596–97).
- New material on **document design** includes advice about typefaces, illustrations, and other elements (p. 749).
- For **computers in business writing**, we offer a contemporary résumé (p. 739) and extensive discussion of electronic mail (p. 742).
- A new appendix provides basic tips for **word processing** (p. 753), guidelines for **writing collaboratively on computers** (p. 755), and suggestions for **creating hypertext documents** (p. 758).

English as a second language

As before, the material for nonnative English speakers is thoroughly integrated into the main text, so that students do not have to distinguish between ESL problems and those they share with native speakers. At the same time, a small colour block (ESL) highlights the material so that it can be easily consulted or easily skipped. (See pp. 231 and 247 for examples.)

Critical thinking and the writing process

The book's Introduction and Chapters 1–2 have seen important additions besides those dealing with computers:

- A much longer section on **journals** details the uses of a journal and offers encouragement (p. 33).

- New material on the **thesis sentence** (p. 41) and **organization** (p. 45) makes these key topics more accessible and practical for students.
- A new **checklist for revision** (p. 61) stresses key concerns (purpose, thesis, and so on), and a new **checklist for editing** (p. 66) highlights the most common errors.
- Throughout the discussion of the writing process, we continue to show a student's **work in progress,** signalled by the notebook image shown here.

Research writing

In addition to the changes addressing electronic research, the chapters on research writing have been strengthened in several ways:

- **Evaluating and synthesizing sources** receive more attention (p. 541), including a procedure for synthesis (p. 545) and, as mentioned earlier, tips for evaluating electronic sources (p. 544).
- The expanded discussion of **integrating quotations,** with additional examples, now focuses more on alterations in quotations and placement of signal phrases (p. 568).
- A new **general introduction to documenting sources** discusses academic standards and styles (p. 575).
- Besides a thorough treatment of electronic sources, coverage of **MLA documentation** includes new models of in-text citations (p. 576) and new models of works-cited entries (p. 581).
- For **other disciplines,** the expansions are similar. The handbook adds new documentation models and sample page formats for all three styles (Chicago, p. 680; APA, p. 692; CBE, p. 715).

Other additions

Several further improvements increase the handbook's usefulness for students both in and out of English courses:

- The chapter on **writing about literature,** contributed by Sylvan Barnet and Reid Gilbert, now includes a discussion of critical approaches to literature (p. 653) and a new student paper on drama (p. 669) to complement the papers on fiction and poetry.
- The chapter on **essay exams** includes two annotated sample essays on the same question, one a successful answer and one not (p. 730).
- A new appendix on **oral presentations** offers advice for preparing and delivering a talk or speech (p. 764).
- We have added or expanded discussions of many key topics,

such as **transitions** (pp. 89, 112, 363), **comma splices** (p. 263), and the trickier uses of the **ellipsis mark** (p. 414).
- We have greatly expanded the coverage of **biased language** to emphasize not just sexist language but also stereotypes of race, age, religion, and other characteristics (p. 449).

Continuing features

We want to put in a word for what has *not* changed in this second edition:

- Text **explanations** are clear and practical, assuming little or no knowledge of terms and concepts and emphasizing the essentials of writing.
- **Examples** represent subjects from across the curriculum, reflect students' diverse backgrounds, and, above all, illustrate concepts clearly. **Annotations** on the examples demonstrate concepts with more immediacy than do text explanations.
- Plentiful **exercises** encourage students to tackle writing from many angles. Sentence exercises are always in **connected discourse** so that students work at the level of the paragraph rather than the isolated sentence. **End-of-part revision exercises** ask students to revise brief essays containing a range of errors, not just one type.
- *The Little, Brown Handbook* is **accessible.** The uncluttered **design** invites students in and clarifies the relationship of elements. More than 140 **boxes** highlight important information. **Cross-references** give page numbers, not code numbers. Two extensive **glossaries** before the index answer usage questions and define terms. And the **index** itself is the most comprehensive available, listing not only terms but problem expressions.

Supplements

An extensive package of supplements accompanies *The Little, Brown Handbook,* some for instructors and some for students. An asterisk (*) precedes any item or items that are complimentary to qualified adopters of the handbook.

For instructors

- *The Instructor's Manual for *The Little, Brown Handbook* (Second Canadian Edition), revised and updated by Kathryn McArthur of the University of Waterloo.
- *Teaching Online: Internet Research, Conversation, and Composition* is an accessible introduction to Internet resources for teaching writing. Written by Daniel Anderson, Bret Benjamin, Chris Busiel, and Bill Paredes-Holt of the University of Texas at Austin, the book offers basic definitions and information on

Internet access and shows how to integrate a variety of Internet tools in writing courses.

- *An extensive **assessment package** includes diagnostic tests and TASP and CLAST exams. All tests are keyed to the handbook, and all are available both in print and on computer software. In addition, the software versions can be customized and used on a network for online testing.
- *Two books contain photo-reproducible material that can be distributed to students: ***Eighty Practices,*** a collection of grammar and usage exercises, and ***Model Research Papers from Across the Disciplines,*** a collection of student papers in the humanities, social sciences, and natural sciences.
- *The series **Longman Resources for Instructors** includes four valuable works: *Teaching in Progress: Theories, Practices, and Scenarios,* by Josephine Koster Tarvers; *Teaching Writing to the Non-Native Speaker,* by Jocelyn Steer; the videos *Writing, Teaching, and Learning,* by David Jolliffe, and *Writing Across the Curriculum: Making It Work,* produced by Robert Morris College and the Public Broadcasting System.

For students

- ***The Little, Brown Workbook,*** by Donna Gorrell, St. Cloud University, and Kathryn McArthur, University of Waterloo, parallels the handbook's organization but provides briefer text and many more exercises. This edition includes a new sample research paper.
- ***ESL Worksheets,*** by Jocelyn Steer, provides nonnative speakers with extra practice in the areas that tend to be most troublesome for them.
- *A new guide for students, ***Researching Online and Off,*** combines research and documentation information from *The Little, Brown Handbook* with information on Internet access and resources from *Teaching Online* in a handy format.
- **The Writer's Workshop,*** keyed to the handbook, is a heuristics program that helps students explore, form, and express their ideas while writing arguments, research papers, and literary analyses. A new feature, Paper-in-Progress, follows one paper through successive stages to show how one student drafted and revised in response to peer and instructor comments. Also included is a tool for formatting source citations (MLA or APA documentation style) and an online version of *The Little, Brown Handbook,* Seventh Edition. (IBM and Macintosh.)
- A CD-ROM, ***Electric Library,*** co-produced by Longman and Infonautics, gives access to full-text electronic sources from a large collection of newspapers, magazines, and books available online through Prodigy. This powerful and easy-to-use researching tool allows keyword searching on the daily-updated

database. With the purchase of *Electric Library* comes one free month of Prodigy.

- **Supershell* provides a self-paced grammar and usage tutorial for IBM-compatible computers.
- ****Reading Critically: Text, Charts, and Graphs,*** Second Edition, by Judith Olson-Fallon, complements the handbook's Introduction. It provides a framework for developing critical reading questions and gives detailed information on preparing reading notes, study summaries, and graphic organizers.
- *Two guides to **collaborative learning,** both by Tori Haring-Smith, help students work together in groups: *Learning Together* discusses the advantages and varieties of collaborative work; and *Student Manual for Peer Evaluation,* with a new introduction by Helon Raines, contains forms to guide students' peer editing.
- ***Eighty Readings,*** Second Edition, is a versatile collection of professional and student essays organized thematically, with an alternate rhetorical table of contents. The new edition raises the issues that confront today's students.
- A **dictionary** can be packaged with the handbook: *The New American Webster Handy Dictionary,* Third Edition.
- Two guides to **writing with a word processor,** *Using WordPerfect in Composition* and *Using Microsoft Word in Composition,* help students master word-processing functions while they develop their own writing processes.

Acknowledgments to seventh American edition

Over the life of *The Little, Brown Handbook,* thousands of teachers have talked with sales representatives and editors, answered questionnaires, participated in focus groups, sent us personal notes, and written detailed reviews. The handbook remains fresh and useful because of this communication, and we are grateful for it.

For the seventh edition, the following instructors offered welcome insights from their rich experience with students: Joseph A. Alvarez, Central Piedmont Community College; Crystal Bacon, Gloucester County College; Cynthia Bates, University of California, Davis; Russell Bignano, Pennsylvania State University, Beaver; Nancy Blattner, Southeast Missouri State University; Kay Bosgraaf, Montgomery College; Phyllis Brotemarkle, Frostburg State University; Larry Brunner, Hardin-Simmons University; Ellen Burke, Casper College; Terrence Burke, Cuyahoga Community College; Peggy Cole, Arapahoe Community College; Geraldine DeLuca, Brooklyn College; Nancy Enright, Seton Hall University; Tom Ezzy, Dawson College; Richard Fabrizio, Pace University; Stuart Foreman, Millersville University; Rob Friedman, New Jersey Institute of Technology; Judith Gallagher, Tarrant County Junior College; Barbara Granger, Thomas Nelson Community College; Ida Hagman, College of DuPage; Marcia

Halio, University of Delaware; Carol Hammond, Yavapai College; Judy Hemmington, San Joaquin Delta College; Maurice Hunt, Baylor University; Peggy Jolly, University of Alabama, Birmingham; Michael Keller, South Dakota State University; Malcolm Kiniry, Rutgers University, Newark; James Scott King, Delaware State University; Paul Kleinpoppen, Florida Community College at Jacksonville, South Campus; Richard N. Lewis, Jr., Sandhills Community College; Rob Little, Rend Lake College; Dara Llewellyn, Florida Atlantic University; Mike Matthews, Tarrant County Junior College; Patricia M. Medeiros, Scottsdale Community College; Troy D. Nordman, Butler County Community College; George Redman, Benedict College; Ken Risdon, University of Minnesota, Duluth; Joan K. Robertson, North Central Technical College; Jan Schmidt, SUNY, New Paltz; Jeff Schonberg, Hardin-Simmons University; Marilyn Schultz, Lincoln University; Eileen Schwartz, Purdue University, Calumet; Richard Sisk, Mount San Jacinto College; Paul Sladky, Augusta College; Frances Smith, Grand Canyon University; Linda Tappmeyer, Southwest Baptist University; Patricia Terry, Gonzaga University; Donald Tighe, Valencia Community College; Warren Westcott, Francis Marion University; Sherri Winans, Whatcom Community College.

A number of instructors also gave very useful comments on the Instructor's Annotated Edition: Jane Allwardt, North Central Technical College; Jan Anderson, Clackamas Community College; Jerrie Callan, Baylor University; Susan Lang, Southern Illinois University; Lynn Langer Meeks, Utah State University; Leonard Sanazaro, City College of San Francisco; Bruce W. Speck, University of Memphis; Alison Warriner, Sacred Heart University.

In addition to these thoughtful critics, a group of creative people helped substantially with parts of the book. Andrew Christensen, David Gibbs, and Deborah A. Person contributed ideas and research support. Isa Engleberg, Prince George's Community College, offered advice for oral presentations, drawing on her text *The Principles of Public Presentation.* Kathleen Shine Cain, Merrimack College, provided crucial material for the research-writing chapters. Susan Lang, Southern Illinois University, advised us on electronic composition and research. And Sylvan Barnet, Tufts University, helped us revise his chapter, "Reading and Writing About Literature," adapted from his *Short Guide to Writing About Literature* and *Introduction to Literature* (with Morton Berman, William Burto, and William E. Cain). We are grateful to all these contributors.

From Longman, the publisher, we had not only support but camaraderie. Patricia Rossi, the editor and captain, was, as always, clever, patient, and true. Her assistant, Lynne Cattafi, apparently found no request too urgent or tiresome. Thomas Maeglin, assisted by Reka Simonsen, led the authors through development with keen intelligence and gentle strength. Robert Ginsberg deftly managed the myriad details and challenges of production. Kathryn Graehl copyedited with precision and tact. And Dorothy Bungert yet again provided creative solutions in design and page make-up. To all, our deep thanks.

Acknowledgments to second Canadian edition

Many people helped with this edition. I would like to thank Deane Downey and Barbara Pell for their exemplary work on the first Canadian edition. Special thanks to Brian Henderson at Addison Wesley Longman for his help in taking on a project already under way. Thanks to Linda Scott for her invaluable work as Managing Editor. Thanks to Michael Young for involving me in the first place. Very special thanks to my wife Kathryn McArthur for her many contributions to this text and her work on the ancillary materials. Thanks to Jane Aaron for her advice and encouragement. Thanks to Kathleen Venema, Norma Snyder, and all the others at the University of Waterloo who contributed.

Many thanks, also, to the following instructors for reviewing the text at various stages. Elizabeth Koper, Champlain College; Don Hair, University of Western Ontario; Carolyn Pittenger, McGill University; Tom Ezzy, Dawson College; Elaine Bander, Dawson College; Pat Rogin, Durham College; Colleen Cassano, University of Windsor; Sabrina Reed, Mount Royal College; Diana Patterson, Mount Royal College; Scott Sneddon, Seneca College; Zsolt Alapi, Marianapolis College; and Jack Robinson, Grant MacEwan College.

But above all, thanks to the students of my English 109, now numbering in the thousands, who have taken this course with me from its first edition in the Fall of 1986.

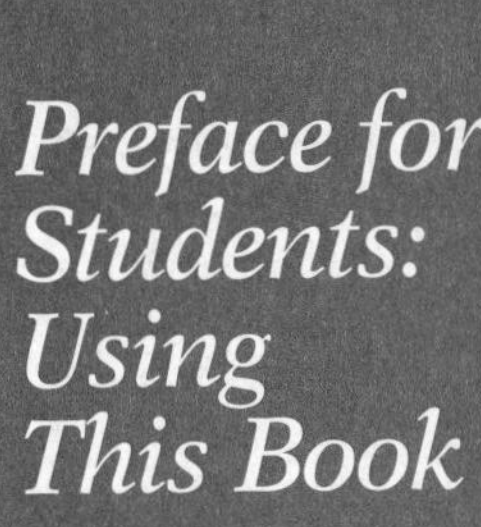

Preface for Students: Using This Book

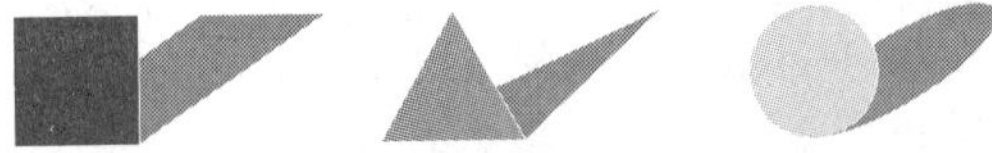

The Little, Brown Handbook is a basic resource that will answer almost any question you have about writing. Here you can find out how to get ideas, punctuate quotations, search the Internet, cite sources, or write a résumé. The handbook can help you not only in writing courses but in other courses and beyond school.

Don't let the size of the handbook put you off. You need not read the whole book to get something out of it, and no one expects you to know everything included. Primarily a reference tool, the handbook is written and arranged to help you find the answers you need when you need them, quickly and easily.

Using this book will not by itself make you a good writer; for that, you need to care about your work at every level, from finding a subject to spelling words. But learning how to use the handbook and the information in it can give you the means to write *what* you want in the *way* you want.

Organization and content

An overview of the handbook appears inside the front cover. Briefly, the book divides into the following sections:

- The Introduction lays a foundation with the essential skills of critical thinking, reading, and writing.
- Chapters 1–4 deal with the big picture: the writing process, paragraphs, and argument.
- Chapters 5–19 cover sentence basics: the system of English grammar and its conventions, errors that affect clarity, and techniques of effective sentences.

- Chapters 20–30 treat two technical elements of sentences and words: punctuation and mechanics (meaning capital letters, underlining, and the like).
- Chapters 31–34 move to words—how to choose them, look them up, learn them, spell them.
- Chapters 35–38 cover research writing from planning through revising, with a complete guide to citing sources.
- Chapters 39 and 40 introduce writing about literature and writing in the other academic disciplines.
- Chapters 41 and 42 contain practical information on taking essay exams and writing business letters and job applications.
- Appendixes A, B, and C provide information on formatting and designing documents, writing with a computer (word processing, collaborating, and creating hypertext documents), and making oral presentations.
- Two glossaries—one of problem words and expressions, the other of terms—and a detailed index finish the book.

Finding information

How you use the handbook will depend on your instructor's wishes and your own inclinations. Your instructor may assign whole sections of the book and discuss them in class or may use comments on your papers to direct you to particular sections. He or she will certainly encourage you to look things up on your own whenever you have a question. To help you do that, the handbook provides many ways of finding information quickly. Some of these surround the main text:

- The **Plan of the Book,** inside the front cover, displays the book's entire contents in abbreviated form. This plan also shows the system of coded headings (explained opposite).
- The **Contents,** immediately after this preface, gives a more detailed version of the book's plan.
- The **ESL Guide,** inside the back cover, indexes the book's topics for students using English as a second language.
- The list of **Editing Symbols,** also inside the back cover, gives the abbreviations often used to mark papers (see p. xvi).
- The list of **Useful Lists and Summaries,** just before the back endpapers, indexes topics that students frequently ask about.
- The **Index,** on the last pages of the book, lists every term and concept and every problem word or expression mentioned in the book. It is very detailed so that you can locate the precise point you seek and the page number where the point is discussed.

Many of the handbook's reference and learning aids appear on the text pages themselves, as illustrated by the reduced samples opposite. On these pages notice especially the heading code in

1. Running head (header): the topic being discussed on this page
2. Section heading in colour. The boxed code (**8b**) consists of the chapter number (**8**) and section letter (**b**).
3. Page tab in colour, containing the nearest section code (**8b**) and the editing symbol for the topic being discussed (**agr**).
4. Examples, always indented, often showing revision.
5. Box in light colour, containing a summary or checklist.
6. Pointer for students using English as a second language, flagged with a small light coloured box.
7. Subsection heading in colour, with heading number in triangle.
8. Exercise with light coloured vertical line.

---

1 **234** Agreement

2 **8b** **Make pronouns and their antecedents agree in person, number, and gender.**

3 agr 8b

The **antecedent** of a pronoun is the noun or other pronoun it refers to.

Home *owners* fret over *their* tax bills.
antecedent pronoun

4 *Its* constant increases make the tax *bill* a dreaded document.
pronoun antecedent

Since a pronoun derives its meaning from its antecedent, the two must agree in person, number, and gender.

5 **Person, number, and gender in pronoun-antecedent agreement**

PERSON	NUMBER: *Singular*	*Plural*
First	*I*	*we*
Second	*you*	*you*
Third	*he, she, it* indefinite pronouns singular nouns	*they* plural nouns

GENDER	
Masculine	*he,* nouns naming males
Feminine	*she,* nouns naming females
Neuter	*it,* all other nouns

6 NOTE ESL The gender of a pronoun should match its antecedent, not a noun that the pronoun may modify: *Sanjay* sent *his* (not *her*) *sister a birthday present.* Also, nouns in English have only neuter gender unless they specifically refer to males or females. Thus nouns such as *book, table, sun,* and *earth* take the pronoun *it.*

7 1 **Antecedents joined by *and* usually take plural pronouns.**

Two or more antecedents joined by *and* usually take a plural pronoun, whether one or all of the antecedents are singular.

The old group have gone *their* separate ways.

In the last example, note that the verb and pronoun are consistent in number (see also p. 230).

4 INCONSISTENT The old group *has* gone *their* separate ways.
CONSISTENT The old group *have* gone *their* separate ways.

8 **Exercise 2**
Revising: Pronoun-antecedent agreement

Revise the following sentences so that pronouns and their antecedents agree in person and number. Some items have more than one possible answer. Try to avoid the generic *he* (see above). If you change the subject of a sentence, be sure to change verbs as necessary for agreement. If the sentence is already correct as given, circle the number preceding it.

Example:
Each of the Boudreaus' children brought their laundry home at Thanksgiving.
Each of the Boudreaus' children brought *his or her* laundry home at Thanksgiving. *Or: All* of the Boudreaus' children brought *their* laundry home at Thanksgiving.

1. Each child in the school hopes that they will be the one chosen to attend the Youth Parliament in Ottawa.

both colour boxes (**8b** in the samples) and the symbol in the marginal box (**agr** in the samples). Your instructor may use either or both of these to mark specific weaknesses in your papers—for instance, either **8b** or **agr** on your paper would indicate an agreement problem. To discover just what the problem is and how to revise it, you can consult the plan of the book or the list of editing symbols, or you can thumb the book. (A sample student paper marked by an instructor with some codes and symbols appears on pp. 77–79.)

The handbook's reference aids are meant to speed your work, but you need not use any or all of them. You may of course browse or read this book like any other, with no particular goal in mind but seeing what you can learn.

Special symbols

Frequently throughout the handbook, you'll see the following symbols:

- The computer shown here signals tips for using computers productively for all kinds of writing activity, from discovering ideas through citing sources.
- The notebook shown here marks examples from students' work-in-progress, applications of the text's principles in specific writing situations.
- The symbol **ESL** flags material for students using English as a second language, which is integrated throughout the handbook. A guide to the ESL topics appears inside the back cover.

Recommended usage

The conventions described and illustrated in this handbook are those of standard written English—the label given the language of business and the professions. (See also p. 444.) Written English is more conservative than spoken English in matters of grammar and usage, and a great many words and constructions that are widely spoken remain unaccepted in careful writing.

When clear distinctions exist between the language of conversation and that of careful writing, the handbook provides examples of each and labels them *spoken* and *written.* When usage in writing itself varies with the level of formality intended, the handbook labels examples *formal* and *informal.* When usage is mixed or currently changing, the handbook recommends that you choose the more conservative usage because it will be acceptable to all readers.

Contents

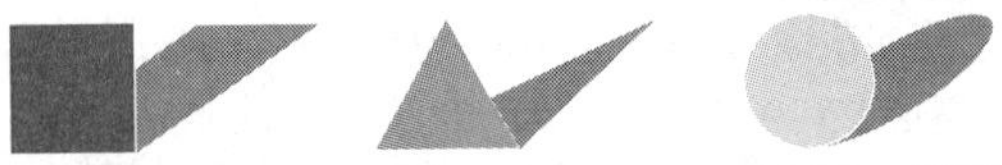

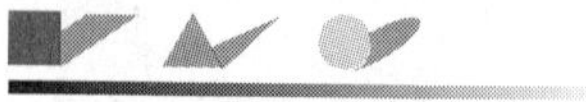

Part III
Clear Sentences 253

Part V
Punctuation *347*

Introduction Critical Thinking, Reading, and Writing

Why does a book on writing begin with an introduction to thinking and reading as well as writing? The answer is that the three can't be separated: thinking underlies reading and writing; writing demands reading; reading and writing clarify and toughen thinking. To get the most out of this book—and your education—you will need to be adept at all three skills.

This Introduction serves as a foundation for several assignments you may encounter in college: writing essays (Chapters 1–2), reading and writing arguments (Chapter 4), writing research papers (Chapters 35–38), reading and writing about literature (Chapter 39), and writing in other disciplines (Chapter 40). All of these assignments require that you foster a critical perspective (section I1), develop a process of critical thinking and reading (I2), and learn to write critically (I3).

I1 Fostering a critical perspective

The kind of thinking, reading, and writing we're concerned with here goes beyond obvious meanings and easy answers. It is called **critical**, meaning "sceptical," "exacting," "creative." When you operate critically, you question, test, and build on what others say and what you yourself think. The word *critical* does not mean "negative" in this context. It comes from Greek words meaning "to separate" and "to discern": a critical thinker, reader, or writer separates a subject into its parts, discerns how the parts work together and how the subject relates to other subjects, and (often) judges the subject's quality and value.

You already operate critically every day of your life, as when you probe a friendship ("What did she mean by that?") or when you discuss a movie you just saw ("Don't you think the villain was too obvious?"). Such questioning helps you figure out why things happen to you or what your experiences mean.

Operating critically in other spheres—school courses, career, our democratic society—expands the subjects and the benefits.

- Critical thinking, reading, and writing improve your ability to learn and to perform as a student and a worker. Your teachers and employers in every field, from the arts to zoology, will expect you to assess what you read and hear and to make a good case for your own ideas.
- Operating critically helps you understand your own actions and ideas, weigh them against opposing views, and persuasively articulate your reasoning and motivations.
- Your very independence and freedom depend on your ability to think, read, and write critically. An open democracy like ours allows as much play for stupid and false claims as for sound ones, and the ones that seem sound often conflict with each other. Whether you are watching the evening news, reading an advertisement, or voting, critical thinking empowers you to decide for yourself what's useful, fair, and wise—and what's not.

There's no denying that critical thinking, reading, and writing require discipline and hard work. Besides channelling your curiosity, paying attention, and probing, you will often need to consult experts, interpreting and evaluating their ideas. Such an approach also requires a healthy tolerance for doubt or uncertainty—that feeling you may have had when the old rules don't seem to apply or when a change is frightening but still attractive. Out of uncertainty, though, comes creativity—the capacity to organize and generate knowledge, to explain, resolve, illuminate, play. Compared to passive, rote learning, creative work is more involving, more productive, and more enjoyable.

I2 Thinking and reading critically

You can think critically about almost anything: an argument you overhear on a bus, a new CD by your favourite solo musician, your roommate's ideas about baseball, even a dog-food commercial. By "separating" and "discerning" any of these, you would be able to understand it better, see its relations to other events or things, and evaluate it.

Of course, in college much of your critical thinking will focus on written texts, such as a short story or a journal article. Like all subjects worthy of critical consideration, written texts operate on at least three levels: (1) what the author actually says, (2) what the author does not say but builds into the text (intentionally or not), and (3) what you think. Discovering the text at each level involves a number of techniques.

Techniques of critical reading

- **Writing:** annotating; taking notes (I2-a)
- **Previewing:** getting background; skimming (I2-b)
- **Reading:** interacting with and absorbing the text (I2-c)
- **Summarizing:** distilling and understanding content (I2-d)
- **Forming your critical response** (I2-e)

Analysing: separating into parts
Interpreting: inferring meaning and assumptions
Synthesizing: reassembling parts; making connections
Evaluating: judging quality and value

Keep in mind that these are techniques, not steps in a firm sequence. You will not use all of them for all the reading you do. On some occasions, even when a close, critical reading is required, you may simply lack the time to preview, read, and reread. (But if your reading time is continually squeezed by your schedule, you may need to rethink your schedule.) On other occasions your reason for reading (your purpose) will determine which techniques you use. For instance, let's say you're reading *People* magazine.

PURPOSE	Learn some gossip while filling time in the dentist's office.
KIND OF READING	Quick, uncritical
PURPOSE	Examine *People* as an artifact of our popular culture that reflects and perhaps even moulds contemporary values.
KIND OF READING	Close, critical

Course assignments, too, differ in their requirements. A book report may require writing, previewing, reading, and summarizing but not intense critical reading. An evaluation of a journal article, in contrast, requires all the techniques listed.

Writing while reading

There are two good reasons to write while you read: to record information and ideas for future use, and to get more out of the text. The first is discussed in detail as part of research writing (see p. 547). The second has more to do with critical reading.

Critical reading is *active* reading. You interact with the text, getting involved with it, bringing to it *your* experiences, ideas, and questions. When you use a pen or pencil while reading, you create writing in response to writing. In this way you "translate" the text into your own words and reconstruct it for yourself.

The writing you do while reading may take several forms. *What* you write will depend on your purpose and your findings during the various stages of reading. *Where* you write will depend on whether you own the material and what kind of thinking you do about it. If you do own the text, you may opt to write directly on the pages as you read them (an illustration of this method appears on p. 6). If you don't own the material, make your notes on a separate sheet or, if the material is brief enough, on a photocopy.

Many readers keep a **reading journal**, a notebook in which they regularly work out questions and thoughts about what they read. One technique for keeping such a journal is to divide a blank page in half, on one side dealing with the text itself (notes, questions, doubts) and on the other side recording what the text makes you think (comparisons with other texts, ideas for writing, and so on). See page 33 for more on keeping a journal.

Previewing the material

Before you begin reading a text word by word, form some expectations about the work and even some preliminary questions. Your reading will be better informed and more fruitful.

One way to preview a text is to **skim** it: go quickly through it looking for clues about its content, its author, and how you will interact with it. Not the same as idly turning pages, skimming is a focused, concentrated activity in which you seek information. Use the questions on the facing page as a guide. In your journal write down any impressions that you may want to return to later.

Reading

Reading is itself more than a one-step process. Your primary goal is to understand the first level on which the text operates—what the author actually says.

Questions for previewing a text

- **Length:** Is the material brief enough to read in one sitting, or do you need more time?
- **Content cues:** What do the title, summary or abstract, headings, illustrations, and other features tell you? What questions do they raise in your mind?
- **Facts of publication:** Does the publisher or publication specialize in a particular kind of material—scholarly articles, say, or popular books? Does the date of publication suggest currency or datedness?
- **Author:** What does the biographical information tell you about the author's publications, interests, biases, and reputation in the field?
- **Yourself:** Do you anticipate particular difficulties with the content? What biases of your own may influence your response to the text—for instance, anxiety, curiosity, boredom, or an outlook similar or opposed to that of the author?

First reading

The first time through new material, read as steadily and smoothly as possible. Try to get the gist of what the author is saying and a sense of his or her tone. Try to enjoy the work, seeking connections between the text and your own experiences, appreciating forceful writing, humour, good examples.

To keep up a steady reading pace, use your pencil or pen sparingly during this reading. Mark or note major stumbling blocks—such as a paragraph you don't understand—so that you can try to resolve them before rereading. But resist any urge to make frequent or extensive notes until your next pass.

NOTE ESL On your first reading, don't stop and look up every unfamiliar word. You will lose more in concentration than you gain in understanding. Instead, try to guess the meanings of words from their contexts (see p. 484), or circle unfamiliar words and look them up later.

Rereadings

After the first reading, plan on at least one other. This time read *slowly*. Your main concern should be to grasp the content and how it is constructed. That means rereading a paragraph if you didn't get the point, or flipping back a few pages to see how ideas are connected, or looking up key words in a dictionary.

Use your pen or pencil freely to annotate the text or make separate notes. If you can write on the material, use any system of annotations that works for you—perhaps "?" in the margin next to passages you don't understand, circles around unfamiliar words, underlining or brackets for main points, "*" for passages you agree with, "!" for those you find startling, "So what?" for those you can't see the point of.

Following is an example of a student's annotations. The passage is from the conclusion to Daniel Yergin's book *The Prize: The Epic Quest for Oil, Money, and Power*. (The passage is part of the longer excerpt from Yergin's book beginning on the facing page.)

> Oil is paramount in the environmental consciousness, for at the top of the concerns are the consequences of hydrocarbon combustion—smog and air pollution, acid rain, global warming, ozone depletion. Some of the most bitterly fought issues concern the opening of new territories to oil and gas production, whether offshore or in Alaska. Great contention also surrounds the siting of new energy facilities, particularly electricity generating plants. The United States and other industrial countries could experience considerable pressure on their electricity supply systems in the 1990s, forcing difficult and contentious choices about how the burgeoning demand for electricity will be met with the least cost to the environment.

"hydrocarbon" oil only?

language of battle, struggle

growing?

Oil vs. the environment

① open new territories to exploration?

② more electric plants? where?

Electricity costs

Of course, you should try to answer the questions you raise in such annotations, and that may take another reading or some digging in other sources, such as dictionaries and encyclopedias. You may find it helpful to summarize the material, as described in the next section (p. 8). Such efforts will resolve any confusion you feel, or they will give you the confidence to say that your confusion is the fault of the author, not the reader.

Exercise 1
Reading

Reprinted on the next two pages is an excerpt from the conclusion of Daniel Yergin's book *The Prize: The Epic Quest for Oil, Money, and Power* (1991). Something of an epic itself at nearly eight hundred pages, *The Prize* examines how petroleum has shaped the mere century and a half since it was first refined for lamp fuel (its uses in generating electricity and powering engines came later). We are now, Yergin says, a "Hydrocarbon Society," "a civilization that would collapse if the world's oil wells suddenly went dry." Yergin holds degrees from Yale and Cambridge universities, has taught at Harvard, has written several books on energy, and runs a consulting firm specializing in energy. His purpose in *The Prize*, as he says in his prologue, is to "illuminate the past, enable us better to understand the present, and help to anticipate the future."

Read this selection at least twice, until you think you understand what the author is saying. Either separately or on these pages, note your questions and reactions in writing. Look up any words you don't know, and try to arrive at answers to your questions. (It may help to discuss the selection with classmates.)

Even as the world continues to move on oil and the economy to live on oil, a new challenge to Hydrocarbon Society has emerged, this time from within, portending a great confrontation that will probably affect the oil industry and, indeed, our way of life in the years ahead. The industrial world is now facing a resurgent wave of the environmental movement. ... It has engendered wide support, cutting across traditional ideological, demographic, and partisan differences. It is an international phenomenon whose concerns include every environmental hazard from the depletion of the tropical rain forests to the disposal of waste products. Its overall concern is no less than the very character of our planet. ... 1

Oil is paramount in the environmental consciousness, for at the top of the concerns are the consequences of hydrocarbon combustion—smog and air pollution, acid rain, global warming, ozone depletion. Some of the most bitterly fought issues concern the opening of new territories to oil and gas production, whether offshore or in Alaska. Great contention also surrounds the siting of new energy facilities, particularly electricity generating plants. The United States and other industrial countries could experience considerable pressure on their electricity supply systems in the 1990s, forcing difficult and contentious choices about how the burgeoning demand for electricity will be met with the least cost to the environment. Among the most important effects of the environmental consensus will be a switch toward natural gas as the least polluting energy source, particularly in electricity generation. And there will be a new emphasis on energy conservation, not only for reasons of security and price, as was the case in the 1970s and early 1980s, but as a way to contain the combustion of hydrocarbons—and to buy time. 2

The new environmental agenda will hardly come to pass without major battles over the accuracy of the science and its predictions, the extent of the risks, the proper remedies—and the costs. Though there is a widespread sentiment that environmental improvement is essentially "free," merely a matter of regulation, this is not likely to be the case. There will be a significant, if not easily calculable, price tag. The environment, like defense or medical care or education, is a social "good," which means that someone has to pay for it; and as the costs emerge, there will be a growing struggle over how the bill is to be divided up among companies, consumers, and governments. Society does not yet know how to allocate costs between the here-and-now—for instance, expensive pollution-control systems on power plants and factories—and the future—the almost incomprehensible costs and disruption in agricultural production and even in human habitation that could result if there is a major climate change. 3

Yet the 1990s began not with another environmental drama, but rather with a struggle over the oil resources of the Persian Gulf, on which the world was again becoming heavily dependent. 4

The Gulf Crisis thrust energy security back onto the political agenda, spurring governments to focus anew on ensuring supplies. It will serve to stimulate oil exploration and development around the world. In the words of a thoughtful observer, Joseph Stanislaw, "The rules of the race between demand growth and production capacity in the 1990s have been changed by the Gulf Crisis. Now secure capacity will count for a lot more." The crisis will rekindle efforts to promote energy development within the industrial countries. Much of the industrial world will find itself caught up in the competition of two great themes—energy and security, and energy and the environment. A far-reaching clash between anxieties about energy security and economic well-being on the one side, and fears about the environment on the other, seems all but inevitable. One point of convergence of the two themes is energy conservation. Another may be greater utilization of natural gas. Aside from that, the consensus necessary to solve environmental problems and at the same time meet the requirements of security, both within and among nations, will undoubtedly be as difficult to achieve as any other form of economic, political, and social cooperation.

But perhaps, just perhaps, all this could eventually point to a 5
new direction for industrial society, and to a beneficent resolution of the conflicts between energy and the environment. Innovation responds to need; and if properly nurtured, research and technology will respond to environmental and energy imperatives. However, until such time as there are new technological breakthroughs, perhaps in solar and renewable energies, industrial society has only three primary clusters of alternatives on which to rely for its new power needs: oil, gas, and coal; nuclear power; and conservation in the form of technological improvements and greater efficiency in the use of energy. In the 1990s, the merits of the various alternatives will be jumbled together in the energy and environmental debate, challenging traditional interests and modes of thought. The clashes will take many forms: lifestyle versus the quality of life, markets versus regulation, controlled versus untrammeled development, economic use versus preservation, dependence versus autonomy, cooperation versus competition among nations—and security and economic growth versus the environment. Great amounts of money will be at stake, as will political standing and power, not only within nations, but in the world arena. And so will be the way we live. Indeed, with the fate of the planet itself seeming to be in question, the hydrocarbon civilization that oil built could be shaken to its foundations.

Summarizing

Before you can see what is beneath the surface of a text and figure out what you think of it, you need to understand exactly what the author is actually saying. A good way to master the content of a text and see its strengths and weaknesses is to **summarize** it: distill it to its main points, in your own words.

Some assignments call for brief summaries, as when you summarize the plot in a critical essay about a novel (p. 660). Summary is also an essential tool in research papers and other writing that draws on sources (p. 549). Here, though, we're concerned with summarizing for yourself—for your own enlightenment.

A summary should state in as few words as possible the main ideas of a passage. When you need to summarize a few paragraphs or a brief article, your summary should not exceed one-fifth the length of the original. For longer works, such as chapters of books or whole books, your summary should be quite a bit shorter in proportion to the original. A procedure for drafting a summary appears in the box below.

Writing a summary

- Work through the text paragraph by paragraph to identify its sections—single paragraphs or groups of paragraphs focused on a single topic. To understand how paragraphs relate to each other, try outlining the text (see p. 49).
- Write a one- or two-sentence summary of each section you identify. Focus on the main point of the section, omitting examples, facts, and other supporting evidence.
- Write a sentence or two stating the author's central idea.
- Write a full paragraph (or more, if needed) that begins with the central idea and supports it with the sentences that summarize sections of the work. The paragraph should concisely and accurately state the thrust of the entire work.
- *Use your own words.* By writing, you re-create the meaning of the work in a way that makes sense for you.

Capturing the essence of even a single paragraph can be tricky. Here is a first attempt to summarize paragraph 1 of the excerpt from Daniel Yergin's *The Prize* (p. 7).

DRAFT SUMMARY

Oil use continues to drive our society, which is a fact the environmental movement objects to.

This sentence "misreads" the paragraph because it places too little emphasis on the environmental movement and understates the movement's concerns about society's dependence on oil. The following revision is a more accurate summary.

REVISED SUMMARY

Our society's dependence on oil has met its match in the environmental movement, a broad-based, worldwide effort to protect the planet.

NOTE When you write a summary, using your own words will ensure that you avoid plagiarism. Even when the summary is in your own words, if you use it in something written for others you must cite the source of the ideas. See pages 555–61.

Exercise 2
Summarizing

Pick up where the preceding summary of Daniel Yergin's first paragraph ends to distill the entire selection reprinted on pages 7–8. Your summary, in your own words, should not exceed one paragraph and should begin with a statement of Yergin's central idea.

Forming your critical response

Once you've got a grip on the content of what you're reading—what the author says—then you can turn to understanding what the author does not say outright but suggests or implies or even lets slip. At this stage you are concerned with the purpose or intention of the author and with how he or she carries it out. Depending on what you are reading and why, you may examine evidence, organization, attitude, use of language, and other elements of the text.

Critical thinking and reading consist of four operations: analysing, interpreting, synthesizing, and (often) evaluating. Although we'll look at them one by one, these operations interrelate and overlap. Indeed, the first three are often combined under the general label *analysis*, and evaluation is sometimes taken for granted as a result of the process.

Analysing

Analysis is the separation of something into its parts or elements, the better to understand it. To see these elements in what you are reading, begin with a question that reflects your purpose in analysing the text: why you are curious about it or what you're trying to make out of it. This question and purpose will provide you with a **framework** for looking at the subject, a kind of lens that highlights some features and not others. Here, for example, are some ways you might look at *People* magazine:

Question reflecting possible purpose for analysis	Framework and elements
Does *People* challenge or perpetuate stereotypes?	Stereotypes: explicit and implicit stereotypes or challenges in the magazine
Does the magazine offer positive role models for its readers?	Role models: text and photographs presenting positive or negative role models
Does the magazine's editorial material (articles and accompanying photographs) encourage readers to consume goods?	Encouragement of buying: references to products, focus on consumers, equation of consumption with happiness or success

The framework concentrates your attention on relevant features and eliminates irrelevant features. For the last example above, you would focus on items about celebrities' well-appointed homes, photographs of designer clothes, and articles on the authors of best-selling books. At the same time, you would skip over uplifting stories about families or the physically challenged.

A difference in analytical framework is a key distinction among academic disciplines. A sociologist neatly outlined the frameworks in three disciplines' approaches to poverty:

> Political science does a wonderful job looking at poverty as a policy issue. Economics does an equally wonderful job looking at it from an income-distribution perspective. But sociology asks how people in poverty live and what they aspire to.

Even within disciplines, analytical frameworks may differ. The sociologist quoted above may focus on how people in poverty live, but another might be more interested in the effects of poverty on cities or the changes in the poor population over the last fifty years. (See Chapters 39 and 40 for more on the disciplines' analytical frameworks.)

Interpreting

Identifying the elements of something is of course only the beginning: you also need to interpret the meaning or significance of the elements and of the whole. Interpretation usually requires you to infer the author's **assumptions**, opinions or beliefs about what is or what could or should be. (**Infer** means to draw a conclusion based on evidence.)

The word *assumption* here has a more specific meaning than it does in everyday usage, where it may stand for expectation ("I assume you'll pay"), speculation ("It was a mere assumption"), or error ("The report was riddled with assumptions"). Defined more strictly as what a person *supposes* to be true, assumptions are unavoidable. We all adhere to certain values and beliefs; we all form opinions. We live our lives by such assumptions.

Though pervasive, assumptions are not always stated outright. Speakers and writers may judge that their audience already understands and accepts their assumptions; they may not even be aware of their assumptions; or they may deliberately refrain from stating their assumptions for fear that the audience will disagree. That is why your job as a critical thinker is to interpret what the assumptions are.

Be careful in making inferences about the assumptions of authors (or, in *People* magazine's case, of publishers). You don't want to take the text at face value, but neither do you want to read too much into it, as in these faulty inferences:

FAULTY — The publishers of *People* do not make decisions based on assumptions about the magazine's readers. [The inference is naive: the magazine brings in hundreds of millions of dollars a year by deliberately appealing to a vast readership of around 3.5 million a week.]

FAULTY — *People*'s publishers deliberately skew the magazine's editorial material to promote products on which they receive kickbacks. [The inference is far-fetched, even absurd. It would be reasonable only if there were hard evidence of kickbacks.]

Faulty inferences like those above are often based on the reader's *own* assumptions about the text or its subject. When thinking and reading critically, you need to look hard at *your* ideas, too.

Your inferences about another's assumptions need to fit the evidence of the text. With the evidence of *People*'s advertisements, the further evidence (from your analysis) of its articles and photographs featuring consumer goods, and your own assumption that the publisher carefully considers what it puts into the magazine, you can make a reasonable inference:

REASONABLE — The publishers of *People* assume that the magazine's readers are consumers who want to see and hear about consumer goods.

Synthesizing

If you stopped at analysis and interpretation, critical thinking and reading might leave you with a pile of elements and possible meanings but no vision of the whole. With **synthesis** you make connections among parts or among wholes. You create a new

Guidelines for analysis, interpretation, and synthesis

- What is the purpose of your reading?
- What questions do you have about the work? Which suggest a promising analytical framework? What elements does the framework highlight for examination? What elements can be ignored as a result?
- How do you interpret the meaning and significance of the elements, both individually and in relation to the whole text? What are your assumptions about the text? What do you infer about the author's assumptions?
- What patterns can you see in (or synthesize from) the elements? How do the elements relate? How does this whole text relate to other texts?
- What do you conclude about the text? What does this conclusion add to the text?

whole by drawing conclusions about relationships and implications. For instance:

> CONCLUSION *People* magazine appeals to its readers' urge to consume by displaying, discussing, and glamorizing consumer goods.

You could also synthesize your critical readings of a number of popular magazines, again drawing your own conclusions:

> CONCLUSION In *People, Us, Vanity Fair,* and other magazines aimed at consumers, the line between advertising and editorial material is sometimes almost invisible.

(Synthesizing several sources is important in research writing. See p. 545.)

Synthesis requires and rewards your own ideas: you create something different from what you started with. At first, *People*'s articles and photographs may have seemed light and rather pointless. On critical examination, though, they have greater significance as (at least in part) a vehicle of our consumer culture.

Evaluating

Many critical reading and writing assignments end at analysis, interpretation, and synthesis: you explain your understanding of what the author says and doesn't say. Only if you are expected to **evaluate** the work will you state and defend the judgments you've made about its quality and its significance. You'll inevitably form such judgments while reading the work: "What a striking series of images," or "That just isn't enough evidence." In evaluating, you collect your judgments, determine that they are generally applicable and are themselves not trivial, and turn them into assertions: "The poet creates fresh, intensely vivid images"; "The author does not summon the evidence to support his case." And you support these statements with citations from the text.

Evaluation takes a certain amount of confidence. You may feel that you lack the expertise to cast judgment on another's writing, especially if the text is difficult or the author well known. True, the more informed you are, the better a critical reader you are. But conscientious reading and analysis will give you the internal authority to judge a work *as it stands* and *as it seems to you,* against your own unique bundle of experiences, observations, and attitudes. The box opposite gives questions that may help you evaluate many kinds of texts. (For arguments and in academic disciplines, you'll require additional, more specific criteria. See Chapters 4, 39, and 40.)

Guidelines for evaluation

- What are your reactions to the text? What in the text are you responding to?
- Is the work unified, with all the parts pertaining to a central idea? Is it coherent, with the parts relating clearly to each other?
- Is the work sound in its general idea? In its details and other evidence?
- Has the author achieved his or her purpose? Is the purpose worthwhile?
- Does the author seem authoritative? Trustworthy? Sincere?
- What is the overall quality of the work? What is its value or significance in the larger scheme of things?
- Do you agree or disagree with the work? Can you support, refute, or extend it?

Exercise 3
Thinking critically

Following are some statements about the communications media. Use systematic critical thinking to understand not only what the statement says but why its author might have said it. As in the example, do your thinking in writing: the act of writing will help you think, and your notes will help you discuss your ideas with your classmates.

Example:

Statement: Every year sees the disappearance of more book publishers because the larger companies gobble up the smaller ones.

Analysis: Why did the author make this statement? Certain words reveal the author's purpose: *disappearance of more book publishers; because; larger companies gobble up smaller ones.*

Interpretation: More book publishers means others have disappeared. *Because* specifies cause. *Gobble up* implies consumption, predator to prey. Author's assumptions: Large publishers behave like predators. The predatory behaviour of large companies causes the disappearance of small companies. The more publishing companies there are, the better.

Synthesis: The author objects to the predatory behaviour of large publishing companies, which he or she holds responsible for eliminating small companies and reducing the total number of companies.

Evaluation: This biased statement against large publishers holds them responsible for the shrinking numbers of book publishers. But are the large companies solely responsible? And why is the shrinking necessarily bad?

1. Violent movies should be rated R to prevent children from seeing and being harmed by them.
2. Newspapers and newsmagazines are better news sources than television because they demand reading, not just viewing.
3. Radio call-in shows are the true democratic forum, giving voice to Canadians of all persuasions.

Exercise 4
Reading critically

Reread the selection from Daniel Yergin's *The Prize* (pp. 7–8) in order to form your own critical response to it. Follow the guidelines for analysis, interpretation, synthesis, and evaluation in the boxes on pages 13 and 14. Focus on any elements suggested by your analytical framework. Assumptions, evidence, organization, use of language, tone, authority, vision of the future—all these elements and more could be considered. Be sure to write while reading and thinking; your notes will help your analysis and enhance your creativity, and they will be essential for writing about the selection (Exercise 7, p. 18).

Exercise 5
Reading critically

Do your own critical reading of *People* or another magazine. What do you see beyond the obvious? What questions does your reading raise? Let the guidelines on pages 13 and 14 direct your response, and do your work in writing. (A writing suggestion based on this exercise appears on p. 18.)

I3 Writing critically

Like critical reading, critical writing is largely influenced by its purpose and by the discipline or profession in which it occurs. Thus the topic is covered more extensively in Chapters 4 (argument), 39 (literature), and 40 (other disciplines), and an example using sources appears in Chapter 38 on research writing. In this introduction we'll look at some fundamentals and an illustration.

It is no doubt obvious by now that critical writing is *not* summarizing. You may write a summary to clarify for yourself what the author says (pp. 8–10) and may briefly summarize a work in your own larger piece of writing. But your job in critical writing is not just to report what a text says; it is to transmit your analysis, interpretation, synthesis, and perhaps evaluation of the text.

The following essay by a student, Dinisha Wade, is a response to the selection on pages 7–8 from Daniel Yergin's *The Prize*. While reading Wade's essay, notice especially the clear structure (highlighted in marginal annotations) and the use of quotations from Yergin's text. Wade does not assume that her readers see the same things in the text or share her views, so she supports her views with evidence in the form of direct quotations from the text. Very brief summaries of long passages or paraphrases of the text author's sentences in your own words may also serve as evidence. (See pp. 549–53 for more on quoting, paraphrasing, and summarizing sources.)

The Right Balance

Introduction: background that readers need to understand Wade's concern

In the final pages of his book *The Prize: The Epic Quest for Oil, Money, and Power*, Daniel Yergin lists some dire results of burning oil: "smog and air pollution, acid rain, global warming, ozone depletion." The author warns that "the fate of the planet itself" may be "in question" because of environmental problems. Yet throughout the pages Yergin maintains a balanced view of the issue of oil versus the environment, siding with neither. Why, when he so clearly recognizes the dangers of oil, does he seem to lack the conviction of a more environmentalist approach? The answer lies in his idea of our "Hydrocarbon Society" and how he sees issues being resolved in our society.

Questions about the text

Answer to question: Wade's central idea

First main point

Yergin calls our contemporary civilization a "Hydrocarbon Society" because it is completely dependent on oil. Some environmentalists speak and write as if they would like to return to the age before oil's uses were discovered in the mid-nineteenth century. Others blame the oil industry and lax government regulation for pollution and all the other bad effects of oil. Yergin, in contrast, takes a more realistic approach. He recognizes that "the world continues to move on oil and the economy to live on oil." It is not just the economic and political empire of the oil industry that keeps us oil dependent: it is our own reliance on the technology that oil makes possible, from the cars we drive to the air conditioners that cool us to the computers that check our spelling. As Yergin says, environmental improvement has a "significant, if not easily calculable, price tag" that we will all have to pay. So far, though, aside from efforts such as recycling some trash, we don't seem aware of the sacrifices ahead or willing to make them.

Evidence for Wade's point: quotation from the text

Yergin's approach is realistic in another way, which is revealed in the words he uses to discuss the issue of oil versus the environment. Throughout his conclusion Yergin uses terms of competition and even war to portray the debate. He predicts a "challenge" to the Hydrocarbon Society and a "great confrontation" from the environmental movement. He describes issues as "bitterly fought" and choices as "contentious." The costs of environmental improvement will be the centre of "a growing struggle." This struggle will generate a "far-reaching clash between anxieties." The conclusion gives a picture of oppositions, culminating in a list of "clashes": "lifestyle versus the quality of life, markets versus regulation, controlled versus untrammelled development, cooperation versus competition among nations—and security and economic growth versus the environment."

Transition to second main point

Evidence: quotations

This language reveals Yergin's assumption that society is made up of competing interests or forces that battle each other for victory. The language also reveals Yergin's faith in society's willingness to debate important issues and its tolerance for the process of debate, no matter how lengthy or complex it is. And Yergin seems guardedly optimistic about the possibility of change through such debate. He finds points of "convergence," speaks of the achievement (however difficult) of "consensus" and "cooperation," and foresees the possibility of "a beneficent resolution of the conflicts."

Statement of second main point

In the end, Daniel Yergin's steady approach to serious environmental issues is not difficult to understand. It's not that he lacks conviction, but that his convictions include a realistic grasp of how dependent we are on oil and how committed we are to our democratic system of competition and consensus. In the difficult matter of oil versus the environment, Yergin sees hard-fought incremental change as the only path to resolution.

Conclusion: two main points drawn together; central idea restated. (A conclusion may also evaluate the text.)

Exercise 6
Responding to critical writing

Read Dinisha Wade's essay carefully. What is her analytical framework? What assumptions does she identify in Daniel Yergin's work? What conclusions does she reach about the work? Do you think her response to the work is accurate and fair? Is it perceptive? Does she provide enough evidence from Yergin's work to convince you of her points? Does she miss anything you would have mentioned? Write your responses in a brief essay.

Exercise 7
Writing critically

Write an essay based on your critical reading of Daniel Yergin's work (Exercise 4, p. 15). Follow the guidelines on pages 16–17 for developing and organizing your essay.

Exercise 8
Writing critically

Write an essay based on your critical response to *People* magazine or another magazine (Exercise 5, p. 15). Follow the guidelines on pages 16–17 for developing and organizing your essay.

Part I

The Whole Paper and Paragraphs

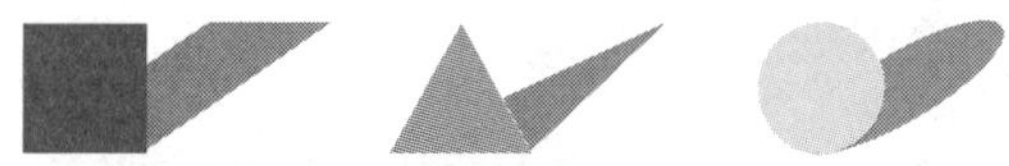

Chapter 1 Developing an Essay

"Writing is easy," snarled the late sportswriter Red Smith. "All you have to do is sit down at the typewriter and open a vein." Most writers would smile in agreement, and so might you. Like anything worthwhile, writing well takes hard work. This chapter and the next will show you some techniques that successful writers use to minimize the discomfort of writing and turn it into gain.

Before you start on these chapters, clear your head of a very common misconception that may be lurking there: *writing is not only, or even mainly, a matter of correctness.* True, any written message will find a more receptive audience if it is correct in grammar, spelling, and similar matters. But these concerns should come late in the process, after you've allowed yourself to discover what you want to say, freeing yourself to make mistakes along the way. As one writer put it, you need to get the clay on the potter's wheel before you can shape it into a bowl, and you need to shape the bowl before you can perfect it. So get your clay on the wheel, and work with it until it looks like a bowl. Then worry about correctness.

1a The writing situation and the writing process

All writing occurs in a context that simultaneously limits and clarifies the writer's choices. Most obviously, context includes the nature of the assignment, the assigned length, and the deadline. But context can also be seen as the **writing situation,** in which you

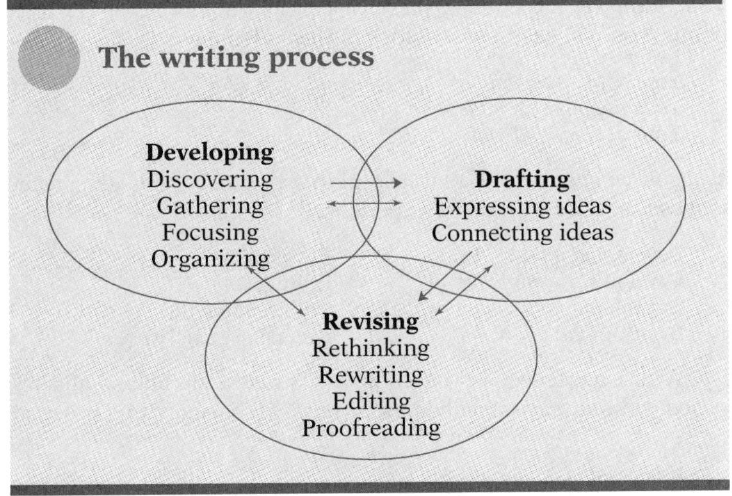

aim to communicate something about a subject to a particular audience of readers. For each writing task, considering the following questions can help you define and make choices:

- What is your subject?
- Who is your audience?
- What is your purpose?
- How can you present yourself and your subject to that audience in order to achieve your purpose?

Understanding the writing situation is an important part of the **writing process**—the term for all the activities, mental and physical, that go into writing what eventually becomes a finished piece of work. Even for experienced writers the process is usually messy, which is one reason that it is sometimes difficult. Though we may get a sense of ease and orderliness from a well-crafted magazine article, we can safely assume that the writer had to work hard to achieve it, struggling to express half-formed thoughts, shaping and reshaping paragraphs to make a point convincingly.

There is no *one* writing process: no two writers proceed in the same way, and even an individual writer adapts his or her process to the task at hand. Still, most experienced writers pass through certain stages that overlap and circle back on each other.

- *Developing or planning:* discovering a subject, gathering information, focusing on a central theme, and organizing material.
- *Drafting:* expressing and connecting ideas.
- *Revising:* rethinking and improving structure, content, style, and presentation.

You, too, will experience these stages as you write. At various points, you will need to take stock of these elements:

Your topic (section 1b)
Your purpose (1c)
Your audience (1d)

And you will probably find it helpful to experiment with some techniques that have worked for experienced writers:

Developing a topic (1e)
Developing a thesis (1f)
Organizing (1g)
Drafting (2a)
Revising (2b)
Editing (2c)
Proofreading (2d)
Receiving criticism (2e)

With experience, as you complete varied assignments and try varied techniques, you will develop your own basic writing process.

Exercise 1
Starting a writing journal

Recall several writing experiences that you have had—a letter you had difficulty with, an essay you enjoyed, an all-nighter spent happily or miserably on a term paper, and so on. What do these experiences reveal to you about writing, particularly your successes and problems with it? For instance:

Do you like to experiment with language?
Are some kinds of writing easier than others?
Do you have trouble getting ideas or expressing them?
Do you worry about grammar and spelling?
Do your readers usually understand what you mean?

Write these thoughts down as the first entry in a continuing journal or log in which you track your experiences as a writer. Specific suggestions for considering your past work appear in Exercises 3, 6, 9, 11, 15, and 19 in Chapter 1; Exercises 2, 5, and 7 in Chapter 2; and Exercises 3, 10, 15, 18, and 20 in Chapter 3. As you complete writing assignments for your composition course and other courses, keep adding to the journal, noting especially which procedures seem most helpful to you. Your aim is to discover your feelings about writing so that you can develop a dependable writing process of your own.

1b Discovering and limiting a subject

For most college, university, and business writing, you will write in response to an assignment. The assignment may specify your subject, or it may leave the choice to you. (If you're stuck, you can use the discovery techniques on pp. 32–40 to think of subjects.) Whether the subject is assigned or not, it will probably need some thought if it is to achieve these aims:

- The subject should be suitable for the assignment.
- It should be neither too general nor too limited for the length of paper and deadline assigned.
- It should be something you care about.

Pursuing your interests and experiences

Some assignments, such as a physics lab report or a business case study, leave you little room to express yourself. But even these assignments provide some leeway—for instance, in how you conduct and write your research. And many other subjects that may seem inflexible actually allow you considerable freedom. If you are assigned a comparison-and-contrast essay on two people you know, the choice of people and the way you compare them could make the difference for you between simply enduring the writing process or enjoying and learning from it.

When no subject is assigned, find one in your experiences, interests, or curiosities.

- What subject do you already know something about or have you been wondering about? Athletic scholarships? Unemployment in your town?
- Have you recently participated in a lively discussion about a controversial topic? About an event in your family's history? About a change in relations between men and women?
- What have you read or seen at the movies or on television? A shocking book? A violent or funny movie? An effective television commercial?
- What topic in the reading or class discussion for a course has intrigued you or seemed especially relevant to your own experiences? A social issue such as homelessness? A psychological problem such as depression?
- What makes you especially happy or especially angry? A hobby? The behaviour of your neighbours?
- Which of your own or others' dislikes and preferences would you like to understand better? A demand for gas-guzzling cars? A taste for raw fish?

Matching subject and assignment

When you receive an assignment, consider the following questions to guide your choice of subject:

- What's wanted from you? Many writing assignments contain words such as *describe, analyse, report, interpret, explain, define, argue,* or *evaluate*. These words specify the way you are to approach your subject, what kind of critical thinking is expected of you, and what your broad purpose is. (See the book's Introduction and pp. 26–27.)
- For whom are you writing? Some assignments will specify your readers, but usually you will have to figure out for yourself whether your audience is the general reading public, your classmates, your boss, the college or university community, your instructor, or some other group or individual. (For more on analyzing your audience, see pp. 28–31.)
- What kind of research is required? Sometimes an assignment specifies the kinds of sources you are expected to consult, and you can use such information to choose your subject. (If you are unsure whether research is required, check with your instructor.)
- What is the length of the paper? The deadline? Having a week to write three pages or three weeks to write six pages can make a big difference in the subject you select (see below).

3 Limiting the subject

Because most assignments leave some room for you to shape the subject, they are usually quite general. The same may be true of your first attempts to make the assigned subject your own or to invent a subject. The achievements of Sir John A. Macdonald, federal and provincial aid to college and university students, corporate support for the arts, summer jobs—all these cover broad areas that whole books might be written about. For a brief paper, you'd need a topic much narrower, much more specific, so that you could provide the facts, examples, and other details that make writing significant and interesting.

The following examples illustrate how broad subjects can be scaled down to one of several manageable **topics**—limited, specific essay subjects.

Broad subjects	Specific topics
Macdonald's achievements as prime minister	Macdonald as a nation builder Macdonald and the Canadian Pacific Railway Macdonald's National Policy
Summer jobs	Kinds of summer jobs for unskilled workers How to find a summer job What a summer job can teach

Federal and provincial aid to college and university students

Which students should be entitled to aid
Kinds of aid available to students
Why the government should (or should not) aid students

Here are some guidelines for narrowing subjects to topics:

- Again, pursue your interests, and consider what the assignment tells you about purpose, audience, sources, length, and deadline (see opposite).
- Break your subject into as many topics as you can think of. Make a list.
- For each topic that interests you and fits the assignment, roughly sketch out the main ideas and consider how many paragraphs or pages of specific facts, examples, and other details you would need to pin those ideas down. This thinking should give you at least a vague idea of how much work you'd have to do and how long the resulting paper might be.
- If an interesting and appropriate topic is still too broad, break it down further and repeat the previous step.

Don't be discouraged if the perfect topic does not leap into your head. You may find that you need to do some planning and writing, exploring different facets of the general subject and pursuing your specific interests, before you hit on the best topic. And the topic you select may require further narrowing or may shift subtly or even dramatically as you move through the writing process.

Exercise 2
Working with assignments

Following are some general writing assignments. Use the given information and your own interests to find specific topics for three of these assignments.

1. For a letter to the editor of the town newspaper, describe the effects of immigration on your community. Length: two pages. Deadline: unspecified.
2. For a course in environmental science, research and evaluate the government's policies for an environmental hazard. Length: five pages. Deadline: three weeks.
3. For a writing course, explain some aspect of campus employment. Length: three pages. Deadline: one week.
4. For the school newspaper, report on an issue in sports. Length: four pages. Deadline: two weeks.

5. For a course in sociology, research and analyse the dynamics of a particular group of people. Length: unspecified. Deadline: four weeks.
6. For a writing course, read and respond to an essay in a text you are using. Length: three pages. Deadline: two weeks.
7. For a government course, consider possible restrictions on legislators. Length: five pages. Deadline: two weeks.

Exercise 3
Considering your past work: Discovering and limiting a subject

Think of something you've recently written—perhaps a business report or a term paper. How did your subject evolve from beginning to end? In retrospect, was it appropriate for your writing situation? How, if at all, might it have been modified?

Exercise 4
Finding a topic for your essay

As the first step in developing a two- to three-page essay for your writing course, choose one of the topics you arrived at in Exercise 2 or some other topic you like. Use the guidelines in the previous section to come up with a topic that is suitably interesting, appropriate, and narrow.

1c Defining your purpose

As a writer, your **purpose** is your chief reason for communicating something about a topic to a particular audience. Purpose thus includes all three elements of the writing situation: you the writer, your topic, and your audience. It ties together both the specific context in which you are working and the goal you hope to achieve.

The purposes for writing

- To entertain readers
- To express your feelings or ideas
- To explain something to readers (exposition)
- To persuade readers to accept or act on your opinion (argument)

Most college, university, and business writing has the primary purpose of explaining or persuading.

- Writing that is mainly explanatory is often called **exposition** (from a Latin word meaning "to explain or set forth"). Almost any topic is suitable for exposition: how to pitch a knuckle ball, why you want to major in business, the implications of a new discovery in computer science, the interpretation of a short story, the causes of an economic slump. Exposition is the kind of writing encountered most often in newspapers, magazines, and textbooks.
- Writing that is primarily persuasive is often called **argument**. A newspaper editorial favouring city council reform, a business proposal for a new personnel policy, a student paper recommending more required courses or defending a theory about human psychological development—all these are arguments. (Chapter 4 discusses argument in some detail and provides illustrative essays.)

Often a writing assignment will specify or imply your purpose: when assigned a report on a physics experiment, for instance, you know the purpose is to explain; when assigned an editorial presenting a case for or against expanding your school's health facilities, you know the purpose is to persuade. If the assignment leaves your purpose up to you, then try to define it soon after you have your topic, to give yourself some direction. Don't despair if you aren't successful, though. Sometimes you may not discover your purpose until you begin drafting, or you may find that your initial sense of purpose changes as you move through the writing process.

Exercise 5
Finding purpose in assignments

For each of your narrowed topics in Exercise 2 (p. 25), suggest a likely purpose (entertainment, self-expression, explanation, persuasion).

Exercise 6
Considering your past work: Defining a purpose

Look over two or three things you've written in the past year or so. What was your purpose in each one? How did that purpose influence your writing? Did you achieve your purpose?

Exercise 7
Defining a purpose for your essay

To begin developing a brief essay of your own, select a topic that has particular interest for you. (The topic may come from your answers to Exercise 4, opposite.) Define a purpose for your essay.

1d Considering your audience

Who are your readers? Why are they reading your writing? What do they need and expect from you? These questions are central to the writing process and will crop up again and again, for (except in writing only for yourself) you are always trying to communicate something to readers.

Like purpose, audience is often specified or implied in a writing assignment. When you write an editorial for the student newspaper favouring expansion of the college or university health facilities, your audience is fellow students, who will be reading the paper for information of general and personal interest. When you write a report on a physics experiment, your audience is your physics instructor, who will be reading to evaluate your competence and see if you need help. If no particular audience is specified or implied, then, as with purpose, you are free to decide whom you want to address: your classmates? your boss and others at work? those who drive cars? Whatever the audience, it can help you decide what to say about your topic and how to say it.

1 Knowing what readers need

As a reader yourself, you know what readers need:

- *Context:* a link between what they read and their own knowledge and experiences.
- *Predictability:* an understanding of the writer's purpose and how it is being achieved.
- *Information:* the specific facts, examples, and other details that make the subject clear, concrete, interesting, and convincing.
- *Respect:* a sense that the writer respects their values and beliefs, their background, and their intelligence.
- *Voice:* a sense that the writer is a real person.
- *Clarity and correctness:* writing free of unnecessary stumbling blocks and mistakes.

For much academic and business writing, the needs and expectations of readers are specifically prescribed; thus Chapters 39, 40, and 42 discuss the special concerns of writing in various disciplines and in business. But even in these areas, you must make many choices based on audience. In other areas where the conventions of structure and presentation are vaguer, the choices are even more numerous. The box opposite contains questions that can help you define and make these choices.

Questions about audience

- Who *are* my readers?
- Why are readers going to read my writing? What will they expect?
- What do I want readers to know or do after reading my work, and how should I make that clear to them?
- What characteristic(s) of readers are relevant for my topic and purpose? For instance:

  Age or sex
  Occupation: students, professional colleagues, etc.
  Social or economic role: adult children, car buyers, potential employers, etc.
  Economic or educational background
  Ethnic background
  Political, religious, or moral beliefs and values
  Hobbies or activities
- How will the characteristic(s) of readers influence their attitudes toward my topic?
- What do readers already know and *not* know about my topic? How much do I have to tell them?
- If my topic involves specialized language, how much should I use and define?
- What ideas, arguments, or information might surprise readers? excite them? offend them? How should I handle these points?
- What misconceptions might readers have of my topic and/or my approach to the topic? How can I dispel these misconceptions?
- What is my relationship to my readers? What role and tone should I assume?
- What will readers do with my writing? Should I expect them to read every word from the top, to scan for information, to look for conclusions? Can I help with a summary, headings, or other aids?

Writing for a specific audience

Your sense of your audience will influence three key elements of what you write:

- The specific information you use to gain and keep the attention of readers and to guide them to accept your conclusions. This information may consist of concrete details, facts, examples, or any other evidence that makes your ideas clear, supports your assertions, and suits your readers' background, biases, and special interests.
- The role you choose to play in relation to your readers. Depending on your purpose and your attitude toward your

topic, you will want readers to perceive you and your attitude in a certain way. The possible roles are many and varied—for instance, portrait painter, storyteller, lecturer, guide, reporter, advocate, inspirer.

- The tone you use. **Tone** in writing is like tone of voice in speaking: words and sentence structures on the page convey some of the same information as pitch and volume in the voice. Your tone will say a lot about your attitude, whether forceful, calm, warm, irritated, or bored.

To see how these three elements may change for different audiences, consider the following two memos. Both are by a student who works part-time in a small company and wants to get the company to conserve paper. The first is addressed to his fellow clerical workers, the second to the managers of the company.

> Ever notice how much paper collects in your trash basket every day? Well, most of it can be recycled with little effort, I promise. Basically, all you need to do is set a bag or box near your desk and deposit wastepaper in it. I know, space is cramped in these little cubicles. But what's a little more crowding when the earth's at stake? . . .

Information: how employees could handle recycling; no mention of costs

Role: cheerful, equally harried colleague

Tone: informal, personal (*Ever notice; you; what's; Well; I know, space is cramped*)

> In my four months here, I have observed that all of us throw out baskets of potentially recyclable paper every day. Considering the drain on our forest resources and the pressure on landfills that paper causes, we could make a valuable contribution to the environmental movement by helping to recycle the paper we use. At the company where I worked before, the employees separate clean wastepaper from other trash at their desks. The maintenance staff collects trash in two receptacles, and the trash hauler (the same one we use here) makes separate pickups. I do not know what the hauler charges for handling recyclable material. . . .

Information: specific reasons; view of company as a whole; reference to another company; problem of cost

Role: serious, thoughtful, responsible employee

Tone: formal, serious (*Considering the drain; forest resources; valuable contribution;* no *you* or contractions)

Typically for business reports and memos, the information grows more specific and the tone more formal as the rank and number of readers rises.

Of course, much of your college or university writing may have only one reader besides you: the instructor of the course you are writing for. In a composition course your instructor is likely to read your work as a representative of a general audience and respond to it in the additional role of helpful critic (see p. 70). That means you should not assume specialized interest in or knowledge of your topic, nor should you expect the patience of a doting parent who fills in what his or her child can't (or won't) express. If something about your topic would need to be said to a classmate or a reader of your local newspaper, say it clearly and carefully.

In academic courses such as literature, psychology, management, and chemistry, your writing will be addressed to a specialized audience of practitioners of the discipline, represented by your instructor. If you are writing a paper on the economic background of the War of 1812 for a Canadian history course, you may assume your instructor's familiarity with the key events, players, and published interpretations. Your job is to show your own command of them and their relevance to your topic while assuming an appropriate academic role and tone.

- Present yourself as a serious and competent student of the subject you are writing in.
- Demonstrate that you have at least a basic understanding of the discipline's research methods, vocabulary, and principles.
- Be specific.
- Write clearly and concisely.
- Avoid undue informality.

These requirements allow considerable room for your own voice, as these two passages on the same topic prove:

> One technique for heightening the emotional appeal of advertisements is "colour engineering." Adding colour to a product or the surrounding advertisement can increase sales despite the fact that the colour serves no practical purpose. For example, until the 1920s fountain pens were made of hard black rubber. When colourful pens were suddenly introduced, sales rose dramatically.

> "Colour engineering" can intensify the emotional appeal of advertisements. New colour in a product or the surrounding ad can boost sales even when the colour serves no other use. In the 1920s, for example, fountain pens that had been hard black rubber suddenly became colourful, and sales shot up.

As you gain experience with academic writing, you will develop the flexibility to write in your voice while also respecting the conventions of the various disciplines.

Exercise 8
Considering audience

Choose one of the following topics and, for each audience specified, ask the questions on page 29. Decide on four points you would make, the role you would assume, and the tone you would adopt for each audience. Then write a paragraph for each based on your decisions.

1. The effects of smoking: for elementary school students and for adult smokers
2. Your opinion of welfare: for someone who is on welfare and for someone who is not and who opposes it
3. Why your neighbours should remove the wrecked truck from their yard: for your neighbours and for your town zoning board

Exercise 9
Considering your past work: Writing for a specific audience

How did audience figure in a piece of writing you've done in the recent past—perhaps a paper for a course? Who were your readers? How did your awareness of them influence your choice of information, your role, and your tone? At what point in the writing process did you find it most productive to consider your readers consciously?

Exercise 10
Analysing the audience for your essay

Use the questions on page 29 to determine as much as you can about the probable readers of your essay-in-progress (see Exercise 7). What does your analysis reveal about the specific information your readers need? What role do you want to assume, and what tone will best convey your attitude toward your topic?

1e Developing your topic

To develop your topic means to generate the ideas and information that will help you achieve your purpose. Sometimes ideas will tumble forth on paper, especially if your topic is very familiar or personal. But when they do not, you shouldn't wait around for inspiration to strike. Instead, use a technique for freeing ideas. Anything that gets your mind working is appropriate: if you like to make drawings or take pictures, for instance, then try it.

The following pages describe some strategies for generating ideas. These strategies are to be selected from, not followed in sequence: some may help you during early stages of the writing process, even before you're sure of your topic; others may help you later on; and one or two may not help at all. Experiment to discover which strategies work best for you. *Whatever strategy or strategies you use, do your work in writing, not just in your head.* Your work will be retrievable, and the act of writing will help you concentrate and lead you to fresh, sometimes surprising, insights.

Techniques for developing a topic

- Keep a journal (1e-1).
- Observe your surroundings (1e-2).
- Freewrite (1e-3).
- Make a list or brainstorm (1e-4).
- Cluster (1e-5).
- Read (1e-6).
- Ask the journalist's questions (1e-7).
- Use the patterns of development (1e-8).
- Think critically (1e-9).

Keeping a journal

A place to record thoughts and observations, a **journal** can be a good source of ideas for writing. It is a kind of diary, but one more concerned with ideas than with day-to-day events. *Journal* comes from the Latin for "daily," and many journal keepers do write faithfully every day; others make entries less regularly, when the mood strikes or an insight occurs or they have a problem to work out.

A journal gives you a place to record your reactions to movies, books, television, and concerts. It gives you an outlet when you need some relief from the pressures of family, friends, studies, and work. It gives you a private place to confide your dreams. Journal keepers often become dependent on the process for the writing practice it gives them and the concentrated thought it encourages. Usually for the same reasons, teachers of writing and other subjects sometimes require students to keep journals.

The following passage comes from the journal of a student, Sandra Lee, whose writing process we follow in this chapter and the next. (The notebook in the margin signals stages in Lee's writing.) Lee was responding to the day's events.

> At school, everyone wanted to be the same as everyone else, yet also different. You wanted to fit in to a group—dress the same, talk the same, listen to the same music. But you also wanted to be your own self, not like anybody else. Maybe things are always like that for everyone. And maybe that is not such a bad thing, especially in a country like this where there are so many groups.

If you write in a journal every day, even for just a few minutes, the routine will loosen up your writing muscles and improve your confidence. And the writing you produce can supply ideas when you are seeking an essay topic or developing an essay. With your assignment or topic in mind, scan your journal entries for relevant ideas. A thought you recorded months ago about a chemistry lab may provide direction for a research paper. Two entries about arguments with your brother may suggest what you need to anchor a psychology paper on sibling relations.

Observing your surroundings

Sometimes you can find a good subject or good ideas by looking around you, not in the half-conscious way most of us move from place to place in our daily lives but deliberately, all senses alert. On a bus, for instance, are there certain types of passengers? What seems to be on the driver's mind? On campus, which buildings stand out? Are bicyclists and pedestrians at peace with each other?

To get the most from observation, you should have a tablet and pen or pencil handy for notes and sketches. If you have a camera, you may find that the lens sees things your unaided eyes do not notice. (When observing or photographing people, though, keep some distance, take photographs quickly, and avoid staring. Otherwise, your subjects will feel uneasy.) Back at your desk, study your notes, sketches, or photographs for oddities or patterns that you'd like to explore further.

Freewriting

Another way to find a subject is to write your way into it: write without stopping for a certain amount of time (say, ten minutes) or to a certain length (say, one page). The goal of this **freewriting** is to generate ideas and information from *within* yourself by going around the part of your mind that doesn't want to write or can't think of anything to write. You let words themselves suggest other words. *What* you write is not important; that you *keep* writing is. Don't stop, even if that means repeating the same words until new words come. Don't go back to reread, don't censor ideas that seem dumb or repetitious, and above all don't stop to edit: grammar, punctuation, spelling, and the like are irrelevant at this stage.

In the physical act of freewriting, you may gain access to ideas you were unaware of. For example, the following freewriting by a student, Robert Benday, gave him the subject of writing as a disguise.

> Write to write. Seems pretty obvious, also weird. What to gain by writing? never anything before. Writing seems always—always— Getting corrected for trying too hard to please the teacher, getting corrected for not trying hard enuf. Frustration, nail biting, sometimes getting carried away making sentences to tell stories, not even true stories, *esp.* not true stories, *that* feels like creating some-

thing. Writing just pulls the story out of me. The story lets me be someone else, gives me a disguise.

(A later phase of Benday's writing appears on p. 37.)

Focused freewriting is more concentrated: you start with your topic and write about it without stopping for, say, fifteen minutes or one full page. As in all freewriting, you push to bypass mental blocks and self-consciousness, not debating what to say or editing what you've written. With focused freewriting, though, you let the physical act of writing take you into and around your subject.

An example of focused freewriting can be found in the work of Sandra Lee, whose journal entry appears on page 33. In a writing course, Lee and her classmates read and discussed an unsigned editorial titled "Multicultural Realities" in their local newspaper. The editorial argued that the multicultural nature of Canadian society "pressures people to be the same and to be different" and that this double pressure was eroding the Canadian mosaic. Their instructor gave them the following assignment:

> Respond to the editorial with a limited and well-supported argument of your own about multiculturalism in Canada. Your paper should be 500–700 words. The first draft is due Friday for discussion in class.

Lee disagreed with the editorialist's position, but she knew that merely saying so was not much of an argument. She recalled that she had written about these kinds of pressures in her journal, and this thought prompted the following freewriting.

> Two pressures on all Canadians—to be the same and to be different. Bad and good things in both. Same: all being forced to be the same is bad, assimilation, it's called. While shared values and a common language, English or French, are good things. Different: conflict between cultures is bad—everyone in own little world or ghetto—while many cultures together is great. To be purely the same or different is the problem. There has to be a way to combine the positive of both pressures.

With this freewriting, Lee discovered some interesting complexity in her topic, something she could craft into an argument: when isolated the pressures to be the same and to be different can be negative, when combined they can create something much more positive.

Making a list

Like focused freewriting, list making requires opening yourself to everything that seems even remotely connected to your topic, without concern for order or repetition or form of expression. You can let your topic percolate for a day or more, recording thoughts on it whenever they occur. (For this approach to work, you need to keep a notebook and pen or pencil with you at all times.) Or, in a method more akin to freewriting, you can **brainstorm** about the topic—that is, focus intently on the topic for a fixed amount of time (say, fifteen minutes), pushing yourself to list every idea and detail that comes to mind.

Like freewriting, brainstorming requires turning off your internal editor so that you keep moving ahead instead of looping back over what you have already written to correct it. It makes no difference whether the ideas and details are expressed in phrases or complete sentences. It makes no difference if they seem silly or irrelevant. Just keep pushing.

Here is an example of brainstorming by a student, Johanna Abrams, on what a summer job can teach:

summer work teaches—

how to look busy while doing nothing
how to avoid the sun in summer
seriously: discipline, budgeting money, value of money

which job? Tim Horton's cashier? baby sitter? mail-room clerk?
mail room: how to sort mail into boxes: this is learning??
how to survive getting fired—humiliation, outrage
Mrs. King! the mail-room queen as learning experience
the shock of getting fired: what to tell parents, friends?
Mrs. K was so rigid—dumb procedures
Mrs. K's anger, resentment: the disadvantages of being smarter than your boss
The odd thing about working in an office: a world with its own rules for how to act
what Mr. D said about the pecking order—big chick (Mrs. K) pecks on little chick (me)
probably lots of Mrs. Ks in offices all over—offices are all barnyards
Mrs. K a sad person, really—just trying to hold on to her job, preserve her self-esteem
a job can beat you down—destroy self-esteem, make you desperate enough to be mean to other people
how to preserve/gain self-esteem from work??
if I'd known about the pecking order, I would have been less show-offy, not so arrogant

(A later phase of Abrams's writing appears on p. 48.)

 5 Clustering

Like freewriting and list making, **clustering** also draws on free association and rapid, unedited work. But it also emphasizes the *relations* between ideas by combining writing and nonlinear drawing. When clustering, you radiate outward from a centre point—your topic. When an idea occurs, you pursue related ideas in a branching structure until they seem exhausted. Then you do the same with other ideas, staying open to connections, continuously branching out or drawing arrows.

The example of clustering below shows how Robert Benday used the technique for ten minutes to expand on the topic of creative writing as a means of disguise, an idea he arrived at through freewriting (see pp. 34–35). Though he ventured into several dead ends, Benday also came to the interesting possibility (at the bottom) that the fiction writer is like a god who forgives himself by creating characters that represent his good and bad qualities.

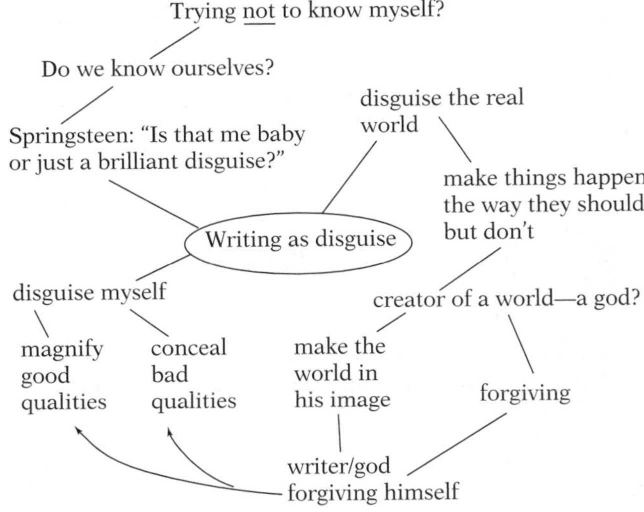

 Reading

Many assignments require reading. To respond to the editorial on multiculturalism, for instance, Sandra Lee had to digest the editorialist's argument. And essays on literary works as well as research papers demand reading. But even when reading is not required by an assignment, it can help you locate or develop your topic by introducing you to ideas you didn't know or expanding on what you do know. (See pp. 510–36 for techniques of library research that you can use to locate readings on a topic.)

People often read passively, absorbing content like blotters, not interacting with it. To read for ideas, you need to be more active, probing text and illustrations with your mind, nurturing any sparks they set off. Read with a pen or pencil in your hand and (unless the material is yours to mark up) with a pad of paper by your side. Then you will be able to keep notes on what you read and—more important—on what the reading makes you *think*. If you haven't done so already, consult this book's Introduction, which discusses the process of active reading in some detail.

NOTE Whenever you use the information or ideas of others in your writing, you must acknowledge your sources in order to avoid the serious offence of plagiarism. (See p. 555.)

Using the journalist's questions

Asking yourself a set of questions about your topic—and writing out the answers—can help you look at the topic objectively and see fresh possibilities in it. Asking questions can also provide some structure to the development of ideas.

One such set of questions is that posed by a journalist with a story to report:

Who was involved?
What happened and what were the results?
When did it happen?
Where did it happen?
Why did it happen?
How did it happen?

These questions can also be useful in probing an essay topic, especially if you are telling a story or examining causes and effects. (See also the following section.)

Using the patterns of development

The **patterns of development**—such as narration, definition, and comparison and contrast—are ways we think about and understand a vast range of subjects, from our own daily experiences to the most complex scientific theories. They also serve as strategies for writing about these subjects. Asking questions based on the patterns can help you view your topic from many angles. Not all these questions will be productive, but at least a few should open up new possibilities.

How did it happen?

In **narration** you develop the topic as a story, with important events usually arranged chronologically (as they occurred in time): for instance, an exciting basketball game or the steps leading to a war.

How does it look, sound, feel, smell, taste?

In **description** you use sensory details to give a clear impression of a person, place, thing, or feeling, such as a friend, a favourite room, a building, or an experience.

What are examples of it or reasons for it?

The pattern of **illustration** or **support** suggests development with one or more examples of the topic (one couple's efforts to adopt a child, say, or three television soap operas) or with the reasons for believing or doing something (three reasons for majoring in English, four reasons for driving defensively).

What is it? What does it encompass, and what does it exclude?

These questions lead to **definition:** specifying what the topic is and is not to give a precise sense of its meaning. Abstract terms—such as *justice, friendship,* and *art*—especially need defining. (See p. 454.)

What are its parts or characteristics?

Using the pattern of **division** or **analysis,** you separate a subject into its elements and examine the relations between elements. The first step in critical thinking, analysis is also discussed on the next page.

What groups or categories can it be sorted into?

Classification involves separating a large group (such as cars) into smaller groups (subcompact, compact, and so on) based on the characteristics of the individual items (the sizes of the cars). Another example: academic, business, personal, literary, and other types of writing.

How is it like, or different from, other things?

With **comparison and contrast,** you point out the similarities and differences between ideas, objects, people, places, and so on: the differences between two similar computer systems, for instance, or the similarities between two opposing political candidates.

Is it comparable to something that is in a different class but more familiar to readers?

This question leads to **analogy,** an extended comparison of unlike subjects. Analogy is often used to explain a topic that may be unfamiliar to readers (for instance, the structure of a government) by reference to a familiar topic (the structure of a family).

Why did it happen, or what results did it have?

With **cause-and-effect analysis,** you explain why something happened or what its consequences were or will be, or both: the causes of cerebral palsy, the effects of a Supreme Court decision, the causes *and* effects of a gradual change in the climate.

How do you do it, or how does it work?

In **process analysis** you explain how the topic is accomplished (how to write an essay) or how it happens (how a plant grows, how a robot works).

As you will see later, the patterns of development also provide a means of introducing information in paragraphs (pp. 94–104, with paragraph-length examples). Further discussion of how the patterns may combine in an essay appears on pages 112–15.

Thinking critically

Like the other strategies discussed in this section, the method of critical thinking, explained in the Introduction to this book (pp. 1–18), can help you produce creative ideas about your topic because it leads you to see what is not obvious. Unlike some of the other strategies, though, critical thinking can also lead you systematically to conclusions about the topic.

Sandra Lee, writing about multiculturalism in Canada, used the operations of critical thinking to explore her topic.

- **Analysis:** What are the subject's elements or characteristics? Lee broke down the pressures of multiculturalism into their negative and positive elements.
- **Interpretation:** Lee then worked out both the significance of these elements and the meaning of these elements in particular instances.
- **Synthesis:** How do the elements relate to each other, or how does this subject relate to another one? Lee worked out how the positive elements could be combined or synthesized to provide a much more positive vision of multicultural possibilities.
- **Evaluation:** What is the value or significance of the subject? Lee concluded that a clearer understanding of multicultural possibilities was essential for understanding the meaning and local life of multiculturalism.

Exercise 11

Considering your past work: Developing a topic

In the past how have you generated the ideas for writing? Have you used any of the techniques described on the preceding pages (perhaps not called by the same names)? Have you found the process of generating ideas to be especially enjoyable or difficult? If some writing tasks have been easier than others, what do you think made the difference?

Exercise 12
Using freewriting, brainstorming, or clustering

If you haven't tried any of them before, experiment with freewriting (p. 34), brainstorming (p. 35), or clustering (p. 36). Continue with the topic you selected in Exercise 4 (p. 26), or begin with a new topic. Write or draw for at least ten minutes without stopping to reread and edit. When you finish, examine what you have written for ideas and relationships that could help you develop the topic. What do you think of the technique you tried? Did one or another help you loosen up and generate ideas?

Exercise 13
Developing your topic

Use at least two of the discovery techniques discussed on the preceding pages to develop the topic you selected in Exercise 4 (p. 26). (If you completed Exercise 12, then use one additional technique.) Later exercises for your essay-in-progress will be based on the ideas you generate in this exercise.

1f Developing your thesis

Your readers will expect an essay you write to be focused on a central idea, or **thesis,** to which all the essay's paragraphs, all its general statements and specific information, relate. The thesis is the controlling idea, the main point.

The thesis will not usually leap fully formed into your head. Even when you begin with an idea you want to communicate, you will need to refine that idea to fit the realities of the paper you write. And often you will have to write and rewrite before a central, controlling idea emerges. Still, it's wise to try to pin down your thesis when you have a fairly good stock of ideas. Then it can help you start drafting, help keep you focused, and serve as a point of reference when changes inevitably occur.

1 Conceiving your thesis sentence

A good way to develop your thesis is to frame it in a **thesis sentence.** The thesis sentence gives you a vehicle for expressing your thesis at an early stage, and eventually it or (more likely) a revised version may be placed in the introduction of your final essay as a signal to your readers.

As an expression of the thesis, the thesis sentence serves two crucial functions and one optional one:

Functions of the thesis sentence

- It narrows the topic to a single idea that you want readers to gain from your essay.
- It names the topic and asserts something about it, conveying your purpose, your opinion, and your attitude.
- It often provides a concise preview of how you will arrange your ideas in the essay.

Here are some examples of topics and corresponding thesis sentences:

Topic	Thesis sentence
The pecking order in an office	Two months working in a large government agency taught me that an office's pecking order should be respected.
Why there should be a policy of universal accessibility to Canadian universities and colleges	If Canada hopes to compete economically among the industrialized nations, post-secondary education must be accessible for any student who qualifies academically.
The effects of strip-mining	Strip-mining should be tightly controlled in this region to reduce its pollution of water resources, its permanent destruction of the land, and its devastating effects on people's lives.
My city neighbourhood	The main street of my neighbourhood contains enough variety to make almost any city dweller feel at home.
Macdonald's National Policy	Macdonald introduced the National Policy of tariffs in 1879 to protect Canadian manufacturing interests, primarily against American imports.
The dynamics of single-parent families	In families consisting of a single parent and a single child, the boundaries between parent and child often disappear so that the two interact as siblings or as a married couple.

What public relations is	Although most of us are unaware of the public relations campaigns directed at us, they can significantly affect the way we think and live.

2 Writing and revising your thesis sentence

To draft a thesis sentence, ask these questions:

- What central idea emerges from the work I have done so far?
- How can I frame that idea as an assertion about my topic?
- How can I convey my purpose and attitude in that assertion?

Answering these questions in a sentence can take more than one attempt, sometimes over one or more drafts of the essay.

Sandra Lee went through a common procedure in writing and revising her thesis sentence on multiculturalism in Canada. First she turned her topic into an assertion, a statement about the topic.

> Multiculturalism is not about being purely the same or different.

This sentence focused on Lee's topic but did not specify what the pressures to be the same or different really are. Nor did it convey Lee's attitude to the topic, what she saw as the meaning of multiculturalism. Realizing this, Lee rewrote the sentence.

> The meaning of multiculturalism is not to be found in assimilation or ghettos.

In this sentence, Lee articulated the negative pressures more concretely but did not balance them with the positive aspects of multiculturalism, aspects that Lee, in fact, wanted to emphasize. She rewrote the sentence adding those positive aspects.

> The meaning of multiculturalism is not to be found in assimilation or ghettos but in the mixing of shared values and cultural diversity.

With this sentence, Lee succeeded in stating her topic succinctly and specifically, while also conveying her attitude and purpose. The focus of the sentence is on the *mixing* of positive pressures that was the origin of her essay. In the structure of the sentence, Lee also forecast or predicted the general organization of her essay.

When you are writing and revising your thesis sentence, check it against the following questions.

Checklist for revising the thesis sentence

- Does it make an *assertion* about your topic?
- Does it convey your *purpose,* your *opinion,* and your *attitude?*
- Is it *limited* to an assertion of only one idea?
- Is the assertion *specific?*
- Is the sentence *unified* so that the parts relate to each other?

Here are other examples of thesis sentences revised to meet these requirements:

Faulty original	Revised
This new product brought in over $300 000 last year. [A statement of fact, not an assertion: what is significant about the product's success?]	This new product succeeded because of its innovative marketing campaign.
People should not go on fad diets. [A vague statement that needs limiting with one or more reasons: what's wrong with fad diets?]	Fad diets can be dangerous when they deprive the body of essential nutrients or rely on excessive quantities of potentially harmful foods.
Televised sports are different from live sports. [A general statement that needs to be made more specific: how are they different, and why is the difference significant?]	Although television cannot transmit all the excitement of being in a crowd during a game, its close-ups and slow-motion replays more than compensate.
Seat belts can save lives, but now car makers are installing air bags. [Not unified: how do the two parts of the sentence relate to each other?]	If drivers more often used life-saving seat belts, car makers might not need to install air bags.

Exercise 14
Evaluating thesis sentences

Evaluate the following thesis sentences, considering whether each one is sufficiently limited, specific, and unified. Rewrite the sentences as necessary to meet these goals.

1. Aggression usually leads to violence, injury, and even death, and we should use it constructively.
2. Gun control is essential.

3. One evening of a radio talk show amply illustrates both the appeal of such shows and their silliness.
4. Good manners make our society work.
5. The poem is about motherhood.
6. City people are different from country people.
7. Television is a useful baby sitter and an escape for people who do not want to think about their own problems.
8. I liked history in high school, but not in university.
9. We are encouraged to choose a career in high school, but people change jobs frequently.
10. Drunken drivers, whose perception, coordination, and reaction time are impaired, should receive mandatory suspensions of their licences.

Exercise 15
Considering your past work: Developing a thesis

Have you been aware in the past of focusing your essays and other writing on a central idea or thesis? Have you found it more efficient generally to try to pin down your idea early or to let it evolve during drafting? To what extent has a thesis helped or hindered you in shaping your draft?

Exercise 16
Drafting and revising your own thesis sentence

Continuing from Exercise 13 (p. 41), write a limited, specific, and unified thesis sentence for your essay-in-progress.

1g Organizing your ideas

An effective essay has a recognizable shape—an arrangement of parts that guides readers, helping them see how ideas and details relate to each other and contribute to the whole. You may sometimes let an effective organization emerge over one or more drafts. But many writers find that organizing ideas to some extent before drafting can provide a helpful sense of direction, as a map can help a driver negotiate a half-familiar system of roads. If you feel uncertain about the course your essay should follow or have a complicated topic with many parts, devising a shape for your material can clarify your options.

Before you begin organizing your material, look over all the writing you've done so far—freewriting, notes from reading, lists, whatever. Pull together a master list of all the ideas and details you think you may want to include, leaving blank margins for further notes, connecting arrows, and other additions that will occur to you as you think about shape.

Distinguishing the general and the specific

To organize material for an essay, you need to distinguish general and specific ideas and see the relations between ideas. **General** and **specific** refer to the number of instances or objects included in a group signified by a word. The following "ladder" illustrates a general-to-specific hierarchy.

MOST GENERAL

↑ life form
plant
flowering plant
rose
John Cabot rose
↓ Uncle Dan's prize-winning John Cabot rose

MOST SPECIFIC

Here are some tips for arranging your ideas:

- Underline or circle the most general ideas. (Your thesis sentence may help you identify your most important points.) Then connect each general idea by arrows to the specific ideas and details that support it.
- If the preceding technique proves too messy, start over with a fresh sheet of paper. Write each general idea down with space beneath it, and add specific information in the appropriate spaces.
- As you sort ideas, respect their meanings. Otherwise, your hierarchies could become jumbled, with *rose* illogically subordinated to *animal*, or *life form* somehow subordinated to *rose*.
- Once you have sorted out general ideas and specific supporting information, delete information that has no place, or fill in holes where support is skimpy.

Choosing an organizing tool

Some writers view outlines as chores and straitjackets, but they need not be dull or confining. There are many different kinds of outlines, some more flexible than others. All of them can enlarge and clarify your thinking, showing you patterns of general and specific, suggesting proportions, highlighting gaps or overlaps in coverage.

Many writers use outlines for another purpose as well—to check the underlying structure of a draft when revising it (see p. 59). No matter when it's made, though, an outline can change to reflect changes in your thinking. You should view any outline you make as a tentative sketch, not as a fixed paint-by-numbers diagram.

Using a scratch or informal outline

For many essays, especially those with a fairly straightforward structure, a simple listing of ideas and perhaps their support may provide adequate direction for your writing. A **scratch outline** lists the key points of the paper in the order they will be covered.

Here is Sandra Lee's scratch outline for her essay on multiculturalism in Canada.

THESIS SENTENCE

The meaning of multiculturalism is not to be found in assimilation or ghettos but in the mixing of shared values and cultural diversity.

SCRATCH OUTLINE

Pressures to be same and different—
  Same
    —assimilation—example
    —shared values—example
  Different
    —ghettos: pressure from without and within
    —cultural diversity: mixing identities

Lee put more into this outline than its simplicity might indicate. She worked out the order in which she would cover the pressures and the meaning of multiculturalism. Under the two types of pressure, she placed first the negative and then the positive aspects and examples. Lee might have begun drafting from this outline, but she opted to expand it first into a detailed formal outline (see p.49).

An **informal outline** is usually more detailed than a scratch outline, including key general points and the specific evidence for them. Here is a student's informal outline:

THESIS SENTENCE

The main street of my neighbourhood contains enough variety to make almost any city dweller feel at home.

INFORMAL OUTLINE

The beginning of the street
  high-rise condominium occupied by well-to-do people
  ground floor of building: an art gallery
  across the street: a delicatessen
  above the delicatessen: a tailor's shop, a camera-repair shop, a lawyer's office
The middle of the street
  four-storey brick apartment buildings on both sides
  at ground level: an Italian bakery and a Greek taverna
  people sitting on steps
  children playing

The end of the street
 a halfway house for drug addicts
 a boarding house for retired men
 a discount drugstore
 an expensive department store
 a beer store
 another high-rise condominium

Using a tree diagram

In a **tree diagram,** ideas and details branch out in increasing specificity. Like any outline, the diagram can warn of gaps, overlaps, and digressions. But unlike more linear outlines, it can be supplemented and extended indefinitely, so it is easy to alter for new ideas and arrangements discovered during drafting and revision.

Following is Johanna Abrams's tree diagram, based on her earlier list of ideas on a summer job (p. 36). Each main part of the four-part diagram represents a different general idea about the summer-job experience. Within each part, information grows more specific as it branches downward.

THESIS SENTENCE

Two months working in a large government agency taught me that an office's pecking order should be respected.

TREE DIAGRAM

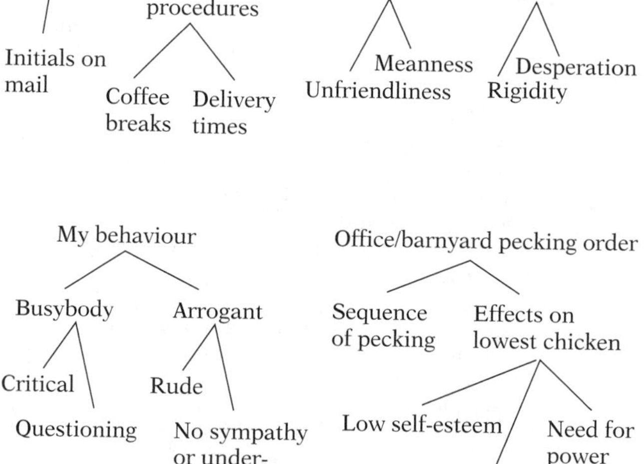

Using a formal outline

For complex topics requiring complex arrangements of ideas and support, you may want or be required to construct a **formal outline.** More rigidly arranged and more detailed than other outlines, a formal outline not only lays out main ideas and their support but also shows the relative importance of all the essay's elements and how they connect with each other.

NOTE Because of its structure, a formal outline can be an excellent tool for checking a draft before revising it. See page 59.

On the basis of her scratch outline (p. 47), Sandra Lee prepared this formal outline for her essay on multiculturalism in Canada.

THESIS SENTENCE

The meaning of multiculturalism is not to be found in assimilation or ghettos but in the mixing of shared values and cultural diversity.

FORMAL OUTLINE

I. Pressure to be the same
  A. Assimilation
    1. Pressure on recent immigrants
    2. Command for sameness
    3. Melting pot of compulsory assimilation
  B. Shared values
    1. Respect for law and order
    2. Debate over Mountie uniform and turban
II. Pressure to be different
  A. Ethnic ghettos
    1. Pressure of established communities
    2. Command for difference
    3. Fracturing mosaic of ethnic difference
  B. Cultural diversity
    1. Keeping cultural identities
    2. Mixing identities
    3. Bonding through common language and political framework

Lee's outline illustrates several principles of outlining that can help ensure completeness, balance, and clear relationships. (These principles largely depend on distinguishing between the general and the specific. See p. 46.)

- All the outline's parts are systematically indented and labelled: Roman numerals (I, II) for primary divisions of the essay; indented capital letters (A, B) for secondary divisions; further indented Arabic numerals (1, 2) for principal supporting examples. A level of detail below the Arabic numbers would be indented further still and labelled with small letters (a, b). Each succeeding level contains more specific information than the one before it.

Principles of the formal outline

- Labels and indentions indicate order and relative importance.
- Sections and subsections reflect logical relationships.
- Topics of equal generality appear in parallel headings.
- Each subdivision has at least two parts.
- Headings are expressed in parallel grammatical form.
- The introduction and conclusion may be omitted (though not, of course, from the essay).

- The outline divides the material into several groups. An uninterrupted listing of ideas like the one following would indicate a need for tighter, more logical relationships among ideas. (Compare this example with part II of Lee's actual outline.)

  II. Pressure to be different
      A. Pressure of established communities
      B. Command for difference
      C. Fracturing mosaic of ethnic difference
      D. Keeping cultural identities
      E. Mixing identities
      F. Bonding through common language and political framework

- Within each part of the outline, distinct topics of equal generality appear in parallel headings (with the same indention and numbering or lettering). In the following example, points C and D are more specific than point B, not equally general, so they should be subheadings 1 and 2 under it. (See section IB of Lee's outline.)

  B. Shared values
  C. Respect for law and order
  D. Debate over Mountie uniform and turban

- All subdivided headings in the outline break into at least two parts because a topic cannot logically be divided into only one part. The following example violates this principle.

  B. Shared values: respect for law and order
      1. Debate over Mountie uniform and turban

  Any single subdivision should be matched with another subdivision (as in part IB of Lee's outline), combined with the heading above it, or rechecked for its relevance to the heading above it.
- All headings are expressed in parallel grammatical form. Lee's is a topic outline, in which each heading consists of a noun plus modifiers. In a sentence outline, all headings are expressed as full sentences, as in this rewrite of section IB of Lee's outline.

B. The positive pressure comes from our shared values.
   1. We all have respect for law and order.
   2. The Mountie uniform and turban debate was about shared values.

- The outline covers only the body of the essay, omitting the introduction and the conclusion (see below, 1g-3). The beginning and the ending are important in the essay itself, but you need not include them in the outline unless you are required to do so or anticipate special problems with their organization.

Choosing a structure

Most essays share a basic shape consisting of an introduction, a body, and a conclusion.

- The **introduction** draws readers into the world of the essay, stating the topic and often the thesis sentence. It makes a commitment that the rest of the essay delivers on. (See pp. 106–09.)
- The **conclusion** generally gives readers something to take away from the essay—a summary of ideas, for instance, or a suggested course of action. (See pp. 109–10.)
- The **body** of the essay is its centre, the part offering ideas and supporting details, examples, and reasons to develop the thesis and thus fulfil the commitment of the introduction. In an essay of two or three pages, the body may contain three to five substantial paragraphs, each presenting and supporting a part of the thesis.

In almost any writing situation, at least one of the schemes listed below will be appropriate for organizing the body of your essay. These schemes are so familiar that readers expect them and look for them. Thus the schemes both help you arrange your material and help readers follow you.

Schemes for organizing ideas in an essay

- Space
- Time
- Emphasis

  General to specific
  Specific to general
  Increasing importance (climactic)
  Decreasing familiarity
  Increasing complexity

Organizing by space or time

Two organizational schemes—spatial and chronological—grow naturally out of the topic. A **spatial organization** is especially appropriate for essays that describe a place, an object, or a person. Following the way people normally survey something, you move through space from a chosen starting point to other features of the subject. Describing a friend, for instance, you might begin with his shoes and move upward or begin with his face and move downward. The informal outline on pages 47–48 illustrates a spatial organization, moving from one end of the street to the other.

A **chronological organization** reports events as they occurred in time, usually from first to last. This pattern, like spatial organization, corresponds to readers' own experiences and expectations. It suits essays in which you recount a sequence of events, explain a process from beginning to end (for instance, how to run a marathon), or tell a personal story. A chronological organization structures the essay on pages 73–74.

Organizing for emphasis

Some organizational schemes must be imposed on ideas and information to aid readers' understanding and achieve a desired emphasis. Two of these depend on the distinction between the general and the specific, discussed on page 46. The **general-to-specific scheme** is common in expository and argumentative essays that start with a general discussion of the main points and then proceed to specific examples, facts, or other evidence. The following thesis sentence forecasts a general-to-specific organization:

> If it hopes to compete in the global economy, Canada must make higher education possible for any student who qualifies academically.

The body of the essay might first elaborate on the basic argument and then provide the supporting data.

In some expository or argumentative essays, a **specific-to-general scheme** can arouse readers' interest in specific examples or other evidence, letting the evidence build to more general ideas. The following thesis sentence could be developed in this way.

> Although most of us are unaware of the public relations campaigns directed at us, they can significantly affect the way we think and live.

The writer might devote most of the essay to a single specific example of a public relations campaign and then explain more generally how the example typifies public relations campaigns.

In a **climactic organization,** ideas unfold in order of increasing drama or importance to a climax. For example, the following thesis sentence lists three effects of strip-mining in order of their increasing severity, and the essay would cover them in the same order.

> Strip-mining should be tightly controlled in this region to reduce its pollution of water resources, its permanent destruction of the land, and its devastating effects on people's lives.

As this example suggests, the climactic organization works well in arguments because it leaves readers with the most important point freshest in their minds. In exposition, such an arrangement can create suspense and thus hold readers' attention.

Expository essays can also be arranged in variations of the climactic pattern. An essay on the effects of air pollution might proceed from **most familiar to least familiar**—from effects readers are likely to know to ones they may not know. Similarly, an essay on various computer languages might proceed from **simplest to most complex,** so that the explanation of each language provides a basis for readers to understand the more difficult one following.

4 Checking for unity and coherence

In conceiving your organization and writing your essay, you should be aware of two qualities of effective writing that relate to organization: unity and coherence. When you perceive that someone's writing "flows well," you are probably appreciating these two qualities. An essay has **unity** if all its parts relate to and support the thesis sentence. Check for unity with these questions:

- Is each main section relevant to the main idea (thesis) of the essay?
- Within main sections of the outline, does each example or detail support the principal idea of that section?

An essay has **coherence** if readers can see the relations among parts and move easily from one thought to the next. Check for coherence with these questions:

- Do the ideas follow in a clear sequence?
- Are the parts of the essay logically connected?
- Are the connections clear and smooth?

A unified and coherent outline will not necessarily guide you to a unified and coherent essay, because so much can change during drafting. Thus you shouldn't be too hard on your outline, in case a seemingly wayward idea proves useful. But do cut obvious digressions and rearrange material that clearly needs moving.

The unity and coherence of an essay begin in its paragraphs, so the two are treated in greater detail in Chapter 3 (pp. 76 and 82).

Exercise 17
Organizing ideas

The following list of ideas was extracted by a student from free-writing he did for a brief paper on professional hockey in Canada. Using his thesis sentence as a guide, pick out the general ideas and arrange the relevant specific points under them. In some cases you may have to invent general ideas to cover specific points in the list.

THESIS SENTENCE

To ensure that professional hockey flourishes in the country that produces the majority of players, the NHL will have to work with its partners to provide a level playing field for small market Canadian franchises.

LIST OF IDEAS

The difference between the American and Canadian dollar is crucial.
Small market National Football League teams do well because all franchisees share TV money equally.
The Canadian Major Junior League is still the biggest and best development league for the NHL.
More that sixty percent of all NHL players come from Canada.
Governments should find ways to stop big market Canadian teams from monopolizing areas that could support more than one franchise.
The NHL should pay more for the development of players, money that could go into franchise development.
Rivalry between franchises in big market Canadian areas (like Southern Ontario) would only increase interest in areas that are already hockey mad and generate more revenues for all.

Exercise 18
Creating a formal outline

Use your arrangement of general ideas and specific points from Exercise 17 as the basis for a formal topic or sentence outline. Follow the principles given on pages 49–51.

Exercise 19
Considering your past work: Organizing ideas

What has been your experience with organizing your writing? Many writers find it difficult. If you do, too, can you say why? What kinds of outlines or other organizing tools have you used? Which have been helpful and which not?

Exercise 20
Organizing your own essay

Continuing from Exercise 16 (p. 45), choose an appropriate organization for your essay-in-progress. Then, experiment with organizing tools by preparing a tree diagram or a scratch, informal, or formal outline.

Chapter 2 Drafting and Revising the Essay

The separation of drafting and revising from the planning activities discussed in Chapter 1 is somewhat artificial because the stages almost always overlap during the writing process. Eventually, though, your primary goal will shift from planning toward forming connected sentences and paragraphs in a draft and then restructuring and rewriting the draft.

2a Writing the first draft

The only correct drafting style is the one that works for you. Generally, though, the freer and more fluid you are, the better. Some writers draft and revise at the same time, but most let themselves go during drafting and *especially* do not worry about errors. Drafting is the occasion to find and convey meaning through the act of writing. If you fear making mistakes while drafting, that fear will choke your ideas. You draft only for yourself, so errors do not matter. Write freely until you have worked out what you want to say; *then* focus on any mistakes you may have made.

Starting to draft sometimes takes courage, even for seasoned professionals. Students and pros alike find elaborate ways to procrastinate—rearranging shelves, napping, lunching with friends. Such procrastination may actually help you if you let ideas for writing simmer at the same time. At some point, though, enough is enough: the deadline looms; you've got to get started. If the blankness still stares back at you, then try one of the following techniques for unblocking.

Ways to start drafting

- Read over what you've already written—notes, outlines, and so on—and immediately start your draft with whatever comes to mind.
- Freewrite (see 1e-3).
- Write scribbles or type nonsense until words you can use start coming.
- Pretend you're writing to a friend about your topic.
- Conjure up an image that represents your topic—a physical object, a facial expression, two people arguing over something, a giant machine gouging the earth for a mine, whatever. Describe that image.
- Write a paragraph on what you think your essay will be about when you finish it.
- Skip the opening and start in the middle. Or write the conclusion.
- Using your outline, divide your essay into chunks—say, one for the introduction, another for the first example or reason, and so on. Start writing the chunk that seems most eager to be written, the one you understand best or feel most strongly about.

You should find some momentum once you've started writing. If not, however, or if your energy flags, try one or more of these techniques to keep moving ahead.

Ways to *keep* drafting

- Set aside enough time for yourself. (For a brief essay, a first draft is likely to take at least an hour or two.)
- Work in a place where you won't be interrupted.
- Make yourself comfortable.
- If you must stop working, jot a note before leaving the draft about what you expect to do next. Then you can pick up where you left off with minimal disruption.
- Be as fluid as possible, and don't worry about mistakes. Spontaneity will allow your attitudes toward your subject to surface naturally in your sentences. It will also make you receptive to ideas and relations you haven't seen before.

- Keep going. Skip over sticky spots; leave a blank if you can't find the right word. If an idea pops out of nowhere but doesn't seem to fit in, quickly jot it down on a separate sheet, or write it into the draft and bracket it for later attention.
- Resist self-criticism. Don't worry about your style, grammar, spelling, punctuation, and the like. Don't worry about what your readers will think. These are very important matters, but save them for revision.
- Use your thesis sentence and outline to remind you of your planned purpose, organization, and content.
- But don't feel constrained by your thesis and outline. If your writing leads you in a more interesting direction, follow.

To accommodate later changes, write or type your first draft only on one side of the paper, leave wide margins, and double- or triple-space all lines. Then you will find it easy to change words or whole sentences and to cut the draft apart and rearrange it. If you draft on a word processor, print out the finished draft so that you'll have a paper copy to work on.

Sandra Lee's first draft on multiculturalism in Canada appears below. (Her earlier work appears on pp. 33, 35, 40, 43, 47, and 49.)

First draft

Title?

In an editorial entitled "Multicultural Realities," the author argues that society "pressures people to be the same and to be different." Being the same means assimilation, and being different produces ghettos. The meaning of multiculturalism is not to be found in assimilation or in ghettos but in the mixing of shared values and cultural diversity.

The pressure to be the same is really directed at recent immigrants. It is the command that "everyone must be the same" that leads to full assimilation. Assimilation is something you can choose like you choose your clothes. But wouldn't it all be awful if we all wore the same thing. Societies or groups that are forced to dress all the same, the same tunic or business suit or dress, are so dull. I had to wear a uniform for public school, and your uniqueness as a person just gets lost. But shared values are what holds a society together. All Canadians share an immense respect for law and order. The debate over whether Sikh officers could wear a turban instead of a stetson largely took place over this sameness in difference issue.

Real differences can also be reinforced from within established immigrant communities. "Stick with your own kind," goes this command. Ethnic groups should not only live and work together, this view says, but also try to live and work as they did in the old country. Fortunately, these self-imposed ghettos are rarely possible in our multi-ethnic streets and neighbourhoods.

Critics of the fact of multiculturalism and immigration often argue that this situation should lead to assimilation or could lead to the social fragmentation of ghettos. Neither extreme view provides the real meaning of multiculturalism. The real meaning is in the mixing of our neighbourhoods, people, and cultures, and we need to see more of it.

Exercise 1
Analysing a first draft

Compare Lee's draft with the previous step in her planning (her formal outline) on page 49. List the places in the draft where the act of drafting led Lee to rearrange her information, add or delete material, or explore new ideas.

Exercise 2
Considering your past work: Drafting

Think back over a recent writing experience. At what point in the writing process did you begin drafting? How did drafting go—smoothly, haltingly, painfully, painlessly? If you had difficulties, what were they? If you didn't, why?

Exercise 3
Drafting your own essay

Prepare a draft of the essay you began in Chapter 1. Use your thesis sentence and your outline as guides, but don't be unduly constrained by them. Concentrate on opening up options, not on closing them down. Do not, above all, worry about mistakes.

2b Revising the first draft

Revision literally means "re-seeing"—looking anew at ideas and details, their relationships and arrangement, the degree to which they work or don't work for the thesis. While drafting, you have been focused inwardly, concentrating on pulling your topic out of yourself. In revising, you look out to your readers, trying to anticipate how they will see your work. You adopt a critical perspective toward your work (see p. 1), examining your draft as a pole-vaulter or dancer would examine a videotape of his or her performance.

Reading your own work critically requires that you create some distance between it and yourself—not always an easy task. The techniques below may help.

Ways to gain distance from your work

- Take a break after finishing the draft to pursue some other activity. A few hours may be enough; a whole night or day is preferable. The break will clear your mind, relax you, and give you some objectivity.
- Ask someone to read and react to your draft. Many writing instructors ask their students to submit their first drafts so that the instructors and, often, the other members of the class can serve as an actual audience to help guide revision. (See also 2e on receiving and benefiting from criticism.)
- Outline your draft. A formal outline, especially, with its careful structure and many possible levels of detail, can show where organization is illogical or support is skimpy. (See 1g-2 for a discussion of outlining.)
- Listen to your draft: read it out loud, read it into a tape recorder and play the tape, or have someone read the draft to you. Experiencing your words with ears instead of eyes can alter your perceptions.
- Ease the pressure. Don't try to re-see everything in your draft at once. Use a checklist like the one on page 61, making a separate pass through the draft for each item.

Strictly speaking, revision includes editing—refining the manner of expression to improve clarity or style or to correct errors. In this chapter, though, revision and editing are treated separately to stress their differences: in revision you deal with the underlying meaning and structure of your essay; in editing you deal with its surface. You can avoid the temptation to substitute editing for revision and prevent them from interfering with each other by making at least two separate drafts beyond the first: a revised one and then an edited one (p. 65).

Set aside at least as much time to revise your essay as you took to draft it. Plan on going through the draft several times to answer the questions in the checklist opposite and to resolve any problems. (If you need additional information on any of the topics in the checklist, refer to the handbook sections given in parentheses.) Note that the checklist can also help you if you have been asked to comment on another writer's draft (see p. 70).

A note on titling your essay

The revision stage is a good time to consider a title because attempting to sum up your essay in a phrase can focus your attention sharply on your topic, purpose, and audience.

Here are some suggestions for titling an essay:

- A **descriptive title** is almost always appropriate and is often expected for academic writing. It announces the topic clearly, accurately, and as briefly as possible. The title that Lee finally chose, "The Pressures of Multiculturalism," is an example. Other examples: "The Trickster Figure in Native Drama"; "Home and Away in Maritime Satire"; "The Myth of the Railway in Canadian History."
- A **suggestive title**—the kind often found in popular magazines—may be appropriate for more informal writing. Examples include "Winning the Peace" (for an essay on the global economy) and "Sold Glory" (for an essay on Canadian-American trade disputes). For a more suggestive title, Lee might have chosen "Mixing Identities." Such a title conveys the writer's attitudes and main concerns but not the precise topic, thereby pulling readers into the essay to learn more. A source for such a title may be a familiar phrase, a fresh image, or a significant expression from the essay itself.
- A title tells readers how big the topic is. For Lee's essay, the title "Sameness and Difference" or "Cultural Diversity" would have been too broad, whereas "Shared Values" or "Self-Imposed Ghettos" would have been too narrow.

Checklist for revision

See also specific revision checklists for arguments (p. 147), research papers (p. 572), and literary analyses (p. 660).

- Does the body of the essay carry out the purpose and central idea expressed by the thesis sentence (1f)?
  Is the reason for writing apparent, not only in the thesis sentence but throughout the essay?
  If the body of the essay does not carry out the thesis sentence, is the problem more with the thesis sentence (because it does not reflect a new and better direction in the draft) or with the body (because it wanders)?
- Are there adequate details, examples, or reasons to support each of the ideas (1d, 1e)?
  Do readers need more information at any point to understand the meaning or appreciate the point of view?
- Does the tone of the writing convey a clear and appropriate attitude toward the topic (1d-3)?
  Is the tone appropriate for the purpose and audience?
  Is it consistent throughout the essay?
- Is the essay unified (1g-4)?
  Does each paragraph and sentence relate clearly to the thesis sentence?
- Is the essay coherent (1g-4)?
  Is the sequence of ideas clear?
  Are the relationships within and among parts apparent?
- Is each paragraph in the body unified (3a), coherent (3b), and well developed (3c)?
- Does the title state or hint at the essay's scope and approach (see opposite)?
  Does the introduction engage and focus readers' attention (3c-1)?
  Does the conclusion provide a sense of completion (3c-2)?

- A title should not restate the assignment or the thesis sentence, as in "The Meaning of Multiculturalism" or "Mixing Values and Diversity."

For more information on essay titles, see pages 748 (the format of a title in the final paper) and 424 (capitalizing words in a title).

In revising her first draft, Sandra Lee had the help of her instructor and several of her classmates, to whom she showed the draft as part of her assignment. (See p. 70 for more on this kind of collaboration.) Based on the revision checklist, she felt that she wanted to stick with her initial purpose and thesis sentence and that they had held up well in the draft. But she also knew without being told that her introduction was too hurried and that the body of the essay was thin: she hadn't supplied enough details to support her ideas and convince her readers.

Lee's readers confirmed her self-criticism: some were confused by the introduction; others were unconvinced by her essay; everyone asked for more examples. And among other comments, her readers raised additional points that she had not considered. They are reflected in this comment by a classmate:

> I think you are basically right. Assimilation is something you can choose to do. Everyone should be free to choose. But I think assimilation or, what's it called, conformity is something different from school uniforms. I think that is a bad example. And I think you need to recognize even more the complexities of these pressures. That's what you are trying to do, but maybe you could take it further.

While revising, Lee made many changes directly on the draft, but she also inserted new passages. Her revision begins on the next page. The principal changes are explained below and keyed to the revisions by numbers (some numbers are used more than once).

1. Lee added a descriptive title to give her readers a clearer sense of her topic and to bring into focus for herself what she was actually writing about.
2. Lee rewrote and expanded the previous abrupt introduction to supply a context for the quotation about multicultural pressures from the newspaper and for her thesis about the mixing of positive pressures.
3. She began to add examples and other details to support her general statements. This and the following category of changes occupied most of her attention during revision.
4. In response to her classmate's comments, Lee further defined and clarified her conception of a key idea, assimilation.
5. After some consideration, Lee cut what she now saw as a digression about clothing that the same classmate had found distracting and irrelevant.
6. Lee added some concessions and assertions that developed further her representation of the complexities of multiculturalism.
7. Her classmates had not commented on her conclusion. However, Lee thought it needed development, and she filled out her final vision of the positive mixing of multiculturalism with more concrete examples.

Revised first draft

~~Title?~~ The Pressures of Multiculturalism 1

As a glance into any classroom in this country will show, Canada does not 2
have a population all the same.. Canadians come from around the globe from
Asia, Africa, Europe, North and South America, even Australia. All of these 3
differences create certain pressures. They also provide certain opportunities
and advantages.

In ~~an editorial entitled~~ "Multicultural Realities,"
editorialist
the ~~author~~ argues that society "pressures people to be the
same and to be different." Being the same means assimilation, and being different produces ghettos. The meaning of multiculturalism is not to be found in assimilation or in ghettos but in the mixing of shared values and cultural diversity.

The pressure to be the same is really directed at
Those most recent to Canada feel most the pressure to conform.
recent immigrants. ~~It is~~ ~~t~~The command that "everyone must
or the loss of group identity 4
be the same" ~~that~~ leads to full assimilation. Assimilation
and should not have ~~forced on you~~
is something you can choose ~~like you choose your clothes~~.
~~Any individual can assimilate to the mainstream, but a whole group~~
~~But wouldn't it be awful if we all wore the same thing.~~
would lose its identity in a melting pot sameness
~~Societies or groups that are forced to dress the same, the~~ 5
~~same tunic or business suit or dress, are so dull. I had~~
~~to wear a uniform for public school, and your uniqueness~~
~~as a person just gets lost. But~~ ¶ ~~s~~Shared values are what
, not sameness , for example,
holds a society together. All Canadians share an immense
After all, the most widely recognized symbol of Canada is a police officer, the mountie 3
respect for law and order. The debate over whether Sikh
officers could wear a turban instead of a stetson largely
took place over this sameness in difference issue. Clearly,
the Sikh officer would enforce all the same laws; only his appearance would be different.

, however,
Real differences ^ can also be reinforced from within established immigrant communities. "Stick with your own kind," goes this command. Ethnic groups should not only live and work together, this view says, but also try to
Without any active mixing with other groups, this kind of pressure can also 6
live and work as they did in the old country. ^ ~~Fortunately,~~
be negative. It breaks our mosaic up into isolated tiles. The opposite of
~~these self-imposed ghettos are rarely possible in our~~
the melting pot, but just as bad.
~~multi-ethnic streets and neighbourhoods.~~ The cultural diversity 6
that comes from mixing identities is also balanced by a strong common language and political system. New and established Canadians may not always agree and may have conflicts. Yet we are bound together by English and/or French and by respect for a parliamentary system of government and for our Charter of Rights and Freedoms.

Critics of the fact of multiculturalism and immigration
unless all groups assimilate to sameness the pressures
often argue that ^ ~~this situation should lead to assimila-~~
of difference will lead to fragmentation.
~~tion or could lead to the social fragmentation of ghettos.~~
is
Neither extreme ~~view provides~~ the real meaning of multiculturalism. The real meaning is in the mixing of our 7
people, our cultures, and especially our neighbourhoods. On these streets we
~~neighbourhoods, people, and cultures, and we need to see~~
sometimes party together, we sometimes argue. We sometimes work
~~more of it.~~
together, we sometimes pull apart. Nonetheless, the meaning is in the mixing.

Exercise 4
Analysing a revised draft

Compare Lee's revised draft with her first draft on pages 57–58. Based on the discussion of her intentions for revision (pp. 61–62), can you see the reasons for most of her changes? Where would you suggest further revisions, and why?

Exercise 5
Considering your past work: Revising

In the past, have you usually revised your drafts extensively? Do you think your writing would benefit from more revision of the sort described in this chapter? Why or why not? Many students who don't revise much explain that they lack the time. Is time a problem for you? Can you think of ways to resolve the problem?

Exercise 6
Revising your own draft

Revise your own first draft from Exercise 3 (p. 59). Use the checklist for revision on page 61 as a guide. Concentrate on purpose, content, and organization, leaving smaller problems for the next draft.

2c Editing the revised draft

Editing for style, clarity, and correctness may come second to more fundamental revision, but it is far from unimportant. A carefully developed essay will still fall flat with readers if you overlook awkwardness and errors.

When you have revised your first draft, try the following approaches to editing.

Ways to find what needs editing

- Recopy, retype, or print out your revision so that you can read it easily and have plenty of room for changes.
- As you read the new draft, imagine yourself encountering it for the first time, as a reader will.
- Have a friend or relative read your work. Or, if you share your work in class, listen to the responses of your classmates or instructor. (See 2e.)
- As when revising, read the draft aloud, preferably into a tape recorder, listening for awkward rhythms, repetitive sentence patterns, and missing or clumsy transitions.
- When reading aloud or silently, be careful to read what you actually see *on the page,* not what you may have intended to write but didn't.
- Learn from your own experience. Keep a record of the problems that others have pointed out in your writing. (See p. 72 for a suggested format.) When editing, check your work against this record.

In your editing, work for clarity and a smooth movement among sentences and for correctness. Use the questions in the checklist below to guide your editing. (Chapter numbers in parentheses indicate where you can look in the handbook for more information.) Note that the checklist may also serve as a guide if you are commenting on another writer's paper (see p. 70).

Checklist for editing

- Are the sentences grammatical?
  Do they avoid errors in case (6), verb form (7), agreement (8), and adjectives and adverbs (9)?
- Are the sentences clear?
  Do they avoid sentence fragments (10), comma splices and fused sentences (11), errors in pronoun reference (12), shifts (13), misplaced or dangling modifiers (14), and mixed or incomplete constructions (15)?
- Are the sentences effective?
  Do they use subordination and coordination (16) and parallelism (17) appropriately?
  Are they emphatic (18) and varied (19)?
- Is the use of commas, semicolons, colons, periods, and other punctuation correct (20–25)?
- Are the sentences mechanically correct in the use of capitals, italics, abbreviations, numbers, and hyphens (26–30)?
- Are the words appropriate to the writing situation (31a)?
  Do the words exactly convey meaning and feeling (31b)?
  Is the writing concise (31c)?
- Are the words spelled correctly (34)?

In response to these questions and her own sense of clarity and effectiveness, Sandra Lee edited the revised draft of her essay. The first paragraph appears below.

Edited draft (excerpt)

As a glance into any classroom in this country will
homogeneous
show, Canada does not have a ^ population ~~all the same.~~
: f
Canadians come from around the globe/ ^ From Asia, Africa,
the s,
Europe, ~~North and South~~ ^ America ^ even Australia. All of
tensions and ; t
these differences create certain ^ pressures ^ They also
provide certain opportunities and advantages. In "Multi-
the specific nature of Canadian
cultural Realities," the editorialist argues that ^ society

```
"pressures people to be the same and to be different."
```

~~Being~~ But to be entirely the same means assimilation, and ~~being~~ to be entirely different produces ghettos. The meaning of multiculturalism is not to be found in assimilation or in ghettos but in the mixing of shared values and cultural diversity.

Exercise 7
Considering your past work: Editing

How do you find what needs editing in your drafts? What kinds of changes do you make most often? Have you tried focusing on particular kinds of changes, such as correcting mistakes you made in previous writing? If your readers often comment on editing concerns in your work, what can you do to reduce such comments?

Exercise 8
Editing your own draft

Use the checklist for editing (p. 66) and your own sense of your essay's needs to edit the revised draft you prepared in Exercise 6 (p. 65).

2d Proofreading and submitting the final draft

After editing your essay, recopy, retype, or print it once more for submission to your instructor. Follow the guidelines in Appendix A or the wishes of your instructor for an appropriate manuscript form. Be sure to proofread the final essay several times to spot and correct errors. To increase the accuracy of your proofreading, you may need to experiment with ways to keep yourself from

Techniques for proofreading

- Read the paper aloud, very slowly, and distinctly pronounce exactly what you see.
- Place a ruler under each line as you read it.
- Read "against copy," comparing your final draft one sentence at a time against the edited draft you copied it from.
- Read the essay backward, end to beginning, examining each sentence as a separate unit. (This technique will help keep the content of your writing from distracting you.)

relaxing into the rhythm of your prose. The box on the previous page gives a few tricks used by professional proofreaders.

Sandra Lee's final essay, along with her instructor's comments, follows. The instructor pointed out the strengths he saw in the essay as well as the flaws remaining in it. He used a combination of written comments, correction symbols (from inside the back cover of this handbook), and correction codes (from inside the front cover).

Final draft with instructor's comments

The Pressures of Multiculturalism

As a glance into any classroom in this country will show, Canada does not have a homogeneous population. Canadians come from around the globe: from Asia, Europe, the Americas, even Australia. All of these differences create certain tensions and pressures; they also provide certain opportunities and advantages. In "Multicultural Realities," the editorialist argues that the specific nature of Canadian society "pressures people to be the same and to be different." But to be entirely the same means assimilation, and to be entirely different produces ghettos. The meaning of multiculturalism is not to be found in assimilation or in ghettos but in the mixing of shared values and cultural diversity.

CS

strong, clear thesis

The pressure to be the same is really directed at recent immigrants. Those most recent to Canada feel most the pressure to conform. The command that "everyone must be the same" leads to full assimilation or the loss of group identity. Assimilation is something you can choose and should not have forced on you. Any individual can assimilate to the mainstream, but a whole group would lose it's identity in a melting pot sameness.

2/a

ap it's=it is

Shared values are what hold a society together, not sameness. All Canadians, for example, share an immense respect for law and order. After all, the most widely recognized symbol of Canada is a police officer, the Mountie. The debate over whether Sikh officers could wear a turban instead of a stetson largely took place over this sameness in difference issue. Clearly, the Sikh officer would enforce all the same laws and represent the same values; only his appearance would be different. *correct use of semicolon*

Real differences, however, can also be reinforced from within established immigrant communities. "Stick with your own kind," goes with this command. Ethnic groups should not only live and work together, this view holds, but also try to live and work as they did in the old country. Without any active mixing with other groups, this kind of pressure can also be negative. It breaks our mosaic up into isolated tiles. The opposite of the melting pot, but just as bad. *frag*

¶ Fortunately, these self-imposed ghettos are rarely possible in our multi-ethnic neighbourhoods. The cultural diversity that comes from mixing identities is also balanced by a strong common language and political system. New and established Canadians may not always agree and may have conflicts. Yet we are bound together by English and/or French and by a respect for a parliamentary system of government and for our Charter of Rights and Freedoms. *Break this very long ¶*

Critics of multiculturalism often argue that unless all groups assimilate to sameness the pressures of difference will lead to fragmentation. Neither extreme is the real meaning of multiculturalism. The real meaning is in the mixing of our peoples, our cultures, and especially our neighbourhoods. On these streets, *(21b)* we sometimes party together, *(CS)* we sometimes argue. We sometimes work together, *(CS)* we sometimes pull apart. Nonetheless, the meaning is in the mixing.

You did a fine job of adding details and recognizing complexities in the issue. Your introduction and conclusion are much stronger. This essay is well done.

In your next assignment, pay close attention to the use of commas. Review Chapter 11 (comma splices), 21 (comma), and 22 (semicolon). Punctuation errors mar the clarity of your sentences, especially the strong sentences at the end.

Exercise 9
Proofreading

Proofread the following passage, using any of the techniques listed on page 67 to bring errors into the foreground. There are ten errors in the passage: missing and misspelled words, typographical errors, and the like. If you are in doubt about any spellings, consult a dictionary.

An envirnmental group, National Resources Defence Council, has estimated that 5500 to 6200 children who are preschool today may contract cancer durng their lives becuase of the pesticides they consume in their food In addition, these children will be at greater risk for kidney damage, problems with immunity, and other serious imparments. The government bases it pesticide-safety standards on adults, but childen consume much more the fruits and fruit products likely to contain pestcides.

Exercise 10
Revising an essay

To become familiar with the symbols and codes of this handbook, revise Lee's essay wherever her instructor has used a symbol or code to mark a problem.

Exercise 11
Preparing your final draft

Prepare the final draft of the essay you have been working on throughout Chapters 1 and 2. Proofread carefully and correct all errors before submitting your essay for review.

2e Receiving and giving criticism

Almost all the writing you do in college or university will generate responses from an instructor. In writing courses you may submit early drafts as well as your final paper, and your readers may include your classmates as well as your instructor. Indeed, like Sandra Lee's, many writing courses feature **collaborative learning,** in which students work together on writing, from completing exercises to commenting on each other's work to producing whole papers. Collaboration is common in business, where workers often meet to solve problems and generate ideas. Whether you participate in collaborative learning as a writer or as a writing "coach," you stand to gain experience in reading written work critically and in reaching others through writing.

If you are the reader of someone else's writing, keep the following principles in mind.

Guidelines for criticizing others' work

- Be sure you know what the writer is saying. If necessary, summarize the paper to understand its content. (See pp. 8–10.)
- Read closely and critically. (See pp. 2–14.)
- Unless you have other instructions, address only the most significant problems in the work. If you point out every flaw you detect, the writer may have trouble sorting out the important from the unimportant.
- Use the revision checklist on page 61 as a guide to what is significant in a piece of writing.
- Be specific. Explain the *reasons* for your confusion or *why* you disagree with a conclusion.
- Remember that you are the reader, not the writer. Resist the temptation to edit sentences, add details, or otherwise assume responsibility for the paper.
- Word your comments supportively. Question the writer in a way that emphasizes the effect of the work on *you,* the reader ("I find this paragraph confusing"), and avoid measuring the work against a set of external standards ("This essay is poorly organized"; "Your thesis sentence is inadequate").
- Be positive as well as honest. Instead of saying "This paragraph doesn't interest me," say "You have a really interesting detail here that seems buried in the rest of the paragraph." And tell the writer what you like about the paper.

When you *receive* the comments of others, whether your classmates or your instructor, you will get more out of the process if you follow the guidelines at the top of the next page

Reading and listening to what others have to say will help you see and keep track of the flaws in your work so that you can concentrate on eliminating them. One device for tracking problems is a chart like the one at the bottom of the next page, with a vertical column for each assignment (or draft) and a horizontal row for each weakness. The handbook section is noted for each problem, and check marks indicate how often the problem occurs in each essay. The chart also provides a convenient place to keep track of words you misspell so that you can master their spellings.

Guidelines for benefiting from criticism

- Think of your readers as counsellors or coaches who will help you see the virtues and flaws in your work and sharpen your awareness of readers' needs.
- Read or listen to comments closely.
- Make sure you know what the critic is saying. If you need more information, ask for it, or consult the appropriate section of this handbook. (See "Using This Book," p. xiii, for a guide to the handbook.)
- Don't become defensive. Letting comments offend you will only erect a barrier to improvement in your writing. As one writing teacher advises, "Leave your ego at the door."
- When comments seem appropriate, revise your work in response to them, whether or not you are required to do so. You will learn more from the act of revision than from just thinking about changes.
- Though you should be open to suggestions, you are the final authority on your paper. You are free to decline advice when you think it is inappropriate.
- Keep track of problems that recur in your work so that you can give them special attention in new essays. In this way your learning on one assignment will carry over to the next one.

	Assignment			
Problems	1	2	3	
not enough details for readers (1d)	✓	✓	✓	
unity—wanders away from thesis (1g)	✓			
parallelism (17)	✓✓	✓	✓	
agreement (8a)	✓		✓	
comma splice (11)	✓✓	✓	✓	
misspellings	among deceive	rebel seize	omission cruelty	

Exercise 12
Analysing an essay

Carefully read the essay below by Johanna Abrams. (Abrams's earlier work on this essay appears on pp. 36 and 49.) Answer the following questions about the essay:

1. What is Abrams's purpose?
2. Who do you think constitutes Abrams's intended audience? What role does she seem to be assuming? What does the tone reveal about her attitude toward the topic?
3. How well does the thesis sentence convey Abrams's purpose and attitude? What assertion does the thesis sentence make? How specific is the sentence? How well does it preview Abrams's ideas and organization?
4. What organization does Abrams use? Is it clear throughout the essay?
5. What details, examples, and reasons does Abrams use to support her ideas? Where is supporting evidence skimpy?
6. How successful is Abrams in making you care about the topic and her views of it?

Working in the Barnyard

Until two months ago I thought summer jobs occupied time and helped pay the next year's tuition but otherwise provided no useful training. Then I took a temporary job in a large government agency. Two months there taught me the very valuable lesson that the hierarchy of supervisor to employee should be respected.

Last May I was hired by the personnel department of the agency to fill in for vacationing workers in the mail room. I had seven coworkers and a boss, Mrs. King. Our job was to sort the huge morning and afternoon mail shipments into four hundred slots, one for every employee in the agency. Then we delivered the sorted mail out of grocery carts that we wheeled from office to office along assigned corridors, picking up outgoing mail as we went along. Each mail delivery took an entire half-day to sort and deliver.

My troubles began almost as soon as I arrived. Hundreds of pieces of mail were dumped on a shallow table against a wall of mail slots. I was horrified to see that the slots were labelled not with people's names but with their initials—whereas the incoming letters, of course, contained full names. Without thinking, I asked why this was a good idea, only to receive a sharp glance from Mrs. King. So I repeated the question. This time Mrs. King told me not to question what I didn't understand. It was the first of many such exchanges, and I hadn't been on the job a half-hour.

I mastered the initials and the sorting and delivery procedures after about a week. But the longer I worked at the job, the more I saw how inefficient all the procedures were, from delivery routes to times for coffee breaks. When I asked Mrs. King about the procedures, however, she always reacted the same way: it was none of my business.

I pestered Mrs. King more and more over the next seven weeks, but my efforts were fruitless, even counterproductive. Mrs. King began calling me snide names. Then she began picking on my work and singling me out for reprimands, even though I did my best and worked faster than most of the others.

Two months after I had started work, the personnel manager called me in and fired me. I objected, of course, calling up all the deficiencies I had seen in Mrs. King and her systems. The manager interrupted to ask if I had ever heard of the barnyard pecking order: the top chicken pecks on the one below it, the second pecks on the third, and so on all the way down the line to the lowliest chicken, whose life is a constant misery. Mrs. King, the manager said, was that lowliest chicken at the bottom of the pecking order in the agency's management. With little education, she had spent her entire adult life building up her small domain, and she had to protect it from everyone, especially the people who worked for her. The arbitrariness of her systems was an assertion of her power, for no one should doubt for a moment that she ruled her roost.

I had a month before school began again to think about my adventure. At first it irritated me that I should be humiliated while Mrs. King continued on as before. But eventually I saw how arrogant, and how unsympathetic, my behaviour had been. In my next job, I'll learn the pecking order before I become a crusader, *if* I do.

Chapter 3

Writing and Revising Paragraphs

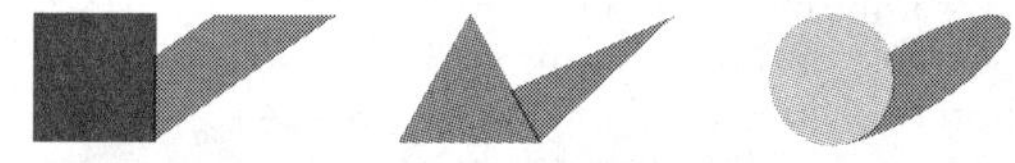

A **paragraph** is a group of related sentences set off by a beginning indention or, sometimes, by extra space. For you and your readers, paragraphs provide breathers from long stretches of text and indicate key changes in your development of ideas. In the body of your essay, you may use paragraphs for any of these purposes:

- To introduce one of the main points supporting your essay's central idea (its thesis) and to develop the point with examples, facts, or other supporting evidence. (See pp. 41–44 for a discussion of an essay's thesis.)
- To shift approach—for instance, from pros to cons, from problem to solution, from questions to answers.
- To mark movement in a sequence, such as from one reason or step to another.
- Within a group of paragraphs centring on one main point, to introduce and develop a key example or other important evidence.

In addition, you will sometimes use paragraphs for special purposes:

- To introduce or to conclude an essay. (See pp. 106 and 109.)
- Occasionally, to give strong emphasis to an important point or mark a significant change in direction. (See p. 111.)
- In dialogue, to indicate that a new person has begun speaking. (See p. 111.)

The following paragraph illustrates simply how an effective body paragraph works to help both writer and reader. The thesis of

¶ un
3a

the essay in which this paragraph appears is that the geography of Vancouver contributes to its personality.

> All this beautiful scenery does, however, make for some interesting logistical challenges. Everywhere you go in Vancouver you have to get on a bridge to get somewhere else. The downtown core is in effect an island, with five of the six accesses to it by bridge or viaduct. This naturally shapes the traffic routes, the traffic mentality and, eventually, the *personality* of the city. One of the newspaper chains recently decided against establishing a third paper in Vancouver because its research showed a community chopped up by water, creating pockets of tinier communities rather than a homogeneous whole.
>
> —ALLAN FOTHERINGHAM

General statement relating to thesis: topic sentence

Four sentences developing the topic in specific examples

While you are drafting, conscious attention to the requirements of the paragraph may sometimes help pull ideas out of you or help you forge relationships. But don't expect effective paragraphs like Fotheringham's to flow from your fingertips while you are grappling with what you want to say. Instead, use the following checklist to guide your revision of paragraphs so that they work to your and your readers' advantage.

Checklist for revising paragraphs

- Is the paragraph **unified?** Does it adhere to one general idea that is either stated in a **topic sentence** or otherwise apparent? (See 3a.)
- Is the paragraph **coherent?** Do the sentences follow a clear sequence (3b-1)? Are the sentences linked as needed by parallelism (3b-2), repetition or restatement (3b-3), pronouns (3b-4), consistency (3b-5), and transitional expressions (3b-6)?
- Is the paragraph **developed?** Is the general idea of the paragraph well supported with specific evidence such as details, facts, examples, and reasons? (See 3c.)

3a Maintaining paragraph unity

Readers generally expect a paragraph to explore one idea. They will be alert for that idea and will patiently follow its development. In other words, they will seek and appreciate paragraph **unity,** clear identification and clear elaboration of one idea and of that idea only.

In an essay the thesis sentence often asserts the main idea as a commitment to readers (see p. 41). In a paragraph a **topic sentence** often alerts readers to the essence of the paragraph by asserting the central idea and expressing the writer's attitude toward it. In a brief essay each body paragraph will likely treat one main point supporting the essay's thesis sentence; the topic sentences simply elaborate on parts of the thesis. In longer essays paragraphs tend to work in groups, each group treating one main point. Then the topic sentences will tie into that main point, and all the points together will support the thesis.

Focusing on the central idea

Like the thesis sentence, the topic sentence is a commitment to readers, and the rest of the paragraph delivers on that commitment. Look again at Fotheringham's paragraph on Vancouver: the opening statement conveys the author's promise that he will describe how the scenery or geography contributes to the personality of the city, and the following sentences keep the promise. But what if he had written this paragraph instead?

> All this beautiful scenery does, however, make for some interesting logistical challenges. Everywhere you go in Vancouver you have to get on a bridge to get somewhere else. The downtown core is in effect an island, with five of the six accesses to it by bridge or viaduct. They don't make bridges like they used to. Bridges used to define a city, gave it a style and a signature. Nor, for that matter, do they make viaducts like they used to. Toronto may be the only city with a signature viaduct. But, of course, Toronto doesn't have any famous bridges: they suffer from bridge envy.

Topic sentence: general statement

Two sentences developing the topic

Digression

In this altered version, the topic of Vancouver's geography is forgotten midway. In Fotheringham's original, by contrast, every sentence after the first develops the meaning of the topic sentence with examples.

You should expect digressions while you are drafting: if you allow yourself to explore ideas, as you should, then of course every paragraph will not be tightly woven, perfectly unified. But spare your readers the challenge and frustration of repeatedly shifting focus to follow your rough explorations: revise each paragraph so that it develops a single idea.

Placing the topic sentence

The topic sentence of a paragraph and its supporting details may be arranged variously, depending on how you want to direct readers' attention and how complex your central idea is. In the most common arrangements, the topic sentence comes at the beginning of the paragraph, comes at the end, or is not stated at all but is nonetheless apparent.

Topic sentence at the beginning

When the topic sentence appears first in a paragraph, it can help you select the details that follow. For readers, the topic-first model establishes an initial context in which all the supporting details can be understood. Look again at Fotheringham's paragraph on page 76 to see how easily we readers relate each detail or example back to the point made in the first sentence.

The topic-first model is common not only in expository paragraphs, such as Fotheringham's, but also in argument paragraphs, such as the one following.

> Canadians, as a people, are no better and no worse than anyone else. We were slavers in the eighteenth and early nineteenth centuries, and our treatment of minorities, from Indians to Jehovah's Witnesses, is only marginally different from that of the Americans. We have staged some of the bigger and more bloody-minded riots on the continent, from the Bytown Riots of the 1840s ("Them Bytown days was fightin' days") to the Kenora race riots of 1974. We have not only passed, but applauded, viciously repressive legislation, and our gun laws, to take only one example of wrong-headed self-congratulation, are in fact looser and dumber than those in most U.S. states.
>
> —WALTER STEWART, *But Not in Canada*

Topic sentence: correction of misconception

Development of correction through examples

Topic sentence at the end

In some paragraphs the central idea may be stated at the end, after supporting sentences have made a case for the general statement. Since this model leads the reader to a conclusion by presenting all the evidence first, it can prove effective in argument. And because the point of the paragraph is withheld until the end, this model can be dramatic in exposition too, as illustrated by the following example. In the sentence before the paragraph, the author says that the television game show *Wheel of Fortune* provides a "scenario" of material success.

> The terminology of the rules of the game are consistent with the scenario being played out. A contestant *"earns* the right to buy a prize" by solving a puzzle and accumulating money by spinning The Wheel. If you win the game, you take the money you have accumulated and then go shopping, at the "actual retail prices," for the prizes offered until you have exhausted your account. You can also elect to bank your money, hoping that you can solve another puzzle without hitting "bankrupt," which wipes out all you've earned but not your merchandise, "because once you buy a prize, it's yours to keep." So whether you can spend only $200 for a framed print or $15,000 for a Mustang convertible depends upon a combination of common sense, basic literacy and luck. It is, plain and simple, a microcosm of the mechanisms operating in the American ideology of an open society and the work ethic.
>
> —GLORIA NAYLOR, "Sexual Equality in a TV Fantasy"

Transition from preceding paragraph

Information supporting and building to topic sentence

Topic sentence

Expressing the central idea at the end of the paragraph does not eliminate the need to unify the paragraph. The idea in the topic sentence must still govern the selection of all the preceding details.

Central idea not stated

Occasionally, a paragraph's central idea will be stated in the previous paragraph or will be so obvious that it need not be stated at all. The following is from an essay on the actor Humphrey Bogart.

> Usually he wore the trench coat unbuttoned, just tied with the belt, and a slouch hat, rarely tilted. Sometimes it was a captain's cap and a yachting jacket. Almost always his trousers were held up by a cowboy belt. You know the kind: one an Easterner waiting for a plane out of Phoenix buys just as a joke and then takes a liking to. Occasionally, he'd hitch up his slacks with it, and he often jabbed his thumbs behind it, his hands ready for a fight or a dame.
>
> —PETER BOGDANOVICH, "Bogie in Excelsis"

Details adding up to the unstated idea that Bogart's character could be seen in the details of his clothing

Paragraphs in descriptive writing (like the one above) and in narrative writing (relating a sequence of events) often lack stated topic sentences. But a paragraph without a topic sentence still should have a central idea, and its details should develop that idea.

Exercise 1
Finding the central idea

What is the central idea of each paragraph below? In what sentence or sentences is it expressed?

1. Like lessons of this sort, those about the north are taught by 1
precept and example, but also, more enjoyably, by cautionary
nasty tale. There is death by blackfly, the one about the fellow who 2
didn't have his shirt cuffs tight enough in the spring and undressed
at night only to find he was running with blood, the ones about the
lost travellers who bloated up from too many bites and who, when
found, were twice the size, unrecognizable, and dead. There is 3
death from starvation, death by animal, death by forest fire; there
is death from something called "exposure," which used to confuse
me when I heard about men who exposed themselves: why would
they intentionally do anything that fatal? There's death by thunder- 4
storm, not to be sneered at: on the open lake, in one of the exces-
sive northern midsummer thunderstorms, a canoe or a bush plane
is a vulnerable target. The north is full of Struwwelpeter-like sto- 5
ries about people who didn't do as they were told and got struck by
lightning. Above all, there are death by freezing and death by 6
drowning. Your body's heat-loss rate in the water is twenty times 7
that in air, and northern lakes are cold. Even in a life jacket, even 8
holding on to the tipped canoe, you're at risk. Every summer the 9
numbers pile up. —MARGARET ATWOOD, "True North"

2. Though they do not know why the humpback whale sings, sci- 1
entists do know something about the song itself. They have mea- 2
sured the length of a whale's song: from a few minutes to over half
an hour. They have recorded and studied the variety and complex 3
arrangements of low moans, high squeaks, and sliding squeals that
make up the song. And they have learned that each whale sings in 4
its own unique pattern. —JANET LIEBER (student), "Whales' Songs"

Exercise 2
Revising a paragraph for unity

The following paragraph contains ideas or details that do not support its central idea. Identify the topic sentence in the paragraph and delete the unrelated material.

In the northern part of the province, some people still live much 1
as they did a century ago. They use coal- or wood-burning stoves for 2
heating and cooking. Their homes do not have electricity or indoor 3
bathrooms or running water. The towns can't afford to put in sewers 4
or power lines, because they don't receive adequate funding from the
provincial and federal governments. Beside most homes there is a 5
garden where fresh vegetables are gathered for canning. Small pas- 6
tures nearby support livestock, including cattle, pigs, horses, and
chickens. Most of the people have cars or trucks, but the vehicles are 7
old and beat-up from travelling on unpaved roads.

Exercise 3
Considering your past work: Paragraph unity

For a continuing exercise in this chapter, choose a paper you've written in the past year. Examine the body paragraphs for unity. Do they have clear topic sentences? If not, are the paragraphs' central ideas still clear? Are the paragraphs unified around their central ideas? Should any details be deleted for unity? Should other, more relevant details be added in their stead?

Exercise 4
Writing a unified paragraph

Develop the following topic sentence into a unified paragraph by using the relevant information in the statements below it. Delete each statement that does not relate directly to the topic, and then rewrite and combine sentences as appropriate.

TOPIC SENTENCE

Mozart's accomplishments in music seem remarkable even today.

SUPPORTING INFORMATION

Wolfgang Amadeus Mozart was born in 1756 in Salzburg, Austria.

He began composing music at the age of five.

He lived most of his life in Salzburg and Vienna.

His first concert tour of Europe was at the age of six.

On his first tour he played harpsichord, organ, and violin.

He published numerous compositions before reaching adolescence.

He married in 1782.

Mozart and his wife were both poor managers of money.

They were plagued by debts.

Mozart composed over six hundred musical compositions.

His most notable works are his operas, symphonies, quartets, and piano concertos.

He died at the age of thirty-five.

Exercise 5
Turning topic sentences into unified paragraphs

Develop three of the following topic sentences into detailed and unified paragraphs.

1. Men and women are different in at least one important respect.
2. AIDS should be everybody's concern.
3. Fans of country music (or rock music, classical music, jazz) come in [number] varieties.

4. Professional sports have (or have not) been helped by extending the regular season with championship play-offs.
5. Working for good grades can interfere with learning.

3b Achieving paragraph coherence

A paragraph is unified if it holds together—if all its details and examples support the central idea. A paragraph is **coherent** if readers can see *how* the paragraph holds together—how the sentences relate to each other—without having to stop and reread. Coherent paragraphs convey relations in the ways summarized below.

Ways to achieve paragraph coherence

- Organize effectively (3b-1).
- Use parallel structures (3b-2).
- Repeat or restate words and word groups (3b-3).
- Use pronouns (3b-4).
- Be consistent in nouns, pronouns, and verbs (3b-5).
- Use transitional expressions (3b-6).

Incoherence gives readers the feeling of being yanked around, as the following example shows.

> The ancient Egyptians were masters of preserving dead people's bodies by making mummies of them. Mummies several thousand years old have been discovered nearly intact. The skin, hair, teeth, finger- and toenails, and facial features of the mummies were evident. It is possible to diagnose the diseases they suffered in life, such as smallpox, arthritis, and nutritional deficiencies. The process was remarkably effective. Sometimes apparent were the fatal afflictions of the dead people: a middle-aged king died from a blow on the head, and polio killed a child king. Mummification consisted of removing the internal organs, applying natural preservatives inside and out, and then wrapping the body in layers of bandages.

Topic sentence

Sentences related to topic sentence but disconnected from each other

The paragraph as it was actually written is much clearer. The writer organized information and linked sentences to help readers move easily from one sentence to the next.

The ancient Egyptians were masters of preserving dead people's bodies by making mummies of them. Basically, mummification consisted of removing the internal organs, applying natural preservatives inside and out, and then wrapping the body in layers of bandages. And the process was remarkably effective. Indeed, mummies several thousand years old have been discovered nearly intact. Their skin, hair, teeth, finger- and toenails, and facial features are still evident. Their diseases in life, such as smallpox, arthritis, and nutritional deficiencies, are still diagnosable. Even their fatal afflictions are still apparent: a middle-aged king died from a blow on the head; a child king died from polio.

—MITCHELL ROSENBAUM (student), "Lost Arts of the Egyptians"

Here is the same paragraph annotated to show its shape and its connections.

The ancient Egyptians were masters of preserving dead people's bodies by (making mummies) of them. [Basically,] (mummification) consisted of removing the internal organs, applying natural preservatives inside and out, and then wrapping the body in layers of bandages. [And] (the process) was remarkably effective. [Indeed,] (mummies) several thousand years old have been discovered nearly intact. (Their) skin, hair, teeth, finger- and toenails, and facial features are [still] evident. (Their) diseases in life, such as smallpox, arthritis, and nutritional deficiencies, are [still] diagnosable. [Even] (their) fatal afflictions are [still] apparent: a middle-aged king died from a blow on the head; a child king died from polio.

Topic sentence

Circled words: pronouns; repeated or restated key terms

Boxed words: links between sentences

Point 1: what mummification is

Point 2: why the Egyptians were masters

Specific examples

Underlined phrases: parallel form for parallel content

Though some of the connections in this paragraph were added in revision, the writer attended to them while drafting as well. Not only superficial coherence but also an underlying clarity of relationships can be achieved by tying each sentence to the one before—generalizing from it, clarifying it, qualifying it, adding to it, illustrating it. Each sentence in a paragraph creates an expectation of some sort in the mind of the reader, a question such as "How was a mummy made?" or "How intact are the mummies?" or "What's another example?" When you recognize these expectations and try to fulfil them, readers are likely to understand relationships without struggle.

Organizing the paragraph

The paragraphs on mummies illustrate an essential element of coherence: information must be arranged in an order that readers can follow easily and that corresponds to their expectations. The common organizations for paragraphs correspond to those for entire essays (see pp. 51–53): by space, by time, and for emphasis. (In addition, the patterns of development also suggest certain arrangements. See pp. 94–104.)

Organizing by space or time

A paragraph organized **spatially** focuses readers' attention on one point and scans a person, object, or scene from that point. The movement usually parallels the way people actually look at things, from top to bottom, from side to side, from near to far. Virginia Woolf follows the last pattern in the following paragraph.

> The sun struck straight upon the house, making the white walls glare between the dark windows. Their panes, woven thickly with green branches, held circles of impenetrable darkness. Sharp-edged wedges of light lay upon the window-sill and showed inside the room plates with blue rings, cups with curved handles, the bulge of a great bowl, the criss-cross pattern in the rug, and the formidable corners and lines of cabinets and bookcases. Behind their conglomeration hung a zone of shadow in which might be a further shape to be disencumbered of shadow or still denser depths of darkness.
>
> —VIRGINIA WOOLF, *The Waves*

Description moving from outside (closer) to inside (farther)

Central idea implied: sunlight barely penetrated the house's secrets

Another familiar way of organizing the elements of a paragraph is **chronologically**—that is, in order of their occurrence in time. In a chronological paragraph, as in experience, the earliest events come first, followed by more recent ones.

> Nor can a tree live without soil. A hurricane-born mangrove island may bring its own soil to the sea. But other mangrove trees make their own soil—and their own islands—from scratch. These are the ones which interest me. The seeds germinate in the fruit on

Topic sentence [brackets: "But other mangrove trees make their own soil—and their own islands—from scratch. These are the ones which interest me."]

> the tree. The germinated embryo can drop anywhere—say, onto a dab of floating muck. The heavy root end sinks; a leafy plumule unfurls. The tiny seedling, afloat, is on its way. Soon aerial roots shooting out in all directions trap debris. The sapling's networks twine, the interstices narrow, and water calms in the lee. Bacteria thrive on organic broth; amphipods swarm. These creatures grow and die at the tree's wet feet. The soil thickens, accumulating rainwater, leaf rot, seashells, and guano; the island spreads.
>
> —ANNIE DILLARD, "Sojourner"

Details in order of their occurrence

Organizing for emphasis

Some organizational schemes are imposed on paragraphs to achieve a certain emphasis. In the **general-to-specific** scheme, the topic sentence generally comes first and then the following sentences become increasingly specific. The paragraph on mummies (p. 83) illustrates this organization: each sentence is either more specific than the one before it or at the same level of generality. Here is another illustration:

> Perhaps the simplest fact about sleep is that individual needs for it vary widely. Most adults sleep between seven and nine hours, but occasionally people turn up who need twelve hours or so, while some rare types can get by on three or four. Rarest of all are those legendary types who require almost no sleep at all; respected researchers have recently studied three such people. One of them—a healthy, happy woman in her seventies—sleeps about an hour every two or three days. The other two are men in early middle age, who get by on a few minutes a night. One of them complains about the daily fifteen minutes or so he's forced to "waste" in sleeping.
>
> —LAWRENCE A. MAYER, "The Confounding Enemy of Sleep"

Topic sentence

Supporting examples, increasingly specific

In the **specific-to-general** organization, the elements of the paragraph build to a general conclusion.

> It's disconcerting that so many college women, when asked how their children will be cared for if they themselves work, refer with vague confidence to "the day care center" as though there were some great amorphous kiddie watcher out there that the state

Common belief

provides. But such places, adequately funded, well run, and available to all, are still scarce in this country, particularly for middle-class women. And figures show that when she takes time off for family-connected reasons (births, child care), a woman's chances for career advancement plummet. In a job market that's steadily tightening and getting more competitive, these obstacles bode the kind of danger ahead that can shatter not only professions, but egos. A hard reality is that there's not much more support for our daughters who have family-plus-career goals than there was for us; there's simply a great deal more self and societal pressure.

Actual situation

General conclusion: topic sentence

—JUDITH WAX, *Starting in the Middle*

When your details vary in significance, you can arrange them in a **climactic** order, from least to most important or dramatic.

Nature has put many strange tongues into the heads of her creatures. There is the frog's tongue, rooted at the front of the mouth so it can be protruded an extra distance for nabbing prey. There is the gecko lizard's tongue, so long and agile that the lizard uses it to wash its eyes. But the ultimate lingual whopper has been achieved in the anteater. The anteater's head, long as it is, is not long enough to contain the tremendous tongue which licks deep into anthills. Its tongue is not rooted in the mouth or throat: it is fastened to the breastbone.

Topic sentence

Least dramatic example

Most dramatic example

—ALAN DEVOE, "Nature's Utmost"

In other organizations, details are arranged according to readers' likely understanding of them. In discussing the virtues of public television, for instance, you might proceed from **most familiar to least familiar,** from a well-known program your readers have probably seen to less well-known programs they may not have seen. Or in defending the right of government employees to strike, you might arrange your reasons from **simplest to most complex,** from the employees' need to be able to redress grievances to more subtle consequences for employer-employee relations.

Using parallel structures

Another way to achieve coherence, although not necessarily in every paragraph, is through **parallelism**—the use of similar grammatical structures for similar elements of meaning within a sentence or among sentences. (See Chapter 17 for a detailed discussion of parallelism.) Parallel structures help tie together the last three sentences in the paragraph on mummies (p. 83). In the following paragraph, underlining highlights the parallel structures linking sentences. Aphra Behn (1640–89) was the first Englishwoman to write professionally.

> In addition to her busy career as a writer, Aphra Behn also found time to briefly marry and spend a little while in debtor's prison. She found time to take up a career as a spy for the English in their war against the Dutch. She made the long and difficult voyage to Suriname [in South America] and became involved in a slave rebellion there. She plunged into political debate at Will's Coffee House and defended her position from the stage of the Drury Lane Theatre. She actively argued for women's rights to be educated and to marry whom they pleased, or not at all. She defied the seventeenth-century dictum that ladies must be "modest" and wrote freely about sex. —ANGELINE GOREAU, "Aphra Behn"

3 Repeating or restating words and word groups

Repeating or restating key words or word groups is an important means of achieving paragraph coherence and of reminding your readers what the topic is. In the next example, notice how the circled words tie the sentences together and stress the important ideas of the paragraph.

> Having listened to both Chinese and English, I also tend to be suspicious of any comparisons between the two languages. Typically, one language—that of the person doing the comparing—is often used as the standard, the benchmark for a logical form of expression. And so the language being compared is always in danger of being judged deficient or superfluous, simplistic or unnecessarily complex, melodious or cacophonous. English speakers point out that Chinese is extremely difficult because it relies on variations in tone barely discernible to the human ear. By the same token, Chinese speakers tell me English is extremely difficult because it is inconsistent, a language of too many broken rules, of Mickey Mice and Donald Ducks. —AMY TAN, "The Language of Discretion"

NOTE Though planned repetition can be effective, careless or excessive repetition weakens prose (see pp. 463–64).

Using pronouns

Pronouns, such as *she, he, it, they,* and *who,* refer to and function as nouns (see p. 155). Thus pronouns naturally help relate sentences to one another. In the following paragraph the pronouns are circled.

> After dark, on the warrenlike streets of Brooklyn where I live, I often see women who fear the worst from me. They seem to have set their faces on neutral, and with their purse straps strung across their chests bandolier-style, they forge ahead as though bracing themselves against being tackled. I understand, of course, that the danger they perceive is not a hallucination. Women are particularly vulnerable to street violence, and young black males are drastically overrepresented among the perpetrators of that violence. Yet these truths are no solace against the kind of alienation that comes of being ever the suspect, a fearsome entity with whom pedestrians avoid making eye contact.
>
> —Brent Staples, "Black Men and Public Space"

Being consistent

Being consistent is the most subtle way to achieve paragraph coherence because readers are aware of consistency only when it is absent. Consistency (or the lack of it) occurs primarily in the tense of verbs and the number and person of nouns and pronouns (see Chapter 13). Although some shifts will be necessary because of meaning, inappropriate shifts, as in the following passages, will interfere with a reader's ability to follow the development of ideas.

Shifts in tense

In the Hopi religion, water *is* the driving force. Since the Hopi *lived* in the Arizona desert, they *needed* water urgently for drinking, cooking, and irrigating crops. Their complex beliefs *are* focused in part on gaining the assistance of supernatural forces in obtaining water. Many of the Hopi kachinas, or spirit essences, *were* directly concerned with clouds, rain, and snow.

Shifts in number

Kachinas represent spiritually the things and events of the real world, such as cumulus clouds, mischief, cornmeal, and even death. A *kachina* is not worshipped as a god but regarded as an interested friend. *They* visit the Hopi from December through July in the form of men who dress in kachina costumes and perform dances and other rituals.

SHIFTS IN PERSON

Unlike the man, the Hopi *woman* does not keep contact with kachinas through costumes and dancing. Instead, *one* receives a tihu, or small effigy, of a kachina from the man impersonating the kachina. *You* are more likely to receive a tihu as a girl approaching marriage, though a child or older woman sometimes receives one, too.

6 Using transitional expressions

Specific words and word groups, called **transitional expressions,** can connect sentences whose relationships may not be instantly clear to readers. Notice the difference in these two versions of the same paragraph:

> Medical science has succeeded in identifying the hundreds of viruses that can cause the common cold. It has discovered the most effective means of prevention. One person transmits the cold viruses to another most often by hand. An infected person covers his mouth to cough. He picks up the telephone. His daughter picks up the telephone. She rubs her eyes. She has a cold. It spreads. To avoid colds, people should wash their hands often and keep their hands away from their faces.

Paragraph coherent but choppy and hard to follow

> Medical science has [thus] succeeded in identifying the hundreds of viruses that can cause the common cold. It has [also] discovered the most effective means of prevention. One person transmits the cold viruses to another most often by hand. [For instance,] an infected person covers his mouth to cough. [Then] he picks up the telephone. [Half an hour later,] his daughter picks up the [same] telephone. [Immediately afterward,] she rubs her eyes. [Within a few days,] she, [too,] has a cold.

Transitional expressions (boxed) remove choppiness and spell out relationships

And thus it spreads. To avoid colds, therefore, people should wash their hands often and keep their hands away from their faces.

—KATHLEEN LAFRANK (student),
"Colds: Myth and Science"

Following is a partial list of transitional expressions, arranged by the functions they perform. (For a discussion of transitions *between* paragraphs, see pp. 111 and 112–15.)

Transitional expressions

TO ADD OR SHOW SEQUENCE

again, also, and, then, besides, equally important, finally, first, further, furthermore, in addition, in the first place, last, moreover, next, second, still, too

TO COMPARE

also, in the same way, likewise, similarly

TO CONTRAST

although, and yet, but, but at the same time, despite, even so, even though, for all that, however, in contrast, in spite of, nevertheless, notwithstanding, on the contrary, on the other hand, regardless, still, though, yet

TO GIVE EXAMPLES OR INTENSIFY

after all, an illustration of, even, for example, for instance, indeed, in fact, it is true, of course, specifically, that is, to illustrate, truly

TO INDICATE PLACE

above, adjacent to, below, elsewhere, farther on, here, near, nearby, on the other side, opposite to, there, to the east, to the left

TO INDICATE TIME

after a while, afterward, as long as, as soon as, at last, at length, at that time, before, earlier, formerly, immediately, in the meantime, in the past, lately, later, meanwhile, now, presently, shortly, simultaneously, since, so far, soon, subsequently, then, thereafter, until, when

TO REPEAT, SUMMARIZE, OR CONCLUDE

all in all, altogether, as has been said, in brief, in conclusion, in other words, in particular, in short, in simpler terms, in summary, on the whole, that is, therefore, to put it differently, to summarize

TO SHOW CAUSE OR EFFECT

accordingly, as a result, because, consequently, for this purpose, hence, otherwise, since, then, therefore, thereupon, thus, to this end, with this object

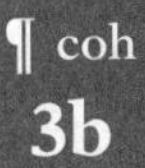

Combining devices to achieve coherence

The devices we have examined for achieving coherence rarely appear in isolation in effective paragraphs. As any example in this chapter shows, writers usually combine sensible organization, parallelism, repetition, pronouns, consistency, and transitional expressions to help readers follow the development of ideas. And the devices also figure, naturally, in the whole essay (see pp. 112–15 for an example of paragraphs linked in an essay).

Exercise 6
Analysing paragraphs for coherence

Study the paragraphs by Janet Lieber (p. 80), Hillary Begas (p. 95), and Freeman Dyson (pp. 96–97) for the author's use of various devices to achieve coherence. Look especially for organization, parallel structures and ideas, repetition and restatement, pronouns, and transitional expressions.

Exercise 7
Arranging sentences coherently

After the topic sentence (sentence 1), the sentences in the paragraph below have been deliberately scrambled to make the paragraph incoherent. Using the topic sentence and other clues as guides, rearrange the sentences in the paragraph to form a well-organized, coherent unit.

The animal is an eating machine, even if it is not always hun- 1
gry. It *must* chaw continually with its chisel-like teeth or it will per- 2
ish. Trees up to forty-two inches in diameter have been felled by 3
these determined lumber-rats, their heads tilted as they chew
against the grain, spitting out the chips. The incisors can chop 4
their way through a six-inch tree in five minutes. Its four self- 5
sharpening incisors, coated with bright orange enamel, can grow
up to a length of seven inches and if not worn down by constant
gnawing will eventually pierce the beaver's skull.

-PETER NEWMAN, *Company of Adventurers*

Exercise 8
Eliminating inconsistencies

The following paragraph is incoherent because of inconsistencies in person, number, or tense. Identify the inconsistencies and revise the paragraph to give it coherence.

The Hopi tihu, or kachina effigy, is often called a "doll," but its owner, usually a girl or woman, does not regard them as a plaything. Instead, you treated them as a valued possession and hung them out of the way on a wall. For its owner the tihu represents a connection with the kachina's spirit. They are considered part of the kachina, carrying a portion of the kachina's power.

Exercise 9
Using transitional expressions

Transitional expressions have been removed from the following paragraph at the numbered blanks. Fill in each blank with an appropriate transitional expression (1) to contrast, (2) to intensify, and (3) to show effect. Consult the list on page 90 if necessary.

All over the country people are swimming, jogging, weightlifting, dancing, walking, playing tennis—doing anything to keep fit. ___(1)___ this school has consistently refused to construct and equip a fitness centre. The school has ___(2)___ refused to open existing athletic facilities to all students, not just those playing organized sports. ___(3)___ students have no place to exercise except in their rooms and on dangerous public roads.

Exercise 10
Considering your past work: Paragraph coherence

Continuing from Exercise 3 (p. 81), examine the body paragraphs of your essay to see how coherent they are and how their coherence could be improved. Do the paragraphs have a clear organization? Do you use parallelism, repetition and restatement, pronouns, and transitional expressions to signal relationships? Are the paragraphs consistent in person, number, and tense? Revise two or three paragraphs in ways you think will improve their coherence.

Exercise 11
Writing a coherent paragraph

Write a coherent paragraph from the following information, combining and rewriting sentences as necessary. First, begin the paragraph with the topic sentence given and arrange the supporting sentences in a climactic order. Then combine and rewrite the supporting sentences, helping the reader see connections by introducing parallelism, repetition and restatement, pronouns, consistency, and transitional expressions.

Topic sentence

Hypnosis is far superior to drugs for relieving tension.

Supporting information

Hypnosis has none of the dangerous side effects of the drugs that relieve tension.

Tension-relieving drugs can cause weight loss or gain, illness, or even death.

Hypnosis is nonaddicting.

Most of the drugs that relieve tension do foster addiction.

Tension-relieving drugs are expensive.

Hypnosis is inexpensive even for people who have not mastered self-hypnosis.

Exercise 12
Turning topic sentences into coherent paragraphs

Develop three of the following topic sentences into coherent paragraphs. Organize your information by space, by time, or for emphasis, as seems most appropriate. Use parallelism, repetition and restatement, pronouns, consistency, and transitional expressions to link sentences.

1. The most interesting character in the book (or movie) was ________.
2. Of all my courses, ________ is the one that I think will serve me best throughout life.
3. Although we Canadians face many problems, the one we should concentrate on solving first is ________ .
4. The most dramatic building in town is the ________ .
5. Children should not have to worry about the future.

3c Developing the paragraph

In an essay that's understandable and interesting to readers, you will provide plenty of solid information to support your general statements. The place where you work that information into the essay is in the paragraph, as you build up each point relating to the thesis. A paragraph may be unified and coherent but still be inadequate if you skimp on details. For instance:

> Despite complaints from viewers, television commercials aren't getting any more realistic. Their makers still present idealized people in unreal situations. And the advertisers also persist in showing a version of male-female relationships that can't exist in more than two households. What do the advertisers know about us, or about how we see ourselves, that makes them continue to plunge millions of dollars into these kinds of commercials?

General statements needing examples to be convincing

This paragraph lacks **development,** completeness. It does not provide enough information for us to evaluate or even care about the writer's assertions.

¶ dev
3c

Using specific information

If they are sound, the general statements you make in any writing will be based on what you have experienced, observed, read, and thought. Readers will assume as much and will expect you to provide the evidence for your statements—sensory details, facts, statistics, examples, quotations, reasons. Whatever helps you form your views you need, in turn, to share with readers.

Here is the actual version of the preceding sample paragraph. With examples, the paragraph is interesting and convincing.

> Despite complaints from viewers, television commercials aren't getting any more realistic. Their makers still present idealized people in unreal situations. Friendly shopkeepers stock only their favourite brand of toothpaste or coffee or soup. A mother cleans and buffs her kitchen floor to a mirror finish so her baby can play on it. A rosy-cheeked pregnant woman uses two babies, two packaged diapers neatly dissected, and two ink blotters to demonstrate one diaper's superior absorbency to her equally rosy-cheeked and pregnant friend. The advertisers also persist in showing a version of male-female relationships that can't exist in more than two households. The wife panics because a meddlesome neighbour points out that her husband's shirt is dirty. Or she fears for her marriage because her finicky husband doesn't like her coffee. What do the advertisers know about us, or about how we see ourselves, that makes them continue to plunge millions of dollars into these kinds of commercials?
>
> —Kelly Phelps (student), "Television Advertising"

Examples supporting general statements about idealized people and false relationships

Using a pattern of development

If you have difficulty developing an idea or shaping your information, then try using one of the patterns of development. (They correspond to the patterns of essay development discussed on pp. 38–40.) Ask yourself a series of questions about an idea.

How did it happen? (Narration)

Narration retells a significant sequence of events, usually in the order of their occurrence (that is, chronologically).

> Jill's story is typical for "recruits" to religious cults. She was very lonely in university and appreciated the attention of the nice young men and women who lived in a house near campus. They persuaded her to share their meals and then to move in with them. Between intense bombardments of "love," they deprived her of sleep and sometimes threatened to throw her out. Jill became increasingly confused and dependent, losing touch with any reality besides the one in the group. She dropped out of school and refused to see or communicate with her family. Before long she, too, was preying on lonely university students.
>
> —HILLARY BEGAS (student), "The Love Bombers"

Important events in chronological order

As this paragraph illustrates, a narrator is concerned not just with the sequence of events but also with their consequence, their importance to the whole. Thus a narrative rarely corresponds to real time; instead, it collapses transitional or background events and focuses on events of particular interest. In addition, writers often rearrange events, as when they simulate the workings of memory by flashing back to an earlier time.

How does it look, sound, feel, smell, taste? (Description)

Description details the sensory qualities of a person, place, thing, or feeling. You use concrete and specific words to convey a dominant mood, to illustrate an idea, or to achieve some other purpose. Some description is **subjective:** the writer filters the subject through his or her biases and emotions. In Virginia Woolf's subjective description on page 84, the *glare* of the white walls, the *impenetrable darkness,* the *bulge of a great bowl,* and the *formidable corners and lines* all indicate Woolf's feelings about what she describes.

In contrast to subjective description, journalists and scientists often favour description that is **objective,** conveying the subject without bias or emotion.

> The two toddlers, both boys, sat together for half an hour in a three-metre-square room with yellow walls (one with a two-way mirror for observation) and a brown carpet. The room was unfurnished except for two small chairs and about two dozen toys. The boys' interaction was generally tense. They often struggled physically and verbally over several toys, especially a large red beach ball and a small wooden fire engine. The larger of the

Objective description: specific record of sensory data without interpretation

two boys often pushed the smaller away or pried his hands from the desired object. This larger boy never spoke, but he did make grunting sounds when he was engaging the other. In turn, the smaller boy twice uttered piercing screams of "No!" and once shouted "Stop that!" When he was left alone, he hummed and muttered to himself.

—RAY MATTISON (student), "Case Study: Play Patterns of Toddlers"

What are examples of it or reasons for it? (Illustration or support)

Some ideas can be developed simply by **illustration or support**—supplying detailed examples or reasons. The writer of the paragraph on television commercials (p. 94) developed her idea with several specific examples of each general statement. You can also supply a single extended example.

The language problem that I was attacking loomed larger and larger as I began to learn more. When I would describe in English certain concepts and objects enmeshed in Korean emotion and imagination, I became slowly aware of nuances, of differences between two languages even in simple expression. The remark "Kim entered the house" seems to be simple enough, yet, unless a reader has a clear visual image of a Korean house, his understanding of the sentence is not complete. When a Korean says he is "in the house," he may be in his courtyard, or on his porch, or in his small room! If I wanted to give a specific picture of entering the house in the Western sense, I had to say "room" instead of house—sometimes. I say "sometimes" because many Koreans entertain their guests on their porches and still are considered to be hospitable, and in the Korean sense, going into the "room" may be a more intimate act than it would be in the English sense. Such problems!

[Topic sentence (assertion to be illustrated)]
[Single detailed example]

—KIM YONG IK, "A Book-Writing Venture"

Sometimes you can develop a paragraph by providing your reasons for stating a general idea. For instance:

There are three reasons, quite apart from scientific considerations, that mankind needs to travel in space. The first reason is the need

[Topic sentence]

for garbage disposal: we need to transfer industrial processes into space, so that the earth may remain a green and pleasant place for our grandchildren to live in. The second reason is the need to escape material impoverishment: the resources of this planet are finite, and we shall not forgo forever the abundant solar energy and minerals and living space that are spread out all around us. The third reason is our spiritual need for an open frontier: the ultimate purpose of space travel is to bring to humanity not only scientific discoveries and an occasional spectacular show on television but a real expansion of our spirit.

Three reasons arranged in order of increasing drama and importance

—FREEMAN DYSON, "Disturbing the Universe"

What is it? What does it encompass, and what does it exclude? (Definition)

A **definition** says what something is and is not, specifying the characteristics that distinguish the subject from the other members of its class. You can easily define concrete, noncontroversial terms in a single sentence: *A knife is a cutting instrument* (its class) *with a sharp blade set in a handle* (the characteristics that set it off from, say, scissors or a razor blade). But defining a complicated or controversial topic often requires extended explanation, and you may need to devote a whole paragraph or even an essay to it. Such a definition may provide examples to identify the subject's characteristics. It may also involve other methods of development discussed below, such as classification or comparison and contrast.

The following definition of the word *quality* comes from an essay asserting that "quality in product and effort has become a vanishing element of current civilization."

In the hope of possibly reducing the hail of censure which is certain to greet this essay (I am thinking of going to Alaska or possibly Patagonia in the week it is published), let me say that quality, as I understand it, means investment of the best skill and effort possible to produce the finest and most admirable result possible.

General definition

Its presence or absence in some degree characterizes every man-made object, service, skilled or unskilled labor—laying bricks, painting a picture, ironing shirts, practicing medicine, shoemaking, scholarship, writing a book.

Activities in which quality may figure

You do it well or you do it half-well. Materials are sound and durable or they are sleazy; method is pain-

¶ dev
3c

staking or whatever is easiest. Quality is achieving or reaching for the highest standard as against being satisfied with the sloppy or fraudulent. It is honesty of purpose as against catering to cheap or sensational sentiment. It does not allow compromise with the second-rate.

—BARBARA TUCHMAN, "The Decline of Quality"

Contrast between quality and nonquality

What are its parts or characteristics? (Division or analysis)

Division and **analysis** both involve separating something into its elements, the better to understand it. Here is a simple example:

A typical daily newspaper compresses considerable information into the top of the first page, above the headlines. The most prominent feature of this space, the newspaper's name, is called the *logo* or *nameplate.* Under the logo and set off by rules is a line of small type called the *folio line,* which contains the date of the issue, the volume and issue numbers, copyright information, and the price. To the right of the logo is a block of small type called a *weather ear,* a summary of the day's forecast. And above the logo is a *skyline,* a kind of advertisement in which the paper's editors highlight a special feature of the issue.

—KANSHA STONE (student), "Anatomy of a Paper"

The subject being divided

Elements of the subject, arranged spatially

Generally, analysis goes beyond simply identifying elements. Often used as a synonym for *critical thinking,* analysis also involves interpreting the elements' meaning, significance, and relationships. You identify and interpret elements according to your particular interest in the subject, your own framework for analysis. (See pp. 10–14 for more on critical thinking and analytical frameworks.)

The following paragraph comes from an essay about soap operas. The analytical framework of the whole essay is the way soap operas provide viewers with a sense of community missing from their own lives. The paragraph itself has a narrower framework related to the broader one.

The surface realism of the soap opera conjures up an illusion of "liveness." The domestic settings and easygoing rhythms encourage the viewer to believe that the drama, however ridiculous, is simply an extension of daily life. The conversation is so slow that some have called it "radio with pictures." (Advertisers have always assumed that

Topic and framework: how "liveness" seems an extension of daily life

Elements:

Slow conversation

busy housewives would listen, rather than watch.) Conversation is casual and colloquial, as though one were eavesdropping on neighbors. There is plenty of time to "read" the character's face; close-ups establish intimacy. The sets are comfortably familiar: well-lit interiors of living rooms, restaurants, offices, and hospitals. Daytime soaps have little of the glamour of their prime-time relations. The viewer easily imagines that the conversation is taking place in real time.

—RUTH ROSEN, "Search for Yesterday"

Casual conversation

Intimate close-ups

Familiar sets

Absence of glamour

Appearance of real time

What groups or categories can it be sorted into? (Classification)

Classification involves sorting many things into groups based on their similarities. Using the pattern, we scan a large group composed of many members that share at least one characteristic—office workers, say—and we assign the members to smaller groups on the basis of some principle—salary, perhaps, or dependence on computers. Here is an example:

In my experience, the parents who hire daytime sitters for their school-age children tend to fall into one of three groups. The first group includes parents who work and want someone to be at home when the children return from school. These parents are looking for an extension of themselves, someone who will give the care they would give if they were at home. The second group includes parents who may be home all day themselves but are too disorganized or too frazzled by their children's demands to handle child care alone. They are looking for an organizer and helpmate. The third and final group includes parents who do not want to be bothered by their children, whether they are home all day or not. Unlike the parents in the first two groups, who care for their children whenever and however they can, these parents are looking for a permanent substitute for themselves.

—NANCY WHITTLE (student), "Modern Parenting"

Topic sentence

Three groups:

Alike in one way (all hire sitters)

No overlap in groups (each has a different attitude)

Classes arranged in order of increasing drama

How is it like, or different from, other things? (Comparison and contrast)

Asking about similarities and differences leads to **comparison and contrast:** comparison focuses on similarities, whereas contrast focuses on differences. The two may be used separately or together to develop an idea or to relate two or more things. Commonly, comparisons are organized in one of two ways. In the first, **subject by subject,** the two subjects are discussed separately, one at a time.

> A house is all right for a man to work in. He brings his work into the house, a place is cleared for it; the house rearranges itself as best it can around him. Everybody recognizes that his work exists. He is not expected to answer the telephone, to find things that are lost, to see why the children are crying, or to feed the cat. He can shut his door. Imagine (I said) a mother shutting her door, and the children knowing she is behind it; why, the very thought of it is outrageous to them. A woman who sits staring into space, into a country that is not her husband's or her children's is likewise known to be an offense against nature. So a house is not the same for a woman. She is not someone who walks into the house to make use of it, and will walk out again She is the house; there is no separation possible.
>
> —ALICE MUNRO, "The Office"

[Margin annotations: A man in a house; A woman in a house]

In the second comparative organization, **point by point,** the two subjects are discussed side by side and matched feature for feature.

> The first electronic computer, ENIAC, went into operation not even fifty years ago, yet the differences between it and today's home computer are enormous. ENIAC was enormous itself, consisting of forty panels, each approximately half a metre wide and a metre deep. Today's PC or Macintosh, by contrast, fits easily on a small table. ENIAC had to be configured by hand, with its programmers taking up to two days to reset switches and cables. Today, the average home user can change programs in an instant. And for all its size and inconvenience, ENIAC was also slow. In its time, its operating speed of 100 000 pulses per second seemed amazingly fast. However, today's home machine can operate at 4 million pulses per second or faster.
>
> —SHIRLEY KAJIWARA (student), "The Computers We Deserve"

[Margin annotations: Subjects: ENIAC and home computer; Size: ENIAC, home computer; Ease of programming: ENIAC, home computer; Speed: ENIAC, home computer]

The following examples show the two organizing schemes in outline form. The one on the left corresponds to the point-by-point paragraph immediately above. The one on the right uses the same information but reorganizes it to cover the two subjects separately, first one, then the other.

POINT BY POINT	SUBJECT BY SUBJECT
I. Size	I. ENIAC
A. ENIAC	A. Size
B. Home computer	B. Ease of programming
II. Ease of programming	C. Speed
A. ENIAC	II. Home computer
B. Home computer	A. Size
III. Speed	B. Ease of programming
A. ENIAC	C. Speed
B. Home computer	

Is it comparable to something that is in a different class but more familiar to readers? (Analogy)

Whereas we draw comparisons and contrasts between elements in the same general class (audiences, computers), we link elements in different classes with a special kind of comparison called **analogy.** Most often in analogy we illuminate or explain an unfamiliar, abstract class of things with a familiar and concrete class of things.

> We might eventually obtain some sort of bedrock understanding of cosmic structure, but we will never understand the universe in detail; it is just too big and varied for that. If we possessed an atlas of our galaxy that devoted but a single page to each star system in the Milky Way (so that the sun and all its planets were crammed on one page), that atlas would run to more than ten million volumes of ten thousand pages each. It would take a library the size of Harvard's to house the atlas, and merely to flip through it, at the rate of a page per second, would require over ten thousand years.
> —TIMOTHY FERRIS, *Coming of Age in the Milky Way*

Abstract subject: the universe, specifically the Milky Way

Concrete subject: an atlas

Why did it happen, or what results did it have? (Cause-and-effect analysis)

When you use analysis to explain why something happened or what is likely to happen, then you are determining causes and effects. **Cause-and-effect analysis** is especially useful in writing about social, economic, or political events or problems. In the next paragraph the author looks at the causes of Japanese collectivism, which he elsewhere contrasts with American individualism.

> The *shinkansen* or "bullet train" speeds across the rural areas of Japan giving a quick view of cluster after cluster of farmhouses

Effect: pattern of Japanese farming

surrounded by rice paddies. This particular pattern did not develop purely by chance, but as a consequence of the technology peculiar to the growing of rice, the staple of the Japanese diet. The growing of rice requires the construction and maintenance of an irrigation system, something that takes many hands to build. More importantly, the planting and the harvesting of rice can only be done efficiently with the cooperation of twenty or more people. The "bottom line" is that a single family working alone cannot produce enough rice to survive, but a dozen families working together can produce a surplus. Thus the Japanese have had to develop the capacity to work together in harmony, no matter what the forces of disagreement or social disintegration, in order to survive.

—William Ouchi, *Theory Z: How American Business Can Meet the Japanese Challenge*

Causes: Japanese dependence on rice, which requires collective effort

Effect: working in harmony

Cause-and-effect paragraphs tend to focus either on causes, as Ouchi's does, or on effects, as the next paragraph does.

The War of 1812 thus tended to bring British North America together and strengthened the bond with Britain. Any common feelings among the colonists, however, were largely directed against the United States. This anti-American spirit was still a narrow basis on which to build a Canadian nationalism. Anti-Americanism was particularly evident in Upper Canada. Further American settlement was largely prevented there, and American settlers already in the province were in danger of persecution—the Loyalists' case in reverse—if their declarations of British sentiments were not loud enough. Nevertheless, on the whole these reactions to the strain of the War of 1812 were understandable and not an extreme price to pay for the survival of British North America.

—J. M. S. Careless, *Canada: A Story of Challenge*

Cause: War of 1812

Effects: Anti-Americanism

Examples

How does one do it, or how does it work? (Process analysis)

When you analyze how to do something or how something works, you explain the steps in a **process.** Paragraphs developed by process analysis are usually organized chronologically or spatially, as the steps in the process occur. Some process analyses tell the reader how to do a task.

> As a car owner, you waste money when you pay a mechanic to change the engine oil. The job is not difficult, even if you know little about cars. All you need is a wrench to remove the drain plug, a large, flat pan to collect the draining oil, plastic bottles to dispose of the used oil, and fresh oil. First, warm up the car's engine so that the oil will flow more easily. When the engine is warm, shut it off and remove its oil-filler cap (the owner's manual shows where this cap is). Then locate the drain plug under the engine (again consulting the owner's manual for its location) and place the flat pan under the plug. Remove the plug with the wrench, letting the oil flow into the pan. When the oil stops flowing, replace the plug and, at the engine's filler hole, add the amount and kind of fresh oil specified by the owner's manual. Pour the used oil into the plastic bottles and take it to a waste-oil collector, which any garage mechanic can recommend.
>
> —ANTHONY ANDREAS (student), "Do-It-Yourself Car Care"

Process: changing oil

Equipment needed

Steps in process

Other process analyses explain how processes are done or how they work in nature. Annie Dillard's paragraph on mangrove islands (pp. 84–85) is one example. Here is another:

> What used to be called "laying on of hands" is now practised seriously by nurses and doctors. Studies have shown that therapeutic touch, as it is now known, can aid relaxation and ease pain, two effects that may in turn cause physiological healing. A "healer" must first concentrate on helping the patient. Then, hands held a few centimetres from the patient's body, the healer moves from head to foot. The state of concentration allows the healer to detect energy disturbances in the patient that indicate localized tension, pain, or sickness. With further hand movements, the healer can redirect the energy. Patients report feeling heat from the healer's hands, perhaps indicating an energy transfer between healer and patient.
>
> —LISA KUKLINSKI (student), "Old Ways to Noninvasive Medicine"

Process: therapeutic touch

Benefits

Steps in process

How process works

Combining patterns of development

Whatever pattern you choose as the basis for developing a paragraph, other patterns may also prove helpful. We have seen combined patterns often in this section: Dyson analyses causes and effects in presenting reasons (pp. 96–97); Tuchman uses contrast to define *quality* (pp. 97–98); Kajiwara uses description to compare (p. 100); Ouchi uses process analysis to explain causes (pp. 101–02).

As you will see in 3e, the paragraphs within an essay inevitably will be developed with a variety of patterns, even when one controlling pattern develops and structures the entire essay.

Checking length

The average paragraph contains between 100 and 150 words, or between four and eight sentences. These numbers are averages, of course. The actual length of a paragraph depends on its topic, the role it plays in developing the thesis of the essay, and its position in the essay. Nevertheless, very short paragraphs are often inadequately developed; they may leave readers with a sense of incompleteness. And very long paragraphs often contain irrelevant details or develop two or more topics; readers may have difficulty sorting out or remembering ideas.

When you are revising your essay, reread the paragraphs that seem very long or very short, checking them especially for unity and adequate development. If the paragraph wanders, cut everything from it that does not support your main idea (such as sentences that you might begin with *By the way*). If it is underdeveloped, supply the specific details, examples, or reasons needed, or try one of the methods of development we have discussed here.

Exercise 13
Analysing paragraph development

Examine the paragraphs by Gloria Naylor (p. 79), Margaret Atwood (p. 80), and Judith Wax (pp. 85–86) to discover how the authors achieve paragraph development. What pattern or patterns of development does each author use? Where does each author support general statements with specific evidence?

Exercise 14
Analysing and revising skimpy paragraphs

The following paragraphs are not well developed. Analyse them, looking especially for general statements that lack support or leave questions in your mind. Then rewrite one into a well-developed paragraph, supplying your own concrete details or examples.

1. One big difference between successful and unsuccessful teachers is the quality of communication. A successful teacher is sensitive to students' needs and excited by the course subject. In contrast, an unsuccessful teacher seems uninterested in students and bored by the subject.

2. Gestures are one of our most important means of communication. We use them instead of speech. We use them to supplement the words we speak. And we use them to communicate some feelings or meanings that words cannot adequately express.

3. Children who have been disciplined too much are often easy to spot. Their behaviour toward adults may reflect the harsh treatment they have received from adults. And their behaviour toward other children may be uncontrolled.

Exercise 15
Considering your past work: Paragraph development

Continuing from Exercises 3 (p. 81) and 10 (p. 92), examine the development of the body paragraphs in your writing. Where does specific information seem adequate to support your general statements? Where does support seem skimpy? Revise the paragraphs as necessary so that readers will understand and appreciate your ideas. It may help you to pose the questions on pages 94–102.

Exercise 16
Writing with the patterns of development

Write at least three unified, coherent, and well-developed paragraphs, each one developed with a different pattern. Draw on the topics provided here, or choose your own topics.

1. *Narration*
   An experience of public speaking
   A disappointment
   Leaving home
   Waking up
2. *Description (objective or subjective)*
   Your room
   A crowded or deserted place
   A food
   An intimidating person
3. *Illustration or support*
   Why study
   Having a headache
   The best sports event
   Usefulness (or uselessness) of a self-help book
4. *Definition*
   Humour
   An adult
   Fear
   Authority
5. *Division or analysis*
   A television news show
   A barn
   A set for a movie or play
   A piece of music
6. *Classification*
   Factions in a campus controversy
   Styles of playing poker
   Types of street people
   Kinds of teachers
7. *Comparison and contrast*
   Driving a friend's car and driving your own car
   AM and FM radio announcers
   Junior and professional hockey
   Movies on TV and in a theatre
8. *Analogy*
   Paying taxes and giving blood
   The Charter of Right and Freedoms and a building's foundation
   Graduating from high school and being released from prison

9. *Cause-and-effect analysis*
   Connection between tension and anger
   Causes of failing a course
   Connection between credit cards and debt
   Causes of a serious accident

10. *Process analysis*
    Preparing for a job interview
    Making a cabinet
    Protecting your home from burglars
    Making a jump shot

3d Writing special kinds of paragraphs

Several kinds of paragraphs do not always follow the guidelines for unity, coherence, development, and length because they serve special functions. These are the essay introduction, the essay conclusion, the transitional or emphatic paragraph, and the paragraph of spoken dialogue.

1 Opening an essay

Most of your essays will open with a paragraph that draws readers from their world into your world. A good opening paragraph usually satisfies several requirements:

- It focuses readers' attention on your subject and arouses their curiosity about what you have to say.
- It specifies what your topic is and implies your attitude.
- Often it states your thesis sentence.
- It is concise and sincere.

To grab readers' attention, you have a number of options.

Some strategies for opening paragraphs

- State the subject.
- Use a quotation.
- Relate an incident.
- Create an image.
- Ask a question.
- State an opinion.
- Make a historical comparison or contrast
- Describe a problem or dilemma.

The most common introduction forms a kind of funnel: it starts generally with a statement or question about the subject, clarifies or narrows the subject in one or more sentences, and then, in the thesis sentence, asserts the central idea of the essay (see pp. 41–44). Here are two examples:

We Canadians love our doughnut shops. From coast to coast, in country and in city, you will find Canadians gathering in doughnut shops. We gather there not just to eat and drink but also to talk, to discuss, to see and be seen. What the cafe is to French public life, what the pub is to the English neighbourhood, so the doughnut shop is to the Canadian strip mall.

—TERRY PELLETIER (student), "Doughnut Dominion"

Subject related to reader's experience

Development of subject

Thesis sentence

Can your home or office computer make you sterile? Can it strike you blind or dumb? The answer is: probably not. Nevertheless, reports of side effects relating to computer use should be examined, especially in the area of birth defects, eye complaints, and postural difficulties. Although little conclusive evidence exists to establish a causal link between computer use and problems of this sort, the circumstantial evidence can be disturbing.

—THOMAS HARTMANN, "How Dangerous Is Your Computer?"

Subject related to reader's experience

Clarification of subject: bridge to thesis sentence

Thesis sentence

Several other types of introduction can be equally effective, though they are sometimes harder to invent and control. You can begin with a quotation that leads into the thesis sentence:

"It is difficult to speak adequately or justly of London," wrote Henry James in 1881. "It is not a pleasant place; it is not agreeable, or cheerful, or easy, or exempt from reproach. It is only magnificent." Were he alive today, James, a connoisseur of cities, might easily say the same thing about New York or Paris or Tokyo, for the great city is one of the paradoxes of history. In countless different ways, it has almost always been an unpleasant, disagreeable, cheerless, uneasy and reproachful place; in the end, it can only be described as magnificent. —*Time*

You can relate an incident or create an image that sets the stage for the thesis:

Canada is pink. I knew that from the map I owned when I was six. On it, New York was green and brown, which was true as far as I could see, so there was no reason to distrust the map maker's portrayal of Canada. When my parents took me across the border and we entered the immigration booth, I looked excitedly for the pink earth. Slowly it dawned on me; this foreign, "different" place

¶ 3d

was not so different. I discovered that the world in my head and the world at my feet were not the same.

—ROBERT ORNSTEIN, *Human Nature*

You can open with a startling question or opinion:

> Caesar was right. Thin people need watching. I've been watching them for most of my adult life, and I don't like what I see. When these narrow fellows spring at me, I quiver to my toes. Thin people come in all personalities, most of them menacing. You've got your "together" thin person, your mechanical thin person, your condescending thin person, your tsk-tsk thin person. All of them are dangerous. —SUZANNE BRITT, "That Lean and Hungry Look"

When some background to the essay is useful, you can begin with a historical comparison or contrast:

> Throughout the first half of this century, the American Medical Association, the largest and most powerful medical organization in the world, battled relentlessly to rid the country of quack potions and cure-alls; and it is the AMA that is generally credited with being the single most powerful force behind the enactment of the early pure food and drug laws. Today, however, medicine's guardian seems to have done a complete about-face and become one of the pharmaceutical industry's staunchest allies—often at the public's peril and expense.
>
> —MAC JEFFERY, "Does Rx Spell Rip-off?"

An effective introductory paragraph need not be long, as the following opener shows.

> I've often wondered what goes into a hot dog. Now I know and I wish I didn't. —WILLIAM ZINSSER, *The Lunacy Boom*

When writing and revising an introductory paragraph, avoid the following approaches that are likely to bore readers or make them question your sincerity or control.

Opening paragraphs to avoid

- Don't reach back too far with vague generalities or truths, such as those beginning "Throughout human history . . ." or "In today's world. . . ." You may have needed a warm-up paragraph to start drafting, but your readers can do without it.
- Don't start with "The purpose of this essay is . . . ," "In this essay I will . . . ," or any similar flat announcement of your intention or topic.
- Don't refer to the title of the essay in the first sentence—for example, "This is my favourite activity" or "This is a big problem."
- Don't start with "According to Webster . . ." or a similar phrase leading to a dictionary definition. A definition can be an effective

springboard to an essay, but this kind of lead-in has become dull with overuse.

- Don't apologize for your opinion or for inadequate knowledge with "I'm not sure if I'm right, but I think . . . ," "I don't know much about this, but . . . ," or similar lines.

2 Closing an essay

Most of your essays will end with a closing statement or conclusion, a signal to readers that you have not simply stopped writing but have actually finished. The conclusion completes the essay, bringing it to a climax while assuring readers that they have understood your intention. Usually set off in its own paragraph, the conclusion may consist of a single sentence or a group of sentences. It may take one or more of the approaches below.

Some strategies for closing paragraphs

- Create an image.
- Strike a note of hope or despair.
- Use a quotation.
- Give a symbolic or powerful fact or other detail.
- Recommend a course of action.
- Summarize the paper.
- Echo the introduction.
- Restate the thesis in a fresh way.

The following paragraph concludes the essay on the doughnut shop whose introduction is on page 107.

> Thus, the little circle of fried dough draws us together: police and citizen, senior and student, anglophone and francophone. [Summary] By day and by night, through summer's heat and winter's snow, the doughnut shop is there for us, our second home, our national refuge. [Conclusion]
>
> —TERRY PELLETIER (student), "Doughnut Dominion"

Maxine Hong Kingston uses a different technique—a vivid image—to conclude an essay on her aunt, a suicide by drowning.

> My aunt haunts me—her ghost drawn to me because now, after fifty years of neglect, I alone devote pages of paper to her, though not origamied into houses and clothes. I do not think she always means me well. I am telling on her, and she was a spite suicide, [Summary]

drowning herself in the drinking water. The Chinese are always very frightened of the drowned one, whose weeping ghost, wet hair hanging and skin bloated, waits silently by the water to pull down a substitute.

Image

—MAXINE HONG KINGSTON, "No Name Woman"

In the next paragraph the author concludes an essay on environmental protection with a call for action.

Until we get the answers, I think we had better keep on building power plants and growing food with the help of fertilizers and such insect-controlling chemicals as we now have. The risks are well known, thanks to the environmentalists. If they had not created a widespread public awareness of the ecological crisis, we wouldn't stand a chance.

Summary and opinion

But such awareness by itself is not enough. Flaming manifestos and prophecies of doom are no longer much help, and a search for scapegoats can only make matters worse. The time for sensations and manifestos is about over. Now we need rigorous analysis, united effort and very hard work.

Call for action

—PETER F. DRUCKER, "How Best to Protect the Environment"

These three paragraphs illustrate ways of avoiding several pitfalls of conclusions.

Closing paragraphs to avoid

- Don't simply restate your introduction—statement of subject, thesis sentence, and all. Presumably the paragraphs in the body of your essay have contributed something to the opening statements, and it's that something you want to capture in your conclusion.
- Don't start off in a new direction, with a subject different from the one your essay has been about. If you arrive at a new idea, this may be a signal to start fresh with that idea as your thesis.
- Don't conclude more than you reasonably can from the evidence you have presented. If your essay is about your frustrating experience trying to clear a parking ticket, you cannot reasonably conclude that *all* local police forces are tied up in red tape.
- Don't apologize for your essay or otherwise cast doubt on it. Don't say, "Even though I'm no expert," or "This may not be convincing, but I believe it's true," or anything similar. Rather, to win your readers' confidence, display confidence.

Using short emphatic or transitional paragraphs

A short, emphatic paragraph can give unusual stress to an important idea, in effect asking the reader to pause and consider before moving on.

> In short, all those who might have taken responsibility ducked it, and catastrophe was inevitable.

A transitional paragraph, because it is longer than a word or phrase and set off by itself, moves a discussion from one point to another more slowly or more completely than does a single transitional expression or even a transitional sentence attached to a larger paragraph.

> These, then, are the causes of the current expansion in hospital facilities. But how does this expansion affect the medical costs of the government, private insurers, and individuals?
>
> So the debates were noisy and emotion-packed. But what did they accomplish? Historians agree on at least three direct results.

Use transitional paragraphs rarely—only to shift readers' attention when your essay makes a significant turn. A paragraph like the following one betrays a writer who is stalling.

> Now that we have examined these facts, we can look at some others that are equally central to an examination of this important issue.

Writing dialogue

When recording a conversation between two or more people, start a new paragraph for each person's speech. The paragraphing establishes for the reader the point at which one speaker stops talking and another begins.

> The dark shape was indistinguishable. But once I'd flooded him with light, there he stood, blinking.
>
> "Well," he said eventually, "you're a sight for sore eyes. Should I stand here or are you going to let me in?"
>
> "Come in," I said. And in he came.
>
> —Louise Erdrich, *The Beet Queen*

Though dialogue appears most often in fictional writing (the source of the preceding example), it may occasionally freshen or enliven narrative or expository essays. (For guidance in using quotation marks and other punctuation in passages of dialogue, see pp. 398–99.)

Exercise 17
Analysing an introduction and conclusion

Analyse the introductory and concluding paragraphs in the first and final drafts of the student essay in Chapter 2, pages 57–58 and 68–70. What is wrong with the first-draft paragraphs? Why are the final-draft paragraphs better? Could they be improved still further?

Exercise 18
Considering your past work: Introductions and conclusions

Most writers struggle over introductions and conclusions. Have you devised any strategies that help you with these paragraphs? If you have problems with them, what are the difficulties?

Examine the opening and closing paragraphs of the essay you've been analysing in Exercises 3, 10, and 15. Do the paragraphs fulfil the requirements and avoid the pitfalls outlined on pages 106–10? Revise them as needed for clarity, conciseness, focus, and interest.

3e Linking paragraphs in the essay

Your paragraphs do not stand alone: each one is a key unit of a larger piece of writing. Though you may draft paragraphs or groups of paragraphs almost as mini-essays, you will eventually need to stitch them together into a unified, coherent, well-developed whole. The techniques parallel those for linking sentences in paragraphs:

- Make sure each paragraph contributes to your thesis.
- You will probably use varied patterns of development for individual paragraphs, even when the whole essay is developed and structured by some other pattern. Just be sure to follow through on your overall pattern.
- Arrange the paragraphs in a clear, logical order. See pages 45–53 for advice on essay organization.
- Create links between paragraphs. Use repetition and restatement to stress and connect key terms, and use transitional expressions or even transitional sentences to indicate sequence, direction, contrast, and other relationships.

The following essay illustrates the way effective paragraphs can build an effective essay. The overall pattern of development is analysis. The overall organization is climactic. Sentences and paragraphs are linked by repetition and restatement (circled words), transitional expressions (boxed words), and transitional sentences, pronouns, and parallelism (noted in annotations).

A Picture of Hyperactivity

A hyperactive committee member can contribute to efficiency. A hyperactive salesperson can contribute to profits. When a child is hyperactive, though, people—even parents—may wish he had never been born. A collage of those who must cope with hyperactivity in children is a dark picture of frustration, anger, and loss.

Thesis sentence

The first part of the collage is the doctors. In their terminology the word *hyperactivity* is short for H-LD, a hyperkinesis-learning disability syndrome. They apply the word to children who are "abnormally or excessively busy." But doctors do not fully understand the problem and thus differ over how to treat it. For example, some recommend a special diet; others, behaviour-modifying drugs; and still others, who do not consider hyperactivity to be a medical problem, a psychiatrist for the entire family. The result is a merry-go-round of tests, confusion, and frustration for the parents and the child.

Transitional topic sentence

Pronouns

Paragraph developed by definition, example, and cause-and-effect analysis

As the parent of a hyperactive child, I can say what the word *hyperactivity* means to the parents who form the second part of the collage. It means a worry that is deep and enduring. It means a despair that is a companion on dark and sleepless nights. It means a fear that is heart twisting and constant, for the hyperactive child is most destructive toward himself. It means a mixture of frus-

Transitional topic sentence

Pronouns and parallelism

Paragraph developed by definition and cause-and-effect analysis

¶ 3e

tration, guilt, and anger. And finally, since there are times when that anger goes out of control and the child is in danger from the parent, it means self-loathing.

The weight of hyperactivity, however, rests not on the doctors or the parents but on the child. For him is reserved the final and darkest part of the collage because he is most affected. From early childhood he is dragged from doctor to doctor, is attached to strange and frightening machines, and is tested or discussed by physicians, parents, neighbours, teachers, peers. His playmates dislike him because of his temper and his unwillingness to follow rules; and even his pets fear and mistrust him, for he treats them erratically, often hurting them without meaning to. As time goes on, he sees his parents more and more often in tears and anger, and he knows that he is the cause. Though he is highly intelligent, he does poorly when he enters school because of his short attention span. He is fond of sports and games but never joins the other children on the playground because he has an uncontrollable temper and poor coordination. By the time he reaches age seven or eight, he is obsessed with one thought: "Mama," my son asks me repeatedly, "why do I have to be hyperactive?"

At last the collage is completed, and it is dark and sombre. *Hyperactivity,* as applied to children, is a word with uncertain, unattrac-

Transitional sentence

Topic sentence

Pronouns

Paragraph developed by narration and cause-and-effect analysis

Transitional sentence

tive, and bitter associations. But the picture does have a bright spot, for inside every hyperactive child is a loving, trustful, calm person waiting to be recognized.

—LINDA DEVEREAUX (student)

Exercise 19
Analysing paragraphs in essays

Analyse the ways in which paragraphs combine in the two student essays in Chapter 2, pages 68 and 73. With what techniques, if any, does each writer link paragraphs to the thesis sentence and to each other? Where, if at all, does the writer seem to stray from the thesis or fail to show how paragraphs relate to it? How would you revise the essays to solve any problems they exhibit?

Exercise 20
Considering your past work: Paragraphs in the essay

Examine the overall effect of the essay you've been analysing in Exercises 3, 10, 15, and 18. Do all the paragraphs relate to your thesis? Are they arranged clearly and logically? How do repetition and restatement, transitional expressions, or transitional sentences connect the paragraphs? Can you see ways to improve the essay's unity, coherence, and development?

Chapter 4 Reading and Writing Arguments

Argument is writing that attempts to change readers' minds or move readers to action. A good argument is neither a cold exercise in logic nor an attempt to beat others into submission. It is a work of negotiation and problem solving in which both writer and reader search for the knowledge that will create common ground between them.

Of course, not all arguments are "good." Whether deliberately or not, some are unclear, incomplete, misleading, or downright false. The negotiation fails; the problem remains unsolved. This chapter will help you recognize good arguments when you read them (4a–4b) and write good arguments when you need to (4b–4g).

4a Reading arguments critically

Few arguments are an easy read. Most demand the attentive critical reading discussed in this book's Introduction. (If you haven't read pp. 1–16, you should do so before continuing.) As a reader of argument, your purpose and analytical framework (pp. 10–11) will almost always be the same: you'll want to know whether you should be convinced by the argument. The framework focuses your attention on the elements that make an argument convincing, or not.

In one simple scheme an argument has three parts:

1. **Assertions:** positive statements that require support. In an argument the central assertion is stated outright as the **thesis** (see p. 41): it is what the argument is about. For instance:

   The university needs a new chemistry laboratory to replace the existing outdated lab.

   Several minor assertions, such as that the present equipment is inadequate, will contribute to the central assertion.
2. **Evidence:** the facts, examples, expert opinions, and other information that support the assertions. Evidence to support the preceding example might include the following:

   The present lab's age
   An inventory of equipment
   The testimony of chemistry professors

   Like the assertions, the evidence is always stated outright.
3. **Assumptions:** opinions or beliefs held by the writer that tie the evidence to the assertions. For instance, the following assumption might connect the evidence of professors' testimony with the assertion that a new lab is needed:

   Chemistry professors are the most capable of evaluating the present lab's quality.

In the following pages, we'll examine each of these elements and the ways they are put together.

Questions for critically reading an argument

- What kind of **assertions** does the writer make? (4a-1)
- What kind and quality of **evidence** does the writer use? (4a-2)
- What **assumptions** is the writer making? (4a-3)
- What is the writer's **tone?** How does the writer use **language?** (4a-4)
- Is the writer **reasonable?** (4a-5)
- Is the argument logical? Has the writer committed any **fallacies?** (4b)
- Are you convinced? Why or why not?

Testing assertions

The assertions in an argument carry specific burdens: they should state arguable opinions, and they should define their terms.

Fact, opinion, belief, and prejudice

Most statements we hear, read, or make in speaking and writing are assertions of fact, opinion, belief, or prejudice. In an argument the acceptability of an assertion depends partly on which of these categories it falls into.

A **fact** is verifiable—that is, one can determine whether it is true. It may involve numbers or dates:

> World War II ended in 1945.
> The football field is 110 yards long.

The numbers may be implied:

> The earth is closer to the sun than Saturn is.
> The cost of medical care is rising.

Or the fact may involve no numbers at all:

> The city council adjourned without taking a vote.
> The Senate delayed the bill.

Facts provide crucial evidence for the assertions of an argument, and as evidence they may be problematic because they can be misinterpreted or distorted (see p. 121). But they are ultimately verifiable, so they do not make worthwhile arguments by themselves.

An **opinion** is a judgment *based* on facts, an honest attempt to draw a reasonable conclusion from evidence. For example:

> Mandatory drug testing in workplaces is essential to increase employees' productivity.
>
> Mandatory drug testing in workplaces does not substantially increase employees' productivity.
>
> Mandatory drug testing in workplaces violates constitutional freedoms.

All three of these opinions share certain features:

- They express viewpoints based on an interpretation of facts.
- They are arguable. Indeed, they argue with each other, though each writer had access to the same facts.
- They are potentially changeable. With more evidence the writers might alter their opinions partly or wholly.

The main assertion, or thesis, of an argument is always an opinion. Other, more specific assertions of opinion generally form the backbone of the argument supporting the thesis. By themselves, however, opinions do not make arguments. As a critical reader, you must satisfy yourself that the writer has specified the evidence and that the assumptions linking assertions and evidence are clear and believable.

An opinion is not the same as a **belief,** a conviction based on cultural or personal faith, morality, or values:

> Capital punishment is legalized murder.
>
> The primary goal of government should be to provide equality of opportunity for all.

Such statements are often called opinions because they express viewpoints, but they are not based on facts and other evidence. Since they cannot be disproved by facts or even contested on the basis of facts, they cannot serve as the central assertion of an argument. (Statements of belief do figure in argument, however: they can serve as a kind of evidence, and they often form the assumptions linking assertions and evidence. See pp. 121 and 123.)

One kind of assertion that has no place in argument is **prejudice,** an opinion based on insufficient or unexamined evidence:

> Women are bad drivers.
> Fat people are jolly.
> Teenagers are irresponsible.

Unlike a belief, a prejudice is testable: it can be contested and disproved on the basis of facts. Very often, however, we form prejudices or accept them from others—parents, friends, the communications media—without questioning their meaning or testing their truth. Writers who display prejudice do not deserve the confidence and agreement of readers. Readers who accept prejudice are not thinking critically.

Defined terms

In any argument, but especially in arguments about abstract ideas, clear and consistent definition of terms is essential. In the following assertion the writer is not clear about what she means by the crucial term *justice.*

> Over the past few decades, justice has deteriorated so badly that it almost does not exist anymore.

The word *justice* is **abstract:** it does not refer to anything specific or concrete and in fact has varied meanings. (The eight definitions in the *Gage Canadian Dictionary* include "rightfulness; lawfulness; well-founded reason" and "the exercise of power to maintain what is just and right.") When the writer specifies her meaning, her assertion is much clearer.

> If by *justice* we mean treating people fairly, punishing those who commit crimes, and protecting the victims of those crimes, then justice has deteriorated badly over the past few decades.

Writers who use highly abstract words such as *justice, equality, success,* and *maturity* have a responsibility to define them. If the word is important to the argument, such a definition may take an entire paragraph. As a reader, you have the obligation to evaluate the writer's definitions before you accept his or her assertions. (See Chapter 3, pp. 97–98, for more on definition and a paragraph defining the abstract word *quality.*)

2 Weighing evidence

In argument, evidence demonstrates the validity of the writer's assertions. If the evidence is inadequate or questionable, the assertions are at best doubtful.

Kinds of evidence

Writers draw on several kinds of evidence to support their assertions.

Evidence for argument

- **Facts:** verifiable statements
- **Statistics:** facts expressed in numbers
- **Examples:** specific cases
- **Expert opinions:** the judgments of authorities
- **Appeals to readers' beliefs or needs**

Facts are statements whose truth can be verified by observation or research (see p. 118).

> Quebec is almost three times the size of France.
> By law, seatbelts must be worn in a majority of the provinces.

Facts employing numbers are **statistics.**

> Of those polled, 62 percent stated a preference for a flat tax.
>
> In 1994 there were 85 000 men and women in the Canadian armed forces.
>
> The average Canadian household consists of 3.1 persons.

Examples are specific instances of the point being made, including historical precedents. The passage below uses a personal narrative as partial support for the assertion in the first sentence.

> Besides broadening students' knowledge, required courses can also introduce students to possible careers that they otherwise would

> have known nothing about. Somewhat reluctantly, I enrolled in a psychology course to satisfy the social science requirement. But what I learned in the course about human behaviour has led me to consider becoming a clinical psychologist instead of an engineer.

Expert opinions are the judgments formed by authorities on the basis of their own examination of the facts. In the following passage the writer cites the opinion of an expert to support the assertion in the first sentence.

> Despite tremendous advancements in our century, science is powerless, by itself, to solve the world's escalating problems of overpopulation and environmental destruction. Dr. David Suzuki, a well-known geneticist from the University of British Columbia who has fostered public awareness of the relation between science and society, maintains that "solutions to the environmental crisis will not come from science but will be political and socio-economic" (52).

As this passage illustrates, a citation of expert opinion should always refer the reader to the source, here indicated by the page number in parentheses, "(52)." Such a citation is also generally accompanied by a reference to the expert's credentials. See page 570.

Appeals to beliefs or needs are statements that ask readers to accept an assertion in part because it states something they accept as true without evidence or because it coincides with their needs. Each of the following examples combines such an appeal (second sentence) with a summary of factual evidence (first sentence).

> Thus the chemistry laboratory is outdated in its equipment. In addition, its shabby, antiquated appearance shames the school, making it seem a second-rate institution. [Appeals to readers' belief that their school is or should be first-rate.]
>
> That police foot patrollers reduce crime has already been demonstrated. Such officers might also restore our sense that our neighbourhoods are orderly, stable places. [Appeals to readers' need for order and stability.]

(For more on beliefs, see p. 119. For more on appeals to emotion, see pp. 142–44.)

The reliability of evidence

To support assertions and convince readers, evidence must be reliable. The tests of reliability for appeals to readers' beliefs and needs are specific to the situation: whether they are appropriate for the argument and correctly gauge how readers actually feel (see pp. 142–44). With the other kinds of evidence, the standards are more general, applying to any argument.

Criteria for weighing evidence

- Is it **accurate:** trustworthy, exact, undistorted?
- Is it **relevant:** authoritative, pertinent, current?
- Is it **representative:** true to context?
- Is it **adequate:** plentiful, specific?

Accurate evidence is true:

- It is drawn from trustworthy sources.
- It is quoted exactly.
- It is presented with the original meaning undistorted.

In an essay favouring gun control, the writer should not rely exclusively on procontrol sources, which are undoubtedly biased. Instead, the writer should also cite anticontrol sources (representing the opposite bias) and neutral sources (attempting to be unbiased). If the writer quotes an expert, the quotation should present the expert's true meaning, not just a few words that happen to support the writer's argument. (As a reader, you may have difficulty judging the accuracy of quotations if you are not familiar with the expert's opinions.)

Not just opinions but also facts and examples may be misinterpreted or distorted. Suppose you were reading an argument for extending a three-year-old law allowing the police to stop vehicles randomly as a means of apprehending drunk drivers. If the author cited statistics showing that the number of drunk-driving accidents dropped in the first two years of the law, but failed to note that the number rose back to the previous level in the third year, then the evidence would be distorted and thus inaccurate. You or any reader would be justified in questioning the entire argument, no matter how accurate the rest seemed.

Relevant evidence pertains to the argument:

- It comes from sources with authority on the subject.
- It relates directly to the point the writer is making.
- It is current.

In an argument against a method of hazardous-waste disposal, a writer should not offer his aunt's opinion as evidence unless she is an authority on the subject and her expertise is up to date. If she is an authority on Method A and not Method B, the writer should not use her opinion as evidence against Method B.

Representative evidence is true to its context:

- It reflects the full range of the sample from which it is said to be drawn.
- It does not overrepresent any element of the sample.

In an essay arguing that residences should stay open during school holidays, a writer might say that "the majority of the school's students favour leaving the residences open." But that writer would mislead you and other readers if the statement were based only on a poll of her roommates and residence neighbours. A few residents could not be said to represent the entire student body, particularly the nonresident students. To be representative, the poll would have to take in many more students in proportions that reflect the numbers of resident and nonresident students on campus.

Adequate evidence is sufficient:

- It is plentiful enough to support the writer's assertions.
- It is specific enough to support the writer's assertions.

A writer arguing against animal abuse cannot hope to win over readers solely with statements such as *Too many animals are deliberately injured or killed by humans every year.* She needs to supply facts instead of the vague *too many.* How many animals are injured? How many die? She needs to specify the conditions under which animals are injured or killed. And she needs to demonstrate that the actions are deliberate, perhaps with examples of animal abuse.

3 Discovering assumptions

Assumptions connect evidence to assertions: they are the opinions or beliefs that explain why a particular piece of evidence is relevant to a particular assertion. As noted in the book's Introduction on critical thinking (pp. 11–12), assumptions are not flaws in arguments but necessities: we all acquire beliefs and opinions that shape our view of the world. Here are some examples that you, or people you know, may hold:

> Criminals should be punished.
> Hard work is virtuous.
> Teachers' salaries are too low.

Assumptions are inevitable in argument, but they aren't neutral. For one thing, an assumption can weaken an argument. For instance, a writer may claim that real estate development should be prevented in the town. As evidence for this assertion, the writer offers facts about past developments that have replaced older buildings. But the evidence is relevant to the assertion only if you accept the writer's extreme assumptions that old buildings are always worthy and new development is always bad.

In such a case, the writer's bias may not even be stated. Hence a second problem: in arguments both sound and unsound, assumptions are not always explicit. Here, for example, is a summary of a reasonable argument. What is the unstated assumption?

Assertion

The town should create a plan to manage building preservation and new development.

Evidence

Examples of how such plans work; expert opinions on how and why both preservation and development are needed.

In this instance the assumption is that neither uncontrolled development nor zero development is healthy for the town. If you can accept this assumption, you should be able to accept the writer's claim (though you might still disagree over particulars).

Here are some tips for dealing with assumptions.

Guidelines for analysing assumptions

- What are the assumptions underlying the argument? How does the writer connect assertions with evidence?
- Are the assumptions believable? Do they express your values? Do they seem true in your experience?
- Are the assumptions consistent with each other? Is the argument's foundation solid, not slippery?

Watching language, hearing tone

Tone is the expression of the writer's attitudes toward himself or herself, toward the subject, and toward the reader (see p. 30 for a discussion). Tone can tell you quite a bit about the writer's intentions, biases, and trustworthiness. For example:

> Some women cite personal growth as a reason for pursuing careers while raising children. Of course, they are equally concerned with the personal growth of the children they relegate to "child-care specialists" while they work.

In the second sentence this writer is being **ironic,** saying one thing while meaning another. The word *relegate* and the quotation marks with *child-care specialists* betray the writer's belief that working mothers may selfishly neglect their children for their own needs. Irony can sometimes be effective in argument, but here it marks the author as insincere in dealing with the complex issues of working parents and child care.

When reading arguments, you should be alert for the author's language. Look for words that **connote,** or suggest, certain attitudes and evoke certain responses in readers. Connotative language is no failure in argument; indeed, the strongest arguments use it skilfully to appeal to readers' hearts as well as their minds (see pp. 142–44). But be suspicious if the language runs counter to the substance of the argument.

Look also for evasive words. **Euphemisms,** such as *attack of a partly sexual nature* for "rape" or *peace-keeping force* for a war-making army, are supposedly inoffensive substitutes for words that may frighten or offend readers (see p. 449). In argument, though, they are sometimes used to hide or twist the truth. An honest, forthright arguer will avoid them.

Finally, watch carefully for sexist, racist, and other biased language that reveals deep ignorance or, worse, entrenched prejudice on the part of the writer. Obvious examples are *broad* for woman and *fag* for homosexual. (See pp. 449–50 for more on such language.)

5 Judging reasonableness

The **reasonableness** of an argument is the sense you get as reader that the author is fair and sincere. The reasonable writer does not conceal or distort facts, hide prejudices, mask belief as opinion, manipulate you with language, or resort to any of dozens of devices used unconsciously by those who don't know better and deliberately by those who do.

Reasonableness involves all the elements of argument examined so far: assertions, evidence, assumptions, and language. In addition, the fair, sincere argument always avoids so-called fallacies (covered in the next section), and it acknowledges the opposition. Judging whether the opposition is adequately dealt with is a fairly simple matter for the reader of argument. By definition, an arguable issue has more than one side. Even if you have no preconceptions about a subject, you will know that another side exists. If the writer pretends otherwise, or dismisses the opposition too quickly, you are justified in questioning the honesty and fairness of the argument. (For the more complicated business of *writing* an acknowledgment of the opposition, see p. 144–45.)

Exercise 1
Reading arguments critically

Following are two brief arguments. The two arguments take different stances on environmental issues in general and on the specific issues involved in the logging of old growth forests in the Temagami region of Northern Ontario, a controversy that has raged for decades. Read each argument critically, following the process outlined in the Introduction (pp. 1–16) and answering the questions in the box on page 117 (questions about assertions, evidence, assumptions, and the other elements of argument). Develop your responses in writing so that you can refer to them for later exercises and class discussion.

Canadian Values and Priorities: A Multiple-use Perspective

The Temagami debate revolves around values which are central to 1
the Canadian experience.

The issues at stake in Temagami are not environmental in nature. 2
The Temagami forest has been logged for about 130 years. The area is riddled with bush roads. There has been no identification to date of significant ecological damage arising from the building or use of roads in the Temagami forest.

Nor are the issues economic. The village of Temagami enjoys a 3
level of economic diversity that is the envy of other small Northern Ontario towns. The district in which it is situated is a world-renowned tourist area. The local economy is further strengthened by forestry, mining, and trapping. As a result of all these factors, unemployment in Temagami has been negligible, which is all the more remarkable given that a land injuction has stifled development for about fifteen years.

The issues are not scientific either. Where are the scientists? Has 4
David Suzuki, our self-proclaimed forestry expert, set up camp with others to study any of the old-growth or other parts of the forest? Where is the university or private-industry research data? Scientists who have been called to the area by government grants have not come to any specific conclusions. Sixty-five scientists asked for a moratorium on logging. When NORTHCARE (Northern Community Advocates for Resource Equity) contacted many of them, several indicated that they did not know where Temagami was. All of the others cited personal beliefs as a reason for their statements, but none had any hard data. In general, it is clear that, despite what some people claim, we don't know everything about the forest with absolute certainty.

How many times do we have to say that the Temagami forest is 5
one of the most protected and regulated areas of Ontario? In terms of its productivity, real and potential, it is probably unrivalled.

No, the issues involve values other than environmental, economic, 6
and scientific ones. Canada is sustained by its small community resource sector, and by the people who work there without the benefit of air-conditioned offices, university tenure, and travel grants to faraway places. In the Temagami area, one thinks of the Keevils and O'Connors (mining), the Goulards and the Fisets (lumber), the Grants and the Fryers (forestry), and of all the families who work with them. These people have built the communities that make up Canada. They also uphold the

values, chief among which is a commitment to hard work and the land, that have made our country what it is.

Without the values of our resource people in the Temagami forest we wouldn't be able to provide the funds for the government office that is coordinating the study of development issues in Temagami. Without the values of the people in the Temagami forest and in forests across Canada we couldn't afford universities and hospitals. These values represent our basic Canadian heritage. So do the values of the prospector, who has been responsible for much of the importance of the Temagami forest, and of the trapper. 7

In recent years the values of people in all the resource sectors—forestry, mining, and trapping—have been effectively ignored, and they continue to be ignored. In the Temagami area, they are now banned from huge areas of our forest even though, without them, there would not be a Tall Pines Project, a Wilderness society, or a canoe-vacation company. But make no mistake: these values hold much of the hope for the future of Temagami. 8

Have our values changed? Canada is still sustained by forestry, mining, agriculture, and fishing. Half of the world's lumber is Canadian. Canada is the world's largest producer of paper. More money is spent on hard-rock mining in the Temagami area than in the rest of Canada or in Australia, Peru, the United States, and Chile. Our values as Canadians have remained nearly the same since Confederation. More than anything, we remain dedicated to land. 9

Are the values of the forest, mining, and trapping communities different from those of the rest of our communities? Do we value the environment any less? Do we value clean air and water any less? Do we value aesthetics any less? Do we value recreation in the forest any less? Absolutely not. No group in Canada can claim to hold the value of our environment more highly than we do in the Temagami region or anywhere in Northern Ontario. 10

The creation of a single-use forest in Temagami would present a serious threat to Ontario as a whole. A huge no-development area with restrictions on roads would severely disrupt settlement patterns and the entire region's economy. Already, old transportation routes are being destroyed by the restrictions imposed on the Temagami forest. The impact is being felt by North Bay, Sudbury, and Timmins. 11

NORTHCARE is committed to local decision-making based on the wise and multiple-use of crown land and water, which constitute over 90 percent of northern Ontario. Multiple-use is a tradition in the north, and we want to maintain that tradition. As a province and as a country, we have to continue using our resources in a common-sense, cooperative way. And we have to work together; the north's values and concerns can't be ignored any longer. 12

We in NORTHCARE favour multiple-use over single-use, employment over recreation, the needs of residents over the needs of visitors. It is our view that the values of the residents of Canadian resource communities must be a priority even though these residents are a minority in the province as a whole. If we examine their values carefully we will see that they include the environment and recreation. We will also see that they encompass the complexity of the land and the realities of Canada at large. 13

—JUDITH SKIDMORE

Temagami: An Environmentalist's Perspective

1 Temagami is probably the most contested piece of land in North America. We are now into the 112th year of the Teme-Augama Anishnabai struggle to regain their homeland. In the past five years alone Temagami has been the subject of seven court decisions, three road blockades, and at least 124 arrests on the Temagami Wilderness Society's blockade of the Red Squirrel road. About one-third of the blockaders have been from Northern Ontario; the remainder have come from as far away as France and Wales. Native people from the area, the Teme-Augama Anishnabai, and even from Malaysia, have been involved. The oldest person arrested was seventy-seven years of age. He insisted on being arrested, in spite of a heart condition, because he felt so strongly about making a personal statement.

2 The Temagami Wilderness Society (TWS) has proposed a wilderness reserve for the area. This reserve would not be a park, but a land trust to be held for the Teme-Augama Anishnabai. There is no provision in either the Provincial Parks Act or the National Parks Act for a wilderness reserve. The proposal is entirely designed for the unique situation in Temagami.

3 The Teme-Augama have lived in Temagami for 6 000 years and have never surrendered their rights. This is the TWS's position and it does not hinge on a court decision. The land belongs to the Teme-Augama.

4 Readers may be familiar with the TWS's Tall Pines Project. It is the largest field study of old-growth forest in Canada. The Tall Pines team discovered that Temagami contains the largest known stand of old-growth red and white pine in Ontario. We did not know this until April 1989. The Ministry of Natural Resources (MNR) did not know it either. Only since then has MNR recognized old growth as a distinct and sensitive feature of the Temagami environment. But even now it has no protection policy, only a logging policy: cut the trees as quickly as possible.

5 There are some myths about old growth that should be dispelled. Old growth does not consist just of emperors of the forest—the big, old trees. Old-growth red- and white-pine ecosystems *do* contain trees at least 140 years of age, but that is not sufficient. The *entire* ecosystem is old. In it there are snags (standing dead trees) and deadfalls, and a thick floor of organic material—the emperors of past generations. In Temagami these pine ecosystems have been evolving for 500 to 700 years. Interestingly, the oldest trees found in Temagami are 375-year-old white pine. They are outside the parks and are unprotected.

6 When a tree dies it is not the end of life, but the beginning. It becomes home to a different set of flora and fauna. Eventually it recycles back into the soil to support new tree growth. We are trying to preserve not the big trees, but the processes of the ecosystems that preserve the forest. Old-growth forests are ancient fortresses of life that have preserved the processes and the species, the blueprints for restoring our lost forests.

7 Unfortunately, Temagami has been undergoing successive destruction at the hands of the Ontario government. The "production policy," as it is called by MNR, is an Ontario-wide effort that is the sum of logging targets set in each district, including Temagami. This policy, which has resulted in doubling Temagami's logging volume since 1980, is based on

a fifty-year rotation. It assumes that the forests of Ontario will be logged over fifty years and all of them will grow back in the same length of time.

But Ontario's forests cannot grow back in fifty years. Nature cannot 8
do it. Even the MNR's Temagami policy states that white and red pine take 120 years to regenerate while jack pine needs eighty years. The fastest growing species in northern Ontario is poplar and it still takes sixty years to grow back. MNR has built into its planning process the ultimate demise of the forest industry.

Half of the ministry's grand theory involves logging and the other 9
half regeneration. It assumes that everything logged is regenerated. In the case of conifers, the theory requires replanting or reseeding. But only 50 percent of Ontario's logged areas are replanted. In the district of Temagami for 1980–87, only 26.5 percent was replanted. In fifty years little of our heritage will be left because MNR is not keeping its promise to our forests, to our industry, to our First Nations, or to the public.

The only independent field audit of replanted areas in Ontario that 10
we have found was conducted by the provincial auditor in 1985. The study found that two-thirds of the audited areas had no commercially viable forest returning. The forests of Temagami will not return because the Ontario government does not know how to bring them back. There is not going to be a forest, an industry, or a future.

But there is hope for the future of the people of Temagami. Mem- 11
bers of the local community are standing up and saying that they intend to create a sustainable future. Look at the Temcor proposal for a destination resort which, local entrepreneurs hope, will create up to 400 permanent jobs. But, of course, it will succeed only if the forests remain.

Recently, in the *Globe and Mail's Report on Business* magazine, I 12
read an interesting comment by Lieutenant Governor David Lam of British Columbia. I want to cite it because BC is similar in so many ways to Northern Ontario: "The unfortunate part of a natural-resource based economy is that it limits one's imagination and flexibility and adaptability. It creates a complacent, fatalistic attitude that says, "Destiny governs, what can I do?" Such an attitude is not conducive to creating a mind geared to the competitive world of the 21st century." I think the people of Temcor and the town of Temagami already know where the future is, and it is not in logging anymore. It is in sustaining our resources.

The people of Temagami are trying to bring together many groups 13
to work on their project for sustainable development, including the Teme-Augama Anishnabai. Until we can come to terms with the people living on the land, we will never come to terms with the other life forms on the land, and we will never protect our environment. —Brian Back

4b Recognizing fallacies

This section is positioned between reading and writing arguments because you'll need to know **fallacies**—errors in argument—as both a reader (to spot them) and a writer (to avoid them). The many common fallacies fall into two groups. Some evade the issue of the argument. Others treat the argument as if it were much simpler than it is.

Checklist of fallacies

EVASIONS

- **Begging the question:** treating an opinion that is open to question as if it were already proved or disproved.
- **Non sequitur** ("it does not follow"): drawing a conclusion from irrelevant evidence.
- **Inappropriate appeals:**

  Appealing to readers' fear or pity.
  Snob appeal: appealing to readers' wish to be like those who are more intelligent, famous, rich, and so on.
  Bandwagon: appealing to readers' wish to be part of the group.
  Flattery: appealing to readers' intelligence, taste, and so on.
  Argument ad populum ("to the people"): appealing to readers' general values, such as patriotism or love of family.
  Argument ad hominem ("to the man"): attacking the opponent rather than the opponent's argument.

OVERSIMPLIFICATIONS

- **Hasty generalization (jumping to a conclusion):** asserting an opinion based on too little evidence. **Absolute statements** and **stereotypes** are variations.
- **Reductive fallacy:** generally, oversimplifying causes and effects.
- **Post hoc fallacy:** assuming that *A* caused *B* because *A* preceded *B*.
- **Either/or fallacy (false dilemma):** reducing a complicated question to two alternatives.
- **False analogy:** exaggerating the similarities in an analogy or ignoring key differences.

1 Recognizing evasions

The central assertion of an argument defines an issue or question: Should real estate development be controlled? Should drug testing be mandatory in the workplace? An effective argument faces the central issue squarely with relevant opinions, beliefs, and evidence. An ineffective argument dodges the issue.

Begging the question

A writer **begs the question** by treating an opinion that is open to question as if it were already proved or disproved. (In essence, the writer begs readers to accept his or her ideas from the start.) For example:

> The university library's expenses should be reduced by cutting subscriptions to useless periodicals. [Begged questions: Are some of the library's periodicals useless? Useless to whom?]
>
> The fact is that the welfare system is too corrupt to be reformed. [Begged questions: How corrupt is the welfare system? Does corruption, even if extensive, put the system beyond reform?]

Non sequitur

A **non sequitur** occurs when no logical relation exists between two or more connected ideas. In Latin *non sequitur* means "it does not follow." In the following sentences the second thought does not follow from the first.

> If high school English were easier, fewer students would have trouble with the university English requirement. [Presumably, if high school English were easier, students would have *more* trouble.]
>
> Kathleen Newsome has my vote for mayor because she has the best-run campaign organization. [Shouldn't one's vote be based on the candidate's qualities, not the campaign organization's?]

Inappropriate appeals

Appeals to readers' emotions are common in effective arguments. But such appeals must be relevant and must supplement rather than substitute for facts, examples, and other evidence.

Writers sometimes ignore the question with **appeals to readers' fear or pity.**

> By electing Susan Clark to the city council, you will prevent the city's economic collapse. [Trades on people's fears. Can Clark single-handedly prevent economic collapse?]
>
> She should not have to pay taxes because she is an aged widow with no friends or relatives. [Appeals to people's pity. Should age and loneliness, rather than income, determine a person's tax obligation?]

Sometimes writers ignore the question by appealing to readers' sense of what other people believe or do. One approach is **snob appeal,** inviting readers to accept an assertion in order to be identified with others they admire.

> As any literate person knows, James Joyce is the best twentieth-century novelist. [But what qualities of Joyce's writing make him a superior novelist?]

A similar tactic invites readers to accept an assertion because everybody else does. This is the **bandwagon approach.**

> As everyone knows, marijuana use leads to heroin addiction. [What is the evidence?]

Yet another diversion involves **flattery** of readers, in a way inviting them to join in a conspiracy.

> We all understand campus problems well enough to see the disadvantages of such a backward policy. [What are the disadvantages of the policy?]

The **argument ad populum** ("argument to the people") asks readers to accept a conclusion based on shared values or even prejudices and nothing else.

> Any concerned Canadian will support the Prime Minister's action. [But why is the action worth taking?]

One final and very common kind of inappropriate emotional appeal addresses *not* the pros and cons of the issue itself but the real or imagined negative qualities of the people who hold the opposing view. This kind of argument is called **ad hominem,** Latin for "to the man."

> One of the scientists has been treated for emotional problems, so his pessimism about nuclear waste merits no attention. [Do the scientist's previous emotional problems invalidate his current views?]

Recognizing oversimplifications

To **oversimplify** is to conceal or ignore complexities in a vain attempt to create a neater, more convincing argument than reality allows.

Hasty generalization

A **hasty generalization** is an assertion based on too little evidence or on evidence that is unrepresentative. (This fallacy is also called **jumping to a conclusion.**) For example:

> People who care about the environment recycle their trash. [Many people who care about the environment may not have the option of recycling.]

A variation of the hasty generalization is the **absolute statement** involving words such as *all, always, never,* and *no one* that allow no exceptions. Rarely can evidence support such terms. Moderate words such as *some, sometimes, rarely,* and *few* are more reasonable.

Another common hasty generalization is the **stereotype,** a conventional and oversimplified characterization of a group of people:

> People who live in cities are unfriendly.
> Albertans are all cowboys.
> Women are emotional.
> Men can't express their feelings.

(See also pp. 449–50 on sexist and other biased language.)

Reductive fallacy

The **reductive fallacy** oversimplifies (or reduces) the relation between causes and their effects. The fallacy (sometimes called **oversimplification**) often involves linking two events as if one caused the other directly, whereas the causes may be more complex or the relation may not exist at all. For example:

> Poverty causes crime. [If so, then why do people who are not poor commit crimes? And why aren't all poor people criminals?]
>
> The better a school's athletic facilities are, the worse its academic programs are. [The sentence assumes a direct cause-and-effect link between athletics and scholarship.]

Post hoc fallacy

Related to the reductive fallacy is the assumption that because *A* preceded *B*, then *A* must have caused *B*. This fallacy is called in Latin *post hoc, ergo propter hoc,* meaning "after this, therefore because of this," or the **post hoc fallacy** for short.

> In the two months since he took office, Mayor Holcomb has allowed crime in the city to increase 2 percent. [The increase in crime is no doubt attributable to conditions existing before Holcomb took office.]
>
> The town council erred in permitting the adult bookstore to open, for shortly afterwards two women were assaulted. [It cannot be assumed without evidence that the women's assailants visited or were influenced by the bookstore.]

Either/or fallacy

In the **either/or fallacy** (also called **false dilemma**), the writer assumes that a complicated question has only two answers, one good and one bad, both bad, or both good.

> City police officers are either brutal or corrupt. [Most city police officers are neither.]

Either we permit mandatory drug testing in the workplace or productivity will continue to decline. [Productivity is not necessarily dependent on drug testing.]

False analogy

An **analogy** is a comparison between two essentially unlike things for the purpose of definition or illustration. (See also p. 101.) In arguing by analogy, a writer draws a likeness between things on the basis of a single shared feature and then extends the likeness to other features. But analogy can only illustrate a point, never prove it: just because things are similar in one respect, they are not *necessarily* alike in other respects. In the fallacy called **false analogy,** the writer assumes such a complete likeness.

The non-human primates such as chimpanzees and gorillas care for their young, clean and groom each other, and defend themselves and sometimes the group from attack. Why, then, must the human primates go so much further—unemployment insurance, child care, welfare, hospital insurance, and so on—to protect the weak? [Taken to its logical extreme, this analogy would lead us to ask why we speak to each other when gorillas do not.]

Exercise 2
Analysing advertisements

Leaf through a magazine or watch television for half an hour, looking for advertisements that attempt to sell a product not on the basis of its worth but by snob appeal, flattery, or other inappropriate appeals to emotions. Be prepared to discuss the advertiser's techniques.

Exercise 3
Identifying and revising fallacies

Identify at least one fallacy illustrated by each of the following sentences. Then revise the sentence to make it more reasonable.

1. A successful marriage demands a maturity that no one under twenty-five possesses.
2. Students' persistent complaints about the grading system prove that it is unfair.
3. World War I was caused by the assassination of Archduke Ferdinand.
4. People watch television because they are too lazy to talk or read or because they want mindless escape from their lives.
5. The North American Free Trade Agreement will eventually destroy our national identity.

Exercise 4
Identifying fallacies in arguments

Analyse the two arguments on pages 126–29 for fallacies. To what extent do any fallacies weaken either argument? Explain.

4c Developing an argument

In composing an argument, you try to illuminate an issue or solve a problem by finding the common ground between you and others who will read your work. Using critical thinking, you develop and test your own ideas. Using a variety of techniques, you engage readers in an attempt to narrow the distance between your views and theirs.

Sections 4c through 4g will be more helpful to you if you have already read Chapters 1 and 2 on the writing process.

Finding a topic and conceiving a thesis

An argument topic must be arguable—that is, reasonable people will disagree over it and be able to support their positions with evidence. This sentence implies several *do*'s and *don't*'s.

Tests for an argument topic

A GOOD TOPIC:

- Concerns a matter of opinion—a conclusion drawn from evidence (see 4a-1).
- Can be disputed: others might take a different position.
- *Will* be disputed: it is controversial.
- Is something you care about and know about, or want to research.
- Is narrow enough to argue in the space and time available (see 1b-3).

A BAD TOPIC:

- Cannot be disputed because it concerns a fact, such as the distance to Saturn or the functions of the human liver.
- Cannot be disputed because it concerns a personal preference or belief, such as a liking for the colour red or a moral commitment to vegetarianism.
- *Will not* be disputed because few if any disagree over it—the virtues of a secure home, for instance.

If you feel uncertain about finding a topic for argument, try some of the techniques listed on page 33 for discovering ideas.

Once you have a topic, you may also have a thesis, or you may need to do some research and writing to find your angle. The **thesis** is the main idea of your paper (see pp. 40–44). In an argument the **thesis sentence** states the assertion that you want your readers to accept or act on. Here are two thesis sentences on the same subject.

> The new room fees are unjustified given the condition of the residences.
>
> The administration should postpone the new room fees at least until conditions in the residences are improved.

Your thesis sentence must satisfy the same requirements as the topic (see the box on p. 135). But it must also specify the grounds of your argument, the general basis for your assertion. In the two thesis sentences above, the grounds for protesting the room fees are that the residences are in bad condition.

Note that the writer of either of these arguments must clarify the definition of *condition(s)* if the argument is to be clear and reasonable. Always take pains to define abstract and general terms that are central to your argument, preferably in or just after the thesis sentence. (See pp. 119–20.)

2 Analysing your purpose and your audience

Your purpose in argument is, broadly, to engage readers in order to convince them of your position or persuade them to act. But arguments have more specific purposes as well. For instance:

To strengthen the commitment of existing supporters
To win new supporters from the undecided
To get the opposition to reconsider
To inspire supporters to act
To deter the undecided from acting

It's no accident that each of these purposes characterizes the audience (*existing supporters, the undecided,* and so on). In argument even more than in other kinds of writing, achieving your purpose depends on the response of your readers, so you need a sense of who they are and where they stand. The "Questions About Audience" on page 29 can help you identify readers' knowledge, beliefs, and other pertinent background information. You also need to know their position on your topic—not only whether they agree or disagree generally, but also which specific assertions they will find more or less convincing.

Your purpose can help you fill in this information. If you decide to address supporters or opponents, you essentially select readers with certain inclinations and ignore other readers who may tune in. If you decide to win new supporters from those who are undecided on your topic, you'll have to imagine sceptical readers who will be convinced only by an argument that is detailed, logical, and fair. Like you when you read an argument critically, these sceptical readers seek to be reasoned with, not manipulated into a position or hammered over the head.

Exercise 5
Finding a topic; conceiving a thesis sentence

Analyse each topic in the following list to determine whether it is appropriate for argument. For each of the topics you deem arguable, draft a thesis sentence that specifies the grounds for an argument. If you prefer, choose five arguable topics of your own and draft a thesis sentence for each one. One thesis sentence should interest you enough to develop into a complete argument.

1. User fees for Medicare
2. Care of automobile tires
3. History of the town park
4. Housing for the homeless
5. Billboards in urban residential areas or in rural areas
6. Animal testing for cosmetics research
7. Cats versus dogs as pets
8. [*Name*] for student-government president (or some other elected office)
9. Ten steps in recycling wastepaper
10. Benefits of being a parent

Exercise 6
Analysing purpose and audience

Specify a purpose and likely audience for the thesis sentence you chose to develop in Exercise 5. What do purpose and audience suggest about the way you should develop the argument?

4d Using reason and evidence

As a reader of argument, you seek evidence for the writer's assertions and clear reasoning about the relationship of evidence to assertions. As a writer of argument, you seek to provide what the reader needs in a way that furthers your case.

1 Reasoning inductively and deductively

The thesis of your argument is a conclusion you reach by reasoning about evidence. Two common processes of reasoning are induction and deduction—methods of thinking that you use all the time even if you don't know their names.

Induction

When you're about to buy a used car, you consult friends, relatives, and consumer guides before deciding what kind of car to buy. Using **inductive reasoning,** you make specific observations about cars (your evidence) and you induce, or infer, a **generalization** that Model X is the most reliable. Writing a term paper on print advertising, you might also use inductive reasoning:

First analyse advertisements in newspapers and magazines (evidence).
Then read comments by advertisers, publishers, and critics (more evidence).
Finally, form a conclusion about print advertising (generalization).

In the framework for analysing arguments discussed earlier (see p. 117), the evidence is connected to the generalization (or assertion) by your assumption that what is true in one set of circumstances (the ads you look at) is true in a similar set of circumstances (other ads). With induction you create new knowledge out of old.

The more evidence you accumulate, the more probable it is that your generalization is true. Note, however, that absolute certainty is not possible. At some point you must *assume* that your evidence justifies your generalization, for yourself and your readers. Most errors in inductive reasoning involve oversimplifying either the evidence or the generalization. See pages 129–34 on fallacies.

Deduction

You use **deductive reasoning** when you proceed from your generalization that Model X is the most reliable used car to your own specific circumstances (you want to buy a used car) to the conclusion that you should buy a Model X car. In deduction your assumption is the generalization you believe to be true. It links the evidence (new information) to the assertion (the conclusion you draw). With deduction you apply old information to new.

Say that you want the school administration to postpone new room fees for one residence. You can base your argument on a deductive **syllogism:**

Premise: The administration should not raise fees on residence rooms in bad condition. [A generalization or belief that you assume to be true.]
Premise: The rooms in Polk Hall are in bad condition. [New information: a specific case of the first premise.]
Conclusion: The administration should not raise fees on the rooms in Polk Hall.

As long as the premises of a syllogism are true, the conclusion derives logically and certainly from them.

The force of deductive reasoning depends on the reliability of the premises and the care taken to apply them in drawing conclusions. The reasoning process is **valid** if the premises lead logically to the conclusion. It is **true** if the premises are believable. Sometimes the reasoning is true but *not* valid:

> *Premise:* The administration should not raise fees on residence rooms in bad condition.
> *Premise:* Tyler Hall is a residence.
> *Conclusion:* The administration should not raise fees on the rooms in Tyler Hall.

Both premises may be true, but the first does not *necessarily* apply to the second, so the conclusion is invalid.

Sometimes, too, the reasoning is valid but *not* true:

> *Premise:* All college administrations are indifferent to students' needs.
> *Premise:* The administration of Eastern Polytechnic is a college administration.
> *Conclusion:* The administration of Eastern Polytechnic is indifferent to students' needs.

This syllogism is valid but useless: because the first premise is an untrue assumption, the entire argument is untrue. Invalid and untrue syllogisms lie behind many of the fallacies discussed on pages 129–34.

A particular hazard of deductive reasoning is the **unstated premise:** the basic assumption linking evidence and conclusion is not stated but implied. Here the unstated premise is believable and the argument is reasonable:

> Ms. Stein has worked with drug addicts for fifteen years, so she knows a great deal about their problems. [Unstated premise: Anyone who has worked fifteen years with drug addicts knows about their problems.]

But when the unstated premise is wrong or unfounded, the argument is false. For example:

> Since Roger Thomas is a member of Parliament, he must receive money illegally from lobbyists. [Unstated premise: All members of Parliament receive money illegally from lobbyists.]

To avoid such false conclusions, you may be tempted to make your assertions sound more reasonable. But even a reasonable-sounding conclusion must be supportable. For instance, changing *must* to *might* modifies the unstated assumption about M.P. Thomas:

Test for inductive and deductive reasoning

Induction

- Have you stated your evidence clearly?
- Is your evidence complete enough and good enough to justify your assertion? What is the assumption that connects evidence and assertion? Is it believable?
- Have you avoided fallacies? (See 4b.)

Deduction

- What are the premises leading to your conclusion? Look especially for unstated premises.
- What does the first premise assume? Is the assumption believable?
- Does the first premise necessarily apply to the second premise?
- Is the second premise believable?
- Have you avoided fallacies? (See 4b.)

> Since Roger Thomas is a member of Parliament, he might receive money illegally from lobbyists. [Unstated premise: *Some* members of Parliament receive money illegally from lobbyists.]

But it does not necessarily follow that M.P. Thomas is one of the "some." The sentence, though logical, is not truly reasonable unless evidence demonstrates that M.P. Thomas should be linked with illegal activities.

Using evidence

Whether your argument is reasonable or not depends heavily on the evidence you marshal to support it. The kinds of evidence and the criteria for evaluating evidence are discussed in detail on pages 120–24). How to find evidence is discussed under research writing on pages 510–36.

The kind and quantity of evidence you use should be determined by your purpose, your topic, and the needs of your audience. Some arguments, such as a plea for volunteer help in a soup kitchen, will rely most heavily on appeals to readers' beliefs. Other arguments, such as a proposal for mandatory air bags in cars, will rely much more on statistics and expert opinions. Most arguments, including these, will mingle facts, examples, expert opinions, and appeals to readers' beliefs and needs (see also p. 143).

In using evidence for argument, you'll need to be especially wary of certain traps that carelessness or zeal can lure you into. These are listed in the following box.

Responsible use of evidence

- **Don't distort.** You mislead readers when you twist evidence to suit your argument—for instance, when you claim that crime in your city occurs five times more often than it did in 1925, without mentioning that the population is also seven times larger.
- **Don't stack the deck.** Ignoring damning evidence is like cheating at cards. You must deal forthrightly with the opposition (see 4e-2).
- **Don't exaggerate.** Watch your language. Don't try to manipulate readers by characterizing your own evidence as *pure* and *rock-solid* and the opposition's as *ridiculous* and *half-baked.* Make the evidence speak for itself.
- **Don't oversimplify.** Avoid forcing the evidence to support more than it can. (See also 4b-2.)
- **Don't misquote.** When you cite experts, quote them accurately and fairly.

Exercise 7
Reasoning inductively

Study the facts below and then evaluate each of the numbered conclusions following them. Which of the generalizations are reasonable given the evidence, and which are not? Why?

> Between the 1981 and 1991 national census, the population of Canada increased 12.9 percent to 28 120 000.
>
> The percentage increase from 1971 to 1981 was 12.8 percent.
>
> The population of Alberta increased 12.9 percent between 1981 and 1991.
>
> The population of Nova Scotia increased only 7.2 percent between 1981 and 1991.

1. Between 1981 and 1991 the population of Canada continued to grow at the same rapid rate as in the 1960s.
2. During the 1980s the population of Alberta increased almost two times more than the population of Nova Scotia.
3. Canadians prefer to live in the climate of the Prairies rather than in the climate of the Maritimes.

arg
4e

Exercise 8
Reasoning deductively

Convert each of the following statements into a syllogism. (You may have to state unstated assumptions.) Use the syllogism to evaluate both the validity and the truth of the statement.

Example:

DiSantis is a banker, so he does not care about the poor.

Premise: Bankers do not care about the poor.
Premise: DiSantis is a banker.
Conclusion: DiSantis does not care about the poor.

The statement is untrue because the first premise is untrue.

1. The mayor opposed pollution controls when he was president of a manufacturing company, so he may not support new controls or vigorously enforce existing ones.
2. Government demands so much honesty that we should not leave it to lawyers and professional politicians.
3. Schroeder is a good artist because she trained at the Nova Scotia College of Art, just like other good artists.
4. Wealthy athletes who use their resources to help others deserve our particular appreciation.
5. Jimson is sexist because she has hired only one woman.

Exercise 9
Using reason and evidence in your argument

Develop the structure and evidence for the argument you began in Exercises 5 and 6 (p. 137). (You may want to begin drafting at this stage.) Is your argument mainly inductive or mainly deductive? Use the box on page 140 to test the reasoning of the argument. Use the boxes on pages 122 and 141 to test your evidence.

4e Reaching your readers

To reach your readers in argument, you appeal directly to their reason and emotions, you account for views opposing yours, and you cast the argument in a clear, logical structure.

1 Appealing to readers

In forming convictions about arguable issues, we generally interpret the factual evidence through the filter of our values, beliefs, tastes, desires, and feelings. You may object to placing the new town dump in a particular wooded area because the facts suggest that the site is not large enough and that prevailing winds will blow odours back through the town. But you may also have fond memories of playing in the wooded area as a child, feelings that colour your interpretation of the facts and strengthen your conviction that the dump should be placed elsewhere. Your conviction is partly rational, because it is based on evidence, and partly emotional, because it is also based on feelings.

In most arguments you will combine **rational appeals** to readers' capacities for reasoning logically from evidence to a conclusion with **emotional appeals** to readers' beliefs and feelings. The following passages, all arguing the same view on the same subject, illustrate how either a primarily rational or a primarily emotional appeal may be weaker than an approach that uses both.

RATIONAL APPEAL

> Advertising should show more physically challenged people. The hundreds of thousands of disabled Canadians have considerable buying power, yet so far advertisers have made no attempt to tap that power. [Appeals to the logic of financial gain.]

EMOTIONAL APPEAL

> Advertising should show more physically challenged people. By keeping the physically challenged out of the mainstream depicted in ads, advertisers encourage widespread prejudice against disability, prejudice that frightens and demeans those who hold it. [Appeals to the sense of fairness, open-mindedness.]

RATIONAL AND EMOTIONAL APPEALS

> Advertising should show more physically challenged people. The hundreds of thousands of disabled Canadians have considerable buying power, yet so far advertisers have made no attempt to tap that power. Further, by keeping the physically challenged out of the mainstream depicted in ads, advertisers encourage widespread prejudice against disability, prejudice that frightens and demeans those who hold it.

The third passage, in combining both kinds of appeal, gives readers both rational and emotional bases for agreeing with the writer.

For an emotional appeal to be successful, it must be appropriate for the audience and the argument.

- It must not misjudge readers' actual feelings.
- It must not raise emotional issues that are irrelevant to the assertions and the evidence. (See pp. 131–32 for a discussion of specific inappropriate appeals, such as bandwagon and ad hominem.)

A third kind of approach to readers, the **ethical appeal,** is the sense you give of being a competent, fair person who is worth heeding. A sound argument backed by ample evidence—a rational appeal—will convince readers of your knowledge and reasonableness. (So will your acknowledging the opposition. See the next section.) Appropriate emotional appeals will demonstrate that you share readers' beliefs and needs. In addition, a sincere and even tone will assure readers that you are a balanced person who wants to reason with them.

A sincere and even tone need not exclude language with emotional appeal—words such as *frightens* and *demeans* at the end of the third passage on page 143. But avoid certain forms of expression that will mark you as unfair:

- Insulting words such as *idiotic* or *fascist.*
- Biased language such as *fags* or *broads.* (See pp. 449–50.)
- Sarcasm—for instance, using the sentence *What a brilliant idea* to indicate contempt for the idea and its originator.
- Exclamation points! They'll make you sound shrill!

See also pages 30–31 on tone.

2 Answering opposing views

A good test of your fairness in argument is how you handle possible objections. Assuming your thesis is indeed arguable, then others can marshal their own evidence to support a different view or views. You need to find out what these other views are and what the support is for them. Then, in your argument, you need to take these views on, refute those you can, grant the validity of others, and demonstrate why, despite their validity, the opposing views are less compelling than your own. The student who wrote the following paragraph first stated an opposing view, then conceded its partial validity, and finally demonstrated its irrelevance.

> The athletic director argues against reducing university support for athletic programs on the grounds that they make money that goes toward academic programs. It is true that here at Northern the surpluses from the football and hockey programs have gone into the general university fund, and some of that money may have made it into academic departments (the fund's accounting methods make it impossible to say for sure). But the athletic director misses the point. The problem is not that the athletic programs cost more than they take in but that they demand too much to begin with. For an institution that hopes to become first-rate academically, too many facilities, too much money, too much

energy, and too many people are tied up in the effort to produce championship sports teams.

Before you draft your essay, list for yourself all the opposing views you can think of. You'll find them in your research, by talking to friends, and by critically thinking about your own ideas. Figure out which opposing views you can refute (do more research if necessary), and prepare to concede those views you can't refute. It's not a mark of weakness or failure to admit that the opposition has a point or two. Indeed, by showing yourself to be honest and fair, you strengthen your ethical appeal and thus your entire argument.

3 Organizing your argument

There are organizing schemes for arguments that relate directly to induction and deduction:

- An **inductive organization** moves from specific evidence to a generalization about the evidence.
- A **deductive organization** begins with a commonly held opinion or belief (the first premise of the syllogism), applies it to a new case (the second premise), and draws a conclusion.

In practice, your sense of purpose and audience may dictate that you vary these schemes—for example, stating your generalization (your thesis) first in an inductive argument to secure readers' attention. Further, your argument may be both inductive and deductive, so that you could not adhere strictly to either scheme.

Because of such variations in subject, purpose, audience, and form of reasoning, arguments can be effectively organized in many different ways. One trusty scheme appears in the box below. Some of the elements can be rearranged.

Organization of an argument

INTRODUCTION

Statement of the significance of the argument; background on the issue; statement of thesis. (See 3d-1 on introductions, 1f and 4c-1 on the thesis sentence.) The introduction may be one or more paragraphs, depending on the complexity of the issue, readers' knowledge of it, and the length of the whole paper.

Body

Assertions relating to the thesis, each developed in one or more paragraphs with the evidence for the assertion. If the argument consists of a string of supporting assertions, they are usually best arranged in order of increasing importance or persuasiveness. Sometimes the body of the argument will break into distinct sections, such as description of a problem, proposal for solving the problem, and advantages of the proposal. However arranged, the body is the meat of the argument and will run as long as needed.

Answering the opposition

Refutation of opposing views, with evidence; concession to views more valid than your own; demonstration of your argument's greater strength (see 4e-2). This material may come elsewhere in the argument, after the introduction or throughout the body. The choice depends mainly on whether you think readers need the opposition to be dealt with right away or can wait.

Conclusion

Restatement of the thesis; summary of the argument; last appeal to readers. (See 3d-2 on conclusions.) The conclusion may be one or more paragraphs, depending on the complexity and the length of your argument.

Exercise 10
Identifying appeals

Identify each passage below as primarily a rational appeal or primarily an emotional appeal. Which passages make a strong ethical appeal as well?

1. Only complacency, indifference, or selfishness could allow us to ignore these people's hunger. We who have so much cannot in good conscience let others starve.
2. Thus the data collected by these researchers indicate that a mandatory sentence for illegal possession of handguns may lead to reduction in handgun purchases.
3. Most broadcasters worry that further government regulation of television programming could breed censorship—certainly, an undesirable outcome. Yet most broadcasters also accept that children's television is a fair target for regulation.
4. Anyone who cherishes life in all its diversity could not help being appalled by the mistreatment of laboratory animals. The so-called scientists who run the labs are misguided.
5. Many experts in constitutional law have warned that the rule violates the right to free speech. Yet other experts have viewed

the rule, however regretfully, as necessary for the good of the community as a whole.

Exercise 11
Reaching your readers

Continuing your argument-in-progress from Exercise 9 (p. 142), analyse whether your assertions are rational or emotional and whether the mix is appropriate for your audience and argument. Analyse your ethical appeal, too, considering whether it can be strengthened. Then make a list of possible opposing views. Think freely at first, not stopping to censor views that seem far-fetched or irrational. When your list is complete, decide which views must be taken seriously and why, and develop a response to each one.

4f Revising your argument

When you revise your argument, do it in at least two stages—revising underlying meaning and structure, and editing more superficial elements. The checklists on pages 61 and 66 can be a guide. Supplement them with the following checklist, which encourages you to think critically about your own argument.

Checklist for revising an argument

1. Is your thesis an arguable assertion (4c-1)?
2. Have you considered your readers' needs for information and their probable beliefs and values (4c-2)?
3. Does your thesis derive from induction, deduction, or both (4d-1)? If induction, have you shown how evidence and generalization are related? If deduction, is your syllogism both true and valid?
4. Is your evidence accurate, relevant, representative, and adequate (4a-2)? Is the evidence fairly presented (4d-2)?
5. Have you combined rational, emotional, and ethical appeals appropriately for your subject, your purpose, and your audience (4e-1)?
6. Have you answered the opposition (4e-2)?
7. Have you organized your argument so that it is clear and effective (4e-3)?
8. Have you avoided logical fallacies (4b)?

4g Examining a sample argument

The following student essay illustrates the principles discussed in this chapter. As you read the essay, notice especially the structure, the relation of assertions and supporting evidence, and the kinds of appeals the writer makes.

Share the Ride

Introduction: identification of problem

Every year we encounter more bad news about the environment, and a good portion of it is due to the private automobile. Respected scientists warn that carbon dioxide emissions, such as those from cars, may produce disastrous global warming. Soot, sulfur, and other automobile emissions are contributing to reduced air quality almost everywhere. The oil that powers cars comes from rapidly depleting reserves, leading to an unhappy choice between imports of foreign oil and exploration, such as offshore drilling, that threatens the environment.

Thesis sentence: proposal for a solution

In its own way Beverly Community College contributes to the problem. School administrators report that campus parking lots are filled with about 1800 cars every weekday, so that means 3600 trips a day are made to and from campus. If just a third of the solo drivers shared rides with one another, the total trips to and from campus would be reduced by at least 600. It is time for the BCC community to make a difficult move toward an organized car-pooling system that would achieve this modest goal.

Explanation of the proposal

The first step in getting car-pools going is to form a task force of administrators, faculty, and students to devise a workable system. School records would be used to connect people who live near each other and would be willing to car-pool. With administration backing, the task force would initiate a school-wide campaign of meetings, rallies, posters, and other public relations efforts to overcome resistance to car-pooling, answer questions, and win converts. The administration would assign staff to help with records and to keep the system current each term, since schedules and the student population change. As soon as administrators thought it was feasible, they could give a big boost to the system by creating monetary incentives to car-pool. Students who participate in car-pooling could receive a tuition rebate—say, $100 a term for full-time students. Faculty and staff could receive equivalent bonuses. In addition, parking fees could be instituted to discourage driving to school.

Support for the proposal: first advantage

The most obvious advantage of this proposal is that it would reduce car trips and thus air pollution and needless use of oil. Burning a single litre of gasoline produces 3 kilograms of carbon dioxide. If the average length of a trip to or from BCC is 10 kilometres (a conservative number) and the average car gets 20 kilometres to the litre (a generous number), then it takes only 2 trips to burn a litre of gasoline. Saving just 600 trips a day would keep 900 kilograms of carbon dioxide out of the air. It would also keep 300 litres of gasoline in the pumps.

Support for the proposal: second advantage

That unused gasoline would also save money for participants. If a full-time student drove half as often as now, the gasoline savings would be about $30 a term, plus the savings in wear and tear on the car. If the school instituted a $100 tuition rebate, the cash savings would rise to $130 a term. If the school instituted a parking fee of, say, $1 a day, the cash savings would rise to more than $160 a term. (All figures assume that car-pools consist of two people who share driving and expenses equally.)

Support for the proposal: third advantage

There are more abstract advantages, too. Individual freedom is a cherished right in our society, but it has no meaning outside the community. Like recycling and other environmental efforts, car-pooling would ask the individual to make a sacrifice on behalf of the community. Car-poolers would be actively participating in something larger than themselves, instead of just furthering their own self-interest.

Probable objection and response

Members of the BCC administration may point out that the proposed program asks for sacrifice from the school as well. They may object that rebates or bonuses and the costs of running the program are not feasible given the school's tight budget. True, $100 rebates or bonuses for an estimated 600 participants would cost $60 000 a term, and administrative time would also cost something. But considerable money could be raised by instituting a dollar parking fee, which could produce as much as $1500 a day, nearly $100 000 a term, in revenue. Furthermore, sponsoring a car-pooling system is no more than many corporations do that encourage their employees to take public transportation by contributing to their monthly passes. Businesses, schools, and other institutions that require their people to assemble in one place should help reduce the environmental cost of commuting.

Probable objection and response

Of course, it is the cost of commuters' convenience that will probably make or break the program. Students and faculty may have to arrive at school earlier than they want or leave later because of their car-pools. While considerable, this inconvenience could over time be turned to an advantage if car-poolers learned to use their extra on-campus time wisely to prepare for classes (work they would have do at home anyway). In addition, this inconvenience might seem worthwhile in exchange for helping the environment and the concrete rewards of a rebate or bonus and savings on parking.

It is no small flaw in the proposal that not all commuters would be able to participate in the program, even if they wanted to. The fact is that many part-time faculty and students have schedules that are too complicated or erratic to permit car-pooling. Many teachers and students must make intermediate stops between their homes and BCC, such as for work. These commuters would not have access to the rebates or bonuses and still would be subject to the parking fee.

Probable objection

This unfairness is regrettable but, for now, unavoidable; we have to start somewhere. A change away from single-passenger cars to car-pools is like all other significant changes we must make on behalf of the environment. The shift in consciousness and responsibility will be halting and prolonged, and the costs and benefits will not always be distributed equally. One thing we can be sure of, however, is that the shift will not occur at all if we don't take the difficult first steps.

Response to probable objection and conclusion

—Lee Morrison (student)

Exercise 12
Critically reading an argument

Analyse the construction and effectiveness of the preceding essay by answering the following questions.

1. Where does the writer make general assertions related to his thesis sentence, and where does he provide statistics or other evidence to support the assertions?
2. Where does the writer appeal primarily to reason, and where does he appeal primarily to emotion? What specific beliefs, values, and desires of readers does the writer appeal to?
3. How would you characterize the writer's ethical appeal?
4. What objections to his plan does the writer anticipate? How does he respond to each one?
5. How effective do you find this argument? To what extent do you agree with the writer about the problems identified in his introduction? To what extent does he convince you that his plan is desirable and workable and would address those problems? Does he fail to anticipate any major objections to his plan?
6. Write a critical evaluation of "Share the Ride." First summarize the writer's views. Then respond to those views by answering the questions posed in item 5 above.

Exercise 13
Writing and revising your argument

Draft and revise the argument you have developed in Exercises 5 and 6 (p. 137), 9 (p. 142), and 11 (p. 147). Use the revision checklists on pages 61 and 147 to review your work.

Part II

Grammatical Sentences

Chapter 5 Understanding Sentence Grammar

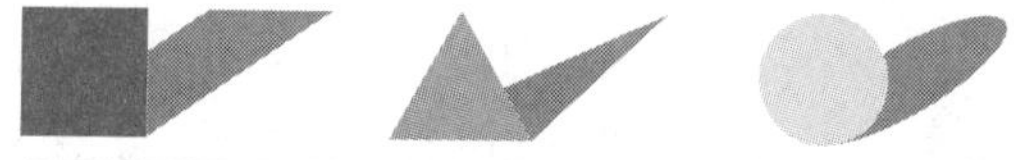

Grammar describes how language works. Following the rules of standard English grammar is what allows you to communicate with others across barriers of personality, region, class, or ethnic origin. If you are a native English speaker, you follow these rules mostly unconsciously. But when you're trying to improve your ability to communicate, it can help to make the rules conscious and learn the language used to describe them.

Grammar tells a lot about a sentence, even if you don't know the meanings of all the words.

> The rumfrums prattly biggled the pooba.

You don't know what this sentence means, but you can infer that some things called *rumfrums* did something to a *pooba.* They *biggled* it, whatever that means, in a *prattly* way. Two grammatical cues, especially, tell you that this sentence is like *The students easily passed the test:*

- Word forms. The ending *-s* means more than one *rumfrum.* The ending *-ed* means that *biggled* is an action that happened in the past. The ending *-ly* means that *prattly* probably describes *how* the rumfrums biggled.
- Word order. *Rumfrums biggled pooba* resembles a common sequence in English: something (*rumfrums*) performed some action (*biggled*) to or on something else (*pooba*). Since *prattly* comes right before the action, it probably describes the action.

This chapter explains how these and other structures work and shows how practising with them can help you communicate more effectively.

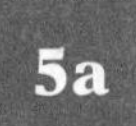

5a Understanding the basic sentence

The **sentence** is the basic unit of thought. Its grammar consists of words with specific forms and functions arranged in specific ways.

1 Identifying subjects and predicates

Most sentences make statements. First they name something; then they make an assertion about or describe an action involving that something. These two sentence parts are the **subject** and the **predicate.**

SUBJECT	PREDICATE
Art	can be controversial.
It	has caused disputes in Parliament and in artists' studios.
Its meaning and value to society	are often the focus of debate.

2 Identifying the basic words: Nouns and verbs

The following five simple sentences consist almost entirely of two quite different kinds of words.

SUBJECT	PREDICATE
The earth	trembled.
The earthquake	destroyed the city.
The result	was chaos.
The government	sent the city aid.
The citizens	considered the earthquake a disaster.

The words in the subject position name things, such as *earth, earthquake,* and *government.* In contrast, the words in the predicate position express actions, such as *trembled, destroyed,* and *sent.*

These two groups of words work in different ways. *Citizen* can become *citizens,* but not *citizened. Destroyed* can become *destroys,* but not *destroyeds.* Grammar reflects such differences by identifying the **parts of speech** or **word classes** shown in the box on the next page. Except for *the* and *a,* which simply point to and help identify the words after them, the five sentences about the earthquake consist entirely of nouns and verbs.

The parts of speech

Nouns name persons, places, things, ideas, or qualities: *Diefenbaker, girl, Kip River, coastline, Koran, table, strife, happiness.* (See below.)

Pronouns usually substitute for nouns and function as nouns: *I, you, he, she, it, we, they, myself, this, that, who, which, everyone.* (See the next page.)

Verbs express actions, occurrences, or states of being: *run, bunt, inflate, become, be.* (See the next page.)

Adjectives describe or modify nouns or pronouns: *gentle, small, helpful.* (See p. 161.)

Adverbs describe or modify verbs, adjectives, other verbs, or whole groups of words: *gently, helpfully, almost, really, someday.* (See p. 161.)

Prepositions relate nouns or pronouns to other words in a sentence: *about, at, down, for, of, with.* (See p. 164.)

Conjunctions link words, phrases, and clauses. **Coordinating conjunctions** and **correlative conjunctions** link words, phrases, or clauses of equal importance: *and, but, or, nor; both . . . and, not only . . . but also, either . . . or.* (See p. 178.) **Subordinating conjunctions** introduce subordinate clauses and link them to main clauses: *although, because, if, whenever.* (See p. 172.)

Interjections express feeling or command attention, either alone or in a sentence: *hey, oh, darn, wow.*

Nouns

Meaning

Nouns name. They may name a person (*Karen Kain, John Candy, astronaut*), a thing (*chair, book, Mt. Logan*), a quality (*pain, mystery, simplicity*), a place (*city, Saint John, ocean, Red Sea*), or an idea (*reality, peace, success*).

Form

Nouns change form to distinguish between singular (one) and plural (more than one). Most nouns add *-s* or *-es* for the plural: *earthquake, earthquakes; city, cities.* Some nouns have irregular plurals: *woman, women; child, children.*

Note ESL Some useful rules for forming noun plurals appear on pages 494–95. The irregular plurals must be memorized.

Most nouns also form the **possessive** to indicate ownership or source. Singular nouns usually add an apostrophe plus *-s* (*Auden's poems*); plural nouns usually add just an apostrophe (*citizens' rights*).

Nouns with *the, a,* and *an*

Nouns are often preceded by *the* or *a* (*an* before a vowel sound: *an apple*). These words are usually called **articles** or **determiners** and always indicate that a noun follows.

Note ESL See pages 247–50 for the rules governing the use of *the, a/an,* or no article at all before a noun.

Verbs

Meaning

Verbs express an action (*bring, change, grow*), an occurrence (*become, happen*), or a state of being (*be, seem*).

Form

Most verbs can be recognized by two changes in form:

- To indicate a difference between present and past time, most verbs add *-d* or *-ed* to the form listed in the dictionary: *They play today. They played yesterday.* Some verbs indicate past time irregularly: *eat, ate; begin, began* (see p. 199).
- When their subjects are singular nouns or some singular pronouns, all present-time verbs except *be* and *have* add *-s* or *-es* to the dictionary form: *The bear escapes. It runs. The woman begins. She sings. The -s* forms of *be* and *have* are *is* and *has.*

(See Chapter 7, pp. 197–99, for more on verb forms.)

Helping verbs

All verbs can combine with the words *do, does, did, can, could, may, might, will, would, shall, should,* and *must: could run, may escape, must help.* These words are called **helping verbs** or **auxiliary verbs.** They and a few others combine with special forms of verbs to make verb phrases such as *will be running, might have escaped,* and *could have been helped.* (See Chapter 7, p. 199.)

A note on form and function

In different sentences an English word may serve different functions, take correspondingly different forms, and belong to different word classes. For example:

> The government sent the city *aid.* [*Aid* functions as a noun.]
> Governments *aid* citizens. [*Aid* functions as a verb.]

Because words can function in different ways, we must always determine how a particular word works in a sentence before we can identify what part of speech it is. **The *function* of a word in a sentence always determines its part of speech in that sentence.**

Pronouns

Most **pronouns** substitute for nouns and function in sentences as nouns do. In the following sentence all three pronouns—*who, they, their*—refer to *nurses.*

Some nurses *who* have families prefer the night shift because *they* have more time with *their* children.

The most common pronouns are the **personal pronouns** (*I, you, he, she, it, we, they*) and the **relative pronouns** (*who, whoever, which, that*). Most of these change form to indicate their function in the sentence—for instance, *He called me. I called him back.* (See Chapter 6 for a discussion of these form changes.)

Exercise 1
Identifying subjects and predicates

Identify the subject and the predicate of each sentence below. Then use each sentence as a model to create a sentence of your own.

Example:

An important scientist spoke at convocation.

subject predicate
An important scientist | spoke at convocation.
The hungry family ate at the diner.

1. The leaves fell.
2. October ends soon.
3. The orchard owners made apple cider.
4. They examined each apple carefully before using it.
5. Over a hundred people will buy cider at the roadside stand.

Exercise 2
Identifying nouns, verbs, and pronouns

In the following sentences identify all words functioning as nouns with *N*, all words functioning as verbs with *V*, and all pronouns with *P*.

Example:

We took the tour through the museum.

P V N N
We took the *tour* through the *museum*.

1. The trees died.
2. They caught a disease.
3. The disease was a fungus.
4. It ruined a grove that was treasured.
5. Our great-grandfather planted the grove in the last century.

Exercise 3
Using nouns and verbs

Identify each of the following words as a noun, as a verb, or as both. Then create sentences of your own, using each word in each possible function.

Example:
fly
Noun and verb.
The *fly* sat on the meat loaf. [Noun.] The planes *fly* low. [Verb.]

1. wish
2. tie
3. swing
4. mail
5. spend
6. label
7. door
8. company
9. whistle
10. glue

Forming sentence patterns with nouns and verbs

We build all our sentences, even the most complicated, on the five basic patterns shown in the box on the next page. As the diagrams indicate, the patterns differ in their predicates because the relation between the verb and the remaining words is different.

Pattern 1: The earth trembled.

In the simplest pattern the predicate consists only of the verb. Verbs in this pattern do not require following words to complete their meaning and thus are called **intransitive** (from Latin words meaning "not passing over").

SUBJECT	PREDICATE
	Intransitive verb
The earth	trembled.
Mosquitoes	buzz.
The hospital	may close.

Pattern 2: The earthquake destroyed the city.

In pattern 2 the predicate consists of a verb followed by a noun that identifies who or what receives the action of the verb. This noun is a **direct object.** Verbs that require direct objects to complete their meaning are called **transitive** ("passing over"): the verb transfers the action from subject to object.

SUBJECT	PREDICATE	
	Transitive verb	*Direct object*
The earthquake	destroyed	the city.
The people	wanted	peace.
Education	opens	doors.

NOTE ESL The distinction between transitive verbs and intransitive verbs like those in pattern 1 is important because only transitive

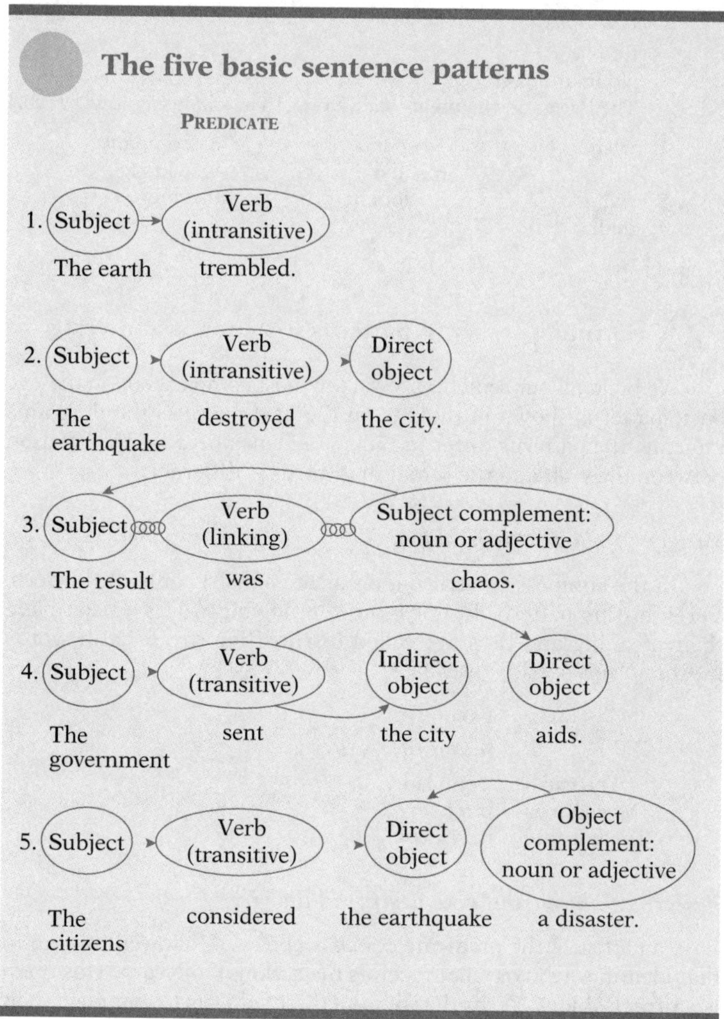

verbs can be used in the passive voice (*The city was destroyed*). (See p. 218.) Your dictionary will indicate whether a verb is transitive or intransitive. For some verbs (*begin, learn, read, write,* and others), it will indicate both uses.

Pattern 3: The result was chaos.

In pattern 3 the predicate also consists of a verb followed by a single noun, but here the noun renames or describes the subject. We could write the sentence *The result = chaos.* The verb serving as an equal sign is a **linking verb** because it links the subject and the following description. The linking verbs include *be, seem, appear, become, grow, remain, stay, prove, feel, look, smell, sound,* and *taste.* The word that describes the subject is called a **subject complement** (it complements, or completes, the subject).

SUBJECT	PREDICATE	
	Linking verb	*Subject complement*
The result	was	chaos.
The trees	are	elms.
The man	became	an accountant.

Subject complements in this sentence pattern may also be adjectives, words such as *tall* and *hopeful* (see p. 161):

SUBJECT	PREDICATE	
	Linking verb	*Subject complement*
The result	was	chaotic.
Rents	are	high.
The apartments	seem	expensive.

Pattern 4: The government sent the city aid.

In sentence 4 the predicate consists of a verb followed by two nouns. The second noun is a direct object, identifying what was sent. But the first noun, *city,* is different. This noun is an **indirect object,** identifying to or for whom the action of the verb is performed. The direct object and indirect object refer to different things, people, or places.

SUBJECT	PREDICATE		
	Transitive verb	*Indirect object*	*Direct object*
The government	sent	the city	aid.
Businesses	gave	the museum	money.
One company	offered	its employees	bonuses.

A number of verbs can take indirect objects, including those above and *allow, bring, buy, deny, find, get, leave, make, pay, read, sell, show, teach,* and *write.*

NOTE ESL Some verbs expressing action done to or for someone must be followed by *to* or *for*. These verbs include *admit, announce, demonstrate, explain, introduce, mention, prove, recommend, say,* and *suggest.*

FAULTY The manual explains workers the new procedure.

REVISED The manual explains the new procedure *to* workers.

Pattern 5: The citizens considered the earthquake a disaster.

In sentence 5 the predicate again consists of a verb followed by two nouns. But in this pattern the first noun is a direct object and the second noun renames or describes it. Here the second noun is an **object complement** (it complements, or completes, the object).

SUBJECT	PREDICATE		
	Transitive verb	*Direct object*	*Object complement*
The citizens	considered	the earthquake	a disaster.
The class	elected	Joan O'Day	president.
Reporters	declared	her	the winner.

Just as a subject complement (pattern 3) renames or describes a subject, so an object complement renames or describes a direct object. Like a subject complement, an object complement may be a noun or an adjective, as below.

SUBJECT	PREDICATE		
	Transitive verb	*Direct object*	*Object complement*
The citizens	considered	the earthquake	disastrous.
The results	proved	Sweeney	wrong.
Success	makes	some people	nervous.

Exercise 4
Identifying sentence patterns

In the following sentences, identify each verb as intransitive, transitive, or linking. Then identify each direct object (DO), indirect object (IO), subject complement (SC), and object complement (OC).

Example:

Children give their parents both headaches and pleasures.
Give is a transitive verb.

Children give their *parents* [IO] both *headaches* [DO] and *pleasures* [DO].

1. Montreal draws many visitors every year.
2. Tourists find Montreal sophisticated and fun.
3. Visitors send friends postcards of the view from Mount Royal.
4. Mount Royal dominates Montreal's landscape.
5. The downtown boulevards are wide and impressive.

Exercise 5
Creating sentences

Create sentences by using each of the following verbs in the pattern indicated. (For the meanings of the abbreviations, see the directions for Exercise 4.) You may want to change the form of the verb.

Example:
give (S–V–IO–DO)
Sam gave his brother a birthday card.

1. laugh (S–V)
2. elect (S–V–DO–OC)
3. steal (S–V–DO)
4. catch (S–V–DO)
5. bring (S–V–IO–DO)
6. seem (S–V–SC)
7. call (S–V–DO–OC)
8. become (S–V–SC)
9. buy (S–V–IO–DO)
10. study (S–V)

5b Expanding the basic sentence with single words

Most of the sentences we read, write, or speak are more complex and also more informative and interesting than those examined so far. Most sentences contain one or more of the following: (1) modifying words; (2) word groups, called phrases and clauses; and (3) combinations of two or more words or word groups of the same kind.

Using adjectives and adverbs

The simplest expansion of sentences occurs when we add modifying words to describe or limit the nouns and verbs. Modifying words add details.

Recently, the earth trembled.
The earthquake *nearly* destroyed the *old* city.
The *federal* government *soon* sent the city aid.
The grant was a *very generous* one but disappeared *too quickly.*

The italicized words represent two different parts of speech:

- **Adjectives** describe or modify nouns and pronouns. They specify which one, what quality, or how many.

old city (adjective noun) — generous one (adjective pronoun) — two pears (adjective noun)

- **Adverbs** describe or modify verbs, adjectives, other adverbs, and whole groups of words. They specify when, where, how, and to what extent.

nearly destroyed (adverb verb) — too quickly (adverb adverb)

very generous (adverb adjective) — Unfortunately, taxes will rise. (adverb word group)

An *-ly* ending often signals an adverb, but not always: *friendly* is an adjective; *never, not,* and *always* are adverbs. The only way to tell whether a word is an adjective or an adverb is to determine what it modifies.

Adjectives and adverbs appear in three forms:

- The **positive** form is the basic form, the one listed in the dictionary: *good, green, angry; badly, quickly, angrily.*
- The **comparative** form indicates a greater degree of the quality named by the word: *better, greener, angrier; worse, more quickly, more angrily.*
- The **superlative** form indicates the greatest degree of the quality named: *best, greenest, angriest; worst, most quickly, most angrily.*

(For further discussion of these forms, see p. 243.)

Using other words as modifiers

Nouns and special forms of verbs may sometimes serve as modifiers of other nouns. In combinations such as *office buildings, Thanksgiving prayer,* and *shock hazard,* the first noun modifies the second. In combinations such as *singing birds, corrected papers,* and *broken finger,* the first word is a verb form modifying the following noun. (These modifying verb forms are discussed in more detail on pp. 167–69.) Again, the part of speech to which we assign a word always depends on its function in a sentence.

Exercise 6
Identifying and using adjectives and adverbs

Identify the adjectives and adverbs in the following sentences. Then use each sentence as a model for creating a sentence of your own.

Example:

The red barn sat uncomfortably among modern buildings.

adjective adverb adjective
The *red* barn sat *uncomfortably* among *modern* buildings.
The little girl complained loudly to her busy mother.

1. The icy rain created glassy patches on the roads.
2. Happily, children played in the slippery streets.
3. Fortunately, no cars ventured out.
4. Wise parents stayed indoors where they could be warm and dry.
5. The dogs slept soundly near the warm radiators.

Exercise 7
Using verb forms as modifiers

Use each of the following verb forms to modify a noun in a sentence of your own.

Example:

smoking
Only a *smoking cigar* remained.

1. scrambled
2. twitching
3. rambling
4. typed
5. painted
6. written
7. charging
8. ripened
9. known
10. driven

Exercise 8
Sentence combining: Single-word modifiers

To practise expanding the basic sentence patterns with single-word modifiers, combine each group of sentences below into one sentence. You will have to delete and rearrange words.

Example:

The speaker told us the facts. The speaker told us calmly. The facts were terrifying.

The speaker *calmly* told us the *terrifying* facts.

1. A painting hung on a wall. The painting was religious. The wall was wooden.
2. The clock ticked. The clock was big. It was a wall clock. It ticked noisily.
3. The parents comforted their children. The parents were departing. The children were nervous.
4. The house sheltered people. The people were homeless. The house was abandoned.
5. Children leave toys. The children are growing. They leave the toys behind. The toys are many. The toys are broken.
6. The car is a Chevrolet. The car is wrecked. The car is silver.
7. We bought our father a knife. We bought the knife recently. It is for carving.
8. The doors open. The doors are brass. They open inward.
9. The oceans are deep. The oceans contain fish. The fish are peculiar.
10. The boy drank the water. The boy was hicupping. He drank the water quickly.

5c Expanding the basic sentence with word groups

Most sentences we read or write contain whole word groups that serve as nouns and modifiers. Such word groups enable us to combine several bits of information into one sentence and to make the relations among them clear, as in this sentence:

subject (skaters) — verb (sought) — object (safety)

When the ice cracked, the skaters, fearing an accident, sought safety at the lake's edge.

Attached to *skaters sought safety*, the skeleton of this sentence, are three groups of words that add related information: *When the ice cracked, fearing an accident,* and *at the lake's edge.* These constructions are phrases and clauses.

- A **phrase** is a group of related words that lacks either a subject or a predicate or both: *fearing an accident, at the lake's edge.*
- A **clause** contains both a subject and a predicate: *When the ice cracked* and *the skaters sought safety* are both clauses, though only the second can stand alone as a sentence.

1 Using prepositional phrases

Prepositions are connecting words. Unlike nouns, verbs, and modifiers, which may change form, prepositions never change form.

Common prepositions

about	beneath	in spite of	round
above	beside	instead of	since
according to	between	into	through
across	beyond	like	throughout
after	by	near	till
against	concerning	next to	to
along	despite	of	toward
along with	down	off	under
among	during	on	underneath
around	except	onto	unlike
as	except for	out	until
aside from	excepting	out of	up
at	for	outside	upon
because of	from	over	with
before	in	past	within
behind	in addition to	regarding	without
below	inside		

A preposition connects a noun or pronoun to another word in the sentence: *Robins nest in trees.* The noun or pronoun so connected (*trees*) is the **object of the preposition.** The preposition plus its object and any modifiers is a **prepositional phrase.**

Preposition	Object
of	spaghetti
on	the surface
with	great satisfaction
upon	entering the room
from	where you are standing

Prepositions normally come before their objects. But in speech and informal writing the preposition sometimes comes after its object: *What do you want to see him about?*

Prepositional phrases usually function as adjectives (modifying nouns) or as adverbs (modifying verbs, adjectives, or other adverbs). As modifiers, they add details that make sentences clearer and more interesting for readers.

Life *on a raft* was an opportunity *for adventure.*
adjective phrase — adjective phrase

Huck Finn rode the raft *by choice.*
adverb phrase

Occasionally, prepositional phrases also function as nouns, though rarely in writing.

subject
Across the river is too far to go for ice cream.

NOTE ESL The meanings and idiomatic uses of English prepositions can be difficult to master; most must be memorized or looked up in a dictionary (a list of ESL dictionaries appears on p. 470). See pages 223–24 for the uses of prepositions in two-word verbs such as *look after* and 455–56 for the uses of prepositions in idioms.

Punctuating prepositional phrases

Since a prepositional phrase lacks a subject and a predicate, it should not be punctuated as a complete sentence. If it is, the result is a **sentence fragment** (Chapter 10):

FRAGMENT Toward the sun.

The phrase must be attached to another group of words containing both a subject and a predicate:

REVISED The plane turned *toward the sun.*

A prepositional phrase that introduces a sentence is set off with punctuation, usually a comma, unless it is short (see 21b).

According to the newspaper and other sources, the mayor has reluctantly decided to veto the bill.

In 1918 the First World War finally ended.

A prepositional phrase that interrupts or concludes a sentence is *not* set off with punctuation when it restricts the meaning of the word or words it modifies (see 21c).

The announcement *of a tuition increase* surprised no one.
Students expected new fees *for the coming year.*

When an interrupting or concluding prepositional phrase does *not* restrict meaning, but merely adds information to the sentence, then it *is* set off with punctuation, usually a comma or commas (see 21c).

> The mayor, *according to the newspaper and other sources*, has reluctantly decided to veto the bill.

As all the preceding examples illustrate, a preposition and its object are not separated by a comma (see 21j-1).

Exercise 9
Identifying prepositional phrases

Identify the prepositional phrases in the following passage. Indicate whether each phrase functions as an adjective or as an adverb, and name the word that the phrase modifies.

Example:

After an hour I finally arrived at the home of my professor.

adverb — adverb — adjective
After an hour I finally arrived *at the home of my professor.*

The woman in blue socks ran from the policeman on horseback. She darted down Bates Street and then into the bus depot. At the depot the policeman dismounted from his horse and searched for the woman. The entrance to the depot and the interior were filled with travellers, however, and in the crowd he lost sight of the woman. She, meanwhile, had boarded a bus on the other side of the depot and was riding across town.

Exercise 10
Sentence combining: Prepositional phrases

To practise writing sentences with prepositional phrases, combine each group of sentences below into one sentence that includes one or two prepositional phrases. You will have to add, delete, and rearrange words. Some items have more than one possible answer.

Example:

I will start working. The new job will pay the minimum wage.
I will start working *at a new job for the minimum wage.*

1. The slow loris protects itself well. Its habitat is Southeast Asia. It possesses a poisonous chemical.
2. To frighten predators, the loris exudes the chemical. The chemical comes from a gland. The gland is on the loris's upper arm.
3. The loris's chemical is highly toxic. The chemical is not like a skunk's spray. Even small quantities of the chemical are toxic.
4. A tiny dose can affect a human. The dose would get in the mouth. The human would be sent into shock.

5. Predators probably can sense the toxin. They detect it at a distance. They use their nasal organs.

Using verbals and verbal phrases

Verbals are special verb forms such as *smoking* or *hidden* or *to win* that can function as nouns (*smoking is dangerous*) or as modifiers (*the hidden money, the urge to win*).

NOTE A verbal *cannot* stand alone as the complete verb in the predicate of a sentence. For example, *The man smoking* and *The money hidden* are not sentences but sentence fragments (see 10a). Any verbal must combine with a helping verb to serve as the predicate of a sentence: *The man was smoking. The money is hidden.*

Because verbals cannot serve alone as sentence predicates, they are sometimes called **nonfinite verbs** (in essence, they are "unfinished"). **Finite verbs,** in contrast, can make an assertion or express a state of being without a helping verb (they are "finished"). Either of two tests can distinguish finite and nonfinite verbs.

Tests for finite and nonfinite verbs (verbals)

TEST 1 Does the word require a change in form when a third-person subject changes from singular to plural?

YES Finite verb: *It sings. They sing.*

NO Nonfinite verb (verbal): *bird singing, birds singing*

TEST 2 Does the word require a change in form to show the difference in present, past, and future?

YES Finite verb: *It sings. It sang. It will sing.*

NO Nonfinite verb (verbal): *The bird singing is/was/will be a robin.*

There are three kinds of verbals: participles, gerunds, and infinitives.

Participles

All verbs have two participle forms, a present and a past. The **present participle** consists of the dictionary form of the verb plus the ending *-ing: beginning, completing, hiding.* The **past participle** of most verbs consists of the dictionary form plus *-d* or *-ed: believed, completed.* Some common verbs have an irregular past participle: *begun, hidden.* (See pp. 199–202.)

Both present and past participles function as adjectives to modify nouns and pronouns.

Shopping malls sometimes frustrate shoppers.

Shoppers may feel *trapped.*

NOTE ESL For verbs expressing feeling, the present and past participles have different meanings: *It was a boring lecture. The bored students slept.* See page 246.

Gerunds

Gerund is the name given to the *-ing* form of the verb when it serves as a noun.

subject
Strolling through stores can exhaust the hardiest shopper.

object
Many children learn to hate *shopping.*

Present participles and gerunds can be distinguished *only* by their function in a sentence. If the *-ing* form functions as an adjective (*a teaching degree*), it is a present participle. If the *-ing* form functions as a noun (*Teaching is difficult*), it is a gerund.

NOTE ESL Always use a gerund rather than any other verb form as the object of a preposition: *Diners are prohibited from smoking.* See also the ESL note below.

Infinitives

The **infinitive** is the *to* form of the verb, the dictionary form preceded by the infinitive marker *to: to begin, to hide, to run.* Infinitives may function as nouns, adjectives, or adverbs.

The question *to answer* is why shoppers endure mall fatigue.
adjective

The solution for mall fatigue is *to leave.*
noun

Still, shoppers find it difficult *to quit.*
adverb

NOTE ESL Infinitives and gerunds may follow some verbs and not others and may differ in meaning after a verb: *The singer stopped to sing. The singer stopped singing.* (See pp. 221–22.)

Verbal phrases

Participles, gerunds, and infinitives—like other forms of verbs—may take subjects, objects, or complements, and they may be modified by adverbs. The verbal and all the words immediately related to it make up a **verbal phrase.** With verbal phrases, we can create concise sentences packed with information.

Like participles, **participial phrases** always serve as adjectives, modifying nouns or pronouns.

Buying things, most shoppers feel themselves in control.

They make selections *determined by personal taste.*

Gerund phrases, like gerunds, always serve as nouns.

subject

Shopping for clothing and other items satisfies personal needs.

object of preposition

Malls are good at *creating such needs.*

Infinitive phrases may serve as nouns, adverbs, or adjectives.

sentence subject — subject complement

To design a mall is *to create an artificial environment.*

noun phrase — noun phrase

Malls are designed *to make shoppers feel safe.*

adverb phrase

The environment supports the impulse *to shop for oneself.*

adjective phrase

Note When an infinitive or infinitive phrase serves as a noun after verbs such as *bear, let, help, make, see,* and *watch,* the infinitive marker *to* is omitted: *We all heard her* (*to*) *tell the story.*

Punctuating verbals and verbal phrases

Verbal phrases punctuated as complete sentences are sentence fragments (Chapter 10). A complete sentence must contain a subject and a finite verb (p. 167).

Fragment *Treating* the patients kindly.

Revised *She treats* the patients kindly.

A verbal or verbal phrase serving as a modifier is almost always set off with a comma when it introduces a sentence (see 21b).

To pay tuition, some students work at two jobs.
Breathing evenly, the cat lay asleep on the rug.

A modifying verbal or verbal phrase that interrupts or concludes a sentence is *not* set off with punctuation when it restricts the meaning of the word or words it modifies (see 21c).

Jobs *paying well* are hard to find.

When an interrupting or concluding verbal modifier does *not* restrict meaning, but merely adds information to the sentence, it *is* set off with punctuation, usually a comma or commas (see 21c).

One job, *paying twelve dollars an hour*, was filled in fifteen minutes.

Exercise 11
Identifying verbals and verbal phrases

The following sentences contain participles, gerunds, and infinitives as well as participial, gerund, and infinitive phrases. First identify each verbal or verbal phrase. Then indicate whether it is used as an adjective, an adverb, or a noun.

Example:

Laughing, the talk-show host prodded her guest to talk.

Adjective / adverb
Laughing, the talk-show host prodded her guest *to talk.*

1. Founded in 1713 on Cape Breton Island, the military outpost of Louisbourg dominated the region.
2. Following the practice of the day, French military engineers created a walled fortress.
3. The fortifications were not strong enough to withstand the sieges of 1745 and 1758.
4. After defeating the defenders of the fort, the conquerors forced the population of the settlement to return to France.
5. Later, the fall of Louisbourg, after Quebec and Montreal were captured in 1759 and 1760, ended France's ability to extend its influence in North America.

Exercise 12
Sentence combining: Verbals and verbal phrases

To practise writing sentences with verbals and verbal phrases, combine each pair of sentences below into one sentence. You will have to add, delete, change, and rearrange words. Each item has more than one possible answer.

Example:

My father took pleasure in mean pranks. For instance, he hid the neighbour's cat.

My father took pleasure in mean pranks such as *hiding the neighbour's cat.*

1. Air pollution is a health problem. It affects millions of Canadians.
2. The air has been polluted mainly by industries and automobiles. It contains toxic chemicals.
3. Environmentalists pressure politicians. They think politicians should pass stricter laws.

4. Many politicians waver. They are not necessarily anti-environment.
5. The problems are too complex. They cannot be solved easily.

Using absolute phrases

Absolute phrases consist of a noun or pronoun and a participle, plus any modifiers.

absolute phrase
Many ethnic groups, *their own place established,* are making way for new arrivals.

absolute phrase / absolute phrase
Their native lands left behind, an uncertain future looming, immigrants face many obstacles.

These phrases are called *absolute* (from a Latin word meaning "free") because they have no specific grammatical connection to any word in the rest of the sentence. Instead, they modify the entire rest of the sentence, adding information or clarifying meaning.

Notice that absolute phrases, unlike participial phrases, always contain a subject. Compare the following.

participial phrase
For many immigrants *learning English,* the language introduces them to Canadian culture.

absolute phrase
The immigrants having learned English, their opportunities widen.

We often omit the participle from an absolute phrase when it is some form of *be,* such as *being* or *having been.*

Two languages (*being*) *at hand,* bilingual citizens, in fact, have many cultural and occupational advantages.

Punctuating absolute phrases

Absolute phrases are always set off from the rest of the sentence with punctuation, usually a comma or commas (see 21d).

Their future more secure, these citizens will make room for new arrivals.

These citizens, *their future more secure,* will make room for new arrivals.

Exercise 13
Sentence combining: Absolute phrases

To practise writing sentences with absolute phrases, combine each pair of sentences below into one sentence that contains an absolute phrase. You will have to add, delete, change, and rearrange words.

Example:

The flower's petals wilted. It looked pathetic.
Its petals wilted, the flower looked pathetic.

1. The First World War began in 1914. Billy Bishop enlisted though he was only seventeen.
2. He was the first Canadian airman to win the Victoria Cross. His record drew attention to itself.
3. He attacked an enemy airfield single-handedly. His exploits became bolder and bolder.
4. He claimed five victories in one day. His greatest achievement came on June 18, 1918.
5. The evidence was lost. His claims were later called into question.

Using subordinate clauses

As we noted earlier, a **clause** is any group of words that contains both a subject and a predicate. There are two kinds of clauses, and the distinction between them is important.

- A **main** or **independent clause** makes a complete statement and can stand alone as a sentence: *The sky darkened.*
- A **subordinate** or **dependent clause** is just like a main clause *except* that it begins with a subordinating word: *when the sky darkened; whoever calls.* The subordinating word reduces the clause to a single part of speech: an adjective, an adverb, or a noun. Because it only modifies or names something, a subordinate clause cannot stand alone as a sentence (see the discussion of punctuation on p. 175).

The following examples show the differences between the two kinds of clauses:

[main clause] [main clause]
The school teaches parents. It is unusual.

[subordinate clause] [main clause]
Because the school teaches parents, it is unusual.

[main clause] [main clause]
Some parents avoid their children's schools. They are often illiterate.

[main clause]
Parents *who are illiterate* often avoid their children's schools.
[subordinate clause]

Two kinds of subordinating words introduce subordinate clauses. **Subordinating conjunctions,** like prepositions, never change form in any way.

Common subordinating conjunctions

after	because	in order that	than	when
although	before	now that	that	whenever
as	even if	once	though	where
as if	even though	rather than	till	whereas
as long as	if	since	unless	wherever
as though	if only	so that	until	while

The second kind of subordinating word is the **relative pronoun.**

Relative pronouns

which	what	who (whose, whom)
that	whatever	whoever (whomever)

Unlike subordinating conjunctions, relative pronouns usually act as subjects or objects in their own clauses, and two of them (*who* and *whoever*) change form accordingly (see p. 193).

Subordinate clauses function as adjectives, adverbs, or nouns.

Adjective clauses

Adjective clauses modify nouns and pronouns, providing necessary or helpful information about them. They usually begin with *who, whom, whose, which,* or *that,* although a few adjective clauses begin with *when* or *where* (standing for *in which, on which,* or *at which*). The pronoun is the subject or object of the clause it begins. The clause ordinarily falls immediately after the noun or pronoun it modifies.

Parents *who are illiterate* often have bad memories of school.

Schools *that involve parents* are more successful with children.

One school, *which is open year-round,* helps parents learn to read.

The school is in a city *where the illiteracy rate is high.*

Adverb clauses

Like adverbs, **adverb clauses** modify verbs, adjectives, other adverbs, and whole groups of words. They usually tell how, why, when, where, under what conditions, or with what result. They always begin with subordinating conjunctions.

> The school began teaching parents *when adult illiteracy gained national attention.*
>
> At first the program was not as successful *as its founders had hoped.*
>
> *Because it was directed at people who could not read,* advertising had to be inventive.

An adverb clause can often be moved around in a sentence with no loss of clarity. Compare the preceding example with this one:

> Advertising had to be inventive *because it was directed at people who could not read.*

Noun clauses

Noun clauses function as subjects, objects, and complements in sentences. They begin with *that, what, whatever, who, whom, whoever, whomever, when, where, whether, why,* or *how.* Unlike adjective and adverb clauses, noun clauses *replace* a word (a noun) within a clause; therefore, they can be difficult to identify.

> sentence subject
> *Whether the program would succeed* depended on door-to-door advertising.
>
> direct object
> Teachers explained in person *how the program would work.*
>
> sentence subject
> *Whoever seemed slightly interested* was invited to an open meeting.
>
> object of preposition
> A few parents were anxious about *what their children would think.*

Elliptical clauses

A subordinate clause that is grammatically incomplete but clear in meaning is an **elliptical clause** (*ellipsis* means "omission"). The meaning of the clause is clear because the missing element can be supplied from the context. Most often the elements omitted are the relative pronouns *that, which,* and *whom* from adjective clauses or the predicate from the second part of a comparison.

> The parents knew their children could read better *than they* (*could read*).
>
> Scepticism and fear were among the feelings (*that*) *the parents voiced.*
>
> *Though* (*they were*) *reluctant at first,* about a third of the parents attended the meeting.

Punctuating subordinate clauses

Subordinate clauses punctuated as complete sentences are sentence fragments (Chapter 10). Though a subordinate clause contains a subject and a predicate and thus resembles a complete sentence, it also begins with a subordinating word that makes it into a single part of speech.

FRAGMENT	Because a door was ajar.
REVISED	A door was ajar.
REVISED	The secret leaked *because a door was ajar.*

A subordinate clause serving as an adverb is almost always set off with a comma when it introduces a sentence (see 21b).

Although the project was almost completed, it lost its funding.

A modifying subordinate clause that interrupts or concludes a main clause is *not* set off with punctuation when it restricts the meaning of the word or words it modifies (see 21c).

The woman *who spoke* is a doctor.
The project lost its funding *because it was not completed on time.*

When an interrupting or concluding subordinate clause does *not* restrict meaning, but merely adds information to the sentence, it *is* set off with punctuation, usually a comma or commas (see 21c).

The project lost its funding, *although it was almost completed.*
The woman, *who is a doctor*, cares for her invalid father.

Exercise 14
Identifying subordinate clauses

Identify the subordinate clauses in the following sentences. Then indicate whether each is used as an adjective, an adverb, or a noun. If the clause is a noun, indicate its function in the sentence.

Example:

The article explained how one could build an underground house.

noun
The article explained *how one could build an underground house.* [Object of *explained.*]

1. Scientists who want to catch the slightest signals from space use extremely sensitive receivers.
2. Even though they have had to fight for funding, these scientists have persisted in their research.
3. The research is called SETI, which stands for Search for Extraterrestrial Intelligence.

4. The supposition is that intelligent beings in space are trying to get in touch with us.
5. The challenge is to guess what frequency these beings would use to send signals.

Exercise 15
Sentence combining: Subordinate clauses

To practise writing sentences with subordinate clauses, combine each pair of main clauses below into one sentence. Use either subordinating conjunctions or relative pronouns as appropriate, referring to the lists on page 173 if necessary. You will have to add, delete, and rearrange words. Each item has more than one possible answer.

Example:

She did not have her tyre irons with her. She could not change her bicycle tyre.

Because she did not have her tyre irons with her, she could not change her bicycle tyre.

1. Moviegoers expect something. Movie sequels should be as exciting as the original films.
2. A few sequels are good films. Most are poor imitations of the originals.
3. A sequel to a blockbuster film arrives in the theatre. Crowds quickly line up to see it.
4. Viewers pay to see the same villains and heroes. They remember these characters fondly.
5. Afterwards, viewers often grumble about filmmakers. The filmmakers rehash tired plots and characters.

Using appositives

An **appositive** is usually a noun that renames another noun before it. (The word *appositive* derives from a Latin word that means "placed near to" or "applied to.") An appositive phrase includes modifiers as well.

Bizen ware, *a dark stoneware,* has been produced in Japan since the fourteenth century.

The name *Bizen* comes from the location of the kilns used to fire the pottery.

All appositives can replace the words they refer to: <u>*A dark stoneware*</u> *has been produced in Japan.*

Appositives are often introduced by words and phrases such as *or, that is, such as, for example,* and *in other words.*

Bizen ware is used in the Japanese tea ceremony, *that is, the Zen Buddhist observance that links meditation and art.*

Appositives are economical alternatives to adjective clauses containing a form of *be.*

Bizen ware, (*which is*) *a dark stoneware,* has been produced in Japan since the fourteenth century.

Although most appositives are nouns that rename other nouns, they may also be and rename other parts of speech.

The pottery is thrown, or *formed on a potter's wheel.*

gr 5c

Punctuating appositives

Appositives punctuated as complete sentences are sentence fragments (see Chapter 10). To correct such fragments, you can usually connect the appositive to the main clause containing the word referred to.

FRAGMENT An exceedingly tall man with narrow shoulders.

REVISED He stood next to a basketball player, *an exceedingly tall man with narrow shoulders.*

An appositive is *not* set off with punctuation when it restricts the meaning of the word it refers to (see 21c).

The verb *howl* comes from the Old English verb *houlen.*

When an appositive does *not* restrict the meaning of the word it refers to, it *is* set off with punctuation, usually a comma or commas (see 21c).

An aged elm, the tree was struck by lightning.
The tree, *an aged elm,* was struck by lightning.
Lightning struck the tree, *an aged elm.*

A nonrestrictive appositive is sometimes set off with a dash or dashes, especially when it contains commas (see 25b-2).

Three people—*Will, Carolyn, and Tom*—object to the new procedure.

A concluding appositive is sometimes set off with a colon (see 25a-1).

Two principles guide the judge's decisions: *justice and mercy.*

Exercise 16
Sentence combining: Appositives

To practise writing sentences with appositives, combine each pair of sentences into one sentence that contains an appositive. You will have to delete and rearrange words. Some items have more than one possible answer.

Example:

The largest land animal is the elephant. The elephant is also one of the most intelligent animals.

The largest land animal, *the elephant,* is also one of the most intelligent animals.

1. Some people perform amazing feats when they are very young. These people are geniuses from birth.
2. John Stuart Mill was a British philosopher. He had written a history of Rome by age seven.
3. Two great artists began their work at age four. They were Paul Klee and Gustav Mahler.
4. Mahler was a Bohemian composer of intensely emotional works. He was also the child of a brutal father.
5. Paul Klee was a Swiss painter. As a child he was frightened by his own drawings of devils.

5d Compounding words, phrases, and clauses

A **compound construction** combines words that are closely related and equally important. It makes writing clearer and more economical because it pulls together linked information.

Headaches can be controlled by biofeedback. Heart rate can be controlled by biofeedback.

compound subject
Headaches and heart rate can be controlled by biofeedback.

Without medication, biofeedback cures headaches. It steadies heart rate. It lowers blood pressure. It relaxes muscles.

compound predicate
Without medication, biofeedback *cures headaches, steadies heart rate, lowers blood pressure, and relaxes muscles.*

1 Using coordinating conjunctions and correlative conjunctions

Two kinds of words create compound constructions: coordinating and correlative conjunctions. **Coordinating conjunctions** are few and do not change form.

Coordinating conjunctions

and	nor	for	yet
but	or	so	

The coordinating conjunctions *and, but, nor,* and *or* always connect words or word groups of the same kind—that is, two or more nouns, verbs, adjectives, adverbs, phrases, subordinate clauses, or main clauses.

> Biofeedback *or* simple relaxation can relieve headaches.
> Biofeedback is effective *but* costly.
> Relaxation also works well, *and* it is inexpensive.

The conjunctions *for* and *so* connect only main clauses. *For* indicates cause; *so* indicates result.

> Biofeedback can be costly, *for* the training involves technical equipment and specialists.
>
> Relaxation can be difficult to learn alone, *so* some people do seek help.

Like *but,* the conjunction *yet* indicates contrast.

> Relaxation instruction does cost, *yet* it is usually cheaper than biofeedback training.

Some coordinating conjunctions pair up with other words to form **correlative conjunctions.**

Common correlative conjunctions

both . . . and	neither . . . nor
not only . . . but also	whether . . . or
not . . . but	as . . . as
either . . . or	

> *Both* biofeedback *and* relaxation can relieve headaches.
>
> The techniques require *neither* psychotherapy *nor* medication.
>
> The headache sufferer learns *not only* to recognize the causes of headaches *but also* to control those causes.

Punctuating compounded words, phrases, and clauses

Two words, phrases, or subordinate clauses that are connected by a coordinating conjunction are *not* separated by a comma (see 21j-2).

> The library needs *renovation and rebuilding.*
>
> The work will begin *after the spring term ends but before the summer term begins.*

When two *main* clauses are joined into one sentence with a coordinating conjunction, a comma precedes the conjunction (see 21a).

> The project will be lengthy, *and* everyone will suffer some inconvenience.

When two main clauses are joined *without* a coordinating conjunction, they must be separated with a semicolon to avoid the error called a comma splice (see 11a).

> The work cannot be delayed; it's already overdue.

The semicolon sometimes separates two main clauses joined by a coordinating conjunction when the clauses are long or contain commas (see 22c). The semicolon *always* separates two main clauses related by a conjunctive adverb (see the next section).

In a series of three or more items, commas separate the items, with *and* usually preceding the last item (see 21f-1).

> The renovated library will feature *new study carrels*, *new shelving*, *and a larger reference section.*

Semicolons sometimes separate the items in a series if they are long or contain commas (see 22d).

The comma also separates two or more adjectives when they modify a noun equally and are not joined by a coordinating conjunction (see 21f-2).

> *Cracked*, *crumbling* walls will be repaired.

The comma does *not* separate adjectives when the one nearer the noun is more closely related to it in meaning (see 21f-2).

> *New reading* lounges will replace the old ones.

Using conjunctive adverbs

One other kind of connecting word, called a **conjunctive adverb,** relates only main clauses, not words, phrases, or subordinate clauses.

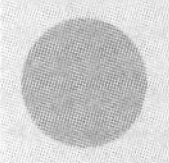

Common conjunctive adverbs

accordingly	furthermore	likewise	otherwise
also	hence	meanwhile	similarly
anyway	however	moreover	still
besides	in addition	namely	then
certainly	incidentally	nevertheless	thereafter
consequently	indeed	next	therefore
finally	in fact	nonetheless	thus
further	instead	now	undoubtedly

It's important to distinguish between conjunctive adverbs and conjunctions (coordinating and subordinating) because they demand different punctuation (see the discussion below). Conjunctive adverbs are *adverbs:* they describe the relation of ideas in two clauses, and, like most adverbs, they can move around in their clause:

> Relaxation techniques have improved; *however,* few people know them.
>
> Relaxation techniques have improved; few people know them, *however.*

In contrast, conjunctions bind two clauses into a single grammatical unit, and they cannot be moved:

> *Although* few people know them, relaxation techniques have improved. [The subordinating conjunction can't be moved: *Few people know them although, relaxation techniques have improved.*]
>
> Relaxation techniques have improved, *but* few people know them. [The coordinating conjunction can't be moved: *Relaxation techniques have improved, few people know them but.*]

Note Some connecting words have more than one use. *After, before, until,* and some other words may be either prepositions or subordinating conjunctions. Some prepositions, such as *behind, in,* and *outside,* can serve also as adverbs, as in *He trailed behind.* And some conjunctive adverbs, particularly *however,* may also serve simply as adverbs in sentences such as *However much it costs, we must have it.* Again, the part of speech of a word depends on its function in a sentence.

Punctuating sentences containing conjunctive adverbs

Because the two main clauses related by a conjunctive adverb remain independent units, they must be separated by a semicolon (see 22b). If they are separated by a comma, the result is a comma splice (Chapter 11):

Comma splice	Interest rates rose, *therefore,* real estate prices declined.
Revised	Interest rates rose; *therefore,* real estate prices declined.

A conjunctive adverb is almost always set off from its clause with a comma or commas.

> The decline was small; *however,* some investors were badly hurt.
> The decline was small; some investors, *however,* were badly hurt.

The comma or commas are optional with some one-syllable conjunctive adverbs (especially *hence, now, then,* and *thus*) and are not used with a few others when they appear inside or at the ends of clauses.

Interest rates rose; *thus,* real estate prices declined.
Interest rates rose; real estate prices, *therefore,* declined.

Exercise 17
Sentence combining: Compound constructions

To practise compounding words, phrases, and clauses, combine each pair of sentences below into one sentence that is as short as possible without altering meaning. Use an appropriate connecting word of the type specified in parentheses, referring to the lists on pages 178–80 if necessary. You will have to add, delete, and rearrange words, and you may have to change or add punctuation.

Example:

The encyclopedia had some information. It was not detailed enough. (*Conjunctive adverb.*)

The encyclopedia had some information; *however,* it was not detailed enough.

1. All too often people assume that old age is not a productive time. Many people in their nineties have made great achievements. (*Conjunctive adverb.*)
2. In his nineties the philosopher Bertrand Russell spoke vigorously for international peace. He spoke for nuclear disarmament. (*Correlative conjunction.*)
3. Grandma Moses did not retire to an easy chair. She began painting at age seventy-six and was still going at one hundred. (*Conjunctive adverb.*)
4. The British general George Higginson published his memoirs after he was ninety. The British archaeologist Margaret Murray published her memoirs after she was ninety. (*Coordinating conjunction.*)
5. The architect Frank Lloyd Wright designed his first building at age twenty. He designed his last building at age ninety. (*Coordinating conjunction.*)

5e Changing the usual order of the sentence

So far, all the examples of basic sentence grammar have been similar: the subject of the sentence comes first, naming the performer of the predicate's action, and the predicate comes second. This arrangement of subject and predicate describes most sentences that occur in writing, but four other kinds of sentences alter the basic pattern.

Forming questions

We form questions in one of several ways. We may invert the normal subject-verb arrangement of statements:

The rate is high. Is the rate high?

We may use a question word such as *how, what, who, when, where, which,* or *why:*

What rate is high?

Or we may use some combination of the two methods:

Why is the rate high?

In each case a question mark signals that the sentence is a question.

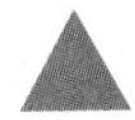

Forming commands

We construct commands even more simply than we construct questions: we merely delete the subject of the sentence, *you.*

Think of options.
Watch the news.
Eat your spinach.
Leave me alone.

Writing passive sentences

When the subject of a sentence performs the action of the verb, the verb is in the **active voice.**

subject / active verb / object
Kyong wrote the paper.

We can change the form of the verb and make the object into the subject. The verb in this new sentence is in the **passive voice** because the subject *receives* the action.

subject / passive verb
The paper was written by Kyong.

Only transitive verbs (verbs that take objects) can be expressed in the passive voice. The passive verb consists of a form of *be* plus the past participle of the main verb (*paper was written, absences were excused*). The actual actor (the person performing the action of the verb) may be expressed in a prepositional phrase (as in the example above: *by Kyong*) or may be omitted entirely if it is unknown or unimportant: *The house was flooded.*

(For more on formation of the passive voice, see Chapter 7, pp. 218–19. Also see p. 220 on overuse of the passive voice.)

Writing sentences with postponed subjects

The subject follows the predicate in two sentence patterns that are not questions, commands, or passive sentences. In one pattern the normal word order is reversed for emphasis:

Henry comes here. [Normal order.]
Here comes Henry. [Reversed order.]

This pattern occurs most often when the normal order is subject–intransitive verb–adverb. Then the adverb moves to the front of the sentence while subject and predicate reverse order.

A second kind of sentence with a postponed subject begins with either *it* or *there,* as in the following:

There *will be* [verb] eighteen *people* [subject] attending the meeting.

It *was* [verb] surprising *that Marinetti was nominated.* [subject]

The words *there* and *it* in such sentences are **expletives.** Their only function is to postpone the sentence subject. Expletive sentences do have their uses (see p. 466), but they can be unemphatic because they add words and delay the sentence subject. Usually, the normal subject-predicate order is more effective: *Eighteen people will attend the meeting. Marinetti's nomination was surprising.*

NOTE ESL Be careful not to omit *there* or *it* from an expletive construction. Only commands and some questions can begin with verbs (see pp. 182–83).

FAULTY No one predicted the nomination. Were no polls showing Marinetti ahead.

REVISED No one predicted the nomination. *There* were no polls showing Marinetti ahead.

Exercise 18
Forming questions and commands

Form a question and a command from the following noun and verb pairs.

Example:

wood, split
Did you *split* all this *wood?*
Split the *wood* for our fire.

1. water, boil
2. music, stop
3. table, set
4. dice, roll
5. telephone, use

Exercise 19
Rewriting passives and expletives

Rewrite each passive sentence below as active, and rewrite each expletive construction to restore normal subject-predicate order. (For additional exercises with the passive voice and with expletives, see pp. 220, 335, and 466.)

1. *The West Wind* was painted by Tom Thomson in 1917.
2. This picture was created with great passion by Thomson.
3. The mystery of the lakes and woods of northern Ontario were captured by the Group of Seven.
4. It is a distinctly Canadian landscape that they depicted.
5. There were many Canadian subjects made possible by their innovations.

5f Classifying sentences

We describe and classify sentences in two different ways: by function (statement, question, command, exclamation, and so forth) or by structure. Four basic sentence structures are possible: simple, compound, complex, and compound-complex.

1 Writing simple sentences

A **simple sentence** consists of a single main clause and no subordinate clause.

main clause
Last summer was unusually hot.

main clause
The summer made many farmers leave the area for good or reduced them to bare existence.

2 Writing compound sentences

A **compound sentence** consists of two or more main clauses and no subordinate clause. The clauses may be joined by a coordinating conjunction and a comma, by a semicolon alone, or by a conjunctive adverb and a semicolon.

main clause — main clause
Last July was hot, but August was even hotter.

main clause — main clause
The hot sun scorched the earth; the lack of rain killed many crops.

3 Writing complex sentences

A **complex** sentence contains one main clause and one or more subordinate clauses.

main clause — subordinate clause
Rain finally came, although many had left the area by then.

main clause — subordinate clause — subordinate clause
Those who remained were able to start anew because the government came to their aid.

Notice that length does not determine whether a sentence is complex or simple; both kinds can be short or long.

4 Writing compound-complex sentences

A **compound-complex sentence** has the characteristics of both the compound sentence (two or more main clauses) and the complex sentence (at least one subordinate clause).

subordinate clause — main clause — main clause
Even though government aid finally came, many people had already been reduced to poverty, and others had been forced to move.

Exercise 20
Identifying sentence structures

Mark the main clauses and subordinate clauses in the following sentences. Identify each sentence as simple, compound, complex, or compound-complex.

Example:

The police began patrolling more often when crime in the neighbourhood increased.

main clause
Complex: The police began patrolling more often
subordinate clause
when crime in the neighbourhood increased.

1. Canada has no true deserts.
2. Some places, however, exhibit distinctive desert-like features.
3. Although they support many life forms, certain areas of the Prairies, for example, have minimal precipitation and semi-arid vegetation.
4. In contrast, the rain forests of British Columbia can have several thousand millimetres of rain per year, and the Maritimes uniformly receive over a thousand millimetres.
5. Since warm air can hold more moisture than cold, southern parts of Canada have more precipitation than northern, but the coasts have more than the central parts.

Exercise 21
Sentence combining: Sentence structures

Combine each set of simple sentences below to produce the kind of sentence specified in parentheses. You will have to add, delete, change, and rearrange words.

Example:

The traffic passed the house. It never stopped. (*Complex.*)
The traffic that passed the house never stopped.

1. Recycling takes time. It reduces garbage in landfills. (*Compound.*)
2. People begin to recycle. They generate much less trash. (*Complex.*)
3. White tissues and paper towels biodegrade more easily than dyed ones. People still buy dyed papers. (*Complex.*)
4. The cans are aluminum. They bring recyclers good money. (*Simple.*)
5. Environmentalists have hope. Perhaps more communities will recycle newspaper and glass. Many citizens refuse to participate. (*Compound-complex.*)

Chapter 6 Case of Nouns and Pronouns

Case is the form of a noun or pronoun that shows the reader how it functions in a sentence—that is, whether it functions as a subject, as an object, or in some other way. As shown in the box on the facing page, only *I, we, he, she, they,* and *who* change form for each case. Thus these pronouns are the focus of this chapter.

The **subjective case** generally indicates that the word is a subject or a subject complement. (See pp. 153 and 159.)

subject
She and Novick discussed the proposal.

subject
The proposal ignores many *who* need help.

subject complement
The disgruntled planners were *she and Novick.*

The **objective case** generally indicates that the word is the object of a verb or preposition:

object of verb
The proposal disappointed *her and Novick.*

object of verb / object of verb
A colleague *whom* they respected let *them* down.

object of proposition
Their opinion of *him* suffered.

The **possessive case** generally indicates ownership or source:

Case forms of nouns and pronouns

	SUBJECTIVE	OBJECTIVE	POSSESSIVE
NOUNS	boy	boy	boy's
	Jessie	Jessie	Jessie's
PERSONAL PRONOUNS			
Singular			
1st person	**I**	**me**	**my, mine**
2nd person	you	you	your, yours
3rd person	**he**	**him**	**his**
	she	**her**	**her, hers**
	it	it	its
Plural			
1st person	**we**	**us**	**our, ours**
2nd person	you	you	your, yours
3rd person	**they**	**them**	**their, theirs**
RELATIVE AND INTERROGATIVE PRONOUNS			
	who	**whom**	**whose**
	whoever	**whomever**	—
	which, that, what	which, that, what	—
INDEFINITE PRONOUNS			
	everybody	everybody	everybody's

Her counterproposal is in preparation.
Theirs is the more defensible position.
The problem is not *his.*

NOTE Do not use an apostrophe to form the possessive of personal pronouns: *yours* (not *your's*); *theirs* (not *their's*). (See p. 391. See also p. 387 for the possessive forms of nouns, which do use apostrophes.)

6a Use the subjective case for all parts of compound subjects and for subject complements.

In compound subjects use the same pronoun form you would use if the pronoun stood alone as a subject.

subject
She and Novick will persist.

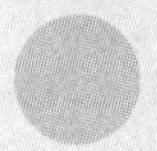

A test for case forms in compound constructions

1. Identify a compound construction (one connected by *and, but, or, nor*).

   (*He, Him*) and (*I, me*) won the prize.
   The prize went to (*he, him*) and (*I, me*).

2. Write a separate sentence for each part of the compound.

   (*He, Him*) won the prize. (*I, Me*) won the prize.
   The prize went to (*he, him*). The prize went to (*I, me*).

3. Choose the pronouns that sound correct.

   He won the prize. *I* won the prize. [Subjective.]
   The prize went to *him*. The prize went to *me*. [Objective.]

4. Put the separate sentences back together.

   He and *I* won the prize.
   The prize went to *him* and *me*.

subject
The others may lend their support when *she and Novick* get a hearing.

If you are in doubt about the correct form, try the test in the box above.

After a linking verb, such as a form of *be,* a pronoun renaming the subject (a subject complement) should be in the subjective case.

subject complement
The ones who care most are *she and Novick.*

subject complement
It was *they* whom the mayor appointed.

If this construction sounds stilted to you, use the more natural order: *She and Novick are the ones who care most. The mayor appointed them.*

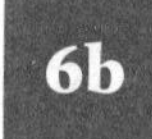

6b Use the objective case for all parts of compound objects.

In compound objects use the same pronoun form you would use if the pronoun stood alone as an object.

direct object
The mayor nominated *Zhu and him.*

indirect object
The mayor gave *Zhu and him* awards.

object of preposition
Credit goes equally to *them and the mayor.*

If you are in doubt about the correct form, try the test in the box opposite.

Exercise 1
Choosing between subjective and objective pronouns

From the pairs in parentheses, select the appropriate subjective or objective pronoun(s) for each of the following sentences.

Example:

"Between you and (*I, me*), the seller said, "this deal is a steal."
"Between you and *me*," the seller said, "this deal is a steal."

1. Jody and (*I, me*) had been hunting for jobs.
2. The best employees at our old company were (*she, her*) and (*I, me*), so (*we, us*) expected to find jobs quickly.
3. Between (*she, her*) and (*I, me*) the job search had lasted two months, and still it had barely begun.
4. Slowly, (*she, her*) and (*I, me*) stopped sharing leads.
5. It was obvious that Jody and (*I, me*) could not be as friendly as (*we, us*) had been.

6c Use the appropriate case when the plural pronoun *we* or *us* occurs with a noun.

The case of the first-person plural pronoun used with a noun depends on the use of the noun.

object of preposition
Freezing weather is welcomed by *us* skaters.

subject
We skaters welcome freezing weather.

6d In appositives the case of a pronoun depends on the function of the word described or identified.

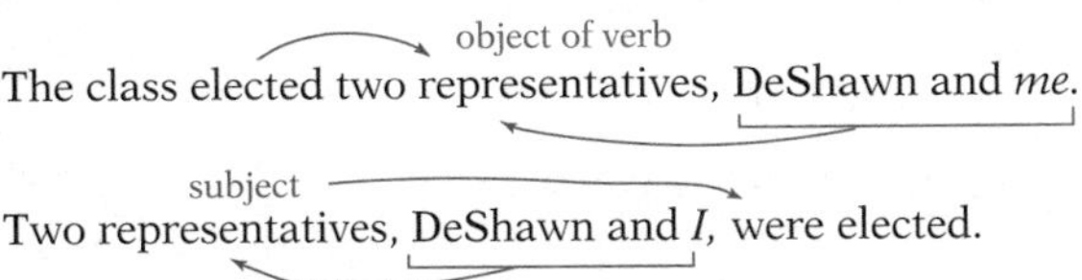

If you are in doubt about case in an appositive, try the sentence without the word the appositive identifies: *The class elected DeShawn and me; DeShawn and I were elected.*

Exercise 2
Choosing between subjective and objective pronouns

From the pairs in parentheses, select the appropriate subjective or objective pronoun for each of the following sentences.

Example:

Convincing (*we, us*) veterans to vote yes will be difficult.
Convincing *us* veterans to vote yes will be difficult.

1. Obtaining enough protein is important to (*we, us*) vegetarians.
2. Instead of obtaining protein from meat (*we, us*) vegetarians get our protein from other sources.
3. Jeff claims to know only two vegetarians, Helena and (*he, him*), who avoid all animal products, including milk.
4. Some of (*we, us*) vegetarians eat fish, which is a good source of protein.
5. (*We, Us*) vegetarians in my family, my parents and (*I, me*), drink milk and eat fish.

6e The case of a pronoun after *than* or *as* in a comparison depends on the meaning.

When a pronoun follows *than* or *as* in a comparison, the case of the pronoun indicates what words may have been omitted. When the pronoun is subjective, it must serve as the subject of an omitted verb.

subject
Some critics like Glass more than *he* (does).

When the pronoun is objective, it must serve as the object of an omitted verb.

object
Some critics like Glass more than (they like) *him*.

6f Use the objective case for pronouns that are subjects or objects of infinitives.

subject of infinitive
The school asked *him* to speak.

object of infinitive
Students chose to invite *him*.

The form of the pronoun *who* depends on its function in its clause.

To choose between *who* and *whom, whoever* and *whomever,* you need to figure out whether the word is a subject or an object.

At the beginning of questions use *who* for a subject and *whom* for an object.

subject →
Who wrote the policy?

object ←
Whom does it affect?

To help find the correct case of *who* in a question, try the test in the following box.

A test for *who* versus *whom* in questions

1. Pose the question.

   (*Who, Whom*) makes that decision?
   (*Who, Whom*) does one ask?

2. Answer the question, using a personal pronoun. Choose the pronoun that sounds correct, and note its case.

   (*She, Her*) makes that decision. *She* makes that decision. [Subjective.]

   One asks (*she, her*). One asks *her.* [Objective.]

3. Use the same case (*who* or *whom*) in the question.

   Who makes that decision? [Subjective.]
   Whom does one ask? [Objective.]

Note In speech the subjective case *who* is commonly used whenever it is the first word of a question, regardless of whether it is a subject or an object. But writing requires a distinction between the forms.

Spoken *Who* should we credit?

object ←
Written *Whom* should we credit?

In subordinate clauses use *who* and *whoever* for all subjects, *whom* and *whomever* for all objects.

The case of a pronoun in a subordinate clause depends on its function in the clause, regardless of whether the clause itself functions as a subject, an object, or a modifier.

subject →
Credit *whoever* wrote the policy.
object ←
Research should reveal *whom* to credit.

If you have trouble determining which form to choose, try the test in the following box.

A test for *who* versus *whom* in subordinate clauses

1. Locate the subordinate clause.

   Few people know (*who, whom*) they should ask.
   They are unsure (*who, whom*) makes the decision.

2. Rewrite the subordinate clause as a separate sentence, substituting a personal pronoun for *who, whom.* Choose the pronoun that sounds correct, and note its case.

   They should ask (*she, her*). They should ask *her.* [Objective.]
   (*She, her*) makes the decision. *She* makes the decision. [Subjective.]

3. Use the same case (*who* or *whom*) in the subordinate clause.

   Few people know *whom* they should ask. [Objective.]
   They are unsure *who* makes the decision. [Subjective.]

NOTE Don't let expressions such as *I think* and *she says* confuse you when they come between the subject *who* and its verb.

subject →
He is the one *who* the polls say will win.

To choose between *who* and *whom* in such constructions, delete the interrupting phrase: *He is the one who will win.*

Exercise 3
Choosing between *who* and *whom*

From the pairs in parentheses, select the appropriate form of the pronoun in each of the following sentences.

Example:

My mother asked me (*who, whom*) I was going out with.
My mother asked me *whom* I was going out with.

1. The school administrators suspended Jurgen, (*who, whom*) they suspected of setting the fire.
2. Jurgen had been complaining to other custodians, (*who, whom*) reported him.
3. He constantly complained of unfair treatment from (*whoever,

whomever) happened to be passing in the halls, including pupils.

4. "(*Who, Whom*) here has heard Mr. Jurgen's complaints?" the police asked.
5. "(*Who, Whom*) did he complain most about?"

Exercise 4
Sentence combining: *Who* versus *whom*

Combine each pair of sentences below into one sentence that contains a clause beginning with *who* or *whom*. Be sure to use the appropriate case form. You will have to add, delete, and rearrange words. Each item may have more than one possible answer.

Example:

David is the candidate. We think David deserves to win.
David is the candidate *who* we think deserves to win.

1. Some children have undetected hearing problems. These children may do poorly in school.
2. They may not hear important instructions and information from teachers. Teachers may speak softly.
3. Classmates may not be audible. The teacher calls on those classmates.
4. Some hearing-impaired children may work harder to overcome their handicap. These children get a lot of encouragement at home.
5. Some hearing-impaired children may take refuge in fantasy friends. They can rely on these friends not to criticize or laugh.

6h Ordinarily, use the possessive form of a pronoun or noun immediately before a gerund.

A **gerund** is the *-ing* form of the verb (*running, sleeping*) used as a noun (p. 168). Like nouns, gerunds are commonly preceded by possessive nouns and pronouns: *our vote* (noun), *our voting* (gerund).

The coach disapproved of *their* lifting weights.

The *coach's* disapproving was a surprise.

A noun or pronoun before an *-ing* verb form is not always possessive. Sometimes the *-ing* form will be a present participle modifying the preceding word.

objective pronoun ← participle
Everyone had noticed *him* weightlifting. [The emphasis is on *him*.]

possessive pronoun → gerund

Everyone had noticed *his* weightlifting. [The emphasis is on the activity.]

Note that a gerund usually is not preceded by the possessive when the possessive would create an awkward construction.

Awkward	A rumour spread about everybody's on the team wanting to quit.
Less awkward	A rumour spread about everybody on the team wanting to quit.
Better	A rumour spread that everybody on the team wanted to quit.

Exercise 5
Revising: Case

Revise all inappropriate case forms in the following paragraph, and explain the function of each case form.

Written four thousand years ago, *The Epic of Gilgamesh* tells of the friendship of Gilgamesh and Enkidu. Gilgamesh was a bored king who his people thought was too harsh. Then he met Enkidu, a wild man whom had lived with the animals in the mountains. Immediately, him and Gilgamesh wrestled to see whom was more powerful. After hours of struggle, Enkidu admitted that Gilgamesh was stronger than him. Now the friends needed adventures worthy of the two strongest men on earth. Gilgamesh said, "Between you and I, mighty deeds will be accomplished, and our fame will be everlasting." Among their acts, Enkidu and him defeated a giant bull, Humbaba, and cut down the bull's cedar forests. Them bringing back cedar logs to Gilgamesh's treeless land won great praise from the people. When Enkidu died, Gilgamesh mourned his death, realizing that no one had been a better friend than him. When Gilgamesh himself died many years later, his people raised a monument praising Enkidu and he for their friendship and their mighty deeds of courage.

Note See page 252 for an exercise involving case along with other aspects of grammar.

Chapter 7 Verbs

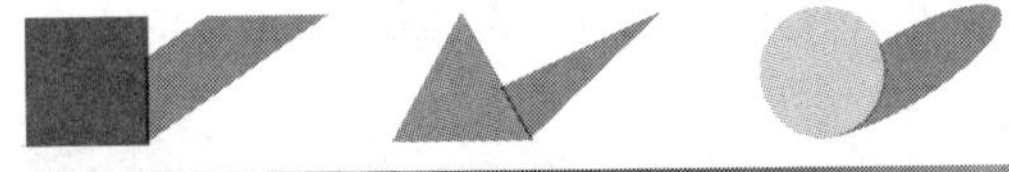

The verb is the most complicated part of speech in English, changing form to express a wide range of information.

VERB FORMS

All verbs except *be* have five basic forms. The first three are the verb's **principal parts.**

- The **plain form** is the dictionary form of the verb. When the subject is a plural noun or the pronoun *I, we, you,* or *they,* the plain form indicates action that occurs in the present, occurs habitually, or is generally true.

  A few artists *live* in town today.
  They *hold* classes downtown.

- The **past-tense form** indicates that the action of the verb occurred before now. It usually adds *-d* or *-ed* to the plain form, although for some irregular verbs it forms in other ways (see p. 199).

  Many artists *lived* in town before this year.
  They *held* classes downtown. [Irregular verb.]

- The **past participle** is usually the same as the past-tense form, except in most irregular verbs. It combines with forms of *have* or *be* (*has climbed, was created*), or by itself it modifies nouns and pronouns (*the sliced apples*).

Terms used to describe verbs

FORM

The spelling of the verb that conveys time, mood, and other information. *Kick, kicked, kicking,* and *kicks* are forms of *kick.* (See p. 197.)

TENSE

The time of the verb's action—for instance, present (*kick*), past (*kicked*), future (*will kick*). (See p. 208.)

MOOD

The attitude of the verb's speaker or writer—the difference, for example, in *I kick the ball, Kick the ball,* and *I suggest that you kick the ball.* (See p. 216.)

VOICE

The distinction between the **active,** in which the subject performs the verb's action (*I kick the ball*), and the **passive,** in which the subject is acted upon (*The ball is kicked by me*). (See p. 218.)

PERSON

The verb form that reflects whether the subject is speaking (*I/we kick the ball*), spoken to (*You kick the ball*), or spoken about (*She kicks the ball*). (See 7c, 8a.)

NUMBER

The verb form that reflects whether the subject is singular (*The girl kicks the ball*) or plural (*Girls kick the ball*). (See 7c, 8a.)

Artists have *lived* in town for decades.
They have *held* classes downtown. [Irregular verb.]

- The **present participle** adds *-ing* to the verb's plain form. It combines with forms of *be* (*is buying*), modifies nouns and pronouns (*the boiling water*), or functions as a noun (*Running exhausts me*).

  A few artists are *living* in town today.
  They are *holding* classes downtown.

- The **-*s* form** ends in *-s* or *-es.* When the subject is a singular noun, a pronoun such as *everyone,* or the personal pronoun *he, she,* or *it,* the *-s* form indicates action that occurs in the present, occurs habitually, or is generally true.

  The artist *lives* in town today.
  She *holds* classes downtown.

The verb *be* has eight forms rather than the five forms of most other verbs.

Verb forms

PLAIN FORM Close, run
PAST TENSE Closed, ran
PAST PARTICIPLE Closed, run
PRESENT PARTICIPLE Closing, running
-S FORM Closes, runs

PLAIN FORM	be		
PRESENT PARTICIPLE	being		
PAST PARTICIPLE	been		
	I	*he, she, it*	*we, you, they*
PRESENT TENSE	am	is	are
PAST TENSE	was	was	were

Helping verbs

Helping verbs, also called **auxiliary verbs,** combine with some verb forms to indicate time and other kinds of meaning, as in *can run, was sleeping, had been eaten.* These combinations are **verb phrases.** Since the plain form, present participle, or past participle in any verb phrase always carries the principal meaning, it is sometimes called the **main verb.**

VERB PHRASE	
Helping	*Main*
Artists *can*	*train* others to draw.
The techniques *have*	*changed* little.

These are the helping verbs:

can	may	must	shall	will
could	might	ought	should	would

Forms of *be:* be, am, is, are, was, were, been, being
Forms of *have:* have, has, had, having
Forms of *do:* do, does, did

See pages 204–07 for more on helping verbs.

7a Use the correct form of regular and irregular verbs.

Most verbs are **regular;** that is, they form their past tense and past participle by adding *-d* or *-ed* to the plain form.

PLAIN FORM	PAST TENSE	PAST PARTICIPLE
live	lived	lived
act	acted	acted

Since the past tense and past participle are created simply by adding to the plain form and since the two are identical, the forms of regular verbs do not often cause problems in speech and writing (but see p. 203).

About two hundred English verbs are **irregular;** that is, they form their past tense and past participle in some irregular way. For example:

PLAIN FORM	PAST TENSE	PAST PARTICIPLE
begin	began	begun
break	broke	broken
sleep	slept	slept

Check a dictionary under the plain form if you have any doubt about a verb's principal parts. If no other forms are listed, the verb is regular: both the past tense and the past participle add *-d* or *-ed* to the plain form. If the verb is irregular, the dictionary will list the plain form, the past tense, and the past participle in that order (*go, went, gone*). If the dictionary gives only two forms (as in *think, thought*), then the past tense and the past participle are the same.

The following list includes the most common irregular verbs. (When two forms are possible, as in *dove* and *dived,* both are included.)

Principal parts of common irregular verbs

PLAIN FORM	PAST TENSE	PAST PARTICIPLE
arise	arose	arisen
become	became	become
begin	began	begun
bid	bid	bid
bite	bit	bitten, bit
blow	blew	blown
break	broke	broken
bring	brought	brought
burst	burst	burst
buy	bought	bought
catch	caught	caught
choose	chose	chosen
come	came	come
cut	cut	cut

Plain form	Past tense	Past participle
dive	dived, dove	dived
do	did	done
draw	drew	drawn
dream	dreamed, dreamt	dreamed, dreamt
drink	drank	drunk
drive	drove	driven
eat	ate	eaten
fall	fell	fallen
find	found	found
flee	fled	fled
fly	flew	flown
forget	forgot	forgotten, forgot
freeze	froze	frozen
get	got	got, gotten
give	gave	given
go	went	gone
grow	grew	grown
hang (suspend)	hung	hung
hang (execute)	hanged	hanged
hear	heard	heard
hide	hid	hidden
hold	held	held
keep	kept	kept
know	knew	known
lay	laid	laid
lead	led	led
leave	left	left
lend	lent	lent
let	let	let
lie	lay	lain
lose	lost	lost
pay	paid	paid
prove	proved	proved, proven
ride	rode	ridden
ring	rang	rung
rise	rose	risen
run	ran	run
say	said	said
see	saw	seen
set	set	set
shake	shook	shaken
shrink	shrank, shrunk	shrunk, shrunken
sing	sang, sung	sung
sink	sank, sunk	sunk
sit	sat	sat
slide	slid	slid

(continued)

Principal parts of common irregular verbs *(continued)*

PLAIN FORM	PAST TENSE	PAST PARTICIPLE
speak	spoke	spoken
spring	sprang, sprung	sprung
stand	stood	stood
steal	stole	stolen
swim	swam	swum
take	took	taken
tear	tore	torn
throw	threw	thrown
wear	wore	worn
write	wrote	written

Exercise 1
Using irregular verbs

For each irregular verb in parentheses, give either the past tense or the past participle, as appropriate, and identify the form you used.

Example:

Though we had (*hide*) the cash box, it was (*steal*).

Though we had *hidden* the cash box, it was *stolen.* [Two past participles.]

1. The world population has (*grow*) by two-thirds of a billion people in less than a decade.
2. Recently it (*break*) the 5 billion mark.
3. Experts have (*draw*) pictures of a crowded future.
4. They predict that the world population may have (*slide*) up to as much as 16 billion by the year 2100.
5. Though the food supply (*rise*) in the last decade, the share to each person (*fall*).

7b Distinguish between *sit* and *set, lie* and *lay,* and *rise* and *raise.*

The forms of *sit* and *set, lie* and *lay,* and *rise* and *raise* are easy to confuse.

PLAIN FORM	PAST TENSE	PAST PARTICIPLE
sit	sat	sat
set	set	set
lie	lay	lain
lay	laid	laid

PLAIN FORM	PAST TENSE	PAST PARTICIPLE
rise	rose	risen
raise	raised	raised

In each of these confusing pairs, one verb is **intransitive** (it does not take an object) and one is **transitive** (it does take an object). (See p. 157 for more on this distinction.)

INTRANSITIVE

The patients *lie* in their beds. [*Lie* means "recline" and takes no object.]

Visitors *sit* with them. [*Sit* means "be seated" or "be located" and takes no object.]

Patients' temperatures *rise*. [*Rise* means "increase" or "get up" and takes no object.]

TRANSITIVE

Orderlies *lay* the dinner trays on tables. [*Lay* means "place" and takes an object, *trays*.]

Orderlies *set* the trays down. [*Set* means "place" and takes an object, *trays*.]

Nursing aides *raise* the shades. [*Raise* means "lift" or "bring up" and takes an object, *shades*.]

Exercise 2
Distinguishing *sit/set, lie/lay, rise/raise*

Choose the correct verb from the pair given in parentheses. Then supply the past tense or past participle, as appropriate.

Example:

After I washed all the windows, I (*lie, lay*) down the squeegee and then I (*sit, set*) the table.

After I washed all the windows, I *laid* down the squeegee and then I *set* the table.

1. Yesterday afternoon the child (*lie, lay*) down for a nap.
2. The child has been (*rise, raise*) by her grandparents.
3. Most days her grandfather has (*sit, set*) with her, reading her stories.
4. She has (*rise, raise*) at dawn most mornings.
5. Her toys were (*lie, lay*) out on the floor.

7c Use the -*s* and -*ed* forms of the verb when they are required.

Speakers of some English dialects and nonnative speakers of English sometimes omit verb endings required by standard English. One such omission is the *-s* ending of the verb when the subject is *he, she, it,* or a singular noun and the verb's action occurs in the present. (The correct form below is in parentheses.)

The roof *leak* (*leaks*).
Harry *live* (*lives*) in town.
He *don't* (*doesn't*) care.
Nobody *have* (*has*) a car.
She *be* (*is*) happy.

Another omitted ending is the *-ed* or *-d* ending when (1) the verb's action occurred in the past (*we bagged*), (2) the verb form functions as a modifier (*used cars*), or (3) the verb form combines with a form of *be* or *have* (*was supposed, has asked*). (The correct form below is in parentheses.)

We *bag* (*bagged*) groceries.
He was *suppose* (*supposed*) to call.
I bought a *use* (*used*) book.
Sue has *ask* (*asked*) for help.

Exercise 3
Using *-s* and *-ed* verb endings

Supply the correct form of each verb in parentheses. Be careful to include *-s* and *-ed* (or *-d*) endings where they are needed for standard English.

A teacher sometimes (*ask*) too much of a student. In high school I was once (*punish*) for being sick. I had (*miss*) some school, and I (*realize*) that I would fail a test unless I had a chance to make up the class work. I (*discuss*) the problem with the teacher, but he said I was (*suppose*) to make up the work while I was sick. At that I (*walk*) out of the class. I (*receive*) a failing grade then, but it did not change my attitude. Today I still balk when a teacher (*make*) unreasonable demands or (*expect*) miracles.

7d Use helping verbs with main verbs appropriately.

Helping verbs combine with some verb forms to form verb phrases (see p. 199).

1 Use helping verbs when they are required.

Some English dialects omit helping verbs required by standard English. In the sentences below, the helping verbs in parentheses are essential.

The owl (*is*) *hooting.*
I (*have*) *taken* French.
Sara (*has*) *been* at home.
That (*would*) *be* awful.

Often, the omission of a helping verb creates an incomplete sentence, or **sentence fragment,** because a present participle (*hooting*) or an irregular past participle (*taken, been*) cannot stand alone as the only verb in a sentence (see Chapter 10).

FRAGMENTS	Some people *smoking.* The sign *broken.*
REVISED	Some people *were smoking.* The sign *was broken.*

Combine helping verbs and main verbs appropriately for your meaning. ESL

Helping verbs combine with main verbs in specific ways.

Form of be + *present participle*

The **progressive tenses** indicate action in progress (see p. 210). Create them with *be, am, is, are, was, were,* or *been* followed by the main verb's present participle.

She *is working* on a new book.

Be and *been* require additional helping verbs to form the progressive tenses.

can	might	should	be working	have	been working
could	must	will		has	
may	shall	would		had	

When forming the progressive tenses, be sure to use the *-ing* form of the main verb.

FAULTY	Her ideas are *grow* more complex. She is *developed* a new approach to ethics.
REVISED	Her ideas are *growing* more complex. She is *developing* a new approach to ethics.

Form of be + *past participle*

The **passive voice** of the verb indicates that the subject *receives* the action of the verb (see p. 218). Create the passive voice with *be, am, is, are, was, were, being,* or *been* followed by the main verb's past participle.

Her latest book *was completed* in four months.

Be, being, and *been* require additional helping verbs to form the passive voice.

have	*been* completed	am	was	*being* completed
has		is	were	
had		are		

will *be* completed

Be sure to use the main verb's past participle for the passive voice.

FAULTY Her next book will be *publish* soon.

REVISED Her next book will be *published* soon.

NOTE Use only transitive verbs to form the passive voice.

FAULTY A philosophy conference *will be occurred* in the same week. [*Occur* is not a transitive verb.]

REVISED A philosophy conference *will occur* in the same week.

See page 220 for advice on when to use and when to avoid the passive voice.

Forms of have

Four forms of *have* serve as helping verbs: *have, has, had, having*. One of these forms plus the main verb's past participle creates one of the **perfect tenses,** those expressing action completed before another specific time or action (see p. 210).

Some students *have complained* about the laboratory.
Others *had complained* before.

Will and other helping verbs sometimes accompany forms of *have* in the perfect tenses.

Several more students *will have complained* by the end of the week.

Forms of do

Always with the plain form of the main verb, three forms of *do* serve as helping verbs: *do, does, did. Do* has three uses:

- To pose a question: *Whom did the officers arrest?*
- To emphasize the main verb: *They did arrest someone.*
- To negate the main verb, along with *not* or *never: The suspect did not escape.*

Be sure to use the main verb's plain form with any form of *do*.

FAULTY They did *captured* someone.

REVISED They did *capture* someone.

Modals

The modals and their main uses are illustrated below:

- *Can* and *could:*

Yuen *can* speak English well. [Ability.]
No one *could* smoke at the meeting. [Permission.]
Could you help us? [Polite request.]

- *May* and *might:*

  May Hector come? [Permission.]
  Hector *might* come if you ask. [Possibility.]

- *Must:*

  You *must* hurry. [Necessity or obligation.]
  The doors *must* have closed. [Probability.]

- *Should* and *ought to:*

  It *should* rain soon. [Expectation.]
  We *ought to* bring umbrellas. [Advisability.]

- *Will* and *would:*

  All the guests *will* come. [Promise or agreement.]
  Would you like to come? [Polite request.]

Exercise 4
Using helping verbs

Add helping verbs in the following sentences where they are needed for standard English.

1. Each year thousands of new readers been discovering Agatha Christie's mysteries.
2. The books written by a prim woman who had worked as a nurse during the First World War.
3. Christie never expected that her play *The Mousetrap* be performed for decades.
4. During her life Christie always complaining about movie versions of her stories.
5. Readers of her stories been delighted to be baffled by her.

Exercise 5
Revising: Helping verbs plus main verbs ESL

Revise the following sentences so that helping verbs and main verbs are used correctly.

Example:

The university testing service has test as many as 500 students at one time.

The university testing service has *tested* as many as 500 students at one time.

1. A report from Statistics Canada has indicate the cause of the problem.
2. High interest rates have keeping potential homeowners from buying.
3. Lending agencies have been suggest for some time that the Bank of Canada ease rates.
4. A lower interest rate will stimulates the economy.

5. A stronger economy will be producing more investment and will be creating more jobs.

TENSE

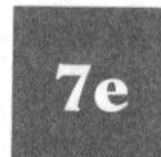

Tense shows the time of a verb's action. The table on the facing page defines and illustrates the tense forms for a regular verb in the active voice. (See pp. 199 and 218 on regular verbs and voice.)

7e Use the appropriate tense to express your meaning.

Many errors in verb tense are actually errors in verb form like those discussed earlier. Still, the present tense, the perfect tenses, and the progressive tenses can cause problems.

1 Observe the special uses of the present tense.

The present tense has several uses.

To indicate action occurring now

She *understands* the problem.
The car *needs* work.

To indicate habitual or recurring action

Horton *goes* to Moncton every Friday.
The store *opens* at ten o'clock.

To state a general truth

The mills of the gods *grind* slowly.
The earth *is* round.

To discuss the content of literature, film, and so on (see also p. 660)

Anne of Green Gables *has* adventures we all envy.
In that article the author *examines* several causes of crime.

To indicate future time

Our friends *arrive* tomorrow.
Ted *leaves* in an hour.

(Time is really indicated here by *tomorrow* and *in an hour*.)

Tenses of a regular verb (active voice)

Present Action that is occurring now, occurs habitually, or is generally true

Simple present Plain form or *-s* form

I *walk.*
You/we/they *walk.*
He/she/it *walks.*

Present progressive *Am, is,* or *are* plus *-ing* form

I *am walking.*
You/we/they *are walking.*
He/she/it *is walking.*

Past Action that occurred before now

Simple past Past-tense form (*-d* or *-ed*)

I/he/she/it *walked.*
You/we/they *walked.*

Past progressive *Was* or *were* plus *-ing* form

I/he/she/it *was walking.*
You/we/they *were walking.*

Future Action that will occur in the future

Simple future Plain form plus *will*

I/you/he/she/it/we/they *will walk.*

Future progressive *Will be* plus *-ing* form

I/you/he/she/it/we/they *will be walking.*

Present perfect Action that began in the past and is linked to the present

Present perfect *Have* or *has* plus past participle (*-d* or *-ed*)

I/you/we/they *have walked.*
He/she/it *has walked.*

Present perfect progressive *Have been* or *has been* plus *-ing* form

I/you/we/they *have been walking.*
He/she/it *has been walking.*

Past perfect Action that was completed before another past action

Past perfect *Had* plus past participle (*-d* or *-ed*)

I/you/he/she/it/we/they *had walked.*

Past perfect progressive *Had been* plus *-ing* form

I/you/he/she/it/we/they *had been walking.*

Future perfect Action that will be completed before another future action

Future perfect *Will have* plus past participle (*-d* or *-ed*)

I/you/he/she/it/we/they *will have walked.*

Future perfect progressive *Will have been* plus *-ing* form

I/you/he/she/it/we/they *will have been walking.*

Observe the uses of the perfect tenses.

The perfect tenses generally indicate action completed before another specific time or action. (The term *perfect* derives from the Latin *perfectus,* "completed.") The present perfect tense also indicates action begun in the past and continued into the present. The perfect tenses consist of a form of *have* plus the verb's past participle.

> present perfect
> The dancer *has performed* here only once. [The action is completed at the time of the statement.]
>
> present perfect
> Critics *have written* about the performance ever since. [The action began in the past and continues now.]
>
> past perfect
> The dancer *had trained* in Asia before his performance. [The action was completed before another past action.]
>
> future perfect
> He *will have performed* here again by next month. [The action begins now or in the future and will be completed by a specified time in the future.]

NOTE ESL With the present perfect tense, the words *since* and *for* are followed by different information. After *since,* give a specific point in time: *Canada has been a member of the United Nations since 1945.* After *for,* give a span of time: *Canada has been a member of the United Nations for over half a century.*

Observe the uses of the progressive tenses. ESL

The progressive tenses indicate continuing (therefore progressive) action. They consist of a form of *be* plus the verb's *-ing* form (present participle). (The words *be* and *been* must be combined with other helping verbs. See p. 205.)

> present progressive
> The economy *is improving.*
>
> past progressive
> Last year the economy *was stagnating.*
>
> future progressive
> Economists *will be watching* for signs of growth.
>
> present perfect progressive
> The government *has been expecting* an upturn.
>
> past perfect progressive
> Various indicators *had been suggesting* improvement.
>
> future perfect progressive
> By the end of this year, investors *will have been watching* the markets nervously for nearly a decade.

Note Verbs that express mental states or activities rather than physical actions do not usually appear in the progressive tenses. These verbs include *adore, appear, believe, belong, care, hate, have, hear, know, like, love, need, prefer, remember, see, taste, think, understand,* and *want.*

Faulty She *is wanting* to study ethics.

Revised She *wants* to study ethics.

7f Use the appropriate sequence of verb tenses.

The term **sequence of tenses** refers to the relation between the verb tense in a main clause and the verb tense in a subordinate clause or phrase. The tenses need not be identical as long as they reflect changes in actual or relative time: in *He had left before I arrived,* the verbs are in clear sequence. The difficulties with tense sequence are discussed below. (For a discussion of tense shifts—changes *not* required by meaning—see pp. 280–81).

1 Use the appropriate tense sequence with infinitives.

The tense of an infinitive is determined by the tense of the verb in the predicate. The **present infinitive** is the verb's plain form preceded by *to* (see p. 168). It indicates action *at the same time* as or *later* than that of the verb.

present present
The researcher *expects to see* change.

present perfect present
She *would have liked to see* (not *to have seen*) more change before.

The verb's **perfect infinitive** consists of *to have* followed by the past participle, as in *to have talked, to have won.* It indicates action *earlier* than that of the verb.

present perfect
Other researchers *would like* (not *would have liked*) *to have seen* change as well.

present perfect
They *judge* the data *to have been interpreted* correctly.

2 Use the appropriate tense sequence with participles.

The tense of a participle is determined by the tense of the verb in the predicate. The present participle shows action occurring *at the same time* as that of the verb.

present / past perfect
Testing a large group, the researcher *had posed* multiple-choice questions.

The past participle and the present perfect participle show action occurring *earlier* than that of the verb.

past / past
Prepared by earlier failures, she *knew* not to ask open questions.

present perfect / past
Having tested many people, she *understood* the process.

Use the appropriate tense sequence when the verb in the main clause is past or past perfect.

When the verb in the main clause is in the past or past perfect tense, the verb in the subordinate clause must also be past or past perfect.

past / past
The researchers *discovered* that people *varied* widely in their knowledge of public events.

past / past perfect
The variation *occurred* because respondents *had been born* in different decades.

past perfect / past
None of them *had been born* when John Diefenbaker *was* prime minister.

Exception Always use the present tense for a general truth, such as *The earth is round.*

past / present
Few *understood* that popular politicians *are* not necessarily good prime ministers.

Use the appropriate tense sequence in conditional sentences. ESL

A **conditional sentence** states a factual relation between cause and effect, makes a prediction, or speculates about what might happen. Such a sentence usually consists of a subordinate clause beginning with *if, when,* or *unless* along with a main clause stating the result. The three kinds of conditional sentences use distinctive verbs.

Factual relation

For statements that something always or usually happens whenever something else happens, use the present tense in both clauses.

present / present
When a voter *casts* a ballot, he or she *has* complete privacy.

If the linked events occurred in the past, use the past tense in both clauses.

past / past
When voters *were enumerated*, they *had* to identify their occupation.

Prediction

For a prediction, generally use the present tense in the subordinate clause and the future tense in the main clause.

present / future
Unless citizens *regain* faith in politics, they *will* not *vote.*

Sometimes the verb in the main clause consists of *may, can, should,* or *might* plus the verb's plain form: *If citizens regain faith, they might vote.*

Speculation

Speculations are mainly of two kinds, each with its own verb pattern. For events that are possible in the present, though unlikely, use the past tense in the subordinate clause and *would, could,* or *might* plus the verb's plain form in the main clause.

past / would + verb
If voters *had* more confidence, they *would vote* more often.

Use *were* instead of *was* when the subject is *I, he, she, it,* or a singular noun. (See 7g for more on this distinctive verb form.)

past / would + verb
If the voter *were* more confident, he or she *would vote* more often.

For events that are impossible in the present, that are contrary to fact, use the same forms as above (including the distinctive *were* when applicable).

past perfect / might + verb
If Sir John A. Macdonald *were* available, he *might inspire* enthusiasm.

For events that were impossible in the past, use the past perfect tense in the subordinate clause and *would, could,* or *might* plus the present perfect tense in the main clause.

past perfect / might + present perfect
If Sir Wilfrid Laurier *had lived* longer, he *might have helped* unify the country.

Use the appropriate tense sequence with indirect quotations. ESL

AN INDIRECT QUOTATION reports what someone said or wrote but not in the exact words and not in quotation marks: *Pierre Trudeau said that reason had made him* (quotation "Reason made me"). Indirect quotations generally appear in subordinate clauses (underlined above), with certain conventions governing verb tense in most cases.

When the verb in the main clause is in the present tense, the verb in the indirect quotation (subordinate clause) is in the same tense as the original quotation.

> present / present
> Ericson *says* that Macdonald *is* our preeminent national figure. [Quotation: "Macdonald *is* our preeminent national figure."]
>
> present / past
> He *says* that Macdonald *was* a brilliant motivator. [Quotation: "Macdonald *was* a brilliant motivator."]

When the verb in the main clause is in the past tense, the verb in the indirect quotation usually changes tense from the original quotation. Present tense changes to past tense.

> past / past
> An adviser to Laurier *said* that the prime minister *was* always thoughtful. [Quotation: "The prime minister *is* always thoughtful."]

Past tense and present tense change to past perfect tense. (Past perfect tense does not change.)

> past / past perfect
> Trudeau *said* that reason *had made* him. [Quotation: "Reason *made* me."]

When the direct quotation states a general truth or reports a situation that is still true, use the present tense in the indirect quotation regardless of the verb in the main clause.

> past / present
> Trudeau *said* that a lack of power *corrupts*. [Quotation: "A lack of power *corrupts*."]

NOTE As several of these examples show, an indirect quotation differs in at least two additional ways from the original quotation: (1) the indirect quotation is usually preceded by *that,* and (2) the indirect quotation changes pronouns, especially from forms of *I* or *we* to forms of *he, she,* or *they.*

Exercise 6
Adjusting tense sequence: Past or past perfect tense

The tenses in each sentence below are in correct sequence. Change the tense of one verb as instructed. Then change the tense of infinitives, participles, and other verbs to restore correct sequence. Some items have more than one possible answer.

Example:

He will call when he reaches his destination. (*Change will call to called.*)

He called when he *reached* (or *had reached*) his destination.

1. Diaries that Adolf Hitler is supposed to have written have surfaced in Germany. (*Change have surfaced to had surfaced.*)

2. Many people believe that the diaries are authentic because a well-known historian has declared them so. (*Change* believe *to* believed.)
3. However, the historian's evaluation has been questioned by other authorities, who call the diaries forgeries. (*Change* has been questioned *to* was questioned.)
4. They claim, among other things, that the paper is not old enough to have been used by Hitler. (*Change* claim *to* claimed.)
5. Eventually, the doubters will win the debate because they have the best evidence. (*Change* will win *to* won.)

Exercise 7
Revising: Tense sequence with conditional sentences ESL

Supply the appropriate tense for each verb in parentheses below.

Example:

If Maurice Richard or Dave Keon (*be*) athletes today, they (*remind*) us that even sports heroes must contend with a harsh reality.

If Maurice Richard or Dave Keon *were* athletes today, they *might* (or *could* or *would*) *remind* us that even sports heroes must contend with a harsh reality.

1. When an athlete (*turn*) professional, he or she commits to a gruelling regimen of mental and physical training.
2. If athletes (*be*) less committed, they (*disappoint*) teammates, fans, and themselves.
3. If professional athletes (*be*) very lucky, they may play until age forty.
4. Unless an athlete achieves celebrity status, he or she (*have*) few employment choices after retirement.
5. If professional sports (*be*) less risky, athletes (*have*) longer careers and more choices after retirement.

Exercise 8
Using verb tenses in indirect quotations ESL

Each passage below comes from the British essayist Charles Lamb (1775–1834). Indirectly quote each passage in a sentence of your own, using the words given in parentheses.

Example:

"The greatest pleasure I know is to do a good action by stealth and to have it found out by accident." (*Charles Lamb said that. . . .*)

Charles Lamb said that the greatest pleasure he *knew was* to do a good action by stealth and to have it found out by accident.

1. "Coleridge holds that a man cannot have a pure mind who refuses apple-dumplings." (*Lamb cited Coleridge's observation that. . . .*)

2. "The human species, according to the best theory I can form of it, is composed of two distinct races, the men who borrow, and the men who lend." (*Lamb wrote that. . . .*)
3. "Nothing puzzles me more than time and space; and yet nothing troubles me less, as I never think about them." (*He muses that. . . .*)
4. "When I am not walking, I am reading; I cannot sit and think." (*He admitted that. . . .*)
5. "Sentimentally I am disposed to harmony. But organically I am incapable of a tune." (*He confesses that. . . .*)

MOOD

Mood in grammar is a verb form that indicates the writer's or speaker's attitude toward what he or she is saying. The **indicative mood** states a fact or opinion or asks a question.

The theatre *needs* help. [Opinion.]
The ceiling *is falling* in. [Fact.]
Will you *contribute* to the theatre? [Question.]

The **imperative mood** expresses a command or gives a direction. It omits the subject of the sentence, *you.*

Help the theatre. [Command.]
Send contributions to the theatre. [Direction.]

The **subjunctive mood** expresses a suggestion, a requirement, or a desire, or it states a condition that is contrary to fact (that is, imaginary or hypothetical). The subjunctive mood uses distinctive verb forms.

- *Suggestion or requirement:* plain form with all subjects.

  The manager asked that he *donate* money. [Suggestion.]
  Rules require that every donation *be* mailed. [Requirement.]

- *Desire or present condition contrary to fact:* past tense; for *be,* the past tense *were.*

  We wish that the theatre *had* more money. [Desire.]

  It would be in better shape if it *were* better funded. [Present condition contrary to fact.]

- *Past condition contrary to fact:* past perfect.

  The theatre could have been better funded if it *had been* better managed.

With conditions contrary to fact, the verb in the main clause also expresses the imaginary or hypothetical with the helping verb *could* or *would,* as in the last two sample sentences above.

(For a discussion of keeping mood consistent within and among sentences, see p. 281.)

7g Use the subjunctive verb forms appropriately.

Contemporary English uses distinctive subjunctive verb forms only in a few constructions and idioms. (For the sequence of tenses in many subjunctive sentences, see pp. 212–13.)

Use the subjunctive in contrary-to-fact clauses beginning with *if* or expressing desire.

If the theatre *were* saved, the town would benefit.
We all wish the theatre *were* not so decrepit.

NOTE The indicative form *was* (*We all wish the theatre was not so decrepit*) is common in speech and in some informal writing, but the subjunctive *were* is usual in formal English.

Not all clauses beginning with *if* express conditions contrary to fact. In the sentence *If Joe is out of town, he hasn't heard the news,* the verb *is* is correct because the clause refers to a condition presumed to exist.

Use *would* or *could* only in the main clause of a conditional statement.

The helping verb *would* or *could* appears in the main clause of a sentence expressing a condition contrary to fact. The helping verb does *not* appear in the subordinate clause beginning with *if*.

NOT Many people would have helped if they *would have* known.

BUT Many people would have helped if they *had* known.

Use the subjunctive in *that* clauses following verbs that demand, request, or recommend.

Verbs such as *ask, demand, insist, mandate, require, recommend, request, require, suggest,* and *urge* indicate demand or suggestion. They often precede subordinate clauses beginning with *that* and containing the substance of the demand or suggestion. The verb in such a *that* clause should be in the subjunctive mood.

The board urged that everyone *contribute.*
The members insisted that they themselves *contribute.*
They suggested that each *donate* both time and money.

NOTE These constructions have widely used alternative forms that do not require the subjunctive, such as *The board urged everyone to contribute* or *The members insisted on donating.*

Use the subjunctive in some set phrases and idioms.

Several English expressions commonly use the subjunctive. For example:

Come rain or *come* shine.
Be that as it may.
The people *be* damned.

Exercise 9
Revising: Subjunctive mood

Revise the following sentences with appropriate subjunctive verb forms.

Example:

I would help the old man if I was able to reach him.
I would help the old man if I *were* able to reach him.

1. If John Hawkins would have known of the dangerous side-effects of smoking tobacco, would he have introduced the dried plant to England in 1565?
2. Hawkins noted that if a Florida Indian was to travel for several days, he would have smoked tobacco to satisfy his hunger and thirst.
3. Early tobacco growers feared that their product would not gain acceptance unless it was perceived as healthful.
4. In 1646 the General Court of Massachusetts passed a law requiring that a colonist smoked tobacco only if he was five miles from any town.
5. In 1647 Connecticut passed a law mandating that one's smoking of tobacco was limited to once a day by oneself in one's own home.

VOICE

The **voice** of a verb tells whether the subject of the sentence performs the action (**active voice**) or is acted upon (**passive voice**). See the illustrations in the box opposite. In the passive voice, the actual actor may be named in a prepositional phrase (such as *by the city*) or may be omitted.

NOTE ESL A passive verb always consists of a form of *be* plus the past participle of the main verb: *rents are controlled, people were inspired.* Other helping verbs must also be used with *be, being,* and *been: rents have been controlled, people would have been inspired.* Only a transitive verb (one that takes an object) may be used in the passive voice. (See pp. 157–58.)

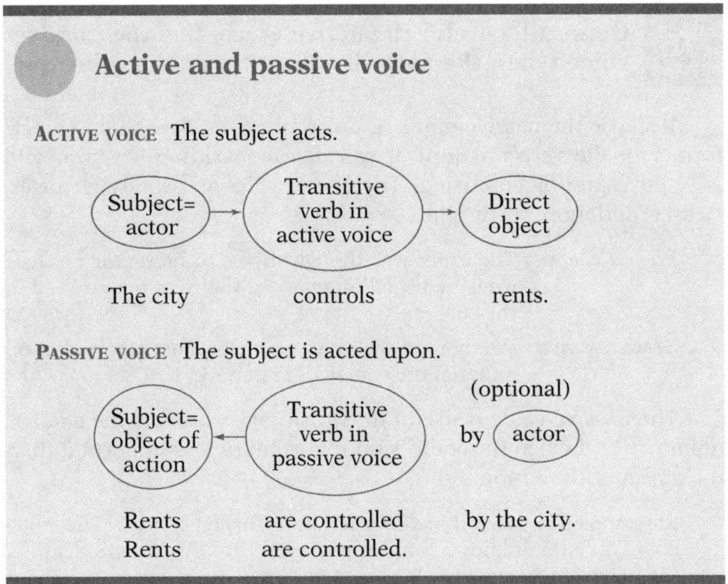

Converting active to passive

To change a transitive verb from active to passive voice, convert either an indirect object or a direct object into the subject of the sentence, and use the passive verb form.

	subject	transitive verb	indirect object	direct object
ACTIVE	The city	gives	tenants	leases.
	new subject	passive verb	direct object	
PASSIVE	Tenants	are given	leases.	
	new subject	passive verb	indirect object	old subject
	Leases	are given	tenants	by the city.

Converting passive to active

To change a passive verb to active, name the verb's actor as subject, use an active verb form, and convert the old subject into an object.

	subject	passive verb	
PASSIVE	Tenants	are protected	by leases.
	new subject	active verb	old subject = object
ACTIVE	Leases	protect	tenants.

7h Generally, prefer the active voice. Use the passive voice when the actor is unknown or unimportant.

Because the passive omits or de-emphasizes the actor (the performer of the verb's action), it can deprive writing of vigour and is often vague or confusing. The active voice is usually stronger, clearer, and more forthright.

WEAK PASSIVE The exam was thought by us to be unfair because we were tested on material that was not covered in the course.

STRONG ACTIVE We thought the exam unfair because it tested us on material the course did not cover.

The passive voice is useful in two situations: when the actor is unknown and when the actor is unimportant or less important than the object of the action.

> Ray Appleton *was murdered* after he returned home. [The murderer may be unknown, and in any event Ray Appleton's death is the point of the sentence.]
>
> In the first experiment acid *was added* to the solution. [The person who added the acid, perhaps the writer, is less important than the fact that acid was added. Passive sentences are common in scientific writing.]

Except in such situations, however, you should prefer the active voice in your writing.

Exercise 10
Converting active and passive voices

To practise using the two voices of the verb, convert the following sentences from active to passive or from passive to active. (In converting from passive to active, you may have to add a subject for the new sentence.) Which version of each sentence seems more effective, and why? (For additional exercises with the passive voice, see pp. 184, 335, and 466.)

Example:

The aspiring actor was discovered in a nightclub.
A *talent scout discovered* the aspiring actor in a nightclub.

1. When the Eiffel Tower was built in 1889, it was thought by the French to be ugly.
2. At that time many people still resisted industrial technology.
3. The tower's naked steel construction epitomized this technology.
4. Beautiful ornament was expected to grace fine buildings.
5. Further, the tower could not even be called a building because it had no solid walls.

OTHER COMPLICATIONS

7i Use a gerund or an infinitive after a verb as appropriate. ESL

Gerunds and infinitives may follow certain verbs but not others. And sometimes the use of a gerund or infinitive with the same verb changes the meaning of the verb. (For definitions of *gerund* and *infinitive*, see p. 168.)

Either gerund or infinitive

A gerund or an infinitive may follow these verbs with no significant difference in meaning:

begin	hate	love
can't bear	hesitate	prefer
can't stand	intend	pretend
continue	like	start

The pump began *working*.
The pump began *to work*.

Meaning change with gerund or infinitive

With four verbs, a gerund has quite a different meaning from an infinitive.

forget	stop
remember	try

The engineer stopped *eating*. [He no longer ate.]
The engineer stopped *to eat*. [He stopped in order to eat.]

Gerund, not infinitive

Do not use an infinitive after these verbs:

admit	dislike	miss	resent
adore	enjoy	postpone	resist
appreciate	escape	practise	risk
avoid	finish	put off	suggest
deny	imagine	quit	tolerate
detest	keep	recall	understand
discuss	mind	recollect	

FAULTY He finished *to eat* lunch.

REVISED He finished *eating* lunch.

Infinitive, not gerund

Do not use a gerund after these verbs:

agree	decide	mean	refuse
ask	expect	offer	say
assent	have	plan	wait
beg	hope	pretend	want
claim	manage	promise	wish

FAULTY He decided *checking* the pump.

REVISED He decided *to check* the pump.

Noun or pronoun + infinitive

Some verbs may be followed by an infinitive alone or by a noun or pronoun and an infinitive. The presence of a noun or pronoun changes the meaning.

ask	need	would like
expect	want	

He expected *to watch.*
He expected *his workers to watch.*

Some verbs *must* be followed by a noun or pronoun before an infinitive:

admonish	dare	oblige	require
advise	encourage	order	teach
allow	forbid	permit	tell
cause	force	persuade	train
challenge	hire	remind	urge
command	instruct	request	warn
convince	invite		

He instructed *his workers to watch.*

Do not use *to* before the infinitive when it follows one of these verbs and a noun or pronoun:

feel	make ("force")
have	see
hear	watch
let	

He let his workers *learn* by observation.

Exercise 11
Revising: Verbs plus gerunds or infinitives

Revise the following sentences so that gerunds or infinitives are used correctly with verbs.

Example:

A politician cannot avoid to alienate some voters.
A politician cannot avoid *alienating* some voters.

1. The Royal Commission promised investigating the allegations.
2. The Commission had planned to make witnesses to take an oath.
3. The witnesses were instead just asked being cooperative.
4. The first witness, however, refused revealing his income.
5. Another witness claimed protecting his source.

7j Use the appropriate particles with two-word verbs. ESL

Some verbs consist of two words: the verb itself and a **particle,** a preposition or adverb that affects the meaning of the verb. For example:

Look up the answer. [Research the answer.]
Look over the answer. [Examine the answer.]

The meanings of these two-word verbs are often quite different from the meanings of the individual words that make them up. (There are some three-word verbs, too, such as *put up with* and *run out of.*) A good ESL dictionary, such as those listed on page 470, will define two-word verbs for you. It will also tell you whether the verbs may be separated in a sentence, as explained below.

NOTE Many two-word verbs are more common in speech than in more formal academic or business writing. For formal writing, consider using *research* instead of *look up, examine* or *inspect* instead of *look over.*

Inseparable two-word verbs

Verbs and particles that may not be separated by any other words include the following:

catch on	go over	play around	stay away
come across	grow up	run into	stay up
get along	keep on	run out of	take care of
give in	look into	speak up	turn up at

FAULTY Children *grow* quickly *up.*

REVISED Children *grow up* quickly.

Separable two-word verbs

Most two-word verbs that take direct objects may be separated by the object.

Parents *help out* their children.
Parents *help* their children *out.*

If the direct object is a pronoun, the pronoun *must* separate the verb from the particle.

FAULTY Parents *help out* them.

REVISED Parents *help* them *out.*

The separable two-word verbs include the following:

bring up	give back	make up	throw out
call off	hand in	point out	try on
call up	hand out	put away	try out
drop off	help out	put back	turn down
fill out	leave out	put off	turn on
fill up	look over	take out	turn up
give away	look up	take over	wrap up

Exercise 12
Revising: Verbs plus particles ESL

Identify any two- or three-word verbs in the sentences below, and indicate whether each is separable (S) or inseparable (I). Then fill the blank with the correct option for placing nouns or pronouns with verbs and particles. Consult an ESL dictionary if necessary.

Example:

Hollywood producers never seem to come up with entirely new plots, but they also never ____ to present the old ones.

a. run out of new ways
b. run new ways out of
c. Either a or b

Hollywood producers never seem to *come up with* (I) entirely new plots, but they also never (a) *run out of new ways* to present the old ones.

1. American movies treat everything from going out with someone to making up an ethnic identity, but few people ____.

   a. look into their significance
   b. look their significance into
   c. Either a or b

2. While some viewers stay away from topical films, others ____ simply because a movie has sparked debate.

   a. turn up at the theatre
   b. turn at the theatre up
   c. Either a or b

3. Some movies aroused such strong responses that theatres were obliged to ____.

   a. throw out rowdy spectators
   b. throw rowdy spectators out
   c. Either a or b

4. Filmmakers have always been eager to ____ to the public.

   a. point out their influence
   b. point their influence out
   c. Either a or b

5. Everyone agrees that filmmakers will ____, if only because it can fill up theatres.

   a. keep on creating controversy
   b. keep creating controversy on
   c. Either a or b

Exercise 13
Revising: Verb forms, tense, mood

Circle all the verbs and verbals in the following paragraph and correct their form, tense, or mood if necessary.

For centuries the natives of Melanesia, a group of islands laying northeast of Australia, have practise an unusual religion. It began in the eighteenth century when European explorers first have visited the islands. The natives were fascinated by the rich goods or "cargo" possessed by the explorers. They saw the wealth as treasures of the gods, and cargo cults eventually had arised among them. Over the centuries some Melanesians turned to Christianity in the belief that the white man's religion will bring them the white man's treasures. During World War II, American soldiers, having arrived by boat and airplane to have occupied some of the islands, introduced new and even more wonderful cargo. Even today some leaders of the cargo cults insist that the airplane is worship as a vehicle of the Melanesians' future salvation.

Note See page 252 for an exercise involving verbs along with other aspects of grammar.

Chapter 8 Agreement

Agreement helps readers understand the relations between elements in a sentence. Subjects and verbs agree in number and person:

More *Acadians live* in New Brunswick than in any other province.
subject verb

Acadia was the name of the first French colony in Canada.
subject verb

Pronouns and their **antecedents**—the words they refer to—agree in person, number, and gender.

Ashley MacIsaac plays *his* fiddle with élan.
antecedent pronoun

Cape Bretoners value *their* Celtic heritage.
antecedent pronoun

8a Make subjects and verbs agree in number.

Most subject-verb agreement problems arise when endings are omitted from subjects or verbs or when the relation between sentence parts is uncertain.

Person and number in subject-verb agreement

	Number	
Person	*Singular*	*Plural*
First	I eat.	We eat.
Second	You eat.	You eat.
Third	He/she/it eats.	They eat.
	The bird eats.	Birds eat.

The *-s* and *-es* endings work differently for nouns and verbs.

An *-s* or *-es* ending does opposite things to nouns and verbs: it usually makes a noun *plural,* but it always makes a present-tense verb *singular.* Thus if the subject noun is plural, it will end in *-s* or *-es* and the verb will not. If the subject is singular, it will not end in *-s* and the verb will.

Singular	Plural
The boy plays.	The boys play.
The bird soars.	The birds soar.

The only exceptions to these rules involve the nouns that form irregular plurals, such as *child/children, woman/women.* The irregular plural still requires a plural verb: *The children play.*

Writers often omit *-s* and *-es* endings from nouns or verbs because they are not pronounced clearly in speech (as in *asks* and *lists*) or because they are not used regularly in some English dialects. However, the endings are required in standard English.

Nonstandard The voter *resist* change.
Standard The voter *resists* change.

Remember that the verb *be* is irregular.

Present tense

he, she, it, singular nouns	*is*	all plurals	*are*

Past tense

he, she, it, singular nouns	*was*	all plurals	*were*

Note In a verb phrase (main verb plus helping verb), the helping verb sometimes reflects the number of the subject and some-

Summary of subject-verb agreement

- Basic subject-verb agreement (8a-1):

SINGULAR	PLURAL
The kite fli*es*.	The kite*s* fly.

- Words between subject and verb (8a-2):
  The kite with two tails *flies* badly. The tails of the kite *compete.*
- Subjects joined by *and* (8a-3):
  The kite and the bird *are* almost indistinguishable.
- Subjects joined by *or* or *nor* (8a-4):
  The kite or the bird *dives.* Kites or birds *fill* the sky.
- Indefinite pronouns as subjects (8a-5):
  No one *knows.* All the spectators *wonder.*
- Collective nouns as subjects (8a-6):
  A flock *appears.* The flock *disperse.*
- Inverted word order (8a-7):
  Is the kite or the bird blue? *Are* the kite and the bird both blue?
- Linking verbs (8a-8):
  The kite *is* a flier and a dipper.
- *Who, which, that* as subjects (8a-9):
  The kite that *flies* longest wins. Kites that *fall* lose.
- Subjects with plural form and singular meaning (8a-10):
  Aeronautics *plays* a role in kite flying.
- Titles and words named as words (8a-11):
  Kite Dynamics *is* one title. Vectors *is* a key word.

times does not: *The car does run. The cars do run. The car/cars will run.* The main verb (*run*) does not change in any way.

Subject and verb should agree even when other words come between them.

When the subject and verb are interrupted by other words, make sure the verb agrees with the subject.

> A catalogue of courses and requirements often *baffles* (not *baffle*) students.

> The requirements stated in the catalogue *are* (not *is*) unclear.

Note Phrases beginning with *as well as, together with, along with,* and *in addition to* do not change the number of the subject.

> The president, as well as the deans, *has* (not *have*) agreed to revise the catalogue.

If you really mean *and* in such a sentence, use it. Then the subject is compound, and the verb should be plural: *The president and the deans have agreed to revise the catalogue.*

Subjects joined by *and* usually take plural verbs.

Two or more subjects joined by *and* usually take a plural verb, whether one or all of the subjects are singular.

> Gretzky and Kurri *were* linemates.

> Roy, Dryden, Parent, and Tretiak *are* among the great goaltenders.

Exceptions: When the parts of the subject form a single idea or refer to a single person or thing, they take a singular verb.

> Avocado and bean sprouts *is* a California sandwich.

When a compound subject is preceded by the adjective *each* or *every,* the verb is usually singular.

> Each man, woman, and child *has* a right to be heard.

But a compound subject *followed* by *each* takes a plural verb.

> The man and the woman each *have* different problems.

When parts of a subject are joined by *or* or *nor,* the verb agrees with the nearer part.

When all parts of a subject joined by *or* or *nor* are singular, the verb is singular; when all parts are plural, the verb is plural.

> Either the painter or the carpenter *knows* the cost.

> The cabinets or the bookcases *are* too costly.

When one part of the subject is singular and the other plural, avoid awkwardness by placing the plural part closer to the verb so that the verb is plural.

AWKWARD Neither the owners nor the contractor *agrees.*

REVISED Neither the contractor nor the owners *agree.*

When the subject consists of nouns and pronouns of different person requiring different verb forms, the verb agrees with the nearer part of the subject. Reword if this construction is awkward.

AWKWARD Either Juarez or I *am* responsible.

REVISED Either Juarez *is* responsible, or I *am.*

5 Generally, use singular verbs with indefinite pronouns.

An **indefinite pronoun** is one that does not refer to a specific person or thing.

Common indefinite pronouns

all	each	neither	one
any	either	nobody	some
anybody	everybody	none	somebody
anyone	everyone	no one	someone
anything	everything	nothing	something

Most indefinite pronouns are singular in meaning (they refer to a single unspecified person or thing), and they take singular verbs.

Something *smells.* Neither *is* right.

A few indefinite pronouns such as *all, any, none,* and *some* may take either a singular or a plural verb depending on the meaning of the word they refer to.

All of the money *is* reserved for emergencies.

All of the funds *are* reserved for emergencies.

6 Collective nouns take singular or plural verbs depending on meaning.

A **collective noun** has singular form but names a group of individuals or things—for example, *army, audience, committee,* *crowd, family, group, team.* As a subject, a collective noun may take a singular or plural verb, depending on the context. When the group acts as one unit, use a singular verb.

The group *agrees* that action is necessary.

Any band *sounds* good in that concert hall.

But when considering the group's members as individuals who act separately, use the plural form of the verb.

The old group *have* gone their separate ways.

The band *do* not agree on where to play.

The collective noun *number* may be singular or plural. Preceded by *a,* it is plural; preceded by *the,* it is singular.

A number of people *are* in debt.

The number of people in debt *is* very large.

NOTE ESL Certain collective nouns are always considered plural: *clergy, military, people, police.* If you mean one representative of the group, use a singular noun such as *police officer.*

The verb agrees with the subject even when the normal word order is inverted.

Inverted subject-verb order occurs mainly in questions and in constructions beginning with *there* or *it* and a form of *be.*

Is voting a right or a privilege?

Are a right and a privilege the same thing?

There *are* differences between them.

In constructions beginning with *there, is* may be used before a compound subject when the first element in the subject is singular.

There *is* much work to do and little time to do it.

Word order may sometimes be inverted for emphasis. The verb still agrees with its subject.

From the mountains *comes* an eerie, shimmering light.

A linking verb agrees with its subject, not the subject complement.

A linking verb such as *is* or *are* should agree with its subject, usually the first element in the sentence, not with the noun or pronoun serving as a subject complement (see p. 159).

Henry's sole support *is* his mother and father.

Henry's mother and father *are* his sole support.

Who, which, and *that* take verbs that agree with their antecedents.

When used as subjects, *who, which,* and *that* refer to another word in the sentence, called the **antecedent.** The verb agrees with the antecedent.

Mayor Garber ought to listen to the people who *work* for her.

Bardini is the only aide who *has* her ear.

Agreement problems often occur with relative pronouns when the sentence includes *one of the* or *the only one of the.*

Bardini is one of the aides who *work* unpaid. [Of the aides who work unpaid, Bardini is one.]

Bardini is the only one of the aides who *knows* the community. [Of the aides, only one, Bardini, knows the community.]

NOTE ESL In phrases like those above beginning with *one of the,* be sure the noun is plural: *Bardini is one of the aides (not aide) who work unpaid.*

Nouns with plural form but singular meaning take singular verbs.

Some nouns with plural form (that is, ending in *-s*) are usually regarded as singular in meaning. They include *athletics, economics, linguistics, mathematics, measles, mumps, news, physics, politics,* and *statistics,* as well as place names such as *Athens, Wales,* and *United States.*

After so long a wait, the news *has* to be good.

Statistics *is* required of psychology majors.

Measurements and figures ending in *-s* may also be singular when the quantity they refer to is a unit.

Three years *is* a long time to wait.

Three-fourths of the library *consists* of reference books.

Note These words take plural verbs when they describe individual items rather than whole bodies of activity or knowledge.

The statistics *prove* him wrong.

11 Titles and words named as words take singular verbs.

When your sentence subject is the title of a corporation or a work (such as a book) or a word you are defining or describing, the verb should be singular even if the title or the word is plural.

Hakada Associates *is* a new firm.

Dream Days *remains* a favourite book.

Folks *is* a down-home word for people.

Exercise 1
Revising: Subject-verb agreement

Revise the verbs in the following sentences as needed to make subjects and verbs agree in number. If the sentence is already correct as given, circle the number preceding it.

Example:

Each of the job applicants type sixty words per minute.
Each of the job applicants *types* sixty words per minute.

1. Weinstein & Associates are a consulting firm that try to make businesspeople laugh.
2. Statistics from recent research suggests that humour relieves stress.
3. Reduced stress in businesses in turn reduce illness and absenteeism.
4. Reduced stress can also reduce friction within an employee group, which then work together more productively.
5. In special conferences held by one consultant, each of the participants practise making the others laugh.
6. One consultant to many companies suggest cultivating office humour with practical jokes such as a rubber fish in the water cooler.

7. When employees or their manager regularly post cartoons on the bulletin board, office spirit usually picks up.
8. When someone who has seemed too easily distracted is entrusted with updating the cartoons, his or her concentration often improves.
9. In the face of levity, the former sourpuss becomes one of those who hides bad temper.
10. Every one of the consultants caution, however, that humour has no place in life-affecting corporate situations such as employee layoffs.

8b Make pronouns and their antecedents agree in person, number, and gender.

The **antecedent** of a pronoun is the noun or other pronoun it refers to.

Home *owners* fret over *their* tax bills.
(*owners* = antecedent; *their* = pronoun)

Its constant increases make the tax *bill* a dreaded document.
(*Its* = pronoun; *bill* = antecedent)

Since a pronoun derives its meaning from its antecedent, the two must agree in person, number, and gender.

Person, number, and gender in pronoun-antecedent agreement

	Number	
Person	***Singular***	***Plural***
First	*I*	*we*
Second	*you*	*you*
Third	*he, she, it* indefinite pronouns singular nouns	*they* plural nouns
Gender		
Masculine	*he,* nouns naming males	
Feminine	*she,* nouns naming females	
Neuter	*it,* all other nouns	

NOTE ESL The gender of a pronoun should match its antecedent, not a noun that the pronoun may modify: *Sanjay* sent <u>*his*</u>

Summary of pronoun-antecedent agreement

- Basic pronoun-antecedent agreement:

  Old Faithful spews *its* columns of water, each of *them* over thirty-five metres high.
- Antecedents joined by *and* (8b-1):

  Old Faithful and Giant are geysers known for *their* height.
- Antecedents joined by *or* or *nor* (8b-2):

  Either Giant or Giantess ejects *its* column the highest.
- Indefinite pronouns as antecedents (8b-3):

  Each of the geysers has *its* own personality. Anyone who visits has *his or her* memories.
- Collective nouns as antecedents (8b-4):

  A crowd amuses *itself* watching Old Faithful. The crowd go *their* separate ways.

(not her) *sister a birthday present.* Also, nouns in English have only neuter gender unless they specifically refer to males or females. Thus nouns such as *book, table, sun,* and *earth* take the pronoun *it.*

1 Antecedents joined by *and* usually take plural pronouns.

Two or more antecedents joined by *and* usually take a plural pronoun, whether one or all of the antecedents are singular.

Mr. Bartos and I cannot settle *our* dispute.

The dean and my adviser have offered *their* help.

Exceptions When the compound antecedent refers to a single idea, person, or thing, then the pronoun is singular.

My friend and adviser offered *her* help.

When the compound antecedent follows *each* or *every,* the pronoun is singular.

Every girl and woman took *her* seat.

When parts of an antecedent are joined by *or* or *nor,* the pronoun agrees with the nearer part.

When the parts of an antecedent are connected by *or* or *nor,* the pronoun should agree with the part closer to it.

Tenants or owners must present *their* grievances.

Either the tenant or the owner will have *her* way.

When one subject is plural and the other singular, the sentence will be awkward unless you put the plural one second.

AWKWARD Neither the tenants nor the owner has yet made *her* case.

REVISED Neither the owner nor the tenants have yet made *their* case.

Generally, use a singular pronoun when the antecedent is an indefinite pronoun.

Indefinite pronouns such as *anybody* and *something* refer to persons or things in general rather than to a specific person or thing. (See p. 230 for a list.) Most indefinite pronouns are singular in meaning. When these indefinite pronouns serve as antecedents to other pronouns, the other pronouns are singular.

Everyone on the team had *her* own locker.

Each of the boys likes *his* teacher.

In speech we commonly use a plural pronoun when the indefinite pronoun means "many" or "all" rather than "one." In writing, however, you should revise sentences to avoid the misuse.

FAULTY Everyone feared for *their* lives.

REVISED *All the riders* feared for *their* lives.

The generic he

The meaning of an indefinite pronoun often includes both masculine and feminine genders, not one or the other. The same is true of other indefinite words such as *child, adult, individual,* and *person.* In such cases tradition has called for *he* (*him, his*) to refer to the antecedent. But this so-called **generic *he*** (or generalized *he*) appears to exclude females. To avoid it, try one of the techniques in the box opposite. (For more on avoiding bias, see p. 449.)

Ways to avoid the generic *he*

GENERIC *HE* None of the students had the credits *he* needed.

- Substitute *he or she.*

  REVISED None of the students had the credits *he or she* needed.

  To avoid awkwardness, don't use *he or she* more than once in several sentences.

- Recast the sentence using a plural antecedent and pronoun.

  REVISED *All the students* in the class lacked the credits *they* needed.

- Rewrite the sentence to avoid the pronoun.

  REVISED None of the students had the *needed credits.*

4 Collective noun antecedents take singular or plural pronouns depending on meaning.

Collective nouns such as *army, committee, family, group,* and *team* have singular form but may be referred to by singular or plural pronouns, depending on the meaning intended. When the group acts as a unit, the pronoun is singular.

The committee voted to disband *itself.*

When the members of the group act separately, the pronoun is plural.

The old group have gone *their* separate ways.

In the last example, note that the verb and pronoun are consistent in number (see also p. 230).

INCONSISTENT The old group *has* gone *their* separate ways.

CONSISTENT The old group *have* gone *their* separate ways.

Exercise 2
Revising: Pronoun-antecedent agreement

Revise the following sentences so that pronouns and their antecedents agree in person and number. Some items have more than one possible answer. Try to avoid the generic *he* (see above). If you change the subject of a sentence, be sure to change verbs as necessary for agreement. If the sentence is already correct as given, circle the number preceding it.

Example:

Each of the Boudreaus' children brought their laundry home at Thanksgiving.

Each of the Boudreaus' children brought *his or her* laundry home at Thanksgiving. *Or: All* of the Boudreaus' children brought *their* laundry home at Thanksgiving.

1. Each child in the school hopes that they will be the one chosen to attend the Youth Parliament in Ottawa.
2. These gatherings are important because it brings young people together from across the country.
3. These young people follow all the rules he has learned about.
4. The Speaker asks each member if they wanted to address the house.
5. Surrounded by her colleagues and their parents, the Prime Minister of the Youth Parliament conducts a mock session for them.

Exercise 3
Adjusting for agreement

In the following sentences subjects agree with verbs, and pronouns agree with antecedents. Make the change specified in parentheses after each sentence, and then revise the sentence as necessary to maintain agreement. Some items have more than one possible answer.

Example:

The student attends weekly conferences with her teacher. (*Change The student to Students.*)

Students *attend* weekly conferences with *their* teacher.

1. A biologist wishes to introduce captive wolves from Alberta into the mountains of Montana in order to increase the wild population of this endangered species. (*Change A biologist to Biologists.*)
2. When freed, the wolf naturally has no fear of humans and thus is in danger of being shot. (*Change wolf to wolves.*)
3. The first experiment to release the wolves was a failure. (*Change experiment to experiments.*)
4. Now researchers pen the wolf puppy in the wooded area that will eventually be its territory. (*Change puppy to puppies.*)
5. The wolf has little contact with people, even its own keeper, during the year of its captivity. (*Change wolf to wolves.*)

Exercise 4
Revising: Agreement

Revise the sentences in the following paragraphs to correct errors in agreement between subjects and verbs or between pronouns and their antecedents. Try to avoid the generic *he* (see p. 236).

Karen Kain and Frank Augustyn, who danced together for many years, shares a background that made their partnership seem fated, if not inevitable. They was born in Hamilton, Ontario, two years apart (Kain in 1951, Augustyn in 1953). Showing early promise of the brilliance to come, they was both recruited by the National Ballet School of Canada where they shone the brightest in their respective classes. Kain joined the National Ballet of Canada in 1969, and she became a principal dancer only two years later. Her first triumph were her role as the Swan Queen in *Swan Lake*. Augustyn joined the National Ballet in 1970 and became a principal in 1971 and a soloist in 1972. In 1973, Kain and Augustyn were awarded the gold medal for the *pas de deux* in the prestigious Moscow International Ballet Competition. The committee were unanimous in their choice.

Kain danced with a sensitive musicality that made her a favourite partner of other brilliant dancers. Her musical sense allowed her to combine a robust athleticism with a keen dramatic representation, a combination that partners finds irresistible. She danced around the world for many years, for example, with Rudolph Nureyev, when he was in his prime. Fans of ballet still says that their performances is among the best they have seen.

Her partnership with Augustyn, however, remain the signature pairing of her early career. Each one brought such energy to their individual performance that together they were unforgettable. In a *pas de deux*, each dancer must be able to rely on his partner: he has to be able to react instinctively. And Kain and Augustyn were that kind of pair.

Note See page 252 for an exercise involving agreement along with other aspects of grammar.

Chapter 9 Adjectives and Adverbs

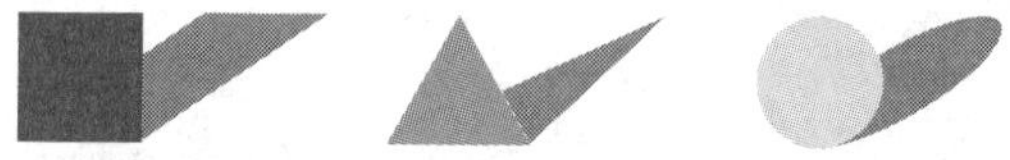

Adjectives and adverbs are modifiers that describe, restrict, or otherwise qualify the words to which they relate.

Functions of adjectives and adverbs

Adjectives modify nouns:	*serious* student
pronouns:	*ordinary* one
Adverbs modify verbs:	*warmly* greet
adjectives:	*only* three people
adverbs:	*quite* seriously
phrases:	*nearly* to the edge of the cliff
clauses:	*just* when we arrived
sentences:	*Fortunately,* she is employed.

Many of the most common adjectives are familiar one-syllable words such as *bad, strange, large,* and *wrong.* Many others are formed by adding endings such as *-al, -able, -ful, -less, -ish, -ive,* and *-y* to nouns or verbs: *optional, fashionable, beautiful, fruitless, selfish, expressive, dreamy.*

Most adverbs are formed by adding *-ly* to adjectives: *badly, strangely, largely, beautifully.* But note that we cannot depend on *-ly* to identify adverbs, since some adjectives also end in *-ly* (*fatherly, lonely*) and since some common adverbs do not end in *-ly* (*always,* *here, not, now, often, there*). Thus the only sure way to distinguish between adjectives and adverbs is to determine what they modify.

9a Use adjectives only to modify nouns and pronouns.

Adjectives modify only nouns and pronouns. Using adjectives instead of adverbs to modify verbs, adverbs, or other adjectives is nonstandard.

NONSTANDARD The groups view family values *different*.

STANDARD The groups view family values *differently*.

The adjectives *good* and *bad* often appear where standard English requires the adverbs *well* and *badly*.

NONSTANDARD Educating children *good* is everyone's focus.

STANDARD Educating children *well* is everyone's focus.

NONSTANDARD Some children suffer *bad*.

STANDARD Some children suffer *badly*.

9b Use an adjective after a linking verb to modify the subject. Use an adverb to modify a verb.

A **linking verb** is one that links, or connects, a subject and its complement: *They are golfers. He is lucky.* (See also p. 159.) Linking verbs are forms of *be*, the verbs associated with our five senses (*look, sound, smell, feel, taste*), and a few others (*appear, seem, become, grow, turn, prove, remain, stay*).

Some of these verbs may or may not be linking, depending on their meaning in the sentence. When the word after the verb modifies the subject, the verb is linking and the word should be an adjective. When the word modifies the verb, however, it should be an adverb.

Two word pairs are especially troublesome in this context. One is *bad* and *badly*.

The weather grew *bad*.
linking verb adjective

Flowers grow *badly* in such soil.
verb adverb

She felt *bad*.
linking verb adjective

The other pair is *good* and *well*. *Good* serves only as an adjective.

Well may serve as an adverb with a host of meanings or as an adjective meaning only "fit" or "healthy."

> Bailey trained *well.*
> verb adverb
>
> He felt *well.*
> linking verb adjective
>
> His health was *good.*
> linking verb adjective

9c After a direct object, use an adjective to modify the object and an adverb to modify the verb.

After a direct object, an adjective modifies the object, whereas an adverb modifies the verb of the sentence. (See p. 157 for more on direct objects.)

> Campus politics made Mungo *angry.*
> adjective
>
> Mungo repeated the words *angrily.*
> adverb

You can test whether a modifier should be an adjective or an adverb by trying to separate it from the direct object. If you can separate it, it should be an adverb: *Mungo angrily repeated the words.* If you cannot separate it, it is probably an adjective.

> The instructor considered the student's work *thorough.* [The adjective can be moved in front of *work* (*student's thorough work*), but it cannot be separated from *work.*]
>
> The instructor considered the student's work *thoroughly.* [The adverb can be separated from *work.* Compare *The instructor thoroughly considered the student's work.*]

9d When an adverb has a short form and an *-ly* form, distinguish carefully between the forms.

Some adverbs have two forms, one with an *-ly* ending and one without. These include the following:

cheap, cheaply	loud, loudly	sharp, sharply
high, highly	near, nearly	slow, slowly
late, lately	quick, quickly	wrong, wrongly

With some of these pairs the choice of form is a matter of idiom, for the two forms have developed entirely separate meanings.

> He went *late.*
> *Lately* he has been eating more.
>
> Winter is drawing *near.*
> Winter is *nearly* here.

In other pairs the long and short forms have the same meaning.

However, the short forms generally occur in informal speech and writing. The *-ly* forms are preferable in formal writing.

INFORMAL Drive *slow.*

FORMAL The funeral procession moved *slowly* through town.

Exercise 1
Revising: Adjectives and adverbs

Revise the following sentences so that adjectives and adverbs are used appropriately. If any sentence is already correct as given, circle the number preceding it.

Example:

The announcer warned that traffic was moving very slow.
The announcer warned that traffic was moving very *slowly.*

1. King George III of England declared Samuel Johnson suitably for a pension.
2. Johnson was taken serious as a critic and dictionary maker.
3. Thinking about his meeting with the king, Johnson felt proudly.
4. Johnson was relieved that he had not behaved badly in the king's presence.
5. After living cheap for over twenty years, Johnson finally had enough money from the pension to eat and dress good.

9e Use the comparative and superlative forms of adjectives and adverbs appropriately.

Adjectives and adverbs can show degrees of quality or amount with the endings *-er* and *-est* or with the words *more* and *most* or *less* and *least.* Most modifiers have three forms.

	ADJECTIVES	ADVERBS
POSITIVE The basic form listed in the dictionary	red awful	soon quickly
COMPARATIVE A greater or lesser degree of the quality named	redder more/less awful	sooner more/less quickly
SUPERLATIVE The greatest or least degree of the quality named	reddest most/least awful	soonest most/least quickly

If sound alone does not tell you whether to use *-er/-est* or *more/most,* consult a dictionary. If the endings can be used, the dictionary will list them. Otherwise, use *more* or *most.*

Use the correct forms of irregular adjectives and adverbs.

The irregular modifiers change the spelling of their positive form to show comparative and superlative degrees.

Degrees of irregular adjectives and adverbs

POSITIVE	COMPARATIVE	SUPERLATIVE
Adjectives		
good	better	best
bad	worse	worst
little	littler, less	littlest, least
many some much	more	most
Adverbs		
well	better	best
badly	worse	worst

Use either *-er/-est* or *more/most,* not both.

A double comparative or double superlative combines the *-er* or *-est* ending with the word *more* or *most.* It is redundant.

Chang was the *wisest* (not *most wisest*) person in town.
He was *smarter* (not *more smarter*) than anyone else.

In general, use the comparative form for comparing two things and the superlative form for comparing three or more things.

She was the *taller* of the two girls. [Comparative.]
Of all those books, *The Yearling* is the *best.* [Superlative.]

In conversation the superlative form is often used to compare only two things: *When two people argue, the angriest one is usually wrong.* But the distinction between the forms should be observed in writing.

Use comparative or superlative forms only for modifiers that can logically be compared.

Some adjectives and adverbs cannot logically be compared—for instance, *perfect, unique, dead, impossible, infinite.* These absolute words can be preceded by adverbs like *nearly* and *almost* that mean "approaching," but they cannot logically be modified by *more* or *most* (as in *most perfect*). This distinction is sometimes ignored in speech, but it should always be made in writing.

NOT	He was the *most unique* teacher we had.
BUT	He was a *unique* teacher.

Exercise 2
Using comparatives and superlatives

Write the comparative and superlative forms of each adjective or adverb below. Then use all three forms in your own sentences.

Example:

heavy: heavier (comparative), heaviest (superlative)

The barbells were too *heavy* for me. The magician's trunk was *heavier* than I expected. Bob Clark was the *heaviest* person on the team.

1. badly
2. great
3. lively
4. steady
5. some
6. often
7. good
8. well
9. elegant
10. understanding

Exercise 3
Revising: Comparatives and superlatives

Revise the sentences below so that the comparative and superlative forms of adjectives and adverbs are appropriate for formal usage.

Example:

Attending classes full-time and working at two jobs was the most impossible thing I ever did.

Attending classes full-time and working at two jobs was *impossible* (or *the hardest thing I ever did*).

1. Charlotte was the older of the three Brontë sisters, all of whom were novelists.
2. Some readers think Emily Brontë's *Wuthering Heights* is the most saddest novel they have ever read.
3. Of the other two sisters, Charlotte and Anne, Charlotte was probably the most talented.
4. Critics still argue about whether Charlotte or Emily wrote more better.
5. Certainly this family of women novelists was the most unique.

9f Avoid double negatives.

A **double negative** is a nonstandard construction in which two negative words such as *no, none, neither, barely, hardly,* or *scarcely* cancel each other out. For instance, *Jenny did not feel nothing* asserts that Jenny felt other than nothing, or something. For the opposite meaning, one of the negatives must be eliminated or changed to a positive: *She felt nothing* or *She did not feel anything.*

FAULTY We could *not hardly* hear the speaker. *None* of her ideas *never* made it to the back of the room.

REVISED We could *hardly* hear the speaker. *None* of her ideas made it to the back of the room.

REVISED We could *not* hear the speaker. Her ideas *never* made it to the back of the room.

9g Use nouns sparingly as modifiers.

We often use one noun to modify another. For example:

child care	flood control	slave trade
father figure	security guard	truth serum

Such phrases can be both clear and concise, but overuse of noun modifiers can lead to flat, even senseless, writing. To avoid awkwardness or confusion, observe two principles. First, prefer possessives or adjectives as modifiers.

NOT A student takes the dental *board* exams to become a *dentist* technician.

BUT A student takes the dental *board's* exams to become a *dental* technician.

Second, use only short nouns as modifiers and use them only in two- or three-word sequences.

CONFUSING Minimex maintains a *plant employee relations improvement* program.

REVISED Minimex maintains a program *for improving* relations *among plant employees.*

9h Distinguish between present and past participles as adjectives. ESL

Both present participles and past participles may serve as adjectives: *a burning bush, a burned bush.* As in the examples, the two participles usually differ in the time they indicate.

But some present and past participles—those derived from verbs expressing feeling—can have altogether different meanings. The present participle refers to something that causes the feeling:

That was a frightening storm. The past participle refers to something that experiences the feeling: *They quieted the frightened horses.*

The following participles are among those likely to be confused:

amazing/amazed	fascinating/fascinated
amusing/amused	frightening/frightened
annoying/annoyed	frustrating/frustrated
astonishing/astonished	interesting/interested
boring/bored	pleasing/pleased
confusing/confused	satisfying/satisfied
depressing/depressed	shocking/shocked
embarrassing/embarrassed	surprising/surprised
exciting/excited	tiring/tired
exhausting/exhausted	worrying/worried

Exercise 4
Revising: Present and past participles ESL

Revise the adjectives in the following sentences as needed to distinguish between present and past participles. If the sentence is already correct as given, circle the number preceding it.

Example:

The subject was embarrassed to many people.
The subject was *embarrassing* to many people.

1. Several critics found Guy Vanderhaeghe's *The Englishman's Boy* to be a fascinated book.
2. One confused critic wished that Vanderhaeghe had set the book more in the past.
3. Another critic argued that although the book contained many depressed episodes, the overall impact was excited.
4. Since other readers found the book annoyed, this critic pointed out its many surprised qualities.
5. In the end most critics agreed that the book was a satisfied novel.

9i Use *a, an, the,* and other determiners appropriately. ESL

Determiners are special kinds of adjectives that mark nouns because they always precede nouns. Some common determiners are *a, an,* and *the* (called **articles**) and *my, their, whose, this, these, those, one, some,* and *any.*

Native speakers of English can rely on their intuition when using determiners, but nonnative speakers often have difficulty with them because many other languages use them quite differently or not at all. In English the use of determiners depends on the context they appear in and the kind of nouns they precede:

- A **proper noun** names a particular person, place, or thing and begins with a capital letter: *February, Joe Allen, Red River.*
- A **count noun** names something that is countable in English and can form a plural: *girl/girls, apple/apples, child/children.*
- A **noncount noun** names something not usually considered countable in English. A noncount noun does not form a plural. Here is a sample of noncount nouns:

advice	happiness	mail	silver
cereal	health	meat	supervision
confidence	homework	money	traffic
courage	information	oil	truth
equipment	intelligence	police	water
evidence	knowledge	pollution	wealth
furniture	legislation	research	weather
hair	love	satisfaction	work

An ESL dictionary will tell you whether a noun is a count noun, a noncount noun, or both. (See p. 470 for recommended dictionaries.)

NOTE Many nouns can be both count and noncount nouns.

> The library has a *room* for readers. [*Room* is a count noun meaning "walled area."]
>
> The library has *room* for reading. [*Room* is a noncount noun meaning "space."]

Use *a, an,* and *the* where they are required.

With singular count nouns

A or *an* precedes a singular count noun when the reader does not already know its identity, usually because you have not mentioned it before.

> *A* scientist in our chemistry department developed *a* process to strengthen metals. [*Scientist* and *process* are being introduced for the first time.]

The precedes a singular count noun that has a specific identity for the reader, usually because (1) you have mentioned it before, (2) you identify it immediately before or after you state it, (3) it is unique (the only one in existence), or (4) it refers to an institution or facility that is shared by a community.

> A scientist in our chemistry department developed a process to strengthen metals. *The* scientist patented *the* process. [*Scientist* and *process* were identified in the preceding sentence.]
>
> *The* most productive laboratory is *the* research centre in the chemistry department. [*Most productive* identifies *laboratory,* and *in the chemistry department* identifies *research centre.*]

The sun rises in *the* east. [*Sun* and *east* are unique.]

Many American men and women aspire to *the* presidency. [*Presidency* is a shared institution.]

The fax machine has changed business communication. [*Fax machine* is a shared facility.]

The is not used before a singular noun that names a general category.

Sherman said that *war* is hell. [*War* names a general category.]

The war in Croatia left many dead. [*War* names a specific war.]

With plural count nouns

A or *an* never precedes a plural noun. *The* does not precede a plural noun that names a general category. *The* does precede a plural noun that names specific representatives of a category.

Men and *women* are different. [*Men* and *women* name general categories.]

The women formed a team. [*Women* refers to specific people.]

With noncount nouns

A or *an* never precedes a noncount noun. *The* does precede a noncount noun that names specific representatives of a general category.

Vegetation suffers from drought. [*Vegetation* names a general category.]

The vegetation in the park withered or died. [*Vegetation* refers to specific plants.]

With proper nouns

A or *an* never precedes a proper noun. *The* generally does not precede proper nouns:

Varma lives in *Flin Flon.*

There are exceptions, however. For instance, we generally use *the* before the names of ships (*the Bluenose*), oceans (*the Pacific*), mountain ranges (*the Alps*), regions (*the Middle East*), rivers (*the Fraser*), and some countries (*the United States, the Netherlands*).

Use other determiners appropriately.

The uses of English determiners besides articles also depend on context and kind of noun. The following determiners may be used with each kind of noun.

With singular count nouns

my, our, your, his, her, its, their, possessive nouns (*boy's, boys'*)
whose, which(*ever*), *what*(*ever*)
this, that
one, any, some, every, each, either, neither, another, the other
the first, the second, and so forth; *the last*

Their bank account is overdrawn.
Every dollar was spent.

With plural count nouns

my, our, your, his, her, its, their, possessive nouns (*boy's, boys'*)
whose, which(*ever*), *what*(*ever*)
these, those
some, any, both, many, enough, more, most, other, the other, such, few, a few, fewer, fewest, several, all, all of the, a lot of
no; two, three, and so forth; *the first, the second,* and so forth; *the last*

Those numbers are incorrect.
Some mistakes were made.

NOTE *Few* means "not many" or "not enough." *A few* means "some" or "a small but sufficient quantity."

Few committee members came to the meeting.
A few members can keep the committee going.

Do not use *much* with a plural count noun.

Many (not *much*) members want to help.

With noncount nouns

my, our, your, his, her, its, their, possessive nouns (*boy's, boys'*)
whose, which(*ever*), *what*(*ever*)
this, that
some, any, much, more, most, enough, other, the other, such, little, a little, less, least, all, all of the, a lot of, a large amount of
no; the first, the second, and so forth; *the last*

That money should be saved.
Would *more* evidence convince you?

NOTE *Little* means "not many" or "not enough." *A little* means "some" or "a small but sufficient quantity."

Little time remains before the conference.
The members need *a little* help from their colleagues.

Do not use *many* with a noncount noun:

Much (not *many*) work remains.

Exercise 5
Revising: Articles ESL

For each blank below, indicate whether *a, an, the,* or no article should be inserted.

In __ nineteenth century, __ name of the Northwest Territories was applied to ____ large parcel of land. ____ parcel included __ area, formerly known as Rupert's Land, owned by the Hudson's Bay Company and Great Britain and ___ arctic islands north of ___ mainland. Later large portions of territories were removed to add to _____ provinces of Manitoba, Saskatchewan, and Alberta and to the Yukon Territories. In twentieth century, __ further chunk was divided and added to Manitoba, Ontario, and Quebec. Even with all ____ portions removed, the Northwest Territories is still __ largest political subdivision in Canada and __ northernmost land mass.

Exercise 6
Revising: Adjectives and adverbs

Revise the following paragraph so that it conforms to formal usage of adjectives and adverbs.

Canadians often argue about which professional sport is better: hockey, football, or baseball. Hockey fans argue that their sport offers more action because the players are constant skating, hitting, and shooting. Because it is played indoors in relatively small arenas, hockey allows fans to be more closer to the action than the other sports do. Fans point to how swift the forwards swoop on the net and how quick the goalie moves to block the shot. Football fanatics say they don't hardly stop yelling once the game begins. They cheer when their team executes a real complicated play good. They roar more louder when the defence stops the opponents in a goal-line stand. They yell loudest when a fullback crashes in for a score. In contrast, the supporters of baseball believe that it might be the most perfect sport played. It combines the one-on-one duel of pitcher and batter struggling valiant with the tight teamwork of double and triple plays. Because the game is played slow and careful, fans can analyse and discuss the manager's strategy. Besides, they don't never know when they might catch a foul ball as a souvenir. However, no matter what the sport, all fans feel happily only when their team wins!

NOTE See the next page for an exercise involving adjectives and adverbs along with other aspects of grammar.

Exercise on Chapters 6–9
Revising: Grammatical sentences

The paragraphs below contain errors in pronoun case, verb forms, subject-verb agreement, pronoun-antecedent agreement, and the forms of adjectives and adverbs. Revise the paragraphs to correct the errors.

Occasionally, musicians become "crossover artists" whom can perform good in more than one field of music. For example, Wynton and Branford Marsalis was train in jazz by their father, the great pianist Ellis Marsalis. Both of the sons has recent became successful classical artists. Branford's saxophone captures the richness of pieces by Ravel and Stravinsky. Wynton's albums of classical trumpet music from the Baroque period has brung him many awards. Still, if he was to choose which kind of music he likes best, Wynton would probable choose jazz. In contrast to the Marsalises, Yo-Yo Ma and Jean Pierre Rampal growed up studying classical music. Then in the 1980s they was invited by Claude Bolling, a French pianist, to record Bolling's jazz compositions. In fact, Rampal's flute blended with Bolling's music so good that the two men have did three albums.

Such crossovers are often more harder for vocalists. Each type of music has their own style and feel that is hard to learn. For example, Luciano Pavarotti and Kiri te Kanawa, two great opera performers, have sang popular music and folk songs in concerts and on albums. On each occasion, their technique was the most perfect, yet each sounded as if he was simply trying to sing proper. It is even more difficulter for pop or country vocalists to sing opera, as Linda Ronstadt and Gary Morris founded when they appear in *La Bohème.* Each of them have a clear, pure voice, but a few critics said that him and her lacked the vocal power necessary for opera. However, Bobby McFerrin been successful singing both pop and classical pieces. He won a Grammy award for his song "Don't Worry, Be Happy." But he is equal able to sing classical pieces *a cappella* (without musical accompaniment). His voice's remarkable range and clarity allows him to imitate many musical instruments.

No matter how successful, all of these musicians has shown great courage by performing in a new field. They are willing to test and stretch their talents, and us music fans benefits.

Part III

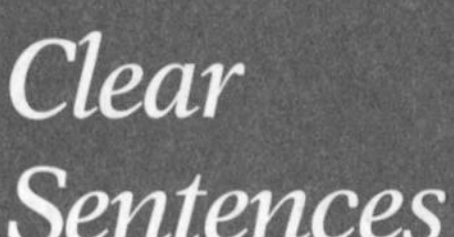

Clear Sentences

Chapter 10 Sentence Fragments

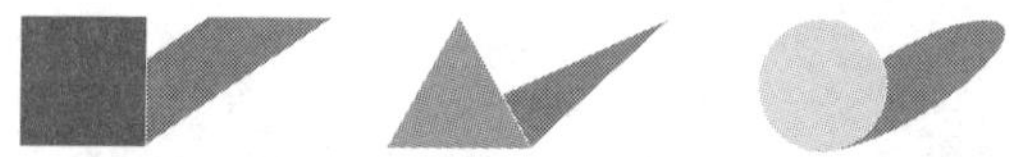

A **sentence fragment** is part of a sentence that is set off as if it were a whole sentence by an initial capital letter and a final period or other end punctuation. Although writers occasionally use fragments deliberately and effectively (see p. 261), readers perceive most fragments as serious errors because, expecting complete sentences, they find partial sentences distracting or confusing. (Before reading further, you may find it helpful to review pp. 153–60 and 172–75 on sentences and clauses.)

Complete sentence versus sentence fragment

A **complete sentence** or **main clause**

- contains a subject and a verb (*The wind blows*)
- and is not a subordinate clause (beginning with a word such as *because* or *who*).

A **sentence fragment**

- lacks a verb (*The wind blowing*)
- or lacks a subject (*And blows*)
- or is a subordinate clause not attached to a complete sentence (*Because the wind blows*).

NOTE ESL Some languages other than English allow the omission of the subject or verb. Except in commands (*Close the door*), English always requires you to state the subject and verb.

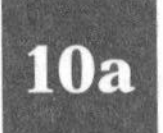

10a Test your sentences for completeness, and revise any fragments.

The following three tests will help you determine whether a word group punctuated as a sentence is actually a complete sentence. If the word group does not pass *all three* tests, it is a fragment and needs to be revised.

Tests for sentence fragments

A sentence is complete only when it passes *all three* tests.

1. Find the verb.
2. Find the subject.
3. Make sure the clause is not subordinate.

Test 1: Find the verb.

Look for a verb in the group of words. If you do not have one, the word group is a fragment.

FRAGMENT The baboon with a stick in his mouth. [Compare a complete sentence: *The baboon held a stick in his mouth.*]

Any verb form you find must be a **finite verb,** one that changes form as indicated below. A verbal does not change; it cannot serve as a sentence verb without the aid of a helping verb.

	FINITE VERBS IN COMPLETE SENTENCES	VERBALS IN SENTENCE FRAGMENTS
SINGULAR	The baboon *looks.*	The baboon *looking.*
PLURAL	The baboons *look.*	The baboons *looking.*
PRESENT	The baboon *looks*	
PAST	The baboon *looked.*	The baboon *looking.*
FUTURE	The baboon *will look.*	

Test 2: Find the subject.

If you find a finite verb, look for its subject by asking who or what performs the action or makes the assertion of the verb. The subject of the sentence will usually come before the verb. If there is no subject, the word group is probably a fragment.

FRAGMENT And eyed the guard nervously. [Compare a complete sentence: *And the baboon eyed the guard nervously.*]

In one kind of complete sentence, a command, the subject *you* is understood.

(You) Move away from the cage.

Test 3: Make sure the clause is not subordinate.

A subordinate clause usually begins with a subordinating word.

SUBORDINATING CONJUNCTIONS			RELATIVE PRONOUNS	
after	once	until	that	who/whom
although	since	when	which	whoever/whomever
as	than	where		whose
because	that	whereas		
if	unless	while		

Subordinate clauses serve as parts of sentences (nouns or modifiers), not as whole sentences.

FRAGMENT When the next cage rattled. [Compare a complete sentence: *The next cage rattled.*]

FRAGMENT The rival that the baboon hated. [This construction is a noun (*rival*) plus its modifier. Compare a complete sentence: *The rival that the baboon hated rattled the cage.*]

NOTE Questions beginning with *how, what, when, where, which, who, whom, whose,* and *why* are not sentence fragments: *Who rattled the cage? Where was the rival?*

Revising sentence fragments

Almost all sentence fragments can be corrected in one of two ways, the choice depending on the importance of the information in the fragment.

Revision of sentence fragments

- Rewrite the fragment as a complete sentence.
- Combine the fragment with the appropriate main clause.

Rewriting the fragment as a complete sentence gives the information in the fragment the same importance as that in other complete sentences.

Fragment The animals acted out a rivalry. *Which mystified their keepers.*

Revised The animals acted out a rivalry. *It* mystified their keepers.

Two main clauses may be separated by a semicolon instead of a period (see 22a).

The second method of correcting a fragment, combining it with a main clause, subordinates the information in the fragment to the information in the main clause.

Fragment The baboon stared at his challenger. *Poised for combat.*

Revised The baboon, poised for combat, stared at his challenger.

In this example, commas separate the inserted phrase from the rest of the sentence because the phrase does not restrict the meaning of any word in the main clause but simply adds information (see 21c). When a phrase or subordinate clause *does* restrict the meaning of a word in the main clause, a comma or commas do *not* separate the two elements.

Fragment The challenger was a newcomer. *Who was unusually fierce.*

Revised The challenger was a newcomer who was unusually fierce.

Sometimes a fragment may be combined with the main clause using a colon or a dash (see 25a and 25b, respectively).

Fragment The rivalry may have begun with a specific cause. *Territory, dominance, or a female baboon.*

Revised The rivalry may have begun with a specific cause: territory, dominance, or a female baboon.

Fragment Now the rivalry was constant and vicious. *A threat to both animals.*

Revised Now the rivalry was constant and vicious—a threat to both animals.

Exercise 1
Identifying and revising sentence fragments

Apply the tests for completeness to each of the following word groups. If a word group is a complete sentence, circle the number preceding it. If it is a sentence fragment, revise it in two ways: by making it a complete sentence, and by combining it with a main clause written from the information given in other items.

> *Example:*
>
> And could not find his money.
>
> The word group has a verb (*could . . . find*) but no subject.
>
> Revised into a complete sentence: And *he* could not find his money.
>
> Combined with a new main clause: *He was lost* and could not find his money.

1. In an interesting article about vandalism against works of art.
2. The motives of the vandals varying widely.
3. Those who harm artwork are usually angry.
4. But not necessarily at the artist or the owner.
5. For instance, a man who hammered at Michelangelo's *Pietà*.
6. And knocked off the Virgin Mary's nose.
7. Because he was angry at the Roman Catholic Church.
8. Which knew nothing of his grievance.
9. Although many damaged works can be repaired.
10. Usually even the most skilful repairs are forever visible.

10b A subordinate clause is not a complete sentence.

Subordinate clauses contain both subjects and verbs, but they always begin with a subordinating conjunction (*although, if,* and so on) or a relative pronoun (*who, which, that*). (See p. 256.) Subordinate clauses serve as nouns or modifiers, but they cannot stand alone as complete sentences.

To correct a subordinate clause set off as a sentence, combine it with the main clause or remove or change the subordinating word to create a main clause.

FRAGMENT Many pine trees bear large cones. *Which appear in August.*

REVISED Many pine trees bear large cones, which appear in August.

REVISED Many pine trees bear large cones. *They* appear in August.

10c A verbal phrase or a prepositional phrase is not a complete sentence.

A **verbal phrase** consists of an infinitive (*to choose*), a past participle (*chosen*), or a present participle or gerund (*choosing*) together with any objects and modifiers it may have (see p. 167). A verbal phrase is a noun or modifier and cannot serve as the verb in a complete sentence.

FRAGMENT She backed closer and closer to the end of the diving board. *At last falling into the water.*

REVISED She backed closer and closer to the end of the diving board, at last falling into the water.

REVISED She backed closer and closer to the end of the diving board. At last *she fell* into the water.

A **prepositional phrase** consists of a preposition (such as *in, on, to,* and *with*) together with its object and any modifier (see p. 164). A prepositional phrase cannot stand alone as a complete sentence.

FRAGMENT Falling gave her confidence. *In her strength.*

REVISED Falling gave her confidence in her strength.

REVISED Falling gave her confidence. *She learned to trust* her strength.

10d Any word group lacking a subject or a verb or both is not a complete sentence.

We often follow a noun with a modifier. No matter how long the noun and its modifier are, they cannot stand alone as a sentence.

FRAGMENTS *People waving flags and cheering. Lined the streets for the parade.*

REVISED People waving flags and cheering lined the streets for the parade.

FRAGMENT *Aboriginal veterans who fought in Korea.* They are finally being honoured.

REVISED *Aboriginal* veterans who fought in Korea are finally being honoured.

Appositives are nouns, or nouns and their modifiers, that rename or describe other nouns (see p. 176). They cannot stand alone as sentences.

FRAGMENT When I was a child, my favourite adult was an old uncle. *A retired sea captain who always told me long stories of wild adventures in faraway places.*

REVISED When I was a child, my favourite adult was an old uncle, a retired sea captain who always told me long stories of wild adventures in faraway places.

Compound predicates are predicates made up of two or more verbs and their objects, if any (see p. 157). A verb or its object cannot stand alone as a sentence.

FRAGMENT Uncle Marlon drew out his tales. *And embellished them.*

REVISED Uncle Marlon drew out his tales and embellished them.

FRAGMENT He described characters he had met. *And storms at sea.*

REVISED He described characters he had met and storms at sea.

NOTE Beginning a sentence with a coordinating conjunction such as *and* and *but* can lead to a sentence fragment. Check every sentence you begin with a coordinating conjunction to be sure it is complete.

Exercise 2
Revising sentence fragments

Correct any sentence fragment below either by combining it with a main clause or by making it a main clause. If an item contains no sentence fragment, circle the number preceding it.

Example:

Jujitsu is good for self-protection. Because it enables one to overcome an opponent without the use of weapons.

Jujitsu is good for self-protection because it enables one to overcome an opponent without the use of weapons.

1. Human beings who perfume themselves. They are not much different from other animals.
2. Animals as varied as insects and dogs release *pheromones*. Chemicals that signal other animals.
3. Human beings have a diminished sense of smell. And do not consciously detect most of their own species' pheromones.
4. The human substitute for pheromones may be perfumes. Especially musk and other fragrances derived from animal oils.
5. Some sources say that humans began using perfume to cover up the smell of burning flesh. During sacrifices to the gods.
6. Perfumes became religious offerings in their own right. Being expensive to make, they were highly prized.
7. The earliest historical documents from the Middle East record the use of fragrances. Not only in religious ceremonies but on the body.
8. In the nineteenth century chemists began synthesizing perfume oils. Which previously could be made only from natural sources.
9. The most popular animal oil for perfume today is musk. Although some people dislike its heavy, sweet odour.
10. Synthetic musk oil would help conserve a certain species of deer. Whose gland is the source of musk.

10e Be aware of the acceptable uses of incomplete sentences.

A few word groups lacking the usual subject-predicate combination are not sentence fragments because they conform to the expectations of most readers. They include exclamations (*Oh no!*); questions and answers (*Where next? To Alberta.*); and commands (*Move along. Shut the window.*). Another kind of incomplete sentence, occurring in special situations, is the transitional phrase (*So much for the causes, now for the results. One final point.*).

Experienced writers sometimes use sentence fragments when they want to achieve a special effect. Such fragments appear more in informal than in formal writing. Unless you are experienced and thoroughly secure in your own writing, you should avoid all fragments and concentrate on writing clear, well-formed sentences.

Exercise 3
Revising: Sentence fragments

Revise the following paragraph to eliminate sentence fragments by combining them with main clauses or rewriting them as main clauses.

Baby red-eared slider turtles are brightly coloured. With bold patterns on their yellowish undershells. Which serve as a warning to predators. The bright colours of skunks and other animals. They signal that the animals will spray nasty chemicals. In contrast, the turtle's colours warn largemouth bass. That the baby turtle will actively defend itself. When a bass gulps down a turtle. The feisty baby claws and bites. Forcing the bass to spit it out. To avoid a similar painful experience. The bass will avoid other baby red-eared slider turtles. The turtle loses its bright colours as it grows too big. For a bass's afternoon snack.

Note See page 304 for an exercise involving sentence fragments along with comma splices, fused sentences, and other sentence errors.

Chapter 11

Comma Splices and Fused Sentences

Two or more consecutive main clauses may be separated from each other in one of four ways:

- With a period:

  The ship was huge. Its mast stood twenty metres high.

- With a semicolon:

  The ship was huge; its mast stood twenty metres high.

- With a comma preceding a coordinating conjunction that joins the clauses and specifies the relation between them:

  The ship was huge, *and* its mast stood twenty metres high.

- Occasionally with a colon when the second clause explains the first (see p. 406):

  The ship was huge: its mast stood twenty metres high.

Two problems commonly occur in punctuating consecutive main clauses. One is the **comma splice,** in which the clauses are joined (or spliced) *only* with a comma.

COMMA SPLICE

The ship was huge, its mast stood twenty metres high.

The other problem is the **fused sentence,** in which no punctuation or coordinating conjunction appears between the clauses.

FUSED SENTENCE

The ship was huge its mast stood twenty metres high.

Comma splices and fused sentences are serious errors because they generally force the reader to reread for sense.

EXCEPTION Experienced writers sometimes use commas between very brief main clauses that are grammatically parallel.

He's not a person, he's a monster.

However, many readers view such punctuation as incorrect. Unless you are certain that your readers will not object to the comma in a sentence like this one, separate the clauses with periods or semicolons, as described in this chapter.

Situations that may produce comma splices and fused sentences

- The first clause is negative; the second, positive.

  SPLICE Petric is not a nurse, she is a doctor.

  REVISED Petric is not a nurse; she is a doctor.

- The second clause amplifies or illustrates the first.

  FUSED She did well in university her average was 3.9.

  REVISED She did well in university: her average was 3.9.

- The second clause contains a conjunctive adverb such as *however, therefore,* or *instead* (see 11b).

  SPLICE She had intended to become a biologist, *however,* medicine seemed more exciting.

  REVISED She had intended to become a biologist; *however,* medicine seemed more exciting.

- The subject of the second clause repeats or refers to the subject of the first clause.

  FUSED Petric is an internist *she* practises in Regina.

  REVISED Petric is an internist. *She* practises in Regina.

- Splicing or fusing is an attempt to link related ideas or to smooth choppy sentences.

  SPLICE She is very committed to her work, she devotes almost all her time to patient care.

  REVISED *Because* she is very committed to her work, she devotes almost all her time to patient care.

COMMA SPLICES

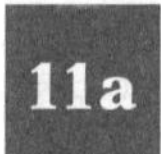

11a Separate two main clauses with a comma *only* when they are joined by a coordinating conjunction.

A comma cannot separate main clauses unless they are linked by a coordinating conjunction (*and, but, or, nor, for, so, yet*). Readers expect the same sentence to continue after a comma. When they find themselves reading a second sentence before they realize they have finished the first, they may have to reread to understand your meaning.

cs 11a

You have four main options for correcting a comma splice. The option you choose depends on the relation you want to establish between the clauses.

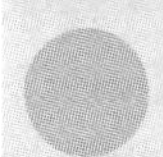

Revision of comma splices

- Make the clauses into separate sentences.
- Insert an appropriate coordinating conjunction after the comma between clauses.
- Insert a semicolon between clauses.
- Subordinate one clause to the other.

Making separate sentences

Revising a comma splice by making separate sentences from the main clauses will always be correct. The period is not only correct but preferable when the ideas expressed in the two main clauses are only loosely related.

COMMA SPLICE	Chemistry has contributed much to our understanding of foods, many foods such as wheat and beans can be produced in the laboratory.
REVISED	Chemistry has contributed much to our understanding of foods. Many foods such as wheat and beans can be produced in the laboratory.

Inserting a coordinating conjunction

When the ideas in the main clauses are closely related and equally important, you may correct a comma splice by inserting the appropriate coordinating conjunction immediately after the comma to join the clauses.

COMMA SPLICE	Some laboratory-grown foods taste good, they are nutritious.
REVISED	Some laboratory-grown foods taste good, *and* they are nutritious.

Using a semicolon

If the relation between the ideas expressed in the main clauses is very close and obvious without a conjunction, you can separate the clauses with a semicolon. (See also 11b.)

COMMA SPLICE	Good taste is rare in laboratory-grown vegetables, they are usually bland.
REVISED	Good taste is rare in laboratory-grown vegetables; they are usually bland.

Subordinating one clause

When the idea in one clause is more important than that in the other, you can express the less important idea in a phrase or a subordinate clause. (See p. 173 for a list of subordinating conjunctions.) Subordination is often more effective than forming separate sentences because it defines the relation between ideas more precisely.

COMMA SPLICE	The vitamins are adequate, the flavour is deficient.
REVISED	The vitamins are adequate. The flavour is deficient. [Both ideas receive equal weight.]
IMPROVED	*Even though* the vitamins are adequate, the flavour is deficient. [Emphasis on the second idea.]

11b Separate main clauses related by *however, thus,* or another conjunctive adverb.

Conjunctive adverbs are modifiers that describe a relation between two clauses:

anyway	hence	meanwhile	still
consequently	however	moreover	then
finally	indeed	nonetheless	therefore
furthermore	instead	otherwise	thus

(See p. 180 for a longer list.)

When two clauses are related by a conjunctive adverb, they must be separated by a period or by a semicolon. The adverb is also generally set off by a comma or commas.

COMMA SPLICE Most Canadians used to live in the country rather than the city, however most now live in an urban area.

REVISED Most Canadians used to live in the country rather than the city. *However*, most now live in an urban area.

REVISED More Canadians used to live in the country rather than the city; *however*, most now live in an urban area.

Note the difference between conjunctive adverbs and coordinating and subordinating conjunctions. Conjunctive adverbs do not join two clauses into a grammatical unit but merely describe the way the clauses relate in meaning. Also, unlike conjunctions, conjunctive adverbs may usually be moved from one place to another in the clause (see p. 181). No matter where in the clause a conjunctive adverb appears, however, the clause must be separated from another main clause by a period or a semicolon.

COMMA SPLICE

The increased time devoted to watching television is not the only cause of the decline in reading ability, however, it is one of the important causes.

PERIOD AND CONJUNCTIVE ADVERB

The increased time devoted to watching television is not the only cause of the decline in reading ability. *However*, it is one of the important causes.

SEMICOLON AND CONJUNCTIVE ADVERB

The increased time devoted to watching television is not the only cause of the decline in reading ability; *however*, it is one of the important causes.

The increased time devoted to watching television is not the only cause of the decline in reading ability; it is, *however*, one of the important causes.

Exercise 1
Identifying and revising comma splices

Correct each comma splice below in *two* of the ways described on pages 264–65. If an item contains no comma splice, circle the number preceding it.

Example:

Carolyn still had a headache, she could not get the child-proof cap off the aspirin bottle.

Carolyn still had a headache *because* she could not get the child-proof cap off the aspirin bottle. [Subordination.]

Carolyn still had a headache, *for* she could not get the child-proof cap off the aspirin bottle. [Coordinating conjunction.]

1. Money has a long history, it goes back at least as far as the earliest records.
2. Many of the earliest records concern financial transactions, indeed, early history must often be inferred from commercial activity.
3. Every known society has had a system of money, though the objects serving as money have varied widely.
4. Sometimes the objects have had real value, in modern times, however, their value has been more abstract.
5. Cattle, fermented beverages, and rare shells have served as money, each one had actual value for the society.

FUSED SENTENCES

11c Combine two main clauses only with an appropriate conjunction or punctuation mark between them.

When two main clauses are joined without a word to connect them or a punctuation mark to separate them, the result is a **fused sentence.** Fused sentences can rarely be understood on first reading, and they are never acceptable in standard written English.

FUSED American foreign policy is not well defined it confuses many countries.

Fused sentences may be corrected in the same ways as comma splices.

Revision of fused sentences

- Make the clauses into separate sentences.
- Insert a comma and an appropriate coordinating conjunction between clauses.
- Insert a semicolon between clauses.
- Subordinate one clause to the other.

SEPARATE SENTENCES

American foreign policy is not well defined. It confuses many countries.

COMMA AND COORDINATING CONJUNCTION

American foreign policy is not well defined, *and* it confuses many countries.

SEMICOLON

American foreign policy is not well defined; it confuses many countries.

SUBORDINATING CONJUNCTION

Because American foreign policy is not well defined, it confuses many countries.

Exercise 2
Identifying and revising fused sentences

Revise each of the fused sentences below in *two* of the four ways shown above.

Example:

Tim was shy he usually refused invitations.
Tim was shy, *so* he usually refused invitations.
Tim was shy; he usually refused invitations.

1. Throughout history money and religion were closely linked there was little distinction between government and religion.
2. The head of state and the religious leader were often the same person all power rested in one ruler.
3. These powerful leaders decided what objects would serve as money their backing encouraged public faith in the money.
4. Coins were minted of precious metals the religious overtones of money were then strengthened.
5. People already believed the precious metals to be divine their use in money intensified its allure.

Exercise 3
Sentence combining: Comma splices and fused sentences

Combine each pair of sentences below into one sentence without creating a comma splice or fused sentence. Combine sentences by (1) supplying a comma and coordinating conjunction, (2) supplying a semicolon, or (3) subordinating one clause to the other. You will have to add, delete, or change words as well as punctuation.

Example:

The sun sank lower in the sky. The colours gradually faded.

As the sun sank lower in the sky, the colours gradually faded. [The first clause is subordinated to the second.]

1. The exact origin of paper money is unknown. It has not survived as coins, shells, and other durable objects have.
2. Perhaps goldsmiths were also bankers. Thus they held the gold of their wealthy customers.
3. The goldsmiths probably gave customers receipts for their gold. These receipts were then used in trade.

4. The goldsmiths were something like modern-day bankers. Their receipts were something like modern-day money.
5. The goldsmiths became even more like modern-day bankers. They began issuing receipts for more gold than they actually held in their vaults.

Exercise 4
Revising: Comma splices and fused sentences

Identify and revise the comma splices and fused sentences in the following paragraph.

All those parents who urged their children to eat broccoli were right, the vegetable really is healthful. Broccoli contains sulforaphane, moreover, this mustard oil can be found in kale and Brussels sprouts. Sulforaphane causes the body to make an enzyme that attacks carcinogens, these substances cause cancer. The enzyme speeds up the work of the kidneys then they can flush harmful chemicals out of the body. Other vegetables have similar benefits however, green, leafy vegetables like broccoli are the most efficient. Thus, wise people will eat their broccoli it could save their lives.

Note See page 304 for an exercise involving comma splices and fused sentences along with other sentence errors.

Chapter 12 Pronoun Reference

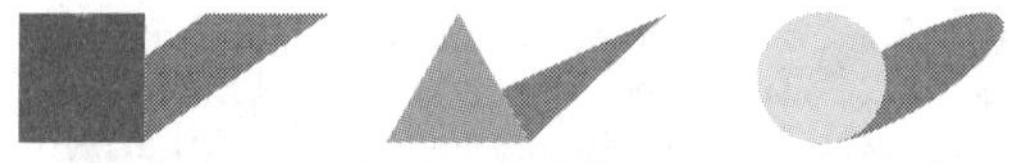

A **pronoun** such as *it* or *they* derives its meaning from its **antecedent,** the noun it substitutes for. Therefore, a pronoun must refer clearly and unmistakably to its antecedent in order for the meaning to be clear. A sentence such as *Jim told Mark he was not invited* is not clear because the reader does not know whether *he* refers to Jim or to Mark.

One way to make pronoun reference clear is to ensure that the pronoun and antecedent agree in person, number, and gender (see p. 234). The other way is to ensure that the pronoun refers unambiguously to a single, close, specific antecedent.

12a Make a pronoun refer clearly to one antecedent.

When either of two nouns can be a pronoun's antecedent, the reference will not be clear.

CONFUSING The workers removed all the furniture from the room and cleaned *it.* ?

Revise such a sentence in one of two ways:

- Replace the pronoun with the appropriate noun.

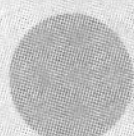

Principal causes of unclear pronoun reference

- More than one possible antecedent (12a):

  CONFUSING To keep birds from eating seeds, soak *them* in blue food colouring.

  CLEAR To keep birds from eating seeds, soak *the seeds* in blue food colouring.

- Antecedent too far away (12b):

  CONFUSING Employees should consult with their supervisor *who* require personal time.

  CLEAR Employees *who* require personal time should consult with their supervisor.

- Antecedent only implied (12c):

  CONFUSING Many children begin reading on their own by watching television, but *this* should be discounted in government policy.

  CLEAR Many children begin reading on their own by watching television, but *such self-instruction* should be discounted in government policy.

See also 12d, 12e, and 12f.

CLEAR The workers removed all the furniture from the room and cleaned *the room* (or *the furniture*).

- Avoid repetition by rewriting the sentence with the pronoun but with only one possible antecedent.

CLEAR After removing all the furniture from *it,* the workers cleaned the room.

CLEAR The workers cleaned all the furniture after removing *it* from the room.

Sentences that report what someone said, using verbs such as *said* or *told,* often require direct rather than indirect quotation.

CONFUSING Juliet Noble told Ann Torre that she was mistaken.

CLEAR Juliet Noble told Ann Torre, "I am mistaken."

CLEAR Juliet Noble told Ann Torre, "You are mistaken."

NOTE Avoid the awkward device of using a pronoun followed by the appropriate noun in parentheses, as in the following example:

WEAK Noble should apologize to Torre, and *she (Noble)* should notify the press.

IMPROVED Noble should apologize to Torre and notify the press.

12b Place a pronoun close enough to its antecedent to ensure clarity.

A clause beginning *who, which,* or *that* generally should fall immediately after the word it refers to.

CONFUSING Jody found a dress in the attic *that* her aunt had worn.

CLEAR In the attic Jody found a dress *that* her aunt had worn.

Even when only one word could possibly serve as the antecedent of a pronoun, the relationship between the two may still be unclear if they are widely separated.

CONFUSING Dawson, where my grandmother grew up, was once the scene of a mad gold rush with fortune seekers, plush opera houses, makeshift hotels, noisy saloons, and dirt streets. When I was a child, *she* often retold the stories she had heard.

CLEAR Dawson, where my grandmother grew up, was once the scene of a mad gold rush with fortune seekers, plush opera houses, makeshift hotels, noisy saloons, and dirt streets. When I was a child, *my grandmother* often retold the stories she had heard.

The confusing separation of pronoun and antecedent is most likely to occur in long sentences and, as illustrated above, in adjacent sentences within a paragraph.

Exercise 1
Revising: Ambiguous and remote pronoun reference

Rewrite the following sentences to eliminate unclear pronoun reference. If you use a pronoun in your revision, be sure that it refers to only one antecedent and that it falls close enough to its antecedent to ensure clarity.

Example:

Saul found an old gun in the rotting shed that was just as his grandfather had left it.

In the rotting shed Saul found an old *gun that* was just as his grandfather had left it.

1. There is a difference between the skating styles of Toller

Cranston and Elvis Stojko; ironically, they both seem somehow out of place for their times.
2. Skating fans still admire Cranston's ground-breaking artistry and skill, even though they were costly.
3. Fans like Cranston for having the courage to be different when it was primarily an athletic sport.
4. They stubbornly refused to accept the judges' low marks and critiques and continued to be artistically innovative.
5. Fans, however frustrated with the final results, still enjoyed it.

12c Make a pronoun refer to a specific antecedent, not an implied one.

A pronoun should refer to a specific noun or other pronoun. When the antecedent is not specifically stated but is implied by the context, the reference can only be inferred by the reader.

1 Use *this, that, which,* and *it* cautiously in referring to whole statements.

The most common kind of implied reference occurs when the pronoun *this, that, which,* or *it* refers to a whole idea or situation described in the preceding clause, sentence, or even paragraph. Such reference, often called **broad reference,** is acceptable only when the pronoun refers clearly to the entire preceding clause. In the following sentence, *which* could not possibly refer to anything but the whole preceding clause.

> I can be kind and civil to people, *which* is more than you can.
> —George Bernard Shaw

But if a pronoun might confuse a reader, you should avoid using it or provide an appropriate noun.

Confusing The faculty agreed on a change in the requirements, but *it* took time.

Clear The faculty agreed on a change in the requirements, but *agreeing* took time.

Clear The faculty agreed on a change in the requirements, but *the change* took time.

Confusing The voyageurs interacted freely with the Aboriginal peoples and travelled wherever furs and the waterways took them. *This* gave the voyageurs a great advantage.

Clear The voyageurs interacted freely with the Aboriginal peoples and travelled wherever furs and the waterways took them. This *freedom and mobility* gave the voyageurs a great advantage.

2 Implied nouns are not clear antecedents.

A noun may be implied in some other word or phrase: *happiness* is implied in *happy, news* in *newspaper.* But a pronoun cannot refer clearly to such an implied noun; it must refer to a specific, stated antecedent.

Confusing In Joan Cohen's advice *she* was not concrete enough.

Clear *Joan Cohen's advice* was not concrete enough.

Confusing She spoke once before, but *it* was sparsely attended.

Clear She spoke once before, but *the speech* was sparsely attended.

3 Titles of papers are not clear antecedents.

The title of a paper is entirely separate from the paper itself, so a pronoun should not be used in the opening sentence of a paper to refer to the title.

Title How to Row a Boat

Not *This* is not as easy as it looks.

But *Rowing a boat* is not as easy as it looks.

12d Use *it* and *they* to refer to definite antecedents. Use *you* only to mean "you, the reader."

In conversation we commonly use expressions such as *It says in the paper* or *In Newfoundland they say.* But such indefinite use of *it* and *they* is inappropriate in writing. The constructions are not only unclear but wordy.

Confusing In Chapter 4 of this book *it* describes the seigneurial system of New France.

Clear *Chapter 4* of this book describes the seigneurial system of New France.

Confusing In the average television drama, *they* present a false picture of life.

CLEAR The average television *drama* presents a false picture of life.

In all but very formal writing, *you* is acceptable when the meaning is clearly "you, the reader." But the context must be appropriate for such a meaning.

INAPPROPRIATE In the fourteenth century *you* had to struggle simply to survive.

REVISED In the fourteenth century *one* (or *a person*) had to struggle simply to survive.

12e Use the pronoun *it* only one way in a sentence.

We use *it* idiomatically in expressions such as *It is raining.* We use *it* to postpone the subject in sentences such as *It is true that more jobs are available to women today.* And we use *it* as a personal pronoun in sentences such as *Joan wanted the book, but she couldn't find it.* All these uses are standard, but two of them in the same passage can confuse the reader.

CONFUSING *It* is true that the Charter of Rights and Freedoms sets limits, but *it* (?) is also flexible.

CLEAR The Charter of Rights and Freedoms does set limits, but *it* is also flexible.

12f Use *who, which,* and *that* for appropriate antecedents.

The relative pronouns *who, which,* and *that* commonly refer to persons, animals, or things. *Who* refers most often to persons but may also refer to animals that have names.

Dorothy is the girl *who* visits Oz.
Her dog, Toto, *who* accompanies her, gives her courage.

Which refers to animals and things.

The Orinoco River, *which* is over 2500 kilometres long, flows through Venezuela into the Atlantic Ocean.

That refers to animals and things and occasionally to persons when they are collective or anonymous.

The rocket *that* failed cost millions.
Infants *that* walk need constant tending.

(See also p. 362 for the use of *which* and *that* in nonrestrictive and restrictive clauses.)

The possessive *whose* generally refers to people but may refer to animals and things to avoid awkward and wordy *of which* constructions.

> The book *whose* binding broke was rare. [Compare *The book of which the binding broke was rare.*]

Exercise 2
Revising: Indefinite and inappropriate pronoun reference

Many of the pronouns in the following sentences do not refer to specific, appropriate antecedents. Revise the sentences as necessary to make them clear.

Example:

In Banff National Park, they have moose, elk, and black bears.

Moose, elk, and black bears live in Banff National Park.

1. "Life begins at forty" is a cliché many people live by, and this may well be true.
2. When she was forty, Pearl Buck's novel *The Good Earth* won the Pulitzer Prize.
3. Buck was a novelist which wrote primarily about China.
4. In *The Good Earth* you have to struggle, but fortitude is rewarded.
5. Buck received much critical praise and earned over $7 million, but she was very modest about it.
6. Kenneth Kaunda, former president of Zambia, was elected to it in 1964, at age forty.
7. When Catherine I became Empress of Russia at age forty, they feared more than loved her.
8. At forty, Paul Revere made his famous ride to warn American revolutionary leaders that the British were going to arrest them. This gave the colonists time to prepare for battle.
9. In the British House of Commons they did not welcome forty-year-old Nancy Astor as the first female member when she entered in 1919.
10. In A.D. 610 Muhammad, age forty, began to have a series of visions that became the foundation of the Muslim faith. Since then, millions of people have become one.

Exercise 3
Revising: Pronoun reference

Revise the following paragraph so that each pronoun refers clearly to a single specific and appropriate antecedent.

In Charlotte Brontë's *Jane Eyre,* she is a shy young woman that takes a job as governess. Her employer is a rude, brooding man named Rochester. He lives in a mysterious mansion, which contributes an eerie quality to Jane's experience. Eerier still are the fires, strange noises, and other unexplained happenings in the house; but Rochester refuses to discuss this. Eventually, they fall in love. On the day they are to be married, however, she learns that he has a wife hidden in the house. She is hopelessly insane and violent and must be guarded at all times, which explains his strange behaviour. Heartbroken, Jane leaves the house, and many years pass before they are reunited.

Note See page 304 for an exercise involving unclear pronoun reference along with sentence fragments, comma splices, and other sentence errors.

Chapter 13 Shifts

Inconsistencies in grammatical elements will confuse your readers and distort your meaning. For instance:

First draft

A bank commonly owes more to its customers than *is held* in reserve. *They kept* enough assets to meet reasonable withdrawals, but panicked customers may demand all their deposits. Then demands will exceed supplies, and *banks failed.* These days, *a person's* losses are not likely to be great because the government insures *your* deposits.

Revised

A bank commonly owes more to its customers than *it holds* in reserve.	*Holds* to match *owes*
It keeps enough assets to meet reasonable withdrawals, but panicked customers may demand all their deposits.	Singular *It* and present tense to match *bank . . . owes*
Then demands will exceed supplies, and *the bank will fail.*	Singular *bank* to match *bank;* future tense to match *will exceed*
These days, *customers'* losses are not likely to be great because the government insures *their* deposits.	Plural *customers'* to match *customers* *Their* to match *customers*

Shifts like those in the first draft are likely to occur while you are trying to piece together meaning during drafting. But you should straighten out your sentences during revision.

13a Keep a sentence or related sentences consistent in person and number.

Person in grammar refers to the distinction among the person talking (first person), the person spoken to (second person), and the person, object, or concept being talked about (third person). **Number** refers to the distinction between one (singular) and more than one (plural).

Shifts in person

Most shifts in person occur because we can refer to people in general, including our readers, either in the third person (*a person, one; people, they*) or in the second person (*you*).

People should not drive when *they* have been drinking.
One should not drive when *one* has been drinking.
You should not drive when *you* have been drinking.

Although any one of these possibilities is acceptable in an appropriate context, a mixture of them is inconsistent.

INCONSISTENT If a *person* works hard, *you* can accomplish a great deal.

REVISED If *you* work hard, *you* can accomplish a great deal.

REVISED If a *person* works hard, *he or she* can accomplish a great deal.

BETTER If *people* work hard, *they* can accomplish a great deal.

Shifts in number

Inconsistency in number occurs most often between a pronoun and its antecedent (see p. 234).

INCONSISTENT If a *student* does not understand a problem, *they* should consult the instructor.

REVISED If a *student* does not understand a problem, *he or she* should consult the instructor.

BETTER If *students* do not understand a problem, *they* should consult the instructor.

Inconsistency in number can also occur between other words (usually nouns) that relate to each other in meaning.

> INCONSISTENT All the *boys* have a good *reputation.*
>
> REVISED All the *boys* have good *reputations.*

The consistency in the revised sentence is called **logical agreement** because the nouns are consistent (the *boys* have *reputations,* not a single *reputation*).

shift
13b

Exercise 1
Revising: Shifts in person and number

Revise the following sentences to make them consistent in person and number.

Example:

A plumber will fix burst pipes, but they won't repair water-logged appliances.

Plumbers will fix burst pipes, but they won't repair water-logged appliances.

1. When a taxpayer is waiting to receive a tax refund from Revenue Canada, you begin to notice what time the mail carrier arrives.
2. If the taxpayer does not receive a refund cheque within six weeks of filing a return, they may not have followed the rules of Revenue Canada.
3. If a taxpayer does not include the Social Insurance Number on a return, you will have to wait for a refund.
4. When taxpayers do not file their return early, he will not get a refund quickly.
5. If one has made errors on the tax form, they might even be audited, thereby delaying a refund even longer.

13b Keep a sentence or related sentences consistent in tense and mood.

Shifts in tense

Within a sentence or from one sentence to another, certain changes in tense may be required to indicate changes in actual or relative time (see pp. 211–14). For example:

> Hoi *will graduate* from university twenty-three years after his father *arrived* in Canada.

But changes that are not required by meaning distract readers.

Unnecessary shifts between past and present in passages narrating a series of events are particularly confusing.

Inconsistent Immediately after Hoi *received* his degree, his father *laughed* with happiness. But his little brother *shouts* his nickname and *embarrasses* him.

Revised Immediately after Hoi *received* his degree, his father *laughed* with happiness. But his little brother *shouted* his nickname and *embarrassed* him.

The present tense is used to describe what an author has written, including the action in literature or a film.

Inconsistent The main character in the novel *suffers* psychologically because he *has* a clubfoot, but he eventually *triumphed* over his handicap.

Revised The main character in the novel *suffers* psychologically because he *has* a clubfoot, but he eventually *triumphs* over his handicap.

Shifts in mood

Shifts in the mood of verbs occur most frequently in directions when the writer moves between the imperative mood (*Unplug the appliance*) and the indicative mood (*You should unplug the appliance*). (See p. 216.) Directions are usually clearer and more concise in the imperative, as long as its use is consistent.

Inconsistent *Cook* the mixture slowly, and *you should stir* it until the sugar is dissolved.

Revised *Cook* the mixture slowly, and *stir* it until the sugar is dissolved.

Exercise 2
Revising: Shifts in tense and mood

Revise the following sentences to make them consistent in tense and mood.

Example:

Lynn ran to first, rounded the base, and keeps running until she slides into second.

Lynn ran to first, rounded the base, and *kept* running until she *slid* into second.

1. When your cholesterol count is too high, adjusting your diet and exercise level reduced it.
2. After you lowered your cholesterol rate, you decrease the chances of heart attack and stroke.
3. First eliminate saturated fats from your diet; then you should consume more whole grains and raw vegetables.

4. To avoid saturated fats, substitute turkey and chicken for beef, and you should use cholesterol-free margarine, salad dressing, and cooking oil.
5. A regular program of aerobic exercise, such as walking or swimming, improves your cholesterol rate and made you feel much healthier.

13c Keep a sentence or related sentences consistent in subject and voice.

When a verb is in the **active voice,** the subject names the actor: *Linda passed the peas.* When a verb is in the **passive voice,** the subject names the receiver of the action: *The peas were passed (by Linda).* (See pp. 218–20.)

A shift in voice may sometimes help focus the reader's attention on a single subject, as in *The candidate campaigned vigorously and was nominated on the first ballot.* However, most shifts in voice also involve shifts in subject. They are unnecessary and confusing.

INCONSISTENT — In the morning the *children rode* their bicycles; in the afternoon *their skateboards were given* a good workout.

REVISED — In the morning the *children rode* their bicycles; in the afternoon *they gave* their skateboards a good workout.

INCONSISTENT — As *we looked* out over the ocean, *ships could be seen* in the distance.

REVISED — As *we looked* out over the ocean, *we could see* ships in the distance.

Exercise 3
Revising: Shifts in subject and voice

Make the following sentences consistent in subject and voice.

Example:

At the reunion they ate hot dogs and volleyball was played.
At the reunion they ate hot dogs and *played volleyball.*

1. If students learn how to study efficiently, much better grades will be made on tests.
2. Conscientious students begin to prepare for tests immediately after the first class is attended.
3. Before each class all reading assignments are completed, and the students outline the material and answer any study questions.
4. In class they listen carefully and good notes are taken.

5. Questions are asked by the students when they do not understand the professor.

Exercise 4
Revising: Shifts

Revise the following paragraph to eliminate unnecessary shifts in person, number, tense, mood, and voice.

Driving in snow need not be dangerous if you practise a few rules. First, one should avoid fast starts, which prevent the wheels from gaining traction and may result in the car's getting stuck. Second, drive more slowly than usual, and you should pay attention to the feel of the car: if the steering seemed unusually loose or the wheels did not seem to be grabbing the road, slow down. Third, avoid fast stops, which lead to skids. One should be alert for other cars and intersections that may necessitate that the brakes be applied suddenly. If you need to slow down, the car's momentum can be reduced by downshifting as well as by applying the brakes. When braking, don't press the pedal to the floor, but it should be pumped in short bursts. If you feel the car skidding, the brakes should be released and the wheel should be turned into the direction of the skid, and then the brakes should be pumped again. If one repeated these motions, the skid would be stopped and the speed of the car would be reduced.

Note See page 304 for an exercise involving shifts along with sentence fragments, comma splices, and other sentence errors.

Chapter 14

Misplaced and Dangling Modifiers

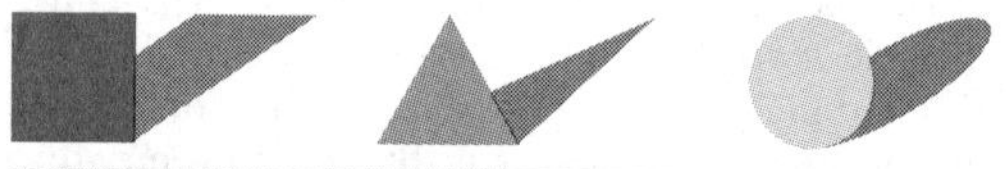

In reading a sentence in English, we depend principally on the arrangement of the words to tell us how they are related. In writing, we may create confusion if we fail to connect modifiers to the words they modify.

MISPLACED MODIFIERS

A modifier is **misplaced** if readers can't easily connect it to the word it modifies. Misplaced modifiers may be awkward, confusing, or even unintentionally funny.

14a Place modifiers where they will clearly modify the words intended.

Readers tend to link a modifying word, phrase, or clause to the nearest word it could modify: *I saw a man in a green hat.* Thus the writer must place the phrase so that it clearly modifies the intended word and not some other.

CONFUSING He served steak to the men *on paper plates.*

REVISED He served the men steak *on paper plates.*

CONFUSING Many dogs are killed by automobiles and trucks *roaming unleashed.*

REVISED Many dogs *roaming unleashed* are killed by automobiles and trucks.

CONFUSING This is the only chocolate chip cookie in a bag that tastes like Mom's. [Actual advertisement.]

REVISED This is the only *bagged* (or *packaged*) chocolate chip cookie that tastes like Mom's.

Exercise 1
Revising: Misplaced clauses and phrases

Revise the following sentences so that prepositional phrases and subordinate clauses clearly modify the words they are intended to modify.

Example:

I came to enjoy flying over time.
Over time I came to enjoy flying.

1. During times of war, women contributed much as defenders, healers, and aids to military strategy in the building of Canada of great value.
2. Françoise-Marie Jacquelin, known as Madame de la Tour, and Marie-Madeleine Jarret de Verchères defended against attackers and cared for the wounded in New France along with others.
3. During the siege of Quebec in 1629, Marie Hébert nursed the sick and helped to ensure the survival of the colony with other women.
4. During the American Revolution, Molly Brant worked as a spy and advisor to the British secretly.
5. Most Canadians know the story of Laura Secord during the War of 1812 with her cow who carried messages through enemy lines.

14b Place limiting modifiers carefully.

Limiting modifiers include *almost, even, exactly, hardly, just, merely, nearly, only, scarcely,* and *simply.* They modify the expressions that immediately follow them. Compare the uses of *just* in the following three sentences:

The instructor *just nodded* to me as he came in.

The instructor nodded *just to me* as he came in.
The instructor nodded to me *just as he came in.*

In speech several of these modifiers frequently occur before the verb, regardless of the words they are intended to modify. In writing, however, these modifiers should fall immediately before the word or word group they modify to avoid any ambiguity.

UNCLEAR They *only* saw each other during meals.

REVISED They saw *only* each other during meals.

REVISED They saw each other *only* during meals.

Exercise 2
Using limiting modifiers

Use each of the following limiting modifiers in two versions of the same sentence.

Example:

only
He is the *only* one I like.
He is the one *only* I like.

1. almost
2. even
3. hardly
4. simply
5. nearly

14c Make each modifier refer to only one grammatical element.

A modifier can modify only *one* element in a sentence—the subject, the verb, or some other element. A **squinting modifier** seems confusingly to refer to either of two words.

SQUINTING Snipers who fired on the soldiers *often* escaped capture.

CLEAR Snipers who *often* fired on the soldiers escaped capture.

CLEAR Snipers who fired on the soldiers escaped capture *often.*

When an adverb modifies an entire main clause, as in the last example, it can usually be moved to the beginning of the sentence: *Often, snipers who fired on the soldiers escaped capture.*

Exercise 3
Revising: Squinting modifiers

Revise each sentence twice so that the squinting modifier applies clearly first to one element and then to the other.

Example:

The work that he hoped would satisfy him completely frustrated him.

The work that he hoped would *completely* satisfy him frustrated him.

The work that he hoped would satisfy him frustrated him *completely.*

1. People who sunbathe often can damage their skin.
2. Sunbathers who apply a sunscreen frequently block some of the sun's harmful ultraviolet rays.
3. Men and women who lie out in the sun much of the time have leathery, dry skin.
4. Doctors tell sunbathers when they are older they risk skin cancer.
5. People who stay out of the sun usually will have better skin and fewer chances of skin cancer.

14d Keep subjects, verbs, and objects together.

The movement from subject to verb to object is so familiar in English that modifiers inserted between these elements can be awkward or confusing.

A subject and verb may be separated by an adjective that modifies the subject: *The wreckers who were to demolish the house started work early.* But an adverb of more than a word usually stops the flow of the sentence:

Awkward The *wreckers,* [subject] soon after they began demolishing the house, [adverb] *discovered* [verb] a large box of coins.

Revised Soon after they began demolishing the house, [adverb] the *wreckers* [subject] *discovered* [verb] a large box of coins.

A modifier between a verb and its direct object is always awkward.

Awkward Three wreckers *lifted,* [verb] with great effort, [adverb] *the heavy box.* [object]

Revised With great effort, [adverb] three wreckers *lifted* [verb] *the heavy box.* [object]

14e Keep parts of infinitives or verb phrases together.

An **infinitive** consists of the marker *to* plus the plain form of a verb: *to produce, to enjoy.* The two parts of the infinitive are widely regarded as a grammatical unit that should not be split.

infinitive

AWKWARD Environment Canada expected temperatures *to* not *rise.*

infinitive

REVISED Environment Canada expected temperatures not *to rise.*

A split infinitive may sometimes be natural and preferable, though it may still bother some readers.

infinitive

Several Canadian industries expect *to* more than *triple* their use of robots.

Here the split infinitive is more economical than the alternatives, such as *Several Canadian industries expect to increase their use of robots by more than three times.*

A **verb phrase** consists of a helping verb plus a main verb, as in *will call, was going, had been writing* (see p. 199). We regularly insert single-word adverbs in them: *Joshua had almost completed the assignment* (see the next page). But when longer adverbs interrupt verb phrases, the result is almost always awkward.

helping verb — adverb — main verb

AWKWARD Many students *had,* by spending most of their time on the assignment, *completed* it.

adverb — verb phrase

REVISED By spending most of their time on the assignment, many students *had completed* it.

verb phrase — adverb

REVISED Many students *had completed* the assignment by spending most of their time on it.

Exercise 4

Revising: Separated sentence parts

Revise the following sentences to connect separate parts (subject-predicate, verb-object, verb phrase, infinitive).

Example:

Most children have by the time they are seven lost a tooth.
By the time they are seven, most children have lost a tooth.

1. The letter carrier returned, after two weeks, the undelievered letter.

2. The lieutenant had given, although he was later accused of dereliction of duty, the correct orders.
3. The girls loved to daily sun beside the pool.
4. Ballet will, if the present interest continues to grow, be one of the country's most popular arts.
5. The beavers, when the new housing construction began, abandoned their dam.

14f Position adverbs with care. ESL

Most adverbs may fall before or after the verb or at the beginning or end of the sentence. One exception is the adverb of frequency, such as *always, never, often, rarely, seldom,* and *sometimes*. These adverbs usually appear before the verb or between the helping verb and the main verb in a verb phrase.

verb phrase adverb
Awkward Robots *have put* sometimes humans out of work.

helping verb adverb main verb
Revised Robots *have* sometimes *put* humans out of work.

adverb verb phrase
Revised Sometimes robots *have put* humans out of work.

Adverbs of frequency always follow the verb *be*.

adverb verb
Awkward Robots often *are* helpful to workers.

verb adverb
Revised Robots *are* often helpful to workers.

When an adverb modifies an adjective or another adverb, it usually falls just before the modified word.

adjective adverb
Awkward In automobile manufacturing, robots have been useful especially.

adverb adjective
Revised In automobile manufacturing, robots have been especially useful.

14g Arrange adjectives appropriately. ESL

English follows distinctive rules for arranging two or three adjectives before a noun. (A string of more than three adjectives before a noun is rare.) The order depends on the meaning of the adjectives, as indicated in the following table.

Determiner	Opinion	Size or shape	Age	Colour	Origin	Material	Noun used as adjective	Noun
many			new				state	laws
one		large				glass	bud	vase
	striking			green	Thai			birds
a	fine				German			camera
this		square				wooden		table
all			recent				business	reports
the				blue		litmus		paper

See page 368 for guidelines on punctuating two or more adjectives before a noun.

Exercise 5
Revising: Placement of adverbs and adjectives ESL

Revise the sentences below to correct the positions of adverbs or adjectives. If a sentence is already correct as given, circle the number preceding it.

Example:

Gasoline high prices affect usually car sales.
High gasoline prices *usually* affect car sales.

1. Some years ago Detroit cars often were singled out for praise.
2. Luxury large cars especially were prized.
3. Then a serious oil shortage led drivers to value small, economical cars with low consumption.
4. Despite gas low prices, consumers have not returned to American large cars.
5. In some areas of the country, seldom one sees a large car.

DANGLING MODIFIERS

14h Relate dangling modifiers to their sentences.

A **dangling modifier** does not sensibly modify anything in its sentence.

DANGLING *Passing the building,* the vandalism became visible. [The modifying phrase seems to describe *vandalism,* but vandalism does not pass buildings. Who was passing the building? Who saw the vandalism?]

Dangling modifiers usually introduce sentences, contain a verb form, and imply but do not name a subject: in the example above, the implied subject is the someone or something passing the building. Readers assume that this implied subject is the same as the subject of the sentence (*vandalism* in the example). When it is not, the modifier "dangles" unconnected to the rest of the sentence.

The modifiers most likely to dangle are listed and illustrated below.

- Participial phrases:

  DANGLING *Passing the building,* the vandalism became visible.

  REVISED *As we passed* the building, the vandalism became visible.

- Infinitive phrases:

  DANGLING *To understand the causes,* vandalism has been extensively investigated.

  REVISED To understand the causes, *researchers have* extensively *investigated* vandalism.

- Prepositional phrases in which the object of the preposition is a gerund:

  DANGLING *After studying the problem,* vandals are now thought to share certain characteristics.

  REVISED After studying the problem, *researchers think* that vandals share certain characteristics.

Identifying and revising dangling modifiers

- If the modifier lacks a subject of its own (e.g., *when in diapers*), identify what it describes.
- Verify that what the modifier describes is in fact the subject of the main clause. If it is not, the modifier is probably dangling.
- Revise a dangling modifier (*a*) by recasting it with a subject of its own or (*b*) by changing the subject of the main clause.

  DANGLING *When in diapers,* my mother remarried. (modifier: *When in diapers*; subject: my mother)

  REVISION A When *I was* in diapers, my mother remarried.

  REVISION B When in diapers, *I attended my mother's second wedding.*

- Elliptical clauses in which the subject and perhaps the verb are omitted:

DANGLING *When destructive,* researchers have learned that vandals are more likely to be in groups.

REVISED When *vandals are* destructive, researchers have learned that *they* are more likely to be in groups.

Dangling modifiers are especially likely when the verb in the main clause is in the **passive voice** instead of the **active voice**—that is, when the verb expresses what is *done to* the subject instead of what the subject *does* (see p. 218). The passive voice appears in the second and third examples above: *vandalism has been investigated; vandals are thought.* The revisions recast the verbs and subjects as active: *researchers have investigated; researchers think.*

Note that a modifier may be dangling even when the sentence elsewhere contains a word the modifier might seem to describe, such as *vandals* below:

DANGLING *When destructive,* researchers have learned that vandals are more likely to be in groups.

In addition, a dangling modifier may fall at the end of a sentence:

DANGLING The vandalism was visible *passing the building.*

Revising dangling modifiers

Revise most dangling modifiers in one of two ways, depending on what you want to emphasize in the sentence.

- Change the subject of the main clause to a word the modifier properly describes.

DANGLING *To express themselves,* graffiti decorate walls.

REVISED To express themselves, *some youths decorate* walls with graffiti.

- Rewrite the dangling modifier as a complete clause with its own stated subject and verb.

REVISED *Because some youths need to express themselves,* graffiti decorate walls.

Exercise 6
Revising: Dangling modifiers

Revise the following sentences to eliminate any dangling modifiers. Each item has more than one possible answer.

Example:

Driving north, the vegetation became increasingly sparse.

Driving north, *we noticed* that the vegetation became increasingly sparse.

As we drove north, the vegetation became increasingly sparse.

1. After many years of playing hockey, Jacques Plante's skill at the game led to a coaching job with the Quebec Nordiques.
2. While still very young, his skills led him to the NHL in 1951.
3. To aid his ability to keep the puck out of the net, his original roaming style of play developed.
4. Many scars marred Plante's face after being struck with both pucks and sticks.
5. Although not severely injured when struck by a puck in 1959, the first protective face mask to be used in the NHL was worn by Plante.

Exercise 7
Sentence combining: Placing modifiers

Combine each pair of sentences below into a single sentence by rewriting one as a modifier. Make sure the modifier applies clearly to the appropriate word. You will have to add, delete, and rearrange words, and you may find that more than one answer is possible in each case.

Example:

Bob demanded a hearing from the faculty. Bob wanted to appeal the decision.

Wanting to appeal the decision, Bob demanded a hearing from the faculty.

1. Evening falls in the Central American rain forests. The tungara frogs begin their croaking chorus.
2. Male tungara frogs croak loudly at night. The "songs" they sing are designed to attract female frogs.
3. But predators also hear the croaking. They gather to feast on the frogs.
4. The predators are lured by their croaking dinners. The frogs are prey to bullfrogs, snakes, bats, and opossums.
5. The frogs hope to mate. Their nightly chorus can result in death instead.

Exercise 8
Revising: Misplaced and dangling modifiers

Revise the following paragraph to eliminate any misplaced or dangling modifiers.

Central American tungara frogs silence several nights a week their mating croaks. When not croaking, the chance that the frogs will be eaten by predators is reduced. The frogs seem to fully believe in "safety in numbers." They more than likely will croak along with a large group rather than by themselves. By forgoing croaking on some nights, the frogs' behaviour prevents the species from "croaking."

NOTE See page 304 for an exercise involving misplaced and dangling modifiers along with other sentence errors.

Chapter 15 Mixed and Incomplete Sentences

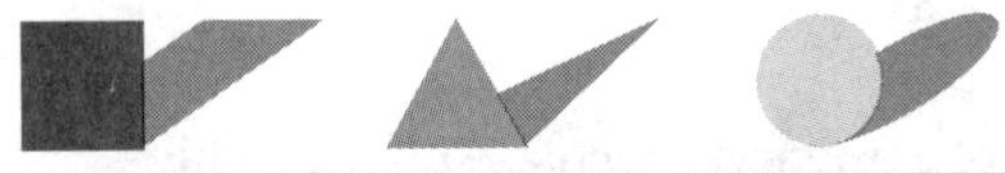

MIXED SENTENCES

A **mixed sentence** contains two or more parts that are incompatible—that is, the parts do not fit together. The misfit may be in grammar or in meaning.

15a Untangle sentences that are mixed in grammar.

Sentences mixed in grammar combine two or more incompatible grammatical structures.

Make sure subject and verb fit together grammatically.

A mixed sentence may occur when you start a sentence with one plan and end it with another.

MIXED In all her efforts to please others got her into trouble.

This mixed sentence makes a prepositional phrase work as the subject of *got,* but prepositional phrases almost never function as sentence subjects. The sentence needs a new subject for *got.*

Revised In all her efforts to please others, *she* got into trouble. [subject: *she*]

Revised *All her efforts* to please others got her into trouble. [subject: *All her efforts* to please others]

Here is another example:

Mixed Although he was seen with a convicted thief does not make him a thief.

Revised *That* he was seen with a convicted thief does not make him a thief. [subject: *That* he was seen with a convicted thief]

Revised Although he was seen with a convicted thief, *he is* not necessarily a thief. [subject + verb: *he is*]

2 State parts of sentences, such as subjects, only once. ESL

In some languages other than English, certain parts of sentences may be repeated. These include the subject in any kind of clause or an object or adverb in an adjective clause. In English, however, these parts are stated only once in a clause.

Repetition of subject

You may be tempted to restate a subject as a pronoun before the verb. But the subject needs stating only once in its clause.

Faulty The *liquid it* reached a temperature of 100°C.

Revised The *liquid* reached a temperature of 100°C.

Faulty *Gases* in the liquid *they* escaped.

Revised *Gases* in the liquid escaped.

Repetition in an adjective clause

Adjective clauses begin with *who, whom, whose, which, that, where,* and *when.* The beginning word replaces another word: the subject (*He is the person who called*), an object of a verb or preposition (*He is the person whom I mentioned*), or a preposition and pronoun (*He knows the office where [in which] the conference will occur*).

Do not state the word being replaced in an adjective clause.

Faulty The technician *whom* the test depended on *her* was burned. [*Whom* should replace *her.*]

Revised The technician *whom* the test depended on was burned.

In adjective clauses beginning with *where* or *when,* no adverb such as *there* or *then* is needed.

FAULTY Gases escaped at a moment *when* the technician was unprepared *then.*

REVISED Gases escaped at a moment *when* the technician was unprepared.

NOTE *Whom, which,* and similar words are sometimes omitted but are still understood by the reader. Thus the word being replaced should not be stated.

FAULTY Accidents rarely happen to technicians the lab has trained *them.* [*Whom* is understood: . . . *technicians whom the lab has trained.*]

REVISED Accidents rarely happen to technicians the lab has trained.

15b Match subjects and predicates in meaning.

In a sentence with mixed meaning, the subject is said to be or do something it cannot logically be or do. Such a mixture is sometimes called **faulty predication** because the predicate conflicts with the subject.

Illogical equation with be

When a form of *be* connects a subject and a word that describes the subject (a complement), the subject and complement must be logically related.

MIXED A *compromise* between the city and the country would be the ideal *place* to live.

REVISED A *community* that offered the best qualities of both city and country would be the ideal *place* to live.

Is when, is where

Definitions require nouns on both sides of *be.* Definition clauses beginning with *when* or *where* are common in speech but should be avoided in writing.

MIXED An *examination* is *when you are tested* on what you know.

REVISED An *examination* is a *test* of what you know.

Reason is because

The commonly heard construction *The reason is because . . .* is redundant since *because* means "for the reason that."

Mixed The *reason* the temple requests donations *is because* the school needs expansion.

Revised The *reason* the temple requests donations *is that* the school needs expansion.

Revised The temple requests donations *because* the school needs expansion.

Other mixed meanings

Faulty predications are not confined to sentences with *be.*

Mixed The *use* of emission controls *was created* to reduce air pollution.

Revised Emission *controls were created* to reduce air pollution.

Mixed The *area* of financial mismanagement *poses* a threat to small businesses.

Revised Financial *mismanagement poses* a threat to small businesses.

In some mixed sentences the combination of faults is so confusing that the writer has little choice but to start over.

Mixed My long-range goal is through law school and government work I hope to deal with those problems I deal with more effectively.

Possible My long-range goal is to go to law school and then work in government so that I can deal more effectively with problems I face.

Exercise 1
Revising: Sentences mixed in grammar or meaning

Revise the following sentences so that their parts fit together both in grammar and in meaning. Each item has more than one possible answer.

Example:

When they found out how expensive pianos are is why they were discouraged.

They were discouraged *because* they found out how expensive pianos are.

When they found out how expensive pianos are, *they* were discouraged.

1. A hurricane is when the winds in a tropical depression rotate counterclockwise at more than 120 kilometres per hour.
2. Because hurricanes can destroy so many lives and so much property is why people fear them.
3. Through high winds, storm surge, floods, and tornadoes is how a hurricane can kill thousands of people.
4. Among the hurricanes in history, they have become less deadly since 1950.
5. The reason for the lower death rates is because improved communication systems and weather satellites warn people early enough to escape the hurricane.

Exercise 2
Revising: Repeated sentence parts ESL

Revise the following sentences to eliminate any unnecessary repetition of sentence parts.

Example:

Over 79 percent of North Americans they have heard of global warming.

Over 79 percent of *North Americans have* heard of global warming.

1. Global warming it is caused by the gradual erosion of the ozone layer that protects the earth from the sun.
2. Scientists who study this problem they say that the primary causes of erosion are the use of fossil fuels and the reduction of forests.
3. Many nonscientists they mistakenly believe that aerosol spray cans are the primary cause of erosion.
4. One scientist whom others respect him argues that North Americans have effectively reduced their use of aerosol sprays.
5. He argues that we will stop global warming only when the public learns the real causes then.

INCOMPLETE SENTENCES

The most serious kind of incomplete sentence is the fragment (see Chapter 10). But sentences are also incomplete when they omit one or more words needed for clarity.

15c Omissions from compound constructions should be consistent with grammar or idiom.

In both speech and writing, we commonly omit words not necessary for meaning, such as those in parentheses in the following examples. Notice that all the sentences contain compound constructions.

By 2000 automobile-emission standards will be tougher, and by 2010 (automobile-emission standards will be) tougher still.

Some cars will run on electricity; some (will run) on methane.

Environmentalists have hopes for alternative fuels and (for) public transportation.

Such omissions are possible only when you omit words that are common to all the parts of a compound construction. When the parts differ in either grammar or idiom, all words must be included in all parts.

One new car *gets* ten kilometres per litre; some old cars *get* as little as five kilometres per litre. [One verb is singular, the other plural.]

Environmentalists *were* invited to submit proposals and *were* eager to do so. [Each *were* has a different grammatical function: the first is a helping verb; the second is a linking verb.]

They believe *in* and work *for* fuel conservation. [Idiom requires different prepositions with *believe* and *work*.]

Notice that in the sentence *My brother and friend moved to Victoria,* the omission of *my* before *friend* indicates that *brother* and *friend* are the same person. If two different persons are meant, the modifier or article must be repeated: *My brother and my friend moved to Victoria.*

(See p. 456 for a list of English idioms and pp. 319–22 for a discussion of grammatical parallelism.)

15d All comparisons should be complete and logical.

Comparisons make statements about the relation between two or more things, as in *Dogs are more intelligent than cats.*

1 State a comparison fully enough to ensure clarity.

A comparison must not omit words needed to clarify meaning.

Unclear Car makers worry about their industry more than environmentalists.

Clear Car makers worry about their industry more than environmentalists *do*.

Clear Car makers worry about their industry more than *they worry about* environmentalists.

2 The items being compared should in fact be comparable.

A comparison is logical only if it compares items that can sensibly be compared.

Illogical The cost of an electric car is greater than a gasoline-powered car. [Illogically compares a cost and a car.]

Revised The cost of an electric car is greater than *the cost of* (or *that of*) a gasoline-powered car.

3 Use *any* or *any other* appropriately in comparisons.

Comparing a person or thing with all others in the same group creates two units: (1) the individual person or thing and (2) all *other* persons or things in the group. The two units need to be distinguished.

Illogical Montreal is larger than *any* city in Quebec. [Since Montreal is itself a city in Quebec, the sentence seems to say that Montreal is larger than itself.]

Logical Montreal is larger than *any other city* in Quebec. [Adding *other* excludes Montreal from the group of the province's other cities.]

Comparing a person or thing with the members of a *different* group assumes separate units to begin with. The two units do not need to be distinguished with *other.*

Illogical Montreal is larger than *any other* city in Manitoba. [The cities in Manitoba constitute a group to which Montreal does not belong.]

Logical Montreal is larger than *any* city in Manitoba. [Omitting the word *other* makes a separate group of the Manitoban cities.]

4 Comparisons should state what is being compared.

Brand X gets clothes *whiter.* [Whiter than what?]
Brand Y is so much *better.* [Better than what?]

15e Include all needed articles, prepositions, and other words.

In haste or carelessness we sometimes omit small words such as articles and prepositions that are needed for clarity.

INCOMPLETE Regular payroll deductions are a type painless savings. You hardly notice missing amounts, and after period of years the contributions can add a large total.

REVISED Regular payroll deductions are a type *of* painless savings. You hardly notice *the* missing amounts, and after *a* period of years the contributions can add *up to* a large total.

Writers whose first language is not English often omit the articles *a, an,* and *the* because their native languages use such words differently or not at all. For guidelines on when to use articles, see pages 247–50.

Be careful not to omit *that* when the omission is confusing.

INCOMPLETE The personnel director expects many employees will benefit from the plan. [*Many employees* seems to be the object of *expects.*]

REVISED The personnel director expects *that* many employees will benefit from the plan.

Attentive proofreading is the only insurance against the kind of omissions described in this section. *Proofread all your papers carefully.* See page 67 for tips.

Exercise 3
Revising: Incomplete sentences

Revise the following sentences so that they are complete, logical, and clear. Some items have more than one possible answer.

Example:

Our house is closer to the courthouse than the subway stop.

Our house is closer to the courthouse than *it is* to the subway stop.

Our house is closer to the courthouse than the subway stop *is.*

1. I get along with my parents better than my sister.
2. Our M.P. not only believes but works for tax reform.
3. Wally believed people who came to him with their problems were using him.

4. His tip was larger than any customer I ever waited on.
5. With an altitude of 5950 metres, the Yukon's Mount Logan is higher than any mountain in Canada.

Exercise 4
Revising: Mixed and incomplete sentences

Revise the following paragraph to eliminate mixed or incomplete constructions.

The Halifax Citadel has overlooked city and its natural harbour for over 130 years. When it was being constructed in the nineteenth century was when design problems were discovered. Because they had to deal with structural problems was why the Royal Engineers took almost thirty years to build it. At a cost exceeding $242 000, the citadel was more expensive than any Canadian fortress. Immediately, however, the introduction of rifled artillery was why the installation became obsolete. The solution of new artillery was installed, and the Citadel housed British garrison until 1906.

inc
15e

NOTE See the next page for an exercise involving mixed and incomplete sentences along with sentence fragments, comma splices, and other sentence errors.

Exercise on Chapters 10–15
Revising: Clear sentences

Clarify meaning in the following paragraphs by revising sentence fragments, comma splices, fused sentences, problems with pronoun reference, awkward shifts, misplaced and dangling modifiers, and mixed and incomplete sentences. Most errors can be corrected in more than one way.

Many people who are physically challenged. They have accomplished much. Which proves that they are not "handicapped." Confined to wheelchairs, successful careers have been forged by Bob Sampson, Stephen Hawking, and Rick Hansen. Despite Sampson's muscular dystrophy, he has earned a law degree he has also worked for United Airlines for more than thirty years. Stephen Hawking most famous for his book *A Brief History of Time.* Unable to speak, Hawking's voice synthesizer allows him to dictate his books and conduct public lectures. And teach mathematics classes at Cambridge University. Rick Hansen went around the world in his wheelchair his theme was the Man in Motion. His tour raised awareness of the capabilities of the physically challenged. For everyone, including the challenged. Hansen was accorded a hero's welcome in his hometown, ending the tour in Vancouver.

Franklin D. Roosevelt, Ann Adams, and Itzhak Perlman all refused let polio destroy their lives. Indeed, Roosevelt led the United States during two of the worst periods of its history as president. The Great Depression and World War II. Reassured by his strong, firm voice, Roosevelt inspired hope and determination in the American public. Ann Adams, who was talented in art before polio paralyzed her, knew she had to continue to be one. Having retrained herself to draw with a pencil grasped in her teeth. She produces sketches of children and pets. That were turned into greeting cards. The profits from the cards sustained her. Roosevelt and Adams were stricken with polio when they were adults; Itzhak Perlman when a child. He was unable to play sports, instead he studied the violin, now many think he is greater than any violinist in the world.

Part IV

Effective Sentences

Chapter 16

Using Coordination and Subordination

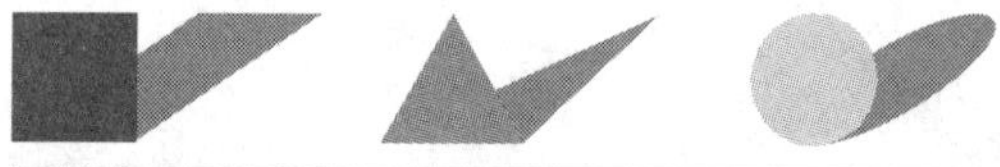

To help readers see the relative importance of ideas, you coordinate or subordinate information in sentences.

- **Coordination** gives ideas equal stress (see pp. 178–82).

  Car and *medical* insurance are modern necessities.
  Car insurance is costly, but *medical insurance* seems *a luxury.*

- **Subordination** de-emphasizes less important ideas so that the more important ones stand out (see pp. 163–77).

  Many people *applying for insurance* are jolted by the cost.
  Because accidents and thefts are frequent, car insurance is expensive.

16a Coordinating to relate equal ideas

By linking equally important information with coordinating conjunctions or conjunctive adverbs, you can emphasize the relations for readers. Compare the following passages.

STRING OF SIMPLE SENTENCES

We should not rely so heavily on oil. Coal and uranium are also overused. We have a substantial energy resource in the moving waters of our rivers. Smaller streams add to the total volume of water. The resource renews itself. Coal and oil are irreplaceable. Uranium is also irreplaceable. The cost of water does not increase much over time. The costs of coal, oil, and uranium rise dramatically.

Principal ways to coordinate and subordinate information in sentences

Use **coordination** to relate ideas of equal importance (16a).

1. Link main clauses with a comma and a coordinating conjunction: *and, but, or, nor, for, so, yet* (p. 178).

   The fortress of Louisbourg is now restored, *but* fifty years ago it was in ruins.

2. Relate main clauses with a semicolon alone or a semicolon and a conjunctive adverb: *however, indeed, thus,* etc. (p. 180).

   The remains of some buildings still existed; *however,* they were piles of stones overgrown with brush.

3. Within clauses, link words and phrases with a coordinating conjunction: *and, but, or, nor* (p. 178).

   The people *and* officials of Cape Breton were indifferent to Louisbourg *or* took its ruin for granted.

Use **subordination** to de-emphasize ideas (16b).

1. Use a subordinate clause beginning with a subordinating conjunction: *although, because, if, whereas,* etc. (p. 178).

   Although the fortress of Louisbourg became a national historic site in 1928, there was no public support for reconstruction.

2. Use a subordinate clause beginning with a relative pronoun: *who, whoever, which, that* (p. 172).

   The first strong step was taken by Parks Canada, *which began to rebuild the fortress in 1961.*

3. Use a prepositional, verbal, or absolute phrase.

   Like most national historic sites, Louisbourg is protected by Parks Canada. [Prepositional phrase. See p. 164.]

   Parks Canada, *supervising many popular tourist sites,* is a highly visible government agency. [Verbal phrase. See p. 167.]

   Visitors can always learn something at National Parks, *the guides being helpful and informative.* [Absolute phrase. See p. 171.]

4. Use an appositive (p. 176).

   A branch of the Department of the Environment, Parks Canada also runs Pacific Rim and other wilderness parks.

5. Use a modifying word.

   At the *grey stone* fortress, guides dressed in *eighteenth-century* costumes protect the *reconstructed* Louisbourg from carelessness and vandalism.

Ideas coordinated

We should not rely so heavily on coal, oil, and uranium, for we have a substantial energy resource in the moving waters of our rivers and streams. Coal, oil, and uranium are irreplaceable and thus subject to dramatic cost increases; water, however, is self-renewing and more stable in cost.

The information in both passages is essentially the same, but the second is shorter and considerably easier to read and understand because it builds connections among coordinate ideas.

Punctuating coordinated words, phrases, and clauses

Most coordinated words, phrases, and subordinate clauses are not punctuated with commas (see 21j-2). The exceptions are items in a series and coordinate adjectives.

We rely heavily on *coal, oil, and uranium.* [A series; see 21f-1.]
Dirty, unhealthy air is one result. [Coordinate adjectives; see 21f-2.]

In a sentence consisting of two main clauses, punctuation depends on whether a coordinating conjunction, a conjunctive adverb, or no connecting word links the clauses.

Oil is irreplaceable, *but* water is self-renewing. [See 21a.]
Oil is irreplaceable; *however,* water is self-renewing. [See 22b.]
Oil is irreplaceable; water is self-renewing. [See 22a.]

1 Using coordination effectively

A string of coordinated elements—especially main clauses—creates the same effect as a string of simple sentences: it obscures the relative importance of ideas and details.

Excessive coordination We were near the end of the trip, and the storm kept getting worse, and the snow and ice covered the windshield, and I could hardly see the road ahead, and I knew I should stop, but I kept on driving, and once I barely missed a truck.

Such passages need editing to stress the important points (*the storm kept getting worse* and *I kept on driving*) and to de-emphasize the less important information.

Revised As we neared the end of the trip, *the storm kept getting worse,* covering the windshield with snow and ice until I could barely see the road ahead. Even though I knew I should stop, *I kept on driving,* once barely missing a truck.

So is often overused as a connector.

EXCESSIVE COORDINATION — The experience was a frightening one, so I am afraid to drive in bad weather, so I had to leave my job, so now I work closer to home.

REVISED — The experience was so frightening that I am afraid to drive in bad weather and had to leave my job for one closer to home.

2 Coordinating logically

Coordinated sentence elements should be logically equal and related, and the relation between them should be the one expressed by the connecting word. If either principle is violated, the result is **faulty coordination.**

FAULTY — John Stuart Mill was a nineteenth-century utilitarian, and he believed that actions should be judged by their usefulness or by the happiness they cause. [The two clauses are not separate and equal: the second expands on the first by explaining what a utilitarian such as Mill believed.]

REVISED — John Stuart Mill, *a nineteenth-century utilitarian,* believed that actions should be judged by their usefulness or by the happiness they cause.

FAULTY — Mill is recognized as a utilitarian, and he did not found the utilitarian school of philosophy. [The two clauses seem to contrast, requiring *but* or *yet* between them.]

REVISED — Mill is recognized as a utilitarian, *but* he did not found the utilitarian school of philosophy.

Sometimes faulty coordination occurs because the writer omits necessary information.

FAULTY — Jeremy Bentham founded the utilitarian school, and Mill was precocious. [The two clauses seem unrelated.]

REVISED — Jeremy Bentham founded the utilitarian school *before Mill was born,* and Mill *joined at the precocious age of twenty.*

coord 16a

Exercise 1
Sentence combining: Coordination

Combine sentences in the following passages to coordinate related ideas in the way that seems most effective to you. You will have to supply coordinating conjunctions or conjunctive adverbs and the appropriate punctuation.

1. Many chronic misspellers do not have the time to master spelling rules. They may not have the motivation. They rely on dictionaries to catch misspellings. Most dictionaries list words under their correct spellings. One kind of dictionary is de-

signed for chronic misspellers. It lists each word under its common *mis*spellings. It then provides the correct spelling. It also provides the definition.

2. Henry Hudson was an English explorer. He captained ships for the Dutch East India Company. On a voyage in 1610 he passed by Greenland. He sailed into a great bay in today's northern Canada. He thought he and his sailors could winter there. The cold was terrible. Food ran out. The sailors mutinied. The sailors cast Hudson adrift in a small boat. Eight others were also in the boat. Hudson and his companions perished.

Exercise 2
Revising: Excessive or faulty coordination

Revise the following sentences to eliminate excessive or faulty coordination. Relate ideas effectively by adding or subordinating information or by forming more than one sentence. Each item has more than one possible answer.

Example:

My dog barks, and I have to move out of my apartment.

Because my dog's barking *disturbs my neighbours,* I have to move out of my apartment.

1. The candidate was a New Democrat, and she disagreed with both the Conservative and the Liberal.
2. He is almost always cheerful, and he has few friends.
3. The dean was furious, and she let the police know it, but they refused to listen, and they began patrolling the campus anyway.
4. The dogs escaped from the pen because the keeper forgot to secure the latch, and the dogs wanted freedom, and they got it by running away, and it took the rest of the day to find them.
5. The weather in March is cold and rainy, but sometimes it is warm and sunny, and the inconsistency makes it impossible to plan outdoor activities, yet everyone wants to be outdoors after the long winter.

16b Subordinating to distinguish main ideas

With **subordination** you use words or word groups to indicate that some elements in a sentence are less important than others. In the following sentence, it is difficult to tell what is most important:

Excessive coordination	In recent years computer prices have dropped, and production costs have dropped more slowly, and computer manufacturers have had to contend with shrinking profits.

The following rewrite places the point of the sentence (shrinking profits) in the main clause and reduces the rest of the information to a subordinate clause:

REVISED *Because* production costs have dropped more slowly than prices in recent years, computer manufacturers have had to contend with shrinking profits.

No rules can specify what information in a sentence you should make primary and what you should subordinate; the decision will depend on your meaning. But, in general, you should consider using subordinate structures for details of time, cause, condition, concession, purpose, and identification (size, location, and the like). Consider the use of subordinate clauses in the following pairs of examples. (Some appropriate subordinating conjunctions and relative pronouns are listed in parentheses. See p. 172 for more on subordinate clauses.)

TIME (*after, before, since, until, when, while*)

The mine explosion killed six workers. The owners adopted safety measures.

After the mine explosion killed six workers, the owners adopted safety measures.

CAUSE (*because, since*)

Jones had been without work for six months. He was having trouble paying his bills.

Because Jones had been without work for six months, he was having trouble paying his bills.

CONDITION (*if, provided, since, unless, whenever*)

Forecasters predict a mild winter. Farmers hope for an early spring.

Whenever forecasters predict a mild winter, farmers hope for an early spring.

CONCESSION (*although, as if, even though, though*)

The horse looked gentle. It proved high-spirited and hard to manage.

Although the horse looked gentle, it proved high-spirited and hard to manage.

PURPOSE (*in order that, so that, that*)

Parliament passed new immigration laws. Illegal immigrants could not enter Canada.

Parliament passed new immigration laws *so that* illegal immigrants could not enter Canada.

IDENTIFICATION (*that, when, where, which, who*)

The old factory now manufactures automobile transmissions. It stands on the south side of town and covers two hectares.

The old factory, *which* stands on the south side of town and covers two hectares, now manufactures automobile transmissions.

Phrases and single words can also indicate the subordinate role of information. Subordinate clauses generally place the greatest emphasis on such information because they are longer and grammatically more like main clauses. Phrases give less weight, and single words the least.

Old barns are common in New Brunswick. They are often painted red. [Separate sentences.]

Old barns, *which are often painted red,* are common in New Brunswick. [Subordinate clause.]

Old barns, *often painted red,* are common in New Brunswick. [Verbal phrase. See p. 167.]

Old *red* barns are common in New Brunswick. [Single word.]

The horse looked gentle. It proved high-spirited and hard to manage. [Separate sentences.]

Although the horse looked gentle, it proved high-spirited and hard to manage. [Subordinate clause.]

Despite its gentle appearance, the horse proved high-spirited and hard to manage. [Prepositional phrase. See p. 164.]

The horse, *a gentle-looking animal,* proved high-spirited and hard to manage. [Appositive. See p. 176.]

The *gentle-looking* horse proved high-spirited and hard to manage. [Single word.]

Punctuating subordinate constructions

A modifying word, phrase, or clause that introduces a sentence is usually set off from the rest of the sentence with a comma (see 21b).

Unfortunately, the company failed.
In a little over six months, the company became insolvent.
When the company failed, many reporters investigated.

A modifier that interrupts or concludes a main clause is *not* set off with punctuation when it restricts the meaning of a word or words in the clause (see 21c).

One article *about the company failure* won a prize.

The article *that won the prize* appeared in the local newspaper.

The reporter wrote the article *because the company failure affected many residents of the town.*

When an interrupting or concluding modifier does *not* restrict meaning, but simply adds information to the sentence, it *is* set off with punctuation, usually a comma or commas (see 21c).

> The company, *over forty years old*, never reopened after its doors were closed.
>
> The company managers, *who were not responsible for the failure*, all found new jobs.
>
> Customers who had paid in advance for goods never recovered all their money, *though most of them tried to do so.*

Like a modifier, an appositive is set off with punctuation (usually a comma or commas) only when it does *not* restrict the meaning of the word it refers to (see 21c-2).

> The company, Northern Food Products, was the oldest in town.
>
> The newspaper, the *Chronicle*, was one of several reporting the story.

A dash or dashes may also be used to set off a nonrestrictive appositive, particularly when it contains commas (see 25b-2). A concluding appositive is sometimes set off with a colon (see 25a-1).

sub 16b

Subordinating logically

Use subordination only for the less important information in a sentence. **Faulty subordination** reverses the dependent relation the reader expects.

FAULTY Ms. Angelo was in her first year of teaching, although she was a better instructor than others with many years of experience. [The sentence suggests that Angelo's inexperience is the main idea, whereas the writer intended to stress her skill *despite* her inexperience.]

REVISED *Although Ms. Angelo was in her first year of teaching,* she was a better instructor than others with many years of experience.

FAULTY Her class, which won a national achievement award, had twenty students. [Common sense says the important fact is the award.]

REVISED Her class *of twenty students* won a national achievement award.

Using subordination effectively

Subordination can do much to organize and emphasize information. But it loses that power when you try to cram too much loosely related detail into one long sentence.

Overloaded The boats that were moored at the dock when the hurricane, which was one of the worst in three decades, struck were ripped from their moorings, because the owners had not been adequately prepared, since the weather service had predicted the storm would blow out to sea, which they do at this time of year.

Such sentences usually have more than one idea that deserves a main clause, so they are best revised by sorting their details into more than one sentence.

Revised Struck by one of the worst hurricanes in three decades, *the boats at the dock were ripped from their moorings. The owners were unprepared* because the weather service had said that hurricanes at this time of year blow out to sea.

A common form of excessive subordination occurs with a string of adjective clauses beginning *which, who,* or *that,* as in the following:

Stringy Adjective Clauses Every Christmas we all try to go to my grandfather's house, which is near Edmonton, which is an attractive city where my parents now live.

To revise such sentences, consider recasting some of the subordinate clauses as other kinds of modifying structures. In the following revision, for example, the clause *which is near Edmonton* has been reduced to a simple modifier, and the clause *which is an attractive city* has been changed to an appositive.

Revised Every Christmas we all try to go to my grandfather's house *near Edmonton, an attractive city where my parents now live.*

Exercise 3
Sentence combining: Subordination

Combine each of the following pairs of sentences twice, each time using one of the subordinate structures in parentheses to make a single sentence. You will have to add, delete, change, and rearrange words.

Example:

During the late eighteenth century, workers carried beverages in brightly coloured bottles. The bottles had cork stoppers. (*Clause beginning that. Phrase beginning with.*)

During the late eighteenth century, workers carried beverages in brightly coloured bottles *that had cork stoppers.*

During the late eighteenth century, workers carried beverages in brightly coloured bottles *with cork stoppers.*

1. The bombardier beetle sees an enemy. It shoots out a jet of chemicals to protect itself. (*Clause beginning when. Phrase beginning seeing.*)
2. The beetle's spray is very potent. It consists of hot and irritating chemicals. (*Phrase beginning consisting. Phrase beginning of.*)
3. The spray's two chemicals are stored separately in the beetle's body and mixed in the spraying gland. The chemicals resemble a nerve-gas weapon. (*Phrase beginning stored. Clause beginning which.*)
4. The tip of the beetle's abdomen sprays the chemicals. The tip revolves like a turret on a World War II bomber. (*Phrase beginning revolving. Phrase beginning spraying.*)
5. The beetle defeats most of its enemies. It is still eaten by spiders and birds. (*Clause beginning although. Phrase beginning except.*)

Exercise 4
Revising: Subordination

Rewrite the following paragraph in the way you think most effective to subordinate the less important ideas to the more important ones. Use subordinate clauses and other subordinate constructions as appropriate.

Many students today are no longer majoring in the liberal arts. I mean by "liberal arts" such subjects as history, English, and the social sciences. Students think a liberal arts degree will not help them get jobs. They are wrong. They may not get practical, job-related experience from the liberal arts, but they will get a broad education, and it will never again be available to them. Many employers look for more than a technical, professional education. They think such an education can make an employee's views too narrow. The employers want open-minded employees. They want employees to think about problems from many angles. The liberal arts curriculum instils such flexibility. The flexibility is vital to the health of our society.

Exercise 5
Revising: Faulty or excessive subordination

Revise the following sentences to eliminate faulty or excessive subordination by reversing main and subordinate ideas, by coordinating ideas, or by making separate sentences. Some items have more than one possible answer.

Example:

Terrified to return home, he had driven his mother's car into a corn field.

Having driven his mother's car into a corn field, he was terrified to return home.

1. Genaro González is blessed with great writing talent, which means that several of his stories and his novel *Rainbow's End* have been published.
2. He loves to write, although he has also earned a doctorate in psychology.
3. His first story, which reflects his growing consciousness of his Aztec heritage and place in the world, is entitled "Un Hijo del Sol."
4. In 1990 González, who writes equally well in English and Spanish, received a large fellowship that enabled him to take a leave of absence from the Pan American University, where he teaches psychology, so that he could write without worrying about an income.
5. González wrote the first version of "Un Hijo del Sol" while he was a sophomore at Pan American, which is in the Rio Grande valley of southern Texas, which González calls "el Valle" in the story.

16c Choosing clear connectors

Most connecting words signal specific and unambiguous relations; for instance, the coordinating conjunction *but* clearly indicates contrast, and the subordinating conjunction *because* clearly indicates cause. A few connectors, however, require careful use, either because they are ambiguous in many contexts or because they are often misused.

1 Using *as* and *while* clearly

The subordinating conjunction *as* can indicate several relations, including comparison and time.

COMPARISON	Technicians work *as* rapidly as possible.
TIME	One shift starts *as* the other stops.

Avoid using *as* to indicate cause. It is unclear.

UNCLEAR	*As* the experiment was occurring, the laboratory was sealed. [Time or cause intended?]
REVISED	*When* the experiment was occurring, the laboratory was sealed. [Time.]
REVISED	*Because* the experiment was occurring, the laboratory was sealed. [Cause.]

The subordinating conjunction *while* can indicate either time or concession. Unless the context makes the meaning of *while* unmistakably clear, choose a more exact connector.

Unclear	*While* technicians work in the next room, they cannot hear the noise. [Time or concession intended?]
Revised	*When* technicians work in the next room, they cannot hear the noise. [Time.]
Revised	*Although* technicians work in the next room, they cannot hear the noise. [Concession.]

Using *as, like,* and *while* correctly

The use of *as* as a substitute for *whether* or *that* is nonstandard (it does not conform to spoken and written standard English).

Nonstandard	They are not sure *as* the study succeeded.
Revised	They are not sure *whether* (or *that*) the study succeeded.

Although the preposition *like* is often used as a conjunction in informal speech and in advertising (*Dirt-Away works like a soap should*), writing generally requires the conjunction *as, as if, as though,* or *that.*

sub
16c

Speech	It seemed *like* it did succeed.
Writing	It seemed *as if* (or *as though*) it did succeed.

The subordinating conjunction *while* is sometimes carelessly used in the sense of *and* or *but,* creating false subordination.

Faulty	The institute will sponsor a new study *while* technicians take new precautions.
Revised	The institute will sponsor a new study, *and technicians will* take new precautions.

Exercise 6
Revising: Clear connectors

Substitute a clear or correct connector in the following sentences where *as, while,* and *like* are ambiguous or misused.

Example:

He looked to me like he had slept in his clothes.
He looked to me *as if* he had slept in his clothes.

1. Many writers use *he* to denote both males and females, while others avoid the usage.
2. Some writers feel like substituting *he* for *a doctor* or *the engineer* insults female members of those professions.
3. As women more frequently enter such fields now, writers can no longer safely use *he* to refer to a white-collar professional.
4. Nor can writers automatically use *she* to refer to a nurse or secretary, like a man would not enter such a career.

5. As they desire to be fair to both genders, many writers prefer plural nouns (for example, *doctors*) and *they*.

Exercise 7
Revising: Coordination and subordination

The following paragraph consists entirely of simple sentences. Use coordination and subordination to combine sentences in the way you think most effective to emphasize main ideas.

Sir Walter Raleigh personified the Elizabethan Age. That was the period of Elizabeth I's rule of England. The period occurred in the last half of the sixteenth century. Raleigh was a courtier and poet. He was also an explorer and entrepreneur. Supposedly, he gained Queen Elizabeth's favour. He did this by throwing his cloak beneath her feet at the right moment. She was just about to step over a puddle. There is no evidence for this story. It does illustrate Raleigh's dramatic and dynamic personality. His energy drew others to him. He was one of Elizabeth's favourites. She supported him. She also dispensed favours to him. However, he lost his queen's good will. Without her permission he seduced one of her maids of honour. He eventually married the maid of honour. Elizabeth died. Then her successor imprisoned Raleigh in the Tower of London. Her successor was James I. Raleigh was charged falsely with treason. He was released after thirteen years. He was arrested again two years later on the old treason charges. At the age of sixty-six he was beheaded.

NOTE See page 346 for an exercise involving coordination and subordination along with parallelism and other techniques for effective sentences.

Chapter 17

Parallelism is a similarity of grammatical form between two or more elements.

The air is dirtied by	factories	belching	smoke
and	cars	spewing	exhaust.

Parallel structure reinforces and highlights a close relation between compound sentence elements, whether words, phrases, or entire clauses.

The principle underlying parallelism is that form should reflect meaning: since the parts of compound constructions have the same function and importance, they should have the same grammatical form.

17a Using parallelism for coordinate elements

Use parallelism in all the situations illustrated in the box on the next page.

Note Parallel elements match each other in structure, as in the example above, but they do not always match word for word.

The pioneers passed	*through the town*
and	*into the vast, unpopulated desert.*

Patterns of parallelism

Use parallel structures for all coordinated elements.

- For elements connected by coordinating conjunctions (*and, but, or,* etc.) or correlative conjunctions (*both . . . and, neither . . . nor,* etc.) (17a-1, 17a-2):

  In 1988 a Greek cyclist, backed up by ‖ *engineers,*
  ‖ *physiologists,*
  and ‖ *athletes,*
  broke the world's record for human flight
  with neither ‖ *a boost*
  nor ‖ *a motor.*

- For elements being compared or contrasted (17a-3):

  ‖ *Pedal power*
  rather than ‖ *horse power*
  propelled the plane.

- For items arranged in a series or outline (17a-4):

  The four-hour flight was successful because
  ‖ (1) *the cyclist was very fit,*
  ‖ (2) *he flew a straight course over water,*
  and ‖ (3) *he kept the aircraft near the water's surface.*

Using parallelism for elements linked by coordinating conjunctions

The coordinating conjunctions *and, but, or, nor,* and *yet* always signal a need for parallelism.

The industrial base is *shifting* and *shrinking.*

Politicians rarely *acknowledge the problem* or *propose alternatives.*

Industrial workers are understandably disturbed *that they are losing their jobs* and *that no one seems to care.*

If sentence elements linked by coordinating conjunctions are not parallel in structure, the resulting sentence will be awkward and distracting.

Nonparallel Three reasons why steel companies keep losing money are that their plants are inefficient, high labour costs, and foreign competition is increasing.

Revised Three reasons why steel companies keep losing money are *inefficient plants, high labour costs,* and *increasing foreign competition.*

All the words required by idiom or grammar must be stated in compound constructions (see also p. 299).

Nonparallel Given training, workers can acquire the skills and interest in other jobs. [*Skills and interest* require different prepositions, so both must be stated.]

Revised Given training, workers can acquire the skills *for* and interest in other jobs.

Often, the same word must be repeated to avoid confusion.

Confusing James stood up for his principles by not taking drugs and leaving the group. [Did he leave the group or not?]

Revised James stood up for his principles by not taking drugs and by leaving the group.

Be sure that clauses beginning *and who* or *and which* are coordinated only with preceding *who* and *which* clauses.

Nonparallel Lisa is a young woman of great ability and who wants to be a professor.

Revised Lisa is a young woman *who has* great ability and who wants to be a professor.

Revised Lisa is a young woman of great ability *who* wants to be a professor.

Using parallelism for elements linked by correlative conjunctions

Correlative conjunctions are pairs of connectors. For example:

both . . . and	neither . . . nor	not only . . . but also
either . . . or	not . . . but	whether . . . or

They stress equality and balance and thus emphasize the relation between elements, even long phrases and clauses. The elements should be parallel to confirm their relation.

Huckleberry Finn *is* not *just a regional statement* but *a larger work, portraying* not *past problems* but *enduring ones.*

At the end of the novel, Huck Finn both *rejects society's values by turning down money and a home* and *affirms his own values by setting out for "the territory."*

Most errors in parallelism with correlative conjunctions occur when the element after the second connector does not match the element after the first connector.

Nonparallel Mark Twain refused either to ignore the moral blindness of his society or spare the reader's sensibilities. [*To* follows *either,* so it must also follow *or.*]

Revised Mark Twain refused either to ignore the moral blindness of his society or *to* spare the reader's sensibilities.

Nonparallel Huck Finn learns not only that human beings have an enormous capacity for folly but also enormous dignity. [The first element includes *that human beings have;* the second element does not.]

Revised Huck Finn learns *that human beings have* not only an enormous capacity for folly but also enormous dignity.

3 Using parallelism for elements being compared or contrasted

Elements being compared or contrasted should ordinarily be cast in the same grammatical form.

It is better *to live rich* than *to die rich.* —Samuel Johnson

Weak The study found that most welfare recipients wanted to work rather than handouts.

Revised The study found that most welfare recipients wanted *work* rather than handouts.

Revised The study found that most welfare recipients wanted to work rather than *to accept handouts.*

4 Using parallelism for items in lists or outlines

The elements of a list or outline that divides a larger subject are coordinate and should be parallel in structure. Parallelism is essential in a formal topic outline (see p. 49).

Faulty	**Improved**
Changes in Renaissance England	Changes in Renaissance England
1. An extension of trade routes	1. The extension of trade routes
2. Merchant class became more powerful	2. The increasing power of the merchant class
3. The death of feudalism	3. The death of feudalism
4. Upsurging of the arts	4. The upsurge of the arts
5. The sciences were encouraged	5. The encouragement of the sciences
6. Religious quarrels began	6. The rise of religious quarrels

Exercise 1
Identifying parallel elements

Identify the parallel elements in the following sentences. How does parallelism contribute to the effectiveness of each sentence?

1. But on St. Urbain, our fathers worked as cutters or pressers or scrap dealers and drifted into cold-water flats, sitting down to supper in their freckled Penman's long winter underwear, clipping their nails at the table. —MORDECAI RICHLER
2. To enter the United States is a matter of crossing an ocean; to enter Canada is a matter of being silently swallowed by an alien continent. —NORTHROP FRYE
3. If [the Scotch] boil their salmon and halibut till no taste remains, if they bake out of their haddock the last drop of moisture, if they serve these ruined fish with a dry, grey potato and (for variation) boiled turnips and sprouts, if they offer for dessert soggy rice pudding with bloated raisins bulging out of it, if they equate a distaste for haggis with disloyalty to Scotland herself—let nobody pity them or wonder why they eat as they do. —HUGH MACLENNAN
4. I don't remember much being made of the sacredness of the life we took, but there was a real emphasis on fair play, much of it codified in law, like shooting game birds only on the wing, like not hunting deer with flashlights at night, like not shooting does. —JANE RULE
5. [I]t is the character who chooses which parts of the personal past, the family past, and the ancestral past have to be revealed in order for the present to be realized and the future to happen. —MARGARET LAURENCE

Exercise 2
Revising: Parallelism

Revise the following sentences to make coordinate, compared, or listed elements parallel in structure. Add or delete words or rephrase as necessary.

Example:

After emptying her bag, searching the apartment, and she called the library, Jennifer realized she had lost the book.

After emptying her bag, searching the apartment, and *calling* the library, Jennifer realized she had lost the book.

1. The ancient Greeks celebrated four athletic contests: the Olympic Games at Olympia, the Isthmian Games were held near Corinth, at Delphi the Pythian Games, and the Nemean Games were sponsored by the people of Cleonae.
2. Each day of the games consisted of either athletic events or holding ceremonies and sacrifices to the gods.

3. In the years between the games, competitors were taught how to box and wrestling and javelin throwing.
4. Competitors participated in running sprints, spectacular chariot and horse races, and running long distances while wearing full armour.
5. The purpose of such events was developing physical strength, demonstrating skill and endurance, and to sharpen the skills needed for war.
6. Events were held for both men and for boys.
7. At the Olympic Games the spectators cheered their favourites to victory, attended sacrifices to the gods, and they feasted on the meat not burned in offerings.
8. The athletes competed less to achieve great wealth than for gaining honour both for themselves and their cities.
9. Of course, exceptional athletes received financial support from patrons, poems and statues by admiring artists, and they even got lavish living quarters from their sponsoring cities.
10. With the medal counts and flag ceremonies, today's Olympians often seem not so much to be demonstrating individual talent as to prove their countries' superiority.

17b Using parallelism to increase coherence

Parallelism makes sentences more coherent by clearly relating paired or opposed units. Consider this sentence:

NONPARALLEL During the early weeks of the term, the course reviews fundamentals, but little emphasis is placed on new material.

Here "the course" is doing two things—or doing one thing and not doing the other—and these are opposites. But the nonparallel construction of the sentence (*the course reviews . . . little emphasis is placed*) does not make the connection clear.

REVISED During the early weeks of the term, the course reviews fundamentals but *places little emphasis* on new material.

Effective parallelism will enable you to combine in a single, well-ordered sentence related ideas that you might have expressed in separate sentences. Compare the following three sentences with the original single sentence written by H. L. Mencken.

> Slang originates in the effort of ingenious individuals to make language more pungent and picturesque. They increase the store of terse and striking words or widen the boundaries of metaphor. Thus a vocabulary for new shades and difference in meaning is provided by slang.

> Slang originates in the effort of ingenious individuals *to make the language* more pungent and picturesque—*to increase the store* of terse and striking words, *to widen the boundaries* of metaphor, and *to provide a vocabulary* for new shades and differences in meaning.
> —H. L. MENCKEN

Parallel structure works as well to emphasize the connections among related sentences in a paragraph.

> *Lewis Mumford stands* high in the company of this century's sages. A scholar of cosmic cultural reach and conspicuous public conscience, a distinguished critic of life, arts, and letters, an unequaled observer of cities and civilizations, *he is* secure in the modern pantheon of great men. *He is* also an enigma and an anachronism. A legend of epic proportions in intellectual and academic circles, *he is* surprisingly little known to the public. —ADA LOUISE HUXTABLE

Here, Huxtable tightly binds her sentences with two layers of parallelism: the subject-verb patterns of all three sentences (italic and underlined) and the appositives of the second and third sentences (underlined). (See p. 87 for another illustration of parallelism among sentences.)

Exercise 3
Sentence combining: Parallelism

Combine each group of sentences below into one concise sentence in which parallel elements appear in parallel structures. You will have to add, delete, change, and rearrange words. Each item has more than one possible answer.

Example:

The new process works smoothly. It is efficient, too.
The new process works smoothly *and efficiently.*

1. People can develop Post-Traumatic Stress Disorder (PTSD). They develop it after experiencing a dangerous situation. They will also have felt fear for their survival.
2. The disorder can be triggered by a wide variety of events. Combat is a typical cause. Similarly, natural disasters can result in PTSD. Some people experience PTSD after a hostage situation.
3. PTSD can occur immediately after the stressful incident. Sometimes it will not appear until many years later.
4. Sometimes people with PTSD will act irrationally. Moreover, they often become angry.
5. Other symptoms include dreaming that one is reliving the experience. They include hallucinating that one is back in the terrifying place. In another symptom one imagines that strangers are actually one's former torturers.

Exercise 4
Revising: Parallelism

Revise the following paragraph to create parallelism wherever it is required for grammar or for coherence.

The great white shark has an undeserved bad reputation. Many people consider the great white not only swift and powerful but also to be a cunning and cruel predator on humans. However, scientists claim that the great white attacks humans not by choice but as a result of chance. To a shark, our behaviour in the water is similar to that of porpoises, seals, and sea lions—the shark's favourite foods. These sea mammals are both agile enough and can move fast enough to evade the shark. Thus the shark must attack with swiftness and noiselessly to surprise the prey and giving it little chance to escape. Humans become the shark's victims not because the shark has any preference or hatred of humans but because humans can neither outswim nor can they outmanoeuver the shark. If the fish were truly a cruel human-eater, it would prolong the terror of its attacks, perhaps by circling or bumping into its intended victims before they were attacked.

Note See page 346 for an exercise involving parallelism along with other techniques for effective sentences.

Chapter 18

Emphasizing Main Ideas

When you emphasize the main ideas in your sentences, you hold and channel readers' attention.

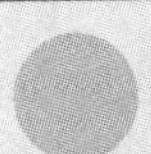

Ways to emphasize ideas

- Put important ideas in the beginnings or endings of sentences (18a-1).
- Arrange series items in order of increasing importance (18a-2).
- Use an occasional balanced sentence (18a-2).
- Carefully repeat key words and phrases (18b).
- Set off important ideas with punctuation (18c).
- Use the active voice (18d).
- Write concisely (18e).

18a Arranging ideas effectively

To arrange ideas emphatically, keep the following two principles in mind:

- The beginning and ending of a sentence are the most emphatic positions, and the ending is generally more emphatic than the beginning.
- A parallel series of words, phrases, or clauses will be more emphatic if the elements are arranged in order of increasing importance.

Using sentence beginnings and endings

Readers automatically seek a writer's principal meaning in the main clause of a sentence—that is, in the subject that names a topic and the predicate that comments on the topic (see p. 153). Thus you can help readers understand your intended meaning by controlling the relation of the main clause and any modifiers attached to it.

The most effective way to call attention to information is to place it first or last in the sentence, reserving the middle for incidentals.

UNEMPHATIC Education remains the most important single means of economic advancement, in spite of its shortcomings. [Emphasizes shortcomings.]

REVISED In spite of its shortcomings, education remains the most important single means of economic advancement. [Emphasizes importance more than shortcomings.]

REVISED Education remains, in spite of its shortcomings, the most important single means of economic advancement. [De-emphasizes shortcomings.]

Many sentences begin with the subject and predicate plus their modifiers and then add more modifiers. Such sentences are called **cumulative** (because they accumulate information as they proceed) or **loose** (because they are not tightly structured).

CUMULATIVE Education has no equal in opening minds, instilling values, and creating opportunities.

CUMULATIVE The Canadian Shield is made up of bare rock, thin soil, and muskeg, in an area extending from Hudson Bay to the Adirondacks and covering about 4.6 million square kilometres, scoured by past glaciers and strewn with countless lakes and rivers.

A cumulative sentence completes its main statement (topic and comment) and then explains, amplifies, or illustrates it. By thus accumulating information, the sentence parallels the way we naturally think.

The opposite kind of sentence, called **periodic,** saves the main clause until just before the end (the period) of the sentence. Everything before the main clause points toward it.

PERIODIC In opening minds, instilling values, and creating opportunities, education has no equal.

PERIODIC In an area extending from Hudson Bay to the Adirondacks and covering about 4.6 million square kilometres, scoured by past glaciers and strewn with countless lakes and rivers, the Canadian Shield is made up of bare rock, thin soils, and muskeg.

A variation of the periodic sentence names the subject at the beginning, follows it with a modifier, and then finishes with the predicate.

> Thirty-eight-year-old Dick Hayne, who works in jeans and loafers and likes to let a question cure in the air for a while before answering it, bears all the markings of what his generation used to call a laid-back kind of guy. —GEORGE RUSH

The periodic sentence creates suspense for the reader by reserving important information for the end. But it requires careful planning so that the reader can remember all the information leading up to the main clause, and the effort should pay off. Most writers save periodic sentences for when their purpose demands climactic emphasis.

emph 18a

2 Arranging parallel elements effectively

Series

With parallelism, you use similar grammatical structures for ideas linked by *and, but,* and similar words (see Chapter 17). In addition, you should arrange the parallel ideas in order of their importance.

UNEMPHATIC The storm ripped the roofs off several buildings, killed ten people, and knocked down many trees in town. [Buries the most serious damage—deaths—in the middle.]

EMPHATIC The storm knocked down many trees in town, ripped the roofs off several buildings, and killed ten people. [Arranges items in order of increasing importance.]

You may want to use an unexpected item at the end of a series for humour or for another special effect.

> Early to bed and early to rise makes a man healthy, wealthy, and dead. —JAMES THURBER

But be careful not to use such a series carelessly. The following series seems thoughtlessly random rather than intentionally humourous.

UNEMPHATIC	The painting has subdued tone, intense feeling, and a length of about a metre.
EMPHATIC	The painting, about a metre long, has subdued tone and intense feeling.

Balanced sentences

A sentence is **balanced** when its clauses are parallel—that is, matched in grammatical structure (pp. 319–20). Read the following examples aloud to hear their rhythm.

> The fickleness of the women I love is equalled only by the infernal constancy of the women who love me. —GEORGE BERNARD SHAW

In a pure balanced sentence two main clauses are exactly parallel: they match item for item.

> Scratch a lover, and find a foe. —DOROTHY PARKER

But the term is commonly applied to sentences that are only approximately parallel or that have only some parallel parts.

> If thought corrupts language, language can also corrupt thought. —GEORGE ORWELL

> As the traveler who has once been from home is wiser than he who has never left his own doorstep, so a knowledge of one other culture should sharpen our ability to scrutinize more steadily, to appreciate more lovingly, our own. —MARGARET MEAD

Balanced sentences are heavily emphatic but require thoughtful planning. When used carefully, they can be an especially effective way to alert readers to a strong contrast between two ideas.

Exercise 1
Sentence combining: Cumulative and periodic sentences

Underline the main clause in each of the following sentences, and identify each sentence as loose or periodic. Then rewrite each loose sentence as a periodic one and each periodic sentence as a loose one.

1. Matthew's children worked two years to get him out of jail—writing letters, seeing lawyers, attending meetings—because they knew him to be honest and believed him to be innocent.
2. Aspiring writers can learn much from waiting on tables, eavesdropping on conversations to sharpen their ear for dialogue and to pick up promising story material.
3. Louis Riel was an obvious leader for the Métis, a man educated in law and theology and deeply committed to the welfare of his people.
4. Finally, early in July 1884, at the request of a group of Saskatchewan Métis led by Gabriel Dumont, Riel arrived at Batoche.
5. In 1885, after the court had found him guilty of treason and the federal Cabinet had been swayed by political considerations, Riel was hanged.

Exercise 2
Revising: Series and balanced elements

Revise the following sentences so that elements in a series or balanced elements are arranged to give maximum emphasis to main ideas.

Example:

The campers were stranded without matches, without food or water, and without a tent.

The campers were stranded without matches, without a tent, and without food or water.

1. Remembering her days as a "conductor" on the Underground Railroad made Harriet Tubman proud, but she got angry when she remembered her years as a slave.
2. Harriet wanted freedom regardless of personal danger, whereas for her husband, John, personal safety was more important than freedom.
3. Harriet proved her fearlessness in many ways: she led hundreds of other slaves to freedom, she was a spy for the North during the Civil War, and she disobeyed John's order not to run away.
4. To conduct slaves to freedom in the northern United States and Canada, Harriet risked being returned to slavery, being hanged for a huge reward, and being caught by Southern patrollers.
5. After the war Harriet worked tirelessly for civil rights and women's suffrage; raising money for homes for needy former slaves was something else she did.

18b Repeating ideas

Careless repetition often clutters and weakens sentences (see p. 463). But planned repetition of key words and phrases can be an effective means of emphasis. Such repetition often combines with parallelism. It may occur in a series of sentences within a paragraph (see p. 87). Or it may occur in a series of words, phrases, or clauses within a sentence, as in the following examples.

> There is something uneasy in the Los Angeles air this afternoon, some unnatural stillness, some tension. —JOAN DIDION

> We have the tools, all the tools—we are suffocating in tools—but we cannot find the actual wood to work or even the actual hand to work it. —ARCHIBALD MACLEISH

18c Separating ideas

When you save important information for the end of a sentence, you can emphasize it even more by setting it off from the rest of the sentence, as in the second example below.

> Mothers and housewives are the only workers who do not have regular time off, so they are the great vacationless class.

> Mothers and housewives are the only workers who do not have regular time off. They are the great vacationless class. —ANNE MORROW LINDBERGH

You can vary the degree of emphasis by varying the extent to which you separate one idea from the others. A semicolon provides more separation than a comma, and a period provides still more separation. Note the use of all three in the following example.

> This revelation was an even greater shock to me; not only was my country owned, but it was owned by the kind of people who carried tin boats across portages and didn't burn their garbage. One doubted their competence. —MARGARET ATWOOD

Sometimes a dash or a pair of dashes will isolate and thus emphasize a part of a statement.

> His schemes were always elaborate, ingenious, and exciting—and wholly impractical.

> Athletics—even winning athletics—have never been a profitable university operation in Canada.

Exercise 3
Emphasizing with repetition or separation

Emphasize the main idea in each sentence or group of sentences below by following the instructions in parentheses: either combine sentences so that parallelism and repetition stress the main idea, or place the main idea in a separate sentence. Each item has more than one possible answer.

Example:

I try to listen to other people's opinions. When my mind is closed, I find that other opinions open it. And they can change my mind when it is wrong. (*Parallelism and repetition.*)

I try to listen to other people's opinions, for they can open my mind when it is closed and they can change my mind when it is wrong.

1. One of the few worthwhile habits is daily reading. One can read for information. One can read for entertainment. Reading can give one a broader view of the world. (*Parallelism and repetition.*)
2. Reading introduces new words. One encounters varied styles of expression through reading. (*Parallelism and repetition.*)
3. Students who read a great deal will write essays that are vivid, well structured, and grammatically correct, for these students will have absorbed the style and sentence structures of other authors. (*Separation.*)
4. Reading gives knowledge. One gets knowledge about other cultures. One will know about history and current events. One gains knowledge about human nature. (*Parallelism and repetition.*)
5. As a result of reading, writers have more resources and more flexibility, and thus reading creates better writers. (*Separation.*)

18d Preferring the active voice

In the **active voice** of the verb, the subject acts: *I peeled the onions.* In the **passive voice** the subject is acted upon: *The onions were peeled by me.* In the passive voice the actor is either relegated to a phrase (*by me*) or omitted entirely: *The onions were peeled.* (See pp. 218–20 for a more detailed explanation of voice.)

The passive voice is indirect because it obscures or removes the actor. The active voice is more direct, vigorous, and emphatic. Further, all sentences turn on their verbs, which give sentences their motion, pushing them along. And active verbs push harder than passive ones.

PASSIVE The new outpatient clinic was opened by the hospital administration and thus ensured that the costs of non-emergency medical care would be reduced.

ACTIVE The hospital *administration opened* the new outpatient clinic and *reduced* the costs of nonemergency medical care.

Sometimes the actor is unknown or unimportant, and many technical writers deliberately omit the actor in order to give impersonal emphasis to what is being acted upon. In these cases the passive voice can be useful.

Wellington was called the "Iron Duke."
Thousands of people are killed annually in highway accidents.
The mixture was then stirred.

Except in these situations, however, rely on the active voice. It is economical and creates movement.

18e Being concise

Conciseness—brevity of expression—aids emphasis no matter what the sentence structure. Unnecessary words detract from necessary words. They clutter sentences and obscure ideas.

WEAK In my opinion the competition in the area of grades is distracting. It distracts many students from their goal, which is to obtain an education that is good. There seems to be a belief among a few students that grades are more important than what is measured by them.

EMPHATIC The competition for grades distracts many students from their goal of obtaining a good education. A few students seem to believe that grades are more important than what they measure.

Because conciseness comes mainly from deleting unneeded words, it receives detailed coverage in Chapter 31, on choosing and using words (see p. 460). The box opposite summarizes that discussion.

Exercise 4
Revising: Active voice; conciseness

Revise the following sentences to make them more emphatic by converting passive to active voice and by eliminating wordiness. (For additional exercises with the passive voice, see pp. 184, 220, and 466.)

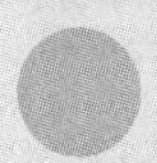

Ways to achieve conciseness

- Cut or shorten empty words or phrases (p. 461).

  Shorten filler phrases, such as *by virtue of the fact that.*
  Cut all-purpose words, such as *area, factor.*
  Cut unneeded qualifiers, such as *in my opinion, for the most part.*
- Cut unnecessary repetition (p. 463).
- Simplify word groups and sentences (p. 465).

  Combine sentences.
  Replace clauses with phrases and phrases with single words.
  Use strong verbs.
  Rewrite passive sentences as active.
  Avoid expletive constructions beginning with *there is* or *it is.*
- Cut or rewrite jargon (p. 467).

Example:

The problem in this particular situation is that we owe more money than we can afford under present circumstances.

The *problem is* that we owe more money than we can afford.

1. As far as I am concerned, customers who are dining out in restaurants in our country must be wary of suggestive selling, so to speak.
2. In suggestive selling, diners are asked by the waiter to buy additional menu selections in addition to what was ordered by them.
3. For each item on the menu, there is another food that will naturally complement it.
4. For example, customers will be asked if they want French fries with a sandwich or salad with a steak dinner.
5. Due to the fact that customers often give in to suggestive selling, they often find that their restaurant meals are more costly than they had intended to pay.

Exercise 5
Revising: Emphasizing main ideas

Drawing on the advice in this chapter, rewrite the following paragraph to emphasize main ideas and to de-emphasize less important information.

In preparing pasta, there is a requirement for common sense and imagination rather than for complicated recipes. The key to success in this area is fresh ingredients for the sauce and perfectly cooked pasta. The sauce may be made with just about any fresh fish, meat, cheese, herb, or vegetable. As for the pasta itself, it may be dried or fresh, although fresh pasta is usually more delicate and flavourful, as many experienced cooks have found. Dried pasta is fine with zesty sauces; with light oil and cream sauces fresh pasta is best used. There is a difference in the cooking time for dried and fresh pasta, with dried pasta taking longer. It is important that the package directions be followed by the cook and that the pasta be tested before the cooking time is up. The pasta is done when the texture is neither tough nor mushy but *al dente,* or "firm to the bite," according to the Italians, who ought to know.

NOTE See page 346 for an exercise involving emphasis along with parallelism and other techniques for effective sentences.

Chapter 19 Achieving Variety

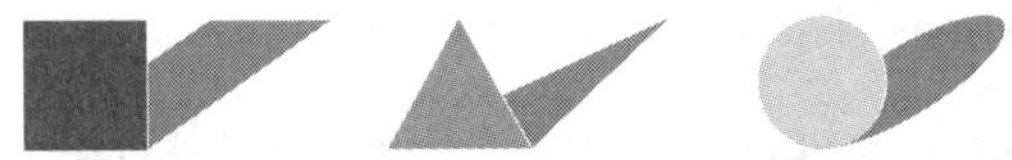

In a paragraph or an essay, your sentences do not stand one by one. Rather, each stands in relation to those before and after it. To make sentences work together effectively, you need to vary their length, structure, and word order to reflect the importance and complexity of ideas. Variety sometimes takes care of itself, but you can practise established techniques for achieving varied sentences.

Ways to achieve variety among sentences

- Vary the length and structure of sentences so that important ideas stand out (19a).
- Vary the beginnings of sentences with modifiers, transitional words and expressions, and occasional expletive constructions (19b).
- Occasionally, invert the normal order of subject, predicate, and object or complement (19c).
- Use an occasional command, question, or exclamation (19d).

A series of similar sentences will prove monotonous and ineffective, as this passage illustrates:

> The armies of the British general James Wolfe and the French general the Marquis de Montcalm fought on 13 September 1759. The battle was on the Plains of Abraham. They were fighting for

> possession of Quebec City and, ultimately, all of what would become Canada. It was one of the most decisive events in our history. Wolfe and Montcalm were contesting the identity and future of our country. Other battles had yet to be fought. Montreal was not captured by the British until the next year. France did not officially yield its colony to England until 1763. Wolfe had already defeated Montcalm, however, in the battle that claimed both their lives, and New France had, in effect, become British North America.

Individually, these nine sentences are perfectly clear and adequately detailed. But together they do not make pleasant reading, and their relative importance is obscure. Their lengths are roughly the same, they are about equally detailed, and they all consist of one or two main clauses beginning with the subject. At the end of the passage we have a sense of names, dates, and events but no sure sense of how they relate.

Now compare the preceding passage with a more effective version.

> When the armies of the British general James Wolfe and the French general the Marquis de Montcalm met on the Plains of Abraham, on 13 September 1759, to fight for possession of Quebec City and, ultimately, all of what would become Canada, it was one of the most decisive events in our history.

Suspenseful periodic sentence (p. 329) focuses attention on meeting. Details of place, time, and cause are in opening subordinate clause.

> These generals were contesting the identity and the future of our country. To be sure, other battles had yet to be fought, for Montreal was not captured by the British until the next year, and France did not officially yield its colony to England until 1763. But, when Wolfe defeated Montcalm in the battle that claimed both their lives, New France in effect became British North America.

Short sentence sums up.

Cumulative sentence (p. 328) describes lingering obstacles.

Short final sentence states the importance of the event.

The rest of this chapter suggests how you can vary your sentences for the kind of interest and clarity achieved in the second passage.

19a Varying sentence length and structure

The sentences of a stylistically effective essay will vary most obviously in their length and the arrangement of main clauses and modifiers. The variation in length and structure makes writing both readable and clear.

Varying length

In most contemporary writing, sentences vary from about ten to about forty words, with an average of fifteen to twenty-five words.

If your sentences are all at one extreme or the other, your readers may have difficulty focusing on main ideas and seeing the relations among them.

- If most of your sentences contain thirty-five words or more, you probably need to break some up into shorter, simpler sentences.
- If most of your sentences contain fewer than ten or fifteen words, you probably need to add details to them or combine them through coordination (p. 306) and subordination (p. 310). Examine your writing particularly for a common problem: strings of main clauses, subjects first, in either simple or compound sentences.

Rewriting strings of brief and simple sentences

A series of brief and simple sentences is both monotonous and hard to understand because it forces the reader to sort out relations among ideas. If you find that you depend on brief, simple sentences, work to increase variety by combining some of them into longer units that emphasize and link new and important ideas while de-emphasizing old or incidental information. (See pp. 306–14 and 327–30.)

The following examples show how a string of simple sentences can be revised into an effective piece of writing.

Monotonous The moon is now drifting away from the earth. It moves away at the rate of about 2.5 centimetres a year. Our days on earth are getting longer. They grow a thousandth of a second longer every century. A month will someday be forty-seven of our present days long. We might eventually lose the moon altogether. Such great planetary movement rightly concerns astronomers. It need not worry us. The movement will take 50 million years.

Revised The moon is now drifting away from the earth *at the rate of about 2.5 centimetres a year. At the rate of a thousandth of a second every century,* our days on earth are getting longer. A month will someday be forty-seven of our present days long, *if we don't eventually lose the moon altogether.* Such great planetary movement rightly concerns astronomers, *but* it need not worry us. It will take 50 million years.

In the revision italics indicate subordinate structures that were simple sentences in the original. With five sentences instead of the original nine, the revision emphasizes the moon's movement, our lengthening days, and the enormous span of time involved.

Rewriting strings of compound sentences

Because compound sentences are usually just simple sentences linked with conjunctions, a series of them will be as weak as a series of brief simple sentences, especially if the clauses of the compound sentences are all about the same length.

MONOTONOUS Physical illness may involve more than the body, for the mind may also be affected. Disorientation is common among sick people, but they are often unaware of it. They may reason abnormally, or they may behave immaturely.

REVISED Physical illness may involve the mind *as well as the body. Though often unaware of it,* sick people are commonly disoriented. They may reason abnormally *or behave immaturely.*

The first passage creates a seesaw effect. The revision, with some main clauses shortened or changed into modifiers (italics), is both clearer and more emphatic. (See p. 308 for more on avoiding excessive coordination.)

Exercise 1
Revising: Varied sentence structures

Rewrite the following paragraphs to increase variety so that important ideas receive greater emphasis than supporting information does. You will have to change some main clauses into modifiers and then combine and reposition the modifiers and the remaining main clauses.

1. Charlotte Perkins Gilman was a leading intellectual in the women's movement during the first decades of this century. She wrote *Women and Economics.* This book challenged Victorian assumptions about differences between the sexes. It explored the economic roots of women's oppression. Gilman wrote little about gaining the vote for women. Many feminists were then preoccupied with this issue. Historians have since focused their analyses on this issue. As a result, Gilman's contribution to today's women's movement has often been overlooked.

2. Nellie McClung was a Canadian reformer and suffragist, and she was raised in Manitoba. She joined the Winnipeg women's rights movement, and she was welcomed by it because of her witty arguments. She fought for female suffrage in Manitoba and Alberta.

Some feminists criticize her support of traditional family values. She was ignored for a decade, but she was rediscovered by the women's movement in the 1960s. Most women's rights advocates now recognize her contribution to the feminist cause.

19b Varying sentence beginnings

Most English sentences begin with their subjects.

The defendant's lawyer relentlessly cross-examined the stubborn witness for two successive days.

However, an unbroken sequence of sentences beginning with the subject quickly becomes monotonous, as shown by the passage on Wolfe and Montcalm that opened this chapter (pp. 337–38). Your final arrangement of sentence elements should always depend on two concerns: the relation of a sentence to those preceding and following it and the emphasis required by your meaning. When you do choose to vary the subject-first pattern, you have several options.

Adverb modifiers

Adverb modifiers can often be placed at a variety of spots in a sentence. Consider these different emphases:

For two successive days, the defendant's lawyer *relentlessly* cross-examined the stubborn witness.

Relentlessly, the defendant's lawyer cross-examined the stubborn witness *for two successive days.*

Relentlessly, for two successive days, the defendant's lawyer cross-examined the stubborn witness.

Notice that the last sentence, with both modifiers at the beginning, is periodic and thus highly emphatic (see p. 329).

Participial phrases

Beginning a sentence with a participial phrase also postpones the subject and sometimes creates a periodic sentence.

The witness was exhausted, and he did not cooperate.
Exhausted, the witness did not cooperate.

Coordinating conjunctions and transitional expressions

When the relation between two successive sentences demands, you may begin the second with a coordinating conjunction or with a transitional expression such as *first, for instance, however, in addition, moreover,* or *therefore.* (See p. 90 for a list of transitional expressions.)

> The witness had expected to be dismissed after his first long day of cross-examination. He was not; the defendant's lawyer called him again the second day.
>
> The witness had expected to be dismissed after his first long day of cross-examination. *But* he was not; the defendant's lawyer called him again the second day.
>
> The price of clothes has risen astronomically in recent years. The cheap cotton shirt that once cost \$6.00 and now costs \$25.00 is an example.
>
> The price of clothes has risen astronomically in recent years. *For example,* a cheap cotton shirt that once cost \$6.00 now costs \$25.00.

Occasional expletive constructions

An expletive construction—*it* or *there* plus a form of *be*—may occasionally be useful to delay and thus emphasize the subject of the sentence.

> His judgment seems questionable, not his desire.
> *It is* his judgment that seems questionable, not his desire.

However, expletive constructions are more likely to flatten writing by adding extra words. You should use them rarely, only when you can justify doing so. (See also p. 466.)

Exercise 2
Revising: Varied sentence beginnings

Follow the instructions in parentheses to revise each pair of sentences below: either create a single sentence that begins with an adverb modifier or a participial phrase, or make one of the two sentences begin with an appropriate coordinating conjunction or transitional expression.

> *Example:*
>
> The *Seabird* took first place. It moved quickly in the wind. (*One sentence with participial phrase beginning* moving.)
>
> *Moving quickly in the wind,* the *Seabird* took first place.

1. Some people are champion procrastinators. They seldom complete their work on time. (*Two sentences with transitional expression.*)
2. Procrastinators may fear criticism. They will delay completing an assignment. (*One sentence with adverb modifier beginning* if.)
3. Procrastinators often desire to please a boss or a teacher. They fear failure so much that they cannot do the work. (*Two sentences with coordinating conjunction.*)

4. Procrastination seems a hopeless habit. It is conquerable. (*One sentence with adverb modifier beginning* although.)
5. Teachers or employers can be helpful as they encourage procrastinators. The teachers or employers can give them the confidence to do good work on time. (*One sentence with participial phrase beginning* helpfully.)

Exercise 3
Revising: Varied sentence beginnings

Revise the following paragraph to vary sentence beginnings by using each of the following at least once: an adverb modifier, a participial phrase, a coordinating conjunction, and a transitional expression.

Scientists in Egypt dug up 40-million-year-old fossil bones. They had evidence of primitive whales. The whale ancestors are called mesonychids. They were small, furry land mammals with four legs. These limbs were complete with kneecaps, ankles, and little toes. Gigantic modern whales have tiny hind legs inside their bodies and flippers instead of front legs. Scientists are certain that these two very different creatures share the same family tree.

19c Inverting the normal word order

Because the word order of subject, verb, and object or complement is so strongly fixed in English, an inverted sentence can be emphatic.

> Voters once had some faith in politicians, and they were fond of incumbents. But now *all politicians,* especially incumbents, *voters seem to detest.*

Inverting the normal order of subject, verb, and complement can be useful in two successive sentences when the second expands on the first.

> Critics of his economic policies were not kind to Prime Minister R. B. Bennett during the Depression. *Particularly harsh was the term* for cars pulled by horses because the owners could not afford gas: Bennett buggies.

Inverted sentences used without need are artificial. Avoid descriptive sentences such as *Up came Larry and down went Cindy's spirits.*

19d Mixing types of sentences

Most written sentences make statements. Occasionally, however, questions, commands, or, more rarely, exclamations may enhance variety.

Questions may set the direction of a paragraph, as in *What does a detective do?* or *How is the percentage of unemployed workers calculated?* More often, though, the questions used in exposition or argument do not require answers but simply emphasize ideas that readers can be expected to agree with. Such **rhetorical questions** are illustrated in the following passage.

> Another word that has ceased to have meaning due to overuse is *attractive. Attractive* has become verbal chaff. Who, by some stretch of language and imagination, cannot be described as attractive? And just what is it that attractive individuals are attracting?
>
> —Diane White

Commands occur frequently in an explanation of a process, particularly in directions, as this passage on freewriting illustrates.

> The idea is simply to write for ten minutes (later on, perhaps fifteen or twenty). Don't stop for anything. Go quickly, without rushing. Never stop to look back, to cross something out, to wonder how to spell something, to wonder what word or thought to use, or to think about what you are doing. —Peter Elbow

Notice that the authors of these examples use questions and commands not merely to vary their sentences but to achieve some special purpose. Variety occurs because a particular sentence type is effective for the context, not because the writer set out to achieve variety for its own sake.

Exercise 4
Writing varied sentences

Imagine that you are writing an essay on a transportation problem at your school. Practise varying sentences by composing a sentence or passage to serve each purpose listed below.

1. Write a question that could open the essay.
2. Write a command that could open the essay.
3. Write an exclamation that could open the essay.
4. For the body of the essay, write an appropriately varied paragraph of at least five sentences, including at least one short and one long sentence beginning with the subject; at least one sentence beginning with an adverb modifier; at least one sentence beginning with a coordinating conjunction or transitional expression; and one rhetorical question or command.

Exercise 5
Analysing variety

Examine the following paragraph for sentence variety. By analysing your own response to each sentence, try to explain why the author wrote each short or long sentence, each cumulative or periodic sentence, each sentence beginning with its subject or beginning some other way, and each question.

> That night in my rented room, while letting the hot water run over my can of pork and beans in the sink, I opened [H. L. Mencken's] *A Book of Prefaces* and began to read. I was jarred and shocked by the style, the clear, clean, sweeping sentences. Why did he write like that? And how did one write like that? I pictured the man as a raging demon, slashing with his pen, consumed with hate, denouncing everything American, extolling everything European or German, laughing at the weaknesses of people, mocking God, authority. What was this? I stood up, trying to realize what reality lay behind the meaning of the words. Yes, this man was fighting, fighting with words. He was using words as a weapon, using them as one would use a club. Could words be weapons? Well, yes, for here they were. Then, maybe, perhaps, I could use them as a weapon? No. It frightened me. I read on and what amazed me was not what he said, but how on earth anybody had the courage to say it. —RICHARD WRIGHT, *Black Boy*

var 19d

Exercise 6
Revising: Variety

The following paragraph consists entirely of simple sentences that begin with their subjects. As appropriate, use the techniques discussed in this chapter to vary sentences so that the paragraph is more readable and its important ideas stand out clearly. You will have to delete, add, change, and rearrange words.

> The Italian volcano Vesuvius had been dormant for many years. It then exploded on August 24 in the year A.D. 79. The ash, pumice, and mud from the volcano buried two busy towns. Herculaneum is one. The more famous is Pompeii. The ruins of both towns lay undiscovered for many centuries. Herculaneum and Pompeii were discovered in 1709 and 1748, respectively. The excavation of Pompeii was the more systematic. It was the occasion for initiating modern methods of conservation and restoration. The methods replaced earlier practices. Herculaneum was simply looted of its most valuable finds. It was then left to disintegrate. Pompeii appears much as it did before the eruption. A luxurious house opens onto a lush central garden. An election poster decorates a wall. A dining table is set for breakfast.

NOTE See the next page for an exercise involving variety along with parallelism and other techniques for effective sentences.

Exercise on Chapters 16–19
Revising: Effective sentences

Revise the paragraphs below to emphasize main ideas, de-emphasize supporting information, and achieve a pleasing, clear variety in sentences. As appropriate, use subordination, coordination, parallelism, and cumulative, periodic, and balanced sentences. Cut wordiness. Use the active voice. Edit the finished product for punctuation.

Modern North Americans owe many debts to Aboriginal peoples. Several pleasures are among the debts. Aboriginal peoples originated two fine junk foods. They discovered popcorn. Potato chips were also one of their contributions.

Aboriginal peoples introduced popcorn to the European settlers. Massasoit provided popcorn at the first Thanksgiving feast. The Aztecs offered popcorn to the Spanish explorer Hernando Cortés. The Aztecs wore popcorn necklaces. So did the peoples of the West Indies. There were three ways that they popped the corn. First, they roasted an ear over the fire. The ear was skewered on a stick. They ate only some of the popcorn. They ate the corn that fell outside the flames. Second, they scraped the corn off the cob. The kernels would be thrown into the fire. Of course, the fire had to be low. Then the popped kernels that did not fall into the fire were eaten. The third method was the most sophisticated. It involved a shallow pottery vessel. It contained sand. The vessel was heated. The sand soon got hot enough. Corn kernels were stirred in. They popped to the surface of the sand and were eaten.

An Aboriginal chef devised the crunchy potato chip. His name was George Crum. In 1853 Crum was cooking at Moon Lake Lodge. The lodge was in Saratoga Springs, New York. Complaints were sent in by a customer. The man thought Crum's French-fried potatoes were too thick. Crum tried a thinner batch. These were also unsuitable. Crum became frustrated. He deliberately made the potatoes thin and crisp. They could not be cut with a knife and fork. Crum's joke backfired. The customer raved about the potato chips. The chips were named Saratoga Chips. Soon they appeared on the lodge's menu. Crum later opened his own restaurant. Of course, he offered potato chips.

Now all North Americans munch popcorn in movies. They crunch potato chips at parties. They gorge on both when alone and bored. They can be grateful to Aboriginal peoples for these guilty pleasures.

eff

Part V *Punctuation*

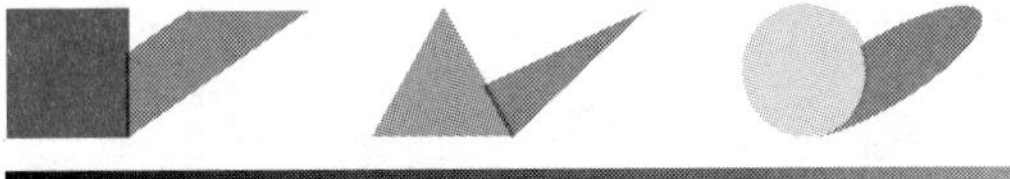

Commas, semicolons, colons, dashes, parentheses

(For explanations, consult the sections in parentheses.)

Sentences with two main clauses

The bus stopped, *but* no one got off. (21a)
The bus stopped; no one got off. (22a)
The bus stopped; *however,* no one got off. (22b)
The mechanic replaced the battery, the distributor cap, and the starter; *but* still the car would not start. (22c)
His duty was clear: he had to report the theft. (25a-1)

Introductory elements

Modifiers (21b)

After the argument was over, we laughed at ourselves.
Racing over the plain, the gazelle escaped the lion.
To dance in the contest, he had to tape his knee.
Suddenly, the door flew open.
With 125 passengers aboard, the plane was half full.
In 1983 he won the Nobel prize.

Absolute phrases (21d)

Its wing broken, the bird hopped around on the ground.

Interrupting and concluding elements

Nonrestrictive modifiers (21c-1)

Jim's car, *which barely runs,* has been impounded.
We consulted the dean, *who had promised to help us.*
The boy, *like his sister,* wants to be a pilot.
They moved across the desert, *shielding their eyes from the sun.*
The men do not speak to each other, *although they share a car.*

Nonrestrictive appositives

The author of "In Flanders Fields," *John McCrae,* served as a medical officer with the Canadian Expenditionary Force during World War I. (21c-2)
The population of the three Prairie provinces—*Alberta, Saskatchewan, and Manitoba*—is approximately 17.5 percent of Canada's total population. (25b-2)
Father demanded one promise: that we not lie to him. (25a-1)

Restrictive modifiers (21j-3)

The car *that hit mine* was uninsured.
We consulted a teacher *who had promised to help us.*
The boy *in the black hat* is my cousin.
They were surprised to find the desert *teeming with life.*
The men do not speak to each other *because they are feuding.*

RESTRICTIVE APPOSITIVES (21j-3)

Shaw's play *Saint Joan* was performed last year.
Their sons *Tony, William, and Steve* all chose military careers, leaving only Joe to run the family business.

PARENTHETICAL EXPRESSIONS

We suspect, *however*, that he will not come. (21c-3)
Jan is respected by many people—including me. (25b-2)
Brian Macdonald (*b. 14 May 1928*) was a brilliant choreographer. (25c-1)

ABSOLUTE PHRASES (21d)

The bird, *its wing broken*, hopped about on the ground.
The bird hopped about on the ground, *its wing broken.*

PHRASES EXPRESSING CONTRAST (21e)

The humidity, *not just the heat*, gives me headaches.
My headaches are caused by the humidity, *not just the heat.*

CONCLUDING SUMMARIES AND EXPLANATIONS

The movie opened to bad notices: *the characters were judged shallow and unrealistic.* (25a-1)
Mrs. McEvoy served us oatcakes, bannocks, and crowberries—*all Cape Breton favourites.* (25b-3)

Items in a series

THREE OR MORE ITEMS

Chimpanzees, gorillas, orangutans, and gibbons are all apes. (21f-1)
The cities singled out for special praise were *Fredericton, New Brunswick; Thunder Bay, Ontario; and Red Deer, Alberta.* (22d)

TWO OR MORE ADJECTIVES BEFORE A NOUN (21f-2)

Dingy, smelly clothes decorated their room.
The luncheon consisted of *one tiny watercress* sandwich.

INTRODUCTORY SERIES (25b-3)

Appropriateness, accuracy, and necessity—these criteria should govern your selection of words.

CONCLUDING SERIES

Every word should be *appropriate, accurate, and necessary.* (25a-3)
Every word should meet three criteria: *appropriateness, accuracy, and necessity.* (25a-1)
Pay attention to your words—*to their appropriateness, their accuracy, and their necessity.* (25b-3)

p

Chapter 20 End Punctuation

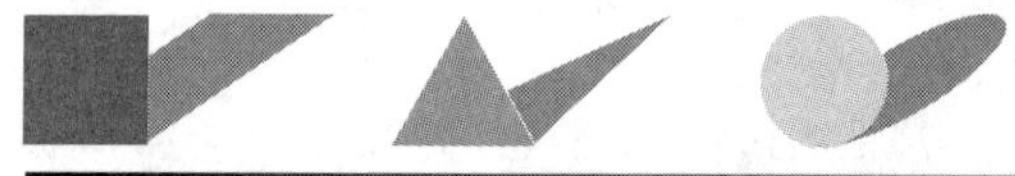

THE PERIOD

20a Use a period to end a statement, mild command, or indirect question.

STATEMENTS

These are exciting and trying times.
The airline went bankrupt.

MILD COMMANDS

Please do not smoke.
Think of the possibilities.

If you are unsure whether to use an exclamation point or a period after a command, use a period. The exclamation point should be used only rarely (see 20f).

An **indirect question** reports what someone has asked but not in the form or exact words of the original.

INDIRECT QUESTIONS

Students sometimes wonder whether their teachers read the papers they write.

Abused children eventually stop asking why they are being punished.

20b Use periods with most abbreviations.

Ordinarily, use periods with abbreviations.

p.	B.C.	B.A.	Mr.
D.C.	A.D.	Ph.D.	Mrs.
M.D.	A.M., a.m.	e.g.	Ms.
Dr.	P.M., p.m.		

(Note that a period follows *Ms.*, even though it is not actually an abbreviation.)

When an abbreviation falls at the end of a sentence, use only one period: *The Queen Charlotte Islands are in B.C.*

Periods are usually dropped from abbreviations for organizations, corporations, and government agencies when more than two words are abbreviated. For example:

IBM	UBC	CFL	NAFTA

Note that **acronyms**—pronounceable words, such as UNESCO, NATO, CUSO, and WHO, formed from the initial letters of the words in a name—never require periods (see p. 432).

Symbols for metric measurements are not followed by a period, although abbreviations of imperial measurements are.

2 m	14 km	8 in.	20 ft.

Exercise 1
Revising: Periods

Revise the following sentences so that periods are used correctly.

Example:

Several times I wrote to ask when my subscription ended?
Several times I wrote to ask when my subscription ended.

1. The instructor asked when Plato wrote *The Republic?*
2. Give the date within one century
3. The exact date is not known, but it is estimated at 370 BC..
4. Dr Arn will lecture on Plato at 7:30 PM.
5. An area of 1600 sq ft is roughly equivalent to 150 m^2

THE QUESTION MARK

20c Use a question mark after a direct question.

DIRECT QUESTIONS

What is the difference between these two people?
Will economists ever really understand the economy?

After indirect questions, use a period: *My father asked why I came in so late.* (See 20a.)

Questions in a series are each followed by a question mark.

> The officer asked how many times the suspect had been arrested. Three times? Four times? More than that?

The use of capital letters for questions in a series is optional (see p. 421).

NOTE Question marks are never combined with other question marks, exclamation points, periods, or commas.

> FAULTY Readers ask, "What is the point?."
>
> REVISED Readers ask, "What is the point?"

20d Use a question mark within parentheses to indicate doubt about the correctness of a number or date.

> The Greek philosopher Socrates was born in 470 (?) B.C. and died in 399 B.C. from drinking poison after having been condemned to death.

NOTE Don't use a question mark within parentheses to express sarcasm or irony. Express these attitudes through sentence structure and diction. (See Chapters 18 and 31.)

> FAULTY Stern's friendliness (?) bothered Crane.
>
> REVISED Stern's *insincerity* bothered Crane.

Exercise 2
Revising: Question marks

Revise the following sentences so that question marks (along with other punctuation marks) are used correctly.

Example:

"When will it end?," cried the man dressed in rags.
"When will it end?" cried the man dressed in rags.

1. In Homer's *Odyssey,* Odysseus took seven years to travel from Troy to Ithaca. Or was it eight years. Or more?
2. Odysseus must have wondered whether he would ever make it home?
3. "What man are you and whence?," asks Odysseus's wife, Penelope.
4. Why does Penelope ask, "Where is your city? Your family?"?
5. Penelope does not recognize Odysseus and asks who this stranger is?

THE EXCLAMATION POINT

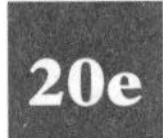

20e Use an exclamation point after an emphatic statement, interjection, or command.

No! We must not lose this election!
Come here immediately!

Follow mild interjections and commands with commas or periods, as appropriate.

No, the response was not terrific.
To prolong your car's life, change its oil regularly.

NOTE Exclamation points are never combined with other exclamation points, question marks, periods, or commas.

FAULTY "This will not be endured!," he roared.

REVISED "This will not be endured!" he roared.

20f Use exclamation points sparingly.

Don't express sarcasm, irony, or amazement with the exclamation point. Rely on sentence structure and diction to express these attitudes. (See Chapters 18 and 31.)

FAULTY After travelling 7 billion kilometres through space, *Voyager 2* was off-target by 33.6 kilometres (!).

REVISED After travelling 7 billion kilometres through space, *Voyager 2* was off-target by *a mere* 33.6 kilometres.

Relying on the exclamation point for emphasis is like crying wolf: the mark loses its power to impress the reader. Frequent exclamation points can also make writing sound overemotional. In the following passage, the writer could have conveyed ideas more effectively by punctuating sentences with periods.

> Our city government is a mess! After just six months in office, the mayor has had to fire four city officials! In the same period the city councillors have done nothing but argue! And city services decline with each passing day!

Exercise 3
Revising: Exclamation points

Revise the following sentences so that exclamation points (along with other punctuation marks) are used correctly. If a sentence is punctuated correctly as given, circle the number preceding it.

Example:

"Well, now!," he said loudly.
"Well, now!" he said loudly.

1. As the firefighters moved their equipment into place, the police shouted, "Move back!"
2. A child's cries could be heard from above: "Help me. Help."
3. When the child was rescued, the crowd called "Hooray."
4. The rescue was the most exciting event of the day!
5. Let me tell you about it.

Exercise 4
Revising: End punctuation

Insert appropriate punctuation (periods, question marks, or exclamation points) where needed in the following paragraph.

When visitors first arrive in Hawaii, they often encounter an unexpected language barrier Standard English is the language of business and government, but many of the people speak Pidgin English Instead of an excited "Aloha" the visitors may be greeted with an excited Pidgin "Howzit" or asked if they know "how fo' find one good hotel" Many Hawaiians question whether Pidgin will hold children back because it prevents communication with the *haoles,* or Caucasians, who run businesses Yet many others feel that Pidgin is a last defence of ethnic diversity on the islands To those who want to make standard English the official language of the state, these Hawaiians may respond, "Just 'cause I speak Pidgin no mean I dumb" They may ask, "Why you no listen" or, in standard English, "Why don't you listen"

NOTE See page 418 for a punctuation exercise combining periods with other marks of punctuation.

Chapter 21 The Comma

Commas usually function within sentences to separate elements (see the box on the next page). Omitting needed commas or inserting needless ones can confuse the reader.

Comma needed	Though very mild-mannered Mackenzie King dominated federal politics for more than twenty years.
Revised	Though very mild-mannered, Mackenzie King dominated federal politics for more than twenty years.
Unneeded commas	The hectic pace of Beirut, broke suddenly into frightening chaos when the city became, the focus of civil war.
Revised	The hectic pace of Beirut broke suddenly into frightening chaos when the city became the focus of civil war.

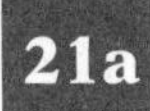

21a Use a comma before *and, but,* or another coordinating conjunction linking main clauses.

The coordinating conjunctions are *and, but, or, nor, for, so,* and *yet.* When these link words or phrases, do not use a comma: *Dugain plays and sings Irish and English folk songs.* However, *do* use a comma when a coordinating conjunction joins main clauses.

Principal uses of the comma

- To separate main clauses linked by a coordinating conjunction (21a).

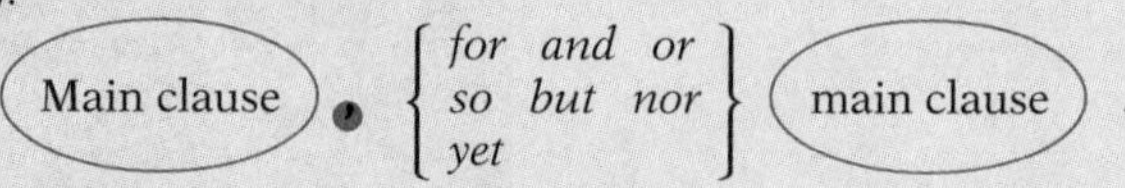

The building is finished, *but* it has no tenants.

- To set off most introductory elements (21b).

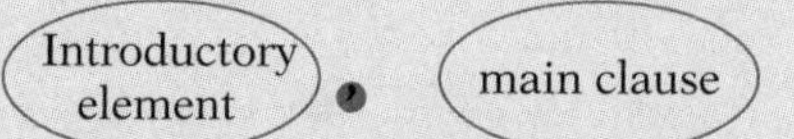

Unfortunately, the only tenant pulled out.

- To set off nonrestrictive elements (21c).

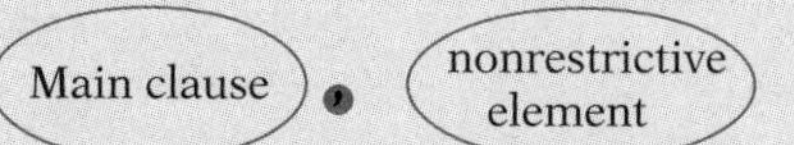

The empty building symbolizes a weak local economy, *which affects everyone.*

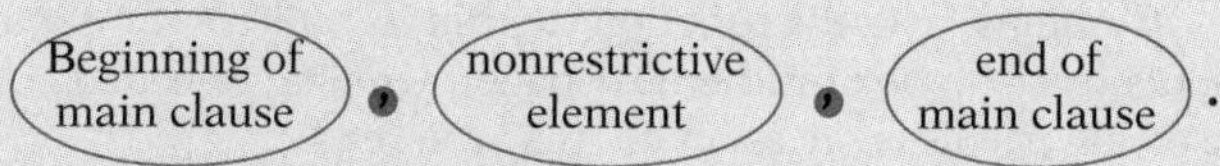

The main cause, *the decline of local industry*, is not news.

- To separate items in a series (21f-1).

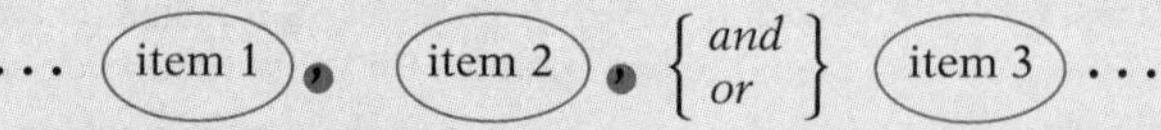

The city needs *healthier businesses*, *new schools*, *and improved housing*.

- To separate coordinate adjectives (21f-2).

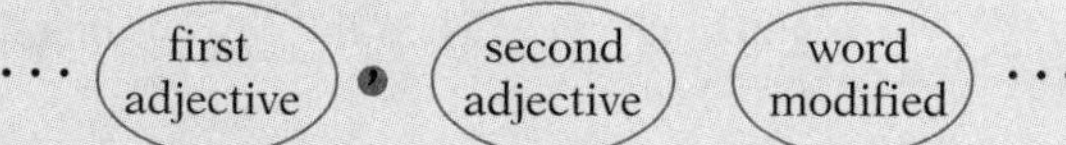

A *tall*, *sleek* skyscraper is not needed.

Other uses of the comma:

To set off absolute phrases (21d).
To set off phrases expressing contrast (21e).
To separate parts of dates, addresses, long numbers (21g).
To separate quotations and identifying words (21h).
To prevent misreading (21i).

See also 21j for when *not* to use the comma.

^
;
21a

A **main clause** has a subject and a predicate (but no subordinating word at the beginning) and makes a complete statement (see p. 172).

> Caffeine can keep coffee drinkers alert, *and* it may elevate their mood.
>
> Caffeine was once thought to be safe, *but* now researchers warn of harmful effects.
>
> Coffee drinkers may suffer sleeplessness, *for* the drug acts as a stimulant to the nervous system.

Exceptions When the main clauses in a sentence are very long or grammatically complicated, or when they contain internal punctuation, a semicolon before the coordinating conjunction will clarify the division between clauses (see p. 383).

> Caffeine may increase alertness, elevate mood, and provide energy; *but* it may also cause irritability, anxiety, stomach pains, and other ills.

When main clauses are very short and closely related in meaning, you may omit the comma between them as long as the resulting sentence is clear.

> Caffeine helps but it also hurts.

If you are in doubt about whether to use a comma in such a sentence, use it. It will always be correct.

Exercise 1
Punctuating linked main clauses

Insert a comma before each coordinating conjunction that links main clauses in the following sentences.

Example:

I would have attended the concert and the reception but I had to baby-sit for my niece.

I would have attended the concert and the reception, but I had to baby-sit for my niece.

1. Parents once automatically gave their children the father's surname but some no longer do.
2. Instead, they bestow the mother's name for they believe that the mother's importance should be recognized.
3. The child's surname may be just the mother's or it may link the mother's and the father's with a hyphen.
4. Sometimes the first and third children will have the mother's surname and the second child will have the father's.
5. Occasionally the mother and father combine parts of their names and a new hybrid surname is born.

Exercise 2
Sentence combining: Linked main clauses

Combine each group of sentences below into one sentence that contains only two main clauses connected by the coordinating conjunction in parentheses. Separate the main clauses with a comma. You will have to add, delete, and rearrange words.

Example:

The circus had come to town. The children wanted to see it. Their parents wanted to see it. (*and*)

The circus had come to town, *and* the children and their parents wanted to see it.

1. Parents were once legally required to bestow the father's surname on their children. These laws have been contested in court. They have been found invalid. (*but*)
2. Parents may now give their children any surname they choose. The arguments for bestowing the mother's surname are often strong. They are often convincing. (*and*)
3. Critics sometimes question the effects of unusual surnames on children. They wonder how confusing the new surnames will be. They wonder how fleeting the surnames will be. (*or*)
4. Children with surnames different from their parents' may suffer embarrassment. They may suffer identity problems. Giving children their father's surname is still very much the norm. (*for*)
5. Hyphenated names are awkward. They are also difficult to pass on. Some observers think they will die out in the next generation. Or they may die out before. (*so*)

21b Use a comma to set off most introductory elements.

An introductory element modifies a word or words in the main clause that follows. These elements are usually set off from the rest of the sentence with a comma.

Subordinate clause (p. 172)

Even when identical twins are raised apart, they grow up very like each other.

Because they are similar, such twins interest scientists.

Verbal or verbal phrase (p. 168)

Explaining the similarity, some researchers claim that one's genes are one's destiny.

Concerned, other researchers deny the claim.

Prepositional phrase (p. 164)

In a debate that has lasted centuries, scientists use identical twins to argue for or against genetic destiny.

Sentence modifier

Of course, scientists can now look directly at the genes themselves.

The comma may be omitted after short introductory elements if its omission does not create confusion. (If you are in doubt, however, the comma is always correct.)

Clear *In a hundred years* genetics may no longer be a mystery.

Confusing Despite intensive research scientists still have more questions than answers.

Clear Despite intensive research, scientists still have more questions than answers.

Note Take care to distinguish verbals used as modifiers from verbals used as subjects. The former almost always take a comma; the latter never do.

modifier
Studying identical twins, geneticists learn about inheritance.

subject
Studying identical twins helps geneticists learn about inheritance.

Exercise 3
Punctuating introductory elements

Insert commas where needed after introductory elements in the following sentences. If a sentence is punctuated correctly as given, circle the number preceding it.

Example:

After the new library opened the old one became a student union.

After the new library opened, the old one became a student union.

1. Moving in a fluid mass is typical of flocks of birds and schools of fish.
2. Because it is sudden and apparently well coordinated the movement of flocks and schools has seemed to be directed by a leader.
3. However new studies have discovered that flocks and schools are leaderless.
4. When each bird or fish senses a predator it follows individual rules for fleeing.
5. Multiplied over hundreds of individuals these responses look as if they have been choreographed.

Exercise 4
Sentence combining: Introductory elements

Combine each pair of sentences below into one sentence that begins with an introductory phrase or clause as specified in parentheses. Follow the introductory element with a comma. You will have to add, delete, change, and rearrange words.

Example:

The girl was humming to herself. She walked upstairs. (*Phrase beginning Humming.*)

Humming to herself, the girl walked upstairs.

1. Scientists have made an effort to explain the mysteries of flocks and schools. They have proposed bizarre magnetic fields and telepathy. (*Phrase beginning In.*)
2. Scientists developed computer models. They have abandoned earlier explanations. (*Clause beginning Since.*)
3. The movement of a flock or school starts with each individual. It is rapidly and perhaps automatically coordinated among individuals. (*Phrase beginning Starting.*)
4. One zoologist observes that human beings seek coherent patterns. He suggests that investigators saw purpose in the movement of flocks and schools where none existed. (*Phrase beginning Observing.*)
5. One may want to study the movement of flocks or schools. Then one must abandon a search for purpose or design. (*Phrase beginning To.*)

^, 21c

21c Use a comma or commas to set off nonrestrictive elements.

Commas around part of a sentence often signal that the element is not essential to the meaning of the sentence. This **nonrestrictive element** may modify or rename the word it refers to, but it does not limit the word to a particular individual or group.

NONRESTRICTIVE ELEMENT

The company, *which is located in Newfoundland,* has an excellent reputation.

In contrast, a **restrictive element** *does* limit the word it refers to: the element cannot be omitted without leaving the meaning too general. Because it is essential, a restrictive element is *not* set off with commas.

RESTRICTIVE ELEMENT

The company rewards employees *who work hard.*

Nonrestrictive elements are *not* essential, but punctuation *is.* Restrictive elements *are* essential, but punctuation is *not.*

Note When a nonrestrictive element falls in the middle of a sentence, be sure to set if off with a pair of commas, one *before* and one *after* the element. Dashes or parentheses may also be used to set off nonrestrictive elements (see pp. 409 and 412).

Meaning and context

The same element in the same sentence may be restrictive or nonrestrictive depending on your intended meaning and the context in which the sentence appears. For example, look at the second sentence in each passage below.

Restrictive

Not all the bands were equally well received, however. The band *playing old music* held the audience's attention. The other groups created much less excitement. [*Playing old music* identifies a particular band.]

Nonrestrictive

A new band called Fats made its debut on Saturday night. The band, *playing old music,* held the audience's attention. If this performance is typical, the group has a bright future. [*Playing old music* adds information about a band already named.]

A test for restrictive and nonrestrictive elements

1. Identify the element.

   Hai Nguyen *who emigrated from Vietnam* lives in Calgary.
   Those *who emigrated with him* live elsewhere.

2. Remove the element. Does the fundamental meaning of the sentence change?

   Hai Nguyen lives in Calgary. **No.**
   Those live elsewhere. **Yes.** [Who are *Those?*]

3. If **no,** the element is nonrestrictive and should be set off with punctuation.

   Hai Nguyen, who emigrated from Vietnam, lives in Calgary.

   If **yes,** the element is *restrictive* and should *not* be set off with punctuation.

   Those who emigrated with him live elsewhere.

Use a comma or commas to set off nonrestrictive clauses and phrases.

Clauses and phrases serving as adjectives and adverbs may be either nonrestrictive or restrictive. Only nonrestrictive clauses and phrases are set off with punctuation. In the following examples the italicized clauses and phrases could be omitted without changing the meaning of the words they modify.

NONRESTRICTIVE

Elizabeth Blackwell was the first woman to graduate from a North American medical school, *in 1849.*

She was a medical pioneer, *helping to found the first medical college for women.*

She taught at the school, *which was affiliated with the New York Infirmary.*

Emily Howard Stowe, *the first Canadian woman to practise medicine in Canada,* graduated from the New York Medical College for Women in 1867.

Stowe was not officially licensed to practise medicine in Canada until 1880, *when she was forty-nine.*

NOTE Most adverb clauses are restrictive because they describe conditions necessary to the main clause. They are set off by a comma only when they introduce sentences (see 21b) and when they are truly nonrestrictive, adding incidental information (as in the last example above) or expressing a contrast beginning *although, even though, though, whereas,* and the like.

^ ;
21c

In the following sentences, the italicized elements restrict the meaning of the words they modify. Removing the elements would leave the meaning too general.

RESTRICTIVE

The history *of aspirin* began *with the ancient Greeks.*

Physicians *who sought to relieve their patients' pains* recommended chewing willow bark.

Willow bark contains a chemical *that is similar to aspirin.*

NOTE Whereas both nonrestrictive and restrictive clauses may begin with *which,* only restrictive clauses begin with *that.* Some writers prefer *that* exclusively for restrictive clauses and *which* exclusively for nonrestrictive clauses. See the Glossary of Usage, page 789, for advice on the use of *that* and *which.*

Use a comma or commas to set off nonrestrictive appositives.

An **appositive** is a noun or noun substitute that renames another noun just before it. (See p. 176.) Many appositives are nonrestrictive; thus they are set off, usually with commas.

NONRESTRICTIVE

Alice Munro's 1986 book of short stories, *The Progress of Love*, won the Governor General's medal for fiction.

Michael Ondaatje's fourth novel, *The English Patient*, won the Booker Prize.

Take care *not* to set off restrictive appositives; like other restrictive elements, they limit or define the word they refer to.

RESTRICTIVE

Ondaatje's novel *In the Skin of a Lion* is about the construction of the Bloor Viaduct in Toronto.

The philosopher *Alfred North Whitehead* once wrote that the history of philosophy was a series of footnotes to Plato.

Use a comma or commas to set off parenthetical expressions.

Parenthetical expressions are explanatory, supplementary, or transitional words or phrases. (Transitional expressions include *however, indeed, consequently, as a result, of course, for example,* and *in fact;* see p. 90 for a longer list.) Parenthetical expressions are often set off by a comma or commas.

Few people would know, *or even guess*, the most celebrated holiday on earth.

That holiday is, *in fact*, New Year's Day.

(Dashes and parentheses may also set off parenthetical elements. See pp. 410 and 412, respectively.)

Use a comma or commas to set off *yes* and *no*, tag questions, words of direct address, and mild interjections.

YES AND *NO*

Yes, the editorial did have a point.
No, that can never be.

TAG QUESTIONS

Jones should be allowed to vote, *should he not?*
They don't stop to consider others, *do they?*

DIRECT ADDRESS

Cody, please bring me the newspaper.
With all due respect, *sir*, I will not do that.

MILD INTERJECTIONS

Well, you will never know who did it.
Oh, they forgot all about the baby.

(You may want to use an exclamation point to set off a forceful interjection. See p. 353.)

Exercise 5
Punctuating restrictive and nonrestrictive elements

Insert commas in the following sentences to set off nonrestrictive elements, and delete any commas that incorrectly set off restrictive elements. If a sentence is correct as given, circle the number preceding it.

Example:

Our language has adopted the words, *garage* and *fanfare,* from the French.

Our language has adopted the words *garage* and *fanfare* from the French.

1. Italians insist that Marco Polo the thirteenth-century explorer did not import pasta from China.
2. Pasta which consists of flour and water and often egg existed in Italy long before Marco Polo left for his travels.
3. A historian who studied pasta places its origin in the Middle East in the fifth century.
4. Most Italians dispute this account although their evidence is shaky.
5. Wherever it originated, the Italians are now the undisputed masters, in making and cooking pasta.
6. Marcella Hazan, who has written several books on Italian cooking, insists that homemade and hand-rolled pasta is the best.
7. Most cooks must buy dried pasta lacking the time to make their own.
8. The finest pasta is made from semolina, a flour from hard durum wheat.
9. Pasta manufacturers choose hard durum wheat, because it makes firmer cooked pasta than common wheat does.
10. Pasta, made from common wheat, tends to get soggy in boiling water.

^
,
21c

Exercise 6
Sentence combining: Restrictive and nonrestrictive elements

Combine each pair of sentences below into one sentence that uses the element described in parentheses. Insert commas as appropriate. You will have to add, delete, change, and rearrange words. Some items have more than one possible answer.

Example:

Mr. Ward's oldest sister helped keep him alive. She was a nurse in the hospital. (*Nonrestrictive clause beginning* who.)

Mr. Ward's oldest sister, *who was a nurse in the hospital,* helped keep him alive.

1. Most sources say it was the Italians. The Italians introduced pasta as a main dish. (*restrictive clause beginning who*)
2. The Italians use the word to mean only tubular pasta. The word is *macaroni*. (*restrictive appositive*)
3. North American manufacturers use *macaroni* to mean all flour-and-water pasta. These manufactures are unlike the Italians. (*non-restrictive phrase beginning unlike*)
4. North Americans also use *spaghetti* for all flour-and-water pasta. The meaning "little strings" in Italian. (*non-restrictive phrase beginning meaning*)
5. North American colonists first imported pasta from the English. The English had discovered it as tourists in Italy. (*non-restrictive clause beginning who*)
6. The English returned from their grand tours of Italy. They were called *macaronis* because of their fancy airs. (*restrictive phrase beginning returning*)
7. A hairstyle was also called *macaroni.* It had elaborate curls. (*restrictive phrase beginning with*)
8. The song "Yankee Doddle" refers to this hairdo. It reports that Yankee Doodle "stuck a feather in his cap and called it macaroni." (*restrictive phrase beginning with when*)
9. The song was actually intended to poke fun at unrefined North American colonists. It was a creation of the English. (non-*restrictive appositive*)
10. The colonists adopted the jolly tune. They turned it to their advantage. (non-*restrictive phrase beginning turning*)

21d Use a comma or commas to set off absolute phrases.

An **absolute phrase** modifies a whole main clause rather than any word in the clause, and it usually consists of at least a participle and its subject (a noun or pronoun). (See p. 171.) Absolute phrases can occur at almost any point in the sentence, and they are always set off by a comma or commas.

Domestic recycling having succeeded, the city now wants to extend the program to businesses.

Many businesses, *their profits already squeezed,* resist recycling.

Exercise 7
Punctuating absolute phrases

Insert commas in the following sentences to set off absolute phrases.

Example:

The recording contract was cancelled the band having broken up.

The recording contract was cancelled, the band having broken up.

1. Prices having risen rapidly the government debated a price freeze.
2. Businesses their profits otherwise made vulnerable would demand a wage freeze as well.
3. Workers their real income having been eaten away by rising prices and taxes would resist any wage freeze.
4. The Prime Minister would have to persuade businesses to accept a price freeze his methods depending on their recalcitrance.
5. No doubt the Prime Minister his advisers having urged it would first try a patriotic appeal.
6. Arm-twisting having worked for previous prime ministers this one might resort to it.

21e Use a comma or commas to set off phrases expressing contrast.

The essay needs less wit, *more pith.*

His generosity, *not his good looks,* won him friends.

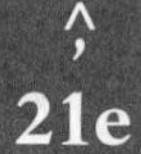

It is not light that is needed, *but fire;* it is not the gentle shower, *but thunder.* —Frederick Douglass

Note Writers often omit commas around contrasting phrases beginning *but: A full, but hazy, moon shone down.*

Exercise 8
Punctuating phrases expressing contrast

Insert commas in the following sentences to set off phrases that express contrast.

Example:

Moira not her sister was the one who attended university in Nova Scotia.

Moira, not her sister, was the one who attended university in Nova Scotia.

1. The expense of heating homes not just the cold makes the winter months difficult in most parts of Canada.
2. Many people must forgo necessities not just luxuries to pay their heating bills.
3. People use their gas ovens more for heat less for cooking.
4. Using a gas oven for heat is extremely dangerous not safe as many people believe.
5. The gas fumes not the flames are the source of danger.

21f Use commas between items in a series and between coordinate adjectives.

Use commas between words, phrases, or clauses forming a series.

Place commas between all elements of a **series**—that is, three or more items of equal importance.

> Anna Spingle *married at the age of seventeen, had three children by twenty-one, and divorced at twenty-two.*
>
> She worked as *a cook, a baby-sitter, and a crossing guard.*

Though some writers omit the comma before the coordinating conjunction in a series (*Breakfast consisted of coffee, eggs, and kippers*), the final comma is never wrong and it always helps the reader see the last two items as separate. Use it consistently and your writing will be clearer, as the following example shows.

CONFUSING	Her new job involves typing, filing and answering correspondence.
CLEAR	Her new job involves typing, filing, and answering correspondence.

EXCEPTION When items in a series are long and grammatically complicated, they may be separated by semicolons. When the items contain commas, they must be separated by semicolons. (See p. 383.)

Use commas between two or more adjectives that equally modify the same word.

When two or more adjectives modify the same word equally, they are said to be **coordinate.** The adjectives may be separated either by *and* or by a comma.

> Spingle's *scratched and dented* car is an eyesore, but it gets her to work.
>
> She has dreams of a *sleek, shiny* car.

Adjectives are not coordinate—and should *not* be separated by commas—when the one nearer the noun is more closely related to the noun in meaning.

> Spingle's children work at *various odd* jobs.
>
> They all expect to go to a *nearby community* college.

NOTE Numbers are not coordinate with other adjectives.

Punctuating two or more adjectives

1. Identify the adjectives.

   She was a *faithful sincere* friend.
   They are *dedicated medical* students.

2. Can the adjectives be reversed without changing meaning?

   She was a *sincere faithful* friend. **Yes.**
   They are *medical dedicated* students. **No.**

3. Can the word *and* be inserted between the adjectives without changing meaning?

   She was a *faithful and sincere* friend. **Yes.**
   They are *dedicated and medical* students. **No.**

4. If **yes** to both questions, the adjectives are coordinate and should be separated by a comma.

   She was a *faithful, sincere* friend.

   If **no** to both questions, the adjectives are *not* coordinate and should *not* be separated by a comma.

   They are *dedicated medical* students.

FAULTY Spingle has *three, teenaged* children.
REVISED Spingle has *three teenaged* children.

Do not use a comma between the final coordinate adjective and the noun.

FAULTY The children hope to avoid their mother's *hard, poor,* life.
REVISED The children hope to avoid their mother's *hard, poor* life.

Exercise 9
Punctuating series and coordinate adjectives

Insert commas in the following sentences to separate coordinate adjectives or elements in series. Circle the number preceding each sentence whose punctuation is already correct.

Example:

Although quiet by day, the club became a noisy smoky dive at night.

Although quiet by day, the club became a noisy, smoky dive at night.

1. Shoes with high heels originated to protect feet from the mud garbage and animal waste in the streets.

2. The first known high heels worn strictly for fashion appeared in the sixteenth century.
3. The heels were worn by men and made of colourful silk brocades soft suedes or smooth leathers.
4. High-heeled shoes received a boost when the short powerful King Louis XIV of France began wearing them.
5. Eventually only wealthy fashionable French women wore high heels.

21g Use commas according to convention in dates, addresses, place names, and long numbers.

When they appear within sentences, dates, addresses, and place names punctuated with commas are also ended with commas.

DATES

July 1, 1867, was the birthday of Confederation.

The signing of the armistice on Monday, November 11, 1918, ended the First World War.

Commas are not used between the parts of a date in inverted order (*15 December 1998*) or in dates consisting of a month or season and a year (*December 1941*).

ADDRESSES AND PLACE NAMES

Use the address 72 Douglas Drive, Saskatoon, Saskatchewan, for all correspondence.

Halifax, Nova Scotia, is the location of Dalhousie University.

Commas are not used between the names of provinces and postal codes in addresses: *Pierrefonds, Quebec H8Z 3H2, is home.*

LONG NUMBERS

Traditionally the comma has been used to separate the figures in long numbers into groups of three, counting from the right. With numbers of four digits, the comma has been optional.

The new assembly plant cost $7,525,000 by to build.

Since Canada adopted the metric system, however, it has become increasingly common to replace the commas in long numbers with small spaces.

The new assembly plant cost $7 525 000 to build.

Exercise 10
Punctuating dates, addresses, place names, numbers

Insert commas as needed in the following sentences.

Example:

One fund-raising event was held on June 24 1997 and the other in late January 1998.

One fund-raising event was held on June 24, 1997, and the other in late January 1998.

1. The Scotia Festival of Music will hold a benefit dinner and performance on September 24 1999 in Halifax.
2. Performers are expected from as far away as St. John's Newfoundland and Thunder Bay Ontario.
3. All inquiries sent to Scotia Festival of Music 1541 Barrington St. Suite 317 Halifax NS B3J 1Z5 will receive a quick response.
4. The deadline for ordering tickets by mail is Friday August 24, 1999.

21h Use commas with quotations according to standard practice.

The words *he said, she replied,* and so on identify the source of a quotation. These identifying words may come before, after, or in the middle of the quotation. They must always be separated from the quotation by punctuation, usually a comma or commas. (See pp. 396–97 for a summary of this and other conventions regarding quotations.)

1 Ordinarily, use a comma with identifying words before or after a quotation.

Eleanor Roosevelt said, "You must do the thing you think you cannot do."

"Knowledge is power," wrote Francis Bacon.

Exceptions Do not use a comma when identifying words following a quotation ending in an exclamation point or a question mark.

"Claude!" Mrs. Harrison called.
"Why must I come home?" he asked.

Do not use commas with a quotation introduced by *that* or with a short quotation that is merely one element in the sentence, not the substance of the sentence.

The warning that "cigarette smoking is dangerous to your health" has fallen on many deaf ears.

People should always say "Excuse me" when they bump into fellow pedestrians.

Use a colon instead of a comma to separate identifying words from a quotation when there is an emphatic break between them in meaning or in grammar or when the quotation is very formal or longer than a sentence. (See also p. 407.)

The 1982 Constitution Act is unequivocal: "English and French are the official languages of Canada and have equality of status and equal rights and privileges as to their use in all institutions of the Parliament and government of Canada."

With an interrupted quotation, precede the identifying words with a comma and follow them with the punctuation required by the quotation.

QUOTATION

"The shore has a dual nature, changing with the swing of the tides."

IDENTIFYING WORDS

"The shore had a dual nature," observes Rachel Carson, "changing with the swing of the tides." [The identifying words interrupt the quotation at a comma and thus end with a comma.]

QUOTATION

"However mean your life is, meet it and live it; do not shun it and call it hard names."

IDENTIFYING WORDS

"However mean your life is, meet it and live it," Thoreau advises in *Walden*; "do not shun it and call it hard names." [The identifying words interrupt the quotation at a semicolon and thus end with a semicolon.]

QUOTATION

"This is the faith with which I return to the South. With this new faith we will be able to hew out of the mountain of despair a stone of hope."

IDENTIFYING WORDS

"This is the faith with which I return to the South," Martin Luther King, Jr., proclaimed. "With this new faith we will be able to hew out of the mountain of despair a stone of hope." [The explanatory words interrupt the quotation at the end of a sentence and thus end with a period.]

NOTE Using a comma instead of a semicolon or a period in the last two examples would result in the error called a comma splice: two main clauses separated only by a comma. (See pp. 262–66.)

Place commas that follow quotations within quotation marks.

"That's my seat," she said coldly.
"You gave it up," I replied evenly, "so you have no right to it."

Exercise 11
Punctuating quotations

Insert commas or semicolons in the following sentences to correct punctuation with quotations. Circle the number preceding any sentence whose punctuation is already correct.

Example:

The shoplifter declared "I didn't steal anything."
The shoplifter declared, "I didn't steal anything."

1. The writer and writing teacher Peter Elbow suggests that an "open-ended writing process . . . can change you, not just your words."
2. "I think of the open-ended writing process as a voyage in two stages" Elbow says.
3. "The sea voyage is a process of divergence, branching, proliferation, and confusion" Elbow continues "the coming to land is a process of convergence, pruning, centralizing, and clarifying."
4. "Keep up one session of writing long enough to get loosened up and tired" advises Elbow "long enough in fact to make a bit of a voyage."
5. "In coming to new land" Elbow says "you develop a new conception of what you are writing about."

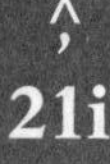

21i Use commas to prevent misreading.

In some sentences words may run together in unintended and confusing ways unless a comma separates them.

CONFUSING	Soon after the business closed its doors.
CLEAR	Soon after, the business closed its doors.

Exercise 12
Punctuating to prevent misreading

Insert commas in the following sentences to prevent misreading.

Example:

To Laura Ann symbolized decadence.
To Laura, Ann symbolized decadence.

1. Though happy people still have moments of self-doubt.
2. In research subjects have reported themselves to be generally happy people.
3. Yet those who have described sufferings as well as joys.
4. Of fifty eight subjects reported bouts of serious depression.
5. For half the preceding year had included at least one personal crisis.

21j Use commas only where required.

Commas can make sentences choppy and even confusing if they are used more often than needed or in violation of rules 21a through 21h.

1 Delete any comma that separates subject and verb or verb and object.

Commas interrupt the movement from subject to verb to object.

FAULTY The returning *athletes, expected* a warmer welcome than they received. [Separation of subject and verb.]

REVISED The returning *athletes expected* a warmer welcome than they received.

Principal misuses of the comma

- Don't separate subject-verb or verb-object (21j-1).

  FAULTY *Anyone* with breathing problems, *should not exercise* during smog alerts.

  REVISED Anyone with breathing problems should not exercise during smog alerts.

- Don't separate a pair of words, phrases, or subordinate clauses joined by *and, or,* or *nor* (21j-2).

  FAULTY Asthmatics are affected by *ozone, and sulfur oxides.*

  REVISED Asthmatics are affected by ozone and sulfur oxides.

- Don't set off restrictive elements (21j-3).

  FAULTY Even people, *who are healthy,* should be careful.

  REVISED Even people who are healthy should be careful.

- Don't set off a series (21j-4).

  FAULTY *Cars, factories, and even bakeries,* contribute to smog.

  REVISED Cars, factories, and even bakeries contribute to smog.

- Don't set off an indirect quotation or a single word that isn't a nonrestrictive appositive (21j-5).

  FAULTY Experts *say, that* the pollutant, *ozone,* is especially damaging.

  REVISED Experts say that the pollutant ozone is especially damaging.

Faulty They had been *chosen, to compete* for their country. [Separation of verb *chosen* and object *to fight.*]

Revised They had been chosen to compete for their country.

Use commas between subject, verb, and object only when other words between these elements require punctuation.

> Canadians, who are preoccupied with other sports, have not developed a strong interest in professional soccer. [Commas set off a nonrestrictive clause.]

Delete any comma that separates a pair of words, phrases, or subordinate clauses joined by a coordinating conjunction.

When linking elements with *and, or,* or another coordinating conjunction, do not use a comma unless the elements are main clauses (see p. 355).

Faulty Banks *could, and should* help older people manage their money. [Compound helping verb.]

Revised Banks could and should help older people manage their money.

Faulty Older people need special assistance *because they live* on fixed incomes, *and because they are not familiar* with new *accounts, and rates.* [Compound subordinate clauses *because . . . because* and compound object of preposition *with.*]

Revised Older people need special assistance because they live on fixed incomes and because they are not familiar with new accounts and rates.

Faulty *Banks, and community groups* can *help* the elderly, *and eliminate* the confusion they often feel. [Compound subject and compound predicate.]

Revised Banks and community groups can help the elderly and eliminate the confusion they often feel.

Delete any commas that set off restrictive elements.

Commas do not set off a restrictive element, which limits the meaning of the word it refers to (see p. 360).

Faulty Margaret Laurence's work, *The Diviners,* is set in her mythical Manitoba town of Manawaka. [The title is essential to distinguish the novel from the rest of Laurence's work.]

Revised Margaret Laurence's work *The Diviners* is set in her mythical Manitoba town of Manawaka.

Faulty The prose style, *that Laurence used,* influenced other novelists. [The clause identifies the prose style.]

Revised The prose style that Laurence used influenced other novelists.

Delete any comma before or after a series unless a rule requires it.

Commas separate the items *within* a series (p. 367) but do not separate the series from the rest of the sentence.

Faulty Among other things, the Europeans brought to the New World, *horses, advanced technology, and new diseases.* [The comma after World separates verb and object.]

Revised Among other things, the Europeans brought to the New World *horses, advanced technology, and new diseases.*

In the following sentence the commas before and after the series are appropriate because the series is a nonrestrictive appositive (see p. 362).

> The three Prairie provinces, *Alberta, Saskatchewan, and Manitoba,* share similar historical and cultural backgrounds.

However, many writers prefer to use dashes rather than commas to set off series functioning as appositives (see pp. 409–10).

Delete any comma setting off an indirect quotation or a single word that isn't a nonrestrictive appositive.

Indirect quotation

Faulty The report *concluded, that* dieting could be more dangerous than overeating.

Revised The report concluded that dieting could be more dangerous than overeating.

Quoted or italicized word

A quoted or italicized word is a restrictive appositive when it limits the word it refers to (see p. 362). Do not use commas around a restrictive appositive.

Faulty James Joyce's story, "Araby," was assigned last year. [The commas imply wrongly that Joyce wrote only one story.]

Revised James Joyce's story "Araby" was assigned last year.

Faulty The word, *open,* can be either a verb or an adjective.

Revised The word *open* can be either a verb or an adjective.

The following sentence requires commas because the quoted title is a nonrestrictive appositive.

Hugh MacLennan's first published novel, *Barometer Rising*, ushered in a new phase in Canadian literary production.

Exercise 13
Revising: Needless or misused commas

Revise the following sentences to eliminate needless or misused commas. Circle the number preceding each sentence that is already punctuated correctly.

Example:

The portrait of the founder, that hung in the dining hall, was stolen by pranksters.

The portrait of the founder that hung in the dining hall was stolen by pranksters.

1. In Greek mythology Theseus is protected by the god, Poseidon.
2. Theseus is an adventurer, and a hero of the Athenians.
3. In one of his adventures Theseus sails, to Crete, to kill the Minotaur, which has been devouring young Athenians.
4. The Minotaur, half-bull and half-human, is kept by the king of Crete, Minos, in his maze-like palace.
5. Each year Minos captures fourteen young Athenians, and throws them to the Minotaur in revenge for the death of his son in Athens.
6. When Theseus arrives in Crete, Minos challenges him by throwing a gold ring into the sea and ordering him to retrieve it.
7. Under the water Theseus meets a woman, who is Poseidon's wife and who hands him the ring to return to Minos.
8. Theseus later meets Minos's only daughter, Ariadne, and she gives him a ball of string so that he can find his way out of the maze.
9. She warns, that the Minotaur's victims have been too exhausted from being lost in the maze to fight for their lives.
10. With a ball of string Theseus can leave a trail behind him, and find his way through, and out of the maze.
11. Theseus does, as Ariadne urges, and conserves the energy, needed to kill the Minotaur.
12. He also rescues some youths, whom the Minotaur has not yet killed.
13. Theseus, the youths, and Ariadne, all flee from Crete in Theseus's ship.
14. They travel to the island, of Naxos, where Theseus deserts Ariadne.
15. One version of the myth explains, that another god, Dionysus, orders Theseus away so that he can have Ariadne for himself.

Exercise 14
Revising: Commas

Insert commas in the following paragraphs wherever they are needed, and eliminate any misused or needless commas.

Canadian sport is indebted to the Aboriginal peoples for the toboggan snowshow lacrosse stick and canoe. The coureurs de bois and the voyageurs through their close contact with the Aboriginal peoples, helped introduce into European settlements the activities, that resulted from the use of these pieces of equipment. Many Aboriginal games had utilitarian purposes related to survival (wrestling jousting archery spear throwing and foot and canoe racing) while activities such as dancing and baggataway ... had religious significance. The Aboriginal peoples also developed a great variety of games such as awl games ring and pole snow snake cat's cradle dice and birchbark cards partly for the sheer love of play, and sometimes for the purpose of gambling. The games of the Inuit, were similarly related to preparing youth for cooperative existence in a harsh environment where one also needed to know one's tolerance limits. Blanket toss tug-of-war dogsled races drum dances spear-throwing and ball games as well as self-testing games, such as arm-pull hand-wrestling and finger-pull helped to fulfil this purpose.

Note See page 418 for a punctuation exercise combining commas with other marks of punctuation.

Chapter 22 The Semicolon

22a Use a semicolon between main clauses not joined by *and, but,* or another coordinating conjunction.

Main clauses contain a subject and a predicate and do not begin with a subordinating word (see p. 172). When you join two main clauses in a sentence, you have two primary options for separating them:

- Insert a comma and a coordinating conjunction: *and, but, or, nor, for, so, yet.* (See p. 355.)

  The drug does little to relieve symptoms, *and* it can have side-effects.

- Insert a semicolon:

  The side-effects are not minor; some leave the patient quite ill.

NOTE If you do not link main clauses with a coordinating conjunction and you separate them only with a comma or with no punctuation at all, you will produce a comma splice or a fused sentence. See Chapter 11.

The box on the next page distinguishes among the principal uses of three often-confused marks: semicolon, comma, and colon. Generally, use the semicolon in sentences like the one above: the first clause creates an expectation, and the second clause fulfils the expectation.

EXCEPTION Writers sometimes use a comma instead of a semicolon between very short and closely parallel main clauses.

> The poor live, the rich just exist.

But a semicolon is safer, and it is always correct.

Distinguishing the comma, the semicolon, and the colon

The **comma** chiefly separates both equal and unequal sentence elements.

- It separates main clauses when they are linked by a coordinating conjunction (21a).

  An airline once tried to boost sales by advertising the tense alertness of its crews, *but* nervous fliers did not want to hear about pilots' sweaty palms.

- It separates subordinate information that is part of or attached to a main clause, such as a nonrestrictive modifier or an introductory element (21b–21h).

  Although the airline campaign failed, many advertising agencies, including some clever ones, copied its underlying message.

The **semicolon** chiefly separates equal and balanced sentence elements.

- It separates complementary main clauses that are *not* linked by a coordinating conjunction (22a).

  The airline campaign had highlighted only half the story; the other half was buried in the copy.

- It separates complementary main clauses that are related by a conjunctive adverb (22b).

  The campaign should not have stressed the pilots' insecurity; *instead,* the campaign should have stressed the improved performance resulting from that insecurity.

The **colon** chiefly separates unequal sentence elements.

- It separates a main clause from a following explanation or summary, which may or may not be a main clause (25a).

  Many successful advertising campaigns have used this message: the anxious seller is harder working and smarter than the competitor.

Exercise 1
Punctuating between main clauses

Insert semicolons to separate main clauses in the following sentences.

Example:

One man at the auction bid prudently another did not.
One man at the auction bid prudently; another did not.

1. More and more musicians are playing computerized instruments more and more listeners are worrying about the future of acoustic instruments.
2. The computer is not the first new technology in music the pipe organ and saxophone were also technological breakthroughs in their day.
3. Musicians have always experimented with new technology audiences have always resisted the experiments.
4. Most computer musicians are not merely following the latest fad they are discovering new sounds and new ways to manipulate sound.
5. Few musicians have abandoned acoustic instruments most value acoustic sounds as much as electronic sounds.

Exercise 2
Sentence combining: Related main clauses

Combine each set of three sentences below into one sentence containing only two main clauses, and insert a semicolon between the clauses. You will have to add, delete, change, and rearrange words. Most items have more than one possible answer.

Example:

Alex Colville's paintings are highly realistic. His subjects are almost always chosen from his immediate environment. Colville's work has dominated the post-war Maritime painting scene.

The subjects of Alex Colville's highly realistic paintings are almost always chosen from his immediate environment; his work has dominated the post-war Maritime painting scene.

1. Electronic instruments are prevalent in jazz. They are also prevalent in rock music. They are less common in classical music.
2. Jazz and rock change rapidly. They nourish experimentation. They nourish improvisation.
3. Traditional classical music does not change. Its notes and instrumentation were established by a composer. The composer was writing decades or centuries ago.
4. Contemporary classical music not only can draw on tradition. It also can respond to innovations. These are innovations such as jazz rhythms and electronic sounds.

5. Much contemporary electronic music is more than just one type of music. It is more than just jazz, rock, or classical. It is a fusion of all three.

22b Use a semicolon between main clauses related by *however, thus,* or another conjunctive adverb.

Conjunctive adverbs include *consequently, hence, however, indeed, instead, nonetheless, otherwise, still, then, therefore,* and *thus.* (See p. 180 for more explanation and a fuller list.) When a conjunctive adverb relates two main clauses, the clauses should be separated by a semicolon.

> Most students now use computers to print their essays; *however,* many still prefer to compose with pen and paper.

The position of the semicolon between main clauses never changes, but the conjunctive adverb may move around within the second clause. When the adverb falls somewhere besides the beginning of the clause, set it off with a comma or commas. (The semicolon remains between clauses.)

> Most students now use computers to print their essays; many still prefer, *however,* to compose with pen and paper.

> Most students now use computers to print their essays; many still prefer to compose with pen and paper, *however.*

Note This rule prevents the errors known as comma splice and fused sentence. See Chapter 11.

; 22b

Exercise 3
Punctuating main clauses related by conjunctive adverbs

Insert a semicolon in each sentence below to separate main clauses related by a conjunctive adverb, and insert a comma or commas where needed to set off the adverb.

Example:

He knew that tickets for the concert would be scarce therefore he arrived at the box office hours before it opened.

He knew that tickets for the concert would be scarce; therefore, he arrived at the box office hours before it opened.

1. Music is a form of communication like language the basic elements however are not letters but notes.
2. Computers can process any information that can be represented numerically consequently they can process musical information.

3. A computer's ability to process music depends on what software it can run furthermore it must be connected to a system that converts electrical vibration into sound.
4. Computers and their sound systems can produce many different sounds indeed the number of possible sounds is infinite.
5. The powerful music computers are very expensive they are therefore used only by professional musicians.

Exercise 4
Sentence combining: Main clauses related by conjunctive adverbs

Combine each set of three sentences below into one sentence containing only two main clauses. Connect the clauses with the conjunctive adverb in parentheses, and separate them with a semicolon. (Be sure conjunctive adverbs are punctuated appropriately.) You will have to add, delete, change, and rearrange words. Each item has more than one possible answer.

Example:

The Albanians censored their news. We got little news from them. And what we got was unreliable. (*therefore*)

The Albanians censored their news; *therefore*, the little news we got from them was unreliable.

1. Most music computers are too expensive for the average consumer. Digital keyboard instruments can be inexpensive. They are widely available. (*however*)
2. Inside the keyboard is a small computer. The computer controls a sound synthesizer. The instrument can both process and produce music. (*consequently*)
3. The person playing the keyboard presses keys or manipulates other controls such as switches. The computer and synthesizer convert these signals. The signals are converted into vibrations and sounds. (*then*)
4. The inexpensive keyboards can perform only a few functions. To the novice computer musician, the range is exciting. The range includes drum rhythms and simulated instruments. (*still*)
5. Would-be musicians can orchestrate whole songs. They start from just the melody lines. They need never again play "Chopsticks." (*thus*)

22c Use a semicolon to separate main clauses if they are long and complex or if they contain commas, even when a coordinating conjunction joins them.

You would normally use a comma with a coordinating conjunction such as *and* or *but* between main clauses. But placing semicolons between clauses punctuated with commas or between long and grammatically complicated clauses makes a sentence easier to read.

> Whatever happens, we shall have to take Layton as he comes and wishes, the good and the bad together**;** *but* that is better than not having him at all. —George Woodcock

Many writers prefer to use a semicolon instead of a comma between main clauses joined by the coordinating conjunctions *so* and *yet,* even when the clauses are not complicated or internally punctuated.

> The day was rainy and blustery**;** *so* the food vendors kept their fruits and vegetables indoors.

> It seemed an unlikely day for shopping**;** *yet* buyers flocked to the market for fresh, inexpensive produce.

22d Use semicolons to separate items in a series if they are long or contain commas.

; 22d

You normally use commas to separate items in a series (see p. 367). But use semicolons instead when the items are long or internally punctuated. The semicolons help the reader identify the items.

> The custody case involved Amy Dalton, the child**;** Ellen and Mark Dalton, the parents**;** and Ruth and Hal Blum, the grandparents.

> One may even reasonably advance the claim that the sort of communication that really counts, and is therefore embodied into permanent records, is primarily written**;** that "words fly away, but written messages endure," as the Latin saying put it two thousand years ago**;** and that there is no basic significance to at least fifty percent of the oral interchange that goes on among all sorts of persons, high and low. —Mario Pei

Exercise 5
Punctuating long main clauses and series items

Substitute commas for semicolons in the following sentences to separate main clauses or series items that are long or contain commas.

Example:

After graduation he debated whether to settle in Vancouver, which was temperate but far from his parents, Toronto, which was exciting but expensive, or Winnipeg, which was close to home but already familiar.

After graduation he debated whether to settle in Vancouver, which was temperate but far from his parents; Toronto, which was exciting but expensive; or Winnipeg, which was close to home but already familiar.

1. The Indian subcontinent is separated from the rest of the world by clear barriers: the Bay of Bengal and the Arabian Sea to the east and west, respectively, the Indian Ocean to the south, and 2500 kilometres of mountain ranges to the north.
2. In the north of India are the world's highest mountains, the Himalayas, and farther south are fertile farmlands, unpopulated deserts, and rain forests.
3. India is a nation of ethnic and linguistic diversity, with numerous religions, including Hinduism, Islam, and Christianity, with distinct castes as well as Aryan, Dravidian, and Mongoloid ethnic groups, and with sixteen languages, including the official Hindi and the "associate official" English.
4. Between the seventeenth and nineteenth centuries the British colonized most of India, taking control of government, the bureaucracy, and industry, and they assumed a social position above all Indians.
5. During British rule the Indians' own unresolved differences and their frustrations with the British erupted in violent incidents such as the Sepoy Mutiny that began on February 26, 1857, and lasted two years, the Amritsar Massacre on April 13, 1919, and violence between Hindus and Moslems during World War II that resulted in the division of India into India and Pakistan.

22e Use the semicolon only where required.

Semicolons do not separate unequal sentence elements and should not be overused.

Delete or replace any semicolon that separates a subordinate clause or a phrase from a main clause.

The semicolon does not separate subordinate clauses and main clauses, or phrases and main clauses.

FAULTY According to African authorities; only about 35 000 Pygmies exist today.

Revised According to African authorities, only about 35 000 Pygmies exist today.

Faulty They are in danger of extinction; because of encroaching development.

Revised They are in danger of extinction because of encroaching development.

Note Many readers regard a phrase or subordinate clause set off with a semicolon as a sentence fragment. See Chapter 10.

Delete or replace any semicolon that introduces a series or explanation.

Colons and dashes, not semicolons, introduce series, explanations, and so forth. (See pp. 406–11.)

Faulty Teachers have heard all sorts of reasons why students do poorly; psychological problems, family illness, too much work, too little time.

Revised Teachers have heard all sorts of reasons why students do poorly: psychological problems, family illness, too much work, too little time.

Revised Teachers have heard all sorts of reasons why students do poorly—psychological problems, family illness, too much work, too little time.

Use the semicolon sparingly.

Use the semicolon only occasionally. Too many semicolons, even when they are required by rule, often indicate repetitive sentence structure. (See p. 337 for tips on revising repetitive structure.)

Semicolon overused

The Make-a-Wish Foundation helps sick children; it grants the wishes of children who are terminally ill. The foundation learns of a child's wish; the information usually comes from parents, friends, or hospital staff; the wish may be for a special toy, perhaps, or a visit to Disneyland. The foundation grants some wishes with its own funds; for other wishes it appeals to those who have what the child desires.

Revised

The Make-a-Wish Foundation grants the wishes of children who are terminally ill. From parents, friends, or hospital staff, the foundation learns of a child's wish for a special toy, perhaps, or a visit to Disneyland. It grants some wishes with its own funds; for other wishes it appeals to those who have what the child desires.

Exercise 6
Revising: Misused or overused semicolons

Revise the following sentences to eliminate misused or overused semicolons, substituting other punctuation as appropriate.

Example:

The doctor gave everyone the same advice; get exercise.
The doctor gave everyone the same advice: get exercise.

1. The main religion in India is Hinduism; a way of life as well as a theology and philosophy.
2. Unlike Christianity and Judaism; Hinduism is a polytheistic religion; with deities numbering in the hundreds.
3. Hinduism is unlike many other religions; it allows its creeds and practices to vary widely from place to place and person to person. Other religions have churches; Hinduism does not. Other religions have principal prophets and holy books; Hinduism does not. Other religions are centred on specially trained priests or other leaders; in Hinduism the individual is his or her own priest.
4. In Hindu belief there are four types of people; reflective, emotional, active, and experimental.
5. Each type of person has a different technique for realizing the true, immortal self; which has infinite existence, infinite knowledge, and infinite joy.

Exercise 7
Revising: Semicolons

Insert semicolons in the following paragraph wherever they are needed. Eliminate any misused or needless semicolons, substituting other punctuation as appropriate.

The set, sounds, and actors in the movie captured the essence of horror films. The set was ideal; dark, deserted streets, trees dipping their branches over the sidewalks, mist hugging the ground and creeping up to meet the trees, looming shadows of unlighted, turreted houses. The sounds, too, were appropriate, especially terrifying was the hard, hollow sound of footsteps echoing throughout the film. But the best feature of the movie was its actors; all of them tall, pale, and thin to the point of emaciation. With one exception, they were dressed uniformly in grey and had grey hair. The exception was an actress who dressed only in black; as if to set off her pale yellow, nearly white, long hair; the only colour in the film. The glinting black eyes of another actor stole almost every scene, indeed, they were the source of all the film's mischief.

Note See page 418 for a punctuation exercise combining semicolons with other marks of punctuation.

Chapter 23 The Apostrophe

Unlike other punctuation marks, which separate words, the apostrophe (') appears as *part* of a word to indicate possession, the omission of one or more letters, or (in a few cases) plural number.

23a Use the apostrophe to indicate the possessive case for nouns and indefinite pronouns.

The **possessive case** shows ownership or possession of one person or thing by another. Possession may be shown with an *of* phrase (*the hair of the dog*); or it may be shown with the addition of an apostrophe and, usually, an *-s* (*the dog's hair*).

NOTE Apostrophes are easy to misuse. For safety's sake, check your drafts to be sure that all words ending in *-s* neither omit needed apostrophes nor add unneeded ones. Also, remember that the apostrophe or apostrophe-plus-*s* is an *addition.* Before this addition, always spell the name of the owner or owners without dropping or adding letters.

1 Add *-'s* to form the possessive case of singular nouns and indefinite pronouns.

Bill *Boughton's* skilful card tricks amaze children.
Anyone's eyes would widen. [Indefinite pronoun.]

Most tricks will pique an *adult's* curiosity, too.

Add -*'s* as well to singular nouns that end in -*s*.

Henry *James's* novels reward the patient reader.
The *business's* customers filed suit.

Exception We typically do not pronounce the possessive -*s* of a few singular nouns ending in an *s* or *z* sound, especially names with more than one *s* sound (*Moses*), names that sound like plurals (*Rivers, Bridges*), and other nouns when they are followed by a word beginning in *s*. In these cases, many writers add only the apostrophe to indicate possession.

Moses' mother concealed him in the bulrushes.
Joan *Rivers'* jokes offend many people.
For *conscience'* sake she confessed her lie.

However, usage varies widely, and the final -*s* is not wrong with words like these (*Moses's*, *Rivers's*, *conscience's*).

Uses and misuses of the apostrophe

Uses

Possessives of nouns and indefinite pronouns (23a)

Singular	Plural
Ms. Park's	the Parks'
everyone's	two weeks'
boy's	boys'

Contractions(23c)

won't shouldn't
they're it's a girl

Plurals of letters, numbers, and words named as words (23d)

C's 6's if's

Misuses

Possessives of personal pronouns (23b)

Not	But
it's toes	its toes
your's	yours
her's	hers

Third-person singulars of verbs (23b)

Not	But
swim's	swims
go's	goes
hope's	hopes

Plurals of nouns (23b)

Not	But
book's are	books are
the Freed's	the Freeds
candy's	candies

’
v
23a

Add *-'s* to form the possessive case of plural nouns *not* ending in *-s*.

The bill establishes *children's* rights.
Publicity grabbed the *media's* attention.

Add only an apostrophe to form the possessive case of plural nouns ending in *-s*.

Workers' incomes have not risen much over the past decade.
Many students benefit from several *years'* work after high school.
The *Jameses'* talents are extraordinary.

Note the difference in the possessives of singular and plural words ending in *-s*. The singular form usually takes *-'s: James's*. The plural takes only the apostrophe: *Jameses'*.

Add *-'s* only to the last word to form the possessive case of compound words or word groups.

The *council president's* address was a bore.
The *brother-in-law's* business failed.
Taxes are always *somebody else's* fault.

When two or more words show individual possession, add *-'s* to them all. If they show joint possession, add *-'s* only to the last word.

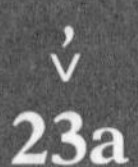

INDIVIDUAL POSSESSION

Youngman's and *Mason's* comedy techniques are similar. [Each comedian has his own technique.]

JOINT POSSESSION

The child recovered despite her *mother and father's* neglect. [The mother and father were jointly neglectful.]

Exercise 1
Forming possessives

Form the possessive case of each word or word group in parentheses.

Example:

The (*men*) blood pressures were higher than the (*women*).
The *men's* blood pressures were higher than the *women's*.

1. In the myths of the ancient Greeks, the (*goddesses*) roles vary widely.
2. (*Demeter*) responsibility is the fruitfulness of the earth.
3. (*Athena*) role is to guard the city of Athens.

4. (*Artemis*) function is to care for wild animals and small children.
5. (*Athena and Artemis*) father, Zeus, is the king of the gods.
6. Even a single (*goddess*) responsibilities are often varied.
7. Over several (*centuries*) time, Athena changes from a (*mariner*) goddess to the patron of crafts.
8. Athena is also concerned with fertility and with (*children*) well-being, since (*Athens*) strength depended on a large and healthy population.
9. Athena often changes into (*birds*) forms.
10. In (*Homer*) *Odyssey* she assumes a (*sea eagle*) form.
11. In ancient Athens the myths of Athena were part of (*everyone*) knowledge and life.
12. A cherished myth tells how Athena fights to retain possession of her (*people*) land when the god Poseidon wants it.
13. (*Athena and Poseidon*) skills are different, and each promises a special gift to the Athenians.
14. At the (*contest*) conclusion, Poseidon has given water and Athena has given an olive tree, for sustenance.
15. The other gods decide that the (*Athenians*) lives depend more on Athena than on Poseidon.

23b Delete or replace any apostrophe in a plural noun, a singular verb, or a possessive personal pronoun.

Not all words ending in -*s* take an apostrophe. Three kinds of words are especially likely to attract unneeded apostrophes.

Plural nouns

The plurals of nouns are generally formed by adding -*s* or -*es* (*boys, Smiths, families, Joneses*). Don’t mistakenly add an apostrophe to form the plural.

FAULTY The unleashed *dog’s* began travelling in a pack.
REVISED The unleashed *dogs* began travelling in a pack.

FAULTY The *Jones’* and *Bass’* were feuding.
REVISED The *Joneses* and *Basses* were feuding.

Singular verbs

Present-tense verbs used with *he, she, it,* and other third-person singular subjects always end in -*s* and *never* take an apostrophe.

FAULTY The subway *break’s* down less often now.
REVISED The subway *breaks* down less often now.

Possessives of personal pronouns

His, hers, its, ours, yours, theirs, and *whose* are possessive forms of the pronouns *he, she, it, we, you, they,* and *who.* They do not take apostrophes.

FAULTY The credit is *her's* not *their's.*

REVISED The credit is *hers,* not *theirs.*

The personal pronouns are often confused with contractions. See the next page.

Exercise 2
Distinguishing between plurals and possessives

Supply the appropriate form—possessive or plural—of each word given in parentheses. Some answers require apostrophes, and some do not.

Example:

A dozen Hawaiian (*shirt*), each with (*it*) own loud design, hung in the window.

A dozen Hawaiian *shirts,* each with *its* own loud design, hung in the window.

1. Demeter may be the oldest of the Greek (*god*), older than Zeus.
2. Many prehistoric (*culture*) had earth (*goddess*) like Demeter.
3. In myth she is the earth mother, which means that the responsibility for the fertility of both (*animal*) and (*plant*) is (*she*).
4. The (*goddess*) festival came at harvest time, with (*it*) celebration of bounty.
5. The (*people*) (*prayer*) to Demeter thanked her for grain and other (*gift*).

’ 23c

23c Use an apostrophe to indicate the omission in a standard contraction.

it is	it's	let us	let's
he is	he's	does not	doesn't
she is	she's	were not	weren't
they are	they're	class of 1987	class of '87
you are	you're	of the clock	o'clock
who is	who's	madam	ma'am

Contractions are common in speech and in informal writing. They may also be used to relax style in more formal kinds of writing, as they are in this handbook. But be aware that many people disapprove of contractions in any kind of formal writing.

NOTE Contractions are easily confused with the possessive personal pronouns.

CONTRACTION	POSSESSIVE PRONOUN
it's	its
they're	their
you're	your
who's	whose

FAULTY Legislators know *their* going to have to trim the budget to eliminate *it's* deficit.

REVISED Legislators know *they're* going to have to trim the budget to eliminate *its* deficit.

Exercise 3
Forming contractions

Form contractions from each set of words below. Use each contraction in a complete sentence.

Example:

we are: we're
We're open to ideas.

1. she would
2. could not
3. they are
4. he is
5. do not
6. she will
7. hurricane of 1962
8. is not
9. we would
10. will not

Exercise 4
Revising: Contractions and personal pronouns

Revise the following sentences to correct mistakes in the use of contractions and personal pronouns. Circle the number preceding any sentence that is already correct.

Example:

The company gives it's employees their birthdays off.
The company gives *its* employees their birthdays off.

1. In Greek myth the goddess Demeter has a special fondness for Eleusis, near Athens, and it's people.
2. She finds rest among the people and is touched by their kindness.
3. Demeter rewards the Eleusians with the secret for making they're land fruitful.
4. The Eleusians begin a cult in honour of Demeter, whose worshipped in secret ceremonies.
5. Its unknown what happened in the ceremonies, for no participant ever revealed their rituals.

23d Use an apostrophe plus *-s* to form the plurals of letters, numbers, and words named as words.

You may cite a character or word as a word rather than use it for its meaning. When such an element is plural, add an apostrophe plus *-s*.

> That sentence has too many *but*'s.
>
> Remember to dot your *i*'s and cross your *t*'s, or your readers may not be able to distinguish them from *e*'s and *l*'s.
>
> At the end of each chapter the author had mysteriously written two *3*'s and two *&*'s.

Notice that the letters, numbers, and words are underlined (italicized) but the apostrophe and added *-s* are not. (See p. 429 on this use of underlining or italics.)

Exception References to the years in a decade are not underlined and often omit the apostrophe. Thus either 1960's or 1960s is acceptable as long as usage is consistent.

Exercise 5
Forming plurals of letters, numbers, words

Form the plural of each letter, number, or word by using an apostrophe and *-s* and by underlining (italicizing) appropriately. Use the new plural in a complete sentence.

> *Example:* x
>
> Erase or white out typing mistakes. Do not use *x*'s.

1. 7
2. q
3. if
4. and
5. stop

Exercise 6
Revising: Apostrophes

In the following paragraph correct any mistakes in the use of the apostrophe or any confusion between contractions and possessive personal pronouns.

Landlocked Chad is among the worlds most troubled countries. The people's of Chad are poor; they're average per capita income equals $205 a year. No more than 15 percent of Chads population is literate, and every thousand people must share only two teacher's. The natural resources of the nation have never been plentiful, and now, as it's slowly being absorbed into the growing Sahara Desert, even water is scarce. Chads political conflicts go back beyond the turn of the century, when the French colonized the land by brutally subduing it's people. The rule of the French—

who's inept government of the colony did nothing to ease tensions among racial, tribal, and religious group's—ended with independence in 1960. But since then the Chadians experience has been one of civil war and oppression, and now their threatened with invasions from they're neighbours.

NOTE See page 418 for a punctuation exercise involving apostrophes along with other marks of punctuation.

Chapter 24 Quotation Marks

Quotation marks—either double (" ") or single (' ')—mainly enclose direct quotations from speech and from writing. The chart on the next two pages summarizes this and other uses.

NOTE Always use quotation marks in pairs, one at the beginning of a quotation and one at the end.

24a Use double quotation marks to enclose direct quotations.

Direct quotations report what someone has said or written in the exact words of the original. Always enclose direct quotations in quotation marks.

> Pierre Elliott Trudeau's famous 1967 statement, "There's no place for the state in the bedrooms of the nation," led to a considerable relaxation of Canada's divorce and anti-homosexual laws.

Indirect quotations report what has been said or written, but not in the exact words of the person being quoted. Indirect quotations are *not* enclosed in quotation marks.

> Pierre Elliott Trudeau's affirmation that the state has no place in the bedrooms of the nation led to a considerable relaxation of Canada's divorce and anti-homosexual laws.

(*Text continues p. 398*)

Handling quotations from speech or writing

(For explanations, consult the sections in parentheses.)

Direct and indirect quotation

Direct quotation (24a)

According to Lewis Thomas, "We are, perhaps uniquely among the earth's creatures, the worrying animal. We worry away our lives."

Quotation within quotation (24b)

Quoting a phrase by Lewis Thomas, the author adds, "We are 'the worrying animal.'"

Indirect quotation (24a)

Lewis Thomas says that human beings are unique among animals in their worrying.

Quotation marks with other punctuation marks

Commas and periods (24g-1)

Human beings are the "worrying animal," says Thomas.
Thomas calls human beings "the worrying animal."

Semicolons and colons (24g-2)

Machiavelli said that "the majority of men live content"; in contrast, Thomas calls us "the worrying animal."

Thomas believes that we are "the worrying animal": we spend our lives afraid and restless.

Question marks, exclamation points, dashes (24g-3)

When part of your own sentence

Who said that human beings are "the worrying animal"?
Imagine saying that we human beings "worry away our lives"!
Thomas's phrase—"the worrying animal"—seems too narrow.

When part of the original quotation

"Will you discuss this with me?" she asked.
"I demand that you discuss this with me!" she yelled.
"Please, won't you—" She paused.

Altering quotations

Brackets for additions (25d)

"We [human beings] worry away our lives," says Thomas.

Brackets for altered capitalization (26a)

"[T]he worrying animal" is what Thomas calls us. He says that "[w]e worry away our lives."

Ellipsis marks for omissions (25e)

"We are . . . the worrying animal," says Thomas.

Our worrying places us "uniquely among the earth's creatures. . . . We worry away our lives."

Punctuating identifying words with quotations

Introductory identifying words (21h-1)

He says, "We worry away our lives."

An answer is in these words by Lewis Thomas: "We are, perhaps uniquely among the earth's creatures, the worrying animal."

Thomas says that "the worrying animal" is afraid and restless.

Concluding identifying words (21h-1)

We are "the worrying animal," says Thomas.
"Who says?" she demanded.
"I do!" he shouted.

Interrupting identifying words (21h-2)

"We are," says Thomas, "perhaps uniquely among the earth's creatures, the worrying animal."

"I do not like the idea," she said; "however, I agree with it."

We are "the worrying animal," says Thomas. "We worry away our lives."

See also:

Special kinds of quoted material

Dialogue (3d-4, 24c)
Poetry (24c)
Prose passages of more than four lines (24c)

Using quotations in your own text

Quotations versus paraphrases and summaries (36b)
Avoiding plagiarism when quoting (36c)
Introducing quotations in your text (36g)
Citing sources for quotations (Chapter 37)

24b Use single quotation marks to enclose a quotation within a quotation.

When you quote a writer or speaker, use double quotation marks (see 24a). When the material you quote contains yet another quotation, distinguish the two by enclosing the second quotation in single quotation marks.

> "[I]n the past century it has come to be generally acknowledged," observed Marshall McLuhan, "that, in the words of Wyndham Lewis, 'The artist is always engaged in writing detailed history of the future because he is the only person aware of the nature of the present.'"

Notice that two different quotation marks appear at the end of the sentence—one single (to finish the interior quotation) and one double (to finish the main quotation).

Exercise 1

Using double and single quotation marks

Insert single and double quotation marks as needed in the following sentences. Circle the number preceding any sentence that is already correct.

Example:

The purpose of this book, explains the preface, is to examine the meaning of the phrase Dance is poetry.

"The purpose of this book," explains the preface, "is to examine the meaning of the phrase 'Dance is poetry.'"

1. Why, the lecturer asked, do we say Bless you! or something else when people sneeze but not acknowledge coughs, hiccups, and other eruptions?
2. She said that sneezes have always been regarded differently.
3. Sneezes feel more uncontrollable than some other eruptions, she said.
4. Unlike coughs and hiccups, she explained, sneezes feel as if they come from inside the head.
5. She concluded, People thus wish to recognize a sneeze, if only with a Gosh.

24c Set off quotations of dialogue, poetry, and long prose passages according to standard practice.

Dialogue

When quoting conversations, begin a new paragraph for each speaker.

"What shall I call you? Your name?" Andrews whispered rapidly, as with a high squeak the latch of the door rose.

"Elizabeth," she said. "Elizabeth."

—GRAHAM GREENE, *The Man Within*

NOTE When you quote a single speaker for more than one paragraph, put quotation marks at the beginning of each paragraph but at the end of only the last paragraph. The absence of quotation marks at the end of each paragraph but the last tells readers that the speech is continuing.

Poetry

When you quote a single line from a poem, a song, or a verse play, run the line into your own text and enclose the line in quotation marks.

```
Dylan Thomas remembered childhood as an idyllic time:
"About the lilting house and happy as the grass was
green" ("Fern Hill" line 2).
```

Poetry quotations of two or three lines may be placed in the text or displayed separately. In the text enclose the quotation in quotation marks and separate the lines with a slash surrounded by space.

```
Margaret Avison begins "The Swimmer's Moment" with a
statement of her universal theme: "For everyone / The
swimmer's moment at the whirlpool comes" (1-2).
```

Quotations of more than three lines of poetry should always be separated from the text with space and an indention. *Do not add quotation marks.*

```
Leonard Cohen rarely needed more than a few lines to
express the complexity of emotion:
          Alas, I cannot travel
          To a love I have so deep
          Or sleep too close beside
          A love I want to keep. ("I Long" 13-16)
```

The *MLA Handbook for Writers of Research Papers,* the standard guide to manuscript format in English and some other disciplines, recommends the following spacings for displayed quotations:

“ ” 24c

- Double-space above and below the quotation.
- Indent the quotation ten spaces from the left margin.
- Double-space the quoted lines.

Unless your instructor specifies otherwise, follow these guidelines for your typewritten or handwritten papers.

NOTE Be careful when quoting poetry to reproduce faithfully all line indentions; space between lines; spelling; capitalization; and punctuation, such as capitals and dashes.

Long prose passages

Separate a prose quotation of more than four typed or handwritten lines from the body of your paper. Follow the guidelines of the *MLA Handbook* in the list above. *Do not add quotation marks.*

> Linda Hutcheon points out the role that separation from the past often plays in self-definition in immigrant literatures:
>
>> For immigrants, the need to resist that dominant culture—however liberal or well meaning—may be intensified because of the weight of cultural tradition, made heavier (not lighter) by distance and time, by memory, by a sense of exile or simple nostalgia. Therefore, the drive towards self-definition may well involve separation from this ethnic past, at least temporarily.

Do not use a paragraph indention when quoting a single complete paragraph or a part of a paragraph. Use paragraph indentions only when quoting two or more complete paragraphs.

24d Put quotation marks around the titles of works that are parts of other works.

Use quotation marks to enclose the titles of short poems, articles in periodicals, short stories, essays, episodes of television and radio programs, the subdivisions of books, and other works that are published or released within larger works. Use quotation marks for

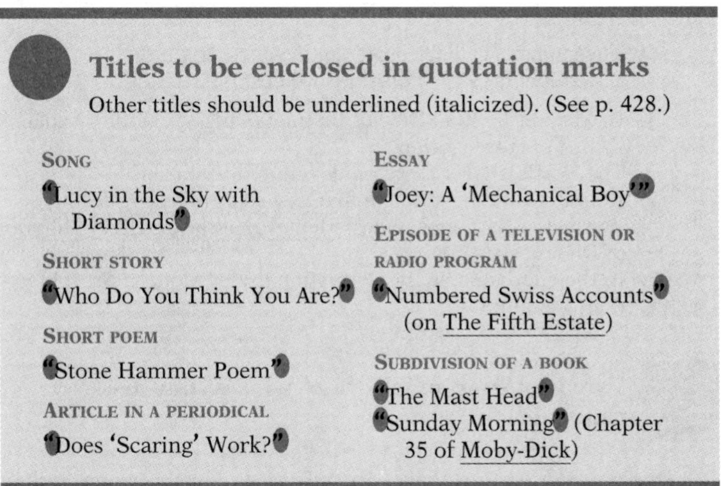

Titles to be enclosed in quotation marks

Other titles should be underlined (italicized). (See p. 428.)

SONG
"Lucy in the Sky with Diamonds"

SHORT STORY
"Who Do You Think You Are?"

SHORT POEM
"Stone Hammer Poem"

ARTICLE IN A PERIODICAL
"Does 'Scaring' Work?"

ESSAY
"Joey: A 'Mechanical Boy'"

EPISODE OF A TELEVISION OR RADIO PROGRAM
"Numbered Swiss Accounts" (on *The Fifth Estate*)

SUBDIVISION OF A BOOK
"The Mast Head"
"Sunday Morning" (Chapter 35 of *Moby-Dick*)

song titles as well. Use underlining (italics) for all other titles, such as books, plays, periodicals, movies, television programs, and works of art. (See p. 428.)

NOTE Use single quotation marks for a quotation within a quoted title and enclose all punctuation in the title within the quotation marks, as in the article title and essay title in the box above.

See page 421 for guidelines on the use of capital letters in titles.

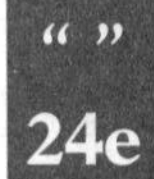

24e Quotation marks may be used to enclose words being defined or used in a special sense.

By "charity" I mean the love of one's neighbour as oneself.

On movie sets movable "wild walls" make a one-walled room seem four-walled on film.

NOTE In definitions, underlining (italics) is more common than quotation marks.

By *charity* I mean the love of one's neighbour as oneself.

Exercise 2
Quoting titles and words

Insert quotation marks as needed for titles and words in the following sentences. If quotation marks should be used instead of underlining, insert them.

Example:

The students call her professor despite her youth.
The students call her “professor” despite her youth.

1. In Chapter 8, titled How to Be Interesting, the author explains the art of conversation.
2. The Beatles' Let It Be reminds him of his uncle.
3. Doom means simply judgment as well as unhappy destiny.
4. The article that appeared in Mental Health was titled Children of Divorce Ask, “Why?”
5. In the encyclopedia the discussion under Modern Art fills less than a column.

24f Use quotation marks only where they are required.

Don't use quotation marks in the titles of your papers unless they contain or are themselves direct quotations.

Title of your paper

Not “Native and Settler in One Poem by Robert Kroetsch”

But Native and Settler in One Poem by Robert Kroetsch

Or Native and Settler in “Stone Hammer Poem”

Common nickname

Not “Gordie” Howe still prefers his nickname to his given name.

But Gordie Howe still prefers his nickname to his given name.

Title of your paper

Quotation marks will not excuse slang or a trite expression that is inappropriate to your writing. If slang is appropriate, use it without quotation marks.

Not His election campaign is “dead in the water” and needs a “jump start.”

But His election campaign has lost momentum and needs to be revived.

(See pp. 447 and 460 for more discussion of slang and trite expressions.)

24g Place other marks of punctuation inside or outside quotation marks according to standard practice.

The position of another punctuation mark inside or outside a closing quotation mark depends on what the other mark is and whether it appears in the quotation.

1 Place commas and periods inside quotation marks.

Commas or periods fall *inside* closing quotation marks, even when (as in the third example) single and double quotation marks are combined.

> Swift uses irony in his essay “A Modest Proposal.”
>
> Many first-time readers are shocked to see infants described as “delicious.”
>
> “‘A Modest Proposal,’” wrote one critic, “is so outrageous that it cannot be believed.”

EXCEPTION When a parenthetical source citation immediately follows a quotation at the end of a sentence, the period follows the source citation. (See also p. 576.)

> One critic calls the essay “outageous” (Olms 26).

(See pp. 370–71 for the use of commas to separate a quotation from words such as *she said.*)

2 Place colons and semicolons outside quotation marks.

> A few years ago the slogan in elementary education was “learning by playing”; now educators are concerned with teaching basic skills.
>
> We all know what is meant by “inflation”: more money buys less.

3 Place dashes, question marks, and exclamation points inside quotation marks only if they belong to the quotation.

When a dash, question mark, or exclamation point is part of the quotation, put it *inside* quotation marks. Don't use any other punctuation such as a period or comma.

"But must you—" Marcia hesitated, afraid of the answer.
Did you say, "Who is she?"
"Go away!" I yelled.

When a dash, question mark, or exclamation point applies only to the larger sentence, not to the quotation, place it *outside* quotation marks—again, with no other punctuation.

One of the most evocative lines in English poetry—"After many a summer dies the swan"—was written by Alfred, Lord Tennyson.

Who said, "Now cracks a noble heart"?

The woman called me "stupid"!

Exercise 3
Revising: Quotation marks

The underlined words in the following sentences are titles or direct quotations. Remove underlining where appropriate, and insert quotation marks. Be sure that other marks of punctuation are correctly placed inside or outside the quotation marks.

Example:

The award-winning essay is Science and Values.

The award-winning essay is "Science and Values."

1. In the title essay of her book The Death of the Moth and Other Essays, Virginia Woolf describes the last moments of a frail and diminutive body.
2. An insect's death may seem insignificant, but the moth is, in Woolf's words, life, a pure bead.
3. The moth's struggle against death, indifferent, impersonal, is heroic.
4. Where else but in such a bit of life could one see a protest so superb?
5. At the end Woolf sees the moth lying most decently and uncomplainingly composed; in death it finds dignity.

Exercise 4
Revising: Quotation marks

Insert quotation marks as needed in the following paragraph.

In one class we talked about two lines from Shakespeare's Sonnet 55:

> Not marble, nor the gilded monuments
> Of princes, shall outlive this powerful rime.

> Why is this true? the teacher asked. Why does Shakespeare's powerful rime indeed live longer than the gilded monuments / Of princes? She then asked if the lines were protected only by Shakespeare's status as our greatest writer. No, said one student. It has more to do with the power of the language. Then another student added, Even though paper is less durable than stone, ideas are more durable than monuments to dead princes. The whole discussion was an eye-opener for those of us (including me) who had never given much credit to rhymes or the words that made them.

Note See page 418 for a punctuation exercise involving quotation marks along with other marks of punctuation.

Chapter 25 Other Punctuation Marks

THE COLON

25a Use the colon to introduce and to separate.

The colon is mainly a mark of introduction: it signals that the words following will explain or amplify. The colon also has several conventional uses, such as in expressions of time.

In its main use as an introducer, a colon is *always* preceded by a complete **main clause**—one containing a subject and a predicate and not starting with a subordinating word (see p. 172). A colon may or may not be followed by a main clause. This is one way the colon differs from the semicolon (see the box on the next page). The colon is often interchangeable with the dash, though the dash is more informal and more abrupt (see 25b).

Note Don't use a colon more than once in a sentence. The sentence should end with the element introduced by the colon.

1 Use a colon to introduce a concluding explanation, series, appositive, or long or formal quotation.

Explanation

Hydrology has a deceptively simple definition**:** the study of water.

Distinguishing the colon and the semicolon

- The **colon** is a mark of introduction that separates elements of *unequal* importance, such as statements and explanations or introductions and quotations. The first element must be a complete main clause; the second element need not be. (See 25a.)

  The business school caters to working students: it offers special evening courses in business writing, finance, and management.

  The school has one goal: to train students to be responsible, competent businesspeople.

- The **semicolon** separates elements of *equal* importance, almost always complete main clauses. (See 22a.)

  Few enrolling students know exactly what they want from the school; most hope generally for a managerial career.

Sometimes a concluding explanation is preceded by *the following* or *as follows* and a colon.

> A more precise definition might be *the following*: the study of the movement of water on or over land, its flows and gatherings, its evaporations and condensations, its interactions with landforms like deltas and coastlines.

SERIES

> Canada has long coastal boundaries on three oceans: the Pacific, the Arctic, and the Atlantic.

APPOSITIVE

> Canada has one salient feature: the longest coastline.

Namely, that is, and other expressions that introduce appositives *follow* the colon: *Canada has one salient feature: namely, the longest coastline.*

LONG OR FORMAL QUOTATION

> One hydrologist has remarked on the importance of the study of this coastline: "We have to know as much as possible about this ecology in order to preserve and protect the immense resources of our coasts."

NOTE Depending on your preference, a complete sentence *after* the colon may begin with a capital letter or a small letter. Just be consistent throughout an essay.

Use a colon to separate titles and subtitles, the subdivisions of time, and the parts of biblical citations.

TITLES AND SUBTITLES

Charles Dickens: An Introduction to His Novels
Eros and Civilization: A Philosophical Inquiry into Freud

TIME

1:30 A.M.
12:26 P.M.

BIBLICAL CITATIONS

Isaiah 28:1–6
1 Corinthians 3:6–7

Use the colon only where required.

Use the colon only at the *end* of a main clause. Avoid using it between a verb and complement, verb and object, or preposition and object.

NOT Two entertaining movies directed by Steven Spielberg are: *E.T.* and *Raiders of the Lost Ark.*

BUT Two entertaining movies directed by Steven Spielberg are *E.T.* and *Raiders of the Lost Ark.*

NOT Shakespeare possessed the qualities of a Renaissance thinker, such as: humanism and a deep interest in classical Greek and Roman literature.

BUT Shakespeare possessed the qualities of a Renaissance thinker, such as humanism and a deep interest in classical Greek and Roman literature.

Exercise 1
Revising: Colons

Insert colons as needed in the following sentences, or delete colons that are misused.

Example:

Mix the ingredients as follows sift the flour and salt together, add the milk, and slowly beat in the egg yolk.

Mix the ingredients as follows: sift the flour and salt together, add the milk, and slowly beat in the egg yolk.

1. In the remote parts of many less developed countries, simple signs mark human habitation a dirt path, a few huts, smoke from a campfire.
2. In the built-up sections of industrialized countries, nature is all but obliterated by signs of human life, such as: houses, factories, skyscrapers, and highways.

3. The spectacle makes many question the words of Ecclesiastes 1:4 "One generation passeth away, and another cometh; but the earth abideth forever."
4. Yet many scientists see the future differently they hold that human beings have all the technology necessary to clean up the earth and restore the cycles of nature.
5. All that is needed is: a change in the attitudes of those who use technology.

THE DASH

25b Use a dash or dashes to indicate sudden changes in tone or thought and to set off some sentence elements.

The dash is mainly a mark of interruption: it signals an insertion or break.

NOTE In handwritten and typewritten papers, form a dash with two hyphens (--). Do not add extra space before, after, or between the hyphens.

1 Use a dash or dashes to indicate sudden shifts in tone, new or unfinished thoughts, and hesitation in dialogue.

— 25b

SHIFT IN TONE

He tells us—does he really mean it?—that he will speak the truth from now on.

UNFINISHED THOUGHT

If she found out—he did not want to think what she would do.

HESITATION IN DIALOGUE

"I was worried you might think I had stayed away because I was influenced by—" He stopped and lowered his eyes.

Astonished, Howe said, "Influenced by what?"

"Well, by—" Blackburn hesitated and for an answer pointed to the table. —LIONEL TRILLING

2 Use a dash or dashes to emphasize nonrestrictive elements.

Dashes may be used in place of commas or parentheses to set off and emphasize nonrestrictive elements. (See the box on the next page.) Dashes are especially useful when these elements are inter-

Distinguishing dashes, commas, and parentheses

Dashes, commas, and parentheses may all set off nonessential information such as nonrestrictive elements.

- **Dashes** give the information the greatest emphasis (25b-2):

  Many students—including some employed by the college—disapprove of the new work rules.

- **Commas** are less emphatic (21c):

  Many students, including some employed by the college, disapprove of the new work rules.

- **Parentheses,** the least emphatic, signal that the information is just worth a mention (25c-1):

  Many students (including some employed by the college) disapprove of the new work rules.

nally punctuated. Be sure to use a pair of dashes when the element interrupts a main clause.

APPOSITIVE

The qualities Monet painted—sunlight, rich shadows, deep colours—abounded near the rivers and gardens he used as subjects.

MODIFIER

Though they are close together—separated by only a few blocks—the two neighbourhoods could be in different countries.

PARENTHETICAL EXPRESSION

At any given time there exists an inventory of undiscovered embezzlement in—or more precisely not in—the country's businesses and banks. —JOHN KENNETH GALBRAITH

Use a dash to set off introductory series and concluding series and explanations.

INTRODUCTORY SERIES

Shortness of breath, skin discolouration or the sudden appearance of moles, persistent indigestion, the presence of small lumps—all these may signify cancer.

A dash sets off concluding series and explanations more informally and more abruptly than a colon does (see pp. 406–07).

CONCLUDING SERIES

The patient undergoes a battery of tests—CAT scan, bronchoscopy, perhaps even biopsy.

CONCLUDING EXPLANATION

Many patients are disturbed by the CAT scan—by the need to keep still for long periods in an exceedingly small space.

Use the dash only where needed.

Don't use the dash when commas, semicolons, and periods are more appropriate. And don't use too many dashes. They can create a jumpy or breathy quality in writing.

NOT In all his life—eighty-seven years—my great-grandfather never allowed his picture to be taken—not even once. He claimed the "black box"—the camera—would rob him of his soul.

BUT In all his eighty-seven years my great-grandfather did not allow his picture to be taken even once. He claimed the "black box"—the camera—would rob him of his soul.

Exercise 2
Revising: Dashes

Insert dashes as needed in the following sentences.

Example:

What would we do if someone like Adolf Hitler that monster appeared among us?

What would we do if someone like Adolf Hitler—that monster—appeared among us?

1. The movie-theatre business is undergoing dramatic changes changes that may affect what movies are made and shown.
2. The closing of independent theatres, the control of theatres by fewer and fewer owners, and the increasing ownership of theatres by movie studios and distributors these changes may reduce the availability of noncommercial films.
3. Yet at the same time the number of movie screens is increasing primarily in multiscreen complexes so that smaller films may find more outlets.
4. The number of active movie screens that is, screens showing films or booked to do so is higher now than at any time since World War II.
5. The biggest theatre complexes seem to be something else as well art galleries, amusement arcades, restaurants, spectacles.

PARENTHESES

25c Use parentheses to enclose nonessential elements within sentences.

Parentheses *always* come in pairs: one before and one after the punctuated material.

Use parentheses to enclose parenthetical expressions.

Parenthetical expressions include explanations, facts, digressions, and examples that may be helpful or interesting but are not essential to meaning. They are emphasized least when set off with a pair of parentheses instead of commas or dashes. (See the box on p. 410.)

> He drove trucks (tractor-trailers, actually) to earn money for technical college tuition.
>
> The population of Montreal (now just over 1.8 million) has declined since 1966.

NOTE Don't put a comma before a parenthetical expression enclosed in parentheses.

> NOT The dungeon, (really the basement) haunted us.
>
> BUT The dungeon (really the basement) haunted us.

A comma or period falling after a parenthetical expression should be placed outside the closing parenthesis.

> We received numerous complaints (125 to be exact), but most harped on the same old theme (namely, high prices).

When it falls between other complete sentences, a complete sentence enclosed in parentheses has a capital letter and end punctuation.

> In general, coaches will tell you that scouts are just guys who can't coach. (But then, so are brain surgeons.) —ROY BLOUNT

Use parentheses to enclose letters and figures labelling items in lists within sentences.

> My father could not, for his own special reasons, even *like* me. He spent the first twenty-five years of my life acting out that painful fact. Then he arrived at two points in his own life: (1) his last years, and (2) the realization that he had made a tragic mistake. —RAY WEATHERLY

When lists are set off from the text, the numbers or letters labelling them are usually not enclosed in parentheses.

Exercise 3
Revising: Parentheses

Insert parentheses as needed in the following sentences.

Example:

Students can find good-quality, inexpensive furniture for example, desks, tables, chairs, sofas, even beds in junk stores.

Students can find good-quality, inexpensive furniture (for example, desks, tables, chairs, sofas, even beds) in junk stores.

1. Many of those involved in the movie business agree that multiscreen complexes are good for two reasons: 1 they cut the costs of exhibitors, and 2 they offer more choices to audiences.
2. Those who produce and distribute films and not just the big studios argue that the multiscreen theatres give exhibitors too much power.
3. The major studios are buying movie theatres to gain control over important parts of the distribution process what gets shown and for how much money.
4. For twelve years 1938–50 the United States government forced the studios to sell all their movie theatres.
5. But because they now have more competition television and videocassette recorders, the studios are permitted to own theatres.

BRACKETS

25d Use brackets only within quotations to indicate your own comments or changes.

If you need to explain, clarify, or correct the words of the writer you quote, place your additions in a pair of brackets.

"That Petro-Canada station [just outside Toronto] is one of the busiest in the nation," said a company spokesperson.

Also use brackets if you need to alter the capitalization of a quotation so that it will fit into your sentence. (See also pp. 420–21.)

"[O]ne of the busiest in the nation" is how a company spokesperson described the station.

You may also use a bracketed word or words to substitute for parts of the original quotation that would otherwise be unclear. In the sentence below, the bracketed word substitutes for *they* in the original.

> "Despite considerable achievements in other areas, [humans] still cannot control the weather and probably will never be able to do so."

The word *sic* (Latin for "in this manner") in brackets indicates that an error in the quotation appeared in the original and was not made by you.

> According to the newspaper report, "The car slammed thru [*sic*] the railing and into oncoming traffic."

But don't use *sic* to make fun of a writer or to note errors in a passage that is clearly nonstandard or illiterate.

THE ELLIPSIS MARK

25e Use the ellipsis mark to indicate omissions within quotations.

The **ellipsis mark** consists of three spaced periods (. . .). It generally indicates an omission from a quotation, as illustrated in the following excerpts from this quotation about the "global village":

ORIGINAL QUOTATION

"McLuhan, of course, coined the phrase the 'global village,' and instructed a generation about the world's interconnectedness in the age of modern communications. For some, interconnectedness reinforces impressions and realities of difference; for others, it enhances a sense of a common humanity. For still others, it provides fleeting and barely relevant images captured by the roving cameras of the western world's television networks. Whatever the individual reaction, the 'global village' does symbolize that previous links among states took a quantum leap in the post-war age. In particular, the 'global village' offers no escape from the cultural trends conveyed daily from news-making, trendsetting centres of the world."

—JEFFREY SIMPSON, *Faultlines*

OMISSION OF THE MIDDLE OF A SENTENCE

"McLuhan . . . instructed a generation about the world's interconnectedness in the age of modern communications."

OMISSION OF THE END OF A SENTENCE

"For some, interconnectedness reinforces impressions and realities of difference. . . ." [The sentence period, closed up to the last word, precedes the ellipsis mark.]

"For some, interconnectedness reinforces impressions and realities of difference. . . ." (Simpson 35). [When the quotation is followed by a parenthetical source citation, as here, the sentence period follows the citation.]

Omission of parts of two sentences

"For some, interconnectedness reinforces impressions and realities of difference; for others, . . . it provides fleeting and barely relevant images captured by the roving cameras of the western world's television networks."

Omission of one or more sentences

"McLuhan, of course, coined the phrase the 'global village,' and instructed a generation about the world's interconnectedness in the age of modern communications. . . . In particular, the 'global village' offers no escape from the cultural trends conveyed daily from news-making, trendsetting centres of the world."

Note these features of the examples:

- The ellipsis mark indicates that material is omitted from the source when the omission would not otherwise be clear. Thus, use an ellipsis mark when the words you quote form a complete sentence that is different in the original (first through fourth examples above). Don't use an ellipsis mark at the beginning or end of a partial sentence: *Simpson argues that interconnectedness offers "no escape."*
- After a grammatically complete sentence, an ellipsis mark usually follows a sentence period and a space (second and last examples). The exception occurs when a parenthetical source citation follows the quotation (third example), in which case the sentence period falls after the citation.

. . .
25e

Note If you omit one or more lines of poetry or paragraphs of prose from a quotation, use a separate line of ellipsis marks across the full width of the quotation to show the omission.

Pauses and unfinished statements in quoted speech may be indicated with an ellipsis mark instead of a dash (p. 409).

"I wish . . ." His voice trailed off.

Exercise 4
Using ellipsis marks

Use ellipsis marks and any other needed punctuation to follow the numbered instructions (next page) for quoting from the following paragraph.

Women in the sixteenth and seventeenth centuries were educated in the home and, in some cases, in boarding schools. Men were educated at home, in grammar schools, and at the universities. The universities were closed to female students. For women, "learning the Bible," as Elizabeth Joceline puts it, was an impetus to learning to read. To be able to read the Bible in the vernacular was a liberating experience that freed the reader from hearing only the set passages read in the church and interpreted by the church. A Protestant woman was expected to read the scriptures daily, to meditate on them, and to memorize portions of them. In addition, a woman was expected to instruct her entire household in "learning the Bible" by holding instructional and devotional times each day for all household members, including the servants. —CHARLOTTE F. OTTEN, *English Women's Voices, 1540–1700*

1. Quote the fifth sentence, but omit everything from *that freed the reader* to the end.
2. Quote the fifth sentence, but omit the words *was a liberating experience that.*
3. Quote the first and fifth sentences.

THE SLASH

25f Use the slash between options and to separate lines of poetry that are run in to the text.

/ 25f

OPTION

I don't know why some teachers oppose pass/fail courses.

When used between options, the slash is not surrounded by extra space.

NOTE The options *and/or* and *he/she* should be avoided. (See the Glossary of Usage, pp. 775 and 782.)

POETRY

A.M. Klein's description of a poet as "the nth Adam taking a green inventory / in world but scarcely uttered" captures the essence of his view of the poet's function in society.

When separating lines of poetry in this way, leave a space before and after the slash. (See p. 399 for more on quoting poetry.)

Exercise 5
Revising: Colons, dashes, parentheses, brackets, ellipsis marks, slashes

Insert colons, dashes, parentheses, brackets, ellipsis marks, or slashes as needed in the following sentences, or remove them where they are not needed. When different marks would be appropriate in the same place, be able to defend the choice you make. Circle the number preceding any sentence that is already correct.

Example:

The residents of the neighbourhood including many who grew up there signed a petition against further development.

The residents of the neighbourhood—including many who grew up there—signed a petition against further development. [The dashes emphasize the parenthetical expression.]

1. Moderate temperatures, spectacular scenery, and the proximity of the sea these are her favourite characteristics of Vancouver.
2. In the March 1958 federal election, John Diefenbaker (affectionately dubbed "Dief the Chief" by his admirers) led the Conservatives to winning 208 seats in the House of Commons the highest number ever held by a single party in Canada up to that time.
3. He has all the qualities of a fine cook he shops patiently for the freshest ingredients, he prepares the food with imagination and care, and he serves the meal elegantly.
4. From the reviewer's sentence "The acting is amazingly incompetent, given that these actors can be powerful," the advertisement extracted praise by using an ellipsis mark: "The acting is amazingly powerful."
5. The bikers—tattooed and draped in chains look more threatening than they really are.
6. "Buy the new Universal Dictionery sic," the ad said. But why would anybody buy a dictionary that can't spell dictionary?
7. James Joyce's Ulysses first published in 1922 is a beautiful, shocking novel.
8. In the letter he quoted two lines of poetry that John Donne once wrote in a letter of his own "Sir, more than kisses, letters mingle souls; For thus friends absent speak."
9. Paying taxes one of life's certainties is only a little less painful than the other certainty.
10. Sylvie Bernier's gold medal in diving the first ever for Canada in that sport was probably the highlight for this country at the 1984 Los Angeles Olympics..

NOTE See the next page for a punctuation exercise combining colons, dashes, and parentheses with other marks of punctuation, such as commas and semicolons.

Exercise on Chapters 20–25
Revising: Punctuation

The following paragraphs are unpunctuated except for end-of-sentence periods. Insert periods, commas, semicolons, apostrophes, quotation marks, colons, dashes, parentheses, or spaces where they are required. When different marks would be appropriate in the same place, be able to defend the choice you make.

Brewed coffee is the most widely consumed beverage in the world. The trade in coffee beans alone amounts to well over $6000000000 a year and the total volume of beans traded exceeds 4250000 tonnes a year. Its believed that the beverage was introduced into Arabia in the fifteenth century AD probably by Ethiopians. By the middle or late sixteenth century the Arabs had introduced the beverage to the Europeans who at first resisted it because of its strong flavour and effect as a mild stimulant. The French Italians and other Europeans incorporated coffee into their diets by the seventeenth century the English however preferred tea which they were then importing from India. Since North America was colonized primarily by the English North Americans also preferred tea. Only after the Boston Tea Party 1773 did North Americans begin drinking coffee in large quantities. Now though the US and Canada are among the top coffee-consuming countries consumption having been spurred on by familiar advertising claims Good till the last drop Rich hearty aroma Always rich never bitter.

Produced from the fruit of an evergreen tree coffee is grown primarily in Latin America southern Asia and Africa. Coffee trees require a hot climate high humidity rich soil with good drainage and partial shade consequently they thrive on the east or west slopes of tropical volcanic mountains where the soil is laced with potash and drains easily. The coffee beans actually seeds grow inside bright red berries. The berries are picked by hand and the beans are extracted by machine leaving a pulpy fruit residue that can be used for fertilizer. The beans are usually roasted in ovens a chemical process that releases the beans essential oil caffeol which gives coffee its distinctive aroma. Over a hundred different varieties of beans are produced in the world each with a different flavour attributable to three factors the species of plant *Coffea arabia* and *Coffea robusta* are the most common and the soil and climate where the variety was grown.

p

Part VI

Mechanics

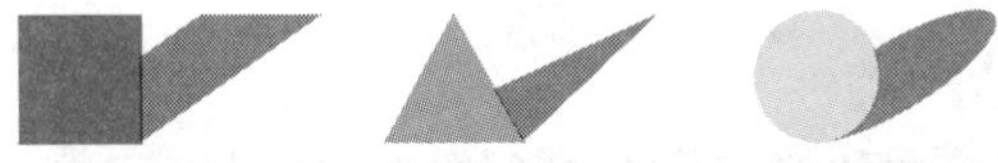

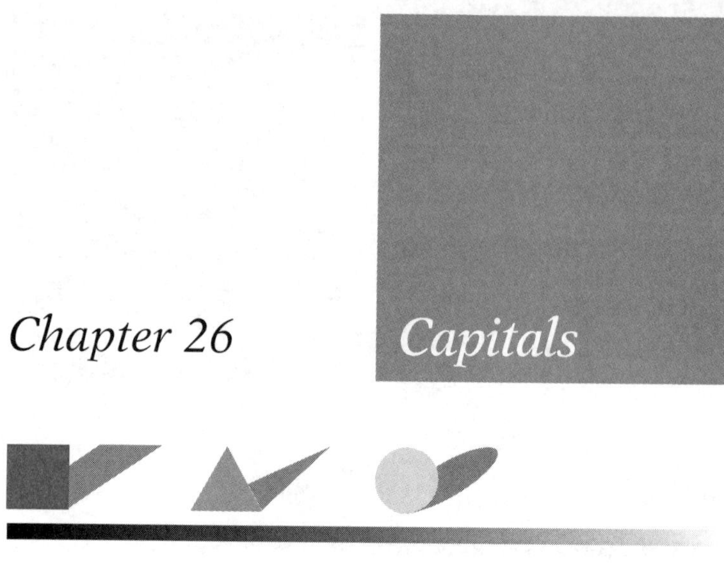

Chapter 26 Capitals

Experienced writers generally agree on when to use capitals, but the conventions are constantly changing. Consult a recent dictionary if you have any doubt about whether a particular word should be capitalized.

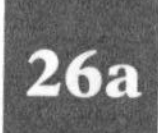

26a Capitalize the first word of every sentence.

Every writer should own a good dictionary.
Will inflation be curbed?
Watch out!

When quoting other writers, you must reproduce the capital letters beginning their sentences or indicate that you have altered the source. Whenever possible, integrate the quotation into your own sentence so that its capitalization coincides with yours.

"Psychotherapists often overlook the benefits of self-deception," the author argues.

The author argues that "the benefits of self-deception" are not always recognized by psychotherapists.

If you need to alter the capitalization in the source, indicate the change with brackets (see p. 413).

> "[T]he benefits of self-deception" are not always recognized by psychotherapists, the author argues.
>
> The author argues that "[p]sychotherapists often overlook the benefits of self-deception."

NOTE Capitalization of questions in a series is optional. Both of the following examples are correct.

> Is the population a hundred? Two hundred? More?
> Is the population a hundred? two hundred? more?

Also optional is capitalization of the first word in a complete sentence after a colon (see p. 407).

26b Capitalize most words in titles and subtitles of works.

In all titles and subtitles of works, capitalize the first and last words and all other words *except* articles (*a, an, the*), *to* in infinitives, and connecting words (prepositions and coordinating and subordinating conjunctions) of fewer than five letters. Capitalize even these short words when they are the first or last word in a title or when they fall after a colon or semicolon.

The Stone Angel	*Nights Below Station Street*
"Courtship Through the Ages"	"Once More to the Lake"
A Diamond Is Forever	*An End to Live For*
"Knowing Whom to Ask"	"Power: How to Get It"
The Last Spike	*File Under Architecture*
"The Truth About AIDS"	*Only when I Laugh*

NOTE Always capitalize the prefix or first word in a hyphenated word within a title. Capitalize the second word only if it is a noun or an adjective or is as important as the first word.

> "Applying Stage Make-up"
> *The Pre-Raphaelites*
> *Through the Looking-Glass*

26c Always capitalize the pronoun *I* and the interjection *O*. Capitalize *oh* only when it begins a sentence.

> I love to stay up at night, but, oh, I hate to get up in the morning.
>
> He who thinks himself wise, O heavens, is a great fool.
> —VOLTAIRE

cap 26c

26d Capitalize proper nouns, proper adjectives, and words used as essential parts of proper nouns.

Proper nouns name specific persons, places, and things: *Shakespeare, Alberta, War of 1812.* **Proper adjectives** are formed from some proper nouns: *Shakespearean, Albertan.*

1 Capitalize proper nouns and proper adjectives.

Capitalize all proper nouns and proper adjectives but not the articles (*a, an, the*) that precede them.

Proper nouns and adjectives to be capitalized

SPECIFIC PERSONS AND THINGS

Peter Mansbridge	SkyDome
Napoleon Bonaparte	the West Edmonton Mall
Doris Lessing	Kenney Dam

SPECIFIC PLACES AND GEOGRAPHICAL REGIONS

New York City	the Mediterranean Sea
China	the Maritimes, the Prairies
Europe	the Northeast, the South
North America	the Rocky Mountains

But: northeast of the city, going south

DAYS OF THE WEEK, MONTHS, HOLIDAYS

Monday	Yom Kippur
May	Christmas
Thanksgiving	Victoria Day

HISTORICAL EVENTS, DOCUMENTS, PERIODS, MOVEMENTS

the Riel Rebellion	the Renaissance
the Constitution	the Romantic Movement
the Treaty of Ghent	the Great Depression
the First World War	the Meech Lake Accord

GOVERNMENT OFFICES OR DEPARTMENTS AND INSTITUTIONS

House of Commons	City of Lethbridge
Parliament	Churchill High School
the Senate	Ontario Provincial Police
Ministry of Labour	Vancouver City Council

POLITICAL, SOCIAL, ATHLETIC, AND OTHER ORGANIZATIONS AND ASSOCIATIONS AND THEIR MEMBERS

Liberal Party, Liberals
Greenpeace
B'nai B'rith
Girl Guides of Canada
Royal Society of Canada
Montreal Canadiens
National Hockey League
Royal Winnipeg Ballet

RACES, NATIONALITIES, AND THEIR LANGUAGES

Aboriginal peoples
African-Canadian
Caucasian
But: blacks, whites
Germans
Swahili
Italian

RELIGIONS, THEIR FOLLOWERS, AND TERMS FOR THE SACRED

Christianity, Christians
Catholicism, Catholics
Judaism, Orthodox Jews
Islam, Muslims
Hinduism, Hindu
God
Allah
Buddha
the Bible (*but* biblical)
the Koran

NOTE Capitalization of pronouns referring to God is optional in most contexts, but it is often used in religious texts and should be used where necessary to avoid confusion.

AMBIGUOUS Our minister spoke of God as though *he* loved every member of our congregation. [Does *he* refer to the minister or to God?]

REVISED Our minister spoke of God as though *He* loved every member of our congregation.

cap 26d

2 Capitalize common nouns used as essential parts of proper nouns.

Common nouns name general classes of persons, places, or things, and they generally are not capitalized. However, capitalize the common nouns *street, avenue, park, river, ocean, lake, company, college, county,* and *memorial* when they are part of proper nouns naming specific places or institutions.

Portage Avenue
Avalon Peninsula
Mackenzie River
Pacific Ocean
Lake Superior
Ford Motor Company
Conestoga College
Lions Gate Bridge

Capitalize trade names.

Trade names identify individual brands of certain products. When a trade name loses its association with a brand and comes to refer to a product in general, it is not capitalized. Refer to a dictionary for current usage when you are in doubt about a name.

Scotch tape
Chevrolet
Xerox
Bunsen burner

But: nylon, thermos

26e Capitalize titles when they precede proper names but generally not when they follow proper names or appear alone.

Professor Otto Osborne	Otto Osborne, a professor of English
Doctor Jane Covington	Jane Covington, a medical doctor
Senator Duff Roblin	Duff Roblin, a senator from Manitoba
the Reverend Wilma Voss	Wilma Voss, the minister

EXCEPTION Many writers capitalize a title denoting very high rank even when it follows a proper name or is used alone.

Romeo LeBlanc, Governor General of Canada
the Prime Minister of Canada

26f Capitalize only when required.

cap 26f

In general, modern writers capitalize fewer words than earlier writers did. Capitalize only when a rule says you must, and especially avoid miscapitalizing in the following situations.

Use small letters for common nouns replacing proper nouns.

UNNECESSARY I am determined to take an Economics course before I graduate from University.

REVISED I am determined to take an economics course before I graduate from university.

REVISED I am determined to take Economics 101 before I graduate from Lakehead University.

Capitalize compass directions only when they refer to specific geographical areas.

The storm blew in from the northeast and then veered south along the coast. [Here *northeast* and *south* refer to general directions.]

People from the West have trouble adjusting to the East's humid summers. [Here *West* and *East* refer to specific regions.]

Use small letters for the names of seasons or the names of academic years or terms.

spring
fall
autumn
summer term
senior year
winter semester

Capitalize the names of relationships only when they form part of or substitute for proper names.

my mother
Makito's brother
the father of my friend

I remember how Father scolded us.

Aunt Annie, Uncle Jake, and Uncle Irvin died within two months of each other.

Exercise
Revising: Capitals

Capitalize words as necessary in the following sentences, or substitute small letters for unnecessary capitals. Consult a dictionary if you are in doubt. If the capitalization in a sentence is already correct, circle the number preceding the sentence.

Example:

The first book on my summer reading list is stephen leacock's *sunshine sketches of a little town.*

The first book on my summer reading list is Stephen Leacock's *Sunshine Sketches of a Little Town.*

1. The new Place des Arts is very imposing. it is made of reinforced concrete and steel.
2. My Grandmother told me stories about my Father and Uncle Gérard.
3. Although Rashid is a muslim, he is very knowledgeable about the bible, especially the old testament.
4. Professor Kellogg recommended that *Sexist and non-sexist language* be a required text for all fall writing courses.
5. The photograph showed senator Davey shaking hands with the Pastor of the largest Church in Toronto.

6. The fraser canyon is in british columbia, between lytton and hope.
7. Colson, the doctor, knew his medicine, but his manner made his patients nervous.
8. Our scavenger-hunt map directed us two blocks Southeast and two blocks Northeast to find an old sink.
9. The Mackenzie river, issuing from the shallow swamps and mud banks of the west arm of Great Slave lake, flows for more than 4000 km through the barren lands of the northwest territories before emptying into the Beaufort sea.
10. The Roy Thompson hall is an acoustical triumph, but, Oh, it was expensive to build.

Note See page 442 for an exercise involving capitals along with underlining (italics) and other mechanics.

Chapter 27 Underlining (Italics)

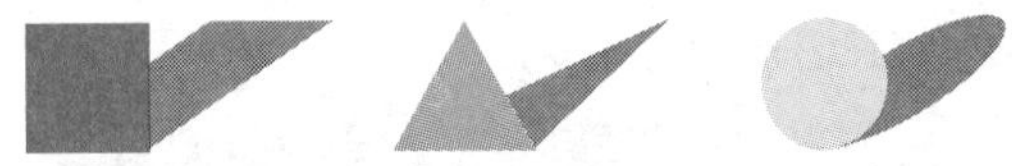

Underlining and *italic type* indicate the same thing: the word or words are being distinguished or emphasized. In your papers use a ruler or the underscore on the keyboard to underline. If your typewriter or word processor can produce italic type, consult your instructor about whether to use it. Many instructors prefer underlining.

27a Underline the titles of works that appear independently.

Many works are published, released, or produced separately from other works: books, some long poems, plays, periodicals, pamphlets, published speeches, long musical works, movies, videotapes, television and radio programs, and works of visual art. Underline the titles of these works. (See the box on the next page.) Use quotation marks for all other titles, such as songs, short poems, short stories, and articles in periodicals (see p. 401).

NOTE Be careful to underline marks of punctuation only if they are part of the title: *Did you read* Survival? (not Survival?). In titles of newspapers underline the name of the city only when it is part of the title.

Titles to be underlined (italicized)

Other titles should be placed in quotation marks. See 24d.

Books

Two Solitudes
War and Peace
The Stone Diaries
Anatomy and Physiology: An Introduction

Long poems

Beowulf
Paradise Lost
Brébeuf and His Brethren

Plays

The Rez Sisters
The Phantom of the Opera

Periodicals

Maclean's
Wired

Pamphlets

The Truth About Alcoholism
On the Vindication of the Rights of Women

Published speeches

Lincoln's *Gettysburg Address*
Pericles's *Funeral Oration*

Long musical works

Tchaikovsky's *Swan Lake*
The Beatles' *Revolver*
But: Symphony in C

Movies and videotapes

Schindler's List
Jesus of Montreal
How to Relax

Television and radio programs

The Royal Canadian Air Farce
Double Exposure
Seinfeld

Works of visual art

Michelangelo's *David*
the *Mona Lisa*
Duchamp's *Standard Stoppages*
Guernica

Manchester *Guardian*
Winnipeg Free Press

When giving the title of a periodical in your text, you need not capitalize or underline the article *the,* even if it is part of the title.

She has the *Winnipeg Free Press* delivered to her in Halifax.

Exceptions Legal documents, the Bible, the Koran, and their parts are generally not underlined.

Not They registered their *deed*.
But They registered their deed.

Not We studied the *Book of Revelation* in the *Bible*.
But We studied the Book of Revelation in the Bible.

27b Underline the names of ships, aircraft, spacecraft, and trains.

Queen Elizabeth 2	Challenger	Orient Express
Spirit of St. Louis	Apollo XI	Montrealer

27c Underline foreign words and phrases that have not been absorbed into English.

English has adopted many foreign words and phrases—such as the French expression "bon voyage"—and these need not be underlined. A foreign phrase should be underlined when it has not been absorbed into our language. A dictionary will say whether a phrase is still considered foreign to English.

> The scientific name for the brown trout is Salmo trutta. [The Latin scientific names for plants and animals are always underlined.]
>
> What a life he led! He was a true bon vivant.
>
> The Latin De gustibus non est disputandum translates roughly as "There's no accounting for taste."

Underline words, letters, numbers, and phrases named as words.

Use underlining to indicate that you are citing a character or word as a word rather than using it for its meaning.

> Some people say th, as in thought, with a faint s or f sound.
> Carved into the column, six metres up, was a mysterious 7.
> Try pronouncing unique North York ten times fast.

und 27e

Underlining may also be used instead of quotation marks in definitions (see p. 401).

> The word syzygy refers to a straight line formed by three celestial bodies, as in the alignment of the earth, sun, and moon.

27e Occasionally, underlining may be used for emphasis.

Underlining can stress an important word or phrase, especially in reporting how someone said something.

> "Why on earth would you do that?" she cried.

But use such emphasis very rarely. Excessive underlining will make your writing sound immature or hysterical.

> The hunters had no food and no firewood. But they were too tired to do anything more than crawl into their sopping sleeping bags. Had it been five degrees colder, they might have frozen to death.

Consult Chapter 18 for other techniques to achieve emphasis.

Exercise
Revising: Underlining (italics)

Underline (italicize) words and phrases as needed in the following sentences, or circle any words or phrases that are underlined unnecessarily. Note that some underlining is correct as given.

Example:

Of Hitchcock's movies, Psycho is the scariest.
Of Hitchcock's movies, Psycho is the scariest.

1. The essay contains many puns and jeux de mots.
2. The author's stories have appeared in such widely diverse periodicals as Saturday Night and Chatelaine.
3. The director warned the writer that the screenplay for The Apprenticeship of Duddy Kravitz had better be finished tout de suite.
4. The map was so out of date that it didn't even show the town Tammy lived in, let alone the street her house was on.
5. According to Books in Canada, Rudy Wiebe's First and Vital Candle is out of print.
6. At one time Canada's second-largest city had two major English language newspapers, the Montreal Star and the Montreal Gazette.
7. Both the Old Testament and the New Testament of the Bible offer profound lessons in human nature.
8. No matter how many times I say it, the word euphemism comes out wrong.
9. Homo sapiens has evolved further than any other species.
10. Whether he's watching Masterpiece Theatre, Sportsweekend, or the silliest situation comedy, Larry is happy in front of the television.

Note See page 442 for an exercise involving underlining (italics) along with capitals and other mechanics.

Chapter 28 Abbreviations

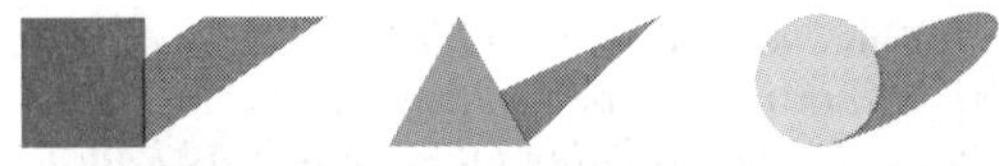

The guidelines on abbreviations in this chapter pertain to nontechnical academic writing and most writing for a general audience. Technical writing, such as in the sciences and engineering, generally uses a great many more abbreviations (see 28f). And abbreviations are common in source citations in all disciplines (see p. 603 for a list).

28a Use standard abbreviations for titles immediately before and after proper names.

BEFORE THE NAME	AFTER THE NAME
Dr. James Hsu	James Hsu, M.D.
Mr., Mrs., Ms., Hon.,	D.D.S., D.V.M., Ph.D.,
St., Rev., Msgr., Gen.	Ed.D., O.S.B., S.J., Sr., Jr.

Use abbreviations such as *Rev., Hon., Prof., Rep., Sen., Dr.,* and *St.* (for *Saint*) only if they appear with a proper name. Spell them out in the absence of a proper name.

FAULTY	We learned to trust the *Dr.*
REVISED	We learned to trust the *doctor.*
REVISED	We learned to trust *Dr. Kaplan.*

Abbreviations for nontechnical writing

- Titles before or after proper names: *Dr. Jorge Rodriguez; Jorge Rodriguez, Ph.D.* (28a).
- Familiar abbreviations and acronyms: *U.S.A., AIDS* (28b).
- *B.C., A.D., A.M., P.M., no.,* and *$* with dates and numbers (28c).
- *I.e., e.g.,* and other Latin abbreviations within parentheses and in source citations (28d).
- *Inc., Bros., Co.,* and *&* with names of business firms (28e).

The abbreviations for academic degrees—*Ph.D., M.A., B.A.,* and the like—may be used without a proper name: *My brother took seven years to get his Ph.D. It will probably take me just as long to earn my B.A.*

28b Familiar abbreviations and acronyms are acceptable in most writing.

An **acronym** is an abbreviation that spells a pronounceable word, such as WHO, NATO, and AIDS. These and other abbreviations using initials are acceptable in most writing as long as they are familiar. Abbreviations of three or more words are usually written without periods.

INSTITUTIONS	UWO, UBC, UPEI
ORGANIZATIONS	CIA, NDP, YMCA, PMO
CORPORATIONS	IBM, CTV, HBC
PEOPLE	JFK, FDR, HRH
COUNTRIES	U.K. (or UK)

(See p. 351 for more on when to use periods in abbreviations.)

NOTE If a name or term (such as *operating room*) appears often in a piece of writing, then its abbreviation (*O.R.*) can cut down on extra words. Spell out the full term at its first appearance, give its abbreviation in parentheses, and use the abbreviation from then on.

28c Use *B.C., A.D., A.M., P.M., no.,* and *$* only with specific dates and numbers.

44 B.C.	8:05 P.M. (*or* p.m.)	no. 36 (*or* No. 36)
A.D. 1492	11:26 A.M. (*or* a.m.)	$7.41

FAULTY Hospital routine is easier to follow in the A.M. than in the P.M.

REVISED Hospital routine is easier to follow in the *morning* than in the *afternoon or evening.*

NOTE The abbreviation B.C. ("before Christ") always follows a date, whereas A.D. (*anno Domini,* Latin for "in the year of the Lord") precedes a date. Increasingly, these abbreviations are being replaced by B.C.E. ("before the common era") and C.E. ("common era"), respectively. Both follow the date.

28d Generally, reserve Latin abbreviations for source citations and comments in parentheses.

i.e. *id est:* that is
cf. *confer:* compare
e.g. *exempli gratia:* for example
et al. *et alii:* and others
etc. *et cetera:* and so forth
N.B. *nota bene:* note well

He said he would be gone a fortnight (i.e., two weeks).
Bloom et al., editors, *Anthology of Light Verse*
Trees, too, are susceptible to disease (e.g., Dutch elm disease).

(Note that these abbreviations are generally not italicized or underlined.)

Some writers avoid these abbreviations in formal writing, even within parentheses.

INFORMAL The cabs of some modern farm machines (e.g., combines) look like airplane cockpits.

FORMAL The cabs of some modern farm machines (for example, combines) look like airplane cockpits.

28e Reserve *Inc., Bros., Co.,* or *&* (for *and*) for official names of business firms.

FAULTY *The Tremblay bros.* operate a large trucking firm in Vancouver and the Lower Mainland.

REVISED *The Tremblay brothers* operate a large trucking firm in Vancouver and the Lower Mainland.

REVISED *Tremblay Bros.* is a large trucking firm that operates in Vancouver and the Lower Mainland.

FAULTY We read about the Hardy Boys & Nancy Drew.

REVISED We read about the Hardy Boys *and* Nancy Drew.

28f Spell out units of measurement and names of places, calendar designations, people, and courses.

Units of measurement, place names, and other elements are usually abbreviated in technical writing but should be spelled out in other academic writing and general writing.

UNITS OF MEASUREMENT

The dog is seventy *centimetres* (not *cm*) high.
Dig a hole two *metres* (not *m*) deep.

EXCEPTION Long phrases such as *kilometres per hour* (km/h) are usually abbreviated, without periods: *The speed limit on that road was once 110 km/h.*

GEOGRAPHICAL NAMES

The publisher is in *Ontario* (not *Ont.* or *ON*).
He came from Auckland, *New Zealand* (not *N.Z.*).
She lived on *University Boulevard* (not *Blvd.*).

EXCEPTIONS The United States is often referred to as the U.S.A. (USA) or the U.S.

NAMES OF DAYS, MONTHS, AND HOLIDAYS

The truce was signed on *Tuesday* (not *Tues.*), *April* (not *Apr.*) 16.
The *Christmas* (not *Xmas*) holidays were uneventful.

NAMES OF PEOPLE

James (not *Jas.*) Bennett ran for that seat.
Robert (not *Robt.*) Kroetsch wrote Prairie poems.

COURSES OF INSTRUCTION

I'm majoring in *political science* (not *poli. sci.*).
Economics (not *Econ.*) is a difficult course.

Exercise
Revising: Abbreviations

Revise the following sentences as needed to correct inappropriate use of abbreviations for nontechnical writing. Circle the number preceding any sentences in which the abbreviations are already appropriate as written.

Example:

One prof. lectured for five hrs.
One *professor* lectured for five *hours*.

1. The kite was flying at about fifty m when the line snapped.
2. Old Montreal, a section of the city south of Dorchester Blvd., contains a number of bldgs. dating from the 18th cent.
3. Jet lag—i.e., disruption of sense of time, place, or well-being—often afflicts air travellers.
4. Upon his inauguration on Fri., Jan. 20, 1961, JFK became the first Roman Catholic President in American history.
5. The relationship between the U.S.A. and the U.S.S.R. is one of the most analysed subjects of the century.
6. Mount Vesuvius erupted in *anno Domini* 79 and buried Pompeii.
7. Mr. and Mrs. Harold Marsh, Jr., donated a new wing for the library.
8. The Lynch bros., Wm. & Robt., went bankrupt in the same year.
9. They asked the rev. to marry them on horseback.
10. There, in the middle of Ch. 6 between pp. 128 & 129, was a leaf my mother had pressed as a child.

NOTE See page 442 for an exercise involving abbreviations along with capitals and other mechanics.

Chapter 29 Numbers

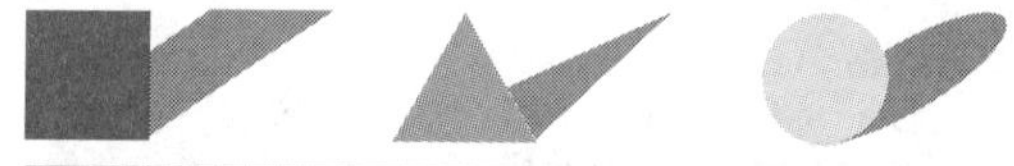

Experienced writers vary in writing numbers out or using figures. In scientific and technical writing, all numbers are usually written as figures. In business writing, all numbers over ten are usually written as figures. In other academic and general writing—the subject of this chapter—numbers are more often spelled out.

29a Use figures for numbers that require more than two words to spell out.

The leap year has *366* days.
The population of Red Deer, Alberta, is about *54 400.*

Spell out numbers of one or two words. (See also 29b.)

That hotel can accommodate no more than *seventy-five* people.
The first writing was done over *six thousand* years ago.
The collection included almost *twelve hundred* drawings.

A hyphenated number between twenty-one and ninety-nine can be considered one word.

The ball game drew *forty-two thousand* people.

Exceptions Round numbers over a million may be expressed in a combination of figures and words: *26 million, 2.45 billion.*

When you use several numbers together, they should be consistently spelled out or consistently expressed in figures.

INCONSISTENT Only *ninety-nine* students attended the first lecture, but the audience increased to *126* for the second lecture and *two hundred* for the third.

REVISED Only *99* students attended the first lecture, but the audience increased to *126* for the second lecture and *200* for the third.

29b Use figures instead of words according to standard practice.

Even when a number requires one or two words to spell out, we conventionally use figures in the following situations:

DAYS AND YEARS

June 18, 1985 A.D. 12 456 B.C. 1999

EXCEPTION The day of a month may be expressed in words when it is not followed by a year (*June fifth; October first*).

PAGES, CHAPTERS, VOLUMES, ACTS, SCENES, LINES

Chapter 9, page 123
Isaiah 28:1 in the Bible
Hamlet, Act 5 (*or* V), Scene 3 (*or* iii), lines 35–40

DECIMALS, PERCENTAGES, AND FRACTIONS

22.5
48% (or 48 percent)
3½

ADDRESSES

432 Marine Drive
Halifax, NS
B3R 1A3

SCORES AND STATISTICS

21 to 7
a mean of 26
a ratio of 8 to 1

EXACT AMOUNTS OF MONEY

$4.50
$3.5 million (*or* $3 500 000)
$2763

THE TIME OF DAY

9:00 A.M.
3:45 A.M.
2:30 P.M.

EXCEPTIONS Round dollar or cent amounts of only a few words may be expressed in words: *seventeen dollars; fifteen hundred dollars; sixty cents.* When the word *o'clock* is used for the time of day, also express the number in words: *two o'clock* (not *2 o'clock*).

29c Always spell out numbers that begin sentences.

For clarity, spell out any number that begins a sentence. If the number requires more than two words, reword the sentence so that the number falls later and can be expressed as a figure.

FAULTY	*103* visitors asked for refunds.
AWKWARD	*One hundred three* visitors asked for refunds.
REVISED	Of the visitors, *103* asked for refunds.

Exercise
Revising: Numbers

Revise the following sentences so that numbers are used appropriately for nontechnical writing. Circle the number preceding any sentence in which numbers are already used appropriately.

Example:

Carol paid two hundred five dollars for used scuba gear.
Carol paid $205 for used scuba gear.

1. The planet Saturn is nine hundred million miles, or nearly one billion five hundred million kilometres, from Earth.
2. Saturn revolves around the sun much more slowly than Earth does: a year on Saturn equals almost thirty of our years.
3. Thus, Saturn orbits the sun only two and four-tenths times during the average human life span.
4. It travels in its orbit at about thirty-four thousand seven hundred and fifty kilometres per hour.
5. 15 to 20 times denser than Earth's core, Saturn's core measures 27 350 kilometres across.
6. The temperature at Saturn's cloud tops is minus seventy-six degrees Celsius.
7. In nineteen hundred thirty-three, astronomers found on Saturn's surface a huge white spot 2 times the size of Earth and 7 times the size of Mercury.
8. Saturn's famous rings reflect almost seventy percent of the sunlight that approaches the planet.
9. The ring system is almost sixty-five thousand kilometres wide, beginning 14 150 kilometres from the planet's visible surface and ending over seventy-five thousand kilometres from that surface.
10. Saturn generates about one hundred thirty trillion kilowatts of electricity.

NOTE See page 442 for an exercise involving numbers along with abbreviations and other mechanics.

Chapter 30

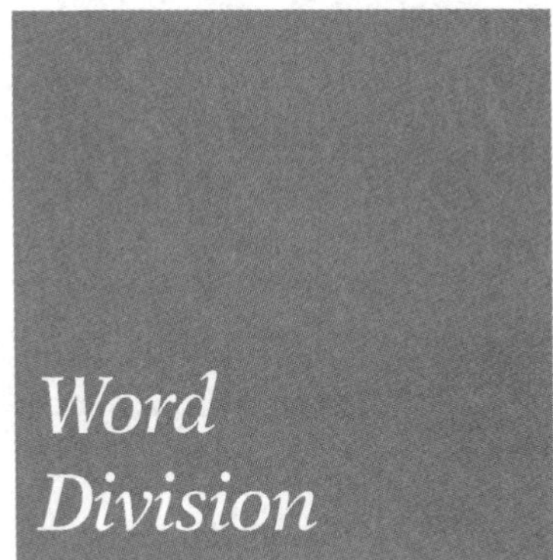

Word Division

As much as possible, avoid dividing words. If you must divide a word between the end of one line and the beginning of the next, follow these guidelines:

- Divide words only between syllables. (Consult a dictionary if necessary.)
- Put a hyphen at the end of the first line, never at the beginning of the second line.
- Try not to divide the last word on a page. In the act of turning the page, the reader may forget the beginning of the word.

Not all syllable breaks are appropriate for word division. Use the following rules to decide when and how to divide words.

30a Any division should leave two or more letters at the end of a line and three or more letters at the beginning of a line.

FAULTY A newspaper or television editorial for or *a-* *gainst* a candidate can sway an election.

REVISED A newspaper or television editorial for or *against* a candidate can sway an election.

FAULTY	Counselling is required for every child *abus- er.*
REVISED	Counselling is required for every child *abuser.*

30b One-syllable words should not be divided.

Since one-syllable words have no break in pronunciation, they should not be divided.

FAULTY	The shiny, spinning space capsule *drop- ped* suddenly from the clouds.
REVISED	The shiny, spinning space capsule *dropped* suddenly from the clouds.

30c Divide compound words only between the words that form them or at fixed hyphens.

Compound words are made up of two or more words (*drawback, homecoming*). Their component words may be separated by a hyphen (*well-paying, cross-reference*), in which case the hyphen is called **fixed.** Compound words should be divided only between their component words and at fixed hyphens.

FAULTY	If you want to have friends, be *good-na- tured.*
REVISED	If you want to have friends, be *good- natured.*

(See pp. 500–02 for guidelines on when to use hyphens in spelling compound words.)

30d Make sure a word division will not confuse readers.

Some word divisions may momentarily confuse readers because the first or second part by itself forms a pronounceable (or unpronounceable) unit that does not fit with the whole. For example: *poi-gnant, read-dress, in-dict.* Avoid word divisions like these.

CONFUSING	Her walking out of class was an act of *her- oism.*
CLEAR	Her walking out of class was an act of *hero- ism.*

Exercise
Revising: Word division

Revise the following sentences to improve inappropriate word divisions. Consult a dictionary if necessary. Circle the number preceding any sentence in which word division is already appropriate.

> *Example:*
>
> I thought Harry's joke was sidesplit-
ting, but no one else even smiled.
>
> I thought Harry's joke was *side-*
splitting, but no one else even smiled.

1. Samuel Johnson, British essayist and poet, com-
piled the first real dictionary of the English language.
2. He followed a method used by dictionary makers ev-
er since.
3. First, he read books about a wide range of sub-
jects.
4. As a result he was probably the most well-edu-
cated man in England.
5. When he discovered a new use for a word, he mark-
ed the passage for his secretary to copy on paper.
6. Since Johnson used a dark pencil to under-
line the passages, the books were damaged.
7. The books' owners were shocked when their well-thumb-
ed and smudged volumes were returned.
8. The words were arranged alphabetical-
ly in large ledger books, with e-
nough room between words for definitions.
9. For each word the definitions were or-
ganized with specialized uses last.
10. Finally, Johnson's secretaries recop-
ied the entries onto clean paper for typeset-
ting.

Note See the next page for an exercise involving word division along with capitals and other mechanics.

Exercise on Chapters 26–30
Revising: Mechanics

Revise the paragraphs below to correct any errors in the use of capital letters, underlining, abbreviations, numbers, and word division. (For abbreviations and numbers follow standard practice for nontechnical writing.) Consult a dictionary as needed.

According to many sources—e.g., the Cambridge An-
cient History and Gardiner's Egypt of the Pharaohs—the
ancient egyptians devoted much attention to making Life
more convenient and pleasurable for themselves.

Our word pharaoh for the ancient egyptian rulers
comes from the egyptian word pr'o, meaning "great house."
Indeed, the egyptians placed great emphasis on family res-
idences, adding small bedrms. as early as 3500 yrs. b.c.
By 3000 b.c., the egyptians made ice through evaporation
of water at night and then used it to cool their homes. A-
bout the same time they used fans made of palm fronds or
papyrus to cool themselves in the day. To light their
homes, the egyptians abandoned the animal-fat lamps Humans
had used for 50 thousand yrs. Instead, around 1300 b.c.
the people of Egt. devised the 1st oil lamps.

Egyptians found great pleasure in playing games. Four
thousand three hundred yrs. ago or so they created one of
the oldest board games known. the game involved racing ivory
or stone pieces across a papyrus playing board. By three
thousand b.c., egyptian children played marbles with semi-
precious stones, some of which have been found in grave-
sites at nagada, EG. Around one thousand three hundred
sixty b.c., small children played with clay rattles cover-
ed in silk and shaped like animals.

To play the game of love, egyptian men and women ex-
perimented with cosmetics applied to skin and eyelids.
Kohl, history's first eyeliner, was used by both sexes
to ward off evil. 5000 yrs. ago egyptians wore wigs
made of vegetable fibres or human hair. In 9 hundred b.c.,
queen Isimkheb wore a wig so heavy that she needed assis-
tance in walking. To adjust their make-up and wigs, e-
gyptians adapted the simple metal mirrors devised
by the sumerians in the bronze age, ornamenting them with
carved handles of ivory, gold, or wood. Feeling that only
those who smelled sweet could be attractive, the egyptians
made deodorants from perfumed oils, e.g., cinnamon and
citrus.

Part VII

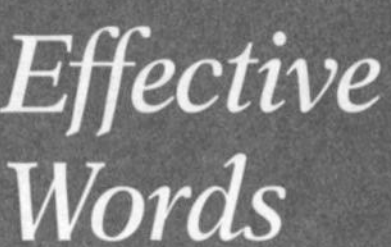

Chapter 31

Choosing and Using Words

Expressing yourself clearly and effectively depends greatly on what words you choose and how you employ them in sentences. English offers an uncommonly rich and extensive vocabulary from which to select the words that precisely suit your meaning and your writing situation (31a and 31b). And the language is uncommonly flexible when it comes to pruning unneeded words that make writing weak or inexact (31c).

31a Choosing the appropriate word

Appropriate words suit your writing situation—your subject, purpose, and audience. Like everyone, you vary your words depending on the context in which you are speaking and writing. Look, for example, at the italicized words in these two sentences:

> Some patients decide to *bag* counselling because their *shrinks* seem *strung out*.
>
> Some patients decide to *abandon* counselling because their *therapists* seem *disturbed.*

The first sentence might be addressed to friends in casual conversation. The second sentence, in contrast, is more formal, more suitable for an academic audience.

Diction in academic and business writing

ALWAYS APPROPRIATE

Standard English (see below)

SOMETIMES APPROPRIATE

Regional words and expressions (31a-2)
Slang (31a-3)
Colloquial language (31a-4)
Neologisms (31a-5)
Technical language (31a-6)
Euphemisms (31a-7)

RARELY OR NEVER APPROPRIATE

Dialect (31a-1)
Archaic and obsolete words (31a-5)
Double talk (31a-7)
Pretentious writing (31a-7)
Biased language: sexist, racist, ethnocentric, etc. (31a-8)

The more formal diction of the second example is typical of what's called **standard English.** This is the written English normally expected and used in school, business, the professions, government, newspapers, and other sites where people of diverse backgrounds must communicate with one another. It is "standard" not because it is better than other forms of English, but because it is accepted as the common language, much as dimes and quarters are accepted as the common currency.

The vocabulary of standard English is huge, allowing expression of an infinite range of ideas and feelings; but it does exclude words that only limited groups of people use, understand, or find inoffensive. Some of those more limited vocabularies should be avoided altogether; others should be used cautiously and in special situations, as when aiming for a special effect with an audience you know will appreciate it. Whenever you doubt a word's status, consult a dictionary (see pp. 475–76).

1 Revising dialect

Like many countries, Canada includes scores of regional, social, or ethnic groups with their own distinct **dialects**, or versions of English: standard English, Newfoundland English, Jamaican English, and the dialect of the Ottawa Valley are examples. All the dialects of English share many features, but each also has its own vocabulary, pronunciation, and grammar.

If you speak a dialect of English besides standard English, you need to be careful about using your dialect in situations where standard English is the norm, such as in academic or business writing. Otherwise, your readers may not understand your meaning, or they may perceive your usage as incorrect. (Dialects are not wrong in themselves, but forms imported from one dialect into another may still be perceived as wrong.)

Your participation in the community of standard English does not mean you should abandon your own dialect. Of course, you will want to use it with others who speak it. You may want to quote it in an academic paper (as when analysing or reporting conversation in dialect). And you may want to use it in writing you do for yourself, such as notes and drafts, which should be composed as freely as possible. But edit your drafts carefully to eliminate dialect expressions, especially those which dictionaries label "nonstandard," such as *eh, inn't, them books, this here rink, right smart, such smart, rink rat, knowed, throwed, could of, ought of, snuck, after saying, didn't never,* and *haven't no.*

2 Using regionalisms only when appropriate

Most national languages vary slightly from one geographical area to another. In American English, regional differences are most marked in pronunciation: a Texan overhearing a conversation between a New Yorker and a Georgian will not mistake either for a fellow Texan.

In a number of instances Canadian pronunciation differs from American, for example, *lieutenant* ("lef ten'ent," not "lü ten'ent"); *been* (rhyming with "bean" rather than "bin"); *shone* (rhyming with "gone," not "bone"); *lever* (as in "beaver," not "sever"); *z* (rhyming with "bed," not "bee"); *route* (rhyming with "suit," not "rout"). (See Walter S. Avis, "Canadian English," reprinted in *Gage Canadian Dictionary*, 1983, pp. xi–xiii.)

appr
31a

Differences in pronunciation are not as marked within Canada, although the conversation of a fisherman from a Newfoundland outport would sound noticeably different from that of one of his British Columbia counterparts. But Canadian regional differences are sometimes reflected in words used mainly in certain areas of the country. Walter Avis gives several examples:

> Other Canadianisms are more or less limited to certain regions—to Newfoundland: *jinker, nunny bag, tickle, tilt*; to the Maritimes: *aboideau, gaspereau, longliner*; to Ontario: *concession road, dew-worm, fire-reels*; to the Prairie Provinces: *bluff* (clump of trees), *grid road, local improvement district*; to British Columbia: *rancherie, skookum, steelhead*; to the Northland: *bush pilot, cat-swing, cheechako*.

Using slang only when appropriate

All groups of people—from musicians and computer scientists to vegetarians and golfers—create novel and colourful expressions called **slang.** The following quotation, for instance, is from an essay on the slang of "skaters" (skateboarders).

> Curtis slashed ultra-punk crunchers on his longboard, while the Rube-man flailed his usual Gumbyness on tweaked frontsides and lofty fakie ollies. —MILES ORKIN, "Mucho Slingage by the Pool"

"Slang," Orkin goes on to say, "is a convenient, creative, mildly poetic, cohesive agent in many subcultures." It reflects the experiences of a group and binds its members.

Some slang gives new meaning to old words, such as *bad* for "good." Some slang comes from other languages, such as *chow* (food) from the Chinese *chao,* "to stir or fry." The slang of a particular group may also spread to other groups, as *out to lunch, put on ice,* and *funky* have spread beyond their African-American origins.

Among those who understand it, slang may be vivid and forceful. It often occurs in dialogue, and an occasional slang expression can enliven an informal essay. Some slang, such as *dropout* (*she was a high school dropout*), has proved so useful that it has passed into the general vocabulary.

But most slang is too flippant and imprecise for effective communication, and it is generally inappropriate for university, college, or business writing. Notice the gain in seriousness and precision achieved in the following revision.

SLANG Many students start out *pretty together* but then *get weird.*

REVISED Many students start out *with clear goals* but then *lose their direction.*

Using colloquial language only when appropriate

appr 31a

Colloquial language designates the words and expressions appropriate to everyday spoken language. Regardless of our backgrounds and how we live, we all try to *get along with* each other. We play with *kids, go crazy* about one thing, *crab* about something else, and in our worst moments try to *get back at* someone who has made us do the *dirty work.*

When you write informally, colloquial language may be appropriate to achieve the casual, relaxed effect of conversation. An occasional colloquial word dropped into otherwise more formal writing can also help you achieve a desired emphasis. But colloquial language does not provide the exactness needed in more formal university, college, business, and professional writing. In such writing you should generally avoid any words and expressions labelled "informal" or "colloquial" in your dictionary. Take special care to avoid **mixed diction,** a combination of standard and colloquial words.

MIXED DICTION According to an Aboriginal myth, the Great Creator *had a dog hanging around with him* when he created the earth.

REVISED According to an Aboriginal myth, the Great Creator *was accompanied by a dog* when he created the earth.

Revising obsolete or archaic words and neologisms

Since our surroundings and our lives are constantly changing, some words pass out of use and others appear to fill new needs. **Obsolete** and **archaic** are dictionary labels for words or meanings of words that we never or rarely use but that appear in older documents and literature still read today. Obsolete words or meanings are no longer used at all—for example, *enwheel* ("to encircle") and *cote* ("to pass"). Archaic words or meanings occur now only in special contexts such as poetry—for example, *fast* ("near," as in *fast by the road*) and *belike* ("perhaps"). Both obsolete and archaic words are inappropriate in nonfiction writing for an academic audience.

Neologisms are words created (or coined) so recently that they have not come into established use. An example is *prequel* (made up of *pre-,* meaning "before," and the ending of *sequel*), a movie or book that takes the story of an existing movie or book back in time. Some neologisms do become accepted as part of our general vocabulary—*motel,* coined from *motor* and *hotel,* is an example. But most neologisms pass quickly from the language. Unless such words serve a special purpose in your writing and are sure to be understood by your readers, you should avoid them.

Using technical words with care

All disciplines and professions rely on special words or give common words special meanings. Chemists speak of *esters* and *phosphatides,* geographers and mapmakers refer to *isobars* and *isotherms,* and literary critics write about *motifs* and *subtexts.* Such technical language allows specialists to communicate precisely and economically with other specialists who share their vocabulary. But without explanation these words are meaningless to nonspecialists. When you are writing for nonspecialists, avoid unnecessary technical terms and carefully define terms you must use.

Revising indirect or pretentious writing

In most writing, small, plain, and direct words are preferable to big, showy, or evasive words. Avoid euphemisms, double talk, and pretentious writing.

A **euphemism** is a presumably inoffensive word that a writer or speaker substitutes for a word deemed potentially offensive or too blunt, such as *passed away* for *died.* Euphemisms appear whenever a writer or speaker wants to bury the truth, as when a premier mentions the *negative growth* (meaning decline) in her province. Use euphemisms only when you know that blunt, truthful words would needlessly hurt or offend members of your audience.

A kind of euphemism that deliberately evades the truth is **double talk** (also called **doublespeak** or **weasel words**): language intended to confuse or to be misunderstood. Today double talk is unfortunately common in politics and advertising—the *revenue enhancement* that is really a tax, the *biodegradable* bags that last decades. Double talk has no place in honest writing.

Euphemism and sometimes double talk seem to keep company with fancy writing. Any writing that is more elaborate than its subject requires will sound **pretentious**—that is, excessively showy. Choose your words for their exactness and economy. The big, ornate word may be tempting, but pass it up. Your readers will be grateful.

PRETENTIOUS	Many institutions of higher education recognize the need for youth at the threshold of maturity to confront the choice of life's endeavour and thus require students to select a field of concentration.
REVISED	Many colleges and universities force students to make decisions about their careers by requiring them to select a major.

Revising sexist and other biased language

Even when we do not mean it to, our language can reflect and perpetuate hurtful prejudices toward groups of people, especially racial, ethnic, religious, age, and sexual groups. In any kind of speech or writing, a word such as *frog, nigger, honky, mick, kike, fag, dyke,* or *broad*—with or without additionally insulting adjectives—reflects poorly on the user, not on the person or persons designated. Unbiased language does not submit to stereotypes. It refers to people as they would wish to be referred to.

Eliminating sexist language

- Avoid occupational or social stereotypes.

Sexist The considerate doctor commends a nurse when she provides his patients with good care.

Revised The considerate doctor commends a nurse *who provides good care for patients.*

Sexist The grocery shopper should save her coupons.

Revised *Grocery shoppers* should save *their* coupons.

- Avoid using *man* or words containing *man* to refer to all human beings. Here are a few alternatives:

businessman	businessperson
chairman	chair, chairperson
craftsman	craftsperson, artisan
fireman	firefighter
layman	layperson
mankind	humankind, humanity, human beings, humans
manmade	handmade, manufactured, synthetic, artificial
manpower	personnel, human resources
policeman	police officer
salesman	salesperson, sales representative

Sexist Man has not reached the limits of social justice.

Revised *Humankind* (or *Humanity*) has not reached the limits of social justice.

Sexist The furniture consists of manmade materials.

Revised The furniture consists of *synthetic* materials

- Avoid using the generic *he* to refer to both genders. (See also p. 119.)

Sexist The person who studies history knows his roots.

Revised The person who studies history knows *his or her* roots.

Revised *People* who study history know *their* roots.

- Avoid demeaning and patronizing language.

Sexist Pushy broads are entering almost every occupation.

Revised *Women* are entering almost every occupation.

Sexist Prime Minister Mulroney came to Mila's defence.

Revised Prime Minister Mulroney came to *Mrs. Mulroney's* defence.

Among the most subtle and persistent biased language is that expressing narrow ideas about men's and women's roles, position, and value in society. This **sexist language** distinguishes needlessly between men and women in such matters as occupation, ability, behaviour, temperament, and maturity. It can wound or irritate readers, and it indicates the writer's thoughtlessness or unfairness. The box on the previous page suggests some ways of eliminating sexist language.

Exercise 1
Revising: Appropriate words

Rewrite the following sentences as needed for standard written English. Consult a dictionary to determine whether particular words are appropriate and to find suitable substitutes.

Example:

If negotiators get hyper during contract discussions, they may mess up chances for a settlement.

If negotiators *become excited or upset* during contract discussions, they may *harm* chances for a settlement.

1. Acquired Immune Deficiency Syndrome (AIDS) is a major deal all over the world.
2. The disease gets around primarily by sexual intercourse, exchange of bodily fluids, shared needles, and blood transfusions.
3. Those who think the disease is limited to homos and druggies are quite mistaken.
4. Stats suggest that one in every five hundred university kids carries the virus.
5. A person with AIDS does not deserve to be subjected to exclusionary behaviour or callousness on the part of his fellow citizens. Instead, he has the necessity for all the compassion, medical care, and financial assistance due those who are in the extremity of illness.

31b Choosing the exact word

To write clearly and effectively, you will want to find the words that fit your meaning exactly and convey your attitude precisely. If, like many people, you feel uncertain about words and their meanings, consult the next two chapters, on using a dictionary (32) and improving your vocabulary (33).

Don't worry too much about choosing exact words while you are drafting an essay. If the right word doesn't come to you, leave a blank. Revision (p. 59) or editing (p. 65) is the stage to consider tone, specificity, and precision.

 Using the right word for your meaning

The precise expression of meaning requires understanding both the denotations and the connotations of words. A word's **denotation** is the thing or idea it refers to, the meaning listed in the dictionary without reference to the emotional associations it may arouse in a reader. Using words according to their established denotations is essential if readers are to grasp your meaning. Here are a few guidelines:

- Become acquainted with a dictionary. Consult it whenever you are unsure of a word's meaning.
- Distinguish between similar-sounding words that have widely different denotations.

  INEXACT Older people often suffer *infirmaries* [places for the sick].

  EXACT Older people often suffer *infirmities* [disabilities].

  Some words, called **homonyms** (from the Greek meaning "same name"), sound exactly alike but differ in meaning: for example, *principal/principle* or *rain/reign/rein.* (See pp. 488–89 for a list of commonly confused homonyms.)
- Distinguish between words with related but distinct denotations.

  INEXACT Television commercials *continuously* [unceasingly] interrupt programming.

  EXACT Television commercials *continually* [regularly] interrupt programming.

In addition to their emotion-free denotations, many words also carry associations with specific feelings. These **connotations** can shape readers' responses and are thus a powerful tool for writers. (At the same time they are a potential snare for readers. See p. 125.) Some connotations are personal: the word *dog,* for instance, may have negative connotations for the letter carrier who has been bitten three times. Usually, though, people agree about connotations. The following word pairs have related denotations but very different connotations.

desire/lust	firm/stubborn	enthusiasm/mania
pride/vanity	lasting/endless	daring/reckless

Understanding connotation is especially important in choosing among **synonyms,** words with approximately, but often not exactly, the same meanings. For instance, *cry* and *weep* both denote the shedding of tears, but *cry* more than *weep* connotes a sobbing sound accompanying the tears. *Sob* itself connotes broken, gasping crying, with tears, whereas *wail* connotes sustained sound, perhaps without tears.

Several resources can help you track down words with the exact connotations you want:

- A dictionary is essential. Many dictionaries list and distinguish among synonyms (see p. 486 for an example).
- A dictionary of synonyms lists and defines synonyms in groups (see p. 472 for a title).
- A thesaurus lists synonyms but does not distinguish among them (see p. 472 for a title). Because it lacks definitions, a thesaurus can only suggest possibilities; you will still need a dictionary to discover the words' connotations.

Exercise 2
Revising: Denotation

Revise the following sentences to replace any italicized word that is not used according to its established denotation. If an underlined word is used correctly, circle it. Consult a dictionary if you are uncertain of a word's precise meaning.

Example:

Sam and Dave are going to Bermuda and Mexico, respectfully, for spring vacation.

Sam and Dave are going to Bermuda and Mexico, *respectively*, for spring vacation.

1. The *inference* of the report from the parents is that the school should care for their children in the afternoon.
2. Burning solid waste is not an *economic* way to generate power, but it eliminates the need for new dumping grounds.
3. The jury did not find the defendant's testimony *credible* and so convicted her.
4. Hospital personnel must wear protective clothing when tending a patient with a highly *communicative* disease.
5. I did not attend the lecture on artificial intelligence because I am *disinterested* in computers.

Exercise 3
Considering the connotations of words

Describe how the connotation of each italicized word in the following sentences contributes to the writer's meaning. Give at least one synonym or related word that the writer could have used instead of the italicized word, and describe how the new word would alter the meaning. Consult a dictionary or thesaurus as necessary.

1. [The river] *slumbers* between broad prairies, *kissing* the long meadow grass, and *bathes* the overhanging boughs of elder bushes and willows or the roots of elms and ash trees and clumps of maples. —NATHANIEL HAWTHORNE
2. The new earth, freshly *torn* from its parent sun, was a ball of *whirling gases*, *intensely* hot, *rushing* through the black spaces of the universe on a path and a speed controlled by *immense* forces. —RACHEL CARSON
3. Summer and winter she *viewed* the town with *sightless* eyes.

[The stone angel] was doubly blind, not only stone *unendowed* with even a *pretense* of sight. Whoever carved her had left the eyeballs blank. It seemed strange to me that she should stand above the town, *harking* us all to heaven without knowing who we were at all. —MARGARET LAURENCE

4. Here and there meadow larks *were suddenly upon* straw stacks, telephone wires, fence posts, their song clear with *ineffable exuberance* that *startled and deepened* the prairie silence—each quick and *impudent* climax of notes leaving behind it a vaster, emptier prairie *world*. The sky was *ideal* blue. —W. O MITCHELL

Balancing the abstract and concrete, the general and specific

To understand a subject as you understand it, your readers need ample guidance from your words. When you describe a building as beautiful and nothing more, you force readers to provide their own conceptions of the features that make a building beautiful. If readers bother (and they may not), they surely will not conjure up the image you had in mind. You'll be much more likely to achieve your purpose if you tell readers what you want them to know, that the beautiful building is *a sleek, silver skyscraper with blue-tinted windows,* for instance, or *a Victorian brick courthouse with tall, arched windows.*

Clear, exact writing balances abstract and general words, which outline ideas and objects, with concrete and specific words, which sharpen and solidify.

- **Abstract words** name qualities and ideas: *beauty, inflation, management, culture, liberal.* **Concrete words** name things we can know by our five senses of sight, hearing, touch, taste, and smell: *sleek, humming, brick, bitter, musty.*
- **General words** name classes or groups of things, such as *buildings, weather,* or *birds,* and include all the varieties of the class. **Specific words** limit a general class, such as *buildings,* by naming one of its varieties, such as *skyscraper, Victorian courthouse,* or *hut.*

exact 31b

Note that *general* and *specific* are relative terms: the same word may be more general than some words but more specific than others.

GENERAL

	↑	
weather		bird
rain		parrot
downpour		cockatoo
sudden downpour	↓	my pet cockatoo Moyshe

SPECIFIC

Abstract and general words are useful in the broad statements that set the course for your writing.

The wild horse in North America has a *romantic* history.

We must be *free* from *government interference* in our *affairs.*

Relations between the sexes today are only a *little* more *relaxed* than they were in the past.

But the sentences following these would have to develop the ideas with concrete and specific details. When your meaning calls for an abstract or general word, make sure you define it, explain it, and narrow it. Look at how concrete and specific information turns vague sentences into exact ones in the examples below.

VAGUE The size of his hands made his smallness real. [How big were his hands? How small was he?]

EXACT Not until I saw his white, doll-like hands did I realize that he stood a full head shorter than most other men.

VAGUE The long flood caused a lot of awful destruction in the town. [How long did the flood last? What destruction did it cause? Why was the destruction awful?]

EXACT The flood waters, which rose swiftly and then stayed stubbornly high for days, killed at least six townspeople and made life a misery for the hundreds who had to evacuate their ruined homes and stores.

Exercise 4
Revising: Concrete and specific words

Make the following paragraph vivid by expanding the sentences with appropriate details of your own choosing. Concentrate especially on substituting concrete and specific words for the abstract and general ones in italics.

I remember *clearly* how *awful* I felt the first time I *attended* Mrs. Murphy's second-grade class. I had *recently* moved from a *small* town in Manitoba to a *crowded* suburb of Toronto. My new school looked *big* from the outside and seemed *dark* inside as I *walked* down the *long* corridor toward the classroom. The class was *noisy* as I neared the door; but when I *entered, everyone* became *quiet* and *looked* at me. I felt *uncomfortable* and *wanted* a place to hide. However, in a *loud* voice Mrs. Murphy *directed* me to the front of the room to introduce myself.

Exercise 5
Using concrete and specific words

For each abstract or general word below, give at least two other words or phrases that illustrate increasing specificity or concreteness. Consult a dictionary as needed. Use the most specific or concrete word from each group in a sentence of your own.

Example:

tired, *sleepy, droopy-eyed*

We stopped for the night when I became so *droopy-eyed* that the road blurred.

1. fabric
2. delicious
3. car
4. narrow-minded
5. reach (*verb*)
6. green
7. walk (*verb*)
8. flower
9. serious
10. pretty
11. teacher
12. nice
13. virtue
14. angry
15. crime

Using idioms

Idioms are expressions in any language whose meanings cannot be determined simply from the words in them or whose component words cannot be predicted by any rule of grammar; often, they violate conventional grammar. Examples of English idioms include *put up with, plug away at,* and *make off with.*

Idiomatic combinations of verbs or adjectives and prepositions can be confusing for both native and nonnative speakers of English. A number of these pairings are listed below.

Idioms with prepositions

abide *by* a rule
abide *in* a place or state

accords *with*
according *to*

accuse *of* a crime

adapt *from* a source
adapt *to* a situation

agree *on* a plan
agree *to* a proposal
agree *with* a person

angry *with*

capable *of*

charge *for* a purchase
charge *with* a crime

concur *in* an opinion
concur *with* a person

contend *for* a principle
contend *with* a person

differ *about* or *over* a question
differ *from* in appearance
differ *with* a person

disappointed *by* or *in* a person
disappointed *in* or *with* a thing

identical *with* or *to*

impatient *at* her conduct
impatient *of* restraint
impatient *for* a raise
impatient *with* a person

independent *of*

infer *from*

inferior *to*

oblivious *of* or *to* one's surroundings
oblivious *of* something forgotten

occupied *by* a person
occupied *in* study
occupied *with* a thing

part *from* a person
part *with* a possession

prior *to*

rewarded *by* the judge
rewarded *for* something done
rewarded *with* a gift

similar *to*

superior *to*

wait *at* a place
wait *for* a train, a person
wait *on* a customer

Note ESL Those learning English as a second language are justified in stumbling over its prepositions. For instance, *at, in,* and *on* have distinctive uses in expressions of time. *At* precedes actual clock time: *She was born at 8:30. In* precedes a month, year, or century: *She was born in 1975. On* precedes a day or date: *She was born on August 31.*

These and other uses of prepositions, such as in two-word verbs (see p. 223), must be memorized. A good ESL dictionary is the best source for idioms; see the recommendations on page 470.

Exercise 6
Using prepositions in idioms

Insert the preposition that correctly completes each idiom in the following sentences. Consult the preceding list or a dictionary as needed.

Example:

I disagree _______ people who say women should not be homemakers.

I disagree *with* people who say women should not be homemakers.

1. He had waited for years, growing impatient _______ her demands and _______ the money that she would leave to him.
2. The writer compared gorilla society _______ human society.
3. They agreed _______ most things, but they differed consistently _______ how to raise their child.
4. I was rewarded _______ my persistence _______ an opportunity to meet the premier.
5. He would sooner part _______ his friends than part _______ his Corvette.

4 Using figurative language

Figurative language (or a **figure of speech**) departs from the literal meanings (the denotations) of words, usually by comparing very different ideas or objects.

Literal: As I try to write, I can think of nothing to say.

Figurative: As I try to write, *my mind is a blank slab of black slate.*

Imaginatively and carefully used, figurative language can capture meaning more precisely and feelingly than literal language.

Figurative language is commonplace in speech. Having *slept like a log,* you may get up to find it *raining cats and dogs* and to discover that the Blue Jays *blanked* the Royals last night. But the rapid exchange of speech leaves little time for inventiveness, and most figures of daily conversation, like those above, are worn and hackneyed. Writing gives you time to reject the tired figure and to search out fresh, concrete words and phrases.

The two most common figures of speech are the **simile** and the **metaphor.** Both compare two things of different classes, often one abstract and the other concrete. A simile makes the comparison explicit and usually begins with *like* or *as.*

> Whenever we grow, we tend to feel it, *as* a young seed must feel the weight and inertia of the earth when it seeks to break out of its shell on its way to becoming a plant. —ALICE WALKER

> The march of social progress is like a large and struggling parade, with the seers and prophets at its head and a smug minority bringing up the rear. —PIERRE BERTON

Instead of stating a comparison, the metaphor implies it, omitting such words as *like* or *as.*

> I cannot and will not cut my conscience to fit this year's fashions. —LILLIAN HELLMAN

> Literature is not only a mirror; it is also a map, a geography of the mind. —MARGARET ATWOOD

Two other figures of speech are **personification** and **hyperbole.** Personification treats ideas and objects as if they were human.

> The economy consumes my money and gives me little in return.
>
> I could hear the whisper of snowflakes, nudging each other as they fell.

Hyperbole deliberately exaggerates.

> She appeared in clouds of billowing chiffon, flashing a rhinestone as big as an ostrich egg.
>
> I'm going to cut him up in small cubes and fry him in deep fat.

To be successful, figurative language must be fresh and unstrained, calling attention not to itself but to the writer's meaning. If readers reject your language as trite or overblown, they may reject your message. One kind of figurative language gone wrong is the **mixed metaphor,** in which the writer combines two or more incompatible figures. Since metaphors often generate visual images in the reader's mind, a mixed metaphor can be laughable.

> MIXED Various thorny problems that we try to sweep under the rug continue to bob up all the same.

To revise a mixed metaphor, follow through consistently with just one image.

IMPROVED Various thorny problems that we try to weed out continue to thrive all the same.

Exercise 7
Analysing figurative language

Identify each figure of speech in the following sentences as a simile or a metaphor and analyse how it contributes to the writer's meaning.

1. All artists quiver under the lash of adverse criticism.

   —CATHERINE DRINKER BOWEN

2. Louisa spends the entire day in blue, limpid boredom. The caressing sting of it appears to be, for her, like the pleasure of lemon, or the coldness of salt water. —ELIZABETH HARDWICK

3. Every writer, in a roomful of writers, wants to be the best, and the judge, or umpire, or referee is soon overwhelmed and shouted down like a chickadee trying to take charge of a caucus of crows. —JAMES THURBER

4. Canadian soldiers had an ambiguous reputation in England at that time; we were supposed to be loyal, furious, hairy fellows who spat bullets at the enemy, but ate women raw.

   —ROBERTSON DAVIES

5. Western sunset opens its sensational act, turning the uppermost third of the Ferris wheel into a burnished bridge, blinding the roller-coaster cowboys as, whooping up, they slingshot out of the shadowy lower depths. —JACK LUDWIG

Exercise 8
Using figurative language

Invent appropriate figurative language of your own (simile, metaphor, hyperbole, or personification) to describe each scene or quality below, and use the figure in a sentence.

Example:

The attraction of a lake on a hot day
The small waves *like fingers beckoned* us irresistibly.

1. The sound of a kindergarten classroom
2. People waiting in line to buy tickets to a rock concert
3. The politeness of strangers meeting for the first time
4. A streetlight seen through dense fog
5. The effect of watching television for ten hours straight

Using fresh expressions

Trite expressions, or **clichés,** are phrases so old and so often repeated that they have become stale. They include the following:

acid test	ladder of success
add insult to injury	moving experience
better late than never	needle in a haystack
beyond the shadow of a doubt	point with pride
brought back to reality	ripe old age
cool, calm, and collected	sadder but wiser
crushing blow	shoulder the burden
dyed in the wool	sneaking suspicion
easier said than done	sober as a judge
face the music	stand in awe
gentle as a lamb	strong as an ox
hard as a rock	thin as a rail
heavy as lead	tired but happy
hit the nail on the head	tried and true
hour of need	wise as an owl

Many of these expressions were once fresh and forceful, but constant use has dulled them. They, in turn, will dull your writing by suggesting that you have not thought about what you are saying and have resorted to the easiest phrase. To prevent clichés from sliding into your writing, be wary of any expression you have heard or used before. Substitute fresh words of your own or restate the idea in plain language.

TRITE A *motley crowd* of the singer's *ardent admirers* awaited her arrival *with bated breath.*

REVISED *Outfitted in wild, colourful costumes,* a crowd of the singer's *fans* awaited her arrival *in tense, eager silence.*

Exercise 9
Revising: Trite expressions

Revise the following sentences to eliminate trite expressions.

Example:

The basketball team had almost seized victory, but it faced the test of truth in the last quarter of the game.

The basketball team *seemed about to win,* but the *real test* came in the last quarter of the game.

1. The disastrous consequences of the war have shaken the small nation to its roots.
2. Prices for food have shot sky high, and citizens have sneaking suspicions that others are making a killing on the black market.
3. Medical supplies are so few and far between that even civilians who are as sick as dogs cannot get treatment.

4. With most men fighting or injured or killed, women have had to bite the bullet and bear the men's burden in farming and manufacturing.
5. Last but not least, the war's heavy drain on the nation's pocketbook has left the economy in a shambles.

31c Writing concisely

Writing concisely means cutting whatever adds nothing to your meaning or the freshness of your writing. It does not mean sacrificing necessary detail or original expression for mere brevity, however. Concise writing does not waste words but still includes the concrete and specific details that make meaning clear. In

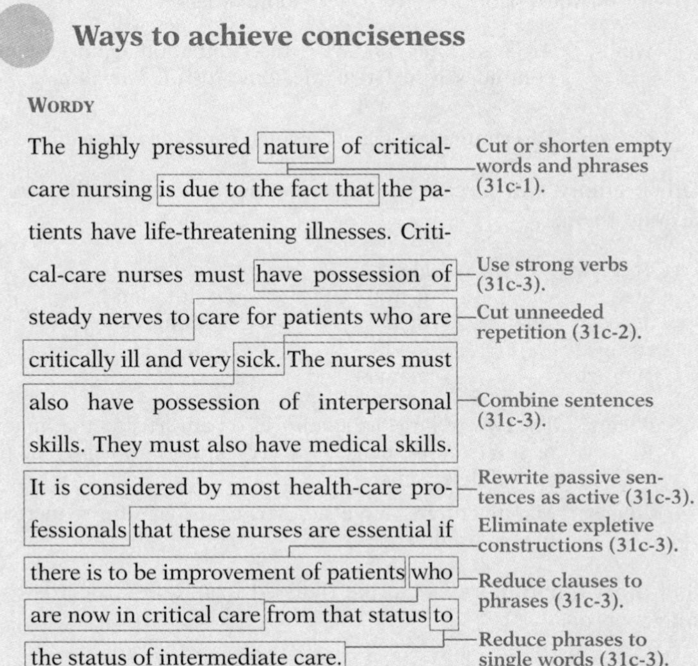

Ways to achieve conciseness

Wordy

The highly pressured nature of critical-care nursing is due to the fact that the patients have life-threatening illnesses. Critical-care nurses must have possession of steady nerves to care for patients who are critically ill and very sick. The nurses must also have possession of interpersonal skills. They must also have medical skills. It is considered by most health-care professionals that these nurses are essential if there is to be improvement of patients who are now in critical care from that status to the status of intermediate care.

Concise

Critical-care nursing is highly pressured because the patients have life-threatening illnesses. Critical-care nurses must possess steady nerves and interpersonal and medical skills. Most health-care professionals consider these nurses essential if patients are to improve to intermediate care.

concise writing the length of an expression is appropriate to the thought.

You should not worry about conciseness while you are drafting. Focus on it during editing.

Cutting or shortening empty words and phrases

Empty words and phrases walk in place, gaining little or nothing in meaning. Shorten them to their essential meaning, or cut them entirely. Your writing will move faster and work harder.

Many empty phrases can be cut entirely:

all things considered	in a manner of speaking
as far as I'm concerned	in my opinion
for all intents and purposes	last but not least
for the most part	more or less

Wordy *As far as I am concerned,* discrimination against women continues to exist in medicine *for all intents and purposes.*

Revised Discrimination against women continues in medicine.

Other empty words can be cut along with some of the words around them:

angle	element	nature
area	factor	situation
aspect	field	thing
case	kind	type
character	manner	

Wordy The *type* of large expenditures on advertising that manufacturers must make is a very important *aspect* of the cost of detergents.

Concise Manufacturers' large advertising expenditures increase the cost of detergents.

Still other empty phrases can be reduced from several words to a single word:

For	Substitute
at all times	always
at the present time	now
at this point in time	now
in the nature of	like
for the purpose of	for
in order to	to
until such time as	until
for the reason that	because

due to the fact that	because
because of the fact that	because
by virtue of the fact that	because
in the event that	if
by means of	by
in the final analysis	finally

WORDY *At this point in time,* the software is expensive *due to the fact that* it has no competition.

REVISED The software is expensive *now because* it has no competition.

Exercise 10
Revising: Empty words and phrases

Revise the following sentences to achieve conciseness by cutting or reducing empty words and phrases.

Example:

I came to university because of many factors, but most of all because of the fact that I want a career in medicine.

I came to university *mainly because* I want a career in medicine.

1. *Gerrymandering* refers to a situation in which the lines of a voting district are redrawn to benefit a particular party or ethnic group.
2. The name is explained by the fact that Elbridge Gerry, the governor of Massachusetts in 1812, redrew voting districts in Essex County.
3. On the map one new district looked in the nature of a salamander.
4. Upon seeing the map, a man who was for all intents and purposes a critic of Governor Gerry's administration cried out, "Gerrymander!"
5. At the present time, a political group may try to change the character of a district's voting pattern by gerrymandering to exclude rival groups' supporters.

Cutting unnecessary repetition

Planned repetition and restatement can make writing more coherent (p. 87) or emphatic (p. 332). But unnecessary repetition weakens sentences.

WORDY Many unskilled workers *without training in a particular job* are unemployed *and do not have any work.*

CONCISE Many unskilled workers are unemployed.

The use of one word two different ways within a sentence is confusing.

CONFUSING Preschool instructors play a *role* in the child's understanding of male and female *roles.*

CLEAR Preschool instructors contribute to the child's understanding of male and female roles.

The simplest kind of useless repetition is the phrase that says the same thing twice. In the following examples, the unneeded words are italicized.

biography *of his life*
circle *around*
consensus *of opinion*
frank and honest exchange
the future *to come*
habitual custom
important (*basic*) essentials
large *in size*
cooperate *together*
few *in number*
final completion
puzzling *in nature*
repeat *again*
return *again*
square (round) *in shape*
surrounding circumstances

NOTE ESL Phrases like those above are redundant because the main word already implies the italicized word or words. The repetition is not emphatic but tedious. A dictionary will tell you what meanings a word implies. *Assassinate,* for instance, means "murder someone well known," so the following sentence is redundant: *Julius Caesar was assassinated and killed.*

Exercise 11
Revising: Unnecessary repetition

Revise the following sentences to achieve conciseness. Concentrate on eliminating repetition and redundancy.

Example:

Because the circumstances surrounding the cancellation of classes were murky and unclear, the editor of the student newspaper assigned a staff reporter to investigate and file a report on the circumstances.

Because the circumstances leading to the cancellation of classes were unclear, the editor of the student newspaper assigned a staffer to investigate and report the story.

1. In today's world in the last quarter of the twentieth century, security has become a more compelling goal than social reform.
2. Deadly nightshade is aptly named. It has small white flowers and deep black fruit. The fruit looks like night, and it also looks like death. The fruit does happen to be poisonous, too.
3. As they embark on the beginning of an operation, all these specialists—the surgeon, the anesthetist, and the operating-room nurses—have specialized tasks to perform.
4. The disastrous drought was devastating to crops, but the farmers cooperated together to help each other out.

5. In deciding whether to choose a career in the field of dentistry, remember that some experts predict a future decline in the incomes of all health professionals.

Simplifying word groups and sentences

Choose the simplest and most direct grammatical construction that fits your meaning. Combine sentences, reduce clauses to phrases and phrases to single words, use strong verbs, use the active voice, and delete expletive constructions.

Combining sentences

Often the information in two or more sentences can be combined into one tight sentence.

WORDY The French and British collaborated on building the Channel Tunnel. The tunnel links France and Britain. The French drilled from Sangatte. The British drilled from Dover.

CONCISE The French and British collaborated on building the Channel Tunnel between their countries, the French drilling from Sangatte and the British from Dover.

A number of exercises in this handbook give you practice in sentence combining. For a list, see "Sentence combining" in the Index.

Reducing clauses to phrases, phrases to single words

Modifiers—subordinate clauses, phrases, and single words—can be expanded or contracted depending on the emphasis you want to achieve. (See pp. 163–74 on phrases and clauses and 310–12 on working with modifiers.) When editing your sentences, consider whether any modifiers can be reduced without loss of emphasis or clarity.

WORDY The tunnel, *which was drilled for thirty-seven kilometres,* runs *through a bed of solid chalk* under the English Channel.

CONCISE The *thirty-seven-kilometre* tunnel runs *through solid chalk* under the English Channel.

Using strong verbs

Weak verbs such as *is, has,* and *make* stall sentences. Strong verbs such as *slice, bicker,* and *stroll* energize sentences, moving them along. Weak verbs usually carry extra baggage, too, such as unneeded prepositional phrases and long, abstract nouns or adjectives.

WORDY The drillers *made slow advancement,* and costs *were over* $5 million a day. The slow progress *was worrisome for* some backers.

CONCISE The drillers *advanced slowly,* and costs *topped* $5 million a day. The slow progress *worried* some backers.

Using the active voice

When a verb is in the **active voice,** the subject of the sentence names the *performer* of the verb's action. When a verb is in the **passive voice,** the subject names the *receiver* of the action.

ACTIVE The *drillers used* huge rotary blades.

PASSIVE Huge rotary *blades were used* by the drillers.

The passive voice is usually wordier than the active voice, simply because it requires a helping verb (*were*) and a prepositional phrase to name the actor (*by the drillers*). Further, passive constructions are indirect, burying the actor or sometimes omitting it entirely (*Huge rotary blades were used*).

Revise a passive construction by changing the verb to the active voice and positioning the actor as the subject. (If you need help with this change, see p. 219.)

WORDY PASSIVE *Over four metres* of chalk an hour *could be chewed through* by the blades.

CONCISE ACTIVE The *blades could chew through* over four metres of chalk an hour.

Eliminating expletive constructions

Expletive constructions begin with *there is* or *it is* and postpone the sentence subject (see p. 184). Expletives can be useful to emphasize the subject (as when introducing it for the first time) or to indicate a change in direction. But most expletives are wordy, limp substitutes for more vigorous sentences.

WORDY *There are more than half a million shareholders who* have invested in the tunnel. *It is they and the banks that* expect to profit.

CONCISE *More than half a million shareholders* have invested in the tunnel. *They and the banks* expect to profit.

Exercise 12
Revising: Simplifying word groups and sentences

Rewrite each passage below into a single concise sentence. As necessary, combine sentences, reduce grammatical structures, replace weak verbs with strong ones, and eliminate passive and expletive constructions.

Example:

He was taking some exercise in the park. Then several thugs were suddenly ahead in his path.

He was *exercising* (or *jogging* or *strolling*) in the park *when* several thugs suddenly *loomed* in his path.

1. Manitoba was founded by Louis Riel. He was one of the Métis leaders who figured centrally in the North-West Rebellion.
2. After he had entered federal politics in 1873, Riel, who was successful in the general election of 1874, made the choice to go to Ottawa and sit in Parliament.
3. Riel was expelled from the House on a motion introduced by the Ontario Orange Leader. The Ontario Orange Leader was Mackenzie Boswell. Boswell became the fifth prime minister of Canada in 1894.
4. In February 1875, a motion was adopted by the federal government to grant amnesty to Riel. The amnesty was conditional on five years of banishment from Canada.
5. Riel suffered a nervous breakdown. Then he was admitted to hospital and was released in 1878 and in 1883 was asked for help by a group of Canadian Métis. They wanted to obtain their legal rights in the Saskatchewan Valley.

Rewriting jargon

Jargon can refer to the special vocabulary of any discipline or profession (see p. 448). But it has also come to describe vague, inflated language that is overcomplicated, even incomprehensible. When it comes from government or business, we call it *bureaucratese.* It sounds almost as if the writer deliberately ignored every suggestion for clear, concise writing.

You may find yourself writing jargon when you are unsure of your subject or when your thoughts are tangled. It's fine, even necessary, to stumble and grope while drafting. But you should straighten out your ideas and eliminate jargon during revision and editing.

JARGON — The necessity for individuals to become separate entities in their own right may impel children to engage in open rebelliousness against parental authority or against sibling influence, with resultant confusion of those being rebelled against.

TRANSLATION — Children's natural desire to become themselves may make them rebel against bewildered parents or siblings.

JARGON	The weekly social gatherings stimulate networking among members of management from various divisions, with the aim of developing contacts and maximizing the flow of creative information.
TRANSLATION	The weekly parties give managers from different divisions a chance to meet and to share ideas.

Exercise 13
Revising: Conciseness

Make the following passage as concise as possible. Cut unneeded or repeated words, and simplify words and grammatical structures. Consult a dictionary as needed. Be merciless.

At the end of a lengthy line of reasoning, he came to the conclusion that the situation with carcinogens [cancer-causing substances] should be regarded as similar to the situation with the automobile. Rather than giving in to an irrational fear of cancer, we should consider all aspects of the problem in a balanced and dispassionate frame of mind, making a total of the benefits received from potential carcinogens (plastics, pesticides, and other similar products) and measuring said total against the damage done by such products. This is the nature of most discussions about the automobile. Rather than responding irrationally to the visual, aural, and air pollution caused by automobiles, we have decided to live with them (while simultaneously working to improve on them) for the benefits brought to society as a whole.

Chapter 32 Using the Dictionary

A dictionary can answer most of the questions about words you may ask. This chapter will show you how to choose a dictionary that suits your purpose and how to read a dictionary without difficulty.

32a Choosing a dictionary

1 Abridged dictionaries

Abridged dictionaries are the most practical for everyday use. Often called desk dictionaries because of their convenient size, they usually list 150 000 to 200 000 words and concentrate on fairly common words and meanings. All of the following abridged dictionaries, listed alphabetically, are dependable.

Gage Canadian Dictionary (1997). This edition is a substantially revised and expanded version of the earlier revised edition of 1983. The introduction to the 1983 dictionary pointed out that it was "the only adult-level dictionary currently available that can be said truly to reflect standard Canadian usage throughout." The introductory essay also goes on to observe that such usage is generally derived from that of Great Britain and the United States, but is often more diverse than that of either country. The 1983 edition was often criticized for not reflecting this diversity enough in its entries; however, the expanded 1997 edition is much more representative of the diversity and specificity of Canadian usages.

ITP Nelson Canadian Dictionary of the English Language (1997). An adaptation of the *American Heritage High School Dictionary*, the *Nelson* is now a rival for the *Gage* in the breadth and depth of its representation of Canadian usage and life and may yet become the senior dictionary of Canadian English. Perhaps even more than the *Gage*, the *Nelson* pays close attention to defining specific Canadianisms. This dictionary also has hundreds of encyclopedia style entries on Canadian nature and culture.

Merriam-Webster's Collegiate Dictionary, 10th edition (1993). This dictionary, based on the unabridged *Webster's Third New International Dictionary* (see opposite), applies usage labels less frequently than do some other dictionaries. It also emphasizes word histories, arranging meanings in order of their appearance in the language and providing the date when a word was first used.

The *Random House Webster's College Dictionary* (1991). Based on the unabridged *Random House Dictionary* (see opposite), this dictionary also lists each word's most common meanings first. The dictionary avoids sexist language in definitions and explanations, and its usage notes indicate words or meanings considered offensive or disparaging to groups such as women and minorities. Appendixes include guidelines for avoiding sexist language.

Webster's New World Dictionary of the American Language, 3rd college edition (1988). This dictionary arranges meanings in order of their appearance in the language. Usage labels (*colloquial, slang,* and so on) are applied liberally, and words and phrases of American origin are starred.

NOTE ESL If English is not your first language, you probably should have a dictionary prepared especially for ESL students in addition to one of the dictionaries listed above. The dictionaries listed below give much more information on such matters as count versus noncount nouns, prepositions with verbs and adjectives, and other concerns of ESL students.

32a

Longman Dictionary of Contemporary English (1987). This dictionary includes 56 000 words and phrases along with usage and study notes. *Longman Dictionary of American English* (1983) is the American abridgment.

Oxford Advanced Learner's Dictionary (1989). This dictionary includes 57 000 words and phrases along with usage notes and illustrations of plants, animals, and other common things. *Oxford ESL Dictionary* (1994) is the American edition.

Unabridged dictionaries

Unabridged dictionaries are the most scholarly and comprehensive of all dictionaries, sometimes consisting of many volumes. They emphasize the history of words and the variety of their uses. An unabridged dictionary is useful when you are studying a word in depth, reading or writing about the literature of another century, or looking for a quotation containing a particular word. The following unabridged dictionaries are available at most libraries.

The *Oxford English Dictionary*, (*OED*), 2nd edition, 20 volumes (1933–89). The first edition is available in a compact, photographically reduced, three-volume edition (1987), as well as a computerized CD-ROM format (1989) produced in cooperation with the University of Waterloo in Ontario. This is the greatest dictionary of our language. Its purpose is to show the histories and current meanings of all words. Its entries illustrate the changes in a word's spelling, pronunciation, and meaning with quotations from writers of every century. Some entries span pages. The second edition integrates the original *OED*, the four supplementary volumes published between 1972 and 1986, and approximately 5000 new words and senses of existing words. While basically British, the *OED* does include some American words and meanings.

The *Random House Dictionary of the English Language,* 2nd edition (1987). This dictionary is smaller (and less expensive) than many unabridged dictionaries. Its entries and definitions are especially up to date, and it includes hundreds of usage notes. Among its appendixes are short dictionaries of French, Spanish, Italian, and German.

Webster's Third New International Dictionary of the English Language (1986). This dictionary attempts to record our language more as it *is* used than as it *should be* used. Therefore, usage labels (such as *slang*) are minimal. Definitions are given in order of their appearance in the language. Most acceptable spellings and pronunciations are provided. Plentiful illustrative quotations show variations in the uses of words.

32a

Special dictionaries

Special dictionaries limit their attention to a single class of word (for example, slang, engineering terms, abbreviations), to a single kind of information (synonyms, usage, word origins), or to a specific subject (Aboriginal cultures, biography, history). (See pp. 515–19 for lists of subject dictionaries.)

Special dictionaries on slang or word origins can help you locate uncommon information, and they make entertaining reading.

For information on slang

Partridge's Concise Dictionary of Slang and Unconventional English. Edited by Paul Beale. 1990.

Wentworth, Harold, and Stuart Berg Flexner. *Dictionary of American Slang.* 2nd supplemented edition. 1975.

For the origins of words

Oxford Dictionary of English Etymology. Edited by Charles T. Onions et al. 1966.

Partridge, Eric. *Origins: A Short Etymological Dictionary of Modern English.* 4th edition. 1966.

For guidance on English usage

The *New Fowler's Modern English Usage*. Edited by R.W. Birchfield. 1996.

Fowler, H. W. *A Dictionary of Modern English Usage.* 2nd edition. Revised and edited by Sir Ernest Gowers. 1965.

Morris, William, and Mary Morris. *Harper Dictionary of Contemporary Usage.* 2nd edition. 1986.

For information about synonyms

Roget's International Thesaurus. 5th edition. Revised by Robert L. Chapman. 1992

Webster's New Dictionary of Synonyms. 1973.

A thesaurus like *Roget's* provides extensive lists of words with related meanings. A dictionary of synonyms like *Webster's* contains discussions and illustrations of shades of meaning.

For information on language usage in a particular region

The *South Shore Phrase Book: A New, Revised and Expanded Nova Scotian Dictionary Complete with Two Appendices.* 2nd edition. Compiled by Lewis J. Poteet. 1988.

Dictionary of Prince Edward Island English. Edited by T. K. Pratt. 1988.

Dictionary of Newfoundland English. 2nd edition. Edited by G. M. Story, W. J. Kirwin, and J. D. A. Widdowson. 1990.

Special scholarly dictionary

Dictionary of Canadianisms on Historical Principles. 1967. Edited by Walter S. Avis, Patrick D. Drysdale, and Matthew H. Scargill. 1967.

32b Working with a dictionary's contents

An abridged dictionary is a quick and accessible reference for all kinds of information. Most dictionaries will tell you the atomic weight of oxygen, Napoleon's birth and death dates, the location of the Orinoco River, the population of Gambia, and similarly varied facts.

Of course a dictionary is most useful on words. Dictionaries use abbreviations and symbols to squeeze a lot of information into a relatively small book. This system of condensed information may at first seem difficult to read. But all dictionaries include in their opening pages detailed information on the arrangement of entries, pronunciation symbols, and abbreviations. And the format is quite similar from one dictionary to another, so becoming familiar with the abbreviations and symbols in one dictionary makes reading any dictionary an easy routine.

Here is a fairly typical entry, from *Merriam-Webster's Collegiate Dictionary,* 10th edition. The labelled parts are discussed on the pages that follow.

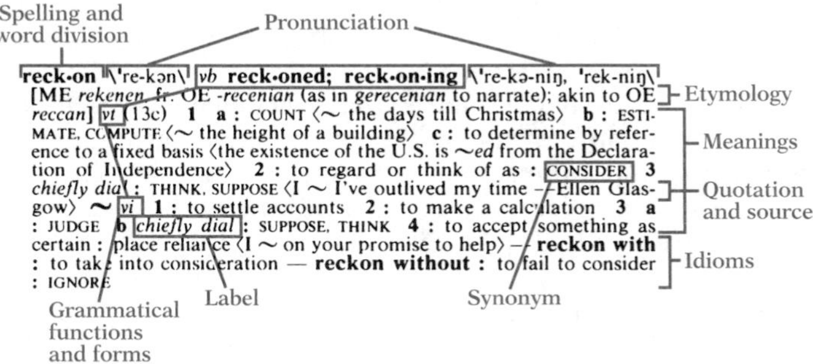

Spelling and word division

The small initial letters for *reckon* indicate that it is not normally capitalized. (In contrast, *Franklin stove* is capitalized in *Merriam-Webster's* because *Franklin* is a proper noun.)

The centred period in **reck·on** shows the division into syllables. If you are writing or typing a word of more than one syllable and need to break it at the end of a line, follow the dictionary's division of the word into syllables. (See also Chapter 30 for general rules about word division.) For a hyphenated compound word, such as *cross-question,* a dictionary shows the hyphen as part of the spelling: **cross-ques·tion.**

Dictionaries provide any variant spellings of a word at the beginning of an entry. For the word *dexterous, Merriam-Webster's* has "**dex·ter·ous** *or* **dex·trous,**" indicating that either spelling is acceptable.

The treatment of foreign words such as *joie de vivre* or *ergo,* which are normally italicized (or underlined) in writing, is more varied. *Webster's New World Dictionary* places a special symbol (‡) before each one. *Gage Canadian Dictionary* (*GCD*) simply designates them as *French* and *Latin,* respectively, therefore indicating they should be italicized.

Dictionaries provide any variant spellings of a word at the beginning of an entry. Thus, for the word *sulphur*, the *GCD* has "**sul·phur** or **sul·fur**," indicating that either spelling is acceptable.

Pronunciation

In *Merriam-Webster's* the pronunciation appears in reversed slashes (\\). The stressed syllable is preceded by an accent mark (ˈre-kən).

Dictionaries use symbols to indicate how to pronounce a word because the alphabet itself does not record all the sounds in the language. (Listen, for example, to the different sounds of *a* in only three words: *far, make,* and *answer.*) Most dictionaries provide a key to the pronunciation symbols at the foot of each page or every two facing pages. The *GCD* puts its "Complete Pronunciation Key" on the inside front and back covers.

Most unabridged and some abridged dictionaries provide variant pronunciations, including regional differences. The *GCD* (1983), for example, provides two pronunciations for the last syllable of *licorice,* and indicates that the word may be pronounced either of three ways: "likʹə rish, likʹrish, or likʹə ris."

Grammatical functions and forms

Dictionaries give helpful information about a word's functions and forms. The *Merriam-Webster's* entry for *reckon* shows the word to be a verb (*vb*), with the past tense and past participle *reckoned* and the present participle *reckoning,* and with both transitive (*vt*) and intransitive (*vi*) meanings. (For the definitions of these terms, see p. 157.)

Most dictionaries provide not only the principal forms of regular and irregular verbs but also the plural forms of irregular nouns and the *-er* and *-est* forms of adjectives and adverbs. An adjective or adverb without *-er* and *-est* forms in the dictionary requires the addition of *more* and *most* to show comparison (see p. 243).

Etymology

32b

Dictionaries provide the **etymology** of a word (its history) to indicate its origin and the evolution of its meanings and forms. The dictionary can compress much information about a word into a small space through symbols, abbreviations, and different typefaces. An explanation of these systems appears in the dictionary's opening pages. *Merriam-Webster's* traces *reckon* back to Old English (OE) by way of Middle English (ME). The notation "(13c)" before the first definition indicates that the first recorded use of *reckon* to mean "count" occurred in the thirteenth century.

Sometimes dictionaries do not give the etymology for a word. Their practices differ (and are explained in their opening pages), but in general they omit etymology when it is obvious, unknown, or available elsewhere in the dictionary.

Meanings

Dictionaries divide the general meaning of a word into particular meanings on the basis of how the word is or has been actually used. They arrange a word's meanings differently, however, explaining the basis of their arrangement in their opening pages. *Merriam-Webster's* and *Webster's New World* list meanings in order of their appearance in the language, earliest first. The *GCD, American Heritage,* and abridged *Random House,* in contrast, usually place the word's most basic or common meaning first. Be sure you know the system of any dictionary you are consulting. Then read through the entire entry before settling on the meaning that fits the context of what you're reading or writing.

The *Merriam-Webster's* entry for *reckon* ends with two uses of the word in idiomatic expressions (*reckon with* and *reckon without*). These phrases are defined because, as with all idioms, their meanings cannot be inferred simply from the words they consist of (see p. 456).

Labels

Dictionaries apply labels to words or to particular meanings that have a special status or use. The labels are usually of four kinds: style, subject, region, and time.

Style labels restrict a word or one of its meanings to a particular level of usage.

- *Slang:* words or meanings inappropriate in writing except for a special effect, such as *crumb* for "a worthless or despicable person."
- *Informal* or *colloquial:* words or meanings appropriate for informal writing but not formal writing, such as *great* to mean "very good," as in *a great movie.*
- *Nonstandard* or *substandard:* words or meanings inappropriate for standard speech and writing, such as *ain't.*
- *Vulgar* or *vulgar slang:* words or meanings considered offensive in speech and writing, as in profanity.
- *Poetic* or *literary:* words or meanings used only in poetry or the most formal writing, such as *eve* for *evening* and *o'er* for *over.*

Subject labels tell us that a word or one of its meanings has a special use in a field of knowledge or a profession. In its entry for *relaxation,* for instance, the *American Heritage* dictionary presents specialized meanings with the subject labels *physiology, physics,* and *mathematics.*

Region labels indicate that a particular spelling, pronunciation, or meaning of a word is not national but limited to some area. A regional difference may be indicated by the label *dialect*. The *GCD* labels as *dialect* the use of *critter* to mean "any living creature" or "an animal, especially a cow, raised as livestock" (as in *Get that critter into the barn*). More specific region labels may designate areas of Canada or other countries. The word *bloke* (meaning "fellow") is labelled as British by most dictionaries. And the *GCD* indicates that in Western Canada, *slough* means "a body of fresh water formed by rain or melted snow" or "a soft, deep, muddy place," while on the Pacific coast of Canada *slough* refers to "a shallow or marshy inlet of the sea."

Time labels indicate words or their meanings that the language, in evolving, has discarded. *Obsolete* designates words or meanings that are no longer used; *archaic* designates words or meanings that are out of date but used occasionally.

See pages 444–51 for further discussion of levels of usage and their appropriateness in your writing.

Synonyms

Synonyms are words whose meanings are approximately the same, such as *small* and *little. Merriam-Webster's Collegiate* defines *reckon* with some words in small capital letters (COUNT, ESTIMATE, CONSIDER, and so on). These are both synonyms and cross-references, in that each word may be looked up in its alphabetical place. Some dictionaries devote separate paragraphs to words with many synonyms. (See pp. 485–86 for a discussion of how to use the synonyms provided by a dictionary to increase your vocabulary.)

Illustrative quotations

Dictionaries are made by collecting quotations showing actual uses of words in all kinds of speech and writing. Some of these quotations, or others that the dictionary makers invent, may appear in the dictionary's entries as illustrations of how a word may be used. Five such quotations illustrate uses of *reckon* in the *Merriam-Webster's* entry (~ in these quotations stands for the word being illustrated).

Unabridged dictionaries usually provide many such quotations, not only to illustrate a word's current uses but also to show the changes in its meanings over time. Abridged dictionaries use quotations more selectively: to illustrate an unusual meaning of the word, to help distinguish between two closely related meanings of the same word, or to show the differences between synonyms.

32b

Exercise
Using a dictionary

Consult your dictionary on five of the following words. First find out whether your dictionary lists the oldest or the most common meanings first in its entries. Then, for each word, write down (*a*) the division into syllables, (*b*) the pronunciation, (*c*) the grammatical functions and forms, (*d*) the etymology, (*e*) each meaning, and (*f*) any special uses indicated by labels. Finally, use the word in at least two sentences of your own.

1. depreciation
2. secretary
3. grammar
4. manifest
5. assassin
6. astrology
7. potlatch
8. plain (*adj.*)
9. ceremony
10. toxic
11. steal
12. obelisk

Chapter 33

Improving Your Vocabulary

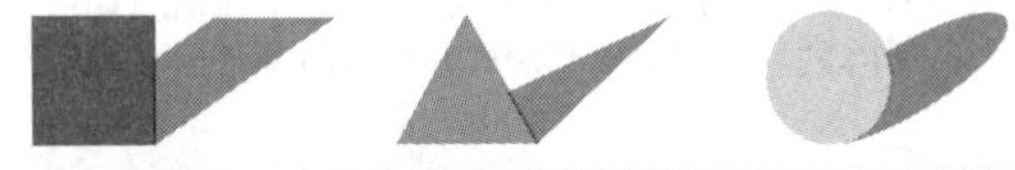

A precise and versatile vocabulary will help you communicate effectively in speech and writing. To a great extent, you can improve your vocabulary by frequent and inquisitive reading, by troubling to notice and learn the interesting or unfamiliar words used by other writers.

This chapter has a twofold purpose: to provide a sense of the potential of English by acquainting you with its history and range of words; and to help you increase the range, versatility, and precision of your own vocabulary.

33a Understanding the sources of English

English has over 500 000 words, probably more than any other language. This exceptional vocabulary and the power and range of expression that accompany it derive from its special mix of word sources. Unlike many other languages, English has borrowed a large number of words.

How English drew on its several sources and acquired its large vocabulary is the story of historical changes. The ancestor of English, Indo-European, was spoken (but not written) perhaps as far back as 5000 B.C., and it eventually spread to cover the area from India west to the British Isles. In what is now England, an

Indo-European offshoot called Celtic was spoken extensively until the fifth century A.D. But over the next few centuries, invaders from the European continent, speaking a dialect of another Indo-European language, Germanic, overran the native Britons. The Germanic dialect became the original source of English.

Old English, spoken from the eighth to the twelfth centuries, was a rugged, guttural language. It used a slightly different alphabet from ours (including the characters ð and þ for *th*), which has been transcribed in the sample below. The sample shows the opening lines of the Lord's Prayer: "Our Father, who art in heaven, hallowed be thy name. Thy kingdom come. Thy will be done on earth as it is in heaven."

> Fæder ure thu the eart on heofonum, si thin nama gehalgod. Tobecume thin rice. Gewurthe thin willa on eorthan swa swa on heofonum.

Many of our nouns, such as *stone, word, gift,* and *foot,* come from Old English. So do most of our pronouns, prepositions, and conjunctions, some (such as *he, under,* and *to*) without any change in spelling. Other Germanic tribes, using a similar dialect but settling on the European continent instead of in England, fostered two other languages, Dutch and German. As a result, Dutch, German, and English are related languages with some similar traits.

In 1066 the Normans, under William the Conqueror, invaded England. The Normans were originally Vikings who had settled in northern France and had forsaken Old Norse for their own dialect of Old French. They made Norman French the language of law, literature, and the ruling class in England. As a result, English acquired many French words, including many military and governmental words such as *authority, mayor, crime, army,* and *guard.* The common English people kept English alive during the Norman occupation, but they adopted many French words intact (*air, point, place, age*). Eventually, the French influence caused the language to shift from Old to Middle English, which lasted from the twelfth through the fifteenth centuries. During this time a great many Latin words also entered English, for Latin formed the background of Norman French and was the language of the Church and of scholars. English words that entered Middle English directly from Latin or from Latin through French include *language, luminous, memory, liberal,* and *sober.*

Middle English, as the following passage from Geoffrey Chaucer's *Canterbury Tales* shows, was much closer to our own language than to Old English.

> A clerk there was of Oxenford also,
> That unto logyk hadde longe ygo.
> As leene was his hors as is a rake,

And he nas nat right fat, I undertake,
But looked holwe, and therto sobrely.

Modern English evolved in the fourteenth and fifteenth centuries as the language's sound and spellings changed. This was the time of the Renaissance in Europe. Ancient Latin and Greek art, learning, and literature were revived, first in Italy and then throughout the continent. English vocabulary expanded rapidly, not only with more Latin and many Greek words (such as *democracy* and *physics*) but also with words from Italian and French. Advances in printing, beginning in the fifteenth century, made publications widely available to an increasingly literate audience. The Modern English of twentieth-century North America is four centuries and an ocean removed from the Modern English of sixteenth-century England, but the two are fundamentally the same. The differences and the similarities are evident in this passage from the King James Bible, published in 1611:

> And the Lord God commanded the man, saying, Of euery tree of the garden thou mayest freely eate. But of the tree of the knowledge of good and euill, thou shalt not eate of it: for in the day that thou eatest thereof, thou shalt surely die.

33b Learning the composition of words

Words can often be divided into meaningful parts. A *handbook*, for instance, is a book you keep at hand (for reference). A *shepherd* herds sheep (or other animals). Knowing what the parts of a word mean by themselves, as you do here, can often help you infer approximately what they mean when combined.

The following explanations of roots, prefixes, and suffixes provide information that can open up the meanings of words whose parts may not be familiar or easy to see. For more information, refer to a dictionary's etymologies, which provide the histories of words (see p. 474).

1 Learning roots

A **root** is the unchanging component of words related in origin and usually in meaning. Both *illiterate* ("unable to read and write") and *literal* ("sticking to the facts or to the first and most obvious meaning of an idea") share the root *liter,* derived from *littera,* a Latin word meaning "letter." A person who cannot understand the letters that make up writing is illiterate. A person who wants to understand the primary meaning of the letters (the words) in a contract is seeking the *literal* meaning of that contract.

At least half our words come from Latin and Greek. The list below includes some common Latin and Greek roots, their meanings, and examples of English words containing them.

Root (source)	Meaning	English words
aster, astr (G)	star	astronomy, astrology
audi (L)	to hear	audible, audience
bene (L)	good, well	benefit, benevolent
bio (G)	life	biology, autobiography
dic, dict (L)	to speak	dictator, dictionary
fer (L)	to carry	transfer, referral
fix (L)	to fasten	fix, suffix, prefix
geo (G)	earth	geography, geology
graph (G)	to write	geography, photography
jur, jus (L)	law	jury, justice
log, logue (G)	word, thought, speech	astrology, biology, neologism
luc (L)	light	lucid, translucent
manu (L)	hand	manual, manuscript
meter, metr (G)	measure	metric, thermometer
op, oper (L)	work	operation, operator
path (G)	feeling	pathetic, sympathy
ped (G)	child	pediatrics
phil (G)	love	philosophy, Anglophile
phys (G)	body, nature	physical, physics
scrib, script (L)	to write	scribble, manuscript
tele (G)	far off	telephone, television
ter, terr (L)	earth	territory, extraterrestrial
vac (L)	empty	vacant, vacuum, evacuate
verb (L)	word	verbal, verbose
vid, vis (L)	to see	video, vision, television

Exercise 1
Learning roots

Define the following italicized words, using the list of roots above and any clues given by the rest of the sentence. Check the accuracy of your meanings in a dictionary.

1. After guiding me through university, my *benefactor* will help me start a career.
2. Always afraid of leading a *vacuous* life, the heiress immersed herself in volunteer work.
3. The posters *affixed* to the construction wall advertised a pornographic movie.
4. After his *auditory* nerve was damaged, he had trouble catching people's words.
5. The child *empathized* so completely with his mother that he felt pain when she broke her arm.

Learning prefixes

Prefixes are standard syllables fastened to the front of a word to modify its meaning. For example, the word *prehistory* is a combination of the word *history,* meaning "based on a written record explaining past events," and the prefix *pre-,* meaning "before." Together, prefix and word mean "before a written record explaining past events," or before events were recorded. Learning standard prefixes can help you improve vocabulary and spelling just as learning word roots can. The following lists group prefixes according to sense so that they are easier to remember. When two or more prefixes have very different spellings but the same meaning, they usually derive from different languages, most often Latin and Greek.

Prefixes showing quantity

MEANING	PREFIXES IN ENGLISH WORDS
half	*semi*annual; *hemi*sphere
one	*uni*cycle; *mon*arch, *mono*rail
two	*bi*nary, *bi*monthly; *di*lemma, *dicho*tomy
three	*tri*angle, *tri*logy
four	*quad*rangle, *quar*tet
five	*quin*tet; *penta*gon
six	*sex*tuplets; *hexa*meter
seven	*sept*uagenarian; *hept*archy
eight	*oct*ave, *octo*pus
nine	*nona*genarian
ten	*dec*ade, *deca*thlon
hundred	*cent*ury; *hecto*litre
thousand	*milli*metre; *kilo*cycle

Prefixes showing negation

MEANING	PREFIXES IN ENGLISH WORDS
without, no, not	*a*sexual; *il*legal, *im*moral, *in*valid, *ir*reverent; *un*skilled
not, absence of, opposing, against	*non*breakable; *ant*acid, *anti*pathy; *contra*dict

MEANING	PREFIXES IN ENGLISH WORDS
opposite to, complement to	*counter*clockwise, *counter*weight
do the opposite of, remove, reduce	*de*horn, *de*vitalize, *de*value
do the opposite of, deprive of	*dis*establish, *dis*arm
wrongly, bad	*mis*judge, *mis*deed

Prefixes showing time

Meaning	Prefixes in English words
before	*ante*cedent; *fore*cast; *pre*cede; *pro*logue
after	*post*war
again	*re*write

Prefixes showing direction or position

Meaning	Prefixes in English words
above, over	*super*vise
across, over	*trans*port
below, under	*infra*sonic; *sub*terranean; *hypo*dermic
in front of	*pro*ceed; *pre*fix
behind	*re*cede
out of	*e*rupt, *ex*plicit; *ec*stasy
into	*in*jection, *im*merse; *en*courage, *em*power
around	*circum*ference; *peri*meter
with	*co*exist, *col*loquial, *com*municate, *con*sequence, *cor*respond; *sym*pathy, *syn*chronize

Exercise 2
Learning prefixes

Provide meanings for the following italicized words, using the lists of prefixes and any clues given by the rest of the sentence. Check the accuracy of your meanings in a dictionary

1. In 1970 the Hudson's Bay Company, the oldest incorporated joint-stock merchandising company in the English-speaking world, celebrated its *tricentennial*.
2. Most poems called sonnets consist of fourteen lines divided into an *octave* and a *sestet*.
3. When the Finance Minister raised federal taxes on old-age security and family allowance benefits, the leader of the New Democratic Party proposed the *countermeasure* of increasing corporate tax rates instead.
4. By suggesting an increase in corporate tax rates, the NDP leader hoped to *forestall* what he predicted as the inevitable dismantling of the universality principle underlying this nation's social programs.
5. Ferdinand Magellan, a Portuguese sailor, commanded the first expedition to *circumnavigate* the globe.

Learning suffixes

Suffixes are standard syllables fastened to the end of a word to modify its meaning and usually its part of speech. The word *popular* is an adjective. With different suffixes, it becomes a different adjective, an adverb, two different verbs, and a noun.

ADJECTIVE	popular popul*ous*	ADVERB	popul*arly*
VERB	popul*ate* popul*arize*	NOUN	popul*ation*

Many words change suffixes in the same way. In fact, suffixes help us recognize what parts of speech many words are, as the following examples show.

Noun suffixes

mis*ery*	min*er*	intern*ship*	random*ness*
refer*ence*	base*ment*	presid*ency*	brother*hood*
relev*ance*	national*ist*	discus*sion*	king*dom*
operat*or*	national*ism*	agita*tion*	

Verb suffixes

hard*en*	pur*ify*
national*ize*	agit*ate*

Adjective suffixes

miser*able*	president*ial*	wonder*ful*	use*less*
ed*ible*	gigant*ic*	fibr*ous*	self*ish*
nation*al*	friend*ly*	adopt*ive*	flatu*lent*

The only suffix regularly applied to adverbs is *-ly: openly, selfishly.*

NOTE Inflectional endings—such as the plural *-s,* the possessive *-'s,* the past tense *-ed,* and the comparative *-er* or *-est*—appear at the ends of words but do not change a word's grammatical function.

Exercise 3
Learning suffixes

Identify the part of speech of each word below, and then change it to the part or parts of speech in parentheses by deleting, adding, or changing a suffix. Use the given word and each created word in a sentence. Check a dictionary, if necessary, to be sure suffixes and spellings are correct.

1. magic (*adjective*)
2. durable (*noun; adverb*)
3. refrigerator (*verb*)
4. self-critical (*noun*)
5. differ (*noun; adjective*)
6. equal (*noun; adverb*)
7. conversion (*verb; adjective*)
8. strictly (*adjective; noun*)
9. assist (*noun*)
10. qualification (*verb; adjective*)

33c Learning to use new words

You can learn a new word not only by understanding its composition but also by examining the context in which it appears and by looking it up in a dictionary—both ways to increase your vocabulary by multiplying and varying your experience with language.

Examining context

Often, you can guess the meaning of an unfamiliar word by looking at the familiar words around it. This technique is helpful when you don't want to interrupt your reading to look up every unfamiliar word. (When you've finished reading, though, check your guesses in your dictionary.)

Parallelism shows you which ideas line up or go together and can often suggest the meaning of a new word. Watch for parallel ideas in the following sentence.

> The kittens see their mother hunt and kill, and they in turn take up *predatory* behaviour.

Context clues suggest the meaning of *predatory:* parallel construction (*kittens see . . . and they . . . take up*); the tip-off phrase *in turn;* and the suggested idea of imitation (kittens watching their mother and taking up her behaviour). These clues lead to the correct conclusion that predatory behaviour consists of hunting and killing.

The phrase *is called* or the word *is* often signals a definition.

> The point where the light rays come together is called the *focus* of the lens.

Sometimes definitions are enclosed in parentheses or set off by commas or dashes.

> In early childhood these tendencies lead to the development of *schemes* (organized patterns of behaviour).

> Many Chinese practise *Tai Chi,* an ancient method of self-defence performed as exercise in slow, graceful motions.

> At *burnout*—the instant a rocket stops firing—the satellite's path is fixed.

Noticing examples can also help you infer the meaning of a word. The expressions *such as, for example, for instance, to illustrate,* and *including* often precede examples.

> Society often has difficulty understanding *nonconformists* such as criminals, inventors, artists, saints, and political protesters.

The examples of people who go beyond the average or beyond the rules suggest that *nonconformists* do not adapt themselves to the usual standards and customs of society.

Sometimes an example that reveals the meaning of an unfamiliar word is not announced by a phrase.

> During the first weeks of *rehabilitation,* Smith exercised as best he could, took his medicine daily, and thought constantly about the physical condition he once possessed.

Guessing the meaning of *rehabilitation* requires considering what occurred during it: (1) exercising "as best he could," as if Smith had some kind of handicap; (2) taking medicine, as if Smith were ill; and (3) thinking about his past physical condition, as if Smith were wishing for the good shape he used to be in. Putting these examples together suggests that *rehabilitation* is returning to a healthy condition, which is one of its meanings.

Exercise 4
Examining context

Use context to determine the meanings of the words italicized below (not including titles). Check the accuracy of your guess by consulting a dictionary.

1. [Canada] ought to have been *obliterated* in the War of 1812, but the Americans were inept, and more important militarily, half-hearted. —RICHARD GWYN
2. A photograph passes for *incontrovertible* proof that a given thing happened. The picture may distort; but there is always a *presumption* that something exists, or did exist, which is like what's in the picture. —SUSAN SONTAG
3. It is not easy to describe or to account for our own culture's particular *predilection* for butter—a loyalty so fierce and so unreasoning that it is called, by those opposed to it, the "butter *mystique.*" —MARGARET VISSER
4. "And this, too, shall pass away." How much [this sentence] expresses! How *chastening* in the hour of pride! How *consoling* in the depths of *affliction!* —ABRAHAM LINCOLN
5. In a community where public services have failed to keep *abreast* of private consumption, . . . in an atmosphere of private *opulence* and public *squalor,* the private goods have full sway. —JOHN KENNETH GALBRAITH

Using the dictionary

33c

The dictionary is a quick reference for the meanings of words (see p. 475). It can give the precise meaning of a word whose general meaning you have guessed by examining the word's context. It can also help you fix the word in your memory by showing its spelling, pronunciation, synonyms, and other features.

Although a dictionary of synonyms is the best source for the precise meanings of similar words (see p. 472), an abridged dictionary will supply much information about synonyms. Most abridged dictionaries list a word's common synonyms and either direct you to the entries for the synonyms or distinguish among them in one place. An example of the latter form is the paragraph below, which follows the main entry for the word *decrease* in the *ITP Nelson Canadian Dictionary of the English Language.* By drawing on this information as you edit, you can substitute a more precise word for *decrease* when your meaning calls for one.

> **Syns:** *decrease, lessen, reduce, dwindle, abate, diminish, subside.* These verbs mean to become or cause to become smaller or less. *Decrease* and *lessen* refer to steady or gradual diminution: *Lack of success decreases confidence. His appetite lessens as his illness progresses. Reduce* emphasizes bringing down in size, degree, or intensity: *The workers reduced their wage demands. Dwindle* suggests decreasing bit by bit to a vanishing point: *Their savings dwindled away. Abate* stresses a decrease in amount or intensity and suggests a reduction of excess: *Toward evening the fire began to abate. Diminish* implies taking away or removal: *The warden's authority diminished after the revolt. Subside* implies a falling away to a more normal level: *Our wild enthusiasm did not subside.*

Exercise 5
Using the dictionary

Consulting the dictionary entry above (and another dictionary if necessary), write five sentences that make precise use of *decrease* and four of its synonyms.

Chapter 34 Spelling

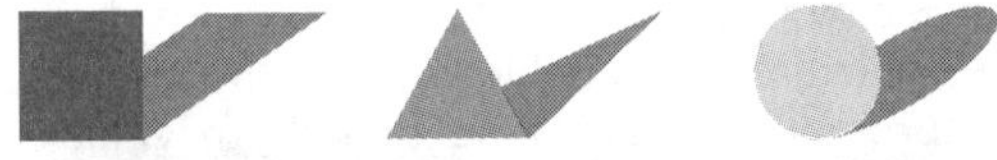

English spelling is difficult, even for some very experienced and competent writers. You can train yourself to spell better, and this chapter will help you. But you can also improve instantly by acquiring three habits:

- Carefully proofread your writing.
- Cultivate a healthy suspicion of your spellings.
- Compulsively check a dictionary whenever you doubt a spelling.

(See 34c for further discussion of these and some other tips.)

NOTE The spelling checkers for computerized word processors can help you find and track spelling errors in your papers. (See p. 755.) But their usefulness is limited, mainly because they can't spot the very common error of confusing words with similar spellings, such as *their/there/they're* or *to/too/two.* A spelling checker can supplement but can't substitute for your own care and attention.

34a Recognizing typical spelling problems

Spelling well involves recognizing situations that commonly lead to misspelling: pronunciation can mislead you in several ways;

different forms of the same word may have different spellings; and some words have more than one acceptable spelling.

1 Being wary of pronunciation

In English, unlike some languages, pronunciation of words is an unreliable guide to their spelling. The same letter or combination of letters may have different sounds in the pronunciation of different words. For an example, say aloud these different ways of pronouncing the letters *ough: tough, dough, cough, through, bough.* Another problem is that some words contain letters that are not pronounced clearly or at all, such as the *ed* in *asked,* the silent *e* in *swipe,* or the unpronounced *gh* in *tight.*

Pronunciation is a particularly unreliable guide to the spelling of **homonyms,** words pronounced the same though they have different spellings and meanings: *great/grate, to/too/two, threw/through.* Some commonly confused homonyms and words with very similar pronunciations, such as *accept/except,* are listed below. (See pp. 497–98 for tips on how to use spelling lists.)

Words commonly confused

accept (to receive)
except (other than)

affect (to have an influence on)
effect (result)

all ready (prepared)
already (by this time)

allude (to refer to indirectly)
elude (to avoid)

allusion (indirect reference)
illusion (erroneous belief or perception)

ascent (a movement up)
assent (agreement)

bare (unclothed)
bear (to carry, or an animal)

board (a plane of wood)
bored (uninterested)

born (brought into life)
borne (carried)

brake (stop)
break (smash)

buy (purchase)
by (next to)

capital (the seat of a government)
capitol (the building where a legislature meets)

cite (to quote an authority)
sight (the ability to see)
site (a place)

desert (to abandon)
dessert (after-dinner course)

discreet (reserved, respectful)
discrete (individual or distinct)

elicit (to bring out)
illicit (illegal)

fair (average, or lovely)
fare (a fee for transportation)

forth (forward)
fourth (after *third*)

gorilla (a large primate)
guerrilla (a kind of soldier)

hear (to perceive by ear)
here (in this place)

heard (past tense of *hear*)
herd (a group of animals)

hole (an opening)
whole (complete)

its (possessive of *it*)
it's (contraction of *it is*)

lead (heavy metal)
led (past tense of *lead*)

lessen (to make less)
lesson (something learned)

meat (flesh)
meet (encounter)

no (the opposite of *yes*)
know (to be certain)

passed (past tense of *pass*)
past (after, or a time gone by)

patience (forbearance)
patients (persons under medical care)

peace (the absence of war)
piece (a portion of something)

plain (clear)
plane (a carpenter's tool, or an airborne vehicle)

presence (the state of being at hand)
presents (gifts)

principal (most important, or the head of a school)
principle (a basic truth or law)

rain (precipitation)
reign (to rule)
rein (a strap for controlling an animal)

raise (to build up)
raze (to tear down)

right (correct)
rite (a religious ceremony)
write (to make letters)

road (a surface for driving)
rode (past tense of *ride*)

scene (where an action occurs)
seen (past participle of *see*)

seam (junction)
seem (appear)

stationary (unmoving)
stationery (writing paper)

straight (unbending)
strait (a water passageway)

their (possessive of *they*)
there (opposite of *here*)
they're (contraction of *they are*)

to (toward)
too (also)
two (following *one*)

waist (the middle of the body)
waste (discarded material)

weak (not strong)
week (Sunday through Saturday)

weather (climate)
whether (*if*, or introducing a choice)

which (one of a group)
witch (a sorcerer)

who's (contraction of *who is*)
whose (possessive of *who*)

your (possessive of *you*)
you're (contraction of *you are*)

Distinguishing between different forms of the same word

Other spelling problems occur when the noun form and the verb form of the same word are spelled differently. For example:

VERB	NOUN	VERB	NOUN
advise	advice	enter	entrance
describe	description	marry	marriage
speak	speech	omit	omission

Sometimes the noun and the adjective forms of the same word differ.

NOUN	ADJECTIVE	NOUN	ADJECTIVE
comedy	comic	height	high
courtesy	courteous	Britain	British
generosity	generous		

The principal parts of irregular verbs are usually spelled differently.

begin, began, begun
break, broke, broken
know, knew, known
ring, rang, rung

Irregular nouns change spelling from singular to plural.

child, children
goose, geese
mouse, mice
shelf, shelves
tooth, teeth
woman, women

Notice, too, that the stem of a word may change its spelling in different forms.

four, forty   thief, theft

sp
34a

Using preferred spellings

Many words have variant spellings as well as preferred spellings (see 32b-2). Often the variant spellings listed in an American dictionary are British spellings. Canadian usage is influenced by the language practices in both the United States and Britain and neither influence predominates. The *Gage Canadian Dictionary,* in its attempt to be descriptive rather than prescriptive, usually lists both American and British alternatives, and lists first the alternative perceived as preferred by the educated Canadian majority. Canadian newspapers, periodicals, and publishing houses tend to use American spellings in the interests of both space economy and consistency, whereas educational institutions tend to use British spellings. The following examples from the dictionary reveal the mixed influences on Canadian spelling.

AMERICAN	BRITISH	CANADIAN (preferred)
analy*z*e	analy*s*e	analy*s*e
cance*l*ed, labe*l*ed, trave*l*ed	cance*ll*ed, labe*ll*ed, trave*ll*ed	cance*ll*ed, labe*ll*ed, trave*ll*ed
catalog	catalog*ue*	catalog*ue*
cent*er*, met*er*, theat*er*	cent*re*, met*re*, theat*re*	cent*re*, met*re*, theat*re*
che*ck*	che*que*	che*que*
col*or*, hum*or*, neighb*or*	col*our*, hum*our*, neighb*our*	col*our*, hum*our*, neighb*our*
conne*ct*ion	conne*x*ion	conne*ct*ion
jail	*gaol*	*jail*
judgment	judg*e*ment	judgment
paraly*z*e	paraly*s*e	paraly*s*e
plo*w*	plo*ugh*	plo*ugh*
reali*z*e	reali*s*e	reali*s*e
ski*ll*ful	ski*l*ful	ski*l*ful
sul*f*ur	sul*ph*ur	sul*ph*ur
wagon	waggon	wagon
woo*l*en	woo*ll*en	woo*ll*en

Most instructors at Canadian educational institutions would probably look for consistency in students' spelling. If in doubt, however, ask your instructor for his or her preferences.

34b Following spelling rules

Misspelling is often a matter of misspelling a syllable rather than the whole word. The following general rules focus on troublesome syllables, with notes for the occasional exceptions.

1 Distinguishing between *ie* and *ei*

Words like *believe* and *receive* sound alike in the second syllable, but the syllable is spelled differently. Use the familiar jingle to distinguish between *ie* and *ei*:

> *I* before *e*, except after *c*, or when pronounced "ay" as in *neighbour* and *weigh*.

i BEFORE *e*	believe	bier	hygiene
	grief	thief	friend
	chief	fiend	

ei AFTER *c*	ceiling receive	conceive deceit	perceive conceit
ei SOUNDED AS "AY"	neighbour sleigh weight	freight eight vein	beige heinous

EXCEPTIONS In some words an *ei* combination neither follows *c* nor is pronounced "ay." These words include *either, neither, foreign, forfeit, height, leisure, weird, seize,* and *seizure.* This sentence might help you remember some of them: *The weird foreigner neither seizes leisure nor forfeits height.*

Exercise 1
Distinguishing between *ie* and *ei*

Insert *ie* or *ei* in the words below. Check doubtful spellings in a dictionary.

1. br__f	5. for__gn	9. l__surely	13. h__ght
2. dec__ve	6. pr__st	10. ach__ve	14. fr__ght
3. rec__pt	7. gr__vance	11. pat__nce	15. f__nt
4. s__ze	8. f__nd	12. p__rce	12. s__ve

2 Keeping or dropping a final *e*

Many words end with an unpronounced or silent *e: move, brave, late, rinse.* Drop the final *e* when adding an ending that begins with a vowel.

advise + able = advisable
force + ible = forcible
surprise + ing = surprising
guide + ance = guidance

Keep the final, silent *e* if the ending begins with a consonant.

battle + ment = battlement
accurate + ly = accurately
care + ful = careful
like + ness = likeness

sp 34b

EXCEPTIONS The silent *e* is sometimes retained before an ending beginning with a vowel. It is kept when *dye* becomes *dyeing,* to avoid confusion with *dying.* It is kept to prevent mispronunciation of words like *shoeing* (not *shoing*) and *mileage* (not *milage*). And the final *e* is often retained after a soft *c* or *g,* to keep the sound of the consonant soft rather than hard.

courageous	changeable	noticeable
outrageous	manageable	embraceable

The silent *e* is also sometimes *dropped* before an ending beginning with a consonant, when the *e* is preceded by another vowel.

argue + ment = argument
due + ly = duly
true + ly = truly

Exercise 2
Keeping or dropping a final *e*

Combine the following words and endings, keeping or dropping final *e*'s as necessary to make correctly spelled words. Check doubtful spellings in a dictionary.

1. malice + ious
2. love + able
3. service + able
4. retire + ment
5. sue + ing
6. virtue + ous
7. note + able
8. battle + ing
9. suspense + ion

Keeping or dropping a final *y*

Words ending in *y* often change their spelling when an ending is added to them. Change the final *y* to an *i* when it follows a consonant.

beauty, beauties	worry, worried	supply, supplies
folly, follies	merry, merrier	deputy, deputize

But keep the *y* when it follows a vowel, when the ending is *-ing,* or when it ends a proper name.

day, days	cry, crying	May, Mays
obey, obeyed	study, studying	Minsky, Minskys

Exercise 3
Keeping or dropping a final *y*

Combine the following words and endings, changing or keeping final *y*'s as necessary to make correctly spelled words. Check doubtful spellings in a dictionary.

1. imply + s
2. messy + er
3. apply + ing
4. delay + ing
5. defy + ance
6. say + s
7. solidify + s
8. Murphy + s
9. supply + ed

Doubling consonants

sp
34b

Words ending in a consonant sometimes double the consonant when an ending is added. Whether to double the final consonant depends first on the number of syllables in the word.

In one-syllable words, double the final consonant when a single vowel precedes the final consonant.

slap, slapping	flat, flatter
tip, tipped	pit, pitted

However, *don't* double the final consonant when two vowels or a vowel and another consonant precede the final consonant.

pair, paired	park, parking
real, realize	rent, rented

In words of more than one syllable, double the final consonant when a single vowel precedes the final consonant and the stress falls on the last syllable of the stem once the ending is added.

submit, submitted	refer, referring
occur, occurred	begin, beginning

But *don't* double the final consonant when it is preceded by two vowels or by a vowel and another consonant, or when the stress falls on other than the stem's last syllable once the ending is added.

refer, reference	despair, despairing
relent, relented	beckon, beckoned

Exercise 4
Doubling consonants

Combine the following words and endings, doubling final consonants as necessary to make correctly spelled words. Check doubtful spellings in a dictionary.

1. repair + ing
2. admit + ance
3. benefit + ed
4. shop + ed
5. conceal + ed
6. allot + ed
7. drip + ing
8. declaim + ed
9. parallel + ing

5 Attaching prefixes

Adding prefixes such as *dis-*, *mis-*, and *un-* does not change the spelling of a word. When adding a prefix, do not drop a letter from or add a letter to the original word.

uneasy	disappoint	misinform
unnecessary	dissatisfied	misstate
antifreeze	defuse	misspell
anti-intellectual	de-emphasize	

(See also p. 501 on when to use hyphens with prefixes.)

6 Forming plurals

Nouns

Most nouns form plurals by adding *-s* to the singular form.

boy, boys	table, tables
carnival, carnivals	Murphy, Murphys

Some nouns ending in *f* or *fe* form the plural by changing the ending to *ve* before adding *-s*.

leaf, leaves	wife, wives
life, lives	yourself, yourselves

Singular nouns ending in *-s, -sh, -ch,* or *-x* form the plural by adding *-es.*

kiss, kisses
wish, wishes
church, churches
Jones, Joneses

(Notice that verbs ending in *-s, -sh, -ch,* or *-x* form the third-person singular in the same way. *Taxes* and *lurches* are examples.)

Nouns ending in *o* preceded by a vowel usually form the plural by adding *-s.*

ratio, ratios
zoo, zoos

Nouns ending in *o* preceded by a consonant usually form the plural by adding *-es.*

hero, heroes
tomato, tomatoes

Exceptions Some very common nouns form irregular plurals.

child, children
mouse, mice
man, men
woman, women

Some English nouns that were originally Italian, Greek, Latin, or French form the plural according to their original language:

analysis, analyses
basis, bases
beau, beaux
crisis, crises
criterion, criteria
datum, data
medium, media
phenomenon, phenomena
piano, pianos
thesis, theses

A few such nouns may form irregular *or* regular plurals: for instance, *index, indices, indexes; curriculum, curricula, curriculums.* The regular plural is more contemporary.

Compound nouns

Form plurals of compound nouns in one of two ways. Add *-s* to the last word when the component words are roughly equal in importance, whether or not they are hyphenated.

city-states
painter-sculptors
breakthroughs
bucket seats
booby traps

Add *-s* to the noun when a noun is combined with other parts of speech.

fathers-in-law
passersby

Note, however, that most modern dictionaries give the plural of *spoonful* as *spoonfuls.*

Exercise 5
Forming plurals

Make correct plurals of the following singular words. Check doubtful spellings in a dictionary.

1. pile	5. kilometre per hour	9. Bales	13. thief
2. donkey	6. box	10. cupful	14. goose
3. beach	7. switch	11. libretto	15. hiss
4. summary	8. sister-in-law	12. video	16. appendix

34c Developing spelling skills

The essential steps in improving spelling skills were listed at the start of this chapter: proofread, be suspicious, and use a dictionary. These and a few additional aids are discussed below.

1 Editing and proofreading carefully

If spelling is a problem for you, give it high priority while editing your writing (p. 65) and again while proofreading, your last chance to catch misspelled words (p. 67). Reading a draft backward, word by word, can help you spot mistakes such as switched or omitted letters in words you know. Because the procedure forces you to consider each word in isolation, it can also highlight spellings you may be less sure of. A sense of uncertainty is crucial in spotting and correcting spelling errors, even for good spellers who make relatively few errors. Listen to your own uncertainty, and let it lead you to the dictionary.

2 Using a dictionary

How can you look up a word you can't spell? Start by guessing at the spelling and looking up your guess. If that doesn't work, pronounce the word aloud to come up with other possible spellings, and look them up. Unless the word is too specialized to be included in your dictionary, trial and error will eventually pay off.

Once you find the correct spelling, check the definition to be sure you have the word you want.

3 Pronouncing carefully

Careful pronunciation is not always a reliable guide to spelling (see p. 488), but it can keep you from misspelling words that are often mispronounced. For example:

aspirin (*not* asprin)	laboratory (*not* labratory)
athletics (*not* atheletics)	library (*not* libary)
disastrous (*not* disasterous)	lightning (*not* lightening)
environment (*not* envirnment)	mischievous (*not* mischievious)
frustrate (*not* fustrate)	nuclear (*not* nucular)
government (*not* goverment)	recognize (*not* reconize)
height (*not* heighth)	representative (*not* representive)
history (*not* histry)	strictly (*not* stricly)
irrelevant (*not* irrevelant)	

4 Tracking and analysing your errors

Keep a list of the words marked "misspelled" or "spelling" or "sp" in your papers. This list will contain hints about your particular spelling problems, such as that you tend to confuse *affect* and *effect* or to form plurals incorrectly. (If you need help analysing the list, consult your writing instructor.) The list will also provide a personalized study guide, a focus for your efforts to spell better. As appropriate, use the suggestions in the next two sections (mnemonics and spellings lists) to master individual words.

5 Using mnemonics

Mnemonics (pronounced with an initial *n* sound) are techniques for assisting your memory. The *er* in *letter* and *paper* can remind you that *stationery* (meaning "writing paper") has an *er* near the end; *stationary* with an *a* means "standing in place." Or the word *dome* with its long *o* sound can remind you that the building in which the legislature meets is spelled *capitol,* with an *o*. If you identify the words you have trouble spelling, you can take a few minutes to think of your own mnemonics, which may work better for you than someone else's.

6 Studying spelling lists

Learning to spell commonly misspelled words will reduce your spelling errors. For general improvement, work with the following list of commonly misspelled words. Study only six or seven words at a time. If you are unsure of the meaning of a word, look it up in a dictionary and try using it in a sentence. Pronounce the word out loud, syllable by syllable, and write the word out. (The list of similar-sounding words on pp. 488–89 should be considered an extension of the one that follows.)

absence
abundance
acceptable
accessible
accidentally
accommodate
accomplish
accumulate
accuracy
accustomed
achieve
acknowledge
acquire
across
actually
address
admission
adolescent
advice
advising
against
aggravate
aggressive
allegiance
all right
all together
almost
already
although
altogether
amateur
among
amount
analysis
analyse
angel
annual
answer
apology
apparent
appearance
appetite
appreciate
appropriate
approximately
argument
arrest
ascend
assassinate
assimilation
assistance
associate
atheist
athlete
attendance
audience
average

bargain
basically
because
beginning
belief
believe
beneficial
benefited
boundary
breath
Britain
bureaucracy
business

calculator
calendar
caricature
carrying
cede
ceiling
cello
cemetery
certain
changeable
changing
characteristic
chief
chocolate
choose
chose
climbed
coarse
column
coming
commercial
commitment
committed
committee
competent
competition
complement
compliment
conceive
concentrate
concert
condemn
conquer
conscience
conscious
consistency
consistent
continuous
controlled
controversial
convenience
convenient
coolly
course
courteous
criticism
criticize
crowd
cruelty
curiosity
curious
curriculum

deceive
deception
decide
decision
deductible
definitely
degree
dependent
descend
descendant
describe
description
desirable
despair
desperate
destroy
determine
develop
device
devise
dictionary
difference
dining
disagree
disappear
disappoint
disapprove
disastrous
discipline
discriminate
discussion
disease
disgusted
dissatisfied
distinction
divide
divine
division
doctor
drawer
easily
ecstasy
efficiency
efficient
eighth
either
eligible
embarrass
emphasize
empty
enemy
entirely
entrepreneur
environment
equipped
especially
essential
every
exaggerate
exceed
excellent
exercise
exhaust
exhilarate
existence
expense
experience
experiment
explanation
extremely

familiar
fascinate
favourite
February
fiery
finally
forcibly
foreign
foresee
forty
forward
friend
frightening
fulfil

gauge
generally
ghost
government
grammar
grief
guarantee
guard
guidance

happily
harass
height
heroes
hideous
humorous
hungry
hurriedly
hurrying
hypocrisy
hypocrite

ideally
illogical
imaginary
imagine
imitation
immediately
immigrant
incidentally
incredible
independence
independent
individually
inevitably
influential
initiate
innocuous
inoculate
insistent
integrate
intelligence
interest
interference
interpret
irrelevant
irresistible
irritable
island

jealousy
judgment

kindergarten
knowledge

laboratory
leisure
length
library
licence
license
lieutenant
lightning
likelihood
literally
livelihood
loneliness
loose
lose
luxury
lying

magazine
maintenance
manageable
marriage
mathematics
meant
medicine
miniature
minor
minutes
mirror
mischievous
missile
misspelled
morale
morals
mortgage
mournful
muscle
mysterious

naturally
necessary
neighbour
neither
nickel
niece
ninety
ninth
noticeable
nuclear
nuisance
numerous

obstacle
occasion
occasionally
occur
occurrence
official
omission
omit
omitted
opinion
opponent
opportunity
opposite
ordinary
originally

paid
panicky
paralleled
parliament
particularly
peaceable
peculiar
pedal
perceive
perception
performance
permanent
permissible
persistence
personnel
perspiration
persuade
persuasion
petal
physical
physiology
physique
pitiful
planning
playwright
pleasant
poison
politician
pollute
possession
possibly
practically
practice
practise
prairie
precede
preference
preferred
prejudice
preparation
prevalent
primitive
privilege
probably
procedure
proceed
process
professor
prominent
pronunciation
psychology
purpose
pursue
pursuit

quandary
quantity
quarter
questionnaire
quiet
quizzes

realistically
realize
really
rebel
rebelled
recede
receipt
receive
recognize
recommend
reference
referred
relief
relieve
religious
remembrance
reminisce
renown
repetition
representative
resemblance
resistance
restaurant
rhyme
rhythm
ridiculous
roommate

sacrifice
sacrilegious
safety
satellite
scarcity
schedule
science
secretary
seize
separate
sergeant
several
sheriff
shining
shoulder
siege
significance

similar
sincerely
sophomore
source
speak
specimen
speech
sponsor
stopping
strategy
strength
strenuous
stretch
strict
studying
succeed
successful
sufficient

summary
superinten-
dent
supersede
suppress
surely
surprise
suspicious

teammate
technical
technique
temperature
tendency
than
then
thorough
though

throughout
together
tomatoes
tomorrow
tragedy
transferred
truly
twelfth
tyranny

unanimous
unconscious
undoubtedly
unnecessary
until
usable
usually

vacuum
vegetable
vengeance
vicious
villain
visible

weather
Wednesday
weird
wherever
whether
wholly
woman
women
writing

yacht

34d Using the hyphen to form compound words

The hyphen (-) is a mark of punctuation used either to divide a word or to form a compound word. Always use a hyphen to divide a word at the end of a line and continue it on the next line, as explained in Chapter 30 on word division. Using a hyphen to form compound words is somewhat more complicated.

Compound words express a combination of ideas. They may be written as a single word, like the noun *breakthrough;* as two words, like the noun *decision making;* or as a hyphenated word, like the noun *cave-in.* Sometimes compound words that include the same element are spelled differently—for example, *cross-reference, cross section,* and *crosswalk.* Several reliable generalizations can be made about using the hyphen for compound words. But if you doubt the spelling of a compound word, consult a dictionary.

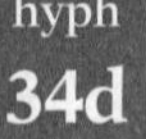

Forming compound adjectives

When two or more words serve together as a single modifier before a noun, a hyphen or hyphens form the modifying words clearly into a unit.

She is a *well-known* actor.
The conclusions are based on *out-of-date* statistics.
No *English-speaking* people were in the room.

When the same compound adjectives follow the noun, hyphens are unnecessary and are usually left out.

The actor is *well-known.*
The statistics were *out-of-date.*
Those people are *English-speaking.*

Hyphens are also unnecessary in compound modifiers containing an *-ly* adverb, even when these fall before the noun: *clearly defined terms; swiftly moving train.*

When part of a compound adjective appears only once in two or more parallel compound adjectives, hyphens indicate which words the reader should mentally join with the missing part.

School-age children should have eight- or nine-o'clock bedtimes.

Writing fractions and compound numbers

Hyphens join the numerator and denominator of fractions.

three-fourths
one-half

The whole numbers twenty-one to ninety-nine are always hyphenated.

Eighteen girls and *twenty-four* boys took the bus.
The total is *eighty-seven*.

Forming coined compounds

Writers sometimes create (coin) temporary compounds and join the words with hyphens.

Muhammad Ali gave his opponent a classic come-and-get-me look.

Attaching some prefixes and suffixes

Prefixes are usually attached to word stems without hyphens: *predetermine, unnatural, disengage.* However, when the prefix precedes a capitalized word or when a capital letter is combined with a word, a hyphen usually separates the two: *un-Canadian, non-European, A-frame.* And some prefixes, such as *self-, all-,* and *ex-* (meaning "formerly"), usually require hyphens no matter what follows: *self-control, all-inclusive, ex-student.* The only suffix that regularly requires a hyphen is *-elect,* as in *president-elect.*

A hyphen is sometimes necessary to prevent misreading, especially when a prefix and stem place the same two vowels together or when a stem and suffix place the same three consonants together.

deemphasize, de-emphasize
antiintellectual, anti-intellectual
trilllike, trill-like

Check a recent dictionary for the current form, particularly for words that join two *e*'s or *i*'s. If the word you seek does not appear in the dictionary, assume that it should be hyphenated.

5 Eliminating confusion

If you wrote the sentence *Doonesbury is a comic strip character,* the reader might stumble briefly over your meaning. Is Doonesbury a character in a comic strip or a comic (funny) character who strips? Presumably you would mean the former, but a hyphen would prevent any possible confusion: *Doonesbury is a comic-strip character.*

Adding prefixes to words can sometimes create ambiguity. *Recreation* (*creation* with the prefix *re-*) could mean either "a new creation" or "diverting, pleasurable activity." The use of a hyphen, *re-creation,* limits the word to the first meaning. Without a hyphen the word suggests the second meaning.

Exercise 6
Using hyphens in compound words

Insert hyphens as needed in the following compounds. Circle all compounds that are correct as given. Consult a dictionary as needed.

1. reimburse
2. deescalate
3. forty odd soldiers
4. little known bar
5. seven eighths
6. seventy eight
7. happy go lucky
8. preexisting
9. premier elect
10. postwar
11. two and six person cars
12. ex songwriter
13. V shaped
14. reeducate

Part VIII

Research Writing

Chapter 35 *Beginning a Research Project*

If you've ever watched a TV detective pursue a culprit, you know that research can be exciting. When an investigator has a goal in sight, the seemingly mundane work of digging through files, interviewing witnesses, and piecing together clues becomes a concentrated and enthusiastic search.

This same excitement can be yours as you conduct research in school. Like many students, you may dread research papers as tedious projects. It is true that responsible, honest research writing demands close attention to details. But tedium is entirely optional, a matter of your choice. You will probably be bored if your project seems a chore and fails to engage you. You will not be bored if you approach research writing as a chance to make discoveries about the world around you and yourself. At the end of such a research project, you will have significant, in-depth knowledge of a subject you care about. You will also have skills that will help you in school, in work, and in life outside work:

- Using the library
- Analysing and evaluating others' work
- Drawing on others' work to form, support, and extend your own opinions
- Documenting your sources

Your investigation will be influenced by whether you are expected mainly to report, to interpret, or to analyse sources.

- In **reporting,** you survey, organize, and objectively present the available evidence about a topic.
- In **interpreting,** you examine a range of views on a topic in order to draw your own conclusions, or you search in varied sources for facts and opinions relevant to your thesis.
- In **analysing,** you attempt to solve a problem or answer a question through critical thinking about texts such as scholarly or literary works. (In this context, *analysis* stands for the entire process of critical reading and writing. See pp. 1–18.)

Reporting, interpreting, and analysing are not exclusive: for instance, a paper analysing a repeated image in a poet's work would also involve a survey of poems and an interpretation of their meaning. Because the three operations overlap, the research and writing process described in this and the next three chapters can generally serve any one of them.

Throughout these chapters at the notebook symbol opposite, we will follow the development of research papers by two students, Mark Shannon and Janice Kowalchuk. Shannon's work, emphasizing interpretation, receives somewhat more attention; Kowalchuk's work, emphasizing analysis, enters the discussion whenever her process differed significantly from Shannon's. Both students followed the same basic process, however.

35a Planning a research project

A thoughtful plan and systematic procedures will help you anticipate and follow through on the diverse and overlapping activities of research writing.

As soon as you receive an assignment for a research project, you can begin developing a strategy for completing it. The first step should be making a schedule that apportions the available time to the necessary work. A possible schedule appears on the next page. In it the research-writing process corresponds to the general writing process discussed in Chapters 1–2: planning or developing (steps 1–8), drafting (step 9), and revising and editing (step 10), plus the additional important stage of documenting the sources you use (steps 11–12). Like any other essay, a research paper evolves gradually, and the steps sometimes overlap and repeat. For instance, while you do research, your reading leads you to organize ideas; and while you organize ideas, you discover where you need to do more research.

Such shifts are inevitable, and allowing for them is one key to successful and rewarding research writing. While working on a proj-

Scheduling steps in research writing

(See the sections in parentheses for discussion of the steps.)

Complete by:

_____ 1. Planning a research project (35a)
_____ 2. Finding and limiting a researchable topic (35b)
_____ 3. Finding information and refining the topic (35c)
_____ 4. Making a working bibliography (35d)

_____ 5. Evaluating and synthesizing sources (36a)
_____ 6. Taking notes using summary, paraphrase, and direct quotation (36b) and avoiding plagiarism (36c)
_____ 7. Developing a thesis sentence (36d)

_____ 8. Creating a structure (36e)
_____ 9. Drafting the paper (36f) and using and introducing summaries, paraphrases, and quotations (36g)

_____ 10. Revising and editing the paper (36h)
_____ 11. Citing sources in your text (37a)
_____ 12. Preparing the list of works cited (37b)
_____ 13. Preparing and proofreading the final manuscript (36i)
_____ Final paper due

Each segment marked off by a horizontal line will occupy *roughly* one-quarter of the total time. The most unpredictable segments are the first two, so it's wise to get started early enough to accommodate the unexpected.

ect, carry index cards or a notebook with you at all times to use as a **research journal,** a place to record your activities and ideas. (See p. 33 on journal keeping.) In the journal's dated entries, you can keep a record of sources you consult, the leads you want to pursue, any dead ends you reach, and, most important, your thoughts about sources, leads, dead ends, new directions, relationships, and anything else that strikes you. Notes on what your sources actually say should be taken and organized separately—for instance, on the note cards discussed on pages 547–53. The research journal is the place for tracking and developing your own ideas. You will probably find that the very act of writing in it opens your mind and clarifies your thinking, making your research increasingly productive and rewarding.

35b Finding and limiting a researchable topic

Before reading this section, you may want to review the suggestions given on pages 22–25 for finding and limiting an essay topic. Generally, the same procedure applies to writing any kind of research paper: take a subject assigned to you, or think of one that interests you, and narrow it to manageable dimensions by making it specific. However, selecting and limiting a topic for a research paper can present special opportunities and problems. If you have questions about your topic anywhere along the line, consult your instructor.

A topic for a research paper has four primary requirements, each with corresponding pitfalls.

1. Ample published sources of information are available on the topic. Other researchers should have had a chance to produce evidence on the topic, weigh the evidence, and publish their conclusions. And the sources should be accessible.

   Avoid (*a*) very recent topics, such as a new medical breakthrough, and (*b*) topics that are removed geographically, such as a minor event in Australian history.

2. The topic encourages research in the kinds and number of sources required by the assignment.

   Avoid (*a*) topics that depend entirely on personal opinion and experience, such as the virtues of your hobby, and (*b*) topics that require research in only one source, such as a straight factual biography or a how-to like "Making Lenses for Eyeglasses." (An exception to *b* is a paper in which you analyse a single work such as a novel or painting.)

Checklist for a good research topic

1. Published sources are ample: the topic is neither too recent nor too removed.
2. Sources are diverse: the topic is neither wholly personal nor wholly factual.
3. Sources can be assessed objectively: the topic is not solely a matter of belief, dogma, or prejudice.
4. Sources can be examined thoroughly in the assigned time and length: the topic is not too broad.

3. The topic will lead you to an assessment of sources and to defensible conclusions. Even when a research paper is intended to persuade, the success of the argument will depend on the balanced presentation of all significant points of view.

   Avoid controversial topics that rest entirely on belief or prejudice, such as when human life begins or why women (or men) are superior. Though these topics may certainly be disputed, your own preconceptions could slant your research or conclusions. Further, your readers are unlikely to be swayed from their own beliefs.

4. The topic suits the length of paper assigned and the time given for research and writing.

   Avoid broad topics that have too many sources to survey adequately, such as a major event in history or the collected works of a poet.

The students Mark Shannon and Janice Kowalchuk took slightly different approaches to finding and limiting topics. For a composition course, Shannon's instructor assigned an interpretation with a persuasive purpose but left the selection of subject to the student. Since Shannon was currently enjoying a course in business management, he decided to take that broad subject as his starting point. Using clustering (see p. 36), he pursued some implications of this subject as illustrated below. An awareness of sex-role stereotyping, developed during a psychology course in high school, encouraged Shannon to give the most thought to the issue of women in management. He posed questions and more questions until he arrived at the one that

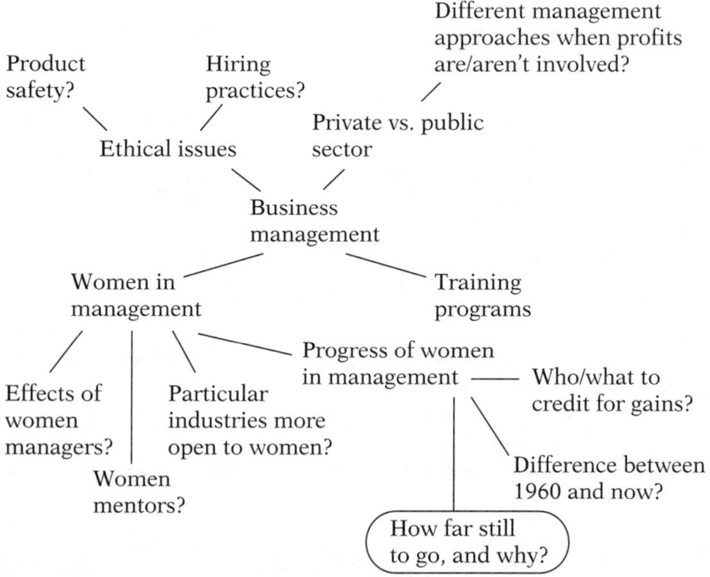

seemed potentially most interesting and fruitful: "How far do women still have to go in management, and why?"

In developing a topic for a paper assigned in a composition course, Janice Kowalchuk followed a somewhat different procedure. The instructor had assigned a persuasive essay on some topic particular to Canadian culture. Janice had recently been reading a book on a sociology course, *Hockey Night in Canada: Sports, Identities, and Cultural Politics,* by Richard Gruneau and David Whitson, that had caused her to look anew at something she had taken completely for granted, hockey in Canadian life. The book had presented hockey as an important example of popular culture and had analysed how popular culture in general, and hockey in particular, is a vehicle for the creation and expression of identity. This idea had allowed her to view her own experience of growing up in Canada in a new way and led her to begin to formulate ideas about the role of popular culture in the creation of identity and how women might more actively use popular culture to their advantage. She wrote the following entry in her journal:

> When I was growing up at home the whole winter world revolved around hockey. My brother's practices, his games, etc. But I played hockey too, real hockey, not ringette. All of these things are part of your identity. I play hockey here too at university, but there is no varsity team, just the club league. Why is that? I should check that out with Athletics. I think I could write a good essay on this topic. What is it about what they called "gender order" in my soc text that makes it like this? And why can't we change it? The same thing works on the professional level. Professional sports is all about money, and women have money, so why don't we have our professional leagues? Hockey is such a good example of all these things in Canada, especially with the Olympics coming and the first medal for women's hockey.

Kowalchuk decided to explore further the role of hockey in popular culture in Canada. To do this, she resolved to find and read several texts on the history of women's hockey in Canada and the role of sports in general in the life of women in North America. She would also do some primary research by consulting the Athletics office of her university to obtain the policies on women's sports.

Exercise 1

Finding and limiting a topic

Choose three of the following subjects and narrow each one to at least one topic suitable for beginning library work on a research paper. Or list and then limit three subjects of your own that you would enjoy investigating. (This exercise can be the first step in a research paper project that continues through Chapters 35–37.)

1. Bilingual education
2. Training of teachers
3. Canadian satire
4. The history of women's suffrage
5. Food additives
6. Immigrants in Canada
7. Space exploration
8. Business espionage

9. The effect of television on professional sports
10. Child abuse
11. Aboriginal land claims
12. Recent developments in cancer research
13. Computer piracy
14. Homelessness
15. The European exploration of North America before Columbus
16. Hazardous substances in the workplace
17. Television evangelism
18. Science fiction
19. Treatment or prevention of AIDS
20. Water pollution
21. Women writers
22. Campaign financing
23. Comic film actors
24. An unsolved crime
25. Genetic engineering
26. Heroes and heroines in modern fiction
27. Computers and the privacy of the individual
28. Gothic or romance novels in the nineteenth and twentieth centuries
29. The social responsibility of business
30. Trends in popular music

35c Finding information and refining the topic

When you investigate a topic, you have access to a wide variety of sources, many of them discussed in this section. (See the index opposite.)

Note If sources you need are not in your library, a librarian may be able to obtain them from another library. But plan ahead: these interlibrary loans can take a week or even several weeks.

Research sources are of two kinds:

- **Primary sources** are firsthand accounts: historical documents (letters, speeches, and so on), eyewitness reports, works of literature, reports on experiments or surveys, or your own interviews, experiments, observations, or correspondence. Whenever possible, you should seek and rely on primary sources, drawing your own conclusions from them.

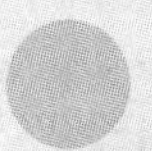

A tip for researchers

If you are unsure of how to locate or use your library's resources, ask a reference librarian. This person is very familiar with all the library's resources and with general and specialized research techniques, and it is his or her job to help you and others with research. Even very experienced researchers often consult reference librarians.

- **Secondary sources** report and analyse information drawn from other sources, often primary ones: a historian's account of a battle, a critic's reading of a poem, a physicist's evaluation of several studies, an encyclopedia or other standard reference work. Secondary sources may contain helpful summaries and interpretations that direct, support, and extend your thinking. However, most research-writing assignments expect your own ideas to go beyond those you find in such sources.

Index to research sources

Conducting electronic searches

Kinds of computerized sources

These days most libraries have at least some research sources on computer. Your library probably has a computerized catalogue of its holdings, at least the more recent ones (see p. 531). The library may also provide some sources on compact disks. Just like music disks, these so-called CD-ROMs (compact disk—read only memory) store data for "reading" but cannot record data. CD-ROMs can store masses of data, as many as 200 000 text pages on a single disk. Many of the reference works, indexes, and other resources described on the following pages are available on CD-ROM.

Before you begin researching your topic, find out what resources your library has available electronically. (A librarian will help you.) A catalogue of CD-ROMs is *CD-ROMs in Print,* but not all the listed works will be available in your library.

In addition to CD-ROMs, many libraries also provide access to information networks and services through telephone connections between computers. The Internet is a huge network of networks linking diverse sources of information, such as publications, businesses, governments, schools, libraries, foundations, and millions of individuals. For access to the Internet, the library subscribes to a service provider that connects the user to the desired source. (Individuals can also subscribe to a service provider, and at some schools the Internet is available to students and teachers on their own computers.) The largest information service, Dialog, also requires subscription and offers hundreds of separate databases (bibliographies, indexes, reports, and so on) in many disciplines. Both the Internet and Dialog generally cost money to use and often require the assistance of a library staffer.

Policies and procedures

Libraries vary widely in their handling of computerized searches. For a catalogue search like that illustrated on pages 533–34, ample terminals, easy-to-follow instructions, and free use should encourage you to work independently (though of course you can ask questions). For other searches, you may opt or be required to obtain a librarian's assistance, and you may be charged a fee. The use of the comprehensive information sources Dialog and the Internet often involves a librarian's time and always costs money for the library if not the researcher; thus libraries sometimes discourage such use for a relatively small-scale research project like a ten- or twenty-page term paper.

Library computers are sometimes attached to printers, allowing you to print out particular records (such as an article listing), whole screens (several listings), or whole documents (entire articles). Printing information is quicker than copying it down and eliminates the risk of mistakes at your end. But there are also risks in accumulating (and losing) dozens of slips of paper in assorted sizes, with assorted information. Especially for source information, try to keep systematic, handy records by taping or transferring the print-out data to a file card (see pp. 537–39).

The ease of printing out the information from computers has led to abuses, and many libraries have disconnected their printers to save money on paper and repairs. You may still be able to avoid laborious hand copying of information by transferring (or downloading) the data from the machine onto your own computer disk. You can then edit and sort the data at your convenience on your computer.

Computer searches

Research by computer is usually faster than research in print sources. The opening screen of a CD-ROM will tell you what databases the disk holds. (Most disks hold more than a single database.) CD-ROMs containing bibliographies and indexes will provide you with *references* to sources but usually not with the actual sources, such as periodical articles. Use the references to find the sources elsewhere (see p. 527).

To conduct a computer search, you'll need to describe your topic using words that correspond to the database's own categories for indexing information. With some databases, you locate subject headings that come as close as possible to your own subject. Most library catalogues, for instance, use the categories listed in *Library of Congress Subject Headings* (see p. 533). Some other databases use this guide, too, but many have their own subject headings. These headings are usually available in the database's thesaurus, stored electronically with the database or located in printed form near the computer or at the reference desk. You can still search a database without the thesaurus by entering your subject headings and asking the computer to show you a list of its own related terms (usually those surrounding yours in alphabetical order). An example of a subject search appears on pages 533–34.

In a more complicated search, you can give the computer keywords to locate within the database, such as in the titles of books and summaries of articles. This kind of search goes beyond the database's menu of subject headings, but unless you carefully define your keywords it can produce a flood of useless references or nothing at all. Mark Shannon, developing his keywords for a computer search, settled on "Women or Female and Executives." The *or* and *and* were important: *or* told the computer to locate references to either synonym, *women* or *female,* while *and* told the computer to locate references to *executives* along with either synonym. The computer thus searched only the equivalent of the coloured areas in the diagram below:

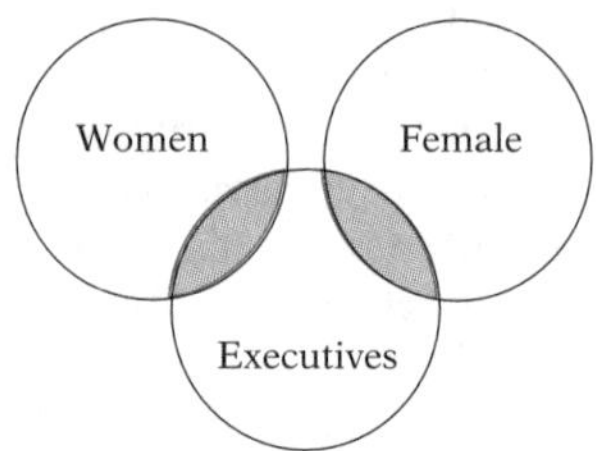

Here are a few guidelines for selecting keywords:

- Keywords should accurately describe your topic. If Mark Shannon had selected "Salaries" or "Executive stress," he probably would not have found the relevant sources he found under "Women or Female and Executives."
- Keywords should not be so narrow that they exclude possibly relevant information. For Shannon, "Women or Female and Executives and Psychology" would have limited the search to only one facet of the topic.
- Keywords should not be so broad that they call up many irrelevant sources. Either "Women or Female" or "Executives" would have generated lengthy lists of sources for Shannon to examine. The more specific "Women or Female and Executives" called up only those sources containing "Women Executives" or "Female Executives."

2 Using reference works

Reference works available in the library (often on computer) include encyclopedias, dictionaries, digests, bibliographies, indexes, atlases, almanacs, and handbooks. Your research *must* go beyond these sources, but they can help you decide whether your topic really interests you and whether it meets the requirements for a research paper (pp. 507–08). Preliminary research in reference works will also direct you to more detailed sources on your topic. For an analysis paper, a specialized encyclopedia can identify the main debates in a field and the proponents of each side.

Mark Shannon's use of reference works illustrates how helpful such sources can be as a starting point. Shannon first consulted *Encyclopedia of Management,* which summarized women's advances since the American Civil Rights Act of 1964. The encyclopedia also listed several books and articles for Shannon to pursue.

The following list gives the types of reference works and suggests when each may be profitable. Once you have a topic, you can scan this list for a reference work to start with. For a more comprehensive catalogue and explanation, consult Eugene P. Sheehy, *Guide to Reference Books,* 10th edition plus supplement (1986, 1992).

General encyclopedias

General encyclopedias give brief overviews and bibliographies. Because they try to cover all fields, they are a convenient, but very limited, starting point. Be sure to consult the most recent edition.

The Canadian Encyclopedia. 2nd edition. 4 volumes.
Collier's Encyclopedia. 24 volumes.
Encyclopedia Americana. 30 volumes.
Encyclopedia International. 20 volumes.
The New Columbia Encyclopedia.
The New Encyclopaedia Britannica. 32 volumes.
Random House Encyclopedia. Revised edition.

Specialized encyclopedias, dictionaries, bibliographies

A specialized encyclopedia, dictionary, or bibliography generally covers an entire field or subject. These works will give you more detailed and more technical information than a general reference book will, and many of them (especially bibliographies) will direct you to particular books and articles on your subject. One general reference work providing information on sources in many of the fields below is the *Essay and General Literature Index* (published since 1900 and now updated semi-annually). It lists tens of thousands of articles and essays that appear in books (rather than periodicals) and that might not be listed elsewhere.

BUSINESS AND ECONOMICS

Canadian Business and Economics: A Guide to Sources of Information/Économique et commerce au Canada: sources d'information
Handbook of Modern Marketing
The New Palgrave: A Dictionary of Economics
Encyclopedia of Advertising
The McGraw-Hill Dictionary of Modern Economics
The Encyclopedia of Management
Encyclopedia of Banking and Finance
Accountant's Handbook
A Dictionary of Economics

History

Guide to Historical Literature
The Study of the Middle East: Research and Scholarship in the Humanities and Social Sciences
Cambridge Ancient History
Cambridge Mediaeval History
Cambridge History of China
Harvard Guide to American History
Oxford Classical Dictionary
An Encyclopedia of Latin-American History
New Cambridge Modern History

Literature, theatre, film, and television

Modern Drama: A Checklist of Critical Literature on Twentieth Century Plays
Film Research: A Critical Bibliography with Annotations and Essays
The Oxford Companion to English Literature
International Television Almnanac
Bibliographical Guide to the Study of the Literature of the U.S.A.
The Oxford Companion to American Literature
The Oxford Companion to the Theatre
A Handbook to Literature
Literary History of Canada: Canadian Literature in English
The Annotated Bibliography of Canada's Major Authors
MLA International Bibliography of Books and Articles on the Modern Languages and Literatures
A Reader's Guide to the Canadian Novel
Reference Sources in English and American Literature: An Annotated Bibliography
The Oxford Companion to Canadian Literature
The Cambridge History of English Literature
New Cambridge Bibliography of English Literature

Music and the visual arts

The Harvard Dictionary of Music
A Handbook of Canadian Film
The Dance Encyclopedia
Encyclopedia of World Art
Encyclopedia of Music in Canada
A Dictionary of Canadian Artists
New Dictionary of Modern Sculpture
Handbook of World Opera
The New Grove Dictionary of Music and Musicians
Encyclopedia of Pop, Rock, and Soul
International Cyclopedia of Music and Musicians
Architecture: From Pre-History to Post-Modernism

PHILOSOPHY AND RELIGION

The Catholic Encyclopedia
The Interpreter's Dictionary of the Bible
The Oxford Dictionary of the Christian Church
The Encyclopedia of Religion
An Encyclopedia of Religion
Eastern Definitions: A Short Encyclopedia of Religions of the Orient
The New Standard Jewish Encyclopedia

SCIENCES

Encyclopedia of Computer Science and Technology
The Encyclopedia of Chemistry
The Encyclopedia of Oceanography
The Encyclopedia of Biological Sciences
Outer Space: Myths, Name Meanings, Calendars from the Emergence of History to the Present Day
The Larousse Encyclopedia of Animal Life
The McGraw-Hill Encyclopedia of Science and Technology
An Introduction to the History of Science
Encyclopaedic Dictionary of Physics

SOCIAL SCIENCES

The Literature of Political Science
Encyclopedia of Psychology
Foreign Affairs Bibliography
Funk and Wagnalls Standard Dictionary of Folklore, Mythology and Legends
A New Dictionary of the Social Sciences
Encyclopedia of Educational Research
Multiculturalism in Canada: Social and Educational Perspective
International Encyclopedia of the Social Sciences
International Bibliography of the Social Sciences
Sources of Information in the Social Sciences: A Guide to the Literature
Dictionary of Anthropology

Unabridged dictionaries and special dictionaries on language

Unabridged dictionaries are more comprehensive than college or abridged dictionaries. Special dictionaries give authoritative information on individual aspects of language. (See Chapter 32 for more on the kinds of dictionaries and how to use them.)

UNABRIDGED DICTIONARIES

The Oxford English Dictionary
The Random House Dictionary of the English Language

Webster's Third New International Dictionary of the English Language

SPECIAL DICTIONARIES

A Dictionary of Canadianisms on Historical Principles. Edited by Walter S. Avis, Patrick D. Drysdale, and Matthew H. Scargill. 1967.
Follett, Wilson. *Modern American Usage: A Guide.* Edited by Jacques Barzun. 1966.
The New Fowler's Modern English. Edited by R. W. Burchfield. 1996.
Lewis, Norman. *The New Roget's Thesaurus of the English Language in Dictionary Form.* 1986.
Morris, William, and Mary Morris. *Harper Dictionary of Contemporary Usage.* 2nd edition. 1985.
The Oxford Dictionary of English Etymology. 1966. Edited by Charles T. Onions, et al.
Partridge, Eric. *A Dictionary of Slang and Unconventional English.* 8th edition. Edited by Paul Beale. 1985.

Biographical reference works

If you want to learn about someone's life, achievements, credentials, or position, or if you want to learn the significance of a name you've come across, consult one of the reference works below. Note, in addition, that more specialized biographical sources are available in fields such as law, health care, and art.

American Men and Women of Science
Contemporary Authors
Current Biography
Dictionary of American Biography
Dictionary of American Negro Biography
Dictionary of Canadian Biography
Dictionary of Literary Biography
Dictionary of National Biography (British)
Dictionary of Scientific Biography
Leading Ladies–Canada 1639–1967
Two Thousand Notable American Women
Webster's New Biographical Dictionary
Who's Who in Canada
World Authors

Atlases and gazetteers

Atlases are bound collections of maps; gazetteers are geographical dictionaries.

Atlas and Gazetteer of Canada
Columbia Lippincott Gazetteer of the World
Cosmopolitan World Atlas
Encyclopaedia Britannica World Atlas International
The National Atlas of Canada
National Geographic Atlas of the World
The Times Atlas of the World

Almanacs and yearbooks

Both almanacs and yearbooks are annual compilations of facts. Yearbooks record information about the previous year in a country, field, or other subject. Almanacs give facts about a variety of fields.

Americana Annual
Britannica Book of the Year
Canada Year Book
Canadian Almanac and Directory
Facts on File Yearbook
U.S. Bureau of the Census. *Statistical Abstract of the United States.*
World Almanac and Book of Facts

3 Using the Internet

The Internet consists of millions of computers around the world that are connected by wires and satellites. Both for refining your topic and for gathering actual sources, the Internet has a number of distinct advantages:

- Since Internet publication is faster than print or even CD-ROM publication, you may find more current information on the Internet than in your library. For example, many government agencies post their data first online, then in print.
- Many scholarly journals are published online. Some are published *only* online, not in print.
- If your school's library has few resources on your subject, you can search catalogues at other libraries.
- If your library does not have some sources—such as government documents—located by your database searches, you can obtain the documents more quickly over the Internet than by interlibrary loan.
- You can get in touch with people who have an interest in your research topic by participating in a discussion group or conducting interviews online.

How do you use the Internet? The following pages introduce the main resources available: the World Wide Web, electronic mail, Listservs, Usenet groups, and synchronous communication such as MOOs and MUDs. Although the amount of material accessible through the Internet has skyrocketed in recent years, gaining access to this material has actually become easier through the document retrieval system known as the World Wide Web, which this chapter focuses on.

NOTE America Online, Prodigy, Sympatico, and other subscription services enable users to send electronic mail across the Internet, participate in discussion groups, read newspapers and magazines linked to the service, and browse the Web. The services

Internet tools in addition to the World Wide Web

The World Wide Web now encompasses many of the older tools for finding and using Internet sources. You may use any of these tools through the Web, through an icon for the application, or through a so-called shell account at your school (activated by typing the application name at a prompt).

Gopher

Until recently, Gopher has been the preferred tool for locating and retrieving text documents over the Internet. It uses menus that are arranged in levels: they begin with general topics and become more specific as you proceed through a system. You can search for documents with the menus, or, using the search engine Veronica or Jughead, you can conduct a keyword search. Gopher remains popular and helpful, but many schools are now phasing it out in favour of the more interactive and flexible Web.

To visit a Gopher site from a shell account, type *gopher* at the shell prompt followed by a space and then the address of the Gopher server you wish to reach. To visit a Gopher site from a Web browser, type *gopher://* and the computer's address in the location window.

File Transfer Protocol (FTP)

FTP allows you to transfer files to and from another computer over a network. The files may be software, documents (from government statistics to the texts of whole books), or graphics, sound, or video. Generally, you transfer files via "anonymous FTP," which lets you copy specified public files without having an account at the remote computer. A search engine named Archie can help you find FTP files by a keyword search of file titles.

With a shell account, type *ftp* followed by a space and the address of the FTP server. When asked to log on to the server, use the name "anonymous" and provide a password, usually your e-mail address. Then use commands to view the files listed at the site and to download them. If you are not working from a shell account, look for an application called Fetch to transfer files. To reach an FTP site with a Web browser, type *ftp://* and the computer's address in the location window. Web browsers have automated access to many FTP sites so that a simple click on a file name will transfer it to your computer or account.

Telnet

Telnet allows you to use a computer at another site on the Internet. You can, for instance, reach government computers or use your school's network from across the country. Often, you must have an account on the remote computer, or *host,* to be able to log on to it, but some hosts, such as libraries, do not require accounts.

To connect to a remote computer with a shell account, type *telnet* followed by a space and the host's address. With a Web browser, type *telnet://* and the address in the location window.

are easy to use, but they do charge for the time spent online. If you plan to conduct much of your research on the Internet, you'll find it more economical to use your school's connection.

Understanding electronic addresses

To get the most from the Web, you need a software program called a **browser:** Netscape Navigator and Microsoft's Internet Explorer are the most popular, and one of them is probably already in use at your school. You also need to understand electronic addresses (called **Uniform Resource Locators,** or **URLs**), which specify a unique location for each online source. A URL has three parts and a fixed form: *protocol://domain/path.* Here is a translation of the address *http://www.uwaterloo.ca/urban/leaders.html:*

- The **protocol** specifies what type of access you are requesting at a particular location. Most Web sites are accessed using *http* (hypertext transfer protocol). The protocol identifier is followed by a colon and two slashes.
- Immediately after the two slashes, the **domain** names the computer (called a **server**) that houses the document you seek. Each server has a unique name, usually referring to the organization that owns it—for instance, *www.uwaterloo.ca (uwaterloo* stands for University of Waterloo; *ca* for Canada—in the United States, educational institutions are indicated by *edu*).
- The **path** specifies the location and name of the document you seek—for instance, */urban/leaders.html* identifies a file (*leaders.html*) within a directory (*urban*). (If you think the directory may contain other files that could be useful as well, you may be able to go there first by omitting the file name from the address—that is, stopping after *urban.*)

Note that an address must be typed exactly as you find it: same capitals and small letters, same punctuation, same spacing.

As you will see, you don't have to know a source's address to find the source: a search engine will find it for you, following your keywords. But you will want to record the address once you have it so that you can return to the source without having to conduct another search. And you must have the address to document any Internet source you use in your final paper.

The World Wide Web

The World Wide Web consists of millions of documents on millions of computers that you can reach easily with your browser. You can travel from document to document and even from computer to computer by clicking on highlighted words or images that provide **hypertext links,** instructions that tell the computer to find and load the new material specified. Besides moving around easily and reading and retrieving text, Web users can also experience sound, images, video, and animation.

To find sources on the Internet, you use a **search engine** that conducts keyword searches (see p. 513–14) or that outlines content in a series of directories. There are over thirty search engines available, all of them accessible via your Web browser by clicking on "Net Search." The box on the facing page describes the most popular engines.

The screen shot below from the Excite search engine shows the features common to most of these tools.

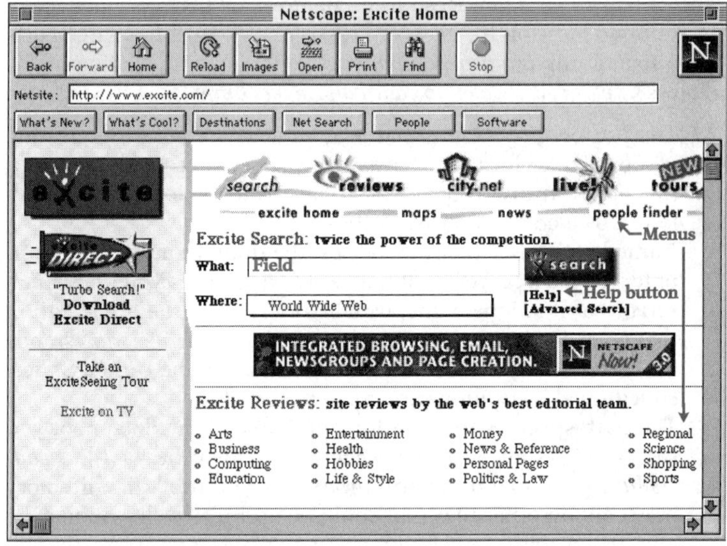

- The field is the place in which you type your keywords. (See pp. 513–14 on developing keywords.)
- Menus let you choose what and how to search—for instance, the entire Web, directories of Web sites, newsgroups, or some other set of directories that the search engine can reach.
- The "Help" button leads you to information on using the search engine:

How to format keyword searches—for instance, whether you need to use *and, not, or,* and symbols such as + or –.

How to link words to search for phrases using parentheses or quotation marks. A few search engines assume that two or more words in a row without any formatting constitute a phrase to search for.

How to interpret the results of the search. When you perform a search using either keywords or a directory, the search engine generates a list of sites that match your search criteria. The matching sites, or **hits,** are listed in order of "relevance," which

Web search engines

Here are six of the most popular search engines for the World Wide Web, with their main features. Click on "Help" whenever you need support from a search engine (see previous page).

ALTA VISTA

Alta Vista lets you search the entire Web with two types of keyword searches. In a simple search, you enter only a keyword or keywords. In an advanced search, you use *and, or,* and several other devices to refine the search. Alta Vista also allows you to specify the keywords that you think most important, so that sites containing those keywords will be listed first in the results. You may also specify starting and ending dates for sources.

EXCITE

Excite allows you to search a directory compiled by a team of people reviewing Internet sites. It also allows simple keyword searches but not advanced searches as on Alta Vista and some other engines. Excite updates addresses frequently and reviews more than sixty thousand Web sites.

INFOSEEK

Infoseek also allows you to search by directory or keyword. In addition, it lets you select the parts of the Internet that you want to search: the Web, Usenet newsgroups, corporate directories, recent news, or e-mail address directories.

LYCOS

Lycos currently claims the largest catalogue of Web sites. It can be searched by directory or by keyword. Additional services include travel maps and reviews of twenty thousand sites. Lycos also indexes sound, photographs, and other media, not just text documents.

MAGELLAN

Magellan also allows you to search by directory or by keyword. You may search the entire Web, or you may limit your search to sites that have been reviewed and rated on the basis of their content, organization, and use of technology.

YAHOO

Yahoo is not actually a search engine but a directory of sites organized by subject. You may search the directory or conduct a keyword search, which is forwarded to and conducted by other search engines. Because you're searching seven or eight engines at once, you increase your chances of finding information; thus Yahoo is especially helpful with obscure topics.

the search engine determines by a combination of the following: the number of times your search terms appear within a document; whether the terms appear at the beginning, middle, or end of a document; whether the terms appear in the title or the address of the document. If there are any special ways the search engine determines relevance, its "Help" information will specify them.

In addition, many search engines allow you to place an optional limit on the number of sources you want the search to return and an optional limit on the range of dates you're interested in. If you specify a date range, the search engine will return only sources posted on the Internet during that time.

When using a search engine, keep the following limitations and cautions in mind:

- No search engine can list every possible source for your keywords. The search engines cannot keep up with the daily additions to and deletions from the Internet.
- Because of constant change, you cannot be sure that the site you found on Monday will contain the same information on Friday. Some sites are designed and labelled as archives: they do not change except with additions. But other sites, such as those for newspapers and magazines, frequently replace old material with new. If you think you'll want to use something from such a site, you should consult it right away. If it seems useful, you should download it to your own computer or take notes from it (see pp. 547–59).
- Anyone with the right hardware and software can place information on the Internet, so your search could turn up sources with widely varying reliability: published articles, government documents, term papers written by high school students, the rantings of crackpots. With Internet sources, you need to be especially careful about evaluating your search and evaluating the individual sources you examine (pp. 542–45).
- Most works on the Internet are copyrighted just as print sources are, and you must acknowledge them when you use them (see p. 559). Keep records of the sources that you find and use online.

Electronic mail

With electronic mail (e-mail), you can send messages to and receive them from most people who use the Internet, as long as you know their addresses. (Some search engines provide the equivalent of telephone books for e-mail accounts, but these are not complete.) If you have little computing experience, using e-mail may be a good way to get started because the terms are mostly familiar: you compose messages, address them to individuals or groups, and send them; your mail is stored in your mailbox; and you can sort, read, reply to, and discard e-mail as you do paper mail. See pages 742–43 for advice on e-mail format and etiquette.

As a research tool, e-mail allows you to communicate with others who are interested in your topic. You may, for instance, carry on an e-mail conversation with a teacher at your school or with other students. Or you may interview an expert in another state to follow up on a scholarly article he or she published. (See pp. 535–36 on conducting interviews.)

Listservs

A **Listserv** (or **discussion group,** or just a **list**) is a group of individuals who discuss a common topic or topics. The Listserv software program acts as a specialized postal service: subscribers to a list send messages to its electronic address, and the software distributes the messages to all of the list's other subscribers via e-mail. Thousands of lists operate on the Internet, each with a particular purpose and audience. Through a Listserv, you may be able to discuss your subject with people the world over, representing diverse experiences and viewpoints.

To find lists that might be relevant to your research topic, use the keywords *list of listservs* (not *listserves*) to search the World Wide Web (p. 521). Your search will locate Web pages with information about subscribing to and using Listservs. When you find a list that interests you, see if it has a compilation of frequently asked questions (FAQs), which will list the topics covered (and *not* covered) by the group and will answer common questions. Spend a week or two reading the list's messages before sending any questions or comments of your own. By reading but not participating (called **lurking**), you can verify whether the list is relevant to your topic (and vice versa) and whether a particular person might be able to answer your questions. Most Listservs are archived, meaning that messages from past months and years are stored online and may be read and downloaded into your own files. Thus you may be able to find information on a topic even if it is not currently under discussion.

Another benefit of Listservs is that they make available subscribers' names and e-mail addresses. Although broad ranging and often very current, the information on Listservs is only as reliable as the subscriber who posts it. Having access to a subscriber list lets you find out who posted a message and communicate directly with that person. (See pp. 544–45 for advice on evaluating online sources.)

Usenet newsgroups

Like Listservs, **Usenet newsgroups** are forums in which people post messages on an enormous range of topics. However, newsgroups are not subscriber-based, and you do not receive postings automatically through your e-mail. Instead, you reach the groups via a Web browser such as Netscape Navigator or via special software. On a Web browser you can obtain a list of groups and other information by using the keywords *list of newsgroups.*

Newsgroups are roughly categorized by subject, indicated by the first letters of the address—for instance, *comp* for computers and computer science, *soc* for social issues, *biz* for business. This prefix will give you an idea of whether the group is relevant to your concerns. When you begin to examine a newsgroup, look for its frequently asked questions (FAQs): like those for Listservs, these documents explain the group's topics and answer common questions. As with Listservs, you should lurk a while before jumping into the discussion to be sure that the group is right for you and that your contributions are relevant.

Because newsgroups, unlike Listservs, are not subscriber-based, anyone can post messages on them, and you may not be able to find out who wrote a particular message. That makes it difficult to evaluate the reliability of a posting (see pp. 544–55 on evaluating sources). Unlike Listservs as well, newsgroups are not always archived, or they may be archived irregularly, so that you cannot read noncurrent postings.

Synchronous communication

With electronic mail, Listservs, and newsgroups, there's a delay between a message you send and any response you receive. But with **synchronous** (or simultaneous) **communication,** you and others can correspond in real time, as you might talk on the phone. As a research tool, synchronous communication can be especially useful for conducting interviews (see pp. 535–36), and you can also participate in academic conferences and debates.

The following are three of the Internet's most popular synchronous programs:

- IRC (Internet Relay Chat) allows people anywhere in the world to talk with each other, either in groups or privately, over "channels." To use IRC, you need special software such as PowWow or IRCLe, which may be installed on your school's computers.
- MUDs and MOOs also provide environments where people can communicate "live." MUDs (multi-user domains or dungeons) started as online versions of role-playing games such as Dungeons and Dragons, but they have expanded well beyond game

playing to scholarly discussion and other uses. A MOO (MUD, object oriented) is a kind of MUD that enables users to create more complex virtual environments in which to play games or hold discussions. Some MUDs and MOOs may be reached via the Web, using the keywords *MUDs and MOOs*. Once you arrive at a site, you generally log on as a guest and receive directions for reaching the site's help files.

While IRC, MUDs, and MOOs can be useful tools, many schools have restricted their use because of their association with games. Check with your computer centre to find out which programs are available to you.

Using periodicals

Periodicals—journals, magazines, and newspapers—are invaluable sources of information in research. The difference between journals and magazines lies primarily in their content, readership, frequency of issue, and page numbering.

- Magazines—such as *Psychology Today, Maclean's,* and *Saturday Night*—are nonspecialist publications intended for diverse readers. Most magazines appear weekly or monthly, and their pages are numbered anew with each issue.
- Journals often appear quarterly or less frequently and contain scholarly, specialized information intended for readers in a particular field. Examples include *English Studies in Canada, Canadian Journal of American Studies,* and *Journal of Chemical Education.* Many journals page each issue separately, but others do not. Instead, the issues for an entire year make up an annual volume, and the pages are numbered continuously throughout the volume, so that issue number 3 (the third issue of the year) may open on page 327. (The method of pagination determines how you cite a journal article in your list of works cited. See p. 591.)

Using indexes to periodicals

Several guides provide information on the articles in journals, magazines, and newspapers. The contents, formats, and systems of abbreviation in these guides vary widely, and they can be intimidating at first glance. But each one includes in its opening pages an introduction and explanation to aid the inexperienced user. Most of the indexes listed on the following pages are available on CD-ROM, so check the library's computerized resources first.

A typical and general periodical guide is the *Readers' Guide to Periodical Literature.* It lists—by author, title, and subject—articles published each year in well over a hundred popular magazines. For a paper on a current topic you should consult at least several years' *Readers' Guide* volumes. Mark Shannon, checking a volume for 1992, found the listing below. (The key elements are labelled.)

WOMEN EXECUTIVES ←Subject heading
See Also
Clothing and dress—Businesswomen
Women entrepreneurs
(Cross-references)
Happy accidents of birth and marriage [women who inherit businesses] S. Nelton. il *Nations's Business* 80:62 O '92.
Mom is the boss [black executives] il *Ebony* 47:72+S '92
Health and hygiene ←Subheading
When you're CEO—and pregnant. A.-M. Corner. il por *Working Woman* 17:39–40 S '92
Article title ↘ **Promotion** ↙Author ↙ Magazine title
Discrimination at the top. M. Gordon. il *Working Woman* 17:68–71 S '92 ←Month (Sept.) and year
Learning to compete with women. A. M. Sheele. il *Working Woman* 17:30–1 N '92
A new interest in cracking the ceiling: women and minorities are getting a fairer shake. S. D. Kaye. il *U.S. News & World Report* 113:80+ O 26 '92
Still seeking a glass slipper [adaptation of address] G. F. Gilder. il *National Review* 44:38–41 D 14 '92
Psychology ↖Volume and page numbers
You've failed. Can you bounce back? A. M. Sheele. il *Working Woman* 17:34+ S '92

Other general indexes to periodicals include the following:

Canadian News Index. Published 1977–79 (vols. 1–3) as *Canadian Newspaper Index*; new title initiated in 1980 as volume 4. Published monthly, with annual accumulations.

Canadian Periodical Index. Published eleven times a year since 1948.

InfoTrac. An index of more than a thousand business, technical, government, and general-interest publications.

NewsBank. An index of more than five hundred newspapers.

The New York Times Index. An index to the most complete U.S. newspaper. The index can serve as a guide to national and international events and can indicate what issues of unindexed newspapers to consult for local reactions to such events.

Nexus. An index of prominent newspapers, such as the *New York Times* and the *Wall Street Journal,* as well as regional newspapers.

Poole's Index to Periodical Literature. An index by subject to British and American periodicals of the nineteenth century.

Popular Periodicals Index. An index to about twenty-five contemporary popular periodicals not listed in major indexes.

Wall Street Journal Index. An index to the leading business newspaper and to *Barron's.*

For scholarly journals, most libraries have a variety of specialized indexes. Shannon also consulted one of these, the *Social Sciences Index.* The listings below appeared in an index volume for 1992:

Women executives ← Subject heading
Perceptions of external barriers and the career success of female managers in Singapore. E. Y. Chi-Ching. bibl *J Soc Psychol* 132:661–74 O '92
Psychology ← Subheading
Perceptions of power: female executives' descriptions of power usage by "best" and "worst" bosses. C. K. Oyster. bibl *Psychol woman* Q16:527–33 D '92 ← Article title
Role reward and role stress in managerial and professional women. M. E. Poole and J. Langan-Fox. *Psychol Rep* 71:851–4 D '92 ptl

Authors
Journal title (abbreviated)
Volume and page numbers
Month (Dec.) and year of publication

The following is a partial list of scholarly indexes.

HUMANITIES

America: History and Life
Art Index
Film Literature Index
Humanities Index
MLA International Bibliography of Books and Articles on the Modern Languages and Literatures
Music Index
Philosopher's Index

LAW AND SOCIAL SCIENCES

Business Periodicals Index
Canadian Education Index
Criminal Justice Periodicals Index
The Education Index
ERIC (Education Resources Information Center). *Current Index to Journals in Education.*
Index to Legal Periodicals
Public Affairs Information Service. *PAIS Bulletin.*
Social Sciences Index

SCIENCES AND TECHNOLOGY

Applied Science and Technology Index
Biological and Agricultural Index
Cumulative Index to Nursing and Allied Health Literature
General Science Index
Index Medicus

Using abstracts and citation indexes

Consulting a collection of article summaries—or **abstracts**—can tell you in advance whether you want to pursue a particular article further. Abstracts are published in many academic disciplines and are also frequently available on computerized databases.

Abstracts of English Studies
America: History and Life (U.S. and Canadian history)
Biological Abstracts
Chemical Abstracts
Communications Abstracts
Criminal Justice and Police Science Abstracts
Dissertation Abstracts International (doctoral dissertations). Before 1969, the title was *Dissertation Abstracts.*
Historical Abstracts (world history)
Human Resources Abstracts
International Political Science Abstracts
LLBA (*Linguistics and Language Behavior Abstracts*)
Psychological Abstracts
Religious and Theological Abstracts
Sociological Abstracts
Urban Affairs Abstracts
Wilson Business Abstracts

When you want to trace what has been written *about* an article or book you are consulting, use a **citation index.** This resource lists references to written works after they are published, as when one scientific article comments on an earlier article. The following is a partial list:

Arts and Humanities Citation Index
Science Citation Index
Social Sciences Citation Index

Finding and using periodicals

Every library lists its holdings of periodicals (usually called *serials*) either in the main catalogue (see the facing page) or in a separate catalogue. The listing for each periodical tells how far back the issues go and where and in what form the issues are stored.

The recent issues of a periodical are usually held in the library's periodical room. Back issues are usually stored elsewhere, in one of three forms: in bound volumes; on **microfilm,** a filmstrip showing pages side by side; or on **microfiche,** a sheet of film with pages arranged in rows and columns. Consulting periodicals stored on microfilm or microfiche requires using a special machine, or "reader," with which you locate the page and project it on a screen. (Some readers are also attached to coin-operated photocopiers.) Any member of the library's staff will show you how to operate the reader.

If the periodical you seek is not available in your library, the librarian may be able to obtain a copy of the article you want through interlibrary loan. The article may arrive by mail or by fax, and there may be a fee for the service. Even with fax transmissions, the process can take several weeks, so place your order early.

5 Using guides to pamphlets and government documents

Organizations such as social-service groups, professional societies, and all branches of government publish booklets, compilations of data, and other sources that usually cannot be retrieved through the library's book catalogue or periodicals listings.

Pamphlets, bulletins, unbound materials, and other miscellaneous items are often stored in file drawers, called **vertical files.** To find out what is available in pamphlet form, consult the *Vertical File Index: A Subject and Title Index to Selected Pamphlet Materials.* If your library does not have the item you seek, the index tells you how to order it from its publisher. You'll need to allow extra time for such orders.

Government documents provide a vast array of data, public records, and other historical and contemporary information. For Canadian government documents, by far the most numerous, consult the *Canadian Research Index*. Your library will have a large collection of government documents only if it is a depository library (that is, designated to receive such documents). If yours is not a depository library, a librarian may be able to help you obtain a needed document from another library.

6 Using guides to books

The library catalogue

The library's catalogue lists books alphabetically by authors' names, titles of books, and subjects. (In some catalogues authors and titles are alphabetized together and subjects are alphabetized separately.) If you are starting research on a subject you don't know very well, begin by looking under subject headings. If you know of an expert in the field and you want to find his or her books, look under the author's name. If you know the title of a relevant book but not the author's name, look for the title.

The library's catalogue may be the familiar card file, held in cabinets of drawers. But to save space and time, most libraries have converted their catalogues to other forms. A printed catalogue in bound volumes contains small reproductions of the cards traditionally found in drawers. A catalogue on microfilm or microfiche (see the previous page) shows the library's collection on film viewed with a special reader.

Increasingly, libraries are computerizing their catalogues. You gain access to the computer's memory by typing a code onto a keyboard along with the name of the author, the title of the work, or the subject heading, as described below. A screen then displays the requested information, along with further instructions.

At this point, many libraries have not yet computerized all their holdings, so older books are still listed only in another catalogue—card, printed, microfilm, or microfiche. Find out whether your library is fully automated and, if not, what the dividing date is between nonautomated and automated listings. If you need books from before that date as well as after, you will have to consult both catalogues.

Seek help from a member of the library's staff if you are uncertain about the location, form, or use of the catalogue. Library staffers can also help you obtain books not in your library by borrowing them from another library. Such interlibrary loans, though usually free or low cost, can take a week or more from the time of your request, so plan accordingly.

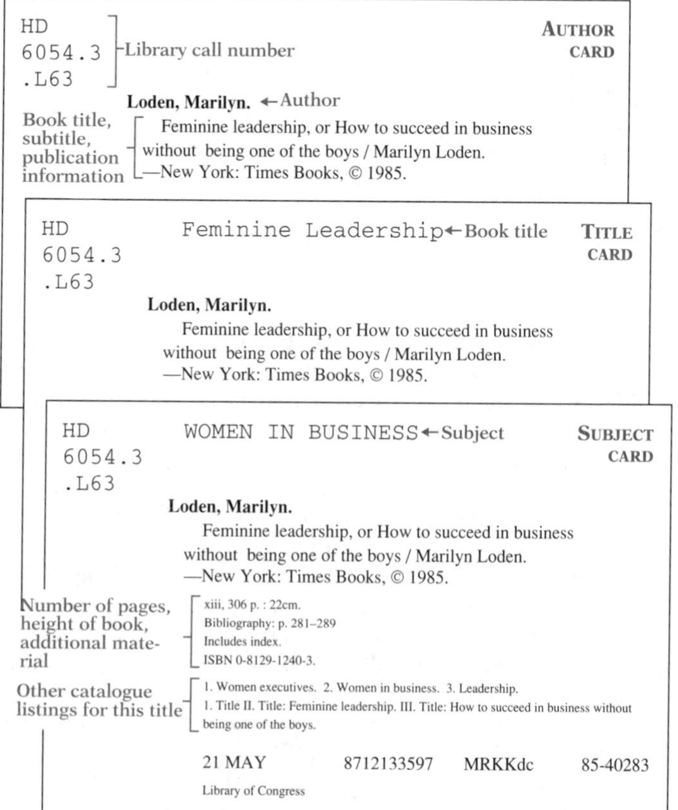

35c

Though the storage systems vary, all book catalogues contain similar information and follow a similar organization. By far the most widely used catalogue format is that of the Library of Congress card. Samples of author, title, and subject cards appear opposite, with notes on their features.

Search strategy

Unless you seek a specific author or title, your search in the library's catalogue will be much more efficient and productive if you zero in on specific words relating to your subject.

In searching the library's book catalogue, you can find such words in *Library of Congress Subject Headings* (*LCSH*). This multivolume work lists headings under which the Library of Congress catalogues books. Consulting this source and following its system of cross-references and headings at different levels of specificity, you will be able to discover the headings most likely to lead to appropriate sources. Mark Shannon used *LCSH* to eliminate the heading of "Women—Employment," which was much too broad for his needs. He isolated the narrower "Women executives," with subcategories such as "Attitudes," "Employment," and "Canada." He then used these words to search the library's computerized catalogue, as illustrated on this and the following page. (For more on selecting keywords for computer searches, see pp. 513–14.)

Note that *LCSH* does not include most proper names of people, places, corporations, associations, government bodies, and the like.

SCREEN 1: KIND OF SEARCH

```
What type of search do you wish to do?
       1. TIL - Title, journal title, series title, etc.
       2. AUT - Author, illustrator, editor, organization, etc.
       3. SUB - Subject heading assigned by library.
       4. NUM - Call number, ISBN, ISSN, etc.
       5. KEY - One word taken from a title, author or subject.
Enter number or code: 3                          Then press SEND
```

SCREEN 2: SUBJECT HEADING (KEYWORDS)

```
Start at the beginning of the Library of Congress subject heading
and enter as many words of the subject heading as you know below.
Choose the most specific subject heading you can.
        Ex: Molecular biology (NOT biology)
        Ex: Bastille Day (NOT France--History)
Enter subject: WOMEN EXECUTIVES                  Then press SEND
```

SCREEN 3: PARTIAL LISTINGS UNDER "WOMEN EXECUTIVES"

```
Your subject: Women executives        matches at least 10 subjects
                                                 No. of citations
                                                 in entire catalogue
  1 Women executives                                                  29
  2 Women executives--Addresses, essays, lectures.                     1
  3 Women executives--Bibilography.                                    6
  4 Women executives--Canada--Bibliography.                            1
  5 Women executives--Congresses.                                      2
  6 Women executives--Denmark--Case studies.                           1
  7 Women executives--Great Britain.                                   3
  8 Women executives--India--Case studies.                             1
  9 Women executives--India--Rajasthan.                                1
 10 Women executives--Job stress.                                      1

Enter number or code, 1                                  Then press SEND
```

SCREEN 4: PARTIAL LISTINGS UNDER "WOMEN EXECUTIVES—CANADA"

```
This subject: Women executives--Canada.              has 29 citations

Ref# Author                           Title                            Date
  23 Political and Economic Plannin   Women in top jobs; four studies in>1988
  24 Powell, Gary N.                  Women & men in management/       1993
  25 Rose, Suzanna.                   Women's careers: pathways and pitf>1988
  26 Schuman, Barbara Jean.           Profile of women leaders in physica>1986
  27 Smith, Mike.                     Development programme for women in>1984
  28 Vicent, Andrea L., 1944-         Career and family, yours/        1979
  29 Williams, Marcille Gray.         New executive women: a guide to bu>1977

Enter number or code: 24                                 Then press SEND
```

SCREEN 5: SPECIFIC SOURCE

```
This subject: Women executives.                       Citation 24 of 29

   AUTHOR Powell, Gary N.
    TITLE Women & men in management/
  EDITION 2nd ed.
PUBLISHER Newbury Park, Calif. : Sage Publications, c1993.

             Loan     Call
Location     Type     Number              Status

MAIN         STACKS   HD6054.3.P69 1993   On Loan   97-08-13 24:00
```

References to books

Two types of reference books can help you identify general books that have information about your topic: publishing bibliographies and digests. Publishing bibliographies tell whether a book is still in print, whether a paperback edition is available, what books were published on a certain topic in a certain year, and so on. Again, several of these are available both in print and on computer.

35c

Books in Print. Books indexed by author, title, and subject.
Canadian Books in Print
Cumulative Book Index
Paperbound Books in Print

You might, for example, want to know if the author of an encyclopedia article has published any relevant books since the date of the encyclopedia. You could look up the author's name in the latest *Books in Print* to find out.

If you want to evaluate a book's relevance to your topic before you search for it, a review index such as the following will direct you to published reviews of the book:

Book Review Digest. Summarizes and indexes reviews of books.
Book Review Index
Current Book Review Citations
Index to Book Reviews in the Humanities
Index to Book Reviews in the Social Sciences
Technical Book Review Index

Generating your own sources

Most of the sources you consult for a research project—and most of the resources of the library—are likely to be secondary sources whose authors draw their information from other authors. However, academic writing will also require you to consult primary sources and to conduct primary research for information of your own. In many papers this primary research will be the sole basis for your writing, as when you analyse a poem or report on an experiment you conducted. In other papers you will be expected to use your research to support, extend, or refute the ideas of others.

Chapters 39 and 40 discuss the textual analyses, surveys, experiments, and other primary sources you may use in writing for various academic disciplines. One primary source not covered there is the personal interview with an expert in the topic you are researching. Because of the give-and-take of an interview, you can obtain answers to questions precisely geared to your topic, and you can follow up instantly on points of confusion and unexpected leads. In addition, quotations and paraphrases from an interview can give your paper immediacy and authority. Mark Shannon used just such an interview in his paper on women executives (see pp. 628–30).

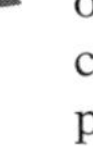

You can conduct an interview in person, over the telephone, or online using electronic mail (see pp. 524–25) or a form of synchronous communication such as Internet Relay Chat (see p. 526). A personal interview is probably preferable if you can arrange it, because you can see the person's expressions and gestures as well as hear his or her tone and words. But telephone and online interviews allow you to interview someone who resists a personal interview or who lives far away from you, while still retaining most advantages of interaction.

A few precautions will help you get the maximum information from an interview with the minimum disruption to the person you are interviewing.

- If you do not already know whom to consult for an interview, ask a teacher in the field or do some telephone or library research. Likely sources, depending on your topic, are those who have written about your topic or something closely related, officials in government, businesspeople, even a relative, if he or she is an expert in your topic because of experience, scholarship, or both.
- Call or write for an appointment. Tell the person exactly why you are calling, what you want to discuss, and how long you expect the interview to take. Be true to your word on all points.
- Prepare a list of open-ended questions to ask—perhaps ten or twelve for a one-hour interview. Plan on doing some research for these questions to discover background on the issues and your subject's published views on the issues.
- Give your subject time to consider your questions. Don't rush into silences with more questions.
- Pay attention to your subject's answers so that you can ask appropriate follow-up questions and pick up on unexpected but worthwhile points.
- Take care in interpreting answers, especially if you are online and thus can't depend on facial expressions, gestures, and tone of voice to convey the subject's attitudes. Ask for clarification when you need it.
- For in-person and telephone interviews, keep careful notes or, if you have the equipment and your subject agrees, tape-record the interview. For online interviews, save the discussion in a file of its own. (A synchronous discussion may require that you activate a "log" or "archive" function before you begin your interview in order to save it afterward.)
- Before you quote your subject in your paper, check with him or her to ensure that the quotations are accurate.
- Send a thank-you note immediately after the interview. Promise your subject a copy of your finished paper, and send the paper promptly.

Exercise 2
Using the library

To become familiar with its layout and resources, visit your library and find the answers to the following questions. (Ask a librarian for help whenever necessary.)

1. Which resources are available on computer? Are the computers attached to printers? Can you transfer data from the com-

puters to your own disks? What fees and other restrictions are there on the use of library computers for research?

2. Where are reference books stored? How are they catalogued and arranged? Which ones are available on computer? Where and in what format(s) are (*a*) *Contemporary Authors,* (*b*) *Encyclopaedia Britannica,* and (*c*) *MLA International Bibliography of Books and Articles on the Modern Languages and Literatures?*
3. Where is the catalogue of the library's periodicals? Where and in what format(s) are the following periodicals stored: (*a*) the *Globe and Mail,* (*b*) *Harper's* magazine, and (*c*) *Dalhousie Review?*
4. Where are the library's periodical indexes? Which ones are available on computer? If computerized indexes are available, what are the library's procedures for using them? Where (and in what formats) are (*a*) the *New York Times Index* and (*b*) the *Social Sciences Index?*
5. What is the format or formats of the library's catalogue of books? If the catalogue is in more than one format, are all formats complete? If any is incomplete, what is not included? If the catalogue (or part of it) is computerized, where are the terminals, and how are they operated?
6. What are the library call numbers of the following books: (*a*) *Obasan,* by Joy Kogawa; (*b*) *Heart of Darkness,* by Joseph Conrad; and (*c*) *The Temptations of Big Bear,* by Rudy Wiebe?

Exercise 3
Finding sources

List at least five sources you can consult for further leads on each of the three topics you produced in Exercise 1 (p. 509) or for three other topics. Use the information provided in the preceding section and additional information at your library.

35d Making a working bibliography

Trying to pursue every source lead as you came across it would prove inefficient and probably ineffective. Instead, you'll want to find out what is available before deciding which leads to follow, and that requires systematically keeping track of where information is and what it is. You can keep track of sources by making a **working bibliography,** a file of the books, articles, and other sources you believe will help you. When you have a substantial file, you can decide which sources seem most promising and look them up first or, if necessary, order them through interlibrary loan.

A working bibliography is your chance to record all the information you need to find your sources. You can use whatever system

Information for a working bibliography

For a book

Library call number
Name(s) of author(s), editor(s), translator(s), or others listed
Title and subtitle
Place of publication
Publisher's name
Date of publication
Other important data, such as edition or volume number

For a periodical article

Name(s) of author(s)
Title and subtitle of article
Title of periodical
Volume number and issue number (if any) in which article appears
Date of issue
Page numbers on which article appears

For other sources

Name(s) of author(s) or others listed, such as a government department or a recording artist
Title of the work
Identifying numbers (if any)
Publisher's or producer's name
Date of publication, release, or production
Format, such as unpublished letter, computer service, or live performance

you like to keep track of information. Some instructors require that the working bibliography be submitted on note cards, with one source to a card, and this system has the advantage of allowing the sources to be shuffled easily. But many researchers have abandoned note cards because computers can print out pages of bibliographic information or even transfer data to the user's own disk. You can combine the two systems by cutting up computer-generated source listings and pasting or taping each source on a note card.

You should have a bibliographic reference for each source you think may be useful. Include all the information listed in the box above. Getting all the information the first time will save you from having to retrace your steps later. Opposite are two samples from Mark Shannon's working bibliography, the first for a periodical and the second for a book.

When you turn in your paper, you will have to attach a list of the sources you have used. So that readers can check or follow up on your sources, your list must include all the information needed to find the sources, in a format readers can understand. Most academic disciplines have special formats used by their practitioners. Several such systems are discussed and illustrated in this handbook:

Bozzi, Vincent. "Assertiveness Breeds Contempt." *Psychology Today* Sept. 1987: 15.

HD
6054.3
.L63

Loden, Marilyn. *Feminine Leadership, or, How to Succeed in Business Without Being One of the Boys.* New York: Times, 1985.

- Modern Language Association (MLA), used in English and some other humanities (pp. 576–97).
- *Chicago Manual of Style* (*CMS*), used in history and some other humanities (pp. 681–87).
- American Psychological Association (APA), used in psychology and other social sciences (pp. 693–703).
- Council of Biology Editors (CBE), used in the biological and other sciences (pp. 716–18).

Before compiling your working bibliography, ask your instructor what documentation style you should use. Then consult the relevant handbook section to determine what kind of information to include and how to arrange it. (Shannon's cards above follow MLA style.)

Exercise 4
Compiling a working bibliography

Prepare a working bibliography of at least ten sources for a research paper on one of the following people or on someone of your own choosing. Begin by limiting the subject to a manageable size, focusing on a particular characteristic or achievement of the person. Then consult reference books, periodical indexes, and the library's catalogue of books. Record complete bibliographic information on note cards.

1. Bob Dylan, or another performer
2. Bertha Wilson, or another Supreme Court justice
3. Sheila Watson, or another writer
4. Wayne Gretzky, or another sports figure
5. Tom Thomson, or another artist

Exercise 5
Compiling a working bibliography

Using one of the topics and the possible references for it from Exercise 3 (p. 537), or starting with a different topic and references, prepare a working bibliography of at least ten sources for your developing research paper.

Chapter 36

Working with Sources and Writing the Paper

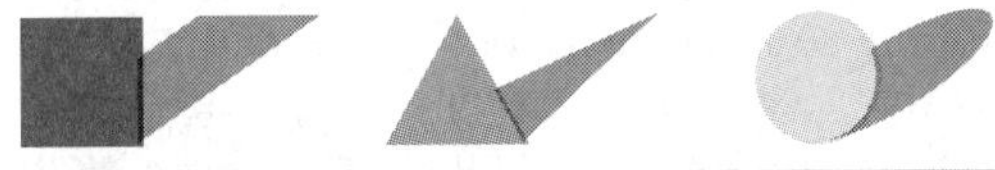

The previous chapter led you through laying the groundwork for a research project. This chapter takes you into the most personal, most intensive, and most rewarding parts of research writing: using the sources you've found, focusing and shaping your ideas, and drafting and revising the paper. In these stages you probe your topic deeply and make it your own.

As before, the work of Mark Shannon and Janice Kowalchuk will illustrate the activity and thought that go into research writing.

36a Evaluating and synthesizing sources

When should you shift gears from *seeking* sources to *using* them? The answer depends on the assigned length of the paper and on the complexity of your subject. You are probably ready to begin reading when your working bibliography suggests that you have explored most aspects of your topic and have found at least some sources that deal directly with your central concern. For a paper of 1800 to 2300 words, 10 to 20 promising titles should give you a good base.

Once you have a satisfactory working bibliography, scan your cards for the sources that are most likely to give you an overview of your topic, and consult those sources first. Mark Shannon, for instance, began investigating titles that indicated a focus on the progress of women in upper corporate management. Janice Kowalchuk began searching for titles on both hockey in Canada, looking for specific books on women's hockey, and the role of sports in general in the life of women in North America

Evaluating sources

When you first examine your sources, your purpose is to evaluate their usefulness and to develop your thinking, not to collect information. Scanning sources—gauging the kind and extent of ideas and information they offer—can help you determine whether your research is on track. For instance, if all your sources are very technical, assuming more background in the subject than you have, then you may need to search in more general-interest books and periodicals; or if all your sources discuss your subject at a very general level, you probably need to broaden your search—or even revise your topic—before proceeding. Scanning can also suggest the subdivisions of your topic, which will eventually help you structure your paper (pp. 563–65).

When evaluating sources, you seek a mix of primary and secondary sources, scholarly and popular sources, older and newer sources, impartial and biased sources. This range reduces to two essential qualities: relevance and reliability.

Both relevance and reliability can be determined in part by consulting works *about* the source you are considering—that is, the works listed in citation indexes (p. 530) or book review indexes (p. 535). But unless you can dismiss the source on the basis of citations or reviews, you will also need to evaluate it yourself.

Relevance

To determine whether sources are relevant, scan the introductions to books and articles and the tables of contents of books. You're looking for opinions and facts that pertain directly to your topic. You're also ensuring that your sources are appropriate in level: you can understand them (if with some effort), and they also expand your knowledge. If you don't see what you need or the source is too high-level or too simple, you can drop it from your list.

36a

 **Guidelines for evaluating sources**

Determine **relevance:**

- Does the source devote some attention to your topic?
- Where in the source are you likely to find relevant information or ideas?
- Is the source appropriately specialized for your needs? Check the source's treatment of a topic you know something about, to ensure that it is neither too superficial nor too technical.
- How important is the source likely to be for your writing?

Judge **reliability:**

- How up to date is the source? Check the publication date.
- Is the author an expert in the field? Look for an author biography, look up the author in a biographical reference (p. 518), or try to trace the author over the Internet (p. 544).
- What is the author's bias? Check biographical information or the author's own preface or introduction. Consider what others have written about the author or the source.
- Whatever his or her bias, does the author reason soundly, provide adequate evidence, and consider opposing views? (See pp. 116–34.)

Reliability

Reliability can be more difficult to judge than relevance. If you haven't already done so, study this book's Introduction and Chapter 4, especially pages 10–14 on analysing and evaluating texts and pages 116–34 on reading an argument critically. When scanning potential sources, think critically, looking for assumptions, evidence, tone, fairness, and other features discussed on the pages cited. In addition, look for information about the author's background to satisfy yourself that the author has sufficient expertise in your subject. Then try to determine what his or her bias is. For instance, a book on parapsychology by someone identified as the president of the National Organization of Psychics may contain an authoritative explanation of psychic powers, but the author's view is likely to be biased. It should be balanced by research in other sources whose authors are more skeptical of psychic powers.

This balance or opposition is important. You probably will not find harmony among sources, for reasonable people often disagree in their opinions. Thus you must deal honestly with the gaps and conflicts in sources. Old sources, superficial ones, slanted ones—these should be offset in your research and your writing by sources that are more recent, more thorough, or more objective.

Evaluating electronic sources

Most books and periodical articles are reviewed before publication, so you can have some confidence in the information they contain. But many Internet sources are self-published by their authors with no preliminary review by others, so you must be the sole judge of reliability. To a great extent, the same critical reading that serves you with books and periodical articles will help you evaluate Internet sources (see the box on the previous page). But you should do some digging as well:

- *Check electronic addresses.* Look for an abbreviation that tells you where the source originates: *edu* (educational institution in the United States), *gov* (government body), *org* (nonprofit organization), or *com* (commercial organization). (Two-letter codes indicate origin other than the United States—for example, *uk* is United Kingdom; *ca* is Canada.) Immediately before this abbreviation, the address will indicate the particular institution, government, or organization: for instance, *gc.ca* is the government of Canada, *ca.gov* is the government of California, *greenpeace.org* is the environmental group Greenpeace, and *ibm.com* is the computer company IBM.
- *Check authorship.* Many sites list the author(s) or group(s) responsible for the site. You can research an author or group through a biographical dictionary, through a work such as the *National Directory of Addresses and Telephone Numbers,* or through a keyword search of the World Wide Web (see p. 521). A site on the Web may provide links to information about, or other work by, an author or group. The author or group may also show up in your other sources.
- *Communicate directly with the author.* For a posting on a Listserv or a Usenet newsgroup, try to reach the author directly to ask about publications and background or to seek further information about your subject. As discussed on page 525, Listservs usually publish subscribers' names and e-mail addresses, so it should be easy to reach an author. Newsgroups (p. 526) are generally more anonymous: you may have to address a posting to the author requesting his or her name and e-mail address. Drop the source from your list if you can't trace the author or the author fails to respond to your requests for information.
- *Check for references or links to reliable sources.* The source may offer as support the titles of sources that you can trace and evaluate—articles in periodicals, other Internet sources, and so on. A Web site may include links to these other sources.

- *Evaluate the source as a whole.* For Web sites, especially, consider the links to other sites. What is the purpose of the site in establishing and organizing links? Are the links worthwhile, or mere window dressing? Is the site trying to sell a particular product, service, or idea? Do some links raise questions about the intentions of the source—because the links are frivolous, say, or indecent?
- *Back up Internet sources.* Always consider Internet sources in the context of other sources so that you can distinguish singular, untested views from more mainstream views that have been subjected to verification. As noted on page 543, only a range of sources will give you a broad and reliable picture of your topic.

2 Synthesizing sources

When you begin to locate the differences and similarities among sources, you move into the most significant part of research writing: forging relationships for your own purpose. This **synthesis,** an essential step in critical reading (pp. 12–13), continues through the drafting and revision of a research paper. As you infer connections—say, between one writer's ideas and another's or between two works by the same author—you create new knowledge.

All kinds of connections may occur to you as you work with sources. Mark Shannon, researching women in management, found several case studies in one source that illustrated an idea proposed by another source. He also found a central disagreement among sources over why women are not more numerous in top management—a disagreement he sought to resolve. Janice Kowalchuk, researching both women's hockey and the role of sport and popular culture in the life of women, found that her ideas about the history of women's hockey were well founded in fact, especially at the university level. She also found that her notions about the importance of sports and popular culture in the life of women had been researched and written about by social scientists. She now knew that she could use women's hockey in Canada as a particular instance of a general pattern in North American life.

First read your sources quickly and selectively to obtain an overview of your topic and a sense of how the sources approach it. Don't get bogged down in taking detailed notes, but *do* write down important connections between sources and general ideas that seem fundamental to your topic. Be especially careful to record ideas of your own, such as your reaction to a writer's theories, because these may not occur to you later. Use your research journal (p. 506).

Exercise 1
Evaluating a source

Imagine that you are researching a paper on the advertising techniques that are designed to persuade consumers to buy products. You have listed the following book in your working bibliography:

Vance Packard, *The Hidden Persuaders,* revised edition, 1981.

On your own or with your classmates (as your instructor wishes), obtain this book from the library and evaluate it as a source for your paper. Use the guidelines on page 543.

Exercise 2
Synthesizing sources

The three passages below address the same issue, the legalization of drugs. What similarities do you see in the authors' ideas? What differences? Write a paragraph of your own in which you use these authors' views as a point of departure for your own view about drug legalization.

Perhaps the most unfortunate victims of drug prohibition laws have been the residents of America's ghettos. These laws have proved largely futile in deterring ghetto-dwellers from becoming drug abusers, but they do account for much of what ghetto residents identify as the drug problem. Aggressive, gun-toting drug dealers often upset law-abiding residents far more than do addicts nodding out in doorways. Meanwhile other residents perceive the drug dealers as heroes and successful role models. They're symbols of success to children who see no other options. At the same time the increasingly harsh criminal penalties imposed on adult drug dealers have led drug traffickers to recruit juveniles. Where once children started dealing drugs only after they had been using them for a few years, today the sequence is often reversed. Many children start using drugs only after working for older drug dealers for a while. . . . Legalization of drugs, like legalization of alcohol in the early 1930s, would drive the drug-dealing business off the streets and out of apartment buildings and into government-regulated, tax-paying stores. It also would force many of the gun-toting dealers out of the business and convert others into legitimate businessmen. —ETHAN A. NADELMANN, "Shooting Up"

All studies show that those most likely to try drugs, get hooked, and die—as opposed to those who suffer from cirrhosis and lung cancer—are young people, who are susceptible to the lure of quick thrills and are terribly adaptable to messages provided by adult society. Under pressure of the current prohibition, the number of kids who use illegal drugs at least once a month has fallen from 39 percent in the late 1970s to 25 percent in 1987, according to the annual survey of high school seniors conducted by the University of Michigan. The same survey shows that attitudes toward drug use have turned sharply negative. But use of legal drugs is still strong. Thirty-eight percent of high school seniors reported getting drunk within the past two weeks, and 27 percent said they

36a

smoke cigarettes every day. Drug prohibition is working with kids; legalization would do them harm.

—MORTON M. KONDRACKE, "Don't Legalize Drugs"

I have to laugh at the debate over what to do about the drug problem. Everyone is running around offering solutions—from making drug use a more serious criminal offense to legalizing it. But there isn't a real solution. I know that. I used and abused drugs, and people, and society, for two decades. Nothing worked to get me to stop all that behavior except just plain being sick and tired. Nothing. Not threats, not ten-plus years in prison, not anything that was said to me. I used until I got through. Period. And that's when you'll win the war. When all the dope fiends are done. Not a minute before.

—MICHAEL W. POSEY, "I Did Drugs Until They Wore Me Out. Then I Stopped."

Exercise 3
Evaluating and synthesizing sources

Look up the sources in the working bibliography you made in Chapter 35, Exercise 5 (p. 540). Evaluate the sources for their relevance and reliability. If the sources seem unreliable or don't seem to give you what you need, expand your working bibliography and evaluate the new sources. In your preliminary notes, jot down the relationships you perceive among sources and the ideas the sources prompt in you.

36b Taking notes using summary, paraphrase, and direct quotation

When you have decided which sources to pursue, you may be ready to gather information, or you may want to step back and get your bearings. Your choice will depend mainly on how familiar you are with the main issues of your topic and whether you have formed a central idea about it.

- If you feel fairly confident that you know what you're looking for in sources, then you might proceed with reading and note taking, as discussed on the following pages.
- If you are attracted to several different main ideas, or you don't see how the various areas of the topic relate, then you might try drafting a thesis sentence to focus your thoughts and making an outline to discover relationships. These steps are discussed on pages 562–63 and 563–64, respectively.

36b

1 Reading and note taking

The most efficient method of reading secondary sources during research is **skimming,** reading quickly to look for pertinent information. (Primary sources usually need to be read more carefully, especially when they are the focus of your paper.) When skimming:

- Read with a specific question in mind, not randomly in hopes of hitting something worthwhile.
- Consult the table of contents, index, or headings to find what you want.
- Concentrate on headings and main ideas, skipping material unrelated to the specific question you are researching.

When you find something relevant, read slowly and carefully to achieve a clear understanding of what the author is saying and to interpret and evaluate the material in the context of your own and others' opinions.

If it is effective, your final paper will show that you have understood and responded critically to your sources—work that can be performed most efficiently in note taking. Taking notes is not a mechanical process of copying from books and periodicals. Rather, as you read and take notes you analyse and organize the information in your sources. Thus your notes both prompt and preserve your thoughts.

Using a system for taking notes helps simplify the process and later makes writing the paper easier. Before you begin, decide on categories that your subject can be divided into. (If you have previously outlined your preliminary ideas, use outline headings for these categories.) Mark Shannon, for instance, divided his general subject of women in top management into these categories:

Data on women in management
Resistance to women's advancement
Sexual stereotypes
Masculine and feminine management styles
Androgynous style
Proposals for change

Headings for your categories will go at the top of each note to cue you about its content.

You can take notes either on note cards or on computer. (Using photocopies from sources is discussed on pp. 553–54.) Note cards have the advantage of being easier to rearrange; computer notes are easier to incorporate into your drafts.

Here are a few guidelines for note cards, illustrated by the sample cards beginning on page 550.

- Use large rather than small cards, to allow yourself more room for notes.
- Write only one fact or idea on a card so that you can easily rearrange information when you want to.
- If the same source gives you more than one idea or fact, make more than one card.
- Near the top of every card, write the author's last name and the

page number(s) of the source so that you will always know where the note came from. (Write a short form of the title as well if you are using two or more sources by the same author.)
- Give the note a brief heading corresponding to one of your categories.

If you use a computer for taking notes from sources, follow these guidelines:

- Create a separate file for each of your categories, and clearly separate each note in a category.
- At the beginning of each note, record the source information: author's last name, title if the author is responsible for two or more sources, and page number(s).
- If a single source provides information relevant to two or more of your headings, sort the information among your files accordingly.
- Print out your notes at regular intervals. Then you'll have a paper copy if your instructor asks to see your notes and when you are away from your computer. (Since most computer monitors show less than a full page of text, print-outs also allow you to scan your notes more quickly.)

Several computer programs are available that will create files and organize your notes automatically once you supply the appropriate commands.

You can use four kinds of notes: summary, paraphrase, direct quotation, and a combination of these methods.

2 Summarizing

When you **summarize,** you condense an extended idea or argument into a sentence or more in your own words. A full discussion of summary appears on pages 8–10, and you should read that section if you have not already.

Mark Shannon summarized the following quotation from one of his sources, Ann Hughey and Eric Gelman, "Managing the Woman's Way," *Newsweek,* page 47:

> Generalizing about male and female styles of management is a tricky business, because stereotypes have traditionally been used to keep women down. Not too long ago it was a widely accepted truth that women were unstable, indecisive, temperamental and manipulative and weren't good team members because they'd never played football. In fighting off these prejudices many women simply tried to adopt masculine traits in the office.

Compare this passage with Shannon's one-sentence summary, in which he picks out the kernel of Hughey and Gelman's idea and expresses it in his own words:

> Masc. and fem. styles
>
> Hughey and Gelman, p. 47
>
> Rather than be labelled with the sexist stereotypes that prevented their promotions, many women adopted masculine qualities.

Summary is most useful when you want to record the gist of an author's idea without the background or supporting evidence.

3 Paraphrasing

When you **paraphrase,** you follow much more closely the author's original presentation, but you still restate it in your own words. Paraphrase is most useful when you want to present or examine an author's line of reasoning but don't feel the original words merit direct quotation.

The following note card shows how Shannon might have paraphrased the passage by Hughey and Gelman given above.

> Masc. and fem. styles
>
> Hughey and Gelman, p.47
>
> Because of the risk of stereotyping, which has served as a tool to block women from management, it is difficult to characterize a feminine management style. Women have been cited for their emotionality, instability, and lack of team spirit, among other qualities. Many women have defended themselves at work by adopting the qualities of men.

Notice how the paraphrase uses different sentence structures and different words to express Hughey and Gelman's idea:

HUGHEY AND GELMAN'S WORDS	SHANNON'S PARAPHRASE
Generalizing about male and female styles of management is a tricky business, because stereotypes have traditionally been used to keep women down.	Because of the risk of stereotyping, which has served as a tool to block women from management, it is difficult to characterize a feminine management style.
Not too long ago it was a widely accepted truth that women were unstable, indecisive, temperamental and manipulative and weren't good team members because they'd never played football.	Women have been cited for their emotionality, instability, and lack of team spirit, among other qualities.
In fighting off these prejudices many women simply tried to adopt masculine traits in the office.	Many women have defended themselves at work by adopting the qualities of men.

Follow these guidelines when paraphrasing:

- Read the material several times to be sure you understand it.
- Restate the main ideas in your own words and sentence structures. You need not put down in new words the whole passage or all the details. Select what is pertinent and restate only that. If complete sentences seem too detailed or cumbersome, use phrases, as in the example below.
- Be careful not to distort meaning. Don't change the source's emphasis or omit connecting words, qualifiers, and other material whose absence will confuse you later or cause you to misrepresent the source.

Mark Shannon might have written this more telegraphic paraphrase of the quotation by Hughey and Gelman:

Masc. and fem. styles

Hughey and Gelman, p. 47

Difficulty of characterizing fem. mgmt. style—risk of stereotypes (emotionality, instability, etc.). Many women's defence: act like men.

If you use such an abbreviated form of note, be sure to cast your notes as complete sentences in your draft.

Using direct quotation

Use direct quotation from secondary sources only when the exact words of the original are important. (See p. 568 for more on when to use quotations.) In a paper analysing primary sources such as literary works, you will use direct quotation extensively to illustrate and support your analysis.

When recording a quotation from a source, take the following precautions to avoid plagiarism or misrepresentation of the source:

- Copy the material *carefully*. Take down the author's exact wording, spelling, capitalization, and punctuation.
- Proofread every direct quotation *at least twice*.
- Use big quotation marks around the quotation so that later you won't confuse it with a paraphrase or summary.
- If you want to add words for clarity, use brackets (see p. 413).
- If you want to omit irrelevant words or sentences, use ellipsis marks, usually three spaced periods (see p. 414).

The note card below shows how Shannon might have quoted Hughey and Gelman, using ellipsis marks and brackets to make the quotation more concise and specific.

> Masc. and fem. styles
>
> Hughey and Gelman, p. 47
>
> "Generalizing about male and female styles of management is a tricky business. . . . Not too long ago it was a widely accepted truth that women were unstable, indecisive, temperamental and manipulative and weren't good team members because they'd never played football. In fighting off these prejudices many women simply tried to adopt masculine traits [such as steadiness and sportsmanship] in the office."

Combining quotation, summary, and paraphrase

Using quotation in combination with summary or paraphrase can help you shape the material to suit your purposes (although you must be careful not to distort the author's meaning). The card following shows how Shannon might have used a combination of quotation and paraphrase to record the statement by Hughey and Gelman. Notice that the quotation marks are clearly visible and that the quotations are absolutely exact.

> Masc. and fem. styles
>
> Hughey and Gelman, p. 47
>
> It is difficult to characterize a feminine style of management "because stereotypes have traditionally been used to keep women down." Women have been cited as "unstable, indecisive, temperamental and manipulative" and have been accused of not being "good team members." Many women defended themselves at work by adopting the qualities of men.

NOTE If the material you are quoting, summarizing, or paraphrasing runs from one page to the next in the source, make a mark (such as a check mark) at the exact spot where one page ends and the next begins. (See p. 633 for an example.) When writing your paper, you may want to use only a part of the material (say, the first or second half). The mark will save you from having to go back to your source to find which page the material actually appeared on.

6 Photocopying or downloading sources

Instead of taking notes, you may want to photocopy sources or download them from the Internet into your own computer or onto a floppy disk. Both photocopying and downloading have distinct advantages:

- They are convenient, particularly when material (such as journal articles) can't be removed from the library or requires too much time to examine closely online. You can also print a downloaded document if you prefer to read text on paper.
- Some researchers believe that photocopying or downloading is preferable to taking notes because it reduces the risk of distorting an author's ideas or introducing errors into quotations. With photocopying you need to write out a quotation only once, into your draft; with downloading you can move the quotation directly from source to draft.

But photocopying and downloading have some disadvantages, too:

- Unlike active note taking on cards or on a computer, photocopying or downloading sources may tempt you to glide through an essential stage of research writing: interpreting, analysing, and synthesizing sources. Once you've run pages through a copier or clicked a mouse to download a file, your work with a source has just begun.
- Photocopying costs money. To economize, copy only sources you definitely want to use.
- Downloading is usually free as long as your Internet account does not charge for time online. However, you should check the source's copyright notice for any restrictions on downloading or requirements for acknowledging the source. (See also p. 559.)

When you photocopy or download a source, take the following additional steps:

- Make sure that you record complete bibliographical information from the source so that you don't have to retrace your steps for it. (Since online sources can change and disappear, retracing your steps may not even be possible.) Write bibliographic information directly on a photocopy, or add it to a downloaded file. See page 538 for a list of what information to record.
- Read the source as thoughtfully as you would any other. Annotate the relevant passages of a photocopy with underlining, circles, and marginal notes about their significance for your topic. You can accomplish the same work with a downloaded document by opening the downloaded file into your word-processing program and inserting highlights and comments at relevant passages.
- Do not import whole blocks of the source into your draft, especially with downloaded sources that you can excerpt electronically. The guidelines on page 568 for judicious use of quotations apply to sources you photocopy or download as well as to those you take notes from.
- To integrate notes on photocopied or downloaded sources into your other notes, make a cross-reference that briefly summarizes the photocopied or downloaded source.

Exercise 4
Summarizing and paraphrasing

Prepare two note cards, one containing a summary of the entire following paragraph and the other containing a paraphrase of the first two sentences (ending with the word *land*). Use the format for a note card provided in the preceding section, omitting only the outline heading.

Thus, an integral part of the history of Canada's federal government is a long series of attempts, both fruitful and fruitless, to overcome the geographic and economic disparities that plague that land. From the official beginning in 1867, a foundation stone of the Canadian Confederation has been the government's professed desire and goal to equalize the different legacies of the land. One of the first such efforts was the new country's promise to British Columbia to overcome its physical separation from the rest of Canada by building a transcontinental railroad through the formidable Rocky Mountains; a century later Pierre Elliott Trudeau, campaigning to become prime minister again, was seeking western Canadian votes by promising to double-track the same single rail line through the same mountains.

—ANDREW H. MALCOLM, *The Canadians,* p. 27

Exercise 5
Combining summary, paraphrase, and direct quotation

Prepare a note card containing a combination of paraphrase or summary and direct quotation that states the major idea of the passage below. Use the format for a note card provided in the preceding section, omitting only the heading.

Most speakers unconsciously duel even during seemingly casual conversations, as can often be observed at social gatherings where they show less concern for exchanging information with other guests than for asserting their own dominance. Their verbal dueling often employs very subtle weapons like mumbling, a hostile act which defeats the listener's desire to understand what the speaker claims he is trying to say (but is really not saying because he is mumbling!). Or the verbal dueler may keep talking after someone has passed out of hearing range—which is often an aggressive challenge to the listener to return and acknowledge the dominance of the speaker. —PETER K. FARB, *Word Play,* p. 107

36c Avoiding plagiarism

Plagiarism (from a Latin word for "kidnapper") is the presentation of someone else's ideas or words as your own. Whether deliberate or accidental, plagiarism is a serious and often punishable offence.

- *Deliberate* plagiarism:

Copying a phrase, a sentence, or a longer passage from a source and passing it off as your own.

Summarizing or paraphrasing someone else's ideas without acknowledging your debt.

Handing in as your own work a paper you have bought, had a friend write, or copied from another student.

- *Accidental* plagiarism:

Forgetting to place quotation marks around another writer's words.
Omitting a source citation for another's idea because you are unaware of the need to acknowledge the idea.
Carelessly copying a source when you mean to paraphrase.

You do not plagiarize, however, when you draw on other writers' material and acknowledge your sources. That procedure is a crucial part of honest research writing, as we have seen. This section shows you how to avoid plagiarism by acknowledging sources when necessary and by using them accurately and fairly.

Checklist for avoiding plagiarism

- What type of source are you using: your own independent material, common knowledge, or someone else's independent material? You must acknowledge someone else's material.
- If you are quoting someone else's material, is the quotation exact? Have you inserted quotation marks around quotations run into the text? Are graphs, statistics, and other borrowed data identical to the source? Have you shown omissions with ellipsis marks and additions with brackets?
- If you are paraphrasing or summarizing someone else's material, have you used your own words and sentence structures? Does your paraphrase or summary employ quotation marks when you resort to the author's exact language? Have you represented the author's meaning without distortion?
- Is each use of someone else's material acknowledged in your text? Are all your source citations complete and accurate? (See 37a.)
- Does your list of works cited include all the sources you have drawn from in writing your paper? (See 37b.)

Knowing what to acknowledge

When you write a research paper, you coordinate information from three kinds of sources: (1) your independent thoughts and experiences; (2) common knowledge, the basic knowledge people share; and (3) other people's independent thoughts and experiences. Of the three, you *must* acknowledge the third, the work of others.

Your independent material

You need not acknowledge your own independent material—your thoughts, compilations of facts, or experimental results, expressed in your words or format—to avoid plagiarism. Such material includes observations from your experience (for example, a conclusion you draw about crowd behaviour by watching crowds at concerts) as well as diagrams you construct from information you gather yourself. Though you generally should describe the basis for your conclusions so that readers can evaluate your thinking, you need not cite sources for them. However, someone else's ideas and facts are not yours; even when you express them entirely in your words and sentence structures, they require acknowledgment.

Common knowledge

Common knowledge consists of the standard information of a field of study as well as folk literature and commonsense observations.

- Standard information includes the major facts of history, such as the dates of Charlemagne's rule as emperor of Rome (800–814). It does not include interpretations of facts, such as a historian's opinion that Charlemagne was sometimes needlessly cruel in extending his power.
- Folk literature, such as the fairy tale "Snow White," is popularly known and cannot be traced to a particular writer. Literature traceable to a writer is not folk literature, even if it is very familiar.
- A commonsense observation is something most people know, such as that inflation is most troublesome for people with low and fixed incomes. An economist's argument about the effects of inflation on Chinese immigrants is not a commonsense observation.

You may treat common knowledge as your own, even if you have to look it up in a reference book. You may not know, for example, the dates of the French Revolution or the standard definition of *photosynthesis,* although these are considered common knowledge. If you do not know a subject well enough to determine whether a piece of information is common knowledge, make a record of the source as you would for any other quotation, paraphrase, or summary. As you read more about the subject, the information may come up repeatedly without acknowledgment, in which case it is probably common knowledge. But if you are still in doubt when you finish your research, always acknowledge the source.

Someone else's independent material

You must always acknowledge other people's independent material—that is, any facts or ideas that are not common knowledge or your own. The source may be anything, including a book, an article, a movie, an interview, a microfilmed document, or a computer program. You must acknowledge not only ideas or facts themselves but also the language and format in which the ideas or facts appear, if you use them. That is, the wording, sentence structures, arrangement of thoughts, and special graphic format (such as a table or diagram) created by another writer belong to that writer just as his or her ideas do.

The following example baldly plagiarizes the original quotation from Jessica Mitford's *Kind and Usual Punishment,* page 9.

> **Original** The character and mentality of the keepers may be of more importance in understanding prisons than the character and mentality of the kept.
>
> **Plagiarism** But the character of prison officials (the keepers) is more important in understanding prisons than the character of prisoners (the kept).

Though the writer has made some changes in Mitford's original and even altered the meaning slightly (by changing *may be* to *is*), she has plagiarized on several counts. She has copied key words (*character, keepers, kept*), duplicated the entire sentence structure, and lifted the idea—all without acknowledging the source. The next example is more subtle plagiarism, because it changes Mitford's sentence structure. But it still uses her words.

> **Plagiarism** In understanding prisons, we should know more about the character and mentality of the keepers than of the kept.

You need to acknowledge another's material no matter how you use it, how much of it you use, or how often you use it. Whether you are quoting a single important word, paraphrasing a single sentence, or summarizing three paragraphs, and whether you are using the source only once or a dozen times, you must acknowledge the original author every time. See page 576 for discussion and examples of how to acknowledge sources in your text.

If you read someone else's material during your research but do not include any of that material in your final draft, you need not acknowledge the source with a citation because you have not actually used the material. However, your instructor may ask you to include such sources in your list of works cited.

Acknowledgment of online sources

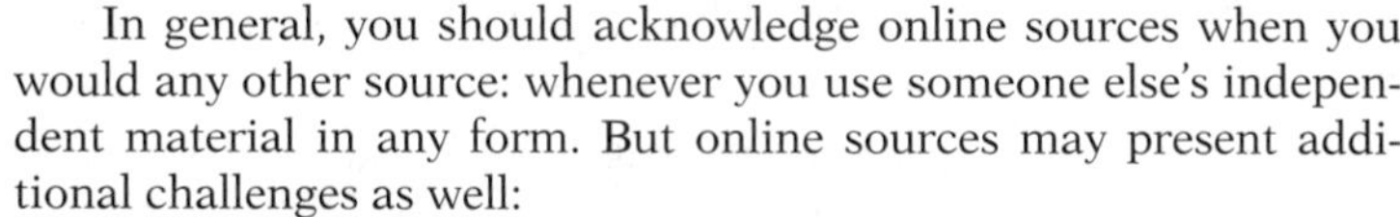

In general, you should acknowledge online sources when you would any other source: whenever you use someone else's independent material in any form. But online sources may present additional challenges as well:

- Keep in mind that online sources may change from one day to the next or even be removed entirely. Be sure to record complete source information each time you consult the source. Without the source information, you *may not* use the source.
- A World Wide Web site may include links to other sites that are copyrighted in their own right and require your acknowledgment. The fact that one person has used a second person's work does not release you from the responsibility to acknowledge the second work.
- If you want to use online material in something you publish online, such as your own site on the World Wide Web, then you may need to seek permission from the copyright holder in addition to citing the source (See pp. 762, 763).
- You may have to do additional research to discover the author of an online source such as a Listserv or newsgroup posting, whether for your citation or for reuse permission. See page 544 for advice on tracing online authors.

2 Quoting, summarizing, and paraphrasing honestly

When using direct quotation, be sure to copy the material from the source accurately and with clear quotation marks. Use the quotation marks in the running text of your paper even if you are quoting only a single word that the original author used in a special or central way. (See pp. 399–400 for the style to use with poetry and long quotations, which are set off from the text and not enclosed in quotation marks.) Acknowledge the source in the manner appropriate for the documentation style you are using. (See p. 576 for the MLA citation style, p. 681 for the *Chicago Manual* style, p. 692 for the APA style, and pp. 716–17 for the CBE style.)

To correct the plagiarism of Mitford's sentence opposite, the writer could place Mitford's exact words in quotation marks and cite the source properly (in this case, in MLA style).

> QUOTATION According to one critic of the penal system, "The character and mentality of the keepers may be of more importance in understanding prisons than the character and mentality of the kept" (Mitford 9).

Or the writer could paraphrase Mitford, using the writer's own words and sentence structure (with no quotation marks) and citing Mitford:

PARAPHRASE One critic of the penal system maintains that we may be able to learn more about prisons from the psychology of the prison officials than from that of the prisoners (Mitford 9).

If you adopt the source's sentence pattern and simply substitute synonyms for key words, or if you use the original words and merely change the sentence pattern, you are not paraphrasing but plagiarizing, even if you acknowledge the source, because both methods use someone else's expression without quotation marks. The inadequate paraphrase below plagiarizes the original source, Frederick C. Crews's *The Tragedy of Manners: Moral Drama in the Later Novels of Henry James,* page 8.

ORIGINAL In each case I have tried to show that all the action in a "Jamesian novel" may be taken as a result of philosophical differences of opinion among the principal characters, and that these differences in turn are explainable by reference to the characters' differing social backgrounds.

PLAGIARISM According to Crews, the action in a "Jamesian novel" comes from philosophical differences of opinion between characters, differences that can be explained by examining the characters' differing social backgrounds (8).

Even though the writer acknowledges the author's work (by giving Crews's name and the parenthetical page number, 8), he plagiarizes because he does not also acknowledge Crews's exact words with quotation marks. The paraphrase below both conveys and acknowledges Crews's meaning without stealing his manner of expression.

PARAPHRASE According to Crews, the characters in Henry James's novels live out philosophies acquired from their upbringing and their place in society (8).

In paraphrasing or summarizing you must not only devise your own form of expression (or place quotation marks around the author's expressions) but also represent the author's meaning exactly, without distorting it. In the following inaccurate summary the writer has not plagiarized but has stated a meaning exactly opposite that of the original. The original quotation, from the artist Henri Matisse, appears in Jack D. Flam, *Matisse on Art,* page 148.

ORIGINAL For the artist creation begins with vision. To see is itself a creative operation, requiring an effort. Everything that we see in our daily life is more or less

> distorted by acquired habits, and this is perhaps more evident in an age like ours when cinema posters and magazines present us every day with a flood of ready-made images which are to the eye what prejudices are to the mind.

INACCURATE SUMMARY Matisse said that the artist can learn how to see by looking at posters and magazines (qtd. in Flam 148).

The revision below combines summary and quotation to represent the author's meaning exactly.

IMPROVED SUMMARY Matisse said that the artist must overcome visual "habits" and "prejudices," particularly those developed in response to popular cultural images (qtd. in Flam 148).

To be sure you acknowledge sources fairly and do not plagiarize, review the checklist on page 556 both before beginning to write your paper and again after you have completed your first draft.

Exercise 6
Recognizing plagiarism

The numbered items below show various attempts to quote or paraphrase the following passage. Carefully compare each attempt with the original passage. Which are plagiarized, inaccurate, or both, and which are acceptable? Why?

> I would agree with the sociologists that psychiatric labelling is dangerous. Society can inflict terrible wounds by discrimination, and by confusing health with disease and disease with badness.
>
> —GEORGE E. VAILLANT, *Adaptation to Life,* p. 361

1. According to George Vaillant, society often inflicts wounds by using psychiatric labelling, confusing health, disease, and badness (361).
2. According to George Vaillant, "psychiatric labelling [such as 'homosexual' or 'schizophrenic'] is dangerous. Society can inflict terrible wounds by . . . confusing health with disease and disease with badness" (361).
3. According to George Vaillant, when psychiatric labelling discriminates between health and disease or between disease and badness, it can inflict wounds on those labelled (361).
4. Psychiatric labels can badly hurt those labelled, says George Vaillant, because they fail to distinguish among health, illness, and immorality (361).
5. Labels such as "homosexual" and "schizophrenic" can be hurtful when they fail to distinguish among health, illness, and immorality.
6. "I would agree with the sociologists that society can inflict terrible wounds by discrimination, and by confusing health with disease and disease with badness" (Vaillant 361).

Exercise 7
Taking notes from sources

Continuing from Exercise 3 (p. 547), as the next step in preparing a research paper, make notes from your sources. Use summary, paraphrase, direct quotation, or a combination as seems appropriate. Be careful to avoid plagiarism or inaccuracy. Mark each note with the author's name, title, and page number as well as with a heading summarizing its content.

36d Developing a thesis sentence

Perhaps earlier in the research-writing process, but certainly once you have taken notes from your sources, you will want to express your central idea and perspective in a thesis sentence—or sentences, if you need more than one. (See p. 41 if you need guidance on developing a thesis sentence.) Drafting a thesis sentence will help you see the overall picture and organize your notes.

Mark Shannon's and Janice Kowalchuk's work on their research papers illustrates how a thesis sentence evolves to become complete and specific. Before finishing his reading on women in management, Shannon wrote the following draft of a thesis sentence:

TENTATIVE THESIS SENTENCE

> Although women have come a long way in their journey up the corporate ladder, they still have a number of obstacles to overcome.

This thesis sentence stated Shannon's preliminary idea that women still have not overcome all obstacles to management. But Shannon's further reading led him to revise this idea: he discovered that women have broken most barriers into middle management but still have difficulty penetrating a "glass ceiling" between themselves and the top jobs. Many of his sources focused on the differences in managerial styles between men and women. Accordingly, Shannon altered his thesis to reflect his growing conviction that businesses create the glass ceiling for women by defining a successful management style as a masculine style.

REVISED THESIS SENTENCE

> If women are ever to break through the glass ceiling in significant numbers, business attitudes will have to change, particularly the definition of successful management styles.

For Janice Kowalchuk, framing a thesis sentence for her paper on women's sports required drawing together (synthesizing) all of her ideas into a single statement. The first draft merely conveys a general sense of her position on women's sports.

TENTATIVE THESIS SENTENCE

Women can share the recognition that men get if we press for equality and use our power.

REVISED THESIS SENTENCE

The recognition always given by society to men's sports can be shared by women if we continue to press for equal opportunity and begin to use our economic power to promote ourselves.

Exercise 8
Developing a thesis sentence

Draft and revise a thesis sentence for your research paper. Make sure the revised version asserts the topic specifically and implies your perspective on it. (If you need help, consult pp. 41–44.)

Creating a structure

Before starting to draft your research paper, organize your ideas and information so that you know the main divisions of your paper, the order you'll cover them in, and the important supporting ideas for each division. The goal is to create a structure that presents your ideas in a sensible and persuasive sequence and that supports ideas at each level with enough explanation and evidence.

Creating a structure involves almost constant synthesis, the forging of relationships among ideas (see p. 545). As you arrange and rearrange your notes, you find connections among ideas and determine which are most important, which are merely supportive, and which are not relevant at all.

To build a structure, follow these guidelines:

- Arrange your notes in groups of related ideas and information according to the subject headings you wrote on your note cards or computer files. Each of these groups should correspond to a main section of your paper: a key idea of your own that supports the thesis and the evidence for that idea.
- Review your research journal for connections between sources, opinions of sources, and other thoughts that can help you organize your paper.
- Look objectively at your groups of notes. If some groups are skimpy, with few notes, consider whether you should drop the category or conduct more research to fill it out. If most of your notes fall into one or two groups, consider whether the categories are too broad and should be divided. (Does any of this rethinking affect your thesis sentence? If so, revise it accordingly.)

- Within each group, distinguish between the main idea of the group (which should be your own) and the supporting ideas and evidence (which should come from your sources).

An outline can help you shape your research and also discover potential problems, such as inadequate support and overlapping or irrelevant ideas. For some research projects, you may find an **informal outline** sufficient. As with the informal outline for an essay (see p. 47), you list main points and supporting information in the order you expect to discuss them. Because of its informality, such an outline can help you try out different arrangements of material, even fairly early in the research process. Mark Shannon experimented with an informal outline while examining his sources, in order to see how his developing ideas might fit together.

How far women have come
—American Civil Rights Act of 1964
—Canadian Employment Equity Act and Federal Contractors Program
—1970s workplace vs. present

Gains made since 1970s
—Success: percentage of women in middle and upper management
—Availability of mentors
—Rise of high-tech and service industries

Obstacles
—Statistics on women at the top
—Breaking the "glass ceiling"
—Last bastion for males
—Conservatism at the top
—"Queen bees" and male clones
—Masculine management style

This informal outline helped Shannon decide not to continue researching women's advances in business (the first two sections) and to concentrate on obstacles to advancement (last section).

Unlike an informal outline, a **formal outline** arranges ideas tightly and in considerable detail, with close attention to hierarchy and phrasing. The example below shows the formal outline's format and schematic content:

I. First main idea
  A. First subordinate idea
    1. First evidence for subordinate idea
      a. First detail of evidence
      b. Second detail of evidence
    2. Second evidence for subordinate idea
  B. Second subordinate idea
II. Second main idea

In this model main ideas are labelled with Roman numerals, the first sublevel with capital letters, the second with Arabic numerals, and the third with small letters. (A fourth sublevel, if needed, is labelled with Arabic numerals enclosed in parentheses.) Each level of the outline is indented farther than the one it supports.

To be an effective organizer for your thoughts, a formal outline should be detailed and should adhere to several principles of logical arrangement, clarity, balance, and completeness. These are discussed in detail and illustrated in Chapter 1, pages 49–51. Briefly:

- The outline should divide material into groups that indicate which ideas are primary and, under them, which are subordinate. A long, undivided list of parallel items probably needs to be subdivided.
- Parallel headings should represent ideas of equal importance and generality and should not overlap one another.
- Single sublevels should be avoided because they illogically imply that something is divided into only one part.

A formal outline is usually written either in phrases—a **topic outline**—or in sentences—a **sentence outline.** A complete topic outline is illustrated in Chapter 1, page 49. A complete sentence outline accompanies Mark Shannon's research paper on pages 608–09. Either is suitable for a research paper, though a sentence outline, because it requires complete statements, conveys more information.

Exercise 9
Creating a structure

Continuing from Exercise 8 (p. 563), arrange your notes into a structure. As specified by your instructor, make an informal outline or a formal sentence or topic outline to guide the drafting of your paper.

36f Drafting the paper

Beginning a draft of what will be a relatively long and complicated paper can be difficult, so it may help to remember that you do not have to proceed methodically from beginning to end. Here are some ideas for writing a draft.

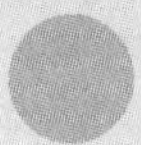

Tips for drafting a research paper

- To get your juices flowing and give yourself a sense of direction, write a quick two- or three-paragraph summary of what the paper will be about. (Pretend you're writing to a friend if that will help loosen you up.)
- Start with the section of the paper you feel most confident about. At first, skip any parts that scare you or give you undue trouble, even the introduction.
- Work in chunks, one unit or principal idea at a time. Fit the sections together only after you begin to see the draft take shape.
- Insert source information (author's name and page number) into the draft as you quote, paraphrase, or summarize.

Working section by section

In writing a first draft, remember that a primary reason for doing a research paper is learning how to interpret and evaluate the evidence in sources, draw your own conclusions from the evidence, and weave the two together in a way that establishes your expertise in your subject. The weaving will be easier if you view each principal idea in your outline as a unit. Depending on the importance of the idea to your scheme, on its complexity, and on the amount of evidence needed to support it, a unit may require a single paragraph or a block of several paragraphs.

Compose the units of your paper as if each will stand alone (though of course you will pull the units together before your draft is complete).

- Begin each unit by stating the idea, which should be a conclusion you have drawn from reading and responding to your sources.
- Follow the statement with specific support from your notes: facts and examples; summaries, paraphrases, or quotations of secondary sources; quotations of passages from primary sources with your analysis.
- If your research focuses on or has uncovered a disagreement among experts, present the disagreement fairly and give the evidence that leads you to side with one expert or another.
- As much as possible, try to remain open to new interpretations or new arrangements of ideas that occur to you.

Proceeding in this way will help you avoid a common trap of research writing: allowing your sources to control you, rather than vice versa. Make sure each unit of your paper centres on an idea of your own, not someone else's, and that your paragraphs are pointed toward demonstrating that idea, not merely presenting sources.

Tracking source citations

As you draft your paper, insert the source of each summary, paraphrase, and quotation in parentheses in the text—for instance, "(Frankel 42)" referring to page 42 in a work by Frankel. If you are conscientious about inserting these notes and carrying them through successive drafts, you will be less likely to plagiarize accidentally and you will have little difficulty citing your sources in the final paper. (Citing sources is discussed in Chapter 37.)

Drafting on a computer

If you write on a word processor, the following suggestions could ease the transition from developing ideas and reading sources to drafting the paper:

- Copy your preliminary outline into your document file, and compose paragraphs directly under headings, deleting the remnants of the outline and adding transitions as you go along.
- If you have kept your source notes on a computer and your word processor can display separate files on the same screen, open both your document file and a copy of your notes file, one above the other. (Leave the original notes file intact in case you accidentally delete a note and need it later.) Then you can import your notes directly into your draft to support your ideas, using the word processor's editing functions to mesh source information into your own ideas and sentences.
- Instead of working with two files on the same screen, you can copy your notes file into your document file (again, leaving the original notes file intact), arrange the notes under your outline headings, and write the parts of the draft that the notes support. Integrate the notes into your own text using the word processor's editing functions.
- If you do import your notes into your draft, you'll need to rewrite and edit the notes so that they work for your ideas and fit into your sentences. Avoid importing many long quotations from your sources. (See the box on the next page.)
- Be sure to include source information for every summary, paraphrase, and quotation, as described on page 538.

36g Using and introducing summaries, paraphrases, and quotations

One of your challenges in writing a research paper will be deciding when, where, and how to introduce summaries, paraphrases, and quotations from your sources into your text.

1 Using borrowed material

The evidence of others' information and opinions should *back up* your conclusions. You don't want to let your evidence overwhelm your own point of view and voice. The point of research writing is to investigate and go beyond sources, to interpret them and convey your interpretations to readers.

Most papers of six to ten pages should not need more than two to four quotations that are longer than a few lines each. Except when you are analysing literature or other primary sources (see below), favour paraphrases and summaries over quotations. For quotations from secondary sources, use the tests below.

In papers analysing literature, historical documents, and other sources, quotations will often be both the target of your analysis and the chief support for your ideas. You may need to quote many brief passages, integrated into your sentences, and then comment on the quotations to clarify your analysis and win readers' agreement with it. Examples of such extensive quotation can be seen in the three literary analyses in Chapter 39 (pp. 661, 666, and 669).

Tests for direct quotations

The author's original satisfies one of these requirements:

- The language is unusually vivid, bold, or inventive.
- The quotation cannot be paraphrased without distortion or loss of meaning.
- The words themselves are at issue in your interpretation.
- The quotation represents and emphasizes the view of an important expert.
- The quotation is a graph, diagram, or table.

The quotation is as short as possible.

- It includes only material relevant to your point.
- It is edited to eliminate examples and other unneeded material. (For editing quotations, see the note that follows.)

NOTE If you need guidance in the mechanics of quotation, see pages 370–71 (punctuating identifying words such as *he insists*), 399–400 (quoting poetry and long prose passages), 413–14 (using brackets for additions to quotations), and 414–15 (using ellipsis marks for deletions from quotations).

Introducing borrowed material

When using summaries, paraphrases, and quotations, integrate them smoothly into your own sentences. In the passage below, the writer has not meshed the structures of her own and her source's sentences.

AWKWARD One editor disagrees with this view and "a good reporter does not fail to separate opinions from facts" (Lyman 52).

REVISED One editor disagrees with this view, maintaining that "a good reporter does not fail to separate opinions from facts" (Lyman 52).

Even when it does not conflict with your own sentence structure, borrowed material will be ineffective if you merely dump it in readers' laps without explaining how you intend it to be understood.

DUMPED Many news editors and reporters maintain that it is impossible to keep personal opinions from influencing the selection and presentation of facts. "True, news reporters, like everyone else, form impressions of what they see and hear. However, a good reporter does not fail to separate opinions from facts" (Lyman 52).

REVISED Many news editors and reporters maintain that it is impossible to keep personal opinions from influencing the selection and presentation of facts. Yet not all authorities agree with this view. One editor grants that "news reporters, like everyone else, form impressions of what they see and hear." But, he insists, "a good reporter does not fail to separate opinions from facts" (Lyman 52).

In the first version, we must figure out for ourselves that the writer's opening sentence and the quotation represent opposite points of view. In the revised version, the writer's additions (underlined) tell us what to expect in the quotation. (A list of verbs for introducing borrowed material appears on the following page.)

You can do even more to integrate a quotation into your text and inform readers why you are using it. If your readers will recognize it, you can provide the author's name in the text:

36g

AUTHOR NAMED . . . Harold Lyman grants that "news reporters, like everyone else, form impressions of what they see and hear." But, Lyman insists, "a good reporter does not fail to separate opinions from facts" (52).

Verbs for introducing summaries, paraphrases, and quotations

Introduce borrowed material with a verb that conveys information about the source author's attitude or approach to what he or she is saying. In the sentence *Smith ____ that the flood might have been disastrous,* filling the blank with *observes, finds,* or *insists* would create different meanings. (Note that all these verbs are in the present tense, the appropriate tense for discussions of others' writings.)

Author is neutral	Author infers or suggests	Author argues	Author is uneasy or disparaging
comments	analyses	claims	belittles
describes	asks	contends	bemoans
explains	assesses	defends	complains
illustrates	concludes	disagrees	condemns
notes	considers	holds	deplores
observes	finds	insists	deprecates
points out	predicts	maintains	derides
records	proposes	**Author agrees**	laments
relates	reveals	admits	warns
reports	shows	agrees	speculates
says	suggests	concedes	
sees	supposes	concurs	
thinks		grants	
writes			

If the source title contributes information about the author or the context of the quotation, you can provide it in the text:

Title given . . . Harold Lyman, in his book *The Conscience of the Journalist,* grants that "news reporters, like everyone else, form impressions of what they see and hear." But, Lyman insists, "a good reporter does not fail to separate opinions from facts" (52).

Finally, if the quoted author's background and experience reinforce or clarify the quotation, you can provide these credentials in the text:

Credentials given . . . Harold Lyman, a newspaper editor for more than forty years, grants that "news reporters, like everyone else, form impressions of what they see and hear." But, Lyman insists, "a good reporter does not fail to separate opinions from facts" (52).

You need not always name the author, source, or credentials in your text. In fact, such introductions may get in the way when you are simply establishing facts or weaving together facts and opinions from varied sources. In the following passage from Mark Shannon's paper, the information is more important than the source, so the name of the source is mentioned only in a parenthetical acknowledgment:

> The fact is, women are still rare in the highest executive positions. In the United States, they represented only about 2 percent of the top executives in *Fortune* 500 companies in 1992 (Dominguez 387).

(See pp. 576–81 for an explanation of the parenthetical form of citation used in this passage and the ones above.)

Exercise 10
Using and introducing borrowed material

Drawing on the ideas in the following paragraph and using examples from your own observations and experiences, write a paragraph about anxiety. Integrate at least one direct quotation and one paraphrase from the following paragraph into your own sentences. In your paragraph identify the author by name and give his credentials: he is a professor of psychiatry and a practising psychoanalyst.

> There are so many ways in which man is different from all the lower forms of animals, and almost all of them make us uniquely susceptible to feelings of anxiousness. Our imagination and reasoning powers facilitate anxiety; the anxious feeling is precipitated not by an absolute impending threat—such as the worry about an examination, a speech, travel—but rather by the symbolic and often unconscious representations. We do not have to be experiencing a potential danger. We can experience something related to it. We can recall, through our incredible memories, the original symbolic sense of vulnerability in childhood and suffer the feeling attached to that. We can even forget the original memory and still be stuck with the emotion—which is then compounded by its seemingly irrational quality at this time. It is not just the fear of death which pains us, but the anticipation of it; or the anniversary of a specific death; or a street, a hospital, a time of day, a color, a flower, a symbol associated with death.
>
> —WILLARD GAYLIN, "Feeling Anxious," p. 23

36h Revising and editing the paper

When you have written a first draft, take a break for at least a day so that you can gain some objectivity about your work and read the draft critically when you begin to revise. Then evaluate your first draft according to the advice and revision checklist on pages 59–61. Be especially attentive to the following:

- Ensure that your thesis sentence accurately describes your topic and your perspective as they emerged during drafting, so that the paper is unified and coherent.
- Be alert for major structural problems that may not have been apparent in your outline:

  Illogical arrangements of ideas.

  Inadequate emphasis of important points and overemphasis of minor points.

  Imbalance between the views of others (support) and your own views (interpretation or analysis).
- Hunt out irrelevant ideas and facts that crept in just because you had notes on them.
- Look for places where supporting evidence is weak.
- Evaluate the reasonableness of your argument (see pp. 137–41).
- Examine your explanations to be sure your readers will understand them. Define terms and clarify concepts that readers may be unfamiliar with.

A computerized word processor simplifies the mechanics of revision, making it possible, for instance, to move blocks of text with a few keystrokes or to make side-by-side comparisons of the same passage or section.

When you complete your revision—and only then—you are ready to edit. If you do not write on a computer, copy or retype the new draft if possible so that you have a clean copy to work on. If you write on a computer, you can edit directly on screen or print a clean copy. (Some writers find it easier to spot errors on paper than on screen.) For editing, consult the advice and checklist on pages 65–66. Try to read the paper from the point of view of someone who has not spent hours planning and researching but instead has come fresh to the paper. Look for lapses in sense, awkward passages, wordiness, poor transitions between ideas and evidence, unnecessary repetition, wrong or misspelled words, errors in grammar, punctuation, or mechanics—in short, anything that is likely to interfere with a reader's understanding of your meaning.

Note Before you prepare and proofread the final draft (next section), you must insert your source citations into the text and prepare your list of sources. See Chapter 37.

Exercise 11
Drafting and revising your paper

Draft the research paper you have been preparing throughout Chapters 35 and 36. Before beginning the first draft, study your research journal and your notes. While drafting, follow your notes, thesis sentence, and outline as closely as you need to, but stay open to new ideas, associations, and arrangements. Then revise and edit thoroughly and carefully, working to improve not only your presentation of ideas but also, if necessary, the ideas themselves.

36i Preparing and proofreading the final manuscript

Prepare the final draft of your paper when you have edited the text (previous page), added the source citations (p. 576), and written the list of works cited (p. 582). Most instructors expect research papers to be neatly typed with clear titling, double spacing, standard margins, and minimal handwritten corrections. Your instructor may have additional requirements, suggested by the discipline you are writing in. This book explains four such document formats:

- In English, foreign languages, and some other humanities, use the format of the *MLA Handbook for Writers of Research Papers.* See Appendix A (pp. 746–52) for a detailed description and the research papers of Mark Shannon and Janice Kowalchuk (pp. 606–47) for illustrations.
- In history, art history, and some other humanities, use the Chicago format. See pages 681–82 and 688 for a description and illustrations.
- In psychology and other social sciences, use the format of the *Publication Manual of the American Psychological Association.* See pages 706 and 707–12 for a description and illustrations.
- In the life sciences, physical sciences, and mathematics, use the format of *Scientific Style and Format: The CBE Manual for Authors, Editors, and Publishers.* See pages 720 and 721–24 for a description and illustration.

In any discipline, you can use a computerized word processor to present your ideas effectively and attractively with readable typefaces, headings, illustrations, and other elements. See pages 749–52 for ideas and illustrations.

Before you submit your paper, proofread it carefully for typographical errors, misspellings, and other slight errors. (See p. 67 for proofreading tips.) Unless the errors are very numerous (more than several on a page), you can correct them by whiting out or crossing out (neatly) and inserting the correction (neatly) in ink (see p. 747). Don't let the pressure of a deadline prevent you from proofreading, for even minor errors can impair clarity or annoy readers and thus negate some of the hard work you have put into your project.

Exercise 12
Preparing and proofreading your final manuscript

After adding source citations and a list of works cited (Chapter 37), prepare the final draft of your research paper. Unless your instructor specifies otherwise, follow the manuscript format recommended in Appendix A. Proofread and correct the final paper before handing it in.

Chapter 37 Documenting Sources

Every time you borrow the words, facts, or ideas of others, you must acknowledge the source so that readers know you borrowed the material and know where you borrowed it from. To cite sources is to **document** them, to supply references (documents) that legitimate your use of borrowed material and support your claims about its origins. Pages 556–59 discuss in detail what kinds of information you must acknowledge.

Editors and teachers in most academic disciplines require special documentation formats (or styles) in their scholarly journals and in students' papers. This book covers four such styles:

- The formats of the Modern Language Association (MLA), used in English, foreign languages, and some other humanities (next page).
- The formats of the *Chicago Manual of Style* (*CMS*), often used in history, art, and some other humanities (p. 681).
- The formats of the American Psychological Association (APA), widely used in the social sciences (p. 693).
- The formats of the Council of Biology Editors (CBE), widely used in the sciences (p. 716).

If your instructor does not assign a particular documentation style, you may opt to consult Kate L. Turabian, *A Manual for Writers of Term Papers, Theses, and Dissertations,* 6th edition, edited by Rev. John Grossman and Alice Bennett (1996). Do follow some system for citing sources so that you provide all the necessary information in a consistent format.

37a Citing sources in your text: MLA style

As you draft your paper, you should note source information for every quotation, summary, and paraphrase. These notes and the information in your working bibliography (p. 538) should give you everything you need to write source citations.

The documentation system of the Modern Language Association is detailed in the *MLA Handbook for Writers of Research Papers,* 4th edition (1995). This style employs brief parenthetical citations within the text that direct readers to the list of works cited. For example:

```
Only one article mentions this discrepancy (Wolfe 62).
```

The name Wolfe directs readers to the article by Wolfe in the list of works cited, and the page number 62 specifies the page in the article on which the cited material appears.

The following pages describe this documentation system: what must be included in a citation (below), where to place citations (p. 580), and when to use footnotes or endnotes in addition to parenthetical citations (p. 581).

Writing parenthetical citations

The in-text citations of sources have two requirements:

- They must include just enough information for the reader to locate the appropriate source in your list of works cited.
- They must include just enough information for the reader to locate the place in the source where the borrowed material appears.

Usually, you can meet both these requirements by providing the author's last name and the page(s) in the source on which the material appears. The reader can find the source in your list of works cited and find the borrowed material in the source itself. Refer to the index opposite to find the form of reference for the kind of source and citation you are using.

1. Author not named in your text

When you have not already named the author in your sentence, provide the author's last name and the page number(s), with no punctuation between them, in parentheses.

Index to MLA parenthetical citations


```
One researcher concludes that "women impose a distinc-
tive construction on moral problems, seeing moral
dilemmas in terms of conflicting responsibilities"
(Gilligan 105).
```

2. Author named in your text

If the author's name is already given in your text, you need not repeat it in the parenthetical citation. The citation gives just the page number(s).

```
One researcher, Carol Gilligan, concludes that "women
impose a distinctive construction on moral problems,
seeing moral dilemmas in terms of conflicting responsi-
bilities" (105).
```

3. A work with two or three authors

If the source has two or three authors, give all their names in the text or in the citation:

```
As Frieden and Sagalyn observe, "The poor and the
minorities were the leading victims of highway and
renewal programs" (29).
```

```
According to one study, "The poor and the minorities
were the leading victims of highway and renewal pro-
grams" (Frieden and Sagalyn 29).
```

4. A work with more than three authors

If the source has more than three authors, you may list all their last names or use only the first author's name followed by "et al."

(the abbreviation for the Latin "and others"). The choice depends on what you do in your list of works cited (see p. 585).

> Lester Pearson was awarded the Nobel Peace Prize for proposing the creation of the United Nations peacekeeping forces (Logan et al. 432).

> Lester Pearson was awarded the Nobel Peace Prize for proposing the creation of the United Nations peacekeeping forces (Logan, Gold, McVey, and Wlosek 432).

5. An entire work (no page numbers)

When you cite an entire work rather than a part of it, the reference will not include any page number. If the author's name appears in the text, no parenthetical reference is needed. But remember that the source must appear in the list of works cited.

> Boyd deals with the need to acknowledge and come to terms with our fear of nuclear technology.

6. A multivolume work

If you consulted only one volume of a multivolume work, your list of works cited will indicate as much (see pp. 587–88), and you can treat the volume as any book. If you consulted more than one volume, give the appropriate volume in your text citation.

> After issuing the Emancipation Proclamation, Lincoln said, "What I did, I did after very full deliberations, and under a very heavy and solemn sense of responsibility" (5: 438).

The number 5 indicates the volume from which the quotation was taken; the number 438 indicates the page number in that volume. If you are referring generally to an entire volume of a multivolume work and are not citing specific page numbers, add the abbreviation "vol." before the volume number, as in `(vol. 5)`. Then readers will not misinterpret the volume number as a page number.

7. A work by an author of two or more works

If your list of works cited includes two or more works by the same author, then your citation must tell the reader which of the author's works you are referring to. Use the appropriate title or a shortened version of it in the parenthetical citation.

> At about age seven, children begin to use appropriate gestures with their stories (Gardner, Arts 144-45).

The title *Arts* is shortened from Gardner's full title, *The Arts and Human Development*. Often, as here, the first main word in the title is enough to direct the reader to the appropriate source.

8. An unsigned work

Anonymous works are alphabetized by title in the list of works cited. In the text they are referred to by full or shortened title.

```
One article notes that young offenders generally
benefit more form personal counselling and vocational
training ("Future").
```

This citation refers to an unsigned article titled "Future Offenders." A page number is unnecessary because the article is no longer than a page (see the entry for the article on p. 592).

9. A government document or a work with a corporate author

If the author of the work is listed as a government body or a corporation, cite the work by that organization's name. If the name is long, work it into the text to avoid an intrusive parenthetical citation.

```
A 1996 report by Statistics Canada predicts a marked
increase in the number of home workplaces (22).
```

10. An indirect source

When you quote or paraphrase one source's quotation of someone else, your citation must indicate as much. In the following citation "qtd. in" ("quoted in") says that Davino was quoted by Boyd.

```
George Davino maintains that "even small children have
vivid ideas about nuclear energy" (qtd. in Boyd 22).
```

The list of works cited then includes only Boyd (the work consulted), not Davino.

11. A literary work

Novels, plays, and poems are often available in many editions, so your instructor may ask you to provide information that will help readers find the passage you cite no matter what edition they consult. For novels, the page number comes first, followed by a semicolon and then information on the appropriate part or chapter of the work.

```
Toward the end of James's novel, Maggie suddenly feels
"the thick breath of the definite--which was the
```

intimate, the immediate, the familiar, as she hadn't had them for so long" (535; pt. 6, ch. 41).

For poems, you can omit the page number and supply the line number(s) for the quotation. To prevent confusion with page numbers, precede the numbers with "line" or "lines" in the first citation; then just use the numbers.

In Shakespeare's Sonnet 73 the speaker identifies with the trees of late autumn, "Bare ruined choirs, where late the sweet birds sang" (line 4). "In me," Shakespeare writes, "thou seest the glowing of such fire / That on the ashes of his youth doth lie" (9-10).

For verse plays, omit a page number and cite the appropriate act (and scene, if any) plus the line number(s). Use Arabic numerals for acts and scenes (3.4) unless your instructor specifies Roman numerals (III.iv).

Later in King Lear Shakespeare has the disguised Edgar say, "The prince of darkness is a gentleman" (3.4.147).

For prose plays, provide the page number followed by the act and scene, if any (see the reference to *Death of a Salesman* opposite).

12. More than one work

If you use a parenthetical citation to refer to more than a single work, separate the references with a semicolon.

Two recent articles point out that a computer badly used can be less efficient than no computer at all (Richards 162; Gough and Hall 201).

Since long citations in the text can distract the reader, you may choose to cite several or more works in an endnote or footnote rather than in the text. See the next page.

2 Placing parenthetical citations

Generally, place a parenthetical citation at the end of the sentence in which you summarize, paraphrase, or quote a work. The citation should follow a closing quotation mark but precede the sentence punctuation. (See the examples in the previous section.)

When a citation pertains to only part of a sentence, place the citation after the borrowed material and at the least intrusive point—usually at the end of a clause.

```
Though Cousineau argues that Canadian cable companies
"did the best that could be expected" in meeting
consumer needs (33), not everyone agrees with her.
```

When a citation appears after a quotation that ends in an ellipsis mark (. . .), place the citation between the closing quotation mark and the sentence period.

```
One observer maintains that "Canadian manufacturers have
adapted well to the global economy . . ." (Honeymaayer 26).
```

When a citation appears at the end of a quotation set off from the text, place it two spaces *after* the punctuation ending the quotation. No additional punctuation is needed.

```
In Arthur Miller's Death of a Salesman, the most
poignant defence of Willie Loman comes from his wife,
Linda:
          He's not the finest character that ever
          lived.  But he's a human being, and a terri-
          ble thing is happening to him.  So attention
          must be paid.  He's not to be allowed to fall
          into his grave like an old dog.  Attention,
          attention must finally be paid to such a
          person.  (56; act 1)
```

(This citation of a play includes the act number as well as the page number. See opposite.)

See the two sample research papers starting on pages 606 and 640 for further examples of placing parenthetical references in relation to summaries, paraphrases, and quotations.

3 Using footnotes or endnotes in special circumstances

Occasionally, you may want to use footnotes or endnotes in place of parenthetical citations. If you need to refer to several sources at once, listing them in a long parenthetical citation could be intrusive. In that case, signal the citation with a numeral raised above the appropriate line of text and write a note with the same numeral to cite the sources:

TEXT At least five subsequent studies have confirmed these results.[1]

NOTE [1] Abbott and Winger 266-68; Casner 27; Hoyenga 78-79; Marino 36; Tripp, Tripp, and Walk 179-83.

You may also use a footnote or endnote to comment on a source or provide information that does not fit easily in the text:

TEXT So far, no one has succeeded in confirming these results.[2]

NOTE [2] Manter reports spending nearly a year trying to replicate the experiment, but he was never able to produce the high temperatures reported by the original experimenters (616).

In a note the raised numeral is indented five spaces and followed by a space. If the note appears as a footnote, place it at the bottom of the page on which the citation appears, set it off from the text with quadruple spacing, and single-space the note itself. If the note appears as an endnote, place it in numerical order with the other endnotes on a page between the text and the list of works cited; double-space all the endnotes. (See pp. 634–35 for examples of endnotes and the format to use in typing a page of endnotes.)

Exercise 1
Citing sources in your text

Using the preceding explanations and illustrations as a guide, prepare MLA-style text citations for your own research paper. (If you are instructed or given the option to do so, you may instead prepare citations in the style of the *Chicago Manual of Style,* p. 681; the American Psychological Association, p. 693; or the Council of Biology Editors, p. 716.)

37b Preparing the list of works cited: MLA style

In the documentation style of the *MLA Handbook,* your in-text parenthetical citations (discussed in 37a) refer the reader to complete information on your sources in a list you title "Works Cited" and place at the end of your paper. The list should include all the

Index to MLA works-cited models

Books

Periodicals

Electronic sources

Other sources

sources you quoted, paraphrased, or summarized in your paper. (If your instructor asks you to include sources you examined but did not cite, title the list "Works Consulted.")

Follow this format for the list of works cited:

- Arrange your sources in alphabetical order by the last name of the author. If an author is not given in the source, alphabetize the source by the first main word of the title (excluding *A, An,* or *The*).
- Type the entire list double-spaced (both within and between entries).
- Indent the second and subsequent lines of each entry five spaces from the left.

For examples of the works-cited format, see the papers by Mark Shannon (p. 636) and Janice Kowalchuk (p. 647).

The index on the previous page directs you to the MLA formats for specific kinds of sources you may use. The arrangement, spacing, and punctuation of information are precisely standardized to convey the most information in the least space.

NOTE You may have to combine formats for particular sources. For example, to list a work by four authors appearing in a monthly periodical, you will have to draw on model 3 ("A book with more than three authors") and model 23 ("A signed article in a monthly or bimonthly magazine"). Generally, arrange information in this order: author; title of part of book or periodical article; title of book or periodical; translator or editor; edition; volume(s) used; series title; publication information; page number(s).

Listing books

The basic format for a book includes the following elements:

```
    (1)                       (2)
Gilligan, Carol. In a Different Voice: Psychological

     Theory and Women's Development. Cambridge: Har-
                                       (3)
                                       (a)          (b)
     vard UP, 1982.
                (c)
```

1. The author's full name: the last name first, followed by a comma, and then the first name and any middle name or initial. Omit any title or degree attached to the author's name on the source, such as Dr. or Ph.D. End the name with a period and two spaces.
2. The full title of the book, including any subtitle. Underline the title, capitalize all important words (see p. 421), separate the main title and the subtitle with a colon and one space, and end the title with a period and one space. When you cite an essay, story, or poem appearing in a book, give the title, in quotation marks, before the underlined book title (see model 17, p. 588).

3. The publication information:
   a. The city of publication, followed by a colon and one space.
   b. The name of the publisher, followed by a comma. Shorten most publishers' names—in many cases to a single word. For instance, use "Knopf" for Alfred A. Knopf and "Little" for Little, Brown. For university presses, use the abbreviation "UP," as in the example.
   c. The date of publication, ending with a period.

All this information can be found on the title page of the book or on the page after the title page. When other information is required for a reference, it is generally placed either between the author's name and the title or between the title and the publication information, as specified in the models below.

1. A BOOK WITH ONE AUTHOR

`Gilligan, Carol. In a Different Voice: Psychological Theory and Women's Development. Cambridge: Harvard UP, 1982.`

2. A BOOK WITH TWO OR THREE AUTHORS

`Knudsten, Peter, and David Suzuki. Wisdom of the Elders. Toronto: Stoddard, 1992.`

Give the authors' names in the order provided on the title page. Reverse the first and last names of the first author *only,* and separate the authors' names with a comma.

3. A BOOK WITH MORE THAN THREE AUTHORS

`Logan, John B., et al. Canada on the World Stage. Toronto: Pathfinder, 1983.`

You may, but need not, give all authors' names if the work has more than three authors. If you choose not to give all names, provide the name of the first author only, and follow the name with a comma and the abbreviation "et al." (for the Latin *et alii,* meaning "and others").

4. TWO OR MORE WORKS BY THE SAME AUTHOR

`Frye, Northrop. The Bush Garden: Essays on the Canadian Imagination. Toronto: Anansi, 1971.`

`---. The Educated Imagination. Toronto: Canadian Broadcasting, 1963.`

Give the author's name only in the first entry. For the second and any subsequent works by the same author, substitute three hyphens for the author's name, followed by a period and two spaces. Within the set of entries for the author, list the sources alphabetically by the first main word of the title. Note that the three hyphens stand for *exactly* the same name or names. If the second source above were by Frye and somebody else, both names would have to be given in full.

5. A BOOK WITH AN EDITOR

Lochhead, D., ed. Made in Canada: New Poems. Ottawa: Oberon, 1970.

The abbreviation "ed.," separated from the name by a comma, identifies Lochhead as the editor of the work.

6. A BOOK WITH AN AUTHOR AND AN EDITOR

Richardson, John. Wacousta, or The Prophecy: A Tale of the Canadas. Ed. Douglas Cronk. Ottawa: Ottawa UP, 1987.

When citing the work of the author, give his or her name first, and give the editor's name after the title, preceded by "Ed." ("Edited by"). When citing the work of the editor, use model 5 for a book with an editor, and give the author's name after the title preceded by "By": Cronk, Douglas, ed. Wacousta, or The Prophecy: A Tale of the Canadas. By John Richardson."

7. A TRANSLATION

Trudeau, P. E. Approaches to Politics. Trans. I. M. Owen. Toronto: Oxford UP, 1970.

When citing the work of the author, give his or her name first, and give the translator's name after the title, preceded by "Trans." ("Translated by"). When citing the work of the translator, give his or her name first, followed by a comma and "trans."; and after the title give the author's name after "By": Owen, I. M., trans. Approaches to Politics. By P. E. Trudeau."

8. A BOOK WITH A CORPORATE AUTHOR

Lorenz, Inc. Research in Social Studies Teaching. Baltimore: Arrow, 1992.

List the name of the corporation, institution, or other body as author.

9. An anonymous book

Merriam-Webster's Collegiate Dictionary. 10th ed. Springfield: Merriam-Webster, 1993.

List the book under its title. Do not use "anonymous" or "anon."

10. A later edition

Bollinger, Dwight L. Aspects of Language. 2nd ed. New York: Harcourt, 1975.

For any edition after the first, place the edition number between the title and the publication information. Use the appropriate designation for editions that are named or dated rather than numbered—for instance, "Rev. ed." for "Revised edition."

11. A republished book

James, Henry. The Golden Bowl. 1904. London: Penguin, 1966.

Place the original date of publication (but not the place of publication or the publisher's name) after the title, and then provide the full publication information for the source you are using.

12. A book with a title in its title

Eco, Umberto. Postscript to The Name of the Rose. Trans. William Weaver. New York: Harcourt, 1983.

When a book's title contains another book title (as here: The Name of the Rose), do not underline the shorter title. When a book's title contains a quotation or the title of a work normally placed in quotation marks, keep the quotation marks and underline both titles: Critical Response to Henry James's "Beast in the Jungle." (Note that the underlining extends under the closing quotation mark.)

13. A work in more than one volume

Lincoln, Abraham. The Collected Works of Abraham Lincoln. Ed. Roy P. Basler. 8 vols. New Brunswick: Rutgers UP, 1953.

Lincoln, Abraham. The Collected Works of Abraham Lincoln. Ed. Roy P. Basler. Vol. 5. New Brunswick: Rutgers UP, 1953. 8 vols.

If you use two or more volumes of a multivolume work, give the work's total number of volumes before the publication information ("8 vols.") in the first example. Your text citation will indicate which volume you are citing (see p. 578). If you use only one volume, give that volume number before the publication information ("Vol. 5" in the second example). You may add the total number of volumes to the end of the entry ("8 vols." in the second example).

14. A work in a series

Newman, Peter C. The Distemper of Our Times. Carleton Library Ser. Toronto: McClelland, 1978.

Place the name of the series (no quotation marks or underlining) after the title.

15. Published proceedings of a conference

Watching Our Language: A Conference Sponsored by the Program in Architecture and Design Criticism. 6-8 May 1994. New York: Parsons School of Design, 1994.

Whether in or after the title of the conference, supply information about who sponsored the conference, when it was held, and who published the proceedings. If you are citing a particular presentation at the conference, treat it as a selection from an anthology (model 17).

16. An anthology

Martin, Richard, ed. The New Urban Landscape. New York: Rizzoli, 1990.

When citing an entire anthology, give the name of the editor (followed by "ed.") and then the title of the anthology.

17. A selection from an anthology

Brooks, Rosetta. "Streetwise." The New Urban Landscape. Ed. Richard Martin. New York: Rizzoli, 1990.38-39.

Give the author and the title of the selection you are citing, placing the title in quotation marks and ending it with a period. Then give the title of the anthology. If the anthology has an editor, add the name after "Ed.," as above. At the end of the entry, give the inclusive page numbers for the entire selection, but do not include the abbreviation "pp."

If the work you cite comes from a collection of works by one author and with no editor, use the following form:

Klein, A. M. "Portrait of the Poet as Landscape." The Collected Poems of A. M. Klein. Toronto: McGraw, 1974. 330-35.

If the work you cite was previously printed elsewhere, provide the complete information for the earlier publication of the piece, followed by "Rpt. in" ("Reprinted in") and the information for the source in which you found the piece.

Gibian, George. "Traditional Symbolism in Crime and Punishment." PMLA 70 (1955): 979-96. Rpt. in Crime and Punishment. By Feodor Dostoevsky. Ed. George Gibian. Norton Critical Editions. New York: Norton, 1964. 575-92.

18. Two or more selections from the same anthology

Brooks, Rosetta. "Streetwise." Martin 38-39.

Martin, Richard, ed. The New Urban Landscape. New York: Rizzoli, 1990.

Plotkin, Mark J. "Tropical Forests and the Urban Landscape." Martin 50-51.

When citing more than one selection from the same source, avoid unnecessary repetition by giving the source in full (as in the Martin entry) and then simply cross-referencing it in entries for the works you used. Thus, instead of full information for the Brooks and Plotkin articles, give Martin's name and the appropriate pages in his book. Note that each entry appears in its proper alphabetical place among other works cited.

19. An introduction, preface, foreword, or afterword

McLuhan, Marshall. Introduction. The Bias of Communication. By Harold Innis. Toronto: U of Toronto P, 1954. vii-xvi.

An introduction, foreword, or afterword is often written by someone other than the book's author. When citing such a work, give its name without quotation marks or underlining. Follow the title of the book with its author's name preceded by "By." Give the inclusive page numbers of the part you cite. (In the example above, the small Roman numerals indicate that the cited work is in the front matter of the book, before page 1.)

When the author of a preface or introduction is the same as the author of the book, give only the last name after the title:

Gould, Stephen Jay. Prologue. The Flamingo's Smile: Reflections in Natural History. By Gould. New York: Norton, 1985. 13-20.

20. An encyclopedia or almanac

"Mammoth." The Columbia Encyclopedia. 1993.

Mark, Herman F. "Polymers." Encyclopaedia Britannica: Macropaedia. 1974.

Give the name of an author only when the article is signed; otherwise, give the title first. If the articles are alphabetized in the reference work, you needn't list the editors of the work itself or any page numbers. For familiar sources like those in the examples, full publication information is not needed. Just provide the year of publication.

Listing periodicals: Journals, magazines, and newspapers

The basic format for an article from a periodical includes the following information:

①
Lever, Janet.
②
"Sex Differences in the Games Children Play."
③
Social Problems (a) 23 (b) (1976): (c) 478-87. (d)

1. The author's full name: last name first, followed by a comma, and then the first name and any middle name or initial. Omit any title or degree attached to the author's name on the source, such as Dr. or Ph.D. End the name with a period and one space.
2. The full title of the article, including any subtitle. Place the title in quotation marks, capitalize all important words in the title (see p. 421), and end the title with a period (inside the final quotation mark) and one space.
3. The publication information:

    a. The underlined title of the periodical (minus any *A, An,* or *The* at the beginning).
    b. The volume or issue number (in Arabic numerals). See the note following.
    c. The date of publication, followed by a colon and a space. See the note following.
    d. The inclusive page numbers of the article (without the abbreviation "pp."). For the second number in inclusive page numbers over 100, provide only as many digits as needed

for clarity (usually two): 87–88, 100–01, 1026–36, 1190–206, 398–401.

NOTE The treatment of volume and issue numbers and publication dates varies depending on the kind of periodical being cited, as the models indicate. For the distinction between journals and magazines, see page 527.

21. A signed article in a journal with continuous pagination throughout the annual volume

Lever, Janet. "Sex Differences in the Games Children Play." <u>Social Problems</u> 23 (1976): 478-87.

Some journals number the pages of issues consecutively throughout a year, so that each issue after the first in a year begins numbering where the previous issue left off—say, at page 132 or 416. For this kind of journal, give the volume number after the title ("23" in the example above) and place the year of publication in parentheses. The page numbers will be enough to guide readers to the appropriate issue.

22. A signed article in a journal that pages issues separately or that numbers only issues, not volumes

Dacey, June. "Management Participation in Corporate Buy-Outs." <u>Management Perspectives</u> 7.4 (1994): 20-31.

Some journals page each issue separately (starting each issue at page 1). For these journals, give the volume number, a period, and the issue number (as in "7.4" in the Dacey entry above). Then readers know which issue of the periodical to consult. When citing an article in a journal that numbers only issues, not annual volumes, treat the issue number as if it were a volume number, as in model 21.

23. A signed article in a monthly or bimonthly magazine

McKenna, Brian. "Comrades-in-Arms." <u>Saturday Night</u> Dec. 1993: 38-41

Follow the magazine title with the month (abbreviated) and the year of publication. Don't place the date in parentheses, and don't provide a volume or issue number.

24. A signed article in a weekly or biweekly magazine

Chisholm, Patricia. "Tycoon of the Tube." <u>Maclean's</u> 27 Nov. 1995: 36-38.

Follow the magazine title with the day, the month (abbreviated), and the year of publication. Don't place the date in parentheses, and don't provide a volume or issue number.

25. A SIGNED ARTICLE IN A DAILY NEWSPAPER

Delacourt, Susan. "The 905 Revolution." Globe and Mail 25 Nov. 1995: D1.

Give the name of the newspaper as it appears on the first page (but without *A, An,* or *The*). Then follow model 24, with one difference if the newspaper is divided into lettered or numbered sections, with each section paged separately. In that case, provide the section designation before the page number when the newspaper does the same (as in "D5" above), or provide the section designation before the colon when the newspaper does not combine the two in its numbering (as in "sec. 1: 1+" below).

26. AN UNSIGNED ARTICLE

"The Right to Die." Time 11 Oct. 1976: 101.

"Regional Development Top Priority." Calgary Herald 19 May 1983, sec. 1: 1+.

Begin the entry for an unsigned article with the title of the article. The page number "1+" indicates that the article does not run on consecutive pages but starts on page 1 and continues later in the issue.

27. AN EDITORIAL OR LETTER TO THE EDITOR

"Keeping Choice on the TV Dial." Editorial. Montreal Gazette 21 Nov. 1995: B2.

Don't use quotation marks or underlining for the word "Editorial." For a signed editorial, give the author's name first.

Dowding, Michael. Letter. Economist 5-11 Jan. 1985: 4.

Don't use quotation marks or underlining for the word "Letter."

28. A REVIEW

Buitenhuis, Peter. "The Wilds of the Past." Rev. of Friend of My Youth, by Alice Munro. Books in Canada May 1990: 19-22.

"Rev." is an abbreviation for "Review." The name of the author of the work being reviewed follows the title of the work, a comma, and "by." If the review has no title of its own, then "Rev. of . . ." (without quotation marks) immediately follows the name of the reviewer.

29. An abstract of a dissertation

```
Steciw, Steven K. "Alterations to the Pessac Project of
     Le Corbusier." U of Cambridge, England. DAI 46
     (1986): 565C.
```

For an abstract appearing in *Dissertation Abstracts* (*DA*) or *Dissertation Abstracts International* (*DAI*), give the author's name and the title, "Diss." (for "Dissertation"), the institution granting the author's degree, and the publication information.

3 Listing electronic sources

MLA formats for electronic sources vary according to the medium (for instance, CD-ROM or online) and whether the source is also published in print. The *MLA Handbook* does not include particular formats for some online sites that you may find useful, so this section supplements MLA style with models endorsed by the Alliance for Computers and Writing (pp. 596–98).

Note Try to locate all the information required in the following models, so that your readers can trace your sources with minimal difficulty. However, if you search for and still cannot find some information, then give what you can find.

30. Electronic mail or a public posting

```
       (1)              (2)               (3)
Millon, Michele. E-mail to the author. 4 May 1997.
```

For e-mail, give the name of the writer (1); describe the transmission, including whom it was sent to (2); and provide the date of posting (3).

For an online posting on a bulletin board or discussion group, such as a Listserv or Usenet newsgroup, provide the author's name (1); the title (2); the date of posting (3); the words "Online posting" (4), without quotation marks or underlining; the name of the bulletin board or group (5); the name of the network (6); and the date of your access to the posting (7):

```
       (1)                     (2)                   (3)
Cramer, Sherry. "Recent Investment Practices." 26 Mar. 1997.
           (4)                      (5)                 (6)
     Online posting. Newsgroup biz.investment.current. Usenet.
         (7)
     3 Apr. 1997.
```

Note that you may have to correspond with the author directly to obtain his or her name. See page 544.

The following model includes (after "Available") the electronic address needed to reach a retrievable source. As discussed on page 596, the address is optional in MLA style: you may add it if your instructor requires it.

> Tourville, Michael. "European Currency Reform." 6 Jan. 1997. Online posting. International Finance Discussion List. Bitnet. 23 Feb. 1997. Available infin@weg.isu.edu.

31. A source on CD-ROM

A periodical CD-ROM with information for a print version:

> Ramirez, Anthony. "Computer Groups Plan Standards." New York Times 14 Dec. 1993, late ed.: D5. New York Times Ondisc. CD-ROM. UMI-ProQuest. June 1994.

If you are citing a source on CD-ROM that's issued periodically (like a journal or magazine), look for information about a print version of the same source. (The information is usually at the beginning of the source.) If there is such information, provide it as in the model above (1), referring to pages 590–93 as needed. Then provide the following information on the CD-ROM version, separating the elements with periods: the title of the CD-ROM (2), underlined; the medium, "CD-ROM" (3), without underlining or quotation marks; the name of the distributor (or vendor) of the CD-ROM (4); and the date of electronic publication (5).

For an abstract of an article or dissertation on CD-ROM, adapt model 29 (p. 593). Provide full information for the article or dissertation and then information for the CD-ROM abstract:

> Steciw, Steven K. "Alterations to the Pessac Project of Le Corbusier." Diss. U. of Cambridge, England, DAI 46 (1986): 565C. Dissertation Abstracts Ondisc. CD-ROM. UMI-ProQuest. Oct. 1992.

A periodical CD-ROM without information for a print version:

> "Vanguard Forecasts." Jan. 1997. Business Outlook. CD-ROM. Information Access. Mar. 1997.

If a source appears only on CD-ROM (not also in print), replace the print publication information with any date for the source (1), set off with periods. Then continue as in the Ramirez model above.

A nonperiodical CD-ROM:

> Shelley, Mary Wollstonecraft. Frankenstein. Classic Library. CD-ROM. Alameda: Andromeda, 1993.

If you cite a single-issue CD-ROM, treat it as a book or a part of a book (pp. 584–90), with these exceptions: after the author (1) and source title (2), give the title of the CD-ROM (3), underlined, and the medium, "CD-ROM" (4), without quotation marks or underlining. Then continue as for a book with the CD-ROM's place of publication, publisher, and date of publication (5). Here is another example, this one without an author and with a reference to a part of the source (in quotation marks):

"Sugar." Concise Columbia Encyclopedia. 3rd ed. Microsoft Bookshelf. 1996-97 ed. CD-ROM. Redmond: Microsoft, 1996.

32. A SOURCE ON DISKETTE OR MAGNETIC TAPE

Project Scheduler 8000. Ver. 3.1. (1) Diskette. (2) Tacoma: Scitor, 1997.

Treat a source on diskette or magnetic tape as you would a book (pp. 584–90), except after the title add any version number (1), which corresponds to a book's edition number, and add the medium, either "Diskette" or "Magnetic tape" (2), without quotation marks or underlining.

33. AN ONLINE SOURCE FROM A COMPUTER SERVICE

A source from a computer service with information for a print version:

Ramirez, Anthony. "Computer Groups Plan Standards." New York Times 14 Dec. 1993, late ed.: D5. (1) New York Times Online. (2) Online. (3) Nexis. (4) 16 July 1994. (5)

Sources available from computer services—such as Dialog, Nexis, and Lexis—are often also published in print. Look for information about a print version at the beginning of the source. If you find it, provide it first (1), following the models for books and articles on pages 584–93. Then provide the following information for the online version, separating the elements with periods: the title of the database you're using (2), underlined; the medium, "Online" (3), without quotation marks or underlining; the name of the service (4), not underlined; and the date you consulted the source (5).

A source from a computer service without information for a print version:

"Vanguard Forecasts." Jan. 1997. (1) Business Outlook. Online. America Online. 27 Mar. 1997.

If print publication information is not available for your source, substitute the date given for the source (1), set off with periods. Then continue as for an online source with print information, above.

34. AN ONLINE SOURCE FROM A COMPUTER NETWORK

An electronic text:

Austen, Jane. Emma. Ed. Ronald Blythe. Harmondsworth: Penguin, 1972. Online. Oxford Text Archive. Internet. 15 Dec. 1994. Available ftp://black.ox.ac.uk.

For a text such as a novel or a historical document available over a computer network, provide the original source information (1) followed by these elements: the medium, "Online" (2), without quotation marks or underlining; the repository of the text (3); the name of the network (4); and the date you consulted the source (5). After the word "Available," you may also provide the electronic address for the source (6). MLA considers the address optional, depending on your instructor's wishes; but you will not be wrong to include it, and it can help readers trace your electronic sources.

NOTE If you include an electronic address and must break it from one line to the next, do not divide words or add any hyphen that is not part of the address. Break addresses *before* periods and *after* slashes, as in several of the examples on the next two pages.

An electronic journal or newsletter:

Palfrey, Andrew. "Choice of Mates in Identical Twins." Modern Psychology 4.1 (1996): 12 pars. Online. Internet. 25 Feb. 1996. Available ftp://modpsy.liasu.edu/palfrey4(1).txt.

For an electronic journal or newsletter, use a model from pages 590–93 for a printed periodical article (1), up to the page numbers (2). For these, substitute the length given by the source in pages (for instance, "5 pp.") or in paragraphs (for instance, "12 pars.," as above)—or say "n. pag.," for "no pagination," if the length is not given. After the length and a period, add the following: the medium, "Online" (3), without quotation marks or underlining; the network name (4); the date of your access to the source (5); and the electronic address (6) if you choose or are required to provide it.

35. ACW MODELS FOR ONLINE SOURCES

To supplement MLA models for online sources, Janice Walker of the University of South Florida prepared styles that have been endorsed by the Alliance for Computers and Writing (ACW). The ACW models are based on MLA style, with a few important differences:

- The medium (such as "Online") and the name of the network (such as "Internet") are omitted. The access mode (such as "http") is evident from the electronic address.

- The electronic address always appears in the entry, but not preceded by the word "Available."
- The address includes only the punctuation needed to reach the source; for example, there's no final period if it's not part of the address. See below for how to break an address from one line to the next.
- The date on which you consulted the source falls at the end of the entry, in parentheses.

Note Ask your instructor whether you should use these ACW models or try to adapt the MLA models on pages 593–96 to your particular online sources.

A site on the World Wide Web:

```
Still, Lucia. "On the Battlefields of Business, Millions of Casual-
     ties." New York Times 3 Mar. 1996. http://www.nytimes.com/
     specials/downsize/03down1.html (17 Aug. 1996).
```

Give the author's name (1); the title (2), in quotation marks; the title of the periodical or other full source (3), underlined; the date of posting (4), if available; the electronic address (5); and the date you consulted the source (6), in parentheses.

An FTP (File Transfer Protocol) site:

```
Clarke, Kirsty. "A 'Near' Contract Experience." E Law--Murdoch
     Electronic Journal of Law. ftp://infolib.murdoch.edu.au/pub/
     subj/law/jnl/elaw/comment/clarke.txt (29 Feb. 1996).
```

Give the author's name (1); the source title (2), in quotation marks; the title of the periodical or other full source (3), underlined; the FTP address (4), including the path needed to obtain the file; and the date you consulted the source (5), in parentheses. Add the date of the source after the full title if it differs from the date of your access.

A Telnet site:

```
Johnson, Earl. "My House: Come On In." Houses of Cyberspace.
     7 Aug. 1996. telnet://edwin.ohms.bookso.com 7777 @go
     #50827, press 10 (11 Aug. 1996).
```

Provide the author's name (1); the source title (2), if available, in quotation marks; the title of the periodical or other full source (3), underlined; the date of the source (4), if available; the Telnet address (5), including information needed to reach the document; and the date you consulted the source (6), in parentheses.

A Gopher site:

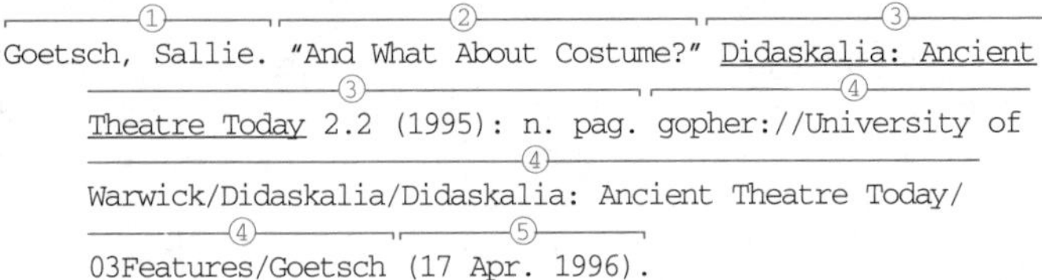

Goetsch, Sallie. "And What About Costume?" Didaskalia: Ancient Theatre Today 2.2 (1995): n. pag. gopher://University of Warwick/Didaskalia/Didaskalia: Ancient Theatre Today/ 03Features/Goetsch (17 Apr. 1996).

Give the author's name (1); the title of the source (2), in quotation marks; other publication information (3), such as periodical title, volume and issue numbers, date of publication, and pagination; the Gopher address (4), including the path needed to reach the document; and the date you consulted the source (5), in parentheses.

A synchronous communication (IRC, MUD, MOO):

Chartreuse_Guest. Tuesday cafe session. gopher://logos.daedalus .com:70/11/Alliance for Computers and Writing/NETORIC/ Tuesday Cafe log 13Feb. (7 Mar. 1996).

Chipault, Dorothy. Personal interview. telnet://hero.village .virginia.edu:7007 (1 July 1996).

Give the author's name (1); the nature of the communication (2); the address (3); and the date (4), in parentheses.

4 Listing other sources

36. A GOVERNMENT DOCUMENT

Ontario. Royal Commission on Learning. For the Love of Learning. Toronto: Queen's Printer for Ontario, 1994.

Canada. Parliamentary Committee on Equality Rights. Equality for All. 33rd Parl., 1st sess. Ottawa: Queen's Printer for Canada, 1984-85.

Unless an author is listed for a government document, give the appropriate agency as author. Begin with the name of the government, then the name of the agency (which may be abbreviated), then the title and publication information. For a parliamentary document (second example), give the committee involved before the title, and give the number and session of Parliament after the title.

37. A PAMPHLET

<u>Medical Answers About AIDS</u>. New York: Gay Men's Health Crisis, 1994.

Most pamphlets can be treated as books. In the example above, the pamphlet has no listed author, so the title comes first. If the pamphlet has an author, list his or her name first, followed by the title and publication information as given here.

38. AN UNPUBLISHED DISSERTATION OR THESIS

Howlett, Linda G. "Narratives of the Franklin Expedition." Diss. U of Saskatchewan, 1971.

The title is quoted rather than underlined. "Diss." stands for "Dissertation." "U of Saskatchewan" is the institution that granted the author's degree.

39. A MUSICAL COMPOSITION OR WORK OF ART

Mozart, Wolfgang Amadeus. Piano Concerto no. 20 in D Minor, K. 466.

Don't underline musical compositions identified only by form, number, and key. Do underline titled operas, ballets, and compositions (<u>Carmen</u>, <u>Sleeping Beauty</u>).

Sargent, John Singer. <u>Venetian Doorway</u>. Metropolitan Museum of Art, New York.

Underline the title of a work of art. Include the name and location of the institution housing the work.

40. A FILM OR VIDEOTAPE

Spielberg, Steven, dir. <u>Schindler's List</u>. Perf. Liam Neeson and Ben Kingsley. Universal, 1993.

Start with the name of the individual whose work you are citing. (If you are citing the work as a whole, start with the title, as in the next example.) Give additional information (writer, lead actors, and so on) as seems appropriate. For a film, end with the film's distributor and date.

<u>Serenade</u>. Chor. George Balanchine. Perf. San Francisco Ballet. Dir. Hilary Bean. 1981. Video-cassette. PBS Video, 1987.

For a videotape, filmstrip, or slide program, include the original release date (if any) and the medium (without underlining or quotation marks) before the distributor's name.

41. A television or radio program

"Swift Kick in the Year End." With Bob Robertson and Linda Cullen. Double Exposure. CBC. CBFT, Vancouver. 31 Dec. 1995.

As in model 40, start with the title of the program or the name of the individual whose work you are citing, and provide other participants' names as seems appropriate. Also give the series title (if any), the broadcasting network (if any), and the local station, city, and date.

42. A performance

The Duchess of Malfi. By John Webster. Dir. William Lloyd Scriven. The Elizabethan and Jacobean Players, Toronto. 18 Mar. 1991.

Ozawa, Seiji, cond. Boston Symphony Orch. Concert. Symphony Hall, Boston. 25 Apr. 1991.

As with films and television programs, place the title first unless you are citing the work of an individual (second example). Provide additional information about participants after the title, as well as the theatre, city, and date. Note that the orchestra concert in the second example is neither quoted nor underlined.

43. A recording

Mitchell, Joni. For the Roses. Asylum, 1972.

Brahms, Johannes. Concerto no. 2 in B-flat, op. 83. Perf. Artur Rubinstein. Cond. Eugene Ormandy. Philadelphia Orch. RCA, 1972.

Begin with the name of the individual whose work you are citing. Then provide the title of the recording (first example) or the title of the work recorded (second example), the names of any artists not already listed, the manufacturer of the recording, the catalogue number, and the date.

44. A letter

Montgomery, Lucy Maud. Letter to Ephraim Weber. 2 March 1908. In Green Gables Letters: From Lucy Maud Montgomery to Ephraim Weber. Ed. Wilfrid Eggleston. Toronto: Ryerson, 1960. 61-64.

A published letter is listed under the writer's name. Specify that the source is a letter and to whom it was addressed, and give the date on which it was written. The remaining information is treated like that for an edited book. (See also model 27, p. 592, for the format of a letter to the editor of a periodical.)

James, Jonathan E. Letter to his sister. 16 Apr. 1970. Jonathan E. James Papers. South Dakota State Archive, Pierre.

For a letter in the collection of a library or archive, specify the writer, recipient, and date, as above, and give the name and location of the archive as well.

Packer, Ann E. Letter to the author. 15 June 1994.

For a letter you receive, give the name of the writer, note the fact that the letter was sent to you, and provide the date of the letter.

45. A LECTURE OR ADDRESS

Carlone, Dennis J. "Urban Design in the 1990s." Sixth Symposium on Urban Issues. City of Cambridge. Cambridge, 16 Oct. 1988.

Give the speaker's name, the title if known (in quotation marks), the title of the meeting, the name of the sponsoring organization, the location of the lecture, and the date. If you do not know the title, replace it with "Lecture" or "Address" but *not* in quotation marks.

46. AN INTERVIEW

Graaf, Vera. Personal interview. 19 Dec. 1993.

Martin, William. Interview. "Give Me That Big Time Religion." Frontline. PBS. WGBH, Boston. 13 Feb. 1984.

Begin with the name of the person interviewed. Then specify "Personal interview" (if you conducted the interview in person), "Telephone interview" (if you conducted the interview over the phone), or "Interview" (if you did not conduct the interview)—without quotation marks or underlining. Finally, provide a date (first example) or provide other bibliographic information and then a date (second example).

47. A MAP OR OTHER ILLUSTRATION

Women in the Armed Forces. Map. Women in the World: An International Atlas. By Joni Seager and Ann Olson. New York: Touchstone, 1992. 44-45.

List the illustration by its title (underlined). Provide a descriptive label ("Map," "Chart," "Table"), without underlining or quotation marks, and the publication information. If the creator of the illustration is credited in the source, put his or her name first in the entry, as with any author.

Exercise 2
Writing works-cited entries

Prepare works-cited entries from the following information. Follow the models of the *MLA Handbook* given in this chapter unless your instructor specifies a different style.

1. An article titled "Credit and Consumer Confidence" by Jocelyn Kim. The article appeared in volume 12, issue 4 of *Adaptation to Change,* a journal that pages issues separately. Volume 12 appeared in 1993. The article began on page 101 and ended on page 106.
2. A book called *Making a Difference: Canadian Multicultural Literature,* published in 1996 by Oxford University Press in Toronto, edited by Smaro Kambourelli.
3. An article in *English Studies in Canada,* volume 12, number 4, published in 1986. The article is "Politics and Religion in Rudy Wiebe's *The Scorched Wood People,*" written by Kenneth Hoeppner, on pages 440 through 450. The journal is paged continuously throughout the annual volume.
4. An article you consulted on March 12, 1997, over the Internet. The article is titled "The Meaning of *The Funeral Elegy*" and is by Jane Downing, Bruce Newell, and Achibo Lauro. It appears in the online journal *Shakespeare,* volume 4, issue 1, published in 1996. The article is thirty-seven paragraphs long. The address for the article is http://www.shakespeare-cambridge.com/downing.html.
5. An article on CD-ROM that is also available in print. The author is Susan Chu. The title is "1996 Election Returns May Widen Gender Gap." The article appears in the January 1997 issue of *Politics and Values,* a monthly magazine, on pages 12 through 26. It also appears on the CD-ROM titled *Resource/One,* released in March 1997 by UMI-ProQuest.

Exercise 3
Preparing your list of works cited

Prepare the final list of works cited for your research paper. Unless your instructor specifies otherwise, follow MLA style, using the models on the preceding pages.

37c Understanding abbreviations

Most disciplines' documentation styles, including that of the MLA, use as few abbreviations as possible. However, they still use some, and you may encounter many more in your reading. The most common abbreviations found in source citations appear below.

anon.	anonymous
bk., bks.	book(s)
c., ca.	*circa* ("about"), used with approximate dates
cf.	*confer* ("compare")
ch., chs.	chapter(s)
col., cols.	column(s)
comp., comps.	compiled by, compiler(s)
diss.	dissertation
ed., eds.	edited by, edition(s), editor(s)
et al.	*et alii* ("and others")
ff.	and the following pages, as in pages 17 ff.
ibid.	*ibidem* ("in the same place")
illus.	illustrated by, illustrator, illustration(s)
l., ll.	line(s)
loc. cit.	*loco citato* ("in the place cited")
ms., mss.	manuscript(s)
n., nn.	note(s), as in p. 24, n. 2
n.d.	no date (of publication)
no., nos.	number(s)
n.p.	no place (of publication), no publisher
n. pag.	no pagination
op. cit.	*opere citato* ("in the work cited")
P	Press (UP = University Press)
p., pp.	page(s)
passim	throughout
q.v.	*quod vide* ("which see")
rev.	revised, revision, revised by, review
rpt.	reprint, reprinted
sec.	section
supp., supps.	supplement(s)
trans.	translator, translated by
univ., U	university (UP = University Press)
vol., vols.	volume(s)

Chapter 38

Two Sample Research Papers

The following pages show the research papers of Mark Shannon and Janice Kowalchuk, whose work we followed in Chapters 35 and 36. (Shannon's paper begins on p. 606, Kowalchuk's on p. 640.) Both students used the documentation style recommended by the *MLA Handbook,* and both typed their papers following the advice on manuscript format in Appendix A of this handbook. Accompanying both students' papers are comments on format, content, documentation, and other matters. The more extensive comments on Shannon's paper are indexed below by text page number (*italic*) and comment number (**boldface**).

Breaking the Glass Ceiling 1

By

Mark Shannon

Prof. C. Mahoney

English 101, Section B

5 April 1997

1. **Title page format.** Provide a separate title page if your instructor requests it or if you are required to submit an outline with your paper. On his title page Shannon includes the title of his paper about a third of the way down the page, his own name (preceded by "By") about 2.5 cm (1") below the title, and, starting about the same distance below his name, some identifying information requested by his instructor (course number, section label, and instructor's name) and the date. He centres all lines in the width of the page and separates them from each other with at least one line of space. If your instructor does not require a title page for your paper, place your name, the identifying information, and the date on the first page of the paper. See Janice Kowalchuk's paper (p. 640) for this alternative format.

NEXT TWO PAGES

2. **Outline format.** If your instructor asks you to include your final outline, place it between the title page and the text, as Shannon does on the following pages. Number the pages with small Roman numerals (i, ii), and place your name just before the page numbers in case the pages of your paper become separated. Place the heading "Outline" 2.5 cm from the top of the first page, and double-space under the heading.
3. **Outline content.** Shannon includes his final thesis sentence as part of his outline so that his instructor can see how the parts relate to the whole.
4. Shannon casts his final outline in full sentences. Some instructors request topic outlines, in which ideas appear in phrases instead of in sentences and do not end with periods.
5. Notice that each main division (numbered with Roman numerals) relates to the thesis sentence and that all the subdivisions relate to their main division.

MLA
38

Shannon i

Outline 2

Thesis sentence: If women are ever to break 3
through the glass ceiling in significant numbers, business attitudes will have to change, particularly the definition of successful management styles.

I. Women face resistance from both men and 4
women in top management.
   A. Women are in a double bind: they are expected to act like men, but are criticized when they do.
   B. Women also face resistance from "queen bees," other women who are already executives.
      1. Queen bees feel that younger women should not have it any easier than they did.
      2. Queen bees interfere with working conditions, morale, and promotions.

II. Business favours a masculine management 5
style over a feminine style.
   A. Kates reports on a 1988 Toronto conference that attempted to come to critical terms with this general trend.

Shannon ii

B. Women are usually not given the option to exercise their own style.

C. When women imitate men, they are subject to sex-role stereotyping and alienation.

1. Brown and Geis found stereotyping in their study.
2. Woman executives pass around a humorous list of characteristics of businessmen versus businesswomen.
3. Loden says that women are less effective when they imitate men.

III. A feminine management style must be accepted in business if women are to make it into top management.

A. An interview with a female manager illustrates a feminine style of cooperation and participation.

B. Loden and others emphasize that a feminine management style takes account of people's emotions, an important part of their lives.

C. A feminine style of management will help not only women but business itself.

Shannon 1

Breaking the Glass Ceiling 6

"You've come a long way, baby." Most 7
people will recognize this slogan from popular cigarette advertisements, but its meaning goes beyond women's freedom to smoke in public. Nowhere are women's gains more clear than in the business world. In the United States, the
Civil Rights Act of 1964 made it illegal to 8
discriminate against women in employment. Twenty years later, women had established themselves firmly in corporations on a number of management levels. Their progress can be measured by what is expected of companies with regard to their treatment of women employees.
According to <u>Business Week</u>'s Irene Pave: 9

> Back in 1966 the mark of a good 10
> company [for women to work in] was 11
> women in at least entry-level management and other non-clerical jobs. In 1976 it was women in middle management. Today a good company has women above that level or in jobs that have remained male turf in most
> companies. (75) 12

Canada lagged more than twenty years behind its U.S. federal counterparts in developing

6. **Title.** Shannon has chosen an intriguing title, just ambiguous enough to make his audience want to read further. A more descriptive title, such as "Why Women Are Still Rare in Top Corporate Management," would also have been appropriate but less interesting. **Paper format**. The margins of the paper are 2.5 cm (1") all around. The title appears on the first page of the paper even if a title page is used. The title is typed 2.5 cm from the top of the page, and it is neither placed in quotation marks nor underlined. The first line of text is typed two lines (double space) below the title. (See Janice Kowalchuk's paper, p. 640, for the format of the first page when a title page is not required.)
7. **Introduction.** Shannon begins with a familiar sentence that calls to mind the strides women have made in the past century. He delays presenting his thesis (end of fourth full paragraph) in order to establish some background: women have indeed made inroads into some levels of management, both in the United States (this paragraph) and Canada (next two paragraphs), yet not into the highest levels (fourth paragraph). The question opening the fourth paragraph sets up the thesis at the end of that paragraph. Note that this introductory material, while quite extensive, is not summarized in the outline..
8. **Common knowledge.** Shannon did not know about the American Civil Rights Act before he began his research, but he found it referred to without documentation in a number of sources. When he realized that it was considered common knowledge, he chose, correctly, not to document it. (See 36c for further discussion of common knowledge.)
9. **Introducing quotations.** Here and elsewhere, Shannon effectively introduces his quotations: he establishes the credentials of each source in an identifying phrase; and he summarizes each source's point of view. (See 36g for a discussion of introducing quotations.)
10. **Format of long quotations.** The Pave quotation exceeds four typed lines, so Shannon sets it off from the text. Such a displayed quotation is set off by double-spacing above and below, is itself double-spaced, and is indented 2.5 cm (1") from the left margin.
11. **Adding to quotations.** Shannon inserts a clarifying phrase so that readers will understand what Pave means by a "good company." The brackets tell the reader that the phrase is added (see 25d).
12. **Reference when the author is named in the text.** Shannon has already mentioned Pave's name in the text, so he does not repeat it in the reference. **Reference with displayed quotation**. The parenthetical reference after the quotation falls *outside* the sentence period and is separated from the period by a space.

legislation to improve business opportunities for women. The Employment Equity Act of 1986 required "all federally regulated companies (banks and transport and communication companies) to set up employment equity programs and to file annual reports on the demographic composition of their workforce" (Kates 60). The first reports were due June 1, 1988. A second government initiative was the Federal Contractors Program, established about the same time, which required every company with one hundred or more employees that wanted to bid on any federal contract over $200 000 "to prove its commitment to gender and minority equity in terms of hiring, training, salary and promotions. No employee equity plan, no federal contract" (Kates 60).

Largely as a result of developments elsewhere, however, particularly in the United States, notable growth in the opportunities for Canadian women to move into management positions had already begun some years earlier. A 1988 paper by analyst Gladys Symons entitled "Women in Power: The Real Threat to Corporate Culture" reported that the percentage of women in management rose from 15 percent in 1971 to 32.3 percent by 1985. By 1993, the number was 42 percent (Powell 1). The rate of rise in numbers of senior managers was somewhat slower, moving from 3.7 percent in 1971 to just 6.4 percent in 1981 (Collins 151). Another sociological analysis, this one by Dorothy Mikolachki, also appearing in 1988, gave more recent figures that confirmed the trend described in Symons's article: "In Canada," Mikolachki noted, "the proportion of women who are in managerial and administrative jobs rose to 8.3 percent from 7.5 percent between 1984 and 1985," adding "hardly an upheaval but evidence that women continue to join the managerial ranks--in spite of an often unfavourable climate for them" (42).

Clearly, women have come far in business. But have they come far enough? The fact is, women are still rare in the highest executive positions. In the United States, they repre-
sented only 2 percent of the top executives in 13
Fortune 500 companies in 1992 (Dominguez 387).
Pave notes that "no one cites 'equal numbers 14
of men and women in top management positions'
as the mark of a good company for women. No

Shannon 4

company would qualify" (76). The situation in
Canada is just as grim. In an article appear-
ing at the end of 1988, James Fleming made the
following observation and prediction:

> . . . the business elite contains
> fewer women than any other ruling
> elite with the exception, perhaps,
> of the Catholic Church. It will be
> at least 10 or 15 years before a
> woman runs one of our 50 largest
> corporations--and that's an opti-
> mistic estimate. (54)

Despite women's persistence in both countries, a
"glass ceiling," or invisible barrier, seemingly
continues to separate women in middle and upper
management from positions in top management.[1] If 15
women are ever to break through the glass ceil-
ing in significant numbers, business attitudes
will have to change, particularly the definition
of successful management styles.

Most experts agree that the main reason 16
women have not broken through the glass
ceiling is, quite simply, that they are
women. Often these women find themselves in
a double bind. On the one hand, they face
resistance from male executives who want

13. **Paraphrasing.** Shannon paraphrases Dominguez because it is the statistic rather than the author's presentation of it that is important. For other instances of paraphrasing, see "Citing a paraphrase" (p. 617) and pages 622 and 627. **Reference when the author is not named in the text**. Because Shannon has not used Dominguez's name in the text, he provides it in the reference.
14. **Quotation within a quotation.** Since he must enclose Pave's words in double quotation marks, Shannon encloses the quotation in single quotation marks (see 24b).
15. **Using an endnote for supplementary information.** Here Shannon helps his readers by briefly defining a key term, "glass ceiling." He provides additional information about the term in a note at the end of the paper. (See p. 634.) **Thesis sentence.** Shannon's introduction has led up to his thesis sentence, which states the idea he will demonstrate in the paper.
16. **Relation to outline.** This paragraph begins part I of Shannon's outline (see p. 608). Part II begins on page 620 and part III on page 628.

their successors to be just like themselves 17
and who, therefore, will not consider women
for top-management positions (Pave 78). On
the other hand, resistance sometimes comes
from men who do not want to see women acting
the role of executive. According to Felice
Schwartz, the founder and president of
Catalyst, a firm that conducts research on
corporate women, "It goes against the grain
of most senior executives to encourage and
welcome the women, so unlike their wives,
who put career before marriage and rearing
children" (185). Thus some women are held 18
back if they behave too much like women,
while others are held back because they
behave too much like men.

As if these two problems were not
enough, women also encounter resistance from
the few women who have made it to the top.
These successful women should be acting as
mentors for those coming up behind them,
serving as role models and providing guid- 19
ance. Instead, many do just the opposite.
David Mathison, an associate professor of
business administration at Loyola Marymount
University, identifies the "queen bee

17. **Paraphrase.** Shannon paraphrases part of a quotation from Pave. His note card is shown below.

> Sexual stereotypes
>
> Pave, p. 78
>
> "Male chauvinism is most crippling to women at the great divide between upper and top management. Senior managers who always pick men for top spots want clones . . . —so women always get locked out."

Citing a paraphrase. Shannon includes Pave's name in the reference because it is not used in the text. In contrast, the reference later in the paragraph to Schwartz does *not* include the name because the text *does*.

18. **Interpreting sources.** In this summary sentence Shannon pulls together information from the two sources cited earlier in the paragraph and shows how the information relates to his point about the double bind women are in. Thus he does not force his readers to guess why he paraphrases and quotes sources, and he clears the way for the next point.

19. **Defining terms.** Shannon slips in a definition of "mentors" after the comma in this sentence. Since his audience would consist of his classmates as well as his instructor, he thought it likely that at least a few readers would not know the term. Yet he opted to abbreviate and downplay the definition in order not to offend any readers who already understood the term. The following is Shannon's edited draft of this passage.

```
These successful women should be acting as mentors/
for those coming up behind them, serving as
^ A mentor is usually an older and professionally
more advanced person who acts as a role model^s and
          ing                    . Instead, many do just the opposite.
provides guidance ^to a younger colleague who is
usually younger and subordinate. Yet often these
successful women are the opposite of mentors.
```

MLA 38

Shannon 6

syndrome": a successful woman feels threatened by the success of other women and resists them as "intrusions" into her territory (qtd. in Bozzi). 20

In a 1986 survey of executive women,
Edith Gilson, with Susan Kane, found that 21
the "queen bee" was thriving in American business: 68 percent of those responding to a questionnaire felt that "their female colleagues were 'unnecessarily competitive' with one another." Some of the respondents exhibited signs of the "queen bee syndrome." One woman declared. "I managed to climb to
my position without any special help. . . . 22
It was tough, but if I did it, why can't
other women?" (184-86). 23

Gilson and Kane emphatically warn against the dangers of this attitude among women.

> Women's undue competitiveness is a major stumbling block to their success. It keeps them awash in anger and fear when their energies could be used more constructively; sets a negative example for lower-level women: creates difficult

20. **Reference to an indirect source.** With the use of "qtd. in," Shannon indicates correctly that he obtained the information on Mathison from the article by Bozzi. **Indirect sources**. The Mathison study is important for Shannon's paper, and the information in Bozzi's article clearly indicated that it had been published in a readily available journal. Instead of relying on a brief summary in a magazine, Shannon should have gone directly to Mathison's article. Use indirect sources (and "qtd. in") only when the original material is not available for you to consult. See, for example, page 627 and comment 32, page 629.
21. **Citation of a book written with an assistant.** The word "with" appears before Kane's name on the cover and title page of the Gilson and Kane book. It indicates that Kane assisted Gilson, the researcher and principal author, probably by helping with the writing. Shannon makes this clear to his readers by using "with" as well. (See also the list of works cited, p. 636, and comment 50, p. 637.) **Introducing and citing a discussion of one work**. By mentioning the names of Gilson and Kane at the beginning of the discussion, Shannon makes it clear that what follows is from their work. The page reference at the very end of the paragraph announces that the citation covers all the intervening material. If, instead, Shannon had placed both parts of the citation together (the page reference in the first sentence or the authors' names in the last sentence), readers might be unsure of how much material the citation covered. **Mixing summary, paraphrase, and quotation**. In the rest of this paragraph, Shannon summarizes, paraphrases, and quotes from several pages of Gilson and Kane's book to give the reader a good sense of one of Gilson's findings.
22. **Editing quotations.** Shannon uses an ellipsis mark to show that he has eliminated irrelevant material from the quotation (see 25e). The ellipsis itself consists of three spaced periods. It is preceded by a sentence period closed up to the last word in the sentence, and it is followed by two spaces.
23. **Placing and punctuating parenthetical citations.** The page reference for all the Gilson and Kane material in this paragraph falls at the end of the paragraph (see comment 21). Since the final quotation ends in a question mark, the reference is followed by a separate period.

Shannon 7

> working conditions for the women
> who are its targets; diminishes
> the effectiveness of teamwork;
> and, in some cases, *actively
> inhibits career progress*. (186-87;
> emphasis added) 24

Like the male executive's reluctance to 25
promote women, the "queen bee syndrome" must
change before women can make serious inroads
into top management.

Even more significant than the atti- 26
tudes described above, however, is the
preference for a masculine rather than
feminine management style. The feminine
management styles seem to have succeeded
quite well at the middle-management level.
But the continued prevalence of the mascu-
line style of management at top levels,
along with the apparent resistance of top
managers to changing that style, is the
single most significant obstacle to women
seeking executive positions.

Characterizing the managerial style of 27
most American industrial corporations, Ann
Hughey and Eric Gelman of *Newsweek* refer to
a "paramilitary form of organization"

24. **Adding emphasis to quotations.** Shannon underlines certain words in the quotation that reinforce his thesis especially clearly. He acknowledges this change inside the parenthetical reference, separated by a semicolon from the page number.
25. **Summary statement.** For three paragraphs Shannon has been discussing the single idea of how sex discrimination by both sexes holds women back. This concluding statement ties the paragraphs together in preparation for a new section of the paper.
26. **Relation to outline.** With this paragraph Shannon begins part II of his outline (see p. 608). **Transitional paragraph**. Shannon devotes a whole paragraph to the shift in direction, briefly summing up the preceding section and then introducing his final and most important point.
27. **Using sources effectively**. In this paragraph Shannon combines material from two sources to support a single point about corporate managerial style. The two sources reinforce each other and strengthen Shannon's conclusion at the end of the paragraph.

Shannon 8

enforced by "rigid, drill-sergeant managers" (46). Marilyn Loden, the author of <u>Feminine Leadership, or, How to Succeed in Business Without Being One of the Boys</u>, borrows a term from the feminist writer Betty Friedan in noting the "masculinism" of the traditional managerial style (23). Its basic premise, Loden says, is competition: the successful manager must conquer his corporate enemies, just as he was trained for victory on the football field or the battlefield; and strategic thinking must take precedence over emotion (24-26). It is no 28
wonder that women--who have been reared to be emotional, cooperative, and generous--encounter difficulties when attempting to adapt to this style.

Despite the difficulties, women are encouraged to imitate men if they want to succeed. Loden surveyed "how to" books written during the 1970s and discovered that virtually all of them gave women exactly that advice (28). Yet women who acquire more masculine traits are then subject to stereotyping. In a 1983 test of people's reactions to videotapes of male and female leaders,

28. **Drawing conclusions**. Shannon correctly places the page reference for Loden after the paraphrase but before the conclusion he draws from the evidence. His conclusion not only spells out the significance of the preceding paragraph but also prepares for the next paragraph. However, Shannon should have found and offered evidence for his understanding that women are "reared to be emotional, cooperative, and generous." The statement may seem self-evident, but many readers would justly criticize it as just the kind of stereotype that Shannon himself is criticizing (see 4b).

Shannon 9

the psychologists Virginia Brown and Flo-
rence Geis found that "[a]lthough both 29
leaders used the same script, the woman was
faulted more than the man for being too
dominating, cold, and insensitive" (822).
Such results reveal that while sex-role
stereotyping may not be as obvious as it was
in a 1971 study (Broverman et al.), it 30
remains pervasive.

Rona Maynard calls similar attention to
this dilemma of the contradictory expecta-
tions often faced by senior women execu-
tives. In a study of what had happened after
ten years to 33 female 1978 MBA graduates
from the University of Western Ontario, she
discovered that a number of these women had
chosen either to drop out of the executive
rat race or to accept a more modest position
in the organization concerned. She summa-
rizes this conflicting pressure on senior
women managers as follows: "On the one hand,
they must demonstrate such 'masculine'
traits as toughness and independence. But if
they go too far, their lack of 'feminine'
submissiveness will unnerve co-workers"
(29). Maynard, noting that one of her

29. **Altering capitalization in quotations**. In the source the word "although" began a sentence and was capitalized. To fit the quotation smoothly into his own sentence, Shannon wanted to use a small letter. The brackets indicate that he altered the capitalization (see 26a).
30. **Reference to a work with more than three authors**. Here and in the list of works cited (see p. 636), Shannon uses "et al." ("and others") to indicate that the work had at least three other authors besides the one named. Shannon could have given all of the authors' names, too. Either form is correct as long as the list of works cited and the text references are consistent.

subjects actually gave up her management position because it required her to deny her feminine identity, concludes, "In her struggle to keep up with men, she felt she was denying her feminine side--the side that tuned in to others' feelings and resisted the ruthlessness that can be required at the top. She already hated to fire people" (29). For similar reasons only one of the ten top Canadian female executives interviewed by Anne Collins aspired to the CEO position in her company (37).

Another dimension of sex stereotyping was examined by Nina Colwill, professor of business administration at the University of Manitoba. Colwill observes that women in business tend to be typecast into one of four traditional roles: mother (the nurturer), seductress (the sex object), pet (the precocious child), or iron maiden (the tough asexual) (qtd. in Kates 63). Colwill remarks that these "guises" may make the woman executive acceptable to men, but it detracts from her competency and effectiveness.

Shannon 11

The dilemma of women is also illustrated in a list comparing businessmen and business-women that made the round of women executives several years ago.

* A businessman is aggressive; a businesswoman is pushy. 31
* A businessman is good on details: she's picky.
* He loses his temper at times because he's so involved in his work; she's temperamental.
* He knows how to follow through; she doesn't know when to quit. (qtd. in
Loden 38) 32

The humour here underlines a serious
problem. Loden observes that if a woman tries 33
to adapt to male business culture without retaining any of her feminine traits, she will end up feeling more rather than less alienated (22). But this is precisely what many women have been expected to do--and in fact have done--in order to succeed. Loden explains that "fraternity pledging"--the term she uses for the first stage of the adaptation process--"causes women to gradually deny what they truly think and feel" (32). Thus, rigid

Shannon 12

insistence on a masculine managerial style is not only detrimental in preventing many women from making it to the top but also harmful in causing those women who do make it to manage less effectively than they might.

Clearly, if business is going to benefit 34
from women's talents, it must accommodate a feminine managerial style. As Hughey and Gelman observe, "the very qualities that men have traditionally denigrated as feminine--sympathy, sensitivity, a lack of the killer instinct--may often be advantages when it comes to getting the best out of people" (46).

A case in point is a story from a woman I 35
interviewed online, Nora Crisi, who is a manager responsible for several departments in a retail organization. A subordinate of hers, Susan, refused to use the guidelines in the company manual to train her own subordinates. In debating how to handle the situation. Crisi says:

> My only real role model was my own boss, a man who kept everyone in line like a drill instructor. He would have called Susan in and given her a stern lecture, complete with

31. **Reproduction of list**. By indenting the list ten spaces like any other long quotation, Shannon indicates that it is indeed a quotation.
32. **Reference to an indirect source**. Shannon's use of "qtd. in" indicates that Loden herself quoted the list. In this case, unlike on page 618, the use of an indirect source is appropriate because the list was available only in Loden's book, not also in another readily available source. (See comment 20, p. 619.)
33. **Selective quotation**. Throughout this paragraph, Shannon chooses quotations carefully. Since he is relying heavily on Loden in this section, he does not simply report what she says but rather uses her ideas and words selectively to support his thesis.
34. **Relation to outline**. At this paragraph Shannon begins part III of his outline (see p. 609).
35. **Primary source: personal interview**. Shannon has tested his ideas by conducting an e-mail interview with a woman in a management position. He weaves together paraphrases and quotations from the interview, after obtaining Crisi's permission. He does not use a parenthetical reference because all the necessary information (Crisi's name) appears in the text.

> threats. I knew I couldn't pull that off; it wasn't my nature.

Instead, Crisi explained to Susan the necessity for common training practices and encouraged the young supervisor to offer suggestions for revising the manual if she found problems with it. Then Crisi emphasized that she would not tolerate any refusal to adhere to company policy. The result was surprising: "You know what? She *thanked* me! I'd been expecting a fight, but I think Susan saw that I respected her, and she appreciated not being treated like a
schoolgirl." Crisi's reliance on her sensi- 36
tivity, coupled with some of the firmness she had learned from her own boss, served her well in a conflict that is common between managers and subordinates.

Crisi's encouragement of feedback on the company's policy illustrates another advantage of a feminine management style: such "participative management," as it is commonly called, permits both emotional and rational assessments of and responses
to business situations.[2] Acknowledgment 37
of the importance of emotion has long

36. **Drawing conclusions**. Again, Shannon does not force readers to figure out the significance of his evidence but states plainly what he got from the interview (and what he wants readers to get).
37. **Using an endnote for supplementary information**. Shannon did not want to do more than mention the term "participative management," whose meaning he thought was clear enough from the words themselves. For readers who might want more information, he provides an endnote with a source to consult.

Shannon 14

been absent from traditional management
styles. But, in the words of Antonia Shusta, 38
an executive with Citibank, "Business is all
people and people in large degree are very
emotional. . . . If you don't understand
emotion, you're missing out on a lot" (qtd.
in Hughey and Gelman 47).

According to Marilyn Loden, "Feminine
leaders see the world through two different
lenses concurrently and, as a result,
respond to situations on both the thinking
and the feeling levels" (61). Loden does not 39
advocate substituting the feminine manage-
ment style for the masculine style (5).
Rather, she argues that business must adopt
both styles. Only then, she claims, will
women achieve true equality in the top
levels of management (277-78).

North American business has been operat- 40
ing on a masculine model since the industrial
revolution. But times have changed, and so has
the business population. Now women as well as
men must be encouraged to break through into
top management. In order for that to happen,
the "old-boy network" must be penetrated, the
"queen bee syndrome" must be cured, and old

38. **Selecting supporting evidence**. Shannon uses two separate sources here to develop his point, mixing the views of a practitioner and an expert.
39. **From note cards to paper**. Shannon wanted to use material from two widely separated passages in Loden's book, both of which he had quoted on his note cards (see below). In the paper, however, he opted for paraphrases of the quotations because he did not want to quote excessively and because he could fit the paraphrases together more smoothly than he could the quotations. Note that on the second card, Shannon inserted a check mark between "knowledge" and "feminine" to indicate the location of a page break in the original source.

Odapting management styles

Loden, p. 5

"[T] he feminine style of leaderships is not a replacement of the traditional style." "

Adapting management styles

Loden, pp. 277-78

"Equality will be achieved only when organizations acknowledge✓ feminine leadership as an acceptable alternative to the traditional style of management."

40. **Conclusion**. In his final paragraph Shannon summarizes the main points of his argument in a way that reminds readers of both what holds women back and what he thinks needs to change. The last sentence—by referring to the title and providing a vivid image—gives the paper a dramatic finish.

Shannon 15

prejudices--women's as well as men's--must be abandoned. Even more important, for women and for business itself, is the adaptation to a more flexible, feminine style of management. Only when these changes are made in business will that glass ceiling finally be broken.

Shannon 16

Notes

[1] "Glass ceiling" is commonly used in 41
articles and books about women in management.
Although I was unable to find any information 42
on the origins of the term, it appears to have
been coined just to describe the situation of
women (not men). One of the best-known exam-
ples of a work employing this term, frequently
referred to by both Canadian and American
analysts, is *Breaking the Glass Ceiling: Can
Women Reach the Top of America's Largest
Corporations?* (1987), by research staff at the
Center for Creative Leadership in Greensboro,
NC.

[2] For further information on women and 43
participative management, see "Special
Talents."

Shannon 17

Works Cited

Bozzi, Vincent. "Assertiveness Breeds Contempt." *Psychology Today* Sept. 1987: 15. 44

Broverman, I. K., et al. "Sex-Role Stereotypes: A Current Appraisal." *Journal of* 45
Social Issues 28.2 (1972): 59-78.

Brown, Virginia, and Florence Geis. "Turning
Lead into Gold: Evaluations of Women and 46
Men Leaders and the Alchemy of Social Consensus." *Journal of Personality and Social Psychology* 46 (1984): 811-24.

Canada. Statistics Canada. "Women in Canada." 47
8 Aug., 1995. Online. Internet. 26 Feb. 1997. Available http://www.statcan.ca/start.html.

Collins, Anne. "'Why We're Not Number One': A 48
Position Paper from Canada's Top Corporate women." *Canadian Business* Nov. 1988: 32-39, 141+.

Crisi, Nora. E-mail interview. 20 Feb. 1997. 49

Dominguez, Cari M. "The Glass Ceiling: Paradox and Promises." *Human Resources Management* 31 (1992): 385-92.

Fleming, James. "Powerful Women." *Report on Business Magazine*. Dec. 1988: 54.

Gilson, Edith, with Susan Kane. *Unnecessary* 50
Choices: The Hidden Life of the Executive Woman. New York: Morrow, 1987.

Hughey, Ann, and Eric Gelman. "Managing the 51
Woman's Way." *Newsweek* 17 Mar. 1986: 46-47.

Kates, Joanne. "Quiet Revolution." *Report on Business Magazine* June 1988: 58-64.

Shannon 18

Lewin, Tamar. "Women in Board Rooms Are Still 52
the Exceptions." New York Times 5 July
1984: C1.

Loden, Marilyn. Feminine Leadership, or, How 53
to Succeed in Business Without Being One
of the Boys. New York: Times Books, 1985.

Maynard, Rona. "Thanks But No Thanks: Ten
Years Ago. . . ." Report on Business Magazine Feb. 1988: 26-32, 34.

Mikolachki, Dorothy. "Women Managers Are Not
Dropping Out, but Moving Up." Editorial.
Financial Times of Canada 6 June 1988: 42.

Pave, Irene. "A Woman's Place Is at GE. Federal Express, P&G. . . ." Business Week
23 June 1986: 75+.

Powell, Gary N. Women in Management. 2nd ed.
Newbury Park: Sage, 1993.

Schwartz, Felice N. "Don't Write Women Off as
Leaders." Fortune 8 June 1987: 185+.

"The Special Talents Women Bring to Partic-
ipative Management." International Man- 54
agement Aug. 1986: 60.

41. **Format of notes**. The word "Notes" is centred 2.5 cm (1") from the top of the page. (The heading would be singular—"Note"—if Shannon had not had more than one note.) The notes begin two lines (one double space) below the heading. The notes themselves are double-spaced. The first line of each is indented 2.5 cm and preceded by a raised number corresponding to the number used in the text. A space separates the number and the note.
42. **Endnotes for additional relevant information**. Shannon's first note provides readers with background information on a definition. His second note refers interested readers to an article on participative management.
43. **Reference to an unsigned article**. Since Shannon is referring to an unsigned article, he uses a shortened form of the title for his citation. Since the article is only one page, he does not include the page number. See the entry for this work in the list of works cited, page 638.
44. **Format of list of works cited.** The heading "Works Cited" is centred 2.5 cm (1") from the top of the page. The first entry is typed two lines (one double space) below the heading, and the entire list is double-spaced. The first line of each entry begins at the left margin; subsequent lines of the same entry are indented 1.25 cm. The entries are alphabetized. **Note**: Some instructors ask students to use the heading "Works Consulted" rather than "Works Cited." Such a list would include all of the sources used with profit during the course of the research project, not just the ones to which the student had directly referred in the paper.
45. Entry for **an article with more than three authors**. A source with more than three authors may be listed with all authors' names or just with the first author's name followed by "et al." ("and others"). As his bibliography card indicates below, Shannon had all the names but opted not to use them. His text reference to the Broverman et al. article is consistent with this decision (see p. 624). The Broverman entry also illustrates a **signed article in a journal that pages issues separately**.

Broverman, I. K., S. R. Vogel, D. M. Broverman, F. E. Clarkson, and P. S. Rosencrantz. "Sex-Role Stereotypes: A Current Appraisal." Journal of Social Issues 28.2 (1972): 59-78.

46. Entry for **a signed article in a journal with continuous pagination throughout an annual volume**.
47. Entry for **a government publication located online**.
48. Entry for **an article in which pagination is not consecutive**. The "+" indicates that the article does not continue on page 142 but farther back in the issue.
49. Entry for **a personal interview on e-mail**.
50. Entry for **a book written with an assistant**. See the discussion of this source in comment 21, p. 619. Note that this entry differs from one for a source with two authors, such as the Hughey and Gelman entry below.
51. Entry for **a signed article in a weekly periodical**.
52. Entry for **a signed article in a daily newspaper**.
53. Entry for **a book with one author**.
54. Entry for **an unsigned article**. The source is alphabetized in the list of works cited by the first main word of its title, "Special." Here is Shannon's bibliography card for this source:

> "The Special Talents Women Bring to Participative Management." *International Management* Aug. 1986: 60.

Kowalchuk 1

Writer's name and page number.

Janice Kowalchuk

Ms. Sachs

English 109

December 4, 1997

Writer's name, course, instructor's name, date not on separate title page.

Everyone's Hockey Night in Canada

Title centred.

In March 1990, Team Canada won the first Women's World Hockey Championship. They came from behind to beat Team USA and win going away 5-2 (McFarlane 152-56). In the stands at the Ottawa Civic Centre, nine thousand fans cheered like crazy and waved the Maple Leaf, and more than one million Canadians watched and cheered also on TSN (185). My family were among that million, and we all cheered stars like France St. Louis and Dawn McGuire, names very few Canadians would recognize now or then the way they recognize the names of Mario Lemieux or Wayne Gretzky. This situation, however, can and will change. The recognition always given by society to men's sports can be shared by women if we continue to press for equal opportunity and begin to use our economic power to promote ourselves.

Double-space throughout.

Citation form: source not named in text.

Thesis sentence.

Some say that sports and leisure activities are not an important concern for women. Male professional athletes are overpaid crybabies, spoiled recipients of "the kind of special treatment," Ken Dryden, former star goalie, notes, "[that] professional athletes have grown accustomed to, and enjoy" ("Game" 168). Women have more important concerns. This objection is true in certain respects. Yet sports has an impact on all women's lives in North America through its place in popular culture and its role in the creation of self- and body image.

Editorial change in quotation in square brackets.

Citation form: two or more works by same author in list of works cited.

In their sociology textbook Hockey Night in Canada, Richard Gruneau and David Whitson define popular culture this way:

> Popular cultures encompass all the various modes of expression, pleasure-seeking, and entertainment through which people negotiate their relationships with one another, with an imagined past and future, and with the institutions and prescriptions of a dominant culture. (28)

Block quotation: quotation over four lines is indented 2.5 cm and double-spaced.

Citation in parentheses follows period and one space.

Gruneau and Whitson argue that all these daily activities, the things that people really like doing, from watching MuchMusic or televised sports to playing in air bands or road hockey, taken together largely determine how we see the world and ourselves (11-30). The "dominant culture," however, determines the shape of a lot of these activities. In televised professional team sports, for example, women are never represented. We may see ourselves playing individual sports like tennis or golf, but we never see ourselves playing together as a team.

In fact, we rarely see ourselves playing sports at all. The four major professional leagues that dominate television--the NFL, NBA, NHL, and Major League Baseball--are all male. This domination continues despite the fact that, as Mariah Burton Nelson, a sociologist and a former professional basketball player, points out, women now form the majority of new participants in organized sports, and more women than men now exercise regularly in leisure fitness programs like swimming or aerobics (25-41). Nelson maintains that the lack of representation and encouragement leads to a lack of participation by girls. This harms what scientists call "'movement literacy'" (28), a key part of the development of body image. Girls, then, almost always start behind, and the older women now working out

Introduction gives source's names and credentials.

Paraphrase of source requires citation.

Punctuation for quotation within quotation.

are rushing to catch up to men and to reclaim their body image (126).

My home town was no different in some respects, except hockey was everything. Hockey was and is popular culture for most from November to March. As Ken Dryden puts it in his story in Home Game about Radisson, Saskatchewan, a town much like mine, "in Canada, hockey is one of winter's expectations" (9). All my brothers were expected to play hockey and did. Girls were traditionally expected not to, largely because of the violence of the game. Gruneau and Whitson explain the basis for this expectation:

> Hockey has come to occupy the place it holds in Canadian culture in part because it provides a public platform for celebrating a very traditional masculine idea. For that reason there are important connections between struggles about violence in and around hockey, and larger struggles over changes in what Australian sociologist Robert Connell calls the gender order: "a historically constructed pattern of power relations between men and women." (191)

Punctuation form: quotation in block quotation.

Kowalchuk 5

In my home town, the change in "gender order" was reflected when we began to play hockey again, women's hockey, without the violence of bodychecking or stickwork.

I say "again" because women have played hockey almost as long as men in this country. In Proud Past, Bright Future, his history of women's hockey in Canada, Brian McFarlane notes that the earliest newspaper account of a woman's hockey game is from 1891 (4). At the university level, women have been playing hockey seriously at schools like McGill, Toronto, Saskatchewan, and Alberta since at least the early 1920s (54, 58). Recent changes, however, in the Canadian Interuniversity Athletic Union (CIAU) promotion of women's athletics reflect the shifts in "gender order." Responding in part to the American Title IX--the federal law that legislates equal distribution of athletic scholarships--the CIAU, where there are no scholarships, has adopted fourteen resolutions (Jollimore). The second resolution--"that the CIAU increase the number of competitive opportunities for women at the national

Citation form: continuing paraphrase of same work.

Citation form: reference to entire work.

championship level by two sports in the next five years" (see Canadian Interuniversity Athletic Union)--will have a great impact on women's hockey because it will likely be one of the sports added to bring the number of women's championships up to the number of men's. Mark Lowry, executive vice-president of the CIAU, confirms that the CIAU recognizes that it now provides more athletic opportunity for men than for women and is moving to rectify the situation (qtd. in Jollimore A12).

The pressure that brings this kind of progress needs to be applied at the professional level as well. Hockey is unique in that it is the only major team sport where a woman has played at the highest professional level. Manon Rheaume has played major junior hockey, minor professional hockey, and a period in an exhibition game between the Tampa Bay Lightning and the St. Louis Blues of the NHL (Gruneau and Whitson 171-72; McFarlane 167-71). Sure, the period in the NHL game was a publicity stunt, and she can play with men because she is a goalie, yet the interest she has raised and the money she makes (more than

Citation form: two or more sources cited.

$500 000 per year [McFarlane 170]) shows what a potential market there is for women in professional team sports. Women have and will have more disposable income. In the future, we can use our money as pressure to create and support our own sports leagues. In the process, we can see ourselves represented. We can promote our self- and body images, and we can see our values and our kind of team play reflected.

Punctuation form: citation within parentheses.

The hockey that I played at home and play here at a club level in university is every bit as competitive as men's hockey. Without the dominating factor of bodychecking, however, there is an even greater emphasis on skills, especially on team skills. This kind of hockey will be on display when women's hockey appears for the first time as a medal sport in the Olympics in Nagano, Japan, in 1998 (McFarlane 202). Imagine the millions watching and cheering. Imagine the stars and the role models that will be created. Imagine the future for women's hockey and for all sports.

Conclusion: recalls introduction and expands on consequences of thesis.

Kowalchuk 8

Works Cited

Canadian Interuniversity Athletic Union. Minutes. September 1995: 76-77.

Dryden, Ken. "The Game." <u>Contest: Essays by Canadian Students</u>. Ed. Robert Hookey, Murray McArthur, and Joan Pilz. 2nd ed. Toronto: Harcourt, 1994. 168-74.

---. <u>Home Game: Hockey and Life in Canada</u>. With Roy MacGregor. Toronto: McClelland, 1989.

Gruneau, Richard, and David Whitson. <u>Hockey Night in Canada: Sports, Identities, and Cultural Politics</u>. Toronto: Garamond, 1993.

Jollimore, Mary. "Evening Out the Numbers." <u>Globe and Mail</u>. 24 June 1995: A12+.

McFarlane, Brian. <u>Proud Past, Bright Future: One Hundred Years of Women's Hockey</u>. Toronto: Stoddart, 1994.

Nelson, Mariah Burton. <u>Are We Winning Yet? How Women Are Changing Sports and Sports Are Changing Women</u>. New York: Random, 1991.

New page for works cited. Heading centred.

Double-spaced throughout.

Two works by same author. After first entry, replace author's name with three hyphens. Alphabetize the works by title.

Sources are alphabetized by author's last name or first word of corporate or group author.

Second and subsequent lines of each source are indented five spaces.

By Sylvan Barnet and Reid Gilbert

Chapter 39 Reading and Writing About Literature

Why read literature? Let's approach this question indirectly by asking why people *write* literature. A thousand years ago a Japanese writer, Lady Murasaki, offered an answer. Here is one of her characters talking about what motivates a writer:

> Again and again something in one's own life or in the life around one will seem so important that one cannot bear to let it pass into oblivion. There must never come a time, the writer feels, when people do not know about this.

When we read certain works—Murasaki's *The Tale of Genji* is one of them—we share this feeling; we are caught up in the writer's world, whether it is the Southern Ontario of Alice Munro, the Labrador coast of the Innuinuit Theatre Company, or the India of Rohinton Mistry. In short, we read literature because it gives us an experience that seems important to us, usually an experience that is both familiar and new. A common way of putting this is to say that reading broadens us and helps us understand our own experience. A less lofty way of putting it is to say that reading gives us pleasure.

39a Reading and responding to literature

When we read nonliterary writings, it may be enough to get the gist of the thesis; in fact, we may have to peer through a good deal of wordiness to find the heart of the matter—say, three arguments against capital punishment. But when we read a story, a poem, or a play, we must pay extremely close attention to what might be called the "feel" of the words. For instance, the word *proposition* in Phyllis Webb's poem, "Proposition," captures the senses of "offer," "mathematical formula," and "sexual advance," and the poem's effect depends upon the interrelationships among these meanings.

Literary authors are concerned with presenting human experience concretely, with *showing* rather than *telling*. Consider the following proverb and an unmemorable paraphrase of it:

> A rolling stone gathers no moss.
>
> If a rock is always moving around, vegetation won't have a chance to grow on it.

The familiar original offers a small but complete world: hard (stone) and soft (moss), inorganic and organic, at rest and in motion. The original is also shapely: each noun (*stone, moss*) has one syllable, and each word of motion (*rolling, gathers*) has two syllables, with the accent on the first of the two. Such relationships unify the proverb into a whole that pleases us and stays in our minds.

Reading a work of literature

Reading literature critically involves interacting with a text. The techniques complement those for critically reading any text, so if you haven't read this book's Introduction on such reading, you should do so. Responding critically is a matter not of making negative judgments but of analysing the parts, interpreting their meanings, seeing how the parts relate, and evaluating significance or quality.

You can preview a literary text somewhat as you can preview any other text (pp. 4, 5). You may gauge the length of the text to determine if you can read it in one sitting, and you may read a biographical note to learn about the author. In a literary text, however, you won't find aids such as section headings or summaries that can make previewing other texts especially informative. You have to dive into the words themselves.

Do write while reading (pp. 4, 5–6). If you own the book you're reading, don't hesitate to underline or highlight passages that especially interest you for one reason or another. Don't hesitate to annotate the margins, indicating your pleasures, displeasures, and uncertainties with remarks such as *Nice detail* or *Do we need this long description?* or *Not believable.* If you don't own the book, make these notes on separate sheets.

An effective way to interact with a text is to keep a **reading journal.** A journal is not a diary in which you record your doings but a place to develop and store your reflections on what you read, such as an answer to a question you may have posed in the margin of the text or a response to something said in class. You may, for instance, want to reflect on why your opinion is so different from that of another student. You may even make an entry in the form of a letter to the author or from one character to another.

Here is a short story by Margaret Atwood. Following are a student's annotations and journal entry on the story.

Margaret Atwood

Marrying the Hangman

She has been condemned to death by hanging. A man may escape this death by becoming the hangman, a woman by marrying the hangman. But at the present time there is no hangman; thus there is no escape. There is only a death, indefinitely postponed. This is not fantasy, it is history.

. . .

To live in prison is to live without mirrors. To live without mirrors is to live without the self. She is living selflessly, she finds a hole in the stone wall and on the other side of the wall, a voice. The voice comes through darkness and has no face. This voice becomes her mirror.

. . .

In order to avoid her death, her particular death, with wrung neck and swollen tongue, she must marry the hangman. But there is no hangman, first she must create him, she must persuade this man at the end of the voice, this voice she has never seen and which has never seen her, this darkness, she must persuade him to renounce his face, exchange it for the impersonal mask of death, of official death which has eyes but no mouth, this mask of a dark leper. She must transform his hands so they will be willing to twist the rope around throats that have been singled out as hers was, throats other than hers. She must marry the hangman or no one, but that is not so bad. Who else is there to marry?

. . .

You wonder about her crime. She was condemned to death for stealing clothes from her employer, from the wife of her employer. She wished to make herself more beautiful. This desire in servants was not legal.

. . .

She uses her voice like a hand, her voice reaches through the wall, stroking and touching. What could she possibly have said that would convince him? He was not condemned to death, freedom awaited him. What was the temptation, the one that worked? Perhaps he wanted to live with a woman whose life he had saved, who had seen down into the earth but had nevertheless followed him back up to life. It was his only chance to be a hero, to one person at least, for the others would now despise him. He was in prison for wounding another man, on one finger of the right hand, with a sword. This too is history.

My friends, who are both women, tell me their stories, which cannot be believed and which are true. They are horror stories and they have not happened to me, they have not yet happened to me, they have happened to me but we are detached, we watch our unbelief with horror. Such things cannot happen to us, it is afternoon and these things do not happen in the afternoon. The trouble was, she said, I didn't have time to put my glasses on and without them I'm blind as a bat, I couldn't even see who it was. These things happen and we sit at a table and tell stories about them so we can finally believe. This is not fantasy, it is history, there is more than one hangman and because of this some of them are unemployed.

. . .

He said: the end of walls, the end of ropes, the opening of doors, a field, the wind, a house, the sun, a table, an apple.

She said: nipple, arms, lips, wine, belly, hair, bread, thighs, eyes, eyes.

They both kept their promises.

. . .

The hangman is not such a bad fellow. Afterwards he goes to the refrigerator and cleans up the leftovers, though he does not wipe up what he accidentally spills. He wants only the simple things: a chair, someone to pull off his shoes, someone to watch him while he talks, with admiration and fear, gratitude if possible, someone in whom to plunge himself for rest and renewal. These things can best be had by marrying a woman who has been condemned to death by other men for wishing to be beautiful. There is a wide choice.

. . .

Everyone said he was a Fool.

Everyone said she was a clever woman.

They used the word *ensnare.*

. . .

What did they say the first time they were alone together in the same room? What did he say when she had removed her veil and he could see that she was not a voice but a body and therefore finite? What did she say when she discovered that she had left one locked room for another? They talked of love, naturally, though that did not keep them busy forever.

The fact is there are no stories I can tell my friends that will make them feel better. History cannot be erased, although we can soothe ourselves by speculating about it. At that time there were no female hangmen. Perhaps there have never been any, and thus no man could save his life by marriage. Though a woman could, according to the law.

. . .

He said: foot, boot, order, city, fist, roads, time, knife.

She said: water, night, willow, rope hair, earth, belly, cave, meat, shroud, open, blood.

They both kept their promises.

"After 29 April 1752, all trace of him and his wife is lost" ("Corolère, Jean," *The Dictionary of Canadian Biography*, Vol. 3).

A student, Janet Chan, made annotations on Atwood's story. Here are notes on the first three segments.

> She has been condemned to death by hanging. A man may escape this death by becoming the hangman, a woman by marrying the hangman. But at the present time there is no hangman; thus there is no escape. There is only a death, indefinitely postponed. This is not fantasy, it is history.

Must a woman marry to gain power?

history or today?

> To live in prison is to live without mirrors. To live without mirrors is to live without the self. She is living selflessly, she finds a hole in the stone wall and on the other side of the wall, a voice. The voice comes through darkness and has no face. This voice becomes her mirror.

Is the self an image in words?

> In order to avoid her death, her particular death, with wrung neck and swollen tongue, she must marry the hangman. But there is no hangman, first she must create him, she must persuade this man at the end of the voice, this voice she has never seen and which has never seen her, this darkness, she must persuade him to renounce his face, exchange it for the impersonal mask of death, of official death which has eyes but no mouth, this mask of a dark leper. She must transform his hands so they will be willing to twist the rope around throats that have been singled out as hers was, throats other than hers. She must marry the hangman or no one, but that is not so bad. Who else is there to marry?

Very strong images

Powerlessness

Writing in her journal, Chan posed a series of questions about the story—critical points, curiosities about characters, possible implications.

> Title—a marriage and a hangman. Weird to put together. Is this history true? Could a woman save herself this way? What does this say about marriage?
>
> Did this woman want too much? What did she want?
>
> Uses voice "like a hand." Can words touch and stroke? Are words contracts? "They both kept their promises."
>
> She disappears into a historical note? Does she have any personal worth?
>
> What is the second story in the present day about?

Freedom? Is she more or less free after she marries?
Irony: freedom is servitude; history continues today.

Chan's journal entry illustrates brainstorming—the discovery technique of listing ideas (or questions) however they occur, without editing (see p. 36). Another productive journal technique is focused freewriting—concentrating on a single issue (such as one of Chan's questions) and writing nonstop for a set amount of time, again without editing (p. 35).

Analysing a work of literature

Like any discipline, the study of literature involves particular frameworks of analysis—particular ways of seeing literary works that help determine what parts the critical reader identifies and how he or she interprets them (see pp. 12–13). Some of the critical frameworks you may encounter in studying literature are these:

- **Historical criticism** focuses on the context in which a literary work was created and how that context affected the work. The critic may examine the author's social, political, and intellectual surroundings or may concentrate on the author's own biography: his or her life experiences or psychological makeup.
- **The New Historicism** has become a widespread critical approach. It suggests there is no fixed "history," but rather a series of narratives particular to time and place. Literature is seen as one of the agencies of power by which "histories" are created and maintained by society.
- **Feminist criticism** has a long tradition. It calls for reappraisal, pointing out the misogynist attitudes of much literature and literary criticism, and urging a new appreciation for women writers, many of whom have been undervalued. There are various schools of feminism: some feminists suggest women use language in a unique manner—an écriture féminine; others deny categories, like "woman." The influence of feminist criticism on contemporary analysis is profound.
- **Gay and lesbian criticism** recognizes that gays and lesbians write and read in unique ways, urges readers to recognize and value gay themes or characters, and—most importantly—suggests that gender is constructed rather than simply biological.
- **Reader-response criticism** focuses on the reactions of an audience to a work of literature, asking why readers respond as they do to a text. In this view the meaning of the text lies not just on the page but in the interaction between the work and its reader.

- **Deconstructive criticism** regards a work of literature sceptically, resisting the obvious meanings and focusing on the ambiguities in the work, especially the internal contradictions. Perceiving that the relationship of words and their meanings is both arbitrary and forever changing—even within the same work—deconstructive critics emphasize multiple meanings and what a text does not say.
- **Postcolonial criticism** examines literature in terms of the historical experience of imperialism, reading work from the former imperial nations and the former colonies and analysing the relationship of power to aesthetic discourse. Today, postcolonial theory also provides useful ways to look at structures of power within race, gender, and class. In Canada, this approach is applied to analysis of national identity and, in fact, exposes the very idea of "nationalism" as part of a larger historical narrative.
- **Formalist criticism** (also called **New Criticism**) focuses primarily on a literary work as a constructed text, as an independent unity understood in itself rather than as an artifact of a particular context or reader response. Beginning with a personal response, the formalist critic tries to account for the response by examining the form of the work (hence *formalist*) and the relations among its elements.

This chapter emphasizes formalist criticism because it engages you immediately in the work of literature itself, without requiring extensive historical or cultural background, and because it introduces the conventional elements of literature that all critical approaches discuss, even though they view the elements differently. The box on the next two pages lists these elements—plot, characters, setting, and so on—and offers questions about each one that can help you think constructively and imaginatively about what you read.

One significant attribute of a literary work is its *meaning,* or what we can interpret to be its meaning. Readers may well disagree over the persuasiveness of someone's argument, but they will rarely disagree over its meaning. With literature, however, disagreements over meaning occur all the time because (as we have seen) literature *shows* rather than *tells:* it gives us concrete images of imagined human experiences, but it usually does not say how we ought to understand the images.

Further, readers bring to their reading not only different critical views, as noted above, but also different personal experiences. To take an extreme case, a woman who has recently been married—or assaulted—may interpret "Marrying the Hangman" differently from most other readers. Or a story that bores a reader at age fifteen may deeply move her at twenty-five. The words on the page remain the same, but their meaning changes.

In writing about literature, then, we can offer only our *interpretation* of meaning rather than *the* meaning. Still, most people agree that there are limits to interpretation: it must be supported by evidence that a reasonable reader finds at least plausible if not totally convincing. For instance, the student who says that in "Marrying the Hangman" the modern woman who tells her friends the story is the literal reincarnation of the imprisoned woman goes beyond the permissible limits because the story offers no evidence for such an interpretation.

Questions for a literary analysis

See later boxes for specific questions on fiction (p. 664), poetry (p. 665), and drama (p. 669).

- **Plot:** the relationships and patterns of events. (Even a poem has a plot—for instance, a change in mood from bitterness to resignation.)

  What actions happen?
  What conflicts occur?
  How do the events connect to each other and to the whole?

- **Characters:** the people the author creates (including the narrator of a story or the speaker of a poem).

  Who are the principal people in the work?
  How do they interact?
  What do their actions, words, and thoughts reveal about their personalities and the personalities of others?
  Do the characters stay the same, or do they change? Why?

- **Point of view:** the perspective or attitude of the speaker in a poem or the voice who tells a story. The point of view may be **first person** (a participant, using *I*) or **third person** (an outsider, using *he, she, it, they*). A first-person narrator may be a major or a minor character in the narrative, and may be **reliable** or **unreliable** (unable to report events wholly or accurately). A third-person narrator may be **omniscient** (knows what goes on in all characters' minds), **limited** (knows what goes on in the mind of only one character), or **objective** (knows only what is external to the characters).

  Who is the narrator (or the speaker of a poem)?
  How does the narrator's point of view affect the narrative?

- **Tone:** the narrator's or speaker's attitude, perceived through the words (for instance, joyful, bitter, or confident).

  What tone (or tones) do you hear? If there is a change, how do you account for it?

Is there an ironic contrast between the narrator's tone (for instance, confidence) and what you take to be the author's attitude (for instance, pity for human overconfidence)?

- **Imagery:** word pictures or visual details involving the senses (sight, sound, touch, smell, taste).

  What images does the writer use? What senses do they draw on?
  What patterns are evident in the images (for instance, religious or commercial images)?
  What is the significance of the imagery?

- **Symbolism:** concrete things standing for larger and more abstract ideas (for instance, the Canadian flag may symbolize home, a singing bird may symbolize happiness, or a dead flower may symbolize mortality).

  What symbols does the author use? What do they seem to signify?
  How does the symbolism relate to the other elements of the work, such as character or theme?

- **Setting:** the place where the action happens.

  What does the locale contribute to the work?
  Are scene shifts significant?

- **Form:** the shape or structure of the work.

  What *is* the form? (For example, a story might divide sharply in the middle, moving from happiness to sorrow.)
  What parts of the work does the form emphasize, and why?

- **Theme:** the main idea, the gist of what the work adds up to.

  How might the theme be stated?
  How do the parts of the work develop the theme?

- **Appeal:** the degree to which the story pleases you.

  What do you especially like or dislike about the work?
  Do you think your responses are unique or common to most readers? Why?

39b Drafting and revising a literary analysis

The process for writing a literary analysis is similar to that for any other kind of essay: once you've done the reading and thought about it, you need to focus your ideas, gather evidence, draft, and revise.

Conceiving a thesis

After reading, rereading, and making notes, you probably will be able to formulate a tentative thesis sentence—a statement of your main point, your argument. Remember that a thesis is a full sentence, not simply a subject waiting for a verb to complete it. When you have thought out the verb or verbs you need, you will have determined what you want to develop. It is the process of creating a full and accurate thesis sentence that helps you organize the whole essay in your mind. (For more on thesis sentences, see pp. 41-44.) Start yourself thinking by glancing over your notes and by jotting down a few especially promising ideas—brief statements of what you think your key points may be and their main support.

At first, Janet Chan considered the idea that the main character of the imprisoned woman was unrealistic. But the more Chan examined the story, the more she believed that several reversals, or ironies, showed that the woman is believable and that she is simply a historical example of a reality that all women face, including contemporary women. Chan explored this idea in her journal.

> Title? Prison of Women (?) Ironical Freedom (?) Ironies for Women (?)
> Thesis: woman escapes but is still imprisoned by man
> Chief irony: woman can only escape by being subservient to a man
> Other ironies: 1. beauty is her crime and weapon
> 2. woman can only "see" herself in him as a mirror
> 3. modern women hearing story are also trapped

From these notes, Chan developed her thesis sentence:

> Although the woman escapes hanging, ironically she continues a life in prison.

This thesis sentence states a specific idea that can be developed and argued from evidence in the story. It has tension within itself. A good thesis will neither state a fact (*The woman in the story can only escape by marrying the hangman*) nor generalize (*All women are forever in prisons*).

Gathering evidence

The evidence for a literary analysis always comes from at least one primary source (the work or works being discussed) and may come from secondary sources (critical and historical accounts about the primary sources). (See pp. 510–11 for more on primary and secondary sources.) For example, if you were writing about Atwood's tale, the primary material would be the story itself, and the

Guidelines for using quotations in literary analysis

- Use quotations to support your assertions. Don't use quotations to pad the paper. Quote at length only when necessary to your argument.
- When you use a quotation, specify how it relates to your idea. Introduce the quotation—for example, *At the outset Atwood conveys the sort of person her protoganist is, "she wished. ..." ". . ."* Sometimes, comment after the quotation. (See pp. 559–61 for more on integrating quotations into your writing.)
- Reproduce spelling, punctuation, capitalization, and all other features exactly as they appear in the source. (See p. 413 for the use of brackets when you need to add something to a quotation, and see p. 414 for the use of an ellipsis mark when you need to omit something from a quotation.)
- Document your sources. (See p. 663.)

secondary material (if you used it) would be histories, *The Dictionary of Canadian Biography,* and critical studies of Atwood and her work.

The bulk of your evidence in writing about literature will usually be quotations from the work, although you will occasionally summarize or paraphrase as well (see pp. 547–52). When using quotations, keep in mind the criteria in the box above.

Your instructor will probably tell you if you are expected to consult secondary sources for an assignment. (If so, see pp. 516 and 529 for lists of reference sources in literature.) Secondary sources can help you understand a writer's work, but your primary concern should always be the work itself, not what critics A, B, and C say about it. In general, then, quote or summarize secondary material sparingly. And always cite your sources. (See p. 663.)

3 Writing a draft

Drafting your essay is your opportunity to develop your thesis or to discover it if you haven't already. (See pp. 55–57 for tips on drafting.) The draft below was actually Janet Chan's second: she deleted some digressions from her first draft and added more evidence for her points. The numbers in parentheses refer to the pages from which the quotations were drawn. Ask your instructor whether you should always give such citations, especially for a short poem or story like Atwood's. (See p. 663 for how to document a paper.)

Ironies for Women

After we know how Margaret Atwood's short story, "Marrying the Hangman," turns out, we find irony at the very start. The story is about a woman who has been condemned to hang because she stole some clothes, because she "wanted to make herself more beautiful" (13). She can escape only by marrying a hangman. So she must first convince a man in the next cell to become the hangman. Then he has to marry her. She does convince him, and she is released from prison.

An irony is that she discovers immediately that she has "left one locked room for another" (14). She is now his wife and she must obey him and keep his house. And she discovers that love "did not keep them busy forever" (14). Although he "is not such a bad fellow," and wants only a simple life, he also wants her to "watch him while he talks, with admiration and fear, gratitude if possible" (14).

A deeper irony is the fact that the woman's crime was wanting to be beautiful. Being beautiful was how she knew herself. It is ironic that she is condemned by the very things that made her clever enough to convince the man and to seduce him. Also, she has to give up her image of herself. She can no longer see her own beauty. She uses him as a mirror. In the prison she uses his voice through a hole in the wall to mirror back to her a sense of her identity. But when she is free, she must continue to use him as her mirror. If she resists, his words become harsh: "foot, boot," "first," "knife" (14). This is her real imprisonment.

The saddest irony in the story is the outer story. Some friends tell the narrator stories about abuse. If we are right that one speaker has been raped, it is horrible that she didn't have "time to put my glasses on" (13) so she couldn't see her attacker. She is like the woman speaking through the hole in the wall who was unable to see the man she had to marry. Atwood tells this ironic historical anecdote to point out the similarity to the contemporary women's lives. "These things happen" (13), she says. The irony is that history repeats itself.

Revising and editing

As in other writing, use at least two drafts to revise and edit, so that you can attend separately to the big structural issues and the smaller surface problems. See pages 61 and 66, respectively, for general revision and editing checklists.

For a literary analysis, revise your paper against the checklist below.

Checklist for revising a literary analysis

- Does the title of the essay consist of more than the title of the work discussed? Your title should give the reader an idea of your topic.
- Does the introductory paragraph avoid openings such as "In this story . . ."? Name the author and the title so that the reader knows exactly what work you are discussing. Develop your thesis a bit so that readers know where they will be going.
- Is the organization effective? The essay should not dwindle or become anticlimactic; rather, it should build up.
- Do quotations provide evidence and let the reader hear the author's voice?
- Is the essay chiefly devoted to analysis, not to summary? Do not summarize the plot in great detail. A couple of sentences may be helpful if your readers are not familiar with the work, but a summary is not an essay.
- Have you used the present tense of verbs to describe both the author's work and the action in the work (for example, *Atwood shows* or *The woman disappears*)?
- If you have used the first-person *I* (for instance, *I find the ending highly plausible*), have you avoided using it so often that you sound egotistical?
- Is your evaluation of the work evident? It may be understood (as in Janet Chan's essay), or it may be explicit. In either case, give the reasons for judging the work to be effective or not, worth reading or not. Remember that it is not enough to express your likes or dislikes; readers will be interested in an evaluation only if you support it with evidence.
- Did you document your sources? (See p. 663.)

An essay on fiction without secondary sources

Janet Chan's final typed draft is not shown, but we show she created it by making changes to an earlier draft. Notice that

1. Chan added a new introduction to set up the paper. It names the story's author and title, introduces the story's overall irony, very briefly summarizes the story, and states Chan's thesis.
2. At many points in both drafts, Chan provides details and quotations to clarify the ironies in the story.
3. Chan carefully adds a Works Cited list. Because she used a reprint of the story she notes the text she actually used, not the original publication; her page references are to the reprinted version. The Works Cited list always appears on a separate, final page.

History Repeats Itself

~~Ironies for Women~~

A rereading of Margaret Atwood's short story, "Marrying the Hangman," reveals layers of irony. The story is about a woman who has been condemned to hang because she stole some clothes, because she wanted to make herself more beautiful (13). She can escape only by marrying a hangman and she must first convince a man in the next cell to become the hangman, then to marry her. She does convince him, by promising him sexual favours ("nipple," "belly," "thighs") (14). She is released from prison. Although the woman escapes hanging, ironically she continues to live in prision and so, it seems, do many women today.

~~After we know how Margaret Atwood's story, "Marrying the Hangman," turns out, we find irony at the very start. The story is about a woman who has been condemned to hang because she stole some clothes, because she "wanted to make herself more beautiful" (13). She can escape only by marrying a hangman. So she must first convince a man in the next cell to become the hangman. Then he has to marry her. She does convince him, and she is released from prison.~~

"Everyone said she was a clever woman," but by clever everyone meant manipulative or sneaky: "They used the word ensnare" (14). ~~It~~ is ironic that she is condemned by the very things that made ~~her clever~~ enough to convince the man and to seduce him.

The central irony ~~An irony~~ is that she discovers immediately that she has "left one locked room for another" (14). She is now a wife who ~~his wife~~ must obey her husband ~~and she must obey him~~ and keep his house. And she discovers that love "did not keep them busy forever" (14). Although he "is not such a bad fellow," and wants only a simple life, he also wants her to "watch him while he talks, with admiration and fear, gratitude if possible" (14).

, perhaps,
A deeper irony ^ is the fact that the woman's crime was wanting to be beautiful. Atwood suggests that her desire for beauty was a way for her to know herself, to give herself worth. Now,
~~Being beautiful was how she knew herself. Also~~, she has to give up her image of herself. She can no longer see her
, but must use her husband
own beauty. ^ ~~She uses him~~ as a mirror. In the prison she uses his voice through a hole in the wall to mirror back to her a sense of her identity. But when she is free, she must con-
see herself through him.
tinue to ~~use him as her mirror~~. If she resists, his words become harsh: "foot, boot," "first," "knife" (14). This is her real imprisonment.

in The women
The saddest irony ~~in the story~~ is ^ the outer story. ~~Some~~
who are telling the narrator horror stories are also afraid, and also can't see themselves
~~friends tell the narrator stories about abuse~~. If we are properly.
right that one speaker has been raped, it is horrible that she didn't have "time to put my glasses on" so she couldn't
In some ways, s
see her attacker. ^ ~~S~~he is like the woman speaking through the
to whom she
hole in the wall who was unable to see the man ~~she had to~~
had to give herself
~~marry~~. Atwood tells this ironic historical anecdote to point
the lives of contemporary women
out the similarity to ~~the contemporary women's lives~~. "These things happen" she says (13). The irony is that history repeats itself.

[New page.]

Work Cited

Atwood, Margaret. "Marrying the Hangman." Selected Poems 1966–1984. Toronto: Oxford UP, 1990. Rpt. in Sylvan Barnet and Reid Gilbert. A Short Guide to Writing about Literature: First Canadian Edition. Don Mills: Addison-Wesley, 1997. 13–14.

Preparing the final draft

Finally, Janet Chan checked over her presentation draft before submitting it. This final stage involves several steps:

- Carefully check the documentation of your sources. Unless your instructor specifies otherwise, use the style of the Modern Language Association (MLA), detailed in Chapter 37. In this style, parenthetical citations in the text of the paper refer to a list of works cited at the end. Sample papers illustrating this style appear in Chapter 38 and on pages 666–68.
- Use MLA format for headings, margins, and other elements. See pages 746–49 for detailed instructions. See pages 606–38 for a full paper in this format. For the special formats of poetry and long prose quotations, see pages 399–400.
- Proofread. See page 67 for tips.

39c Writing about fiction

The "Questions for a literary analysis" on pages 655–56 will help you think about any work of literature, including a story or novel, and find a topic to write on. The box on the following page provides additional questions for thinking about fiction. Not every question is relevant to every story. For an example of writing about fiction, see Janet Chan's essay on Margaret Atwood's "Marrying the Hangman," pages 661–62.

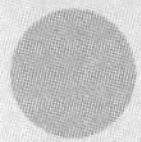

Questions for analysing fiction

- What happens in the story? Summarize the plot (the gist of the happenings). Think about what your summary *leaves out.*
- Is the story told in chronological order, or are there flashbacks or flashforwards? On rereading, what foreshadowing (hints of what is to come) do you detect?
- What conflicts does the work include?
- How does the writer reveal character—for instance, by explicit comment or by letting us see the character in action? With which character(s) do you sympathize? Are the characters plausible? What motivates them? What do minor characters contribute to the work?
- Who tells the story? Is the narrator a character, or does the narrator stand entirely outside the characters' world? (On narrative points of view, see p. 655.)
- What is the setting, the time and place of the action? What does it contribute to the work?
- Do certain characters or settings seem to you to stand for something in addition to themselves—that is, are they symbolic?
- What is the theme—that is, what does the work add up to? Does the theme reinforce values that you hold, or does it challenge them?
- Is the title informative? Did its meaning change for you after you read the work?

39d Writing about poetry

Two types of essays on poetry are especially common. One is an analysis of some aspect of the poem in relation to the whole—for instance, the changes in the speaker's tone or the functions of metre and rhyme. The second is an **explication,** a line-by-line (sometimes almost word-by-word) reading that seeks to make explicit everything that is implicit in the poem. Thus an explication of the first line of P.K. Page's "T-Bar" (the line goes "Relentless, black on white, the cable runs") might call attention to the unending and aggressive nature of the cable run—especially seen as a black line on the white snow—and to the fact that the words are not in the normal order ("The cable runs relentlessly"). These features might support the explanation that the poet is introducing a note of the *un*usual, in preparation for the experience that follows. Although one might conceivably explicate a long poem, in practice explication is confined to short poems or to short passages from long poems.

The "Questions for a literary analysis" on pages 655–56 will help you think about any work of literature, including a poem, and find a topic to write on. The box below provides additional questions for thinking about poetry.

Questions for analysing poetry

- What parts interest or puzzle you? What words seem especially striking or unusual?
- How would you describe the poem's **speaker** (sometimes called the **persona** or the **voice**)? (The speaker may be very different from the author.) What tone or emotion do you detect—for instance, anger, affection, sarcasm? Does the tone change during the poem?
- What is the structure of the poem? Are there stanzas (groups of lines separated by space)? If so, how is the thought related to the stanzas?
- What is the theme of the poem: what is it about? Is the theme stated or implied?
- What images do you find—evocations of sight, sound, taste, touch, or smell? Is there a surprising pattern of images—say, images of business in a poem about love? What does the poem suggest symbolically as well as literally? (Trust your responses. If you don't sense a symbolic overtone, move on. Don't hunt for symbols.)

An essay on poetry without secondary sources

The following sample paper on a short poem by Earle Birney illustrates a literary analysis based on the reader's own response to the work. Here is the poem; the student essay follows:

Earle Birney

The Bear on the Delhi Road

Unreal tall as a myth
by the road the Himalayan bear
is beating the brilliant air
with his crooked arms
About him two men bare
spindly as locusts leap

One pulls on a ring
in the great soft nose His mate
flicks flicks with a stick

up at the rolling eyes

They have not led him here
down from the fabulous hills
to this bald alien plain
and the clamorous world to kill
but simply to teach him to dance

They are peaceful both these spare
men of Kashmir and the bear
alive is their living too
If far on the Delhi way
around him galvanic they dance
it is merely to wear wear
from his shaggy body the tranced
wish forever to stay
only an ambling bear
four-footed in berries

It is no more joyous for them
in this hot dust to prance
out of reach of the praying claws
sharpened to paw for ants
in the shadows of deodars
It is not easy to free
myth from reality
or rear this fellow up
to lurch lurch with them
in the tranced dancing of men

Barbara Gifford

Professor MacGregor

English 101A

March 18, 1997

"These Spare Men of Kashmir"

Earle Birney's poem, "The Bear on the Delhi Road," presents strong images of the captured bear and his captors. No one seems very happy and all are, as Birney puts it, "tranced." These poor men of Kashmir are forced by poverty to bring a bear down from the "fabulous hills" with a "ring/in the great soft nose," but they are also on an "alien plain" and they must "prance" in "hot dust." Although the poem presents exotic images, it is really a poem about poverty and social injustice.

India is a society that has a strong caste system. Although modern India is developing and there is no doubt more opportunity for many people, there is still an enormous population of peasants and uneducated people trapped in centuries-old beliefs and social systems. For these people, the modern world does not exist.

Birney paints a vivid picture of the deprivation in which these men live: they are "bare," meaning partly dressed; they are "spindly," meaning thin; they are like "locusts," meaning they are insect-like. Birney says "it is no more joyous for them" than for the captive bear. They have been forced by economic necessity to give up their home, "in the shadows of deodars," which are aromatic and shady trees, and come down to the "clamorous world" of a more advanced India nearer to the capital, Delhi. They are not participating in the urban life of Delhi, however, but out in the dusty plain.

The actions of the men also show their low status. Although they are by nature "peaceful," they are tormenting the bear by flicking a stick at his eyes because their own poverty necessitates teaching him to dance. They have to keep out of the "praying claws/sharpened to paw for ants." They also have to keep out of the way of the modern world which is steam rollering its way forward without providing any economic security for people like these Kashmir peasants. Because they have no money, they have no power. They can only "lurch, lurch" forward to an uncertain future.

It is words like "lurch" and "tranced" and "spindly" that create the tone of despair and poverty. It is images like "beating the air/with his crooked arms," "the rolling eyes," "to wear, wear/from his shaggy body the tranced wish" that show how worn out and beaten down the bear and the men have become by their plight.

Earle Birney's poem presents foreign images, but the story he tells is true around the world and even in

Canada. Poor people have no power and do whatever they can to survive. If they want to survive, they must attempt to exploit the even more disadvantaged, if any exist. For these men, the only thing lower is a bear. "The Bear on the Delhi Road" is a call for change. The tone of defeat suggests that these conditions cannot continue. The poor have reached the bottom rung and Birney helps us to see the injustice of that fact.

[New page.]

Works Cited

Earle Birney. "The Bear on the Delhi Road" from The Collected Poems of Earle Birney Volume II. Toronto: McClelland & Stewart, 1975. Rpt. in Sylvan Barnet and Reid Gilbert. A Short Guide to Writing about Literature: First Canadian Edition. Don Mills: Addison-Wesley, 1997. 96-97.

39e Writing about drama

Critical writing about a play is somewhat different when you read the play and when you see it in performance.

Analysing drama

Because plays—even some one-act plays—are relatively long, analytic essays on drama usually focus on only one aspect of the play, such as a character's responsibility for his or her fate or the function of a single scene. The essay's introduction usually indicates what the topic and thesis are and why the topic is of some importance. The conclusion often extends the analysis, showing how a study of the apparently small topic helps to illuminate the play as a whole.

The "Questions for a literary analysis" on pages 655–56 will help you think about any work of literature, including a play, and find a topic to write on. The box on the facing page provides additional questions for thinking about drama.

Questions for analysing drama

- Does the plot (the sequence of happenings) seem plausible? If not, is the implausibility a fault? If there is more than one plot, are the plots parallel, or are they related by way of contrast?
- What kinds of conflict are in the play? How are the conflicts resolved? Is the resolution satisfying to you?
- How trustworthy are the characters when they describe themselves or others? Do some characters serve as **foils,** or contrasts, for other characters, thus helping to define the other characters? Do the characters change as the play proceeds? Are the characters' motivations convincing?
- What do you make of the setting, or location? Does it help to reveal character or theme?
- Do certain costumes (dark suits, flowery shawls, stiff collars) or properties (books, pictures, candlesticks) strike you as symbolic?
- If a film has been made of the play, what has been added? What has been omitted?

An essay on drama with secondary sources

The following essay on Judith Thompson's *Lion in the Streets*, written by Christopher Walker when he was in a second year course, examines how Thompson explores evil by the use of language and a kind of magic realism. Walker draws his illustrations from the central play and also from Thompson's earlier play, *White Biting Dog*. He mentions various characters, but, since his concern is with the use of language and states of consciousness, he does not examine any of the characters in detail. Walker is careful not to allow his essay to become a character study or simply a discussion of states of mind: instead, he uses evidence to illustrate how Thompson captures an audience and makes it consider the evil in society.

Christopher Walker

Professor Reid Gilbert

English 210-01

April 5, 1997

A Reality in Dreams:

Thompson's Moral Quest

In an interview with Eleanor Wachtel in Brick, Judith

Thompson reveals the purpose of her plays' focus on evil:

> Well, because it's theatrical, it's what's true, and it's like the purpose the church used to serve: for an hour a week we would confront our spirits.... In the theatre I think what we must do is confront the truth, confront the emotional truth of our lives, which is mixed in the swamp of minutiae, everyday minutiae. (37)

Such a mix occurs in Thompson's White Biting Dog and Lion in the Streets. Thompson captures the audience with poetic dialogue and erratic action that invades the unconscious. Once inside the world she creates, the theatregoer cannot escape her moral attack on the nature of society, and her belief that grace, the freedom of the spirit, is what must be achieved to rid ourselves of evil.

Highly poetic language is what captures the unconscious of the spectators. Kathy Chung, in a review of Lion in the Streets, describes Thompson's dialogue as a place where "her characters seem to lose the division between a private and public self" (132). Chung pinpoints Thompson's ability to show a character's private need to achieve grace and the emotions and thoughts that go along with that need. This need for grace is at the centre of the conflict in a scene in Lion in the Streets when Christine, a reporter, interviews Scarlett, a cerebral palsy patient, and exploits her. Scarlett condemns Christine; Christine physically attacks her and says, "The way you, you, you talked to me like that. Like, like, like you belong. In the world. As if you belong. Where did you get that feeling? I want it. I need it" (Lion 49).

39e

Thompson's language is also very musical. The central Canadian dialect, combined with an acute sense of the rhythms of language, creates hypnotic speech in her plays. A disclaimer at the beginning of White Biting Dog illustrates Thompson's commitment to this kind of dialogue: "Because of the extreme and deliberate musicality of the play, any attempts to go against the textual rhythms... are disastrous" (ii). Interviews reveal the music in Thompson's own speech: "It's acknowledging that, yes, it's a jungle out there, there's a war, but we have our wonderful spirits and great strength, and yes, we have the Force..." (qtd. in Wachtel 41). So, what is it about the exposure of the private self in a musical language that seizes the person experiencing Judith Thompson?

"We do share a collective unconscious and we have as much in common with...the so-called deranged fellow... as you and I have with each other," Thompson tells Wachtel (40). She captures this collective unconscious and burdens it with moral questions in the dream states of her plays. The world of <u>White Biting Dog</u>, for example, consists of such mightmarish things as Glidden covering his stomach in peat moss, the dead dogs being kept in the deep-freeze for years, a talking dog, and action that is in constant, incongruous flux. <u>Lion in the Streets</u> is even more dream-based. Rodney, a gay businessman, acts out an imagined confrontation with his boyhood lover; he kills this man--and the audience witnesses it--but it is just a daydream. Where <u>White Biting Dog</u> is dream-like in dialogue and atmosphere, <u>Lion in the Streets</u> makes the characters' dreams part of the play's reality; reality and dream often get blurred in our own dreams, and this is how Thompson taps into the collective unconscious. Just as a powerful dream can weigh on our minds for days, so do these plays. The difference is that Thompson's plays also have direct access to the conscious mind and thus they are more immediate and permanent than are dreams. She writes in a kind of magic realism.

Central to the conflicts in these two plays is the

inner child. "Children," says Thompson, "are a huge part of ourselves. They're the beautiful, pure god in us...we try to beat it down and make it cower...[but] it takes over in a terrible way, too--the terrible tyrant it can be" (qtd. in Wachtel 40). While Thompson recognizes how tyrannical the inner child can be, she also says of her characters in Lion in the Streets: "All of them have something they find precious and beautiful" (qtd. in Wachtel 40). This ability to see the beauty in things contrasts with the tyrannical and selfish actions that dominate Thompson's work. The characters who are able to see the beauty, and are thus made better, purer, provide a target for the tyranny and thus show its horrible nature. Pony, in White Biting Dog, embodies this wondrous purity: "I was lying on my fold-out in my furnished bachelor on Albany and I got this UNRESISTIBLE urge to get up and go for a walk. And when urges like that come along, I listen to them so I did. I just walked where my feet took me" (White 11). This kind of freedom of self is part of being a child. Pony provides Cape, a character who embodies tyranny, with a means to expose his evil; he, in effect, uses up her goodness to save his own soul.

This evil, found in Cape, is found also in a great many of Thompson's characters. There is something that makes this evil possible, something that Thompson calls "a pathological state of denial" in which we, "as a society, as a culture," are living: "Just having to walk past homeless people, having to--just deny, deny, deny" (qtd. in Wachtel 38). Thompson's characters exhibit the ability to deny compassion to others who are in pain, as do most people in the real world. It is this denial that allows Christine to exploit Scarlett's fantasy on the grounds that "I have a job, Scarlett, I have a child to support..." (Lion 48). The characters are so trapped in states of denial that they become pathological. Cape is so trapped that he cannot love; he cannot have any kind of a genuine mutual relationship with anyone. Thompson describes the kind of person Cape represents: "So, these are people I find Horrifying because they can distance themselves from a person and you think they're laughing with you but actually they're watching you" (qtd. in Tomc 20).

Thompson condemns this tyranny and denial and offers a solution in what she calls "grace." In White Biting Dog grace is a starting point on a path towards resolution. Cape and his mother face the deaths of people who love them and, in their pain and sorrow, may themselves begin to find the ability to love.

In Lion in the Streets, grace is the final resolution. When Isobel tells her murderer that she loves him, she receives grace, and, in turn, sends a message to the audience to seek such peace: "I take my life. I want you all to take your life. I want you all to have your life" (63). She is, in fact, telling people to escape and control their fears, their "lions." Thompson describes to Wachtel what this scene with Isobel means: "It's very hopeful....It's the triumph of the spirit" (40). It is the freedom of the spirit.

Judith Thompson has the ability to make a person come instantly into touch with the evil and the possible virtues of people. She sinks these ideas into the unconscious and the conscious mind through a dream-like atmosphere and the use of a poetic, mesmerizing language that is at once confusing and unavoidable. It is in reaching the collective unconscious that her plays become so powerful. The inner child, it would seem, is the rendezvous point of good and evil; its evil must be controlled and its purity set free. The progression from White Biting Dog to Lion in the Streets shows Thompson's growing ability to control atmosphere and language and to lead the audience to the idea of grace. The confusion within her plays gives way to an exciting and positive experience.

[New page.]

Works Cited

Chung, Kathy. "Emotions and Facts." Canadian Literature 141 (1994): 132-34.

Tomc, Sandra. "Revisions of Probability: An Interview with Judith Thompson." Canadian Theatre Review 59 (1989): 18-23.

Thompson, Judith. White Biting Dog. Toronto: Playwrights Canada, 1984.

---. Lion in the Streets. Toronto: Coach House, 1992.

Wachtel, Eleanor. "An Interview with Judith Thompson." Brick 41 (1991): 37-41.

Chapter 40

Writing in Other Disciplines

Writing in the academic disciplines you study in college or university does much more than simply demonstrate your competence to your instructor. Writing is actually a way you learn concepts, focus ideas, analyse data, uncover assumptions, interpret patterns, and ask and answer questions.

This chapter builds on earlier material: the Introduction on critical thinking, reading, and writing; Chapters 1–2 on the writing process; Chapter 4 on reading and writing arguments; and Chapters

Guidelines for academic writers

- For the discipline you are writing in, become familiar with the methodology and the kinds of evidence considered appropriate and valid.
- Analyse the special demands of the assignment—the kind of research and sources you need. The questions you set out to answer, the assertions you wish to support, will govern how you choose your sources and evidence.
- Become familiar with the specialized tools and language of the discipline.
- Use the style of documentation and the manuscript format customarily used by writers in the discipline.

35–38 on research writing. Study those chapters, if you have not already, because the skills discussed there are fundamental to academic writing.

In this chapter section 40a covers academic writing in general, section 40b covers the humanities besides literature (discussed in Chapter 39), section 40c covers the social sciences, and section 40d covers the natural and applied sciences. For each field, the chapter introduces the basic information that will help you follow the guidelines on the preceding page.

40a Understanding the goals and requirements of the disciplines

Academic disciplines both resemble each other and differ in their methods and evidence, assignments, tools and language, and documentation styles and manuscript formats.

1 Methods and evidence

The **methodology** of a discipline is the way its practitioners study their subjects—that is, how they proceed when investigating the answers to questions. Methodology relates to the framework used to analyse evidence and ideas (see pp. 10–11). For instance, a literary critic and a social historian would probably approach Shakespeare's *Hamlet* through quite different frameworks: the literary critic might study the play for its poetic images; the historian might examine the play's relation to Shakespeare's context, England at the turn of the seventeenth century.

Whatever their analytic framework, academic writers do not compose directly out of their personal experience. Rather, they collect and organize the kinds of evidence appropriate to the discipline, and they base any opinions on that evidence. The evidence comes from research like that described in Chapters 35–36—from primary or secondary sources.

Primary sources are firsthand or original accounts, such as historical documents, works of art, and reports on experiments that the writer has conducted. When you use primary sources, you conduct original research, generating your own evidence. You might analyse a painting and then use examples as evidence for your interpretation of the painting. Or you might conduct a survey of fellow students and then use data from the survey to support your conclusions about students' attitudes. All the sample papers in this chapter and the preceding two chapters depend at least partly on primary sources.

Many primary sources can be found in the library. But more prevalent among a library's holdings are **secondary sources,** books and articles written *about* primary sources. Much academic writing requires that you use such sources to spark, extend, or support your own ideas, as when you review the published opinions and information on your subject before contributing conclusions from your original research.

2 Assignments

For most academic writing, your primary purpose will be either to explain something to your readers or to persuade them to accept your conclusions. To achieve your purpose, you will adapt your writing process to the writing situation, particularly to the kinds of evidence required by the assignment and to the kinds of thinking you are expected to do. Most assignments will contain key words that tell you what these expectations are—words such as *compare, define, analyse,* and *illustrate* that express customary ways of thinking about and organizing a vast range of subjects. Pages 94–103 and 728 explore these so-called patterns of development. You should be aware of them and alert to the wording in assignments that directs you to use them.

3 Tools and language

When you write in an academic discipline, you use the scholarly tools of that discipline, including specialized references such as periodical indexes, abstracts, and computerized databases. (See pp. 510–35 for helpful lists of references.) In addition, you may use the aids developed by practitioners of the discipline for efficiently and effectively approaching research, conducting it, and recording the findings. Many of these aids, such as a system for recording evidence from sources, are discussed in Chapters 35 and 36 and can be adapted to any discipline. Other aids are discussed in later sections of this chapter.

Pay close attention to the texts assigned in a course and any materials given out in class, for these items may introduce you to valuable references and other research aids, and they will use the specialized language of the discipline. This specialized language allows practitioners to write to each other both efficiently and precisely. It also furthers certain concerns of the discipline, such as accuracy and objectivity. Scientists, for example, prefer the verb *indicate* rather than *prove* in discussing their conclusions, because all results are provisional. Some of the language conventions like this one are discussed in the following sections. As you gain experience in a particular discipline, keep alert for such conventions and train yourself to follow them.

Documentation and format

Most disciplines publish journals that require authors to use a certain documentation style and manuscript format. In turn, most instructors in a discipline require the same of students writing papers for their courses.

When you document your sources, you tell readers which ideas and information you borrowed and where they can find your sources. Thus documentation indicates how much knowledge you have and how broad and deep your research was. It also helps you avoid **plagiarism,** the serious offence of presenting the words, ideas, and data of others as if they were your own. (See pp. 555–59 on avoiding plagiarism.)

Manuscript format includes such features as margins and the placement of the title. But it also extends to special elements of the manuscript, such as tables or an abstract, that may be required by the discipline.

The following sections direct you to the style guides published by different disciplines and outline the basic requirements of the ones used most often. If your instructor does not require a particular style, use that of the Modern Language Association, which is described and illustrated at length in Chapter 37 (documentation) and Appendix A (manuscript format).

Writing in the humanities

The humanities include literature, the visual arts, film, history, and philosophy. The preceding chapter discusses the particular requirements of reading and writing about literature. This section concentrates on history. The arts, philosophy, and other humanities have their own concerns, of course, but share many important goals and methods with literature and history.

Methods and evidence in the humanities

Writers in the humanities record and speculate about the growth, ideas, and emotions of human beings. Based on the evidence of written words, artworks, and other human traces and creations, humanities writers explain, interpret, analyse, and reconstruct the human experience.

The discipline of history focuses particularly on reconstructing the past. In Greek the word for history means "to inquire": historians inquire into the past to understand the events of the past. Then they report, explain, analyse, and evaluate those events in their context, asking such questions as what happened before or after the events or how the events were related to the existing political and social structures.

Historians' reconstructions of the past—their conclusions about what happened and why—are always supported with reference to the written record. The evidence of history is mainly primary sources, such as eyewitness accounts and contemporary documents, letters, commercial records, and the like. For history papers, you might also be asked to support your conclusions with those in secondary sources.

In reading historical sources, you need to weigh and evaluate their evidence. If, for example, you find conflicting accounts of the same event, you need to consider the possible biases of the authors or their sources so that you can reject unreliable sources or balance opposing evidence. In general, the more a historian's conclusions are supported by public records such as deeds, marriage licences, and newspaper accounts, the more reliable the conclusions are likely to be.

2 Assignments in the humanities

Papers in the humanities generally perform one or more of the following operations:

- Using **explanation,** you might show how a film director created a particular sequence or clarify a general's role in a battle.
- Using **analysis,** you might examine the elements of a story or painting or break down the causes of a historical event.
- Using **interpretation,** you might infer the meaning of a film from its images or the significance of a historical event from contemporary accounts of it.
- Using **synthesis,** you might find a pattern in a historical period or in a playwright's works.
- Using **evaluation,** you might judge the quality of an architect's design or a historian's conclusions.

Most likely, you will use these operations in combination—say, interpreting and explaining the meaning of a painting and then evaluating it. (These operations are discussed in more detail in the book's Introduction, pp. 10–14.)

Tools and language in the humanities

The tools of the humanities vary according to the discipline. In the arts, for instance, you may ask a series of questions to analyse and evaluate a work (a list of such questions for reading literature appears on pp. 655–56). In addition, a journal—a log of questions, reactions, and insights—can help you discover and record your thoughts.

In history the tools are those of any thorough and efficient researcher, as discussed in Chapters 35 and 36: a system for finding and tracking sources (pp. 510–39); methodical examination of sources, including evaluating and synthesizing them (pp. 541–46); a system for taking notes from sources (pp. 547–54); and a separate system, such as a research journal, for tracking one's own evolving thoughts (pp. 505–06).

When writing about history, it's important to remain as objective as possible. Historians strive for precision and logic; they do not guess about what happened or speculate about "what if." They avoid trying to influence readers' opinions with words having strongly negative or positive connotations, such as *stupid* or *brilliant* (see p. 452). Instead, historians show the evidence and draw conclusions from that. Generally, they avoid using *I:* it tends to draw attention away from the evidence and toward the writer, and it may imply a bias even when there is none.

Writing about history demands some attention to the tenses of verbs to maintain consistency. (See pp. 208–09 for explanations of verb tenses.) Generally, historians use the past tense to refer to events that occurred in the past. They reserve the present tense only for statements about the present or statements of general truths. For example:

> Sir Wilfrid Laurier *died* in 1919. Many of his political and social innovations *persist* in English and French relations in this country.

Source citations and document format in the humanities

Writers in the humanities generally rely on one of the following guides for source-citation style and document format:

Chicago Manual of Style. 14th ed. 1993.

Gibaldi, Joseph. *MLA Handbook for Writers of Research Papers.* 4th ed. 1995.

Turabian, Kate L. *A Manual for Writers of Term Papers, Theses, and Dissertations.* 6th ed. Rev. John Grossman and Alice Bennett. 1996.

The recommendations of the *MLA Handbook* are discussed and illustrated in Chapter 37 and Appendix A. Unless your instructor specifies otherwise, use these recommendations for papers in English and foreign languages. You may also use MLA document format in other humanities as well. However, for source citations many humanities follow the footnote or endnote citation style of the *Chicago Manual of Style* and the student guide adapted from it, Turabian's *Manual for Writers of Term Papers, Theses, and Dissertations.* (These books also discuss another style using in-text parenthetical citations, which is like that of the American Psychological Association, widely used in the social sciences. See pp. 692–705.)

Chicago endnotes or footnotes

The *Chicago Manual* and *A Manual for Writers* detail a source-citation system of raised numerals in the text referring to footnotes (bottoms of pages) or endnotes (end of paper), along with an optional list of works cited at the end of the paper (see the note following).

NOTE The *Chicago Manual* does not require an alphabetical list of works cited if you provide complete source information in your notes. Alternatively, the guide allows you to shorten source information in notes and then provide full information in a list of works cited. *A Manual for Writers,* however, requires both full notes and a full list of works cited. Many instructors have the same requirement, so that the reader has a complete alphabetical list of sources and yet does not have to turn from notes to the works-cited list for full information on a particular text citation. Ask your instructor what he or she requires. The following pages illustrate full notes and works-cited entries as well as shortened notes.

Ask your instructor also whether you should provide footnotes or endnotes. Whichever you use, single-space the notes themselves and double-space between notes. With footnotes, separate the notes from the text with a short line, as shown in the following sample:

```
In 1901, Madras, Bengal, and Punjab were a few of the huge
Indian provinces governed by the British viceroy.6 British
rule, observes Stuart Cary Welch, "seemed as permanent as
Mount Everest."7
____________________  ← Line
5 spaces
     6. Martin Gilbert, Atlas of British History (New   ] Single-
York: Dorset Press, 1968), 96.                          ] space
                                                ← Double-space
     7. Stuart Cary Welch, India: Art and Culture (New  ] Single-
York: Metropolitan Museum of Art, 1985), 421.           ] space

                        ↕ 2.5 cm
```

With endnotes, use the format below for a list of works cited, substituting the heading "NOTES" and numbered entries as for footnotes.

For the list of sources at the end of the paper, use the format below. Arrange the sources alphabetically by the authors' last names.

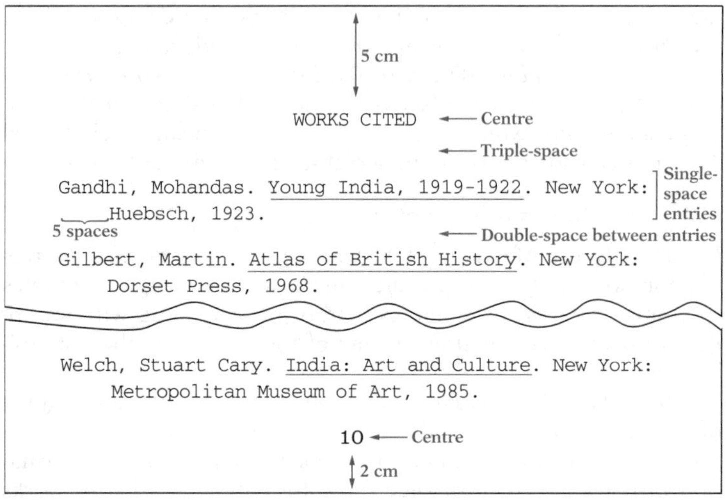

The examples that follow illustrate the essentials of a note and a works-cited entry.

Note

6. Martin Gilbert, Atlas of British History (New York: Dorset Press, 1968), 96.

Index to *CMS* note and works-cited models

WORKS-CITED ENTRY

```
Gilbert, Martin. Atlas of British History. New York:
    Dorset Press, 1968.
```

Notes and works-cited entries share certain features:

- Underline or italicize the titles of books and periodicals (ask your instructor for his or her preference).
- Enclose in quotation marks the titles of parts of books or articles in periodicals.
- Do not abbreviate publishers' names, but omit "Inc.," "Co.," and similar abbreviations.
- Do not use "p." or "pp." before page numbers.

Notes and works-cited entries also differ in important ways:

NOTE	WORKS-CITED ENTRY
Start with a number (typed on the line and followed by a period) that corresponds to the note number in the text.	Do not begin with a number.
Indent the first line five spaces.	Indent the second and subsequent lines five spaces.
Give the author's name in normal order.	Begin with the author's last name.
Use commas between elements such as author's name and title.	Use periods between elements, followed by one space.
Enclose publication information in parentheses, with no preceding punctuation.	Precede the publication information with a period, and don't use parentheses.
Include the specific page number(s) you borrowed from, omitting "p." or "pp."	Omit page numbers except for parts of books or articles in periodicals.

Many computerized word-processing programs will automatically position footnotes at the bottoms of appropriate pages. Some will automatically number notes and even renumber them if you add or delete one or more.

In the following models for common sources, notes and works-cited entries appear together for easy reference. Be sure to use the numbered note form for notes and the unnumbered works-cited form for works-cited entries.

1. A BOOK WITH ONE, TWO, OR THREE AUTHORS

```
     1. Carol Gilligan, In a Different Voice: Psycho-
logical Theory and Women's Development (Cambridge: Har-
vard University Press, 1982), 27.
```

Gilligan, Carol. In a Different Voice: Psychological Theory and Women's Development. Cambridge: Harvard University Press, 1982.

1. Peter Knudsen and David Suzuki, Wisdom of the Elders (Toronto: Stoddard, 1992), 107-211.

Knudsen, Peter, and David Suzuki. Wisdom of the Elders. Toronto: Stoddard, 1992.

2. A book with more than three authors

2. John B. Logan et al., Canada on the World Stage (Toronto: Pathfinder, 1983), 87-105.

Logan, John B., et al. Canada on the World Stage. Toronto: Pathfinder, 1983.

3. A book with an editor

3. D. Lochhead, ed., Made in Canada: New Poems (Ottawa: Oberon, 1970), 313.

Lochhead, D., ed. Made in Canada: New Poems. Ottawa: Oberon, 1970.

4. An anonymous work

4. Merriam-Webster's Collegiate Dictionary, 10th ed. (Springfield: Merriam-Webster, 1993).

Merriam-Webster's Collegiate Dictionary. 10th ed. Springfield: Merriam-Webster, 1993.

5. A later edition

5. Dwight L. Bollinger, Aspects of Language, 2nd ed. (New York: Harcourt Brace Jovanovich, 1975), 20.

Bollinger, Dwight L. Aspects of Language. 2nd ed. New York: Harcourt Brace Jovanovich, 1975.

6. A work in more than one volume

6. Abraham Lincoln, The Collected Works of Abraham

Lincoln, ed. Roy P. Basler (New Brunswick: Rutgers University Press, 1953), 5:426-28.

Lincoln, Abraham. The Collected Works of Abraham Lincoln. Ed. Roy P. Basler. Vol. 5. New Brunswick: Rutgers University Press, 1953.

7. A SELECTION FROM AN ANTHOLOGY

7. Rosetta Brooks, "Streetwise," in The New Urban Landscape, ed. Richard Martin (New York: Rizzoli, 1990), 38-39.

Brooks, Rosetta. "Streetwise." In The New Urban Landscape, ed. Richard Martin, 37-60. New York: Rizzoli, 1990.

8. AN ARTICLE IN A JOURNAL WITH CONTINUOUS PAGINATION THROUGHOUT THE ANNUAL VOLUME

8. Janet Lever, "Sex Differences in the Games Children Play," Social Problems 23 (1976): 482.

Lever, Janet. "Sex Differences in the Games Children Play." Social Problems 23 (1976): 478-87.

9. AN ARTICLE IN A JOURNAL THAT PAGES ISSUES SEPARATELY

9. June Dacey, "Management Participation in Corporate Buy-Outs," Management Perspectives 7, no. 4 (1994): 22.

Dacey, June. "Management Participation in Corporate Buy-Outs." Management Perspectives 7, no. 4 (1994): 20-31.

10. AN ARTICLE IN A POPULAR MAGAZINE

10. Brian McKenna, "Comrades in Arms," Saturday Night, December 1993, 38-41.

McKenna, Brian. "Comrades in Arms." Saturday Night, December 1993, 38-41.

11. An article in a newspaper

11. Susan Delacourt, "The 905 Revolution," Globe and Mail, 25 November 1995, D1.

Delacourt, Susan. "The 905 Revolution." Globe and Mail, 25 November 1995, D1.

12. A work of art

12. John Singer Sargent, In Switzerland, watercolour, 1908, Metropolitan Museum of Art, New York.

Sargent, John Singer. In Switzerland, watercolour, 1908. Metropolitan Museum of Art, New York.

13. A source on CD-ROM or diskette

13. Anthony Ramirez, "Computer Groups Plan Standards," New York Times, 14 December 1993, D5, late edition, New York Times Ondisc [CD-ROM], UMI-ProQuest, June 1994.

Ramirez, Anthony. "Computer Groups Plan Standards." New York Times, 14 December 1993, D5, late edition. New York Times Ondisc [CD-ROM], UMI-ProQuest, June 1994.

When a source is also published in print, as above, give the print information first, followed by the electronic information.

14. An online source

14. Jane Austen, Emma [book online], ed. Ronald Blythe (Harmondsworth: Penguin, 1972), Oxford Text Archive, accessed 15 December 1995; available from ftp://black.ox.ac.uk.

Austen, Jane. Emma [book online]. Ed. Ronald Blythe. Harmondsworth: Penguin, 1972. Oxford Text Archive. Accessed 15 December 1995. Available from ftp://black.ox.ac.uk.

Give the date of your access to the source (after "accessed") as well as the electronic address (after "available from"). When a source is also published in print, give the print information first, as above.

14. Andrew Palfrey, "Choice of Mates in Identical Twins," Modern Psychology 4, no. 1 (1996): pars. 7-8 [journal online], accessed 25 February 1996; available from ftp://modpsy.liasu.edu/palfrey4(1).txt.

Palfrey, Andrew. "Choice of Mates in Identical Twins." Modern Psychology 4, no. 1 (1996) [journal online]. Accessed 25 February 1996. Available from ftp://modpsy.liasu.edu/palfrey4(1).txt.

15. Two or more citations of the same source

To minimize clutter in notes and to give readers a quick sense of how often you acknowledge a source, the Chicago style allows a shortened form for subsequent citations of a source you have already cited fully. The shortened form may also be acceptable for a first citation of a source if you provide full information in a list of works cited. (See the note on p. 681.)

You may use the Latin abbreviation "ibid." (meaning "in the same place") to refer to the same source cited in the preceding note:

8. Janet Lever, "Sex Differences in the Games Children Play," Social Problems 23 (1976): 482.

9. Ibid., 483.

For any source already cited in your notes, not just immediately before, you may use the author's name and (if the author is responsible for more than one cited source) a shortened form of the title.

1. Carol Gilligan, In a Different Voice: Psychological Theory and Women's Development (Cambridge: Harvard University Press, 1982), 27.

2. Carol Gilligan, "Moral Development in the College Years," The Modern American College, ed. A. Chickering (San Francisco: Jossey-Bass, 1981), 286.

3. Gilligan, In a Different Voice, 47.

Omit the title if you are using only one source by the cited author.

The Chicago style recommends in-text parenthetical citations when you cite one or more works repeatedly. This practice allows you to avoid many notes saying "ibid." or giving the same author's name. In the example following, the note number refers to the complete source information in an endnote; the numbers in parentheses are page numbers in the same source.

> British rule, observes Stuart Cary Welch, "seemed as permanent as Mount Everest."[7] Most Indians submitted, willingly or not, to British influence in every facet of life (423-24).

Document format in the humanities

The illustrations on pages 681–82 show several features of the document format recommended by Turabian's *Manual for Writers of Term Papers, Theses, and Dissertations.* The following list supplements those illustrations:

- Use a title page if your instructor requires one. Separate the title, your name, and the course identification and date as illustrated on page 606, but use all-capital letters.
- If your instructor does not require a title page, follow the style of the *MLA Handbook* for positioning your name, course identification, and date (see p. 747).
- Centre your paper title 5 cm (2") from the top of the first page, typed in all-capital letters. Treat section titles, such as "NOTES" or "WORKS CITED," the same way (see pp. 681–82). Triple-space beneath the title or heading.
- Double-space everything except individual footnotes or endnotes and the individual entries in the list of works cited (single-space these as shown on p. 681).
- Number all pages except any preliminary pages (title page, outline) consecutively throughout the paper, including notes and the list of works cited. Place the number at the top of the page, either centred or at the right margin, with one exception: for pages with headings, such as "NOTES," centre the page number at the foot of the page (as shown on p. 682).
- Set long quotations off from your text: poetry quotations of three or more lines and prose quotations of two or more sentences and eight or more lines. (You may display shorter prose quotations to emphasize them or to compare them.) Double-space above and below a displayed quotation, and single-space the quotation itself. Indent the quotation four spaces from the left margin. Do not use quotation marks for a displayed quotation.

40c Writing in the social sciences

The social sciences—including anthropology, economics, education, management, political science, psychology, and sociology—focus on the study of human behaviour. As the name implies, the social sciences examine the way human beings relate to themselves, to their environment, and to each other.

Methods and evidence in the social sciences

Researchers in the social sciences systematically pose a question, formulate a **hypothesis** (a generalization that can be tested), collect data, analyse those data, and draw conclusions to support or disprove their hypothesis. This is the scientific method developed in the natural sciences (see p. 712).

Social scientists gather data in several ways:

- They make firsthand observations of human behaviour and record the observations in writing or on audio- or videotape.
- They interview subjects about their attitudes and behaviour, recording responses in writing or on tape. (See pp. 535–36 for guidelines on conducting an interview.)
- They conduct broader surveys using questionnaires that ask people about their attitudes and behaviour. (See the box on the next page.)
- They conduct controlled experiments, structuring an environment in which to encourage and measure a specific behaviour.

In their writing, social scientists explain their own research or analyse and evaluate others' research.

The research methods of social science generate two kinds of data.

- **Quantitative data** are numerical, such as statistical evidence based on surveys, polls, tests, and experiments. When public-opinion pollsters announce that 47 percent of Canadians polled approve of the Prime Minister's leadership, they are offering quantitative data gained from a survey. Social science writers present quantitative data in graphs, charts, and other illustrations that accompany their text.
- **Qualitative data** are not numerical but more subjective: they are based on interviews, firsthand observations, and inferences, taking into account the subjective nature of human ex-perience. An example is the work of the anthropologist Margaret Mead,

Conducting a survey

- Decide what you want to find out—what your hypothesis is. The questions you ask should be dictated by your purpose.
- Define your population. Think about the kinds of people your hypothesis is about—for instance, college or university men, or five-year-old children. Plan to sample this population so that your findings will be representative.
- Write your questions. Surveys may contain closed questions that direct the respondent's answers (checklists and multiple-choice, true/false, or yes/no questions) or open-ended questions allowing brief, descriptive answers. Avoid loaded questions that reveal your own biases or make assumptions about subjects' answers, such as "Do you want Canada to support democracy in China?" or "How much more money does your father make than your mother?"
- Test your questions on a few respondents with whom you can discuss the answers. Eliminate or recast questions that respondents find unclear, discomforting, or unanswerable.
- Tally the results in actual numbers of answers, including any nonanswers.
- Seek patterns in the raw data that conform or conflict with your hypothesis. Revise the hypothesis or conduct additional research if necessary.

whose experiences among the people of Samoa led to an important description of how adolescent Samoans become aware of adult concerns and rituals. Mead's book *Coming of Age in Samoa* contains few numbers; the data are qualitative.

2 Assignments in the social sciences

Depending on what social science courses you take, you may be asked to complete a variety of assignments.

- A **summary or review of research** reports on the available research literature on a subject, such as infant perception of colour.
- A **case analysis** explains the components of a phenomenon, such as a factory closing.
- A **problem-solving analysis** explains the components of a problem, such as unreported child abuse, and suggests ways to solve it. A problem-solving analysis begins on page 708.
- A **research paper** interprets and sometimes analyses and evaluates the writings of other social scientists about a subject, such as the effect of national appeals in advertising. An example appears in Chapter 38, page 606.

40c

- A **research report** explains the author's own original research or attempt to replicate someone else's research.

Many social science disciplines have special requirements for the content and organization of each kind of paper. The requirements appear in the style guides of the disciplines, such as the *Publication Manual of the American Psychological Association* (APA). (Guides for other disciplines are listed on p. 692.) The APA manual specifies the following outline for the text of a research report:

1. *Abstract:* a summary (about 100 words) of the subject, the research method, the findings, and the conclusions.
2. *Introduction:* a presentation of the problem researched, the research method used, the background (such as other relevant studies), the purpose of the research, and the hypothesis tested.
3. *Method:* a detailed discussion of how the research was conducted, including a description of the research subjects, any materials or tools used (such as questionnaires), and the procedure followed.
4. *Results:* a summary of the data collected and how they were statistically analysed, along with a detailed presentation of the data, often in tables, graphs, or charts.
5. *Discussion:* an interpretation of the data and presentation of conclusions, related to the original hypothesis. (When the discussion is brief, it may be combined with the previous section under the heading "Results and Discussion.")

To this basic text are added a title page and a list of references (the latter described on pp. 696–706).

Because of the differences among disciplines and even among different kinds of papers in the same discipline, you should always ask your instructor what he or she requires for an assignment.

3 Tools and language in the social sciences

Although a **research journal** or **log** may not be required in your courses, such a notebook can be very helpful. Use it to pose preliminary questions as you begin formulating a hypothesis. Then in the field (that is, when conducting research), use the journal to react to the evidence you are collecting, to record changes in your perceptions and ideas, and to assess your progress. To avoid confusing your reflections on the evidence with the evidence itself, keep records of actual data—notes from interviews, observations, surveys, and experiments—separately from the field journal.

Each social science discipline has specialized terminology for concepts basic to the discipline. In sociology, for example, the words *mechanism, identity,* and *deviance* have specific meanings different from those of everyday usage. And *identity* means something different in sociology, where it applies to groups of people, than in psychology, where it applies to the individual. Social scientists also use precise terms to describe or interpret research. For instance, they say *The subject expressed a feeling of . . .* rather than *The subject felt . . .* because human feelings are not knowable for certain; or they say *These studies indicate . . .* rather than *These studies prove . . .* because conclusions are only tentative.

Just as social scientists strive for objectivity in their research, so they strive to demonstrate their objectivity through language in their writing. They avoid expressions such as *I think* in order to focus attention on what the evidence shows rather than on the researcher's opinions. (However, many social scientists prefer *I* to the artificial *the researcher* when they refer to their own actions, as in *I then interviewed the subjects.* Ask your instructor for his or her preferences.) Social scientists also avoid direct or indirect expression of their personal biases or emotions, either in discussions of other researchers' work or in descriptions of research subjects. Thus, one social scientist does not call another's work *sloppy* or *immaculate* and does not refer to his or her own subjects as *drunks* or *innocent victims.* Instead, the writer uses neutral language and ties conclusions strictly to the data.

Documentation and format

As mentioned earlier, some of the social sciences publish style guides that advise practitioners how to organize, document, and type papers. The following is a partial list:

American Psychological Association. *Publication Manual of the American Psychological Association.* 4th ed. 1994.

American Sociological Association. "Editorial Guidelines." Inside front cover of each issue of *American Sociological Review.*

American Anthropological Association. "Style Guide and Information for Authors." *American Anthropologist* (1977): 774–79.

Disciplines that do not have their own style guides may rely on one of those above or may recommend any of several guides. In business, for example, teachers and practitioners often use the *Publication Manual of the American Psychological Association* (APA), listed above; the *MLA Handbook for Writers of Research Papers* (p. 576); *The Chicago Manual of Style* (p. 681); or Turabian's *Manual for Writers of Term Papers, Theses, and Dissertations* (p. 575).

Always ask your instructor in any discipline what style you should use. The APA style and manuscript format are explained and illustrated below because they are by far the most often used in the social sciences and are similar to the styles in sociology, economics, and other disciplines.

Index to APA parenthetical citations

APA parenthetical citations

The APA documentation style is like that of the Modern Language Association in that parenthetical citations within the text refer the reader to a list of sources at the end of the text. The APA style (like the MLA) thus uses footnotes or endnotes only for information that does not fit easily into the text.

APA parenthetical citations contain the author's last name, the date of publication (a key difference from MLA style), and often the page number from which material is borrowed. See above for an index to the models for various kinds of sources.

1. Author not named in your text

```
One critic of Milgram's experiments insisted that the
subjects "should have been fully informed of the
possible effects on them" (Baumrind, 1968, p. 34).
```

When you do not name the author in your text, place in parentheses the author's name, the date of the source, and the page number(s) preceded by "p." or "pp." Separate the elements with commas. Position the reference so that it is clear what material is being documented *and* so that the reference fits as smoothly as possible into your sentence structure. The following would also be correct:

```
In the view of one critic of Milgram's experiments
(Baumrind, 1968, p. 34), the subjects "should have been
fully informed of the possible effects on them."
```


2. Author named in your text

```
Baumrind (1968, p. 34) insisted that the subjects in
Milgram's study "should have been fully informed of the
possible effects on them."
```

When you use the author's name in the text, do not repeat it in the reference. Position the reference next to the author's name. If you cite the same source again in the paragraph, you need not repeat the reference as long as the page number (if any) is the same and it is clear that you are using the same source. Here is a later sentence from the paragraph containing the preceding example.

> Baumrind also criticized the experimenters' rationale.

3. A work with two authors

> Pepinsky and DeStefano (1987) demonstrate that a teacher's language often reveals hidden biases.

> One study (Pepinsky & DeStefano, 1987) demonstrates the hidden biases often revealed in a teacher's language.

When given in the text, two authors' names are connected by "and." In a parenthetical citation, they are connected by an ampersand, "&."

4. A work with three to five authors

> Pepinsky, Dunn, Rentl, and Corson (1983) further demonstrate the biases evident in gestures.

In the first citation of a work with three to five authors, name all the authors, as in the example above. In the second and subsequent references to a work with three to five authors, give only the first author's name, followed by "et al." (Latin for "and others"):

> In the work of Pepinsky et al. (1983), the loaded gestures include head shakes and eye contact.

5. A work with six or more authors

> One study (Rutter et al., 1976) attempts to explain these geographical differences in adolescent experience.

For six or more authors, even in the first citation of the work, give only the first author's name, followed by "et al."

6. A work with a corporate author

> An earlier prediction was even more sombre (Lorenz, Inc., 1990).

For a work with a corporate or group author, treat the name of the corporation or group as if it were an individual's name.

7. An anonymous work

```
One article ("Future Offenders," 1993) noted that young
offenders require individual attention.
```

For an anonymous or unsigned work, use the first two or three words of the title in place of an author's name, excluding an initial *The, A,* or *An.* Underline book and journal titles. Place quotation marks around article titles. (In the list of references, however, do not use quotation marks for article titles. See pp. 701–02.) Capitalize the significant words in all titles cited in the text. (But in the reference list, treat only journal titles this way. See pp. 701–02.)

8. One of two or more works by the same author(s)

```
At about age seven, most children begin to use appro-
priate gestures to reinforce their stories (Gardner,
1973a, pp. 144-145).
```

When you cite one of two or more works by the same author(s), the date will tell readers which source you mean—as long as your reference list includes only one source published by the author(s) in that year. If your reference list includes two or more works published by the same author(s) *in the same year,* the works should be lettered in the reference list (see p. 699). Then your parenthetical citation should include the appropriate letter, as in "1973a" above.

9. Two or more works by different authors

```
Two studies (Herskowitz, 1984; Marconi & Hamblen, 1990)
found that periodic safety instruction can dramatically
reduce employees' accidents.
```

List the sources in alphabetical order by the first author's name. Insert a semicolon between sources.

10. An indirect source

```
Supporting data appear in a study by Wong (cited in
Marconi & Hamblen, 1990).
```

The phrase "cited in" indicates that the reference to Wong's study was found in Marconi and Hamblen. Only Marconi and Hamblen then appears in the list of references.

APA reference list

In APA style, the in-text parenthetical citations refer to the list of sources at the end of the text. This list, titled "References," includes full publication information on every source cited in the paper.

CAUTION The APA style is quite different from that of the *MLA Handbook* (p. 576). Don't confuse the two styles.

The following sample shows the format of the first page of the APA reference list:

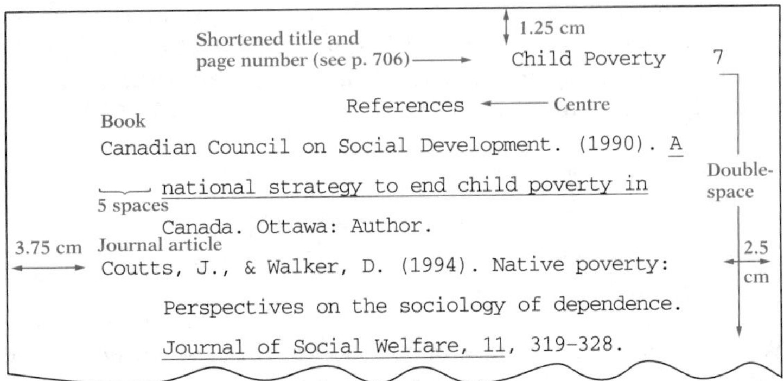

Prepare APA "References" as follows:

- Arrange sources alphabetically by the author's last name or, if there is no author, by the first main word of the title.
- Double-space all entries.
- Use an appropriate indention for each entry. For papers that will be published, the APA recommends indenting the first line of each entry five to seven spaces:

```
     Porter, J. (1965). The vertical mosaic: An analy-
sis of social power and class in Canada. Toronto: Uni-
versity of Toronto Press.
```

When set into type for publication, the initial indentions are then converted into so-called hanging indentions, in which the first line is not indented while the others are. The hanging indention makes it easier for readers to spot authors' names, so the APA recognizes that students who are preparing final copy (not destined for publication) may wish to use the hanging indention for their references:

```
Porter, J. (1965). The vertical mosaic: An analysis of
     social power and class in Canada. Toronto: Univer-
     sity of Toronto Press.
```

Index to APA references

Because it is clearer for readers, the hanging indention is used in the sample page opposite and throughout the following models for references, with a five-space indention for the second and subsequent lines of each entry. Ask your instructor which format he or she prefers.

- List all authors last-name first, separating names and parts of names with commas. Use initials for first and middle names. Use an ampersand (&) before the last author's name.
- In titles of books and articles, capitalize only the first word of the title, the first word of the subtitle, and proper names; all other words begin with small letters. In titles of journals, capitalize all significant words. Underline the titles of books and journals, along with any comma or period following. Do not underline or use quotation marks around the titles of articles.
- For sources that are not periodicals (such as books or government publications), give the city of publication. Canadian and non-American cities can stand alone. The following American cities do not require state names: Baltimore, Boston, Chicago, Los Angeles, New York, Philadelphia, and San Francisco. Follow the city names with a colon. For all other American cities, add a comma after the city name and give the two-letter postal abbreviation of the state. Then put a colon after the state.

- Also for nonperiodical sources, give the publisher's name after the place of publication and a colon. Use shortened names for many publishers (such as "Morrow" for William Morrow), and omit "Co.," "Inc.," and "Publishers." However, give full names for associations, corporations, and university presses (such as "University of Toronto Press"), and do not omit "Books" or "Press" from a publisher's name.
- Use the abbreviation "p." or "pp." before page numbers in books and in newspapers, but *not* in other periodicals. For inclusive page numbers, include all figures: "667–668."
- Separate the parts of the reference (author, date, title, and publication information) with a period and one space.

NOTE You may have to combine models to provide the necessary information on a source—for instance, combining "A book with one author" (1) and "A book with an editor" (3) for a book with only one editor.

1. A BOOK WITH ONE AUTHOR

`Porter, J. (1965).` <u>The vertical mosaic: An analysis of social power and class in Canada.</u> `Toronto: University of Toronto Press.`

The initial "J" appears instead of the author's first name, even though the author's full first name appears on the source. In the title, only the first words of title and subtitle and the proper name are capitalized.

2. A BOOK WITH TWO OR MORE AUTHORS

`Nesselroade, J. R., & Baltes, P. B. (1979).` <u>Longitudinal research in the study of behavioral development</u>. `New York: Academic Press.`

An ampersand (&) separates the authors' names.

3. A BOOK WITH AN EDITOR

`Granatstein, J., & Stevens, P. (Eds.). (1974).` <u>Canada since 1867: A bibliographical guide.</u> `Toronto: Hakkert.`

List the editors' names as if they were authors, but follow the last name with "(Eds.)."—or "(Ed.)." with only one editor. Note the periods inside and outside the final parenthesis.

4. A BOOK WITH A TRANSLATOR

Trudeau, P. E. (1970). Approaches to politics. (I. M. Owen, Trans.). Toronto: Oxford University Press.

The name of the translator appears in parentheses after the title, followed by a comma, "Trans.", a closing parenthesis, and a final period.

5. A BOOK WITH A CORPORATE AUTHOR

Lorenz, Inc. (1992). Research in social studies teaching. Baltimore: Arrow Books.

For a work with a corporate or group author, begin the entry with the corporate or group name. In the references list, alphabetize the work as if the first main word (excluding *The, A,* and *An*) were an author's last name.

6. AN ANONYMOUS BOOK

Merriam-Webster's collegiate dictionary (10th ed.). (1993). Springfield, MA: Merriam-Webster.

When no author is named, list the work under its title, and alphabetize it by the first main word (excluding *The, A, An*).

7. TWO OR MORE WORKS BY THE SAME AUTHOR(S)

Gardner, H. (1973a). The arts and human development. New York: John Wiley.

Gardner, H. (1973b). The quest for mind: Piaget, Lévi-Strauss, and the structuralist movement. New York: Alfred A. Knopf.

When citing two or more works by exactly the same author(s), arrange the sources in order of their publication dates, earliest first. When citing two or more works by exactly the same author(s), published in the same year—as in the examples above—arrange them alphabetically by the first main word of the title and distinguish the sources by adding a letter to the date. Both the date *and* the letter are used in citing the source in the text (see p. 695).

8. A LATER EDITION

Bollinger, D. L. (1975). Aspects of language (2nd ed.). New York: Harcourt Brace Jovanovich.

The edition number in parentheses follows the title and is followed by a period.

9. A work in more than one volume

Lincoln, A. (1953). The collected works of Abraham Lincoln (R. P. Basler, Ed.). (Vol. 5). New Brunswick, NJ: Rutgers University Press.

Lincoln, A. (1953). The collected works of Abraham Lincoln (R. P. Basler, Ed.). (Vols. 1-8). New Brunswick, NJ: Rutgers University Press.

The first entry cites a single volume (5) in the eight-volume set. The second cites all eight volumes. Use the abbreviation "Vol." or "Vols." in parentheses, and follow the closing parenthesis with a period. In the absence of an editor's name, the description of volumes would follow the title directly: The collected works of Abraham Lincoln (Vol. 5).

10. An article or chapter in an edited book

Paykel, E. S. (1974). Life stress and psychiatric disorder: Applications of the clinical approach. In B. S. Dohrenwend & B. P. Dohrenwend (Eds.), Stressful life events: Their nature and effects (pp. 239-264). New York: John Wiley.

Give the publication date of the collection (1974 above) as the publication date of the article or chapter. After the article or chapter title and a period, say "In" and then provide the editors' names (in normal order), "(Eds.)" and a comma, the title of the collection, and the page numbers of the article in parentheses.

11. An article in a journal with continuous pagination throughout the annual volume

Emery, R. E. (1982). Marital turmoil: Interpersonal conflict and the children of discord and divorce. Psychological Bulletin, 92, 310-330.

See page 527 for an explanation of journal pagination. Note that you do not place the article title in quotation marks and that you capitalize only the first words of the title and subtitle. In contrast, you underline the journal title and capitalize all significant words. Separate the volume number from the title with a comma and underline the number. Do not add "pp." before the page numbers.

12. AN ARTICLE IN A JOURNAL THAT PAGES ISSUES SEPARATELY

Dacey, J. (1994). Management participation in corporate buy-outs. Management Perspectives, 7(4), 20-31.

Again, consult page 527 for an explanation of journal pagination. In this case, place the issue number in parentheses after the volume number without intervening space. Do *not* underline the issue number.

13. AN ARTICLE IN A MAGAZINE

Van Gelder, L. (1986, December). Countdown to motherhood: When should you have a baby? Ms., 37-39, 74.

If a magazine has volume and issue numbers, give them as in models 11 and 12. Also give the full date of the issue: year, followed by a comma, month, and day (if any). Give all page numbers even when the article appears on discontinuous pages, without "pp."

14. AN ARTICLE IN A NEWSPAPER

Albert, C. (1995, December 10). Choices diminish for voters. The Kitchener Record, p. A8.

Give month *and* date along with year of publication. Use The in the newspaper name if the paper itself does.

15. AN UNSIGNED ARTICLE

The right to die. (1976, October 11). Time, 121, 101.

List and alphabetize the article under its title, as you would an anonymous book (model 6, p. 699).

16. A REVIEW

Anthony, Elizabeth. (1992, February). Psychodrama. [Review of The secret ring: Freud's inner circles and the politics of psychoanalysis]. Books in Canada, 49-50.

If the review is not titled, use the bracketed information as the title, keeping the brackets.

17. A GOVERNMENT DOCUMENT

House of Commons Task Force on Employment. (1981). Work for tomorrow. Ottawa: Author.

If no individual is listed as author, list the document under the name of the sponsoring agency. When the agency is both the author and the publisher, use "Author" in place of the publisher's name.

18. A SOURCE ON CD-ROM

```
Ramirez, A. (1993, 14 December). Computer groups plan
     standards. The New York Times Ondisc [CD-ROM], p.
     D5. Available: UMI-ProQuest: New York Times Ondisc
     Item: 9340006210
```

Treat an article on CD-ROM as you would a print article from the same type of periodical—journal, newspaper, and so on—but add the medium in brackets after the title, and supply the source and item or file number after "Available:" at the end of the entry.

The following model illustrates citation of an abstract on CD-ROM:

```
Willard, B. L. (1992). Changes in occupational safety
     standards, 1970-1990 [CD-ROM]. Abstract from: Pro-
     Quest File: Dissertation Abstracts Item: 7770763
```

19. AN ONLINE SOURCE

The online models given here are adapted from both the APA *Publication Manual* and *Electronic Style: A Guide to Citing Electronic Information,* by Xia Li and Nancy B. Crane (1993), which adapts APA style to a range of electronic sources and which the *Publication Manual* itself relies on.

NOTE For an online source that is not retrievable by others, the APA requires omitting the source from your list of references and citing it only in your text in parentheses: if the author is not already named, `(G. M. Shay, personal communication, June 6, 1996)`; if the author is already named, `(personal communication, June 6, 1996)`. Such nonretrievable sources generally include personal electronic mail and postings on electronic bulletin boards and discussion groups. However, some discussion groups archive their postings so that they are retrievable (see p. 525), and you may cite an archived posting in your reference list.

The following models illustrate several kinds of online sources. In general, give author and title as you would for a printed source. Between these elements, provide the date of posting given by the source or, if no date is given, provide the date of your access to the source. For an online journal article, add the length (if given) after the article title (see the Palfrey entry below). After the title of the full source, provide the medium in brackets. At the end of the entry, after "Available," provide the electronic address and any other information (such as directory or file name) needed to retrieve the source. Do not add any period that is not part of the electronic address, even at the end of the entry. See page 596 for suggestions on breaking an electronic address from one line to the next.

An article in an online periodical:

Palfrey, A. (1996, January). Choice of mates in identical twins [12 paragraphs]. Modern Psychology [Online serial], 4(1). Available: ftp://modpsy.liasu.edu/palfrey4(1).txt

Ramirez, A. (1993, 14 December). Computer groups plan standards. The New York Times Online [Online], p. D5. Available: Nexis File:NYT

A source on the World Wide Web:

Leppik, P. (1996, January 21). The two rules of Internet security [Online]. Available: http://www.thinck.com/insec.html

An FTP (File Transfer Protocol) site:

Clarke, K. (1996, January). A "near" contract experience. E-Law--Murdoch Electronic Journal of Law [Online serial], 3. Available: ftp://infolib.murdoch.edu.au/pub/subj/law/jnl/elaw/comment/clarke.txt

A Gopher site:

Goetsch, S. (1995). And what about costume? Didaskalia: Ancient Theatre Today [Online serial], 2(2). Available: gopher://University of Warwick/Didaskalia/Didaskalia: Ancient Theatre Today/03Features/Goetsch

A Telnet site:

Johnson, E. (1996, August 11). My house: Come on in. Houses of Cyberspace [Online]. Available: telnet://edwin.ohms.bookso.com 7777 @go #50827, press 10

An archived discussion group:

Campion, D. (1997, January 23). Cincinnati halfway houses. Corrections Alternatives Discussion List [Online]. Available e-mail: coralts@wau.edu

Cite e-mail, discussion-group messages, and other personal communications only in your text unless they are retrievable by others (see p. 703). The Listserv cited above is archived and so may be cited in the list of references.

A synchronous communication (IRC, MUD, MOO):

Chartreuse_Guest. (1996, February 13). Tuesday cafe session [Online]. Available: telnet://logos.daedalus.com:70/11/Alliance for Computers and Writing/NETORIC/Tuesday Cafe log 13Feb.

20. An abstract of an article or dissertation

Emery, R. E. (1982). Marital turmoil: Interpersonal conflict and the children of discord and divorce. Psychological Bulletin, 92, 310-330. (From Psychological Abstracts, 69, Item 1320)

When you cite the abstract of an article, rather than the article itself, give full publication information for the article, followed, in parentheses, by the information for the collection of abstracts, including title, volume number, and either page number or other reference number ("Item 1320" above).

For an abstract of an unpublished doctoral dissertation, give the university and the year of the dissertation in parentheses after the title. Then give the source of the abstract, the volume number, and the page number.

Steciw, S. K. (1986). Alterations to the Pessac project of Le Corbusier (Doctoral dissertation, University of Cambridge, England, 1986). Dissertation Abstracts International, 46, 565C.

21. A report

Gerald, K. (1958). Medico-moral problems in obstetric care (Report No. NP-71). St. Louis, MO: Catholic Hospital Association.

Treat the report like a book, but provide any report number in parentheses immediately after the title, with no punctuation between them.

For a report from the Educational Resources Information Center (ERIC), provide the ERIC document number in parentheses at the end of the entry:

Jolson, M. K. (1981). Music education for preschoolers. (Report No. TC-622). New York: Teachers College, Columbia University. (ERIC Document Reproduction Service No. ED 264 488)

22. An interview

`Brisick, W. C. (1988, July 1). [Interview with Ishmael Reed]. Publishers Weekly, 41-42.`

List a published interview under the interviewer's name. Provide the publication information appropriate for the kind of source the interview appears in (here, a magazine). Immediately after the date, in brackets, specify that the piece is an interview and, if necessary, provide other identifying information. If the interview has its own title, insert it after the date, as with a review (model 16).

Note that interviews you conduct yourself are not included in the list of references. Instead, use an in-text parenthetical citation: if the subject is already named, `(personal communication, July 7, 1996)`; if not, `(L. Kogod, personal communication, July 7, 1996)`.

23. A videotape, recording, or other audiovisual source

`Spielberg, S. (Director). (1993). Schindler's list [Videotape]. Los Angeles: Viacom.`

`Siberry, J. (1995). Caravan. On Maria [CD]. Burbank, CA: Reprise.`

For audiovisual sources such as films, videotapes, television or radio programs, or recordings, begin with the name of the person whose work you are citing, followed by his or her function, if appropriate, in parentheses. Immediately after the title, give the medium in brackets. Then give the location and name of the distributor.

APA manuscript format

In general, the guidelines of the APA for manuscript format coincide with those of the MLA, explained in Appendix A of this book. There are, however, some important differences and additions. The APA *Publication Manual* distinguishes between manuscripts intended for publication (which will be set in type) and those submitted by students (which are the final copy). The following guidelines are appropriate for most undergraduate papers.

- Use a 3.75 cm (1½") margin on the left and 2.5 cm (1") margins on the other sides.
- Number pages consecutively, starting with the title page. Identify each page (including the title page) with a shortened version of the title as well as a page number. For instance:

```
                                    Child Poverty     6

situation of Aboriginal children is especially per-
ilous. More than 50% of Aboriginal children live in
poverty; their life expectancy is eight years less than
the national average; 60% of their homes have no
plumbing.
```

- Put the abstract (if there is one) on a page by itself immediately after the title page, with the centred heading "Abstract".
- Run into your text all quotations of fewer than forty words, and enclose them in quotation marks. For quotations of more than forty words, set them off from your text by indenting all lines five spaces, double-spacing above and below, and double-spacing the quotation itself. Do not use quotation marks around a quotation displayed in this way.
- Do not label the introduction with a heading. For other main sections of your paper, such as "Method" and "Results," centre the heading, type it in capital and small letters, do not underline it, and double-space above and below it. (Start new pages for these sections if they all exceed a few pages.) If you use another level of heading below the main level, begin at the left margin, use capital and small letters, and underline the heading.
- Present any data in tables and figures (graphs or charts), as appropriate. Begin each illustration on a separate page. Number each kind of illustration consecutively and separately from the other (Table 1, Table 2, etc., and Figure 1, Figure 2, etc.). Refer to all illustrations in your text—for instance, "(See Figure 3.)." Generally, place illustrations immediately after the text references to them.
- The reference list starts a new page after the last page of the text, with the heading "References" centred at the top of the page and the entire list typed double-space. (See p. 711.) The references themselves follow the models on pages 698–705.

Because many departments and instructors have their own preferences for manuscript format, you should ask your instructor for his or her wishes before preparing your final draft.

 A sample social science paper

On the following pages are excerpts from a sociology paper. The student followed the APA style of documentation and manuscript format, although page borders are omitted here and only the required page breaks are indicated.

Excerpts from a problem-solving analysis (sociology)

[Title page: centre vertically and horizontally.]

Child Poverty 1

Child Poverty in Canada:

Methods of Evaluation and Courses of Action

Stephen Butterworth

Sociology 272

Professor Marathe

April 7, 1996

[New page.]

Child Poverty 2

Abstract

Child poverty has been identified as a pressing problem for Canadian society. The measurements of poverty, absolute or relative methodologies, are examined and evaluated. The causes of child poverty are identified, and short- and long-term solutions proposed.

[New page.]

Child Poverty in Canada:

Methods of Evaluation and Courses of Action

In November, 1989, Ed Broadbent, then leader of the New Democratic Party, rose to give his final speech in the House of Commons, a speech that prompted the following resolution: "That this house express concern for the more than one million Canadian children currently living in poverty and seek to achieve the goal of eliminating poverty among Canadian children by the year 2000" (cited in Canadian Council on Social Development, 1990, p. 1). Since then, there have been many public and private studies of child poverty in Canada, including some that diminish or even deny the existence of the problem. Child poverty, however, is still with us, and Canada must find solutions or be prepared to pay for the consequences.

Everyone admits that an objective definition of poverty is hard to find. Indeed, the authors of <u>The Canadian Fact Book on Poverty</u> (Ross, Shillington, & Lochhead, 1994, p. 11) list eight commonly used measures of poverty. All these methods divide into either absolute or relative methods (pp. 4-5). Basically, an absolute method takes into account only the actual cost of necessities, but a relative method tries to consider the entire context.

The economist Christopher A. Sarlo (1992, p. 2) uses an absolute or what he calls a "basic needs" method. He argues that relative approaches measure "inequality," not poverty, which he defines as the inability to supply life's basic necessities (pp. 3-13). Using this method, he has come up with a poverty rate that is only a quarter of the most commonly used relative method. This number leads him to argue that poverty "is simply not a major problem in Canada" (p. 2).

The most commonly used relative measure, the one used by the federal government and the basis for Ed Broadbent's motion, is the LICO or Low Income Cut Off set by Statistics Canada:

> There is a LICO for each family size, and LICOs also vary according to the size of the community in which the family lives. In simple terms, each LICO, which is a measure of family income, is set so that all families with less than that amount of income, on average, spend at least 60 percent of their income on the basic necessities of food, clothing and shelter. (Economic Council of Canada, 1992, pp. 1-2)

Using LICO criteria, the Standing Senate Committee on Social Affairs, Sciences, and Technology (1991, p. 4) determined that in 1988 there were 913 000 children under the age of sixteen living in poverty and that with the addition of children aged sixteen and seventeen and Aboriginal children living on reserves, "the figure would exceed one million, hovering at 1.1 million." If this figure is accurate, this means that one in six children in Canada lives below the poverty line.

Roughly 16% of Canadian children, then, are poor. This number may compare favourably with the 20% figure in the United States, but looks less impressive beside Sweden's 5.2% (Standing Senate Committee, 1991, p. 5). This number also does not include the "near poor," those whose family income is only slightly above the LICO (p. 9). The other statistics are bad enough. Over 40% of all users of food banks are children (p. 8). Ross et al. report that the child mortality rate among poor children is twice the national average (1994, p. 2). The situation of Aboriginal children is especially perilous. More than 50% of Aboriginal children live in poverty; their life expectancy is eight years less than the national average; 60% of their homes have no plumbing (Coutts & Walker, 1994, p. 322; Standing Senate Committee, 1991, pp. 9-11).

These last figures demonstrate that disagreements over absolute vs. relative measures are really unimportant for the children themselves, though they may be very important for policy makers, advocacy groups, and others. However you measure the number, however small or large you make it, there are many children suffering from hunger, disease, and death. In order to make the situation better, Canadians have to identify both the causes of child poverty and the short- and long-term solutions.

The obvious immediate cause of child poverty is parent poverty. Poor parents raise poor children, and these parents are not who we think they are. The Canadian Council on Social Development (1990, p. 2) notes that of the 913 000 poor children (1988 figure cited above) 51% lived in two-parent homes, and only 39.1% lived with lone-parent mothers. All these parents need short-term assistance through tax credits, minimum wage adjustments, subsidized housing, retraining and education, and child care. A national child-care policy is especially needed. The CCSD study reports that even though 1.9 million Canadian children needed day care in 1988, only 243 500 spaces were available (p. 6).

These short-term adjustments will work toward the long-term solution, which as the Standing Senate Committee puts it (1991, p. 13), must be "more preventative than curative." The key to ending the cycle of poverty is education. The dropout rate for poor children is 2.5 times the national average (Ross et al., 1994, pp. 1-2). Those who do stay in school are hampered by hunger, exhaustion, and anxiety. Without education and training, poor children become poor adults.

All Canadians pay when this happens. The 187 000 children projected to drop out of high school in the twenty years after 1991 will cost $610 million in unemployment insurance and $710 million in other assistance (Standing Senate Committee, 1991, pp. 5-6). Of all street and residential crime, between 40% and 60% is committed by juveniles (p. 20). As newspaper columnist Barbara Yaffe (1995, p. A7) noted about a string of youth crimes, "Canada's kids are meaner because they are poorer." Why should they respect us or our laws if we let them grow up hungry?

Everyone notes the paradox of one of the wealthiest nations on earth having so many poor children. Yet this situation should not surprise us. The top 40% of families in Canada received 62.4% of the total family income in 1991 (Ross et al., 1994, p. 124). Until wealth is more evenly distributed, Canadians will have poor families with poor children, but we can distribute the wealth more fairly by training and educating people to raise themselves out of the cycle of poverty. Unless we do, we will all continue to pay.

[New page.]

References

Canadian Council on Social Development. (1990). A national strategy to end child poverty in Canada. Ottawa: Author.

Coutts, J., & Walker, D. (1994). Native poverty: Perspectives on the sociology of dependence. Journal of Social Welfare, 11, 319-328.

Economic Council of Canada. (1992). The new faces of poverty: Income security needs of Canadian families. Ottawa: Minister of Supply and Services Canada.

Ross, D. P., Shillington, R. E., & Lochhead, C. (1994). The Canadian fact book on poverty. Ottawa: Canadian Council on Social Development.

Sarlo, C. A. (1992). Poverty in Canada. Vancouver: Fraser Institute.

Standing Senate Committee on Social Affairs, Sciences, and Technology. (1991). Children in poverty: Toward a better future. Ottawa: Minister of Supply and Services Canada.

Yaffee, B. (1995, July 10). No bleeding-heart issue. The Kitchener Record, p. A7.

40d Writing in the natural and applied sciences

The natural and applied sciences include biology, chemistry, physics, mathematics, engineering, computer science, and their branches. Their purpose is to understand natural and technological phenomena. (A *phenomenon* is a fact or event that can be known by the senses.) Scientists conduct experiments and write to explain the step-by-step processes in their methods of inquiry and discovery.

1 Methods and evidence in the sciences

Scientists investigate phenomena by the **scientific method,** a process of continual testing and refinement. (See the box opposite.) Scientific evidence is almost always quantitative—that is, it consists of numerical data obtained from the measurement of phenomena. These data are called **empirical** (from a Greek word for "experience"): they result from observation and experience, generally in a controlled laboratory setting but also (as sometimes in astronomy or biology) in the natural world. Often the empirical evidence for scientific writing comes from library research into other people's reports of their investigations. Surveys of known data or existing literature are common in scientific writing.

The scientific method

- Observe carefully. Accurately note all details of the phenomenon being researched.
- Ask questions about the observations.
- Formulate a **hypothesis,** or preliminary generalization, that explains the observed facts.
- Test the hypothesis with additional observation or controlled experiments.
- If the hypothesis proves accurate, formulate a **theory,** or unified model, that explains *why.* If the hypothesis is disproved, revise it or start anew.

Assignments in the sciences

No matter what your assignment, you will be expected to document and explain your evidence carefully so that anyone reading can check your sources and replicate your research. It is important for your reader to know the context of your research—both the previous experimentation and research on your particular subject (acknowledged in the survey of the literature) and the physical conditions and other variables surrounding your own work.

Assignments in the natural and applied sciences include the following:

- A **summary** distills a research article to its essence in brief, concise form. (Summary is discussed in detail on pp. 8–10.)
- A **critique** summarizes and critically evaluates a scientific report.
- A **laboratory report** explains the procedure and results of an experiment conducted by the writer. (An example begins on p. 720.)
- A **research report** reports on the experimental research of other scientists and the writer's own methods, findings, and conclusions.
- A **research proposal** reviews the relevant literature and explains a plan for further research.

A laboratory report has four or five major sections:

1. *Abstract:* a summary of the report. (See p. 720.)
2. *Introduction* or *Objective:* a review of why the study was undertaken, a summary of the background of the study, and a statement of the problem being studied.
3. *Method* or *Procedure:* a detailed explanation of how the study was conducted, including any statistical analysis.

4. *Results:* an explanation of the major findings (including unexpected results) and a summary of the data presented in graphs and tables.
5. *Discussion:* an interpretation of the results and an explanation of how they relate to the goals of the experiment. This section also describes new hypotheses that might be tested as a result of the experiment. If the section is brief, it may be combined with the previous section in a single section labeled *Conclusions.*

In addition, laboratory or research reports may include a list of references (if other sources were consulted). They almost always include tables and figures (graphs and charts) containing the data from the research (see p. 719).

Tools and language in the sciences

Keeping a journal or notebook can help you reflect on and rethink your ideas for writing, pose and answer questions, or explore your changing attitudes about a subject. In the sciences, a **lab notebook** or **scientific journal** is almost indispensable for accurately recording the empirical data from observations and experiments. Use such a notebook or journal for these purposes:

- Record observations from reading, from class, or from the lab.
- Ask questions and refine hypotheses.
- Record procedures.
- Record results.
- Keep an ongoing record of ideas and findings and how they change as data accumulate.
- Sequence and organize your material as you compile your findings and write your report.

When writing in your notebook, try to observe as well the special conventions of language in the sciences. The main convention is the use of objective language that removes the writer as a character in the situation and events being explained, except as the impersonal agent of change, the experimenter. Although usage is changing, scientists still rarely use *I* in their reports and evaluations, and they often resort to the passive voice of verbs, as in *The mixture was then subjected to centrifugal force.* This conscious objectivity focuses attention (including the writer's) on the empirical data and what they show. It discourages the writer from, say, ascribing motives and will to animals and plants. For instance, instead of asserting that the sea tortoise *evolved* its hard shell *to protect* its body, a scientist would write only what could be observed: that the hard shell *covers and thus protects* the tortoise's body.

Science writers typically change verb tenses to distinguish between established information and their own research. For established information, such as that found in journals and other reliable sources, use the present tense (*Baroreceptors monitor blood pressure*). For your own research, use the past tense (*The bacteria died within three hours*).

As in the social sciences, each discipline in the natural and applied sciences has a specialized vocabulary that permits precise, accurate, and efficient communication. Some of these terms, such as *pressure* in physics, have different meanings in the common language and must be handled carefully in science writing. Others, such as *enthalpy* in chemistry, have no meanings in the common language and must simply be learned and used correctly.

 Source citation and document format in the sciences

Within the natural and applied sciences, the practitioners of each discipline use a slightly different style of documentation and manuscript format. Following are some of the style guides most often consulted:

American Chemical Society. *ACS Style Guide: A Manual for Authors and Editors.* 2nd ed. 1997.
American Institute of Physics. *Style Manual for Guidance in the Preparation of Papers.* 4th ed. 1990.
American Mathematical Society. *A Manual for Authors of Mathematical Papers.* Rev. ed. 1990.
American Medical Association. *Manual of Style.* 8th ed. 1989.
Bates, Robert L., Rex Buchanan, and Marla Adkins-Heljeson, eds. *Geowriting: A Guide to Writing, Editing, and Printing in Earth Science.* 5th ed. 1992.
Council of Biology Editors. *Scientific Style and Format: The CBE Manual for Authors, Editors, and Publishers.* 6th ed. 1994.

Some documentation styles in the sciences closely resemble other styles discussed in this chapter: the Chicago system of in-text raised numerals referring to separate endnotes or footnotes (see p. 681) or the APA system of in-text parenthetical citations and a separate reference list (see p. 693). Ask your instructor what style you should use.

CBE numbered citations

A documentation style common in the health sciences, physics, mathematics, and other disciplines consists of in-text numbers that refer to a list of correspondingly numbered references. A version of this style, described here, appears in *Scientific Style and Format: The CBE Manual for Authors, Editors, and Publishers* (CBE is the Council of Biology Editors). For the text citations, follow the examples and instructions below.

```
Two standard encyclopedias1,2 use this term.

These forms of immunity have been extensively researched.3

According to one report,4 research into some forms of viral
immunity is almost nonexistent.

Hepburn and Tatin2 do not discuss this project.
```

- Within the text, use a raised number or numbers to refer to numbered sources in the reference list at the end of the text.
- The number for each source is based on the order in which you cite the source in the text: the first cited source is 1, the second is 2, and so on.
- When you cite a source you have already cited and numbered, use the original number again (see the last example on the previous page, which reuses the number 2 from the first example). This reuse is the key difference between the CBE numbered citations and numbered references to footnotes or endnotes (pp. 681–88). In the CBE style, each source has only one number, determined by the order in which the source is cited. With notes, in contrast, the numbering proceeds in sequence, so that sources have as many numbers as they have citations in the text.
- When you cite two or more sources at once, arrange their numbers in sequence and separate them with a comma and no space, as in the first example on the previous page.

Note Some versions of the numbered-citation style place citation numbers on the line of type (not raised) and between parentheses:

```
Two standard encyclopedias (1, 2) use this term.
```

CBE numbered references

The list of references for the numbered-citation style begins on a new page at the end of the text. Here is part of the first page:

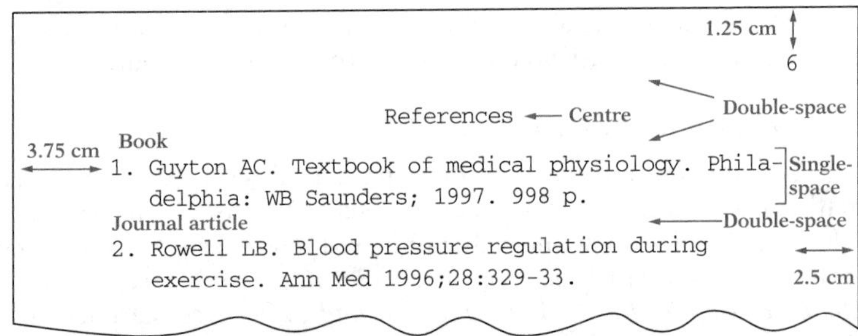

CBE
40d

- Title the list of sources "References."
- Single-space each entry, and double-space between entries.
- Arrange the entries in numerical order—that is, in order of their citation in the text, *not* alphabetically.
- Begin each entry on a new line, and number it. Type the number on the line of type (not raised), and follow it with a period and a space. Indent subsequent lines of each entry directly under the first word of the first line.
- List authors' names with the last name first, followed by initials for first and middle names—for instance, `Guyton AC` in the first entry in the example. Do not use a comma after the last name or periods or space with initials.
- Separate authors' names with commas: `Hepburn PX, Tatin JM.`
- Do not underline or use quotation marks for any titles.
- For journal titles of more than one word, use abbreviations for main words of six or more letters (without periods) and omit most prepositions, articles, and conjunctions. Capitalize each word. For example, *Annals of Medicine* becomes `Ann Med` (see the second entry on the previous page), and *Journal of Chemical and Biochemical Studies* becomes `J Chem Biochem Stud.`
- For book and article titles, capitalize only the first word and any proper nouns (see both entries opposite).
- For books, separate the name of the publisher from the date of publication with a semicolon and a space: `WB Saunders; 1997.` End the reference with the total number of pages in the book: `998 p.`
- For a journal article, put the date of publication after the abbreviated title of the journal, followed by the volume number and the inclusive page numbers for the article (with duplicated digits omitted): `Ann Med 1996;28:329-33.` For a journal that pages each issue separately, add the month (and day, if relevant) after the year, and add the issue number in unspaced parentheses after the volume number: `1993 3 Mar;16(8):16-7.`

Index to CBE references

For all journals, use no punctuation between title and date of publication. Put an unspaced semicolon between the date and volume number. Put an unspaced colon between the volume number (or parenthetical issue number) and the inclusive pages. (See models 6 and 7 following for more examples.)

1. A BOOK WITH ONE AUTHOR

1. Gould SJ. Time's arrow, time's cycle. Cambridge: Harvard Univ Pr; 1987. 222 p.

2. A BOOK WITH MORE THAN ONE AUTHOR

2. Hepburn PX, Tatin JM. Human physiology. 3rd ed. New York: Columbia Univ Pr; 1995. 1026 p.

3. A BOOK WITH AN EDITOR

3. Jonson P, editor. Anatomy yearbook. Los Angeles: Anatco; 1997. 628 p.

4. A SELECTION FROM A BOOK

4. Krigel R, Laubenstein L, Muggia F. Kaposi's sarcoma. In: Ebbeson P, Biggar RS, Melbye M, editors. AIDS: a basic guide for clinicians. 2nd ed. Philadelphia: WB Saunders; 1997. p 100-26.

5. AN ANONYMOUS WORK

5. [Anonymous]. Health care for multiple sclerosis. New York: US Health Care; 1992. 86 p.

6. AN ARTICLE IN A JOURNAL WITH CONTINUOUS PAGINATION THROUGHOUT THE ANNUAL VOLUME

6. Ancino R, Carter KV, Elwin DJ. Factors contributing to viral immunity: a review of the research. Dev Biol 1993;40:156-9.

7. AN ARTICLE IN A JOURNAL THAT PAGES ISSUES SEPARATELY

7. Milbank Symposium. Medical decision making for the dying. Milbank Qtrly 1986 Feb;64(2):26-40.

8. AN ARTICLE IN A NEWSPAPER

8. Immen W. ASA helps heart but hurts brain. Globe and Mail 1996 July 2;Sect A:3(col 2).

9. AN ARTICLE IN A MAGAZINE

9. Van Gelder L. Countdown to motherhood: when should you have a baby? Ms. 1986 Dec:37-39.

10. A GOVERNMENT PUBLICATION

10. Parliamentary Committee on Equality Rights. Equality for all. 33rd Parl., 1st Sess. Queen's Printer Canada; 1984.

11. An electronic source

```
11. Project scheduler 8000 [computer program]. Ver-
    sion 3.1. Orlando (FL): Scitor; 1995. 1 computer
    disk: 3 1/2 in. Accompanied by: 1 manual. System
    requirements: IBM PC or fully compatible com-
    puter; DOS 5.0 or higher; 320K RAM; hard disk
    with a minimum of 2 MB of free space.
12. Grady GF. The here and now of hepatitis B immu-
    nization. Today's Med [serial online] 1993 May
    2;Doc nr 2:[2620 words]. Available from: Public
    Access Computer Systems Forum PACS-L via the In-
    ternet. Accessed 1996 Jan 21.
13. Reich WT, ed. Encyclopedia of bioethics [CD-
    ROM]. New York: Free Pr; 1978.
```

CBE document format

The CBE's *Scientific Style and Format* is not specific about margins, spacing for headings, and other elements of document format. Unless your instructor specifies otherwise, you can use the format of the APA (pp. 705–07). The CBE exception to this style is the list of references, which is described and illustrated on pages 716–17.

The most troublesome aspects of manuscript preparation in the sciences are equations or formulas and illustrations (tables and figures). When typing equations or formulas, be careful to reproduce alignments, indentions, underlining, and characters accurately. If your typewriter or word processor lacks special characters, write them in by hand. (Stationery and art-supply stores also have sheets of transfer type with special characters in different sizes that can be applied to your manuscript by rubbing.)

Because you will be expected to share your data with your readers, most of your writing for the sciences is likely to require illustrations to present the data in concise, readable form. Tables usually summarize raw data (see p. 721 for an example), whereas figures (mainly charts and graphs) recast the data to show noteworthy comparisons or changes. Follow the guidelines in Appendix A (pp. 751–52) for preparing tables, figures, and illustrations.

Sample science paper

The following biology paper illustrates many of the features described in the preceding pages. Some elements, such as page borders and identifiers, have been omitted. Except for the references list in CBE style, the format is APA style, for the reasons explained above.

A laboratory report (biology)

[Title page.]

Exercise and Blood Pressure
Liz Garson
Biology 161
Ms. Traversa
December 13, 1996

[New page.]

Abstract

The transient elevation of blood pressure following exercise was demonstrated by pressure measurements of twenty human subjects before and after exercise.

[New page.]

Exercise and Blood Pressure

Introduction

The purpose of this experiment was to verify the changes in blood pressure that accompany exercise, as commonly reported.[1,2] A certain blood pressure is necessary for the blood to supply nutrients to the body tissues. Baroreceptors near the heart monitor pressure by determining the degree to which blood stretches the wall of the blood vessel.

During exercise, the metabolic needs of the muscles override the influence of the baroreceptors and result in an increase in blood pressure. This increase in blood pressure is observed uniformly (irrespective of sex or race), although men demonstrate a higher absolute systolic pressure than do women.[3] During strenuous exercise, blood pressure can rise to 40 percent above baseline.[1]

Method

The subjects for this experiment were twenty volunteers from laboratory classes, ten men and ten women. All pressure measurements were performed using a standard sphygmomanometer, which was tested for accuracy. To ensure consistency, the same sphygmomanometer was used to take all readings. In addition, all measurements were taken by the same person to avoid discrepancies in method or interpretation.

The first pressure reading was taken prior to exercise as the subject sat in a chair. This pressure was considered the baseline for each subject. All subsequent readings were interpreted relative to this baseline.

In the experiment, the subjects ran up and down stairs for fifteen minutes. Immediately after exercising, the subjects returned to the laboratory to have their pressure measured. Thirty minutes later, the pressure was measured for the final time.

Results

Table 1 contains the blood pressure measurements for the male and female subjects. With the exception of subjects 3 and 14, all subjects demonstrated the expected post-exercise increase in blood pressure, with a decline to baseline or near baseline thirty minutes after exercise. The data for subjects 3 and 14 were invalid because the subjects did not perform the experiment as directed.

[Table on a page by itself.]

Table 1. Blood pressure measurements for all subjects (mmHg)

Subject	Baseline[a]	Post-exercise	30-minute reading
Male			
1	110/75	135/80	115/75
2	125/80	140/90	135/85
3	125/70	125/70	125/70
4	130/85	170/100	140/90
5	120/80	125/95	120/80
6	115/70	135/80	125/75
7	125/70	150/80	130/70
8	130/80	145/85	130/80
9	140/75	180/85	155/80
10	110/85	135/95	115/80
Female			
11	110/60	140/85	115/60
12	130/75	180/85	130/75
13	125/80	140/90	130/80
14	90/60	90/60	90/60
15	115/65	145/70	125/65
16	100/50	130/65	110/50
17	120/80	140/80	130/80
18	110/70	135/80	120/75
19	120/80	140/90	130/80
20	110/80	145/90	120/80

[a]Normal blood pressure at rest: males, 110-130/60-90; females, 110-120/50-80.

Discussion

As expected, most of the subjects demonstrated an increase in blood pressure immediately after exercise and a decline to near baseline levels thirty minutes after exercise. The usual pressure increase was 20-40 mmHg for the systolic pressure and 5-10 mmHg for the diastolic pressure.

In the two cases in which blood pressure did not elevate with exercise (subjects 3 and 14), the subjects simply left the laboratory and returned fifteen minutes later without having exercised. The experimental design was flawed in not assigning someone to observe the subjects as they exercised.

[New page.]

References

1. Guyton AC. Textbook of medical physiology. Philadelphia: WB Saunders; 1997. 998 p.

2. Rowell LB. Blood pressure regulation during exercise. Ann Med 1996;28:329-33.

3. Gleim GW, Stachenfeld NS. Gender differences in the systolic blood pressure response to exercise. Am Heart J 1991;121:524-30.

Part IX

Special Writing Situations

Chapter 41

Essay Examinations

In writing an essay for an examination, you summarize or analyse a topic, usually in several paragraphs or more and usually within a time limit. An essay question not only tests your knowledge of a subject (as short-answer and objective questions do) but also tests your ability to think critically about what you have learned. (If you have not already done so, read this book's Introduction on critical thinking, reading, and writing.)

41a Preparing for an essay examination

To do well on an essay exam, you will need to understand the course content, not only the facts but also the interpretation of them and the relations between them.

- Take careful lecture notes.
- Thoughtfully, critically read the assigned texts or articles. (See pp. 2–14.)
- Review regularly so the material has time to sink in and stimulate your thinking.
- Create summaries that recast others' ideas in your own words and extract the meaning from notes and texts. (See pp. 8–10 for instructions on summarizing.)
- Prepare notes or outlines that reorganize the course material

around key topics or issues: in a business course, the advantages and disadvantages of several approaches to management; in a short-story course, a theme running through all the stories you have read by a certain author or from a certain period; in a psychology course, various theorists' views of what causes a disorder such as schizophrenia. Any one of these is a likely topic for an essay question. Thinking of such categories can help you anticipate the kinds of questions you may be asked and increase your mastery of the material.

41b Planning your time and your answer

When you first receive an examination, take a few minutes to get your bearings and plan an approach. The time spent will not be wasted.

- Always read an exam all the way through at least once before you start answering any questions.
- As you scan the exam, determine which questions seem most important, which ones are going to be most difficult for you, and approximately how much time you'll need for each question. (Your instructor may help by assigning a point value to each question as a guide to its importance or by suggesting an amount of time for you to spend on each question.)

Planning continues when you turn to an individual essay question. Resist the temptation to rush right into an answer without some planning, for a few minutes can save you time later and help you produce a stronger essay.

- Read the question at least twice. You will be more likely to stick to the question and answer it fully.
- Examine the words in the question and consider their implications. Look especially for words such as *describe, define, explain, summarize, analyse, evaluate,* and *interpret,* each of which requires a different kind of response. See the box on the next page and consult earlier discussions of such terms on pages 9–14 and 94–104.
- After you are sure you understand the question, make a brief outline of the main ideas you want to include in your essay. Use the back of the exam sheet or booklet for scratch paper.
- Write a brief thesis sentence for your essay that responds directly to the question and represents your view of the topic. (If you are unsure of how to write a thesis sentence, see pp. 41–44.) Include key phrases that you can expand with supporting evidence for your view.

Sample instructions for essay examinations

SAMPLE INSTRUCTIONS	KEY WORDS	STRATEGIES FOR ANSWERS	EXAMPLES OF WRONG ANSWERS
Define *dyslexia* and compare and contrast it with two other learning disabilities.	Define	Specify the meaning of *dyslexia*—distinctive characteristics, ways the impairment works, etc.	Feelings of children with dyslexia. Causes of dyslexia.
	Compare and contrast	Analyse similarities and differences (severity, causes, treatments, etc.).	Similarities without differences, or vice versa.
Analyse the role of Horatio in *Hamlet.*	Analyse	Break Horatio's role into its elements (speeches, relations with other characters, etc.).	Plot summary of *Hamlet.* Description of Horatio's personality.
Explain the effects of the drug Thorazine on those who take it.	Explain	Set forth the facts and theories objectively.	Argument for or against Thorazine.
	Effects	Analyse the consequences.	Reasons for prescribing Thorazine.
Discuss term limits for elected officials.	Discuss	Explain and compare the main points of view on the issue.	Analysis of one view. Argument for or against one view.

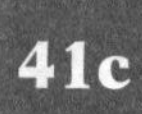

41c Starting the essay

You can begin your essay effectively by stating your thesis immediately and giving an overview of the rest of your essay. Such a capsule version of your answer tells your reader (and grader) generally how much command you have and also how you plan to develop your answer. It also gets you off to a good start.

The opening statement should address the question directly and exactly. The following thesis sentence, in response to the question below, does *not* meet these criteria.

QUESTION

Given humans' natural and historical curiosity about themselves, why did a scientific discipline of anthropology not arise until the twentieth century? Explain, citing specific details.

TENTATIVE THESIS SENTENCE

The discipline of anthropology, the study of humans, actually began in the early nineteenth century and was strengthened by the Darwinian revolution, but the discipline did not begin to take shape until people like Franz Boas and Alfred Kroeber began doing scientific research among nonindustrialized cultures.

This tentative thesis sentence says nothing about *why* anthropology did not arise as a scientific discipline until the twentieth century. Instead, it supplies an unspecific (and unrequested) definition of anthropology, vaguely reasserts the truth implied by the question, and adds irrelevant details about the history of anthropology. The following thesis sentence—revised to address the question directly, to state the writer's view, and to preview the essay—begins the answer more effectively.

REVISED THESIS SENTENCE

Anthropology did not emerge as a scientific discipline until the twentieth century because nineteenth-century Westerners' limited contact with remote peoples and the corresponding failure to see those other people as human combined to overcome natural curiosity and to prevent objective study of different cultures.

This thesis sentence specifies the writer's view of the two main causes of the slow emergence of anthropology—limited contact with remote peoples and, related to that, a narrow definition of humanity—that she will analyse in her essay.

41d Developing the essay

Develop your essay as you would develop any piece of sound academic writing:

- Observe the methods, terms, or other special requirements of the discipline you are writing in (see Chapters 39–40).
- Support your thesis sentence with solid generalizations (each one perhaps the topic sentence of a paragraph).
- Support each generalization with *specific, relevant* evidence (see pp. 120–23).

If you observe a few *don't*'s as well, your essay will have more substance:

- Avoid filling out the essay by repeating yourself.
- Avoid other kinds of wordiness that pad and confuse, whether intentionally or not. (See pp. 461–68.)
- Avoid substituting purely subjective feelings for real definition, analysis, or whatever is asked of you. (It may help to abolish the word *I* from the essay.)

The following essays illustrate a successful and an unsuccessful answer to the sample essay question on the previous page about anthropology. Both answers were written in the allotted time of forty minutes. Marginal comments on each essay highlight their effective and ineffective elements.

Successful essay answer

Anthropology did not emerge as a scientific discipline until the 20th century because of the practical and political motivations behind 19th-century ethnographic studies, the ethnocentric bias of Western researchers, and a strictly material conception of culture.

[Margin: Gets right to the point with thesis statement]

[Margin: Answers question directly and previews three-part response]

Before the 20th century, ethnographic studies were almost always used for practical goals. The study of human culture can be traced back at least as far as Herodotus's investigations of the Mediterranean peoples. Herodotus was like many pre-20th-century "anthropologists" in that he was employed by a government that needed information about its neighbours, just as the colonial nations in the 19th century needed information about their newly conquered subjects. The early politically motivated ethnographic studies the colonial nations sponsored tended to be isolated projects, and they aimed less to advance general knowledge than to solve a specific problem. Frank Hamilton Cushing, who was employed by the American government to study the Zuni tribe of New Mexico, and who is considered one of the pioneers of anthropology, didn't even publish his findings. The political and practical aims of anthropologists and the nature of their research prevented their work from being a scholarly discipline in its own right.

[Margin: Point 1 of thesis: practical aims]

[Margin: Example]

[Margin: Example]

Anthropologists of the 19th century also fell short of the standards of objectivity needed for truly scientific study. This partly had to do with anthropologists' close connection to imperialist governments. But even independent researchers were hampered by the prevailing assumption that Western cultures were inherently superior. While the modern anthropologist believes that a culture must be studied in terms of its own values, early ethnographers were ethnocentric: they judged "primitive" cultures by their own "civilized" values. "Primitive" peoples were seen as uninteresting in their own right. The reasons to study them, ultimately, were to satisfy curiosity, to exploit them, or to prove their inferiority. There was even some debate as to whether so-called savage peoples were human.

Point 2 of thesis: ethnocentricity

Finally, the 19th century tended to conceive of culture in narrow, material terms, often reducing it to a collection of artifacts. When not working for a government, early ethnographers usually worked for a museum. The enormous collections of exotica still found in many museums today are the legacy of this 19th-century object-oriented conception of anthropology, which ignored the myths, symbols, and rituals the objects related to. It was only when the museum tradition was broadened to include all aspects of a culture that anthropology could come into existence as a scientific discipline. When anthropologists like Franz Boas and Bronislaw Malinowski began to publish their findings for others to read and criticize and began to move from the museum to the university, the discipline gained stature and momentum.

Point 3 of thesis (with transition *Finally*): focus on objects

Examples

In brief, anthropology required a whole series of ideological shifts to become modern. Once it broke free of its purely practical bent, the cultural prejudices of its practitioners, and the narrow conception that limited it to a collection of objects, anthropology could grow into a science.

Conclusion restates thesis supported by essay

Unsuccessful essay answer

The discipline of anthropology, the study of humans and their cultures, actually began in the early 20th century and was strengthened by the Darwinian revolution, but the discipline did not begin to take shape until people like Franz Boas and Alfred Kroeber began doing scientific research among nonindustrialized cultures. (Boas, who was born in Germany but emigrated to the US, is the father of the idea of historical particularism.)

Introduction does not answer question

No thesis statement or sense of direction

Irrelevant information

Since the dawn of time, humans have always had a natural curiosity about themselves. Art and literature have always reflected this need to understand human emotions, thought, and behaviour. Anthropology is yet another reflection of this need. Anthropologists have a different way of looking at human societies than artists or writers. Whereas the latter paint an individualistic, impressionistic portrait of the world they see, anthropologists study cultures systematically, scientifically. They are thus closer to biologists. They are *social scientists,* with the emphasis on both words.

Adds cliché to the language of the question without answering the question

Wheel spinning by positioning contemporary anthropology as a scientific discipline

Another reason why anthropology did not develop until the 20th century is that people in the past did not travel very much. The expansion of the automobile and the airplane has played a major role in the expansion of the discipline.

Not *Another reason* but the first reason given.

Assertion without support

Cushing's important work among the Zuni Indians in New Mexico is a good example of the transition between 19th-century and 20th-century approaches to anthropology. Cushing was one of the first to develop the method of *participant observation.* Instead of merely coming in as an outsider, taking notes, and leaving, Cushing actually lived among the Zuni, dressing like them and following their customs. In this way, he was able to build a relationship of trust with his informants, learning much more than someone who would have been seen as an outsider.

Discussion of pioneers shows familiarity with their work but does not answer question

Franz Boas, as mentioned earlier, was another anthropology pioneer. A German immigrant, Boas proposed the idea of *historical particularism* as a response to the prevailing theory of *cultural evolution.* Cultural evolution is the idea that cultures gradually evolve toward higher levels of efficiency and complexity. Historical particularism is the idea that every culture is unique and develops differently. Boas developed his theory to counter those who believed in cultural evolution. Working with the Kwakiutl Indians, he was also one of the first anthropologists to use a an Aboriginal assistant to help him gain access to the culture under study.

Repetition pads

Information has unclear relevance to subject

A third pioneer in anthropology was Malinowski, who developed a theory of *functionalism*—that culture responds to biological, psychological, and other needs. Malinowski's work is extremely important and still influential today.

Vague assertion without support

Anthropologists have made great contributions to society over the course of the past century. One can only hope that they will continue the great strides they have made, building on the past to contribute to a bright new future.

Irrelevant and empty conclusion

41e Rereading the essay

The time limit on an essay examination does not allow for the careful rethinking and revision you would give an essay or research paper. You need to write clearly and concisely the first time. But try to leave yourself a few minutes after finishing the entire exam for rereading the essay (or essays) and doing touchups.

- Correct illegible passages, misspellings, grammatical mistakes, and accidental omissions.
- Verify that your thesis is accurate—that it does, in fact, introduce what you ended up writing about.
- Check to ensure that you have supported all your generalizations. Cross out irrelevant ideas and details, and add any information that now seems important. (Write on another page, if necessary, keying the addition to the page on which it belongs.)

Chapter 42 *Business Writing*

When you write in business, you are addressing busy people who want to see quickly why you are writing and how they should respond to you. A wordy, incoherent letter or memo full of errors in grammar and spelling may prevent you from getting what you want, either because the reader cannot understand your wish or because you present yourself poorly. In business writing, follow these general guidelines:

- State your purpose right at the start.
- Be straightforward, clear, concise, objective, and courteous.
- Observe conventions of grammar and usage, which make your writing clear and impress your reader with your care.

Writing in business demands efficiency, but efficiency does not mean haste. Developing, drafting, and revising—the three overlapping stages of the writing process discussed in Chapters 1 and 2—apply in business writing as much as in academic writing. Except for brief or routine letters and memos, plan what you want to say; work out your meaning freely, unselfconsciously, without stopping to edit; and then revise and edit your draft so that it will achieve your purpose with your reader.

This chapter discusses business letters and job applications (42a), business memos (42b), and the faxes and E-mail of the electronic office (42c).

42a Writing business letters and job applications

The formats of business letters and résumés are fairly standardized and are thus expected by your correspondents.

Using a standard form

Use either unlined white paper measuring 21.5 cm × 28 cm ($8\frac{1}{2}$" × 11") or what is called letterhead stationery with your address printed at the top of the sheet. Type the letter single-spaced (with double space between elements) on only one side of a sheet. The two most common forms for business letters—the full block and the modified block—are illustrated and described on the following pages. (For long and complex letters, you may want to draw on some of the document-design techniques discussed on pp. 749–52.)

The letter

The **return-address heading** of the letter gives your address (but not your name) and the date. (See p. 736 for abbreviations of province and territory names.) If you are using letterhead, you need add only the date. Place your heading at least 2.5 cm from the top of the page, or two lines below the letterhead if there is one. Align all lines of the heading on the left. In the block style, the return-address heading falls at the left margin (see opposite). In the modified block style, it falls to the right of the centre of the paper (see p. 738).

The **inside address** shows the name, title, and complete address of the person you are writing to. (See p. 736 for abbreviations of province, territory, and state names.) Place the address at least two lines below the return-address heading. In both block and modified block styles, the address falls at the left margin of the page.

The **salutation** greets the addressee. In both styles it falls at the left margin, two lines below the inside address and two lines above the body of the letter. It is followed by a colon. If you are not addressing someone whose name you know, use a job title (*Dear Personnel Manager, Dear Customer Service Manager*) or use a general salutation (*Dear Smythe Shoes*). Use *Ms.* as the title for a woman when she has no other title, when you don't know how she prefers to be addressed, or when you know that she prefers to be addressed as *Ms.* If you know a woman prefers to be addressed as *Mrs.* or *Miss,* use the appropriate title.

The **body** of the letter, containing its substance, begins at the left margin in both letter styles. Instead of indenting the first line of

BUSINESS LETTER IN BLOCK STYLE

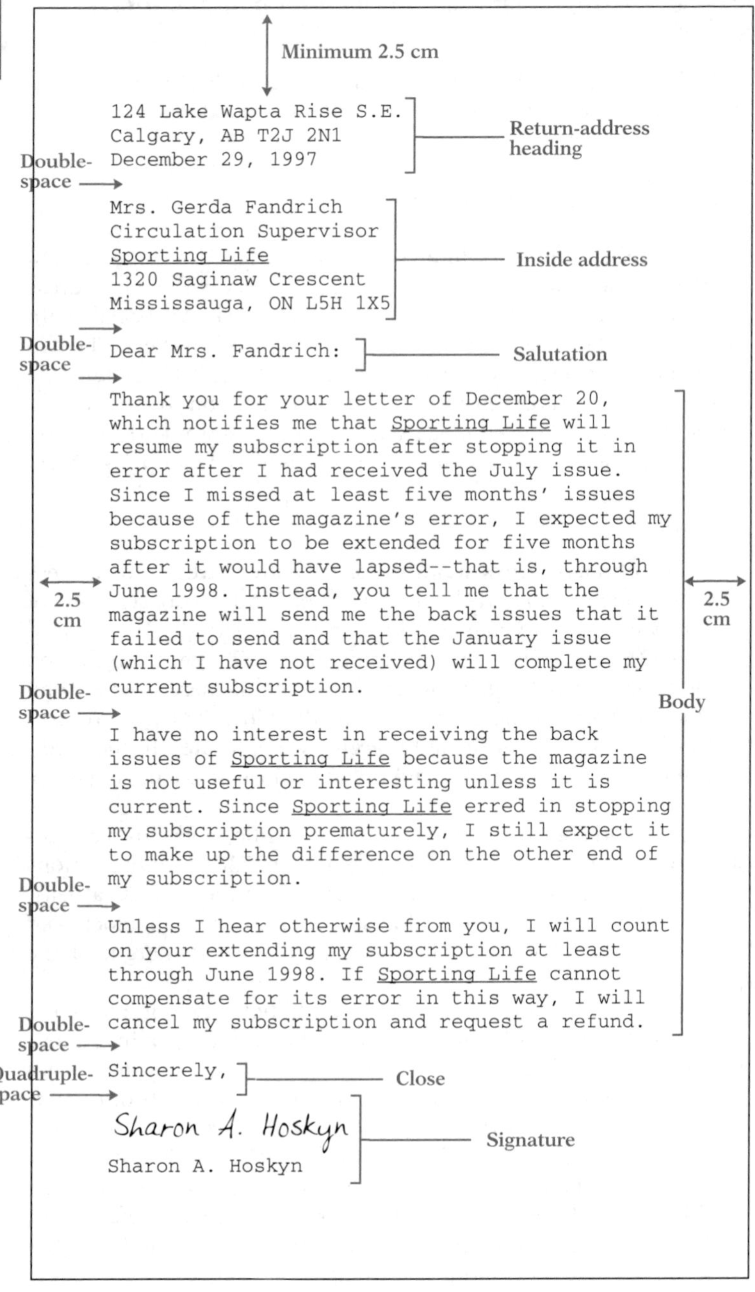

124 Lake Wapta Rise S.E.
Calgary, AB T2J 2N1
December 29, 1997

Mrs. Gerda Fandrich
Circulation Supervisor
Sporting Life
1320 Saginaw Crescent
Mississauga, ON L5H 1X5

Dear Mrs. Fandrich:

Thank you for your letter of December 20, which notifies me that Sporting Life will resume my subscription after stopping it in error after I had received the July issue. Since I missed at least five months' issues because of the magazine's error, I expected my subscription to be extended for five months after it would have lapsed--that is, through June 1998. Instead, you tell me that the magazine will send me the back issues that it failed to send and that the January issue (which I have not received) will complete my current subscription.

I have no interest in receiving the back issues of Sporting Life because the magazine is not useful or interesting unless it is current. Since Sporting Life erred in stopping my subscription prematurely, I still expect it to make up the difference on the other end of my subscription.

Unless I hear otherwise from you, I will count on your extending my subscription at least through June 1998. If Sporting Life cannot compensate for its error in this way, I will cancel my subscription and request a refund.

Sincerely,

Sharon A. Hoskyn

Sharon A. Hoskyn

each paragraph, place an extra line of space between paragraphs so that they are readily visible.

The letter's **close** begins two lines below the last line of the body and aligns with the return-address heading. That is, in the block style the close falls at the left margin (see the preceding page), whereas in the modified block style it falls to the right of the centre of the page (p. 738). The close should reflect the level of formality in the salutation. For formal letters, *Respectfully, Cordially, Yours truly,* and *Sincerely* are common closes. For less formal letters, you may choose to use *Warmest regards, Regards, Best wishes,* or the like. Only the first word of the close is capitalized, and the close is followed by a comma.

The **signature** of a business letter falls below the close and has two parts. One is your name typed on the fourth line below the close. The other is your handwritten signature, which fills the space between the close and your typed name. The signature should consist only of your name, as you sign checks and other documents.

Below the signature at the left margin, you may want to include additional information such as *Enc. 3* (indicating that there are three enclosures with the letter); *cc: Margaret Newton* (indicating that a copy is being sent to the person named); or *CHC/enp* (the initials of the author/the initials of the typist).

The envelope

The envelope of the letter (see below) should show your name and address in the upper-left corner and the addressee's name, title, and address in the center. Use an envelope that will adequately accommodate the letter once it is folded horizontally in thirds.

Canada Post Corporation recommends a format for envelopes that makes them easy for machines to read. As illustrated below, use all capital letters and no punctuation (spaces separate the elements on a line).

```
SHARON A HOSKYN
124 LAKE WAPTA RISE SE
CALGARY AB T2J 2N1

                        MRS GERDA FANDRICH
                        CIRCULATION SUPERVISOR
                        SPORTING LIFE
                        1320 SAGINAW CRES
                        MISSISSAUGA ON L5H 1X5
```

The following are the common Canada Post abbreviations for addresses:

Street names

Avenue	AVE	Expressway	EXPY	Road	RD
Boulevard	BLVD	Freeway	FWY	Square	SQ
Circle	CIR	Lane	LN	Street	ST
Court	CT	Parkway	PKY	Turnpike	TPKE

Compass points

North	N	West	W	Southwest	SW
East	E	Northeast	NE	Northwest	NW

Province and Territory Names

Alberta	AB	Nova Scotia	NS
British Columbia	BC	Ontario	ON
Manitoba	MB	Prince Edward Island	PE
New Brunswick	NB	Quebec	QC
Newfoundland	NF	Saskatchewan	SK
Northwest Territories	NT	Yukon	YT

U.S. State names

Alabama	AL	Kentucky	KY	North Dakota	ND
Alaska	AK	Louisiana	LA	Ohio	OH
Arizona	AZ	Maine	ME	Oklahoma	OK
Arkansas	AR	Maryland	MD	Oregon	OR
California	CA	Massachusetts	MA	Pennsylvania	PA
Colorado	CO	Michigan	MI	Puerto Rico	PR
Connecticut	CT	Minnesota	MN	Rhode Island	RI
Delaware	DE	Mississippi	MS	South Carolina	SC
District of Columbia	DC	Missouri	MO	South Dakota	SD
Florida	FL	Montana	MT	Tennessee	TN
Georgia	GA	Nebraska	NE	Texas	TX
Hawaii	HI	Nevada	NV	Utah	UT
Idaho	ID	New Hampshire	NH	Vermont	VT
Illinois	IL	New Jersey	NJ	Virginia	VA
Indiana	IN	New Mexico	NM	Washington	WA
Iowa	IA	New York	NY	West Virginia	WV
Kansas	KS	North Carolina	NC	Wisconsin	WI
				Wyoming	WY

2 Writing requests and complaints

Letters requesting something—for instance, a pamphlet, information about a product, a T-shirt advertised in a magazine—must be specific and accurate about the item you are requesting. The letter should describe the item completely and, if applicable, include a copy or description of the advertisement or other source that prompted your request.

Letters complaining about a product or a service (such as a wrong billing from the telephone company) should be written in a reasonable but firm tone. (See the sample letter on p. 734.) Assume that the addressee is willing to resolve the problem when he or she has the relevant information. In the first sentence of the letter, say what you are writing about. Then provide as much background as needed, including any relevant details from past correspondence (as in the sample letter). Describe exactly what you see as the problem, sticking to facts and avoiding discourses on the company's social responsibility or your low opinion of its management. In the clearest and fewest possible words and sentences, proceed directly from one point to the next without repeating yourself. Always include your opinion of how the problem can be solved. Many companies are required by law to establish a specific procedure for complaints about products and services. If you know of such a procedure, be sure to follow it.

3 Writing a job application and résumé

In applying for a job or requesting a job interview, send both a résumé and a letter. Both should be on high-quality paper measuring 21.5 cm × 28 cm (8½" × 11"). For the letter follow these guidelines, illustrated in the sample on the facing page.

- Use the block or modified block style (pp. 734, 738).
- Think of the letter as an interpretation of your résumé for a particular job, not as a detailed account of the entire résumé.
- Announce at the outset what job you seek and how you heard about it.
- Include any special reason you have for applying, such as a specific career goal.
- Summarize your qualifications for this particular job, including relevant facts about education and employment history and emphasizing notable accomplishments. Mention that additional information appears in an accompanying résumé.
- At the end of the letter, mention that you are available for an interview at the convenience of the addressee, or specify when you will be available (for instance, when your current job or classes leave you free, or when you could travel to the employer's city).

The résumé that you enclose with your letter of application should follow these guidelines:

JOB-APPLICATION LETTER IN MODIFIED BLOCK STYLE

317 Weber Street
Waterloo, ON N2J 3H8
June 27, 1997

Personnel Manager
Northern Systems Inc.
39 Albert Street
Waterloo, ON N2L 3S1

Dear Personnel Manager:

In response to your posting in the English Department of the University of Waterloo, I am applying for the position of technical writer for the software division of Northern Systems Inc.

I am currently enrolled in my fourth year in the Rhetoric and Professional Writing program at the University of Waterloo. I have worked two terms as a technical writer, one with Bell-Northern in Ottawa and another with the Ontario Ministry of Natural Resources in Cambridge. For several years, I have also written a column for the student newspaper on the difficulties of reading and writing computer manuals. I believe my educational background and my work experience qualify me for the opening you have.

My résumé is enclosed. I am available for an interview at any time and would be happy to show samples of my work. My telephone number is 519-747-7275, and my e-mail address is skeby@watstar.uwaterloo.ca.

Sincerely,

Sylvia K Eby

Sylvia K. Eby

Enc.

- Provide, in table form, your name and address, career objective, and education and employment history, along with information about how to obtain your references. (See the sample opposite.)

RÉSUMÉ

Sylvia K. Eby
317 Weber Street
Waterloo, Ontario N2J 3H8
519-747-7275
e-mail: skeby@watstar.uwaterloo.ca

Position desired
Technical writer.

Education
University of Waterloo, 1994 to present.
Year: fourth
Major: English (Rhetoric and Professional Writing).

Kitchener Collegiate Institute, 1989-1994.
Graduated with OAC standing.

Employment history
The Imprint, student newspaper of University of Waterloo, 1995 to present. Responsibilities include writing weekly column.

Bell-Northern, Ottawa, summer 1996. Responsibilities included writing manuals for telephone equipment.

Ontario Ministry of Natural Resources, Cambridge, summer 1995. Responsibilities included designing and writing pamphlets on conservation.

Special skills:
Fluent in French.
Proficient in Internet research and web design.

References
Available upon request: Placement Office
University of Waterloo
Waterloo, ON N2L 3G1

- Use headings to mark the various sections of the résumé, spacing around them and within sections so that important information stands out.

- Try to limit your résumé to one page so that it can be quickly scanned. However, if your experience and education are extensive, a two-page résumé is preferable to a single cramped, unreadable page.

In preparing your résumé, you may wish to use some of the techniques of document design discussed on pages 749–52, such as variations in spacing and in type sizes and styles. You may also wish to consult one of the many books devoted to application letters, résumés, and other elements of a job search. Two helpful guides are Richard N. Bolles, *What Color Is Your Parachute? A Practical Manual for Job-Hunters and Career Changers,* and Tom Jackson, *The Perfect Résumé.*

42b Writing business memos

Unlike business letters, which address people in other organizations, business memorandums (memos, for short) address people within the same organization. A memo can be quite long, but more often it reports briefly and directly on a very specific topic: an answer to a question, a progress report, an evaluation. Both the form and the structure of a memo are designed to get to the point and dispose of it quickly.

The memo has no return address, inside address, salutation, or close. Instead, as shown in the sample memo on the next page, the heading typically consists of the company's name, the addressee's name, the writer's name, the date, and a subject description or title. Type the body of the memo as you would the body of a business letter: single-spaced, double-spaced between paragraphs, and no paragraph indentions. Never sign a business memo, though you should initial your name in the heading. If copies of the memo need to be sent to people not listed in the "To" line, add a notation two spaces below the last line, and list the persons to whom copies are being sent.

Immerse your reader in your subject at the very beginning of the memo. State your reason for writing in the first sentence, but do not waste words with expressions like "The purpose of this memo is. . . ." Devote the first paragraph to a succinct presentation of your answer, conclusion, or evaluation. In the rest of the memo explain how you arrived at your answer, the facts on which you base your conclusion, and your method of evaluation. The paragraphs may be numbered so that the main divisions of your message are easy to see.

Bigelow Wax Company

TO: Aileen Rosen, Director of Sales
FROM: Patricia Phillips, Territory 12
DATE: March 15, 1997
SUBJECT: 1996 sales of Quick Wax in Territory 12

Since it was introduced in January of 1996, Quick Wax has been unsuccessful in Territory 12 and has not affected the sales of our Easy Shine. Discussions with customers and my own analysis of Quick Wax suggest three reasons for its failure to compete with our product.

1. Quick Wax has not received the promotion necessary for a new product. Advertising--primarily on radio--has been sporadic and has not developed a clear, consistent image for the product. In addition, the Quick Wax sales representative in Territory 12 is new and inexperienced; he is not known to customers, and his sales pitch (which I once overheard) is weak. As far as I can tell, his efforts are not supported by phone calls or mailings from his home office.

2. When Quick Wax does make it to the store shelves, buyers do not choose it over our product. Though priced competitively with our product, Quick Wax is poorly packaged. The container seems smaller than ours, though in fact it holds the same eight ounces. The lettering on the Quick Wax package (red on blue) is difficult to read, in contrast to the white-on-green lettering on the Easy Shine package.

3. Our special purchase offers and my increased efforts to serve existing customers have had the intended effect of keeping customers satisfied with our product and reducing their inclination to stock something new.

Copies: L. Goldberger, Director of Marketing
L. MacGregor, Customer Service Manager

A business memo can be more informal in tone than a business letter, particularly if you know the addressee; but it should not be wordy. Use technical terms if your reader will understand them, but otherwise keep language simple and use short sentences. Provide only the information that your reader needs to know.

See also pages 749–52 for techniques of document design (such as the numbered list in the sample memo) that can improve the readability of a business memo.

42c Communicating electronically

Communicating via electronic devices, especially facsimile (fax) machines and computerized electronic mail (E-mail), speeds up correspondence but also creates new challenges. For both fax transmissions and e-mail, the standards are the same as for other business correspondence: state your purpose at the outset and write straightforwardly, clearly, concisely, objectively, courteously, and correctly.

Faxes

For fax transmissions, follow the format of a letter (p. 734) or memo (p. 741), as appropriate.

- Provide a cover sheet containing the addressee's name, company, and fax number; the date, time, and subject; your own name and fax and telephone numbers (the telephone number is important in case something goes wrong with the transmission); and the total number of pages (including the cover sheet) in the fax.
- Because fax transmissions can go astray, it's often wise to advise your addressee to expect a fax. Such advice is essential if the fax is confidential, because the machine is often shared.
- Transmission by fax can imply that the correspondence is urgent. If yours isn't, consider using the mail. (Swamping your correspondents with needless faxes can make you the boy who cried wolf when you really have an urgent message to transmit.)

E-mail

Postings by electronic mail tend to be more offhand and informal than standard business letters on paper. E-mail can communicate very effectively with a little attention and structure:

- An e-mail posting announces itself in the reader's list of incoming mail, which may be extensive. Give your posting a title that accurately describes the contents, so that your reader knows what priority to assign it.
- Because an e-mail reader must scroll through a posting—and so cannot review two or more screens at once—your posting should be as short as possible. Take a few minutes to condense your draft message before sending it.
- Also because of scrolling, a posting will be more effective if it is tightly structured, with a clear forecast of its contents and a clear division into parts.

- Because many e-mail users cannot display a posting while they are responding to it, your postings should centre on one or two points. Then the reader has a better chance of responding to your whole message.
- When you respond to someone else's posting, you can avoid restating it by excerpting relevant parts in your own message.
- Take the time to edit your posting. Errors in grammar, punctuation, and spelling will interfere with your message.
- E-mail usually does not allow underlining, italics, or boldface, so you can't emphasize or highlight words conventionally. E-mail writers have devised some substitutes, including asterisks before and after words to be emphasized (*I *will not* be able to attend*) or an underscore before and after a book title (*Measurements coincide with those in _Joule's Handbook_*). Don't use all-capital letters for emphasis: they yell too loudly.

Because it is sometimes anonymous as well as immediate, e-mail has been subject to abuses. Its users have developed some basic courtesies:

- The headings in an e-mail message are usually dictated by the network, but for business correspondence you can still address your reader(s) by name and sign off with your own name.
- Most e-mailers consider the medium more immediate than print mail and expect quick responses to their messages.
- E-mail, like faxes, may be broadcast to many recipients at once with a few keystrokes. Avoid flooding your correspondents with irrelevant postings: target your messages only to those who can actually use them.
- E-mail sometimes seems more free and impersonal than telephone conversations or print mail. But that's no justification for flaming, or attacking, correspondents. Address them respectfully and politely, as you would on paper.

Appendix A Preparing a Manuscript

This appendix provides detailed instructions on preparing a manuscript, the final copy of a paper. With more and more writers using word processors, "document design," or page layout, has become increasingly important, even for relatively simple papers. Thus a separate section (p. 749) discusses design basics.

A1 Choosing the appropriate materials

A legible, consistent, and attractive manuscript is a service to readers because it makes reading easier. This appendix discusses the materials necessary for manuscript preparation and some conventions of format adapted from the *MLA Handbook for Writers of Research Papers,* the style guide for English and some other disciplines. Most of these guidelines are standard, but your instructor may request that you follow different conventions in some matters. (The format of the American Psychological Association is detailed on pp. 705–06.)

a Typewritten papers

For papers you produce on a typewriter, use the following guidelines:

- Use 21.5 cm × 28 cm (8½" × 11") white bond paper, not onion-skin sheets, paper torn from notebooks, or coloured paper. Use the same type of paper throughout a project.
- Type on only one side of a sheet.
- Use a black typewriter ribbon that is fresh enough to make a dark impression, and make sure the keys of the typewriter are clean.
- To avoid smudging the page when correcting mistakes, use a liquid correction fluid or a correction tape. Don't use typed hyphens or *x*'s to cross out mistakes, and don't type corrections (strikeovers) on top of mistakes.

Papers produced on a word processor

Word processing offers various options for printers and paper.

- If you use a dot-matrix printer (which forms characters out of tiny dots), make sure the characters are legible and that the tails on letters such as *j, p,* and *y* descend below the line of type, as they do in the typeface used here.
- Be sure the printer's ribbon or cartridge produces a dark impression.
- Use standard-sized (21.5 cm × 28 cm; 8½" × 11") white bond paper.
- If you use continuous paper folded like a fan at perforations, it will also come with a row of holes along each side for feeding the paper into the printer. Before submitting your paper, remove these strips of holes and separate the pages at the folds.

Handwritten papers

When your instructor accepts handwritten papers, follow these guidelines:

- Use regular white paper, 21.5 cm × 28 cm (8½" × 11"), with horizontal lines spaced between .5 cm and 1 cm apart. Don't use paper torn from a notebook, unlined paper, paper with narrow lines, coloured paper, or paper other of a different size (such as legal or stenographer's pads). Use the same type of paper throughout a project.
- Write on only one side of a sheet.
- Use black or dark blue ink, not pencil.
- If possible, use an ink eraser or eradicator to correct mistakes. If you must cross out material, draw a single line through it. Don't scribble over or black out a mistake, and don't write corrections on top of mistakes.

A2 Following a standard format

A consistent physical format makes a manuscript visually effective and prevents confusion. The samples below show the format of a paper.

NOTE For the special formats of source citations and a list of works cited or references, see pages 576–602 (MLA style), 681–88(*CMS* style), 693–706 (APA style), or 715–19 (CBE style).

FIRST PAGE OF PAPER WITH NO TITLE PAGE

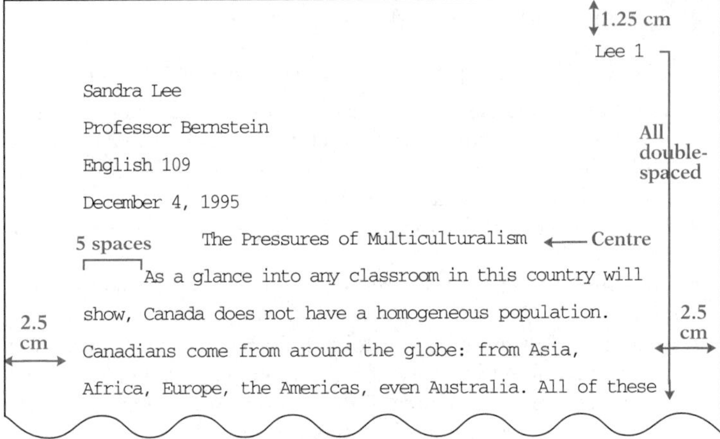

A LATER PAGE OF THE PAPER

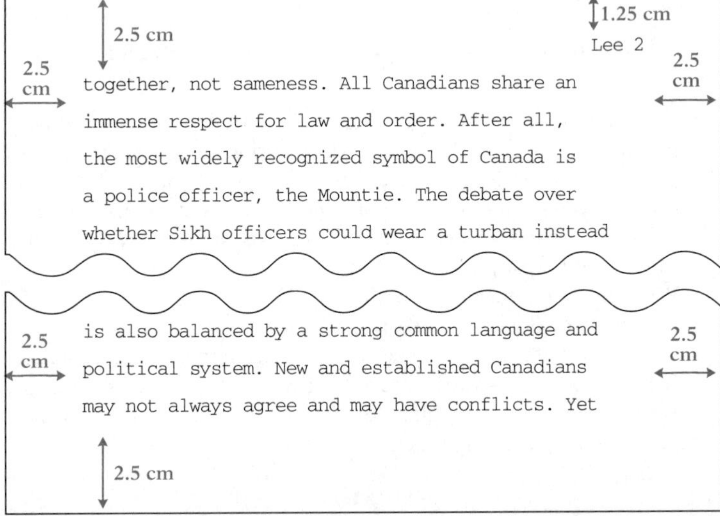

Title and identification

If you do not use a separate title page for an essay, provide your name and the date, plus any other information requested by your instructor, on the first text page. Place this identification 2.5 cm (1") from the top of the page, aligned with the left margin and double-spaced. Double-space again, and centre the title. Don't underline the title or place quotation marks around it, and capitalize the words in the title according to guidelines on page 421. Double-space between the title and the first line of text.

For a research paper, your instructor may ask you to provide a separate title page. If so, follow the guidelines and example on pages 606–07. On the first page of the paper repeat the title, centred 2.5 cm from the top of the page, and double-space between the title and the first line of text. (See p. 610 for an example.)

Text

In text produced on a word processor or typewriter, follow the spacings in the samples above. In addition:

- Leave one space between words.
- Leave one space after all punctuation, with these exceptions:

Dash (two hyphens)	book--its
Hyphen	one-half
Apostrophe within a word	book's
Between two or more adjacent marks	book.")

Leave one space before the three dots of an ellipsis mark (see p. 414):

book . . . in   book. . . . The

- Don't start a line with a mark of punctuation other than a dash, an opening parenthesis, an opening quotation mark, an opening bracket, or an ellipsis mark.
- Don't end a line with an opening quotation mark, parenthesis, or bracket. Close these marks up to the word following.
- Don't break a two-hyphen dash or a three-dot ellipsis mark from one line to the next.
- If you must break a word at the end of a line, follow the guidelines in Chapter 30.
- Use handwriting to make any symbols that are not on your keyboard, leaving two or three spaces and then inserting the symbol in ink.

- Set off quotations of more than four lines of prose or three lines of poetry; two- or three-line poetry quotations may be set off or placed in the text. Indent all lines of a set-off quotation 2.5 cm (1") from the left margin. Double-space above and below the quotation, and double-space the quotation itself. (See pp. 399–400 for samples.)
- For headings within the body of the text, follow the guidelines for document design on pages 750–51.

Most word processors offer a large variety of type styles, sizes, and weights. The section on document design (pp. 749–52) offers some tips for using these options effectively. However, many teachers consider a word processor's variations and embellishments to be a distraction from the work itself, for both reader and writer. Unless you know your instructor accepts alternatives, make your word-processed papers look like typewritten papers, with one size of type, underlining rather than *italics* for emphasis and source citations, and similar conventional elements.

Handwritten text should be reasonably uniform and clear. Be sure letters are easily distinguishable. Cross all *t*'s; dot all *i*'s with dots, not circles; form the loops of letters carefully. Make capital letters and small letters clearly different. Space consistently between words and between sentences. If your handwriting is difficult to read, submit a typed or word-processed paper if possible. If you don't have access to a typewriter and your handwriting is illegible or unusual in size, decoration, or slant, make it more legible or conventional when writing the final manuscript. Indent the first line of every paragraph about 2.5 cm (1"). Write on every line or every other line as specified by your instructor. For displayed quotations, indent all lines 2.5 cm from the left margin.

Margins

Use 2.5 cm margins on all sides of each page. The top margin will contain the page numbers (see p. 749). If the right margin is uneven, it should be no narrower than 2.5 cm. If you have a word processor or electronic typewriter that produces an even (or justified) right margin, use the feature only if it does not leave wide spaces between words and thus interfere with readability. When using a word processor, be sure to instruct the computer to set appropriate margins. Don't let the lines of type run across the perforations on continuous fanfold paper.

 Paging

Whether or not you provide a separate title page, begin numbering your paper on the first text page, and number consecutively through the end. Use Arabic numerals (1, 2, 3), and do not add periods, parentheses, hyphens, or the abbreviation "p." However, place your last name before the page number in case the pages become separated after you submit your paper. Align the page number with the right margin, and position it about 1.25 cm (1/2") from the top of the page, at least two lines above the first line of text.

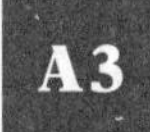 Designing documents

The preceding recommendations for manuscript format will help you produce neat, legible papers, but sometimes your work may call for more. You may need headings to separate and label parts of the work, lists to highlight steps or conclusions, tables or graphs to organize data and show trends.

With computerized word processing, especially desktop publishing, it is possible to produce "documents"—papers, reports, letters, and so on—that look as if they have been professionally typeset and printed, like this book. But even if you work on a typewriter or a very basic word processor, many of the following guidelines can help you produce effective documents. The key elements are white space, type styles and sizes, and illustrations.

 Using white space

The white space on a page eases crowding, distinguishes elements, and focuses readers' attention. On an otherwise full page, just the space of a paragraph indention gives readers a break and reassures them that the author has broken ideas down into manageable chunks. (See p. 104 on paragraph length.)

White space appears mainly in margins and around headings and lists. Use minimum 2.5 cm margins on all sides of the page. Make headings stand out: in double-spaced copy, double- or triple-space above and double-space below; in single-spaced copy, double-space above and below.

If your work contains a list of related items—for example, the steps in a process or the elements in a proposal—then consider indenting the items with numbers or bullets (centred dots). Bulleted lists appear throughout this handbook, as on page 747. A list is easier to read than a paragraph and adds white space to the page. Many word-processing programs can format a numbered or bulleted list automatically.

b Using type styles and sizes

Variations in the size of type and the style (such as CAPITALS, underlining, *italics,* or **boldface**) can affect the readability and the clarity of your work.

For your text, always choose a type size of 10 or 12 points.

```
This is 12-point typewriter type.
This is 10-point typewriter type.
```

Within the text, underlining may be all you need to emphasize key words or sentences. *Italics* provide about the same emphasis and **boldface** somewhat more. (Check with your instructor to be sure you can use italics instead of underlining for source citations and other important elements.)

Varied type sizes and styles may come most into play when you use headings within your text to clarify your organization and the relationships among parts. Plan your headings in advance, using your outline as a guide. (Inconsistent, overlapping, or missing headings do more harm than good.) Keep headings as short as possible while making them specific about the material that follows.

A typewriter with only one size of type can use capital letters, underlining, and positioning to indicate the relative importance of headings.

FIRST-LEVEL HEADING

Second-Level Heading

Third-Level Heading

In these examples the most important heading looks most important. The same principle applies when you have access to more type sizes and styles on a word processor, as in this example:

FIRST-LEVEL HEADING

Second-Level Heading

Third-Level Heading

For academic and business writing (except for promotional pieces), choose type sizes and styles for their ability to communicate, not show off. Avoid extra-large letters and unusual styles (such as outline or shadow type). Keep the appearance simple: most reports or papers shouldn't need more than two type styles or two or three sizes (including the body type).

Using illustrations

Tables and figures (charts, graphs, diagrams) are especially helpful for presenting data, showing changes, explaining processes, and the like. Such illustrations should be as simple as possible, uncluttered, and visually appealing. Whenever you use an illustration, be sure to refer to it in the text. See page 721 for a sample table. Because you will be expected to share your data with your readers, most of your writing for the sciences is likely to require illustrations to present the data in concise, readable form. Tables usually summarize raw data (see p. 721 for an example), whereas figures (mainly charts and graphs) recast the data to show noteworthy comparisons or changes. Follow these guidelines:

- Give each illustration a clear label. Number tables and figures separately (Table 1, Table 2, etc.; Figure 1, Figure 2, etc.).
- Give each illustration a clear title so that readers know what to look for in it. (Generally, a table's label and title are placed above the illustration, whereas a figure's label and title are placed under the illustration.)
- Provide clear labels for all the parts of illustrations, such as columns in a table and bars in a bar graph. Unless your instructor specifically requests abbreviations, avoid them in the interest of clarity.
- If you borrow the data or the whole illustration from another source, provide a second set of numbered references after the one for the text. As in the text citations, give each source a number based on the order in which it is cited in the illustrations.
- Refer to each illustration ("See Figure 6") at the point(s) in the text where readers will benefit by consulting it.
- If your paper includes many illustrations, collect them at the end of the paper, after the reference list. If it includes only a few illustrations, place each one on a page by itself immediately after the page that refers to it.

Many word processors and desktop publishers offer so-called clip art: pointing fingers, smiling faces, banners, and other figures ready to insert into your text. Avoid clip art in serious academic or business writing. It is suitable for light or punchy copy such as an advertisement or newsletter.

A4 Proofreading, correcting, and submitting the final manuscript

Proofread each page of your final work carefully, concentrating on spelling, punctuation, mechanics, and grammar. (See p. 67 for proofreading tips.) Business writing should be free of errors, but there's a little more latitude with most academic writing. If a page has several errors, produce a new, clean page by rewriting, retyping, or correcting on the word processor. If a page has one or two errors and you can't eradicate them, correct them in ink. Draw a single line through a word you want to delete. Don't try to correct a misspelled word without crossing out and rewriting the whole word. To replace a word or mark of punctuation, draw a line through the item, place a caret (^) underneath it, and write the new word or mark in the space above the old one. To add words or marks of punctuation, place a caret underneath the line at the point where you wish to insert the word or mark; then centre the word or mark over the caret in the space above the line.

```
                                  organisms
An ecosystem is a community of ~~arganisms~~ interacting
                                    ^
                          the
with each other and with ^ environment.
```

If you have to add more words than will fit between the lines of text, produce a new, clean page.

When you submit your final paper, be sure the pages will stay together when the paper is shuffled in with others. Depending on the wishes of your instructor, you may fold the paper in half lengthwise, paper-clip or staple the pages in the upper-left corner, or place the paper in a special binder.

Appendix B Writing with a Computer

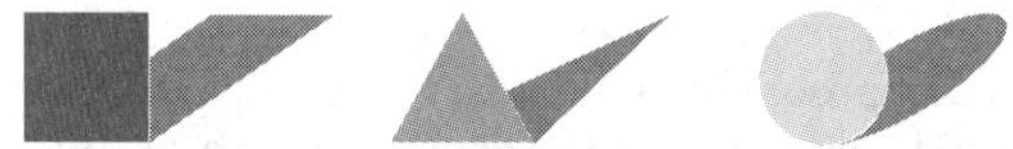

Computers have dramatically changed how we write and even what we write. This appendix offers general advice for word processing (below), guidelines for writing collaboratively with computers (p. 755), and tips for creating a hypertext document such as a page on the World Wide Web (p. 758).

B1 Using a word processor

Writing with a word processor can save time and make writing easier. The advantage of word processing is that you can perform such operations as adding to notes, rearranging outlines, and rewriting first drafts without having to cut pages apart or retype entire pages. The machine will not think for you, but it may leave you more time for the important work of thinking, exploring ideas, focusing and organizing material, and improving content and clarity.

a Word-processing basics

Using a word processor does not require an understanding of computers or expert typing skills. All it takes is a little perseverance and a few hours of practice. When you begin, take some time to examine the materials that explain the system, such as a user's manual or tutorial. Study the keyboard, and make a list of the basic keystrokes you need to perform important commands, such as inserting, deleting, pasting, saving, and printing text. Become familiar with the "Help" menus, usually accessible at the top of the screen. Be adventurous: experiment with commands, and learn by trial and error. Your play will not hurt the machine, and it will help you.

Computers do crash, but you can prevent permanent loss of your work by taking a few precautions:

- Save your work every fifteen minutes or so, either by instructing the computer to do so automatically or by manually saving the text you're working on.
- Label each project with its own file name for easy retrieval.
- Make a backup disk of your work at the end of each word-processing session as insurance against the loss or damage of your working disk.
- Keep your disks in dustproof containers, and store them safely away from heat, cold, or sources of magnetism such as the computer itself or a stereo or television.
- Regularly print paper copies of your work. They serve as second backup copies, and you may find it easier to work on them than on the screen when revising and editing (see pp. 59–67).

b Optional programs

Many word processors either come with optional programs such as spelling checkers or are compatible with optional programs. The programs are often limited, for the reasons given below, but they can support and speed your efforts. The following are the kinds of programs you are most likely to see.

- *Invention or discovery programs* help you develop a topic by prompting you with a structured set of questions or by providing creative analogies that help you think imaginatively. These programs can help you get started, develop new insights, and conceive a purpose for your writing. One example, *The Writer's Workshop,* is available with this handbook.
- *Outlining programs* help you organize your work by providing automatic indentions, easy resequencing, and other features.
- *Documentation programs* help you format your source citations in just about any style. The *Documentor* program that is available with this handbook is one example.
- *Style-checking programs* point out wordy and awkward phrases and incorrect grammar and punctuation. However, these programs can only call your attention to passages that *may* be faulty. They miss many errors because they are not yet capable of analysing the language in all its complexity (for instance,

they can't accurately distinguish a word's part of speech when there are different possibilities, as *light* can be a noun, a verb, and an adjective). And the programs often question passages that don't need editing, such as an appropriate passive verb or an emphatic use of repetition. When you use a style-checking program, you must determine each time it questions something whether a change is needed at all and what change will be most effective. And you must read your text carefully on your own to find any errors the program may have missed.

- *Thesaurus programs* help with word choices by responding to your word with a display of several synonyms (words with similar meanings). A single keystroke allows you to replace your word with a displayed word. Thesaurus programs are limited because they display only some synonyms, not all, and because even a narrow list may contain words that do not suit your meaning. Like a printed thesaurus, an electronic thesaurus is no help if it leads you to misuse words whose meanings you don't know. Before you use a word suggested by a thesaurus, always check its meaning in a dictionary.
- *Spell-checking programs* help you find typographical errors and misspelled words, and they display correct spellings on the screen. They can be valuable proofreading aids. However, they are limited because they cannot store every possible word and thus may identify a word you use as misspelled even though it is correct. More important, they are unreliable because they cannot identify errors such as a confusion between *now* and *not, its* and *it's, your* and *you're,* or *there, their,* and *they're.* Maintain a file of your frequent misspellings and use the search command to check them yourself.

B2 Collaborating using computers

Learning to write collaboratively will help you not only in school but also in work, because much business writing develops collaboratively. Computers, particularly networked computers, simplify some tasks of collaboration (such as making multiple copies of documents), and they open more phases of the writing process to collaboration.

a Possibilities for collaboration

If your classroom has only stand-alone computers (not connected to a network), you can still collaborate electronically by what's called keyboard sharing: all members of the group place their ideas or comments or changes on one computer that everyone has access to and works from individually, returning new drafts and comments to the shared computer.

If the classroom has a number of computers that are linked by a server (a central computer), you and your group will be able to share files. You may be able to retrieve another student's paper from the server, read it and make your comments online, and return the paper, along with your comments, to the server for the author to pick up later.

With a network that allows screen sharing, everyone can work simultaneously on the same material. From their own computers, group members can add text or comments that other members can see and respond to immediately. Revisions and comments can be copied and saved by all group members for later use.

A network also allows you to use personal e-mail or a discussion group for collaboration. Your instructor may create a Listserv—a subscriber-based discussion group (p. 525)—to distribute class assignments and announcements, to further class discussion, or to help students compose together. For example, you and your classmates could exchange experiences with various aspects of the writing process, talk about prospective paper topics, or post papers and evaluations for general class discussions. Listservs may also help you collaborate with students in other classes at your school or at other schools.

You may also have a chance to discuss papers or topics in "real time." Instead of waiting a few hours or days for classmates' responses, you and other members of your group can use a chat environment such as IRC or a MOO to meet and discuss topics as if you were in the same room—although you might be spread across campus or even across the country. (See pp. 526–27 for more on these environments.)

Effective collaboration

Collaborating on computer requires many of the same outlooks and expectations as collaborating in person, so the guidelines on pages 70–72 can help you become an effective computer collaborator. But there are other considerations as well. For one thing, computer communication demands a certain etiquette:

- You wouldn't shout at a fellow student face-to-face, so don't shout by computer either. Temper your comments, and avoid using all-capital letters. (See p. 743 for more about online courtesy.)
- You may not be present to clarify your comments for your

readers when they receive them. If you mean a remark to be taken humorously, you may need to say so. Or use common *emoticons,* combinations of punctuation marks and other symbols that signal emotions: for instance, :-) read sideways shows a smile. You'll also want to avoid inside jokes that only a few group members will understand.

When you are collaborating by personal e-mail or a Listserv, keep these guidelines in mind:

- Discussions by e-mail or on a Listserv take longer than face-to-face discussions. Members of the group may not have the original message that prompted the discussion or may have forgotten important details. Take advantage of the common e-mail feature that allows you to extract portions of the message you are answering and copy them into your own message.
- If you are joining a discussion already in progress, take the time to read all messages so that you don't waste effort and exhaust the goodwill of your collaborators by asking questions or raising issues that have already been discussed. (If you don't know how to obtain past messages, ask your instructor or another group member.) To avoid cluttering everyone else's mailboxes, you may ask that answers to your questions be sent to you "off-list" (just to you, not to all the others on the list).
- If you are responding to another group member's request for information, send the reply off-list unless you think the entire list will benefit from your response.

Collaborating effectively in MOOs or other "live" discussions takes a bit of practice. The pace of these discussions can vary widely because comments appear on all participants' screens as soon as a speaker has composed them and pressed the "Return" or "Enter" key. The conversation may lag if people are spending a few minutes thinking or composing responses that are extended (six or seven sentences or more). Or your screen may fill rapidly with conversation if people are thinking and responding quickly, leaving you little time to read one comment before another appears. A few tips can help you make the most of the discussion:

- Always save a transcript of your MOO session for future reference. Check with your instructor or your computer centre if you don't know how to create a transcript.
- Have a clear sense of what your group's goals are for a MOO or IRC session before beginning. If you sense at first that everyone is waiting for someone else to start, then do so by raising questions about the goals and plans for the session.
- If your group is meeting to comment on a paper, e-mail a copy of the paper to individual participants before the meeting time.

- If you find it impossible to read everyone's comments, pick a thread of conversation that seems most interesting or relevant to you and focus on the comments from the people involved. You can always go back and read the transcripts of other threads.
- Even if you can keep up with a fast-paced conversation, you may not see an opportunity to contribute to it. If you think that a conversation is about to leave you behind, ask the others to slow down for a minute so that you can catch up.
- Remember that you are participating in a conversation, not making a speech. You don't need to have a thought perfectly formed and worded in your mind before trying it out. Sometimes the smallest fragment of a thought may be just what the conversation needs.
- If you notice that some members of the group are not contributing, you may want to ask them what they are thinking to involve them in the conversation. Take the initiative, too, when you think the discussion is stuck or off-track.

B3 Creating hypertext documents

Computers make it possible to compose other types of documents besides the conventional word-processed essay. If you have browsed the World Wide Web, you have encountered **hypertext** documents that provide varied paths through the information they present. Clicking on highlighted links within the site, you may be taken to other spots in the same site (passages of text, video, sound, illustrations, compilations of statistics, and so on), or you may be taken to other sites on the Web. You choose your own path based on the information you want to find. You may also have a chance to interact with a site's author(s) by answering questions, making suggestions, and even adding new information to the text. (For more on the World Wide Web, see pp. 521–24.)

You can create your own hypertext documents, either stored on your computer or posted on the World Wide Web. In some courses you may be asked to create electronic hypertext instead of a conventional printed essay. For example, you might develop a hypertext history project that shows text and images on the same screen and provides links to primary-source documents that are discussed in your main text. Or you might produce a hypertext chemistry project with links to three-dimensional or animated diagrams. Beyond your course work, you can create a hypertext document to share information about a hobby or other special interest or even about yourself. Many job seekers have created hypertext job applications that include a standard résumé (see pp. 737–40) as well as links to recommendations, personal statements, writing samples, and other supporting information.

Technical requirements

If you are preparing a hypertext document for a course, your instructor may recommend specific software and may ask for the document on disk, to be viewed only by the instructor and perhaps other students in the course. The following introduction to creating hypertext documents assumes that you will use generally available software and will post your document on the World Wide Web. (Be aware, however, that some schools discourage students from posting Web pages because of the drain on limited computer facilities.)

- To compose the text of your document, you will need a simple text-editing application such as NotePad (for IBM compatibles) or SimpleText (for Macintoshes). The application should come with your computer. You may also use the word-processing software that you compose conventional essays with, but you will need to save documents as so-called plain text (or ASCII text) so that your Web browser can read them.
- To see what your Web page looks like, you'll need a web browser such as Netscape Navigator or Microsoft's Internet Explorer.
- To create attractive headings, links, and other features of a Web site, you will need a basic knowledge of HTML (HyperText Markup Language). HTML allows you to construct links within the document or with other Web documents and makes it possible to arrange text, images, sound, and video on a page. Using HTML, you code your document with tags, as illustrated in the following excerpt from a coded term project on the subject of electronic mail. The tags are between angle brackets (<>).

```
<html>
<head>
<title>Content Map</title>
</head>
<body>

<h2><center>The Computerized Post Office:<br>Sending and
Receiving Mail in the Late Age of Print</h2></center>
<center>Joyce R. Walker</center><br>
<IMG HEIGHT=5 WIDTH=100% SRC="bar2. jpg"><p>
<center><h3>Content Map</h3></center><p>
<a href= "EC1.html"><IMG Height=20 WIDTH=20 SRC="fire.gif"></a>
Electronic Communications Dynamics<p>
<a href="PP1.html"><IMG height=20 width=20 SRC="book.gif"></a>
Pedagogical Purposes<p>
<a href="DWG1.html"><IMG height=20 width=20
SRC="shakespere.gif"> </a> Dead White Guys and the History of
Letter-Writing Manuals<p>
```

B3

```
<a href="EE1.html"><IMG height=20 width=20
SRC="smiley.gif"></a>   E-mail Etiquette: Online Guides to
Playing Nice<p>

<pre> Some viewing suggestions:</pre>
<UL>
<li>For readers/viewers who feel the insatiable need for the
comfort of boundaries and content control, I've provided a
detailed map of the pages I've created which can be read to
supply the illusion of closure.
<li> When navigating through this essay using the hot buttons
above, a reader/viewer can keep track of the thread he/she
wishes to follow by taking note of the icons and page
backgrounds.
<li>For readers/viewers who wish to have a unique, nonlinear
viewing experience, the four small icons, which correspond to
particular threads, appear on every page of this essay . These
icons are also "hot buttons" which will link to other pages.

<TABLE BORDER=4>
<Center><TR><TD ROWSPAN=1> </TD><TH COLSPAN=3> </TR>
<TR><TD> <a href="linear .html">To View Linear Guide</a></TD>
<TD ALIGN=LEFT><a href="bib.html">To View Bibliography  </a>
</TD><TD ALIGN=CENTER> <a href="connotes1.html">To View
Construction Notes </a></TD></TR></Center>
</TABLE>

</body>
</html>
```

With a Web browser, the page coded above looks like this:

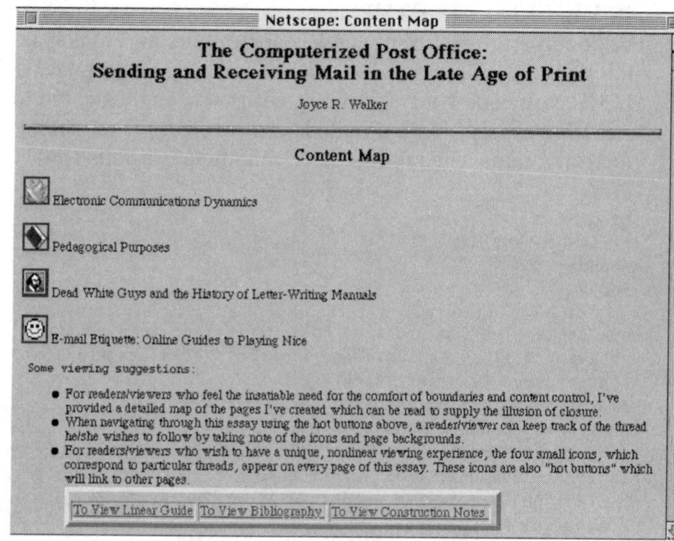

- You can obtain HTML instructions online, using the keywords *HTML and reference.* (See pp. 519–24 if you need help conducting an Internet search.) Bookstores also carry *HTML for Dummies, Teach Yourself HTML in 21 Days,* and other references, some of them packaged with a CD-ROM containing examples of HTML code that you can experiment with to create your own pages.

Effective hypertext documents

To a great extent, creating an effective hypertext document requires the same considerations as creating an effective essay in print: a clear purpose and central idea, a sense of audience, a navigable structure. But its links, its integration of elements (text, image, audio, video), and its wide publication (for a Web page) demand other considerations as well.

Questions during planning

Because of its complexities, hypertext rewards careful planning. Consider the following questions:

- What is your purpose in creating this document? Your choice of links, images, and other features should be geared to this purpose.
- Who is your audience? If you are writing to a specific audience (your instructor, your classmates, prospective employers), you can use the questions on page 29 to analyse the audience's interests, biases, expectations, and so on. But if you're trying to create a site for a wide, unknown audience—anyone who might come across the site in an Internet search—then you need to think more broadly. For instance, you may want to avoid references to incidents or people known only on your campus.
- What do you want your pages to look like? Plan your pages on paper before coding them. Varied headings, text, photographs, video—all these may crowd together (especially on small computer screens) unless you arrange elements attractively, with plenty of space between them.
- What elements will best achieve your purpose? Add elements to your document to further your purpose, not simply for the sake of including them. A single image and a caption may help you illustrate a concept far more efficiently than a page of text alone. Sound or video clips may work as catalysts for discussion or as valuable evidence. But none of these elements should be used as distractions from an otherwise weak document.
- Will the reader be able to download the whole document? If you're posting your document online, consider whether your

readers will have access to all the elements you've included. Text can be downloaded fairly quickly; however, images, sound, and video take much longer, and the reader may choose not to wait for them. Furthermore, the reader's Web browser may not be able to decode complicated graphics, audio, or video. If you think that readers may miss some elements for either of these reasons, consider designing a "light" version of your document that fulfils your purpose without all the elements.

Questions about links

Aside from the technical requirements, probably the trickiest part of creating a hypertext document is making effective links within the document and to other documents. The following questions raise the key issues:

- How does each of your links further your purpose? Your instructor may suggest that your document have a minimum number of links, but don't use this suggestion as an excuse for creating irrelevant links. Each one should add some information that is vital to your central idea.
- Will readers understand the reason for each link? Sometimes your reason for creating a link will be obvious, and you need do no more than provide the highlighted words. Other times you'll need to be more explicit—for instance, "To learn more about the reign of Louis XIV, click here." And occasionally you'll need to explain your links carefully—for instance, giving the reasons for providing a whole text instead of just a relevant excerpt. The point is to think about what readers probably understand and to provide a variety of links geared to their understanding.
- Are the sources of your links clear? You have the same obligation to acknowledge sources in a hypertext document as you do in other academic writing. (See pp. 556–592 on what to acknowledge and pp. 575–76 on citing sources.)
- Have you sought permission for links to copyrighted material? If your hypertext document will be distributed privately (for instance, to your instructor and classmates), then it is enough to acknowledge the use of copyrighted material (see pp. 556–59). But if you are publishing your document on the World Wide Web, then you may be obliged to seek permission for using copyrighted material—just as print publishers do. Another reason for seeking permission is that the computer housing a linked source may not be capable of supporting many simultaneous users or may not be accessible around the clock.

Questions about nontext media

Images, backgrounds, icons, animation, video, and sound can add interest as well as substance to your hypertext document. When using such material, consider these questions:

- What does the element add to your document? A certain amount of window dressing may be appropriate, especially in the use of graphics. But an overloaded text will distract and even annoy readers. As mentioned earlier, nontext elements also increase the download time of your document and cannot always be decoded by Web browsers.
- Can you find the elements you need on the Web? A number of image libraries allow users (especially nonprofit users) to download visual and audio elements without formal permission and to reproduce the elements on the users' own pages. If you reproduce elements from such a source, always acknowledge the source (see pp. 575–76).
- Do you need to seek permission for use of nontext elements? You can download nontext materials from any site on the Web, not just image libraries. But unless the site explicitly allows copying without permission, you should seek permission to publish the material in your own Web document. (Text and nontext material are alike in this respect.) Of course, you must also acknowledge the source in your document (see pp. 575–76).

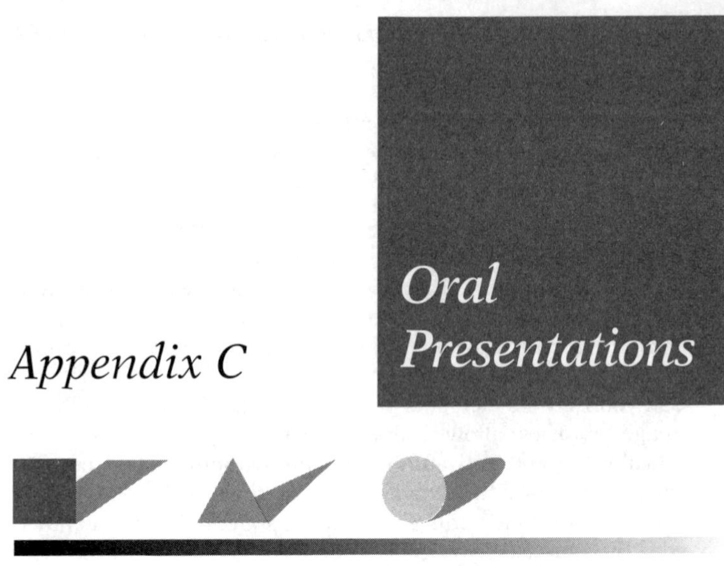

Appendix C Oral Presentations

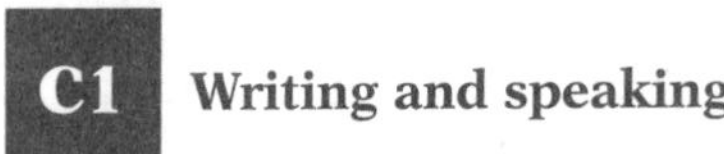

At some point during your education or your work, you will probably be called upon to speak to a group. Oral presentation can be anxiety producing, even for those who are experienced at it. This appendix shows you how you can apply your experiences as a writer to public speaking, and it offers some techniques that are uniquely appropriate for effective oral presentations.

C1 Writing and speaking

Writing and speechmaking have much in common: both require careful consideration of your subject, purpose, and audience. Thus the mental and physical activities that go into the writing process can also help you prepare and present a successful oral presentation.

Despite many similarities, however, writing for readers is not the same as speaking to listeners. Whereas a reader can go back and reread a written message, a listener cannot stop a speech to rehear a section. Several studies have reported that immediately after hearing a short talk, most listeners cannot recall half of what was said.

Effective speakers adapt to their audience's listening ability by reinforcing their ideas through repetition and restatement. They use simple words, short sentences, personal pronouns, contractions, and colloquial expressions. In formal writing, these strategies might seem redundant and too informal; but in speaking, they improve listeners' comprehension.

C2 Considering topic, purpose, and audience

The most important step in developing an oral presentation is to identify your purpose: what do you want your audience to know or do as a result of your speech? Topic and purpose are *not* the same thing. Asking "What am I talking about?" is not the same as asking "Why am I speaking?"

In school and work settings, oral presentations may include anything from a five-minute report before a few peers to an hour-long address before a hundred people. Whatever the situation, you're likely to be speaking for the same reasons that you write in school or at work: to explain something to listeners or to persuade listeners to accept your opinion or take an action. See page 26 for more on these purposes.

Adapting to your audience is a critical task in public speaking as well as in writing. You'll want to consider the questions about audience on page 29. But a listening audience requires additional considerations as well:

- Why is your audience assembled? Is it because these people want to hear you, because they are interested in your topic, because they have been required to attend, or because they always meet in this time and place? Listeners who are required to attend may be more difficult to interest and motivate than listeners who attend because they want to hear you and your ideas.
- How large is your audience? With a small group you can be informal. If you are speaking to a hundred or more people, you may need a public address system, a lectern, special lighting, and audiovisual equipment.
- Where will you speak? Your appearance should match the setting—more casual for a classroom, more formal for an auditorium. If the room is large and the audience small, you may ask the audience to fill in the front section of the room.
- How long are you scheduled to speak and when? A long speech early in the morning or late in the afternoon may find your audience too sleepy to listen well. And keep in mind that audiences lose patience with someone who speaks longer than the assigned time.

When speaking, unlike when writing, you can see and hear your audience's responses during your presentation. Thus you have the luxury and challenge of adapting your presentation to an audience as you speak. If you sense that an audience is bored, try to spice up your presentation. If an audience is restless, consult your watch to make sure you have not gone overtime. If you sense resistance, try to make midspeech adjustments to respond to that resistance.

C3 Organizing the presentation

An effective oral presentation, like an effective essay, has a recognizable shape. The arrangement of sections guides listeners through a presentation and helps them see how ideas and details are related to each other. The advice in Chapter 1 for organizing and outlining an essay serves the speechmaker as well as the writer (see p. 45). Here are additional considerations for the introduction, conclusion, and supporting material.

a The introduction

First impressions count. A strong beginning establishes an important relationship among three elements in an oral presentation: you, your topic, and your audience. More specifically, the beginning of an oral presentation should try to accomplish three goals:

- Gain the audience's attention and interest. When you begin to speak, your listeners may not be ready to pay attention: they may be talking to a neighbour or be preoccupied with other thoughts. To attract listeners' attention, begin with a question, an unusual example or statistic, or a short, relevant story.
- Put yourself in the speech by demonstrating your expertise, experience, or concern. Your audience will be more interested in what you say and more trusting of you.
- Introduce and preview your purpose and topic. By the time your introduction is over, listeners should know what your topic is and the direction in which you wish to take them as you develop your ideas. This information will give them expectations for your speech on which they can pin the specific points that follow.

In addition to these guidelines for beginning a speech, there are some important pitfalls to avoid:

- Don't try to cram too much into your introduction. Giving only a sneak preview of your speech can pique your audience's curiosity about what you have to say.
- Don't begin with an apology. A statement such as "I wish I'd been given more time to get ready for this presentation" will only undermine your listeners' confidence in you.

- Don't begin with "My speech is about...." The statement is dull, and it does little to clarify purpose.

Supporting material

Just as you do when writing, you can and should use facts, statistics, examples, and expert opinions to support spoken arguments (see pp. 139–41). In addition, as a speaker you can draw on other kinds of supporting material:

- Use vivid description to paint a mental image of a scene, a concept, an event, or a person.
- Use well-chosen quotations to add an emotional or humorous moment to your speech.
- Use true or fictional stories to rivet the audience's attention and illustrate your point. Most listeners remember a good story long after they have forgotten other details from a speech.
- Use analogies—comparisons between essentially unlike things, such as a politician and a tightrope walker—to link concepts memorably. (For more on analogy, see p. 101.)

Use a variety of supporting material in your speech. A presentation that is nothing but statistics can bore an audience. Nonstop storytelling may interest listeners but fail to achieve your purpose.

The conclusion

Last impressions count as much as first impressions. You may hope that listeners will remember every detail of your speech, but they are more likely to leave with a general impression and a few ideas about you and your message. You want your conclusion to be clear, of course, but you also want it to be memorable. Remind listeners of how your topic and main idea connect to their needs and interests. If your speech was motivational, tap an emotion that matches your message. If your speech was informational, give some tips on how to remember important details.

C4 Delivering the presentation

Writing and speaking differ most obviously in the form of delivery: the writer is represented in print; the speaker is represented in person. This section describes the methods and techniques of oral presentation (pp. 768–71) as well as some ways of coping with stage fright (pp. 771–72).

Checklist for an oral presentation

- **Purpose:** What do you want your audience to know or do as a result of your presentation? How can your purpose be achieved by an oral presentation in the time and setting you've been given? (See below.)
- **Audience:** What do you know about the characteristics and opinions of your audience? How can this information help you adapt your presentation to your audience's interests, needs, and opinions? (See below.)
- **Organization and content:** How are your ideas arranged? Where might listeners have difficulty following you? What functions do your introduction and conclusion perform? How relevant and interesting is your supporting material for your topic and your audience? (See p. 766.)
- **Method of delivery:** What method of delivery do you plan: extemporaneous? reading from a text? memorized? a mixture? How does your method suit the purpose, setting, and occasion of your presentation? (See below.)
- **Vocal and physical delivery:** In rehearsing your presentation, what do you perceive as your strengths and weaknesses? Is your voice suitably loud for the setting? Are you speaking clearly? Are you able to move your eyes around the room so that you'll be making eye contact during the presentation? Is your posture straight but not stiff? Do your gestures reinforce your ideas? Do you use visual aids appropriately?
- **Confidence and credibility:** What techniques will you use to overcome the inevitable anxiety about speaking? How will you project your confidence and competence? (See p. 771.)

a Methods of delivery

An oral presentation may be delivered impromptu, extemporaneously, from a text, or from memory. No one technique is best for all speeches; indeed, a single speech may include two or more forms or even all four—perhaps a memorized introduction, an extemporaneous body in which quotations are read from a text, and an impromptu response to audience questions during or after the speech.

- *Impromptu* means "without preparation": an impromptu presentation is one you deliver off-the-cuff, with no planning or practice. You may be called on in a class to express your opinion or to summarize something you've written. You may speak up at a neighbourhood meeting. An audience member may ask you a question at the end of an oral presentation. The only way to prepare for such incidents is to be well prepared in general—

to be caught up on course reading, for instance, or to know the facts in a debate.

- Extemporaneous speaking—that done with some preparation, but without reading from a text—is the most common form of presentation, typical of class lectures and business briefings. With extemporaneous speaking, you have time to prepare and practise in advance. Then, instead of following a script of every word, you speak from notes that guide you through the presentation. You can look and sound natural while still covering all the material you want to convey.
- Delivering a presentation from a text involves writing the text out in advance and then reading aloud from it. Unless you have considerable experience writing speeches and reading from a text, try to avoid this form of delivery for an entire presentation. If you do use it, write the text so that it sounds spoken (less formal) rather than written (more formal): for instance, the sentence *Although costs rose, profits remained steady* would sound fine in writing but stiff and awkward in speech because in conversation we rarely use such a structure. In addition, rehearse thoroughly so that you can read with expression and can look up frequently to make eye contact with listeners (see p. 770).
- A memorized presentation has a distinct advantage: complete freedom from notes or a text. However, while you can look at your audience every minute and can move away from a lectern and even into the audience, you risk forgetting your place or a whole passage. When you deliver a memorized presentation, always have some notes at hand to jog your memory.

Vocal delivery

The sound of your voice will influence how your listeners receive you. When rehearsing, consider volume, speed, and articulation.

- Speak loudly. In a meeting with five other people, you can speak in a normal volume. As your audience grows in size, so should your volume. Most speakers can project to as many as a hundred people, but a larger audience may require a microphone. If you can rehearse in the room where you'll be speaking, ask a friend or colleague to sit at the back and tell you what volume is easy to hear. It may seem like shouting to you, but to your audience it will sound confident and clear.
- Speak slowly enough to be understandable. Most audiences prefer speech that's a little fast, around 150 words a minute;

but they have difficulty following too-rapid speech at, say, 190 words a minute.
- Speak clearly and correctly. To avoid mumbling or slurring words, practise articulating. Sometimes it helps to open your mouth a little wider than usual. And to avoid mispronouncing words and names, look up questionable ones or ask someone for the correct pronunciation.

c Physical delivery

You are more than your spoken words when you make an oral presentation. Your face and body also play a role in how your speech is received.

- Make eye contact with listeners. Looking directly in your listeners' eyes conveys your honesty, your confidence, and your control of your material. Don't look above the heads of the audience or at one friendly face. Instead, move your gaze around the entire room, settle on someone, and establish direct eye contact; then move on to someone else.
- Always stand for a presentation, unless it takes place in a small room where standing would be inappropriate. You can see more audience members if you stand, and they in turn can hear your voice and see your gestures more clearly.
- Stand straight, and move around. Turn your body toward one side of the room and the other, step out from behind any lectern or desk, and gesture appropriately, as you would in conversation. Let your gestures and movement support and draw attention to important words and ideas.

Visual aids

Many speakers supplement their oral presentations with visual aids—from words on a chalkboard through posters and models and slides to computer-generated multimedia productions. Visual aids can emphasize key points, organize interrelated concepts, and illustrate complex procedures. They can gain listeners' attention and improve their understanding and memory.

The following guidelines can help you create effective and appropriate visual aids:

- Use visual aids to underscore your points. Short lists of key ideas, illustrations such as graphs or photographs, or objects such as models can make your presentation more interesting and memorable. But use visual aids judiciously: a battery of illustrations or objects will bury your message rather than amplify it.

- Match visual aids and setting. An audience of five people may be able to see a photograph and share a chart; an audience of a hundred will need projected images.
- Coordinate visual aids with your message. Time each visual aid to reinforce a point you're making. Tell listeners what they're looking at—what they should be getting from the aid. Give them enough viewing time so they don't mind turning their attention back to you.

Practise

Practising an oral presentation is the speechmaker's equivalent of editing and proofreading a written text. Good speakers rehearse their presentations exactly as they intend to deliver them before an audience—even in the same room, if possible, certainly with the same audio equipment and visual aids. (Practising an oral presentation silently in your head is not the same as practising it aloud.) With conscientious practice, you can uncover words that are difficult to pronounce or concepts that are unclear. You can tell and retell stories until they sound natural. You can rehearse your introduction so that you can maintain constant eye contact with listeners.

Stage fright

Many people report that speaking in front of an audience is their number-one fear. Even many experienced and polished speakers have some anxiety about delivering an oral presentation, but they use this nervous energy to their advantage, letting it propel them into working hard on each presentation, preparing well in advance, and rehearsing until they're satisfied with their delivery. They know that once they begin speaking and concentrate on their ideas, enthusiasm will quell anxiety. They know, too, that the symptoms of anxiety are usually imperceptible to listeners, who cannot see or hear a racing heart, upset stomach, cold hands, and worried thoughts. Even speakers who describe themselves as nervous usually appear confident and calm to their audiences.

Several techniques can help you reduce your level of anxiety:

- Use simple relaxation exercises, such as deep breathing or tensing and relaxing your stomach muscles, to ease some of the physical symptoms of speech anxiety—stomachache, rapid heartbeat, and shaky hands, legs, and voice.

- Think positively. Try to convert any negative and irrational thoughts about speaking into positive ones about yourself and your behaviour. Instead of worrying about the mistakes you might make, concentrate on how well you've prepared and practised your presentation and how significant your ideas are.
- Don't avoid chances to speak in public. Practice and experience build speaking skills and offer the best insurance for success.

Glossary of Usage

This glossary provides notes on words or phrases that often cause problems for writers. The recommendations for standard written English are based on current dictionaries and usage guides such as the ones listed on pages 469–72. Items labelled **nonstandard** should be avoided in speech and especially in writing. Those labelled **colloquial** and **slang** occur in speech and in some informal writing but are best avoided in the more formal writing usually expected in college and business. (Words and phrases labelled *colloquial* include those labelled by many dictionaries with the equivalent term *informal.*) See Chapter 31, pages 444–51, for further discussion of word choice and for exercises in usage. See pages 475–76 for a description of dictionary labels. Also see pages 488–89 for a list of commonly confused words that are pronounced the same or similarly. The words and definitions provided there supplement this glossary.

Spelling presents a special problem in Canadian English because of the difference between spellings in the United Kingdom and those in the United States. Because of Canada's historical relation to Britain and proximity to the United States, Canadian spelling has tended to waver between the two. The principal forms of the variants are the following (British first): *civilise/civilize; colour/color; centre/center; fulfil/fulfill; defence/defense; travelled/traveled; anaemia/anemia*. A widely recognized authority on Canadian spelling is the *Gage Canadian Dictionary* (1983, revised 1997). In this text, we have followed *Gage* for the most part, preferring the British spellings for *centre, fulfil, defence,* and *travelled,* while preferring the U.S. spellings for *civilize* and *anemia*. We have preserved American spellings as used in quoted material. For more on Canadian spelling practices, see pp. 490–91 and 784 (under "*-ize, -wise*").

This glossary is necessarily brief. Keep a dictionary handy for all your writing, and make a habit of referring to it whenever you doubt the appropriateness of a word or phrase.

a, an Use *a* before words beginning with consonant sounds, including those spelled with an initial pronounced *h* and those spelled with vowels that are sounded as consonants: *a historian, a one-o'clock class, a university.* Use *an* before words that begin with vowel sounds, including those spelled with an initial silent *h: an orgy, an L, an honour.*

The article before an abbreviation depends on how the abbreviation is read: *She was once an AEC undersecretary* (*AEC* is read as three separate letters); *Most Canadians support a NATO presence (NATO* is to be read as one word, *nato).*

For the use of *a/an* versus *the,* see pages 247–49.

accept, except *Accept* is a verb meaning "receive." *Except* is usually a preposition or conjunction meaning "but for" or "other than"; when it is used as a verb, it means "leave out." *I can accept all your suggestions except the last one. I'm sorry you excepted my last suggestion from your list.*

adverse, averse *Adverse* and *averse* both mean "opposed" or "hostile." But *averse* describes the subject's opposition to something, whereas *adverse* describes something opposed to the subject: *The premier was averse to adverse criticism.*

advice, advise *Advice* is a noun, and *advise* is a verb: *Take my advice; do as I advise you.*

affect, effect Usually *affect* is a verb, meaning "to influence," and *effect* is a noun, meaning "result": *The drug did not affect his driving; in fact, it seemed to have no effect at all.* But *effect* occasionally is used as a verb meaning "to bring about": *Her efforts effected a change.* And *affect* is used in psychology as a noun meaning "feeling or emotion": *One can infer much about affect from behaviour.*

aggravate *Aggravate* should not be used in its colloquial meaning of "irritate" or "exasperate" (for example, *We were aggravated by her constant arguing*). *Aggravate* means "make worse": *The Prime Minister was irritated by the Senate's stubbornness because he feared any delay might aggravate the West's disenchantment with Ottawa.*

agree to, agree with *Agree to* means "consent to," and *agree with* means "be in accord with": *How can they agree to a treaty when they don't agree with each other about the terms?*

ain't Nonstandard for *am not, isn't,* or *aren't.*

all, all of Usually *all* is sufficient to modify a noun: *all my loving, all the things you are.* Before a pronoun or proper noun, *all of* is usually appropriate: *all of me, in all of France.*

all ready, already *All ready* means "completely prepared," and *already* means "by now" or "before now": *We were all ready to go to the movie, but it had already started.*

all right *All right* is always two words. *Alright* is a common misspelling.

all together, altogether *All together* means "in unison," or "gathered in one place." *Altogether* means "entirely." *It's not altogether true that our family never spends vacations all together.*

gl/us

allusion, illusion An *allusion* is an indirect reference, and an *illusion* is a deceptive appearance: *Paul's constant allusions to Shakespeare created the illusion that he was an intellectual.*

almost, most *Almost* means "nearly"; *most* means "the greater number (or part) of." In formal writing, *most* should not be used as a substitute for *almost: We see each other almost* (not *most*) *every day.*

a lot *A lot* is always two words, used informally to mean "many." *Alot* is a common misspelling.

among, between In general, use *among* for relationships involving more than two people or things. Use *between* for relationships involving only two or for comparing one thing to a group to which it belongs. *The four of them agreed among themselves that the choice was between Edmonton and Calgary.*

amongst Although sometimes used by Canadian or British writers, *amongst* is an overrefined substitute for *among.*

amount, number Use *amount* with a singular noun that names something not countable (a noncount noun): *The amount of food varies.* Use *number* with a plural noun that names more than one of something countable (a plural count noun): *The number of calories must stay the same.*

an, and *An* is an article (see *a, an*). *And* is a coordinating conjunction. Do not carelessly omit the *d* from *and.*

and etc. *Et cetera* (*etc.*) means "and the rest"; *and etc.* therefore is redundant. See also *et al., etc.*

and/or *And/or* indicates three options: one or the other or both (*The decision is made by the mayor and/or the council*). If you mean all three options, *and/or* is appropriate. Otherwise, use *and* if you mean both, *or* if you mean either.

and which, and who *And which* or *and who* is correct only when used to introduce a second clause beginning with the same relative pronoun: *Jill is my cousin who goes to school here and who* *calls me constantly.* Otherwise, *and* is not needed: *CFCF is my favourite AM radio station, which* (not *and which*) *I listen to every morning.*

ante-, anti- The prefix *ante-* means "before" (*antedate, antebellum*); *anti-* means "against" (*antiwar, antinuclear*). Before a capital letter or *i, anti-* takes a hyphen: *anti-Freudian, anti-isolationist.*

anxious, eager *Anxious* means "nervous" or "worried" and is usually followed by *about. Eager* means "looking forward" and is usually followed by *to. I've been anxious about getting blisters. I'm eager* (not *anxious*) *to get new running shoes.*

gl/us

anybody, any body; anyone, any one *Anybody* and *anyone* are indefinite pronouns; *any body* is a noun modified by *any; any one* is a pronoun or adjective modified by *any. How can anybody communicate with any body of government? Can anyone help Amy? She has more work than any one person can handle.*

any more, anymore *Any more* means "no more"; *anymore* means "now." Both are used in negative constructions: *He doesn't want any more. She doesn't live here anymore.*

anyplace Colloquial for *anywhere.*

anyways, anywheres Nonstandard for *anyway* and *anywhere.*

apt, liable, likely *Apt* and *likely* are interchangeable. Strictly speaking, though, *apt* means "having a tendency to": *Horace is apt to forget his lunch in the morning. Likely* means "probably going to": *Horace is leaving so early today that he's likely to catch the first bus.*

Liable normally means "in danger of" and should be confined to situations with undesirable consequences: *Horace is liable to trip over that hose.* Strictly, *liable* means "responsible" or "exposed to": *The owner will be liable for Horace's injuries.*

are, is Use *are* with a plural subject (*books are*), *is* with a singular subject (*book is*).

as Substituting for *because, since,* or *while, as* may be vague or ambiguous: *As we were stopping to rest, we decided to eat lunch.* (Does *as* mean "while" or "because"?) *As* never should be used as a substitute for *whether* or *who. I'm not sure whether* (not *as*) *we can make it. That's the man who* (not *as*) *gave me directions.*

as, like In formal speech and writing, *like* should not introduce a full clause (with a subject and a verb) because it is a preposition. The preferred choice is *as* or *as if: The plan succeeded as* (not *like*) *we hoped. It seemed as if* (not *like*) *it might fail. Other plans like it have failed.*

When *as* serves as a preposition, the distinction between *as* and *like* depends on meaning. *As* suggests that the subject is equivalent or identical to the description: *She was hired as an engineer. Like* suggests resemblance but not identity: *People like her do well in such jobs.* See also *like, such as.*

as, than In comparisons, *as* and *than* precede a subjective-case pronoun when the pronoun is a subject: *I love you more than he (loves you). As* and *than* precede an objective-case pronoun when the pronoun is an object: *I love you as much as (I love) him.* (See also p. 192.)

assure, ensure, insure *Assure* means "to promise": *He assured us that we would miss the traffic. Ensure* and *insure* often are used interchangeably to mean "make certain," but some reserve *insure* for matters of legal and financial protection and use *ensure* for more general meanings: *We left early to ensure that we would miss the traffic. It's expensive to insure yourself against floods.*

as to A stuffy substitute for *about: The suspect was questioned about* (not *as to*) *her actions.*

at The use of *at* after *where* is wordy and should be avoided: *Where are you meeting him?* is preferable to *Where are you meeting him at?*

at this point in time Wordy for *now, at this point,* or *at this time.*

averse, adverse See *adverse, averse.*

awful, awfully Strictly speaking, *awful* means "awe-inspiring." As intensifiers meaning "very" or "extremely" (*He tried awfully hard*), *awful* and *awfully* should be avoided in formal speech or writing.

a while, awhile *Awhile* is an adverb; *a while* is an article and a noun. Thus *awhile* can modify a verb but cannot serve as the object of a preposition, and *a while* is just the opposite: *I will be gone awhile* (not *a while*). *I will be gone for a while* (not *awhile*).

bad, badly In formal speech and writing, *bad* should be used only as an adjective; the adverb is *badly. He felt bad because his tooth ached badly.* In *He felt bad,* the verb *felt* is a linking verb and the adjective *bad* is a subject complement. See also p. 241.

being as, being that Colloquial for *because,* the preferable word in formal speech or writing: *Because* (not *Being as*) *the world is round, Columbus never did fall off the edge.*

beside, besides *Beside* is a preposition meaning "next to." *Besides* is a preposition meaning "except" or "in addition to" as well as an adverb meaning "in addition." *Besides, several other people besides you want to sit beside Dr. Christensen.*

better, had better *Had better* (meaning "ought to") is a verb modified by an adverb. The verb is necessary and should not be omitted: *You had better* (not *better*) go.

between, among See *among, between.*

bring, take Use *bring* only for movement from a farther place to a nearer one and *take* for any other movement. *First, take these* *books to the library for renewal, then take them to Mr. Daniels. Bring them back to me when he's finished.*

bunch In formal speech and writing, *bunch* (as a noun) should be used only to refer to clusters of things growing or fastened together, such as bananas and grapes. Its use to mean a group of items or people is colloquial; *crowd* or *group* is preferable.

burst, bursted; bust, busted *Burst* is a standard verb form meaning "to fly apart suddenly" (principal parts *burst, burst, burst*). The past-tense form *bursted* is nonstandard. The verb *bust* (*busted*) is slang.

but, hardly, scarcely These words are negative in their own right; using *not* with any of them produces a double negative (see p. 245). *We have but* (not *haven't got but*) *an hour before our plane leaves. I could hardly* (not *couldn't hardly*) *make out her face.*

but, however, yet Each of these words is adequate to express contrast. Don't combine them. *He said he had finished, yet* (not *but yet*) *he continued.*

but that, but what These wordy substitutes for *that* and *what* should be avoided: *I don't doubt that* (not *but that*) *you are right.*

calculate, figure, reckon As substitutes for *expect* or *imagine* (*I figure I'll go*), these words are colloquial.

can, may Strictly, *can* indicates capacity or ability, and *may* indicates permission: *If I may talk with you a moment, I believe I can solve your problem.*

can't help but This idiom is common but redundant. Either *I can't help wishing* or the more formal *I cannot but wish* is preferable to *I can't help but wish.*

case, instance, line Expressions such as *in the case of, in the instance of,* and *along the lines of* are usually unnecessary padding and should be avoided.

censor, censure To *censor* is to edit or remove from public view on moral or some other grounds; to *censure* is to give a formal scolding. *The lieutenant was censured by Major Theriault for censoring the letters her soldiers wrote home from boot camp.*

centre around *Centre on* is more logical than, and preferable to, *centre around.*

climatic, climactic *Climatic* comes from *climate* and refers to weather: *Last winter's temperatures may indicate a climatic change. Climactic* comes from *climax* and refers to a dramatic high point: *During the climactic duel between Hamlet and Laertes, Gertrude drinks poisoned wine.*

complement, compliment To *complement* something is to add to, complete, or reinforce it: *Her yellow blouse complemented her black hair.* To *compliment* something is to make a flattering remark about it: *He complimented her on her hair. Complimentary* can also mean "free": *complimentary tickets.*

compose, comprise *Compose* means "to make up": *The parts compose the whole. Comprise* means "to consist of": *The whole comprises the parts.* Thus, *The band comprises* (not *is comprised of*) *twelve musicians. Twelve musicians compose* (not *comprise*) *the band.*

conscience, conscious *Conscience* is a noun meaning "a sense of right and wrong"; *conscious* is an adjective meaning "aware" or "awake." *Though I was barely conscious, my conscience nagged me.*

contact Often used imprecisely as a verb instead of a more exact word such as *consult, talk with, telephone,* or *write to.*

continual, continuous *Continual* means "constantly recurring": *Most movies on television are continually interrupted by commercials. Continuous* means "unceasing": *Some cable channels present movies continuously without commercials.*

convince, persuade In the strictest sense, to *convince* someone means to change his or her opinion; to *persuade* someone means to move him or her to action. *Convince* thus is properly followed by *of* or *that,* whereas *persuade* is followed by *to: Once he convinced Othello of Desdemona's infidelity, Iago easily persuaded him to kill her.*

could care less The expression is *could not (couldn't) care less. Could care less* indicates some care, the opposite of what is intended.

could of See *have, of.*

couple of Used colloquially to mean "a few" or "several."

credible, creditable, credulous *Credible* means "believable": *It's a strange story, but it seems credible to me. Creditable* means "deserving of credit" or "worthy": *Steve gave a creditable performance. Credulous* means "gullible": *The credulous Claire believed Tim's lies.* See also *incredible, incredulous.*

criteria The plural of *criterion* (meaning "standard for judgment"): *Our criteria are strict. The most important criterion is a sense of humour.*

data The plural of *datum* (meaning "fact"): *Out of all the data generated by these experiments, not one datum supports our hypothesis.* Usually, a more common term such as *fact, result,* or *figure* is preferred to *datum.* Though *data* is often used as a singular noun, most careful writers still treat it as plural: *The data fail* (not *fails*) *to support the hypothesis.*

device, devise *Device* is the noun, and *devise* is the verb: *Can you devise some device for getting his attention?*

differ from, differ with To *differ from* is to be unlike: *The twins differ from each other only in their hair styles.* To *differ with* is to disagree with: *I have to differ with you on that point.*

different from, different than *Different from* is preferred: *His purpose is different from mine.* But *different than* is widely accepted when a construction using *from* would be wordy: *I'm a different person now than I used to be* is preferable to *I'm a different person now from the person I used to be.*

discreet, discrete *Discreet* (noun form *discretion*) means "tactful": *What's a discreet way of telling Maud to be quiet? Discrete* (noun form *discreteness*) means "separate and distinct": *Within a computer's memory are millions of discrete bits of information.*

disinterested, uninterested *Disinterested* means "impartial": *We chose Pete, as a disinterested third party, to decide who was right. Uninterested* means "bored" or "lacking interest": *Unfortunately, Pete was completely uninterested in the question.*

don't *Don't* is the contraction for *do not,* not for *does not: I don't care, you don't care,* but *he doesn't* (not *don't*) *care.*

due to *Due* is an adjective or noun; thus *due to* is always acceptable as a subject complement: *His gray hairs were due to age.* Many object to *due to* as a preposition meaning "because of" (*Due to the holiday, class was canceled*). A rule of thumb is that *due to* is always correct after a form of the verb *be* but questionable otherwise.

due to the fact that Wordy for *because.*

each and every Wordy for *each* or *every.* Write *each one of us* or *every one of us,* not *each and every one of us.*

eager, anxious See *anxious, eager.*

effect See *affect, effect.*

elicit, illicit *Elicit* is a verb meaning "bring out" or "call forth." *Illicit* is an adjective meaning "unlawful." *The crime elicited an outcry against illicit drugs.*

ensure See *assure, ensure, insure.*

enthused Used colloquially as an adjective meaning "showing enthusiasm." The preferred adjective is *enthusiastic: The coach was enthusiastic* (not *enthused*) *about the team's victory.*

especially, specially *Especially* means "particularly" or "more than other things"; *specially* means "for a specific reason." *I especially treasure my boots. They were made specially for me.*

et al., etc. Use *et al.,* the Latin abbreviation for "and other people," only in source citations for works with more than three authors: *Jones et al.* (see pp. 577–78, 585). *Etc.,* the Latin abbreviation for "and other things," should be avoided in formal writing and should not be used to refer to people. When used, it should not substitute for precision, as in *The government provides health care, etc.* See also *and etc.*

everybody, every body; everyone, every one *Everybody* and *everyone* are indefinite pronouns: *Everybody* (*everyone*) *knows Tom steals. Every one* is a pronoun modified by *every,* and *every body* a noun modified by *every.* Both refer to each thing or person of a specific group and are typically followed by *of: The* *game commissioner has stocked every body of fresh water in the province with fish, and now every one of our rivers is a potential trout stream.*

everyday, every day *Everyday* is an adjective meaning "used daily" or "common"; *every day* is a noun modified by *every: Everyday problems tend to arise every day.*

everywheres Nonstandard for *everywhere.*

except See *accept, except.*

except for the fact that Wordy for *except that.*

explicit, implicit *Explicit* means "stated outright": *I left explicit instructions. The movie contains explicit sex. Implicit* means "implied, unstated": *We had an implicit understanding. I trust Marcia implicitly.*

farther, further *Farther* refers to additional distance (*How much farther is it to the beach?*), and *further* refers to additional time, amount, or other abstract matters (*I don't want to discuss this any further*).

fewer, less *Fewer* refers to individual countable items (a plural count noun), *less* to general amounts (a noncount noun, always singular): *Skim milk has fewer calories than whole milk. We have less milk left than I thought.*

field The phrase *the field of* is wordy and generally unnecessary: *Margaret plans to specialize in* (not *in the field of*) *family medicine.*

figure See *calculate, figure, reckon.*

fixing to Avoid this colloquial substitute for "intend to": *The school intends* (not *is fixing*) *to build a new library.*

flaunt, flout *Flaunt* means "show off": *If you have style, flaunt it. Flout* means "scorn" or "defy": *Hester Prynne flouted convention and paid the price.*

flunk A colloquial substitute for *fail.*

former, latter *Former* refers to the first-named of two things, *latter* to the second-named: *I like both skiing and swimming, the former in the winter and the latter all year round.* To refer to the first- or last-named of three or more things, say *first* or *last: I like jogging, swimming, and hang gliding, but the last is inconvenient in the city.*

fun As an adjective, *fun* is colloquial and should be avoided in most writing: *It was a pleasurable* (not *fun*) *evening.*

further See *farther, further.*

get This common verb is used in many slang and colloquial expressions: *get lost, that really gets me, getting on. Get* is easy to overuse; watch out for it in expressions such as *it's getting better* (substitute *improving*) and *we got done* (substitute *finished*).

go As a substitute for *say* or *reply, go* is colloquial: *He says* (not *goes*), *"How do you do, madam?"*

good, well *Good* is an adjective, and *well* is nearly always an adverb: *Larry's a good dancer. He and Linda dance well together.* *Well* is properly used as an adjective only to refer to health: *You look well.* (*You look good,* in contrast, means "Your appearance is pleasing.")

good and Colloquial for "very": *I was very* (not *good and*) *tired.*

had better See *better, had better.*

had ought The *had* is unnecessary and should be omitted: *He ought* (not *had ought*) *to listen to his mother.*

half Either *half a* or *a half* is appropriate usage, but *a half a* is redundant: *Half a loaf* (not *A half a loaf*) *is better than none. I'd like a half-litre* (not *a half a litre*) *of mineral water, please.*

hanged, hung Though both are past-tense forms of *hang, hanged* is used to refer to executions and *hung* is used for all other meanings: *Tom Dooley was hanged* (not *hung*) *from a white oak tree. I hung* (not *hanged*) *the picture you gave me.*

hardly See *but, hardly, scarcely.*

have, of Use *have,* not *of,* after helping verbs such as *could, should, would, may,* and *might: You should have* (not *should of*) *told me.*

he, she; he/she Convention has allowed the use of *he* to mean "he or she": *After the infant learns to creep, he progresses to crawling.* However, many writers today consider this usage inaccurate and unfair because it excludes females. The construction *he/she,* one substitute for *he,* is awkward and objectionable to most readers. The better choice is to use *he or she,* to make the pronoun plural, or to rephrase. For instance: *After the infant learns to creep, he or she progresses to crawling. After infants learn to creep, they progress to crawling. After learning to creep, the infant progresses to crawling.* (See also pp. 236 and 450.)

herself, himself See *myself, herself, himself, yourself.*

hisself Nonstandard for *himself.*

hopefully *Hopefully* means "with hope": *Freddy waited hopefully for a glimpse of Eliza.* The use of *hopefully* to mean "it is to be hoped," "I hope," or "let's hope" is now very common; but since many readers continue to object strongly to the usage, you should avoid it. *I hope* (not *Hopefully*) *Eliza will be here soon.*

idea, ideal An *idea* is a thought or conception. An *ideal* (noun) is a model of perfection or a goal. *Ideal* should not be used in place of *idea: The idea* (not *ideal*) *of the play is that our ideals often sustain us.*

if, whether For clarity, use *whether* rather than *if* when you are expressing an alternative: *If I laugh hard, people can't tell whether I'm crying.*

illicit See *elicit, illicit.*

illusion See *allusion, illusion.*

impact Both the noun and the verb *impact* connote forceful or even violent collision. Avoid the increasingly common diluted meanings of *impact:* "an effect" (noun) or "to have an effect on" (verb). The diluted verb (*The budget cuts impacted social science research*) is bureaucratic jargon.

implicit See *explicit, implicit.*

imply, infer Writers or speakers *imply,* meaning "suggest": *Jim's letter implies he's having a good time.* Readers or listeners *infer,* meaning "conclude": *From Jim's letter I infer he's having a good time.*

in, into *In* indicates location or condition: *He was in the garage. She was in a coma. Into* indicates movement or a change in condition: *He went into the garage. She fell into a coma. Into* is also slang for "interested in" or "involved in": *I am into Zen.*

in . . . A number of phrases beginning with *in* are unnecessarily wordy and should be avoided: *in the event that* (for *if*); *in the neighbourhood of* (for *approximately* or *about*); *in this day and age* (for *now* or *nowadays*); *in spite of the fact that* (for *although* or *even though*); and *in view of the fact that* (for *because* or *considering that*). Certain other *in* phrases are nothing but padding and can be omitted entirely: *in nature, in number, in reality,* and *in a very real sense.* (See also pp. 461–68.)

incredible, incredulous *Incredible* means "unbelievable"; *incredulous* means "unbelieving": *When Nancy heard Dennis's incredible story, she was frankly incredulous.* See also *credible, creditable, credulous.*

individual, person, party *Individual* should refer to a single human being in contrast to a group or should stress uniqueness: *The Charter of Rights and Freedoms places great emphasis on the rights of the individual.* For other meanings *person* is preferable: *What person* (not *individual*) *wouldn't want the security promised in that advertisement? Party* means "group" (*Can you seat a party of four for dinner?*) and should not be used to refer to an individual except in legal documents. See also *people, persons.*

infer See *imply, infer.*

in regards to Nonstandard for *in regard to, as regards,* or *regarding.* See also *regarding.*

inside of, outside of The *of* is unnecessary when *inside* and *outside* are used as prepositions: *Stay inside* (not *inside of*) *the house. The decision is outside* (not *outside of*) *my authority. Inside of* may refer colloquially to time, though in formal English *within* is preferred: *The law was passed within* (not *inside of*) *a year.*

instance See *case, instance, line.*

insure See *assure, ensure, insure.*

irregardless Nonstandard for *regardless.*

is, are See *are, is.*

is because See *reason is because.*

is when, is where These are faulty constructions in sentences that define: *Adolescence is a stage* (not *is when a person is*) *between childhood and adulthood. Socialism is a system in which* (not *is where*) *government owns the means of production.* (See also p. 297.)

its, it's *Its* is the pronoun *it* in the possessive case: *That plant is losing its leaves. It's* is a contraction for *it is: It's likely to die if you don't water it.* Many people confuse *it's* and *its* because possessives are most often formed with *-'s;* but the possessive *its,* like *his* and *hers,* never takes an apostrophe.

-ize, -wise The suffix *-ize* (still occasionally rendered *-ise,* an acceptable variant that reflects the suffix's French origins—though the *-ize* is more common in anglophone Canada) changes a noun or adjective into a verb: *revolutionize, immunize.* The suffix *-wise* changes a noun or adjective into an adverb: *clockwise, otherwise, likewise.* Avoid the two suffixes except in established words: *The two nations are ready to settle on* (not *finalize*) *an agreement. I'm highly sensitive* (not *sensitized*) *to that kind of criticism. Financially* (not *Moneywise*), *it's a good time to buy real estate.*

kind of, sort of, type of In formal speech and writing, avoid using *kind of* or *sort of* to mean "somewhat": *He was rather* (not *kind of*) *tall.*

Kind, sort, and *type* are singular and take singular modifiers and verbs: *This kind of dog is easily trained.* Agreement errors often occur when these singular nouns are combined with the plural adjectives *these* and *those: These kinds* (not *kind*) *of dogs are easily trained. Kind, sort,* and *type* should be followed by *of* but not by *a: I don't know what type of* (not *type* or *type of a*) *dog that is.*

Use *kind of, sort of,* or *type of* only when the word *kind, sort,* or *type* is important: *That was a strange* (not *strange sort of*) *statement.*

later, latter *Later* refers to time; *latter* refers to the second-named of two items. See also *former, latter.*

lay, lie *Lay* means "put" or "place" and takes a direct object: *We could lay the tablecloth in the sun.* Its main forms are *lay, laid, laid. Lie* means "recline" or "be situated" and does not take an object: *I lie awake at night. The town lies east of the river.* Its main forms are *lie, lay, lain.* (See also p. 202.)

leave, let *Leave* and *let* are interchangeable only when followed by *alone; leave me alone* is the same as *let me alone.* Otherwise, *leave* means "depart" and *let* means "allow": *Julia would not let Susan leave.*

less See *fewer, less.*

let See *leave, let.*

liable See *apt, liable, likely.*

lie, lay See *lay, lie.*

like, as See *as, like*

like, such as Strictly, *such as* precedes an example that represents a larger subject, whereas *like* indicates that two subjects are comparable. *Steve has recordings of many great saxophonists such as Ben Webster and Lee Konitz. Steve wants to be a great jazz saxophonist like Ben Webster and Lee Konitz.*

Many writers prefer to keep *such* and *as* together: *Steve admires saxophonists such as . . .* rather than *Steve admires such saxophonists as. . . .*

likely See *apt, liable, likely.*

line See *case, instance, line.*

literally This word means "actually" or "just as the words say," and it should not be used to qualify or intensify expressions whose words are not to be taken at face value. The sentence *He was literally climbing the walls* describes a person behaving like an insect, not a person who is restless or anxious. For the latter meaning, *literally* should be omitted.

lose, loose *Lose* means "mislay": *Did you lose a brown glove? Loose* means "unrestrained" or "not tight": *Ann's canary got loose. Loose* also can function as a verb meaning "let loose": *They loose the dogs as soon as they spot the bear.*

lots, lots of Colloquial substitutes for *very many, a great many,* or *much.* Avoid *lots* and *lots of* in college or business writing. When you use either one informally, be careful to maintain subject-verb agreement: *There are* (not *is*) *lots of fish in the pond.*

may, can See *can, may.*

may be, maybe *May be* is a verb, and *maybe* is an adverb meaning "perhaps": *Tuesday may be a legal holiday. Maybe we won't have classes.*

may of See *have, of.*

media *Media* is the plural of *medium* and takes a plural verb: *All the news media are increasingly visual.*

might of See *have, of.*

moral, morale As a noun, *moral* means "ethical conclusion" or "lesson": *The moral of the story escapes me. Morale* means "spirit" or "state of mind": *Victory improved the team's morale.*

most, almost See *almost, most.*

must of See *have, of.*

myself, herself, himself, yourself The *-self* pronouns refer to or intensify another word or words: *Paul helped himself; Jill herself said so.* The *-self* pronouns are often used colloquially in place of personal pronouns, but that use should be avoided in formal speech and writing: *No one except me* (not *myself*) *saw the accident. Our delegates will be Susan and you* (not *yourself*).

nohow Nonstandard for *in no way* or *in any way.*

nothing like, nowhere near These colloquial substitutes for *not nearly* are best avoided in formal speech and writing: *That program is not nearly* (not *nowhere near*) *as expensive.*

nowheres Nonstandard for *nowhere.*

number See *amount, number.*

of, have See *have, of.*

gl/us

off of *Of* is unnecessary. Use *off* or *from* rather than *off of: He jumped off* (or *from,* not *off of*) *the roof.*

OK, O.K., okay All three spellings are acceptable, but avoid this colloquial term in formal speech and writing.

on, upon In modern English, *upon* is usually just a stuffy way of saying *on.* Unless you need a formal effect, use *on: We decided on* (not *upon*) a location for our next meeting.

on account of Wordy for *because of.*

on the other hand This transitional expression of contrast should be preceded by its mate, *on the one hand: On the one hand, we hoped for snow. On the other hand, we feared that it would harm the animals.* However, the two combined can be unwieldy, and a simple *but, however, yet,* or *in contrast* often suffices: *We hoped for snow. Yet we feared that it would harm the animals.*

outside of See *inside of, outside of.*

owing to the fact that Wordy for *because.*

party See *individual, person, party.*

people, persons In formal usage, *people* refers to a general group: *We the people of Canada. . . . Persons* refers to a collection of individuals: *Will the person or persons who saw the accident please notify. . . .* Except when emphasizing individuals, prefer *people* to *persons.* See also *individual, person, party.*

per Except in technical writing, an English equivalent is usually preferable to the Latin *per: $10 an* (not *per*) *hour; sent by* (not *per*) *parcel post; requested in* (not *per* or *as per*) *your letter.*

percent (per cent), percentage Both these terms refer to fractions of one hundred. *Percent* always follows a numeral (*40 percent of the voters*), and the word should be used instead of the symbol (%) in general writing. *Percentage* usually follows an adjective (*a high percentage*).

person See *individual, person, party.*

persons See *people, persons.*

persuade See *convince, persuade.*

phenomena The plural of *phenomenon* (meaning "perceivable fact" or "unusual occurrence"): *Many phenomena are not recorded. One phenomenon is attracting attention.*

plenty A colloquial substitute for *very: The reaction occurred very* (not *plenty*) *fast.*

plus *Plus* is standard as a preposition meaning *in addition to: His income plus mine is sufficient.* But *plus* is colloquial as a conjunctive adverb: *Our organization is larger than theirs; moreover* (not *plus*), *we have more money.*

practicable, practical *Practicable* means "capable of being put into practice"; *practical* means "useful" or "sensible": *We figured out a practical new design for our kitchen, but it was too expensive to be practicable.*

precede, proceed The verb *precede* means "come before": *My name precedes yours in the alphabet.* The verb *proceed* means "move on": *We were told to proceed to the waiting room.*

prejudice, prejudiced *Prejudice* is a noun; *prejudiced* is an adjective. Do not drop the *-d* from *prejudiced: I was fortunate that my parents were not prejudiced* (not *prejudice*).

pretty Overworked as an adverb meaning "rather" or "somewhat": *He was somewhat* (not *pretty*) *irked at the suggestion.*

previous to, prior to Wordy for *before.*

principal, principle *Principal* is an adjective meaning "foremost" or "major," a noun meaning "chief official," or, in finance, a noun meaning "capital sum." *Principle* is a noun only, meaning "rule" or "axiom." *Her principal reasons for confessing were her principles of right and wrong.*

proceed, precede See *precede, proceed.*

provided, providing *Provided* may serve as a subordinating conjunction meaning "on the condition (that)"; *providing* may not. *The grocer will begin providing food for the soup kitchen provided* (not *providing*) *we find a suitable space.*

question of whether, question as to whether Wordy substitutes for *whether.*

raise, rise *Raise* means "lift" or "bring up" and takes a direct object: *The Kirks raise cattle.* Its main forms are *raise, raised, raised. Rise* means "get up" and does not take an object: *They must rise at dawn.* Its main forms are *rise, rose, risen.* (See also p. 202.)

real, really In formal speech and writing, *real* should not be used as an adverb; *really* is the adverb and *real* an adjective. *Popular reaction to the announcement was really* (not *real*) *enthusiastic.*

reason is because Although colloquially common, this expression should be avoided in formal speech and writing. Use a *that* clause after *reason is: The reason he is absent is that* (not *is because*) *he is sick.* Or: *He is absent because he is sick.*

reckon See *calculate, figure, reckon.*

regarding, in regard to, with regard to, relating to, relative to,

with respect to, respecting Stuffy substitutes for *on, about,* or *concerning: Mr. McGee spoke about* (not *with regard to*) *the plans for the merger.*

respectful, respective *Respectful* means "full of (or showing) respect": *Be respectful of other people. Respective* means "separate": *The French and the Germans occupied their respective trenches.*

rise, raise See *raise, rise.*

scarcely See *but, hardly, scarcely.*

sensual, sensuous *Sensual* suggests sexuality; *sensuous* means "pleasing to the senses." *Stirred by the sensuous scent of meadow grass and flowers, Cheryl and Paul found their thoughts growing increasingly sensual.*

set, sit *Set* means "put" or "place" and takes a direct object: *He sets the pitcher down.* Its main forms are *set, set, set. Sit* means "be seated" and does not take an object: *She sits on the sofa.* Its main forms are *sit, sat, sat.* (See also p. 202.)

shall, will *Will* is the future-tense helping verb for all persons: *I will go, you will go, they will go.* The main use of *shall* is for first-person questions requesting an opinion or consent: *Shall I order a pizza? Shall we dance?* (Questions that merely inquire about the future use *will: When will I see you again?*) *Shall* can also be used for the first person when a formal effect is desired (I *shall expect you around three*), and it is occasionally used with the second or third person to express the speaker's determination (*You shall do as I say*).

should, would *Should* expresses obligation: *I should fix dinner. You should set the table. Jack should wash the dishes. Would* expresses a wish or hypothetical condition: *I would do it. Wouldn't you?* When the context is formal, however, *should* is sometimes used instead of *would* in the first person: *We should be delighted to accept.*

should of See *have, of.*

since *Since* mainly relates to time: *I've been waiting since noon.* But *since* is also often used to mean "because": *Since you ask, I'll tell you.* Revise sentences in which the word could have either meaning, such as *Since you left, my life is empty.*

sit, set See *set, sit.*

situation Often unnecessary, as in *The situation is that we have to get some help* (revise to *We have to get some help*) or *The team was faced with a punting situation* (revise to *The team was faced with punting* or *The team had to punt*).

so Avoid using *so* alone as a vague intensifier: *He was so late. So* needs to be followed by *that* and a clause that states a result: *He was so late that I left without him.*

some *Some* is colloquial as an adverb meaning "somewhat" or "to some extent" and as an adjective meaning "remarkable": *We'll have to hurry somewhat* (not *some*) *to get there in time. Those are remarkable* (not *some*) *photographs.*

somebody, some body; someone, some one *Somebody* and *someone* are indefinite pronouns; *some body* is a noun modified by *some;* and *some one* is a pronoun or an adjective modified by *some. Somebody ought to invent a shampoo that will give hair some body. Someone told Janine she should choose some one plan and stick with it.*

someplace Informal for *somewhere.*

sometime, sometimes, some time *Sometime* means "at an indefinite time in the future": *Why don't you come up and see me sometime? Sometimes* means "now and then": *I still see my old friend Joe sometimes. Some time* means "span of time": *I need some time to make the payments.*

somewheres Nonstandard for *somewhere.*

sort of, sort of a See *kind of, sort of, type of.*

specially See *especially, specially.*

such Avoid using *such* as a vague intensifier: *It was such a cold winter. Such* should be followed by *that* and a clause that states a result: *It was such a cold winter that* Napoleon's troops had to turn back.

such as See *like, such as.*

supposed to, used to In both these expressions, the *-d* is essential: *I used to* (not *use to*) *think so. He's supposed to* (not *suppose to*) *meet us.*

sure Colloquial when used as an adverb meaning *surely: Lester Pearson sure was right about the need for a distinctive flag.* If you merely want to be emphatic, use *certainly: Pearson certainly was right.* If your goal is to convince a possibly reluctant reader, use *surely: Pearson surely was right. Surely Pearson was right.*

sure and, sure to; try and, try to *Sure to* and *try to* are the preferred forms: *Be sure to* (not *sure and*) *buy milk. Try to* (not *Try and*) *find some decent tomatoes.*

take, bring See *bring, take.*

than, as See *as, than.*

than, then *Than* is a conjunction used in comparisons, *then* an adverb indicating time: *Holmes knew then that Moriarty was wilier than he had thought.*

that, which *That* always introduces restrictive clauses: *We should use the lettuce that Susan bought* (*that Susan bought* limits *lettuce* to a particular lettuce). *Which* can introduce both restrictive and nonrestrictive clauses, but many writers reserve *which* only for nonrestrictive clauses: *The leftover lettuce, which is in the refrigerator, would make a good salad* (*which is in the refrig-*

gl/us

erator simply provides more information about the lettuce we already know of). Nonrestrictive clauses (with *which*) are set off by commas; nonrestrictive clauses (with *that* or *which*) are not. (See also pp. 360–62.)

their, there, they're *Their* is the possessive form of *they: Give them their money. There* indicates place (*I saw her standing there*) or functions as an expletive (*There is a hole behind you*). *They're* is a contraction for *they are: They're going fast.*

theirselves Nonstandard for *themselves.*

then, than See *than, then.*

these kind, these sort, these type, those kind See *kind of, sort of, type of.*

this here, these here, that there, them there Nonstandard for *this, these, that,* or *those.*

thru A colloquial spelling of *through* that should be avoided in all academic and business writing.

thusly A mistaken form of *thus.*

till, until, 'til *Till* and *until* have the same meaning; both are acceptable. *'Til,* a contraction of *until,* is an old form that has been replaced by *till.*

time period Since a *period* is an interval of time, this expression is redundant: *They did not see each other for a long time* (not *time period*). *Six accidents occurred in a three-week period* (not *time period*).

to, too, two *To* is a preposition; *too* is an adverb meaning "also" or "excessively"; and *two* is a number. *I too have been to Europe two times.*

too Avoid using *too* as an intensifier meaning "very": *Monkeys are too mean.* If you do use *too,* explain the consequences of the excessive quality: *Monkeys are too mean to make good pets.*

toward, towards Both are acceptable. Use one or the other consistently.

try and, try to See *sure and, sure to; try and, try to.*

type of See *kind of, sort of, type of.* Don't use *type* without *of: It was a family type of* (not *type*) *restaurant.* Or, better: *It was a family restaurant.*

uninterested See *disinterested, uninterested.*

unique *Unique* means "the only one of its kind" and so cannot sensibly be modified with words such as *very* or *most: That was a unique* (not *a very unique* or *the most unique*) *movie.*

until See *till, until, 'til.*

upon, on See *on, upon.*

usage, use *Usage* refers to conventions, most often those of a language: *Is "hadn't ought" proper usage? Usage* is often misused in place of the noun *use: Wise use* (not *usage*) *of insulation can save fuel.*

use, utilize *Utilize* means "make use of": *We should utilize John's talent for mimicry in our play.* In most contexts, *use* is equally or more acceptable and less stuffy.

used to See *supposed to, used to.*

wait for, wait on In formal speech and writing, *wait for* means "await" (*I'm waiting for Paul*), and *wait on* means "serve" (*The owner of the store herself waited on us*).

ways Colloquial as a substitute for *way: We have only a little way* (not *ways*) *to go.*

well See *good, well.*

whether, if See *if, whether.*

which See *that, which.*

which, who *Which* never refers to people. Use *who* or sometimes *that* for a person or persons and *which* or *that* for a thing or things: *The baby, who was left behind, opened the door, which we had closed.* (See also pp. 275–76.)

who's, whose *Who's* is the contraction of *who is: Who's at the door? Whose* is the possessive form of *who: Whose book is that?*

will, shall See *shall, will.*

-wise See *-ize, -wise.*

with regard to, with respect to See *regarding.*

would See *should, would.*

would have Avoid this construction in place of *had* in clauses that begin *if* and state a condition contrary to fact: *If the tree had* (not *would have*) *withstood the fire, it would have been the oldest in town.* (See also p. 217.)

would of See *have, of.*

you In all but very formal writing, *you* is generally appropriate as long as it means "you, the reader." In all writing, avoid indefinite uses of *you,* such as *In one ancient tribe your first loyalty was to your parents.* (See also pp. 274–75.)

your, you're *Your* is the possessive form of *you: Your dinner is ready. You're* is the contraction of *you are: You're bound to be late.*

yourself See *myself, herself, himself, yourself.*

Glossary of Terms

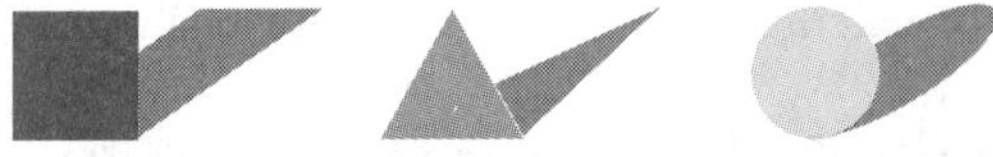

This glossary defines the grammatical, rhetorical, and literary terms used in the text plus a few others that you may come across in discussing writing. Page numbers in parentheses refer you to sections of the text where the term is explained more fully.

absolute phrase A phrase consisting of a noun or pronoun plus the *-ing* or *-ed* form of a verb (a participle): *Our accommodations arranged, we set out on our journey. They will hire a local person, other things being equal.* An absolute phrase modifies a whole clause or sentence (rather than a single word), and it is not joined to the rest of the sentence by a connector. (See p. 171.)

abstract and concrete Two kinds of language. **Abstract** words refer to ideas, qualities, attitudes, and conditions that can't be perceived with the senses: *beauty, guilty, victory.* **Concrete** words refer to objects, persons, places, or conditions that can be perceived with the senses: *Halifax, scratchy, toolbox.* See also *general and specific.* (See p. 454.)

acronym A pronounceable word formed from the initial letter or letters of each word in an organization's title: NATO (North Atlantic Treaty Organization).

active voice See *voice.*

adjectival A term sometimes used to describe any word or word group, other than an adjective, that is used to modify a noun.

Common adjectivals include nouns (*wagon train, railroad ties*), phrases (*fool on the hill*), and clauses (*the man that I used to be*).

adjective A word used to modify a noun (*beautiful*) *morning* or a pronoun (*ordinary one*). (See Chapter 9.) Nouns, some verb forms, phrases, and clauses may also serve as adjectives: *book sale; a used book; sale of old books; the sale, which occurs annually*. (See *clauses, prepositional phrases,* and *verbals and verbal phrases.*)

Adjectives come in several classes:

- A **descriptive adjective** names some quality of the noun: *beautiful morning, dark horse.*
- A **limiting adjective** narrows the scope of a noun. It may be a **possessive** (*my, their*); a **demonstrative adjective** (*this train, these days*); an **interrogative adjective** (*what time? whose body?*); or a **number** (*two boys*).
- A **proper adjective** is derived from a proper noun: *French language, Machiavellian scheme.*

Adjectives also can be classified according to position.

- An **attributive adjective** appears next to the noun it modifies: *full moon.*
- A **predicate adjective** is connected to its noun by a linking verb: *The moon is full.* See also *complement.*

adjective clause See *adjective.*

adjective phrase See *adjective.*

adverb A word used to modify a verb (*warmly greet*), an adjective (*only three people*), another adverb (*quite seriously*), or a whole sentence (*Fortunately, she is employed*). (See Chapter 9.) Some verb forms, phrases, and clauses may also serve as adverbs: *easy to stop, drove by a farm, ploughed the fields when the earth thawed.* (See *clauses, prepositional phrases,* and *verbals and verbal phrases.*)

adverb clause See *adverb.*

adverbial A term sometimes used to describe any word or word group, other than an adverb, that is used to modify a verb, an adjective, another adverb, or a whole sentence. Common adverbials include nouns (*This little piggy stayed home*), phrases (*This little piggy went to market*), and clauses (*This little piggy went wherever he wanted*).

adverbial conjunction See *conjunctive adverb.*

adverb phrase See *adverb.*

agreement The correspondence of one word to another in person, number, or gender. A verb must agree with its subject (*The chef orders egg sandwiches*), a pronoun must agree with its antecedent (*The chef surveys her breakfast*), and a demonstrative adjective must agree with its noun (*She likes these kinds of sandwiches*). (See Chapter 8.)

Logical agreement requires consistency in number between other related words, usually nouns: *The students brought their books* (not *book*). (See p. 280.)

analogy A comparison between members of different classes, such as a nursery school and a barnyard or a molecule and a pair of dancers. Usually, the purpose is to explain something unfamiliar to readers through something familiar. (See p. 101.)

analysis The separation of a subject into its elements. Sometimes called **division,** analysis is fundamental to critical thinking, reading, and writing (pp. 10–11) and a useful tool for developing essays (p. 39) and paragraphs (pp. 98–99).

antecedent The word to which a pronoun refers: *Jonah, who is not yet ten, has already chosen the college he will attend* (*Jonah* is the antecedent of the pronouns *who* and *he*). (See pp. 234–37.)

APA style The style of documentation recommended by the American Psychological Association and used in many of the social sciences. (For discussion and examples, see pp. 691–706.)

appeals Attempts to engage and persuade readers. An **emotional appeal** touches readers' feelings, beliefs, and values. An **ethical appeal** presents the writer as competent, sincere, and fair. A **rational appeal** engages readers' powers of reasoning. (See p. 143.)

appositive A word or phrase appearing next to a noun or pronoun that renames or identifies it and is equivalent to it: *My brother Michael, the best horn player in town, won the provincial competition* (*Michael* identifies which brother is being referred to; *the best horn player in town* renames *My brother Michael*). (See pp. 176–77.)

argument Writing whose primary purpose is to convince readers of an idea or persuade them to act. (See Chapter 4.)

article The word *a, an,* or *the.* Articles are sometimes called **determiners** because they always signal that a noun follows. (See pp. 247–49 for when to use *a/an* versus *the.* See p. 774 for when to use *a* versus *an.*)

assertion A positive statement that requires support. Assertions are the backbone of any argument. (See p. 117.)

assumption A stated or unstated belief or opinion. Uncovering assumptions is part of critical thinking, reading, and writing (see pp. 11–12). In argument, assumptions connect assertions and evidence (see pp. 123–24).

audience The intended readers of a piece of writing. Knowledge of the audience's needs and expectations helps a writer shape writing so that it is clear, interesting, and convincing. (See pp. 28–31, 142–44.)

auxiliary verb See *helping verb.*

balanced sentence A sentence consisting of two clauses with parallel constructions: *Do as I say, not as I do. Befriend all animals; exploit none.* Their balance makes such sentences highly emphatic. (See p. 330.)

belief A conviction based on morality, values, or faith. Statements of belief often serve as assumptions and sometimes as evidence, but they are not arguable and so cannot serve as the thesis in an argument. (See p. 119.)

body In a piece of writing, the large central part where ideas supporting the thesis are presented and developed. See also *conclusion* and *introduction.*

brainstorming A technique for generating ideas about a topic: concentrating on the topic for a fixed time (say, fifteen minutes), you list every idea and detail that comes to mind. (See pp. 35–36.)

cardinal number The type of number that shows amount: *two, sixty, ninety-seven.* Contrast *ordinal number* (such as *second, ninety-seventh*).

case The form of a noun or pronoun that indicates its function in the sentence. Most pronouns have three cases:

- The **subjective case** (*I, she*) for the subject of a verb or for a subject complement.
- The **objective case** (*me, her*) for the object of a verb, verbal, or preposition.
- The **possessive case** to indicate ownership, used either as an adjective (*my, her*) or as a noun (*mine, hers*).

(See p. 189 for a list of the forms of personal and relative pronouns.)

Nouns use the subjective form (*dog, Canada*) for all cases except the possessive (*dog's, Canada's*).

cause-and-effect analysis The determination of why something happened or what its consequences were or will be. See pp. 39 and 101–02.

CBE style A style of documenting sources recommended by the Council of Biology Editors and frequently used in the natural and applied sciences. (For explanation and examples, see pp. 715–19.)

characters The people in a literary work, including the narrator of a story or the speaker of a poem. (See p. 655.)

chronological organization The arrangement of events as they occurred in time, usually from first to last. (See pp. 52, 84.)

citation In research writing, the way of acknowledging material borrowed from sources. Most systems of citation discussed in this handbook are basically similar: a number or brief parenthetical reference in the text indicates that particular material is borrowed and directs the reader to detailed information on the source at the end of the work. The systems do differ, however. (See pp. 576–602 for MLA style, pp. 681–88 for *CMS* style, pp. 693–706 for APA style, and pp. 715–19 for CBE style.)

classification The sorting of many elements into groups based on their similarities. (See pp. 39 and 99.)

clause A group of related words containing a subject and predicate. **A main (independent) clause** can stand by itself as a sentence. **A subordinate (dependent) clause** serves as a single part of speech and so cannot stand by itself as a sentence.

MAIN CLAUSE	*We can go to the movies.*
SUBORDINATE CLAUSE	We can go *if Julie gets back on time.*

A subordinate clause may function as an adjective (*The car that hit Fred was speeding*), an adverb (*The car hit Fred when it ran a red light*), or a noun (*Whoever was driving should be arrested*). (See pp. 172–75.)

clichés See *trite expressions.*

climactic organization The arrangement of material in order of increasing drama or interest, leading to a climax. (See pp. 52–53 and 86.)

clustering A technique for generating ideas about a topic: drawing and writing, you branch outward from a centre point (the topic) to pursue the implications of ideas. (See pp. 36–37.)

***CMS* style** A style of documentation recommended by *The Chicago Manual of Style* and used in history, art, and other humanities. (For discussion and examples, see pp. 681–88.)

coherence The quality of an effective essay or paragraph that helps readers see relations among ideas and move easily from one idea to the next. (See pp. 53 and 82.)

collaborative learning In a writing course, students working together in groups to help each other become better writers and readers. (See pp. 70–72.)

collective noun See *noun.*

colloquial language The words and expressions of everyday speech. Colloquial language can enliven informal writing but is generally inappropriate in formal academic or business writing. See also *formal and informal.* (See p. 447.)

comma splice A sentence error in which two main clauses are separated by a comma with no coordinating conjunction. (See Chapter 11.)

COMMA SPLICE	The book was long, it contained useful information.
REVISED	The book was long; it contained useful information.

REVISED The book was long, *and* it contained useful information.

common noun See *noun.*
comparative See *comparison.*
comparison The form of an adverb or adjective that shows its degree of quality or amount.

- The **positive degree** is the simple, uncompared form: *gross, clumsily.*
- The **comparative degree** compares the thing modified to at least one other thing: *grosser, more clumsily.*
- The **superlative degree** indicates that the thing modified exceeds all other things to which it is being compared: *grossest, most clumsily.*

The comparative and superlative degrees are formed either with the endings *-er* and *-est* or with the words *more* and *most, less* and *least.* (See pp. 243–45.)

comparison and contrast The identification of similarities (comparison) and differences (contrast) between two or more subjects. (See pp. 39 and 99–101.)
complement A word or word group that completes the sense of a subject, an object, or a verb. (See pp. 158–60.)

- A **subject complement** follows a linking verb and renames or describes the subject. It may be an adjective, noun, or pronoun. *I am a lion tamer, but I am not yet experienced* (the noun *lion tamer* and the adjective *experienced* complement the subject *I*). Adjective complements are also called **predicate adjectives.** Noun complements are also called **predicate nouns** or **predicate nominatives.**
- An **object complement** follows and modifies or refers to a direct object. The complement may be an adjective or a noun. *If you elect me president, I'll keep the students satisfied* (the noun *president* complements the direct object *me,* and the adjective *satisfied* complements the direct object *students*).
- A **verb complement** is a direct or indirect object of a verb. It may be a noun or pronoun. *Don't give the chimp that peanut* (*chimp* is the indirect object and *peanut* is the direct object of the verb *give;* both objects are verb complements).

complete predicate See *predicate.*
complete subject See *subject.*
complex sentence See *sentence.*
compound construction Two or more words or word groups serving the same function, such as a **compound subject** (*Harriet and Peter poled their barge down the river*), **compound predicate** (*The scout watched and waited*) or parts of a predi-

cate (*She grew tired and hungry*), and **compound sentence** (*He smiled, and I laughed*). (See pp. 178–82.) **Compound words** include nouns (*featherbrain, make-up*) and adjectives (*two-year-old, downtrodden*).

compound-complex sentence See *sentence.*

compound predicate See *compound construction.*

compound sentence See *sentence.*

compound subject See *compound construction.*

conciseness Use of the fewest and freshest words to express meaning clearly and achieve the desired effect with readers. (See pp. 461–67.)

conclusion The closing of an essay, tying off the writer's thoughts and leaving readers with a sense of completion. (See pp. 109–10 for suggestions.)

A *conclusion* is also the result of deductive reasoning. See *deductive reasoning* and *syllogism.*

concrete See *abstract and concrete.*

conditional statement A statement expressing a condition contrary to fact and using the subjunctive mood of the verb: *If she were mayor, the unions would cooperate.* See also *mood.*

conjugation A list of the forms of a verb showing tense, voice, mood, person, and number. The conjugation of the verb *know* in present tense, active voice, indicative mood is *I know, you know, he/she/it knows, we know, you know, they know.* (See p. 209 for a more complete conjugation.)

conjunction A word that links and relates parts of a sentence.

- **Coordinating conjunctions** (*and, but, or, nor, for, so, yet*) connect words or word groups of equal grammatical rank: *The lights went out, but the doctors and nurses continued caring for their patients.* (See pp. 178–79.)
- **Correlative conjunctions** or **correlatives** (such as *either . . . or, not only . . . but also*) are two or more connecting words that work together: *He was certain that either his parents or his brother would help him.* (See p. 179.)
- **Subordinating conjunctions** (*after, although, as if, because, if, when, while,* and so on) begin a subordinate clause and link it to a main clause: *The seven dwarfs whistle while they work.* (See pp. 172–73.)

conjunctive adverb (adverbial conjunction) An adverb (such as *besides, consequently, however, indeed,* and *therefore*) that relates two main clauses in a sentence: *We had hoped to own a house by now; however, housing costs have risen too fast.* See pp. 180–81. The error known as a comma splice results when two main clauses related by a conjunctive adverb are separated only by a comma. (See pp. 265–66.)

connector (connective) Any word or phrase that links words, phrases, clauses, or sentences. Common connectors include coordinating, correlative, and subordinating conjunctions; conjunctive adverbs; and prepositions.

connotation An association called up by a word, beyond its dictionary definition. Contrast *denotation.* (See p. 452.)

construction Any group of grammatically related words, such as a phrase, a clause, or a sentence.

contraction A condensation of an expression, with an apostrophe replacing the missing letters: for example, *doesn't* (for *does not*), *we'll* (for *we will*). (See p. 391.)

contrast See *comparison and contrast.*

coordinate adjectives Two or more adjectives modifying the same noun or pronoun: *The camera panned the vast, empty desert.* (See pp. 367–68.)

coordinating conjunction See *conjunction.*

coordination The linking of words, phrases, or clauses that are of equal importance, usually with a coordinating conjunction: *He and I laughed, but she was not amused.* Contrast *subordination.* (See pp. 306–09.)

correlative conjunction (correlative) See *conjunction.*

count noun See *noun.*

critical thinking, reading, and writing Looking beneath the surface of words and images to discern meaning and relationships and to build knowledge. (See pp. 1–18.)

cumulative (loose) sentence A sentence in which modifiers follow the subject and verb: *Ducks waddled by, their tails swaying and their quacks rising to heaven.* Contrast *periodic sentence.* (See p. 328.)

dangling modifier A modifier that does not sensibly describe anything in its sentence. (See pp. 290–92.)

DANGLING *Having arrived late,* the concert had already begun.

REVISED Having arrived late, *we* found that the concert had already begun.

declension A list of the forms of a noun or pronoun, showing inflections for person (for pronouns), number, and case. See page 189 for a declension of the personal and relative pronouns.

deductive reasoning Applying a generalization to specific circumstances in order to reach a conclusion. See also *syllogism.* Contrast *inductive reasoning.* (See pp. 137–40.)

definition Specifying the characteristics of something to establish what it is and is not. (See pp. 39 and 97–98.)

degree See *comparison.*

demonstrative adjective See *adjective.*

demonstrative pronoun See *pronoun.*

denotation The main or dictionary definition of a word. Contrast *connotation.* (See p. 452.)

dependent clause See *clause.*

derivational suffix See *suffix.*

description Detailing the sensory qualities of a thing, person, place, or feeling. (See pp. 39 and 95–96.)

descriptive adjective See *adjective.*

determiner A word such as *a, an, the, my,* and *your* which indicates that a noun follows. See also *article.*

developing (planning) The stage of the writing process when one finds a topic, explores ideas, gathers information, focuses on a central theme, and organizes material. Compare *drafting* and *revising.* (See Chapter 1.)

dialect A variety of a language used by a specific group or in a specific region. A dialect may be distinguished by its pronunciation, vocabulary, and grammar. (See p. 445.)

diction The choice and use of words. (See Chapter 31.)

dictionary form See *plain form.*

direct address A construction in which a word or phrase indicates the person or group spoken to: *Have you finished, John? Farmers, unite.*

direct object See *object.*

direct question A sentence asking a question and concluding with a question mark: *Do they know we are watching?* Contrast *indirect question.*

direct quotation (direct discourse) See *quotation.*

division See *analysis.*

documentation In research writing, supplying citations that legitimate the use of borrowed material and support claims about its origins. Contrast *plagiarism.* (See Chapter 37.)

double negative A nonstandard form consisting of two negative words used in the same construction so that they effectively cancel each other: *I don't have no money.* Rephrase as *I have no money* or *I don't have any money.* (See p. 245.)

double possessive A possessive using both the ending *-'s* and the preposition *of: That is a favourite expression of Mark's.*

double talk (doublespeak) Language intended to confuse or to be misunderstood. (See p. 449.)

drafting The stage of the writing process when ideas are expressed in connected sentences and paragraphs. Compare *developing (planning)* and *revising.* (See pp. 55–58.)

editing A distinct step in revising a written work, focusing on clarity, tone, and correctness. Compare *revising.* (See pp. 65–67.)

ellipsis The omission of a word or words from a quotation, indicated by the three spaced periods of an **ellipsis mark:** *"that all . . . are created equal."* (See pp. 414–15.)

elliptical clause A clause omitting a word or words whose meaning is understood from the rest of the clause: *David likes St. John's better than (he likes) Charlottetown.* (See p. 174.)

emotional appeal See *appeals.*

emphasis The manipulation of words, sentences, and paragraphs to stress important ideas. (See Chapter 18.)

essay A nonfiction composition on a single subject and with a central idea or thesis.

ethical appeal See *appeals.*

etymology The history of a word's meanings and forms.

euphemism A presumably inoffensive word that a writer or speaker substitutes for a word deemed possibly offensive or too blunt—for example, *passed beyond* for "died." (See p. 449.)

evaluation A judgment of the quality, value, currency, bias, or other aspects of a work. (See pp. 13–14, 542–43.)

evidence The facts, examples, expert opinions, and other information that support assertions. (See pp. 120–23, 39–40.)

expletive A sentence that postpones the subject by beginning with *there* or *it* and a form of the verb *be: It is impossible to get a ticket. There should be more seats available.* (See p. 184.)

exposition Writing whose primary purpose is to explain something about a topic.

fallacies Errors in reasoning. Some evade the issue of the argument; others oversimplify the argument. (See pp. 129–34.)

faulty predication A sentence error in which the meanings of subject and predicate conflict, so that the subject is said to be or do something illogical: *The installation of an air bag occupies considerable space in a car.* (See pp. 297–98.)

figurative language (figures of speech) Expressions that suggest meanings different from their literal meanings in order to achieve special effects. (See pp. 457–58.) Some common figures:

- **Hyperbole,** deliberate exaggeration: *The bag weighed a tonne.*
- **Irony,** the use of words to signify the opposite of what they usually express. (See p. 804.)
- **Metaphor,** an implied comparison between two unlike things: *The wind stabbed through our clothes.*
- **Personification,** the attribution of human qualities to a thing or idea: *The water beckoned seductively.*
- **Simile,** an explicit comparison, using *like* or *as,* between two unlike things: *The sky glowered like an angry parent.*

A **mixed metaphor** is a confusing or ludicrous combination of incompatible figures: *The wind stabbed through our clothes and shook our bones.*

finite verb Any verb that makes an assertion or expresses a state of being and can stand as the main verb of a sentence or clause: *The moose eats the leaves.* (See p. 167.) Contrast *verbal,* which is formed from a finite verb but is unable to stand alone as the main verb of a sentence: *I saw the moose eating the leaves.*

first person See *person.*

foil A character in a literary work who contrasts with another character and thus helps to define the other character. (See p. 669.)

formal and informal Levels of usage achieved through word choice and sentence structure. More informal writing, as in a letter to an acquaintance or a personal essay, resembles some speech in its colloquial language, contractions, and short, fairly simple sentences. More formal writing, as in academic papers and business reports, avoids these attributes of speech and tends to rely on longer and more complicated sentences.

format In a manuscript such as an essay or research paper, the arrangement and spacing of elements on the page. See Appendix A.

fragment See *sentence fragment.*

freewriting A technique for generating ideas: in a fixed amount of time (say, fifteen minutes), you write continuously without stopping to reread. (See pp. 34–35.)

function word A word, such as an article, conjunction, or preposition, that serves primarily to clarify the roles of and relations between other words in a sentence: *We chased the goat for an hour but finally caught it.* Contrast *lexical word.*

fused sentence (run-on sentence) A sentence error in which two main clauses are joined with no punctuation or connecting word between them. (See pp. 267–68.)

FUSED I heard his lecture it was dull.

REVISED I heard his lecture; it was dull.

future perfect tense See *tense.*

future tense See *tense.*

gender The classification of nouns or pronouns as masculine (*he, boy, handyman*), feminine (*she, woman, actress*), or neuter (*it, typewriter, dog*).

general and specific Terms designating the relative number of instances or objects included in a group signified by a word. The following list moves from most **general** (including the most objects) to most **specific** (including the fewest objects): *vehicle, four-wheeled vehicle, automobile, sedan, Ford Taurus, blue Ford Taurus, my sister's blue Ford Taurus named Hank.* See also *abstract and concrete.* (See p. 454.)

generalization An assertion inferred from evidence. See also *inductive reasoning.* (See p. 138.)

genitive case Another term for possessive case. See *case.*

gerund A verbal that ends in *-ing* and functions as a noun: *Working is all right for killing time* (*working* is the subject of the verb *is; killing* is the object of the preposition *for.*) See also *verbals and verbal phrases.* (See p. 168.)

gerund phrase A word group consisting of a gerund plus any modifiers or objects. See also *verbals and verbal phrases.*

grammar A description of how a language works.

helping verb (auxiliary verb) A verb used with another verb to convey time, obligation, and other meanings: *You should write a letter. You have written other letters.* The **modals** are *can, could, may, might, must, ought, shall, should, will, would.* The other helping verbs are forms of *be, have,* and *do.* (See pp. 199, 204–07.)

homonyms Words that are pronounced the same but have different spellings and meanings, such as *heard/herd* and *to/too/two.* (See pp. 488–89 for a list.)

hyperbole See *figurative language.*

idiom An expression that is peculiar to a language and that may not make sense if taken literally: for example, *dark horse, bide your time,* and *by and large.* See p. 456 for a list of idioms involving prepositions, such as *agree with them* and *agree to the contract.*

illustration or support Supplying examples or reasons to develop an idea. (See pp. 39 and 96.)

imagery Pictures created by words that appeal to the sense of sight, hearing, touch, taste, or smell. (See p. 656.)

imperative See *mood.*

indefinite pronoun See *pronoun.*

independent clause See *clause.*

indicative See *mood.*

indirect object See *object.*

indirect question A sentence reporting a question, usually in a subordinate clause, and ending with a period: *Writers wonder if their work must be lonely.* Contrast *direct question.*

indirect quotation (indirect discourse) See *quotation.*

inductive reasoning Inferring a generalization from specific evidence. Contrast *deductive reasoning.* (See pp. 137–39.)

infinitive A verbal formed from the plain form of the verb plus the **infinitive marker** *to: to swim, to write.* Infinitives and infinitive phrases may function as nouns, adjectives, or adverbs. See also *verbals and verbal phrases.* (See p. 168.)

infinitive marker See *infinitive.*

infinitive phrase A word group consisting of an infinitive plus any subject, objects, or modifiers. See also *verbals and verbal phrases.*

inflection The variation in the form of a word that indicates its function in a particular context. See *declension,* the inflection of nouns and pronouns; *conjugation,* the inflection of verbs; and *comparison,* the inflection of adjectives and adverbs.

inflectional suffix See *suffix.*

informal See *formal and informal.*

intensifier A modifier that adds emphasis to the word(s) it modifies: for example, *very slow, so angry.*

intensive pronoun See *pronoun.*

interjection A word standing by itself or inserted in a construction to exclaim or command attention: *Hey! Ouch! What the heck did you do that for?*

interpretation The determination of meaning or significance—for instance, in a work such as a poem or in the literature on some issue such as job discrimination. (See pp. 11–12, 505.)

interrogative Functioning as or involving a question.

interrogative adjective See *adjective.*

interrogative pronoun See *pronoun.*

intransitive verb A verb that does not take a direct object: *The woman laughed.* (See p. 157.)

introduction The opening of an essay, a transition for readers between their world and the writer's. The introduction often contains a statement of the writer's thesis. (See pp. 106–09 for suggestions.)

invention The discovery and exploration of ideas, usually occurring most intensively in the early stages of the writing process. (See pp. 32–40 for invention techniques.)

inversion A reversal of usual word order in a sentence, as when a verb precedes its subject or an object precedes its verb: *Down swooped the hawk. Our aims we stated clearly.*

irony The use of words to suggest a meaning different from what the words say literally: *What a happy face!* (said to someone scowling miserably); *With that kind of planning, prices are sure to go down* (written with the expectation that prices will rise).

irregular verb A verb that forms its past tense and past participle in some other way than by the addition of *-d* or *-ed* to the plain form: for example, *go, went, gone; give, gave, given.* Contrast *regular verb.* (See pp. 200–02 for a list of irregular verbs.)

jargon In one sense, the specialized language of any group, such as doctors or baseball players. In another sense, jargon is vague, pretentious, wordy, and ultimately unclear writing such as that found in some academic, business, and government publications. (See p. 467.)

journal A personal record of observations, reactions, ideas, and other thoughts. Besides providing a private place to think in writing, a journal can be useful for making notes about reading (pp. 506, 650), discovering ideas for essays (p. 33), and keeping track of a research project (p. 506).

journalist's questions A set of questions useful for probing a topic to discover ideas about it. (See p. 38.)

lexical word A word, such as a noun, verb, or modifier, that carries part of the meaning of language. Contrast *function word.*

linking verb A verb that relates a subject to its complement: *Julie is a New Democrat. He looks harmless. The boy became a man.* Common linking verbs are the forms of *be;* the verbs relating to the senses, such as *look* and *smell;* and the verbs *become, appear,* and *seem.* (See pp. 158–59.)

logical agreement See *agreement.*

logical fallacies See *fallacies.*

main clause See *clause.*

main verb The part of a verb phrase that carries the principal meaning: *had been walking, could happen, was chilled.* See also *verb phrase.*

mass noun Another term for noncount noun. See *noun.*

mechanics The use of capital letters, underlining (italics), abbreviations, numbers, and divided words. (See Chapters 26–30.)

metaphor See *figurative language.*

misplaced modifier A modifier so far from the term it modifies or so close to another term it could modify that its relation to the rest of the sentence is unclear. (See Chapter 14.)

MISPLACED The boys played with firecrackers that they bought illegally *in the field.*

REVISED The boys played *in the field* with firecrackers that they bought illegally.

A **squinting modifier** could modify the words on either side of it: *The plan we considered seriously worries me.*

mixed construction A sentence containing two or more parts that do not fit together in grammar or in meaning. (See pp. 295–98.)

mixed metaphor See *figurative language.*

MLA style The style of documenting sources recommended by the Modern Language Association and used in many of the arts and humanities, including English. (For explanation and examples, see Chapter 37.)

modal See *helping verb.*

modifier Any word or word group that limits or qualifies the meaning of another word or word group. Modifiers include adjectives and adverbs as well as words, phrases, and clauses that act as adjectives and adverbs.

mood The form of a verb that shows how the speaker or writer views the action. (See pp. 216–18.)

- The **indicative mood,** the most common, is used to make statements or ask questions: *The play will be performed Saturday. Did you get the tickets?*
- The **imperative mood** gives a command: *Please get good seats.*
- The **subjunctive mood** expresses a wish, a condition contrary

to fact, a recommendation, or a request: *I wish George were coming with us. Did you suggest that he join us?*

narration Recounting a sequence of events, usually in the order of their occurrence. (See pp. 38 and 94–95.) Literary narration tells a story. (See Chapter 39.)

narrator The speaker in a poem or the voice who tells a story. (See p. 655.)

neologism A word coined recently and not in established use. (See p. 448.)

nominal A noun, a pronoun, or a word or word group used as a noun: *Joan and I talked. The rich owe a debt to the poor* (adjectives acting as subject and object). *Baby-sitting can be exhausting* (gerund acting as subject). *I like to play with children* (infinitive phrase acting as object).

nominative Another term for subjective case. See *case.*

noncount noun See *noun.*

nonfinite verb See *verbals and verbal phrases.*

nonrestrictive element A word or word group that does not limit the term or construction it refers to and that is not essential to the meaning of the sentence's main clause. Nonrestrictive elements are usually set off by commas: *The new apartment building, in shades of tan and gray, will house fifty people* (nonrestrictive adjective phrase). *Sleep, which we all need, occupies a third of our lives* (nonrestrictive adjective clause). *His wife, Patricia, is a chemist* (nonrestrictive appositive). Contrast *restrictive element.* (See pp. 360–63.)

nonstandard Words and grammatical forms not conforming to standard English. (See p. 446.)

noun A word that names a person, place, thing, quality, or idea: *Maggie, Quebec, clarinet, satisfaction, socialism.* Nouns normally form the possessive case by adding *-'s* (*Maggie's*) and the plural by adding *-s* or *-es* (*clarinets, messes*), although there are exceptions (*men, women, children*). The forms of nouns depend partly on where they fit in certain overlapping groups:

- **Common nouns** name general classes and are not capitalized: *book, government, music.*
- **Proper nouns** name specific people, places, and things and are capitalized: *Susan, Athens, the Rideau Canal.*
- **Count nouns** name things considered countable in English (they form plurals): *gram/grams, camera/cameras, person/people.*
- **Noncount nouns** name things not considered countable in English (they don't form plurals): *chaos, fortitude, silver, earth, information.*

- **Collective nouns** are singular in form but name groups: *team, class, family.*

noun clause A word group containing a subject and a verb and functioning as a subject, object, or complement: *Everyone wondered how the door opened. Whoever opened it had left.*

number The form of a noun, pronoun, demonstrative adjective, or verb that indicates whether it is singular or plural: *woman, women; I, we; this, these; runs, run.*

object A noun, pronoun, or word group that receives the action of or is influenced by a transitive verb, a verbal, or a preposition. (See pp. 157, 159, 164.)

- A **direct object** receives the action of a verb or verbal and frequently follows it in a sentence: *We sat watching the stars. Emily caught whatever it was you had.*
- An **indirect object** tells for or to whom something is done: *I lent Stan my car. Reiner bought us all champagne.*
- An **object of a preposition** usually follows a preposition and is linked by it to the rest of the sentence: *They are going to Montreal for the jazz festival.*

gl/tm

object complement See *complement.*

objective See *case.*

opinion A conclusion based on facts; an arguable, potentially changeable assertion. Assertions of opinion form the backbone of any argument. (See p. 118.)

ordinal number The type of number that shows order: *first, eleventh, twenty-fifth.* Contrast *cardinal number* (such as *one, twenty-five*).

paragraph Generally, a group of sentences set off by a beginning indention and developing a single idea. That idea is often stated in a **topic sentence.** (See Chapter 3.)

parallelism Similarity of grammatical form between two or more coordinated elements: *Rising prices and declining incomes left many people in bad debt and worse despair.* (See Chapter 17.)

paraphrase The restatement of source material in one's own words and sentence structures, useful for borrowing the original author's line of reasoning but not his or her exact words. Paraphrases must always be acknowledged in source citations. (See pp. 552–54.)

parenthetical citation In the text of a paper, a brief reference, enclosed in parentheses, indicating that material is borrowed and directing the reader to the source of the material. See also *citation.*

parenthetical element A word or construction that interrupts a sentence and is not part of its main structure, called *partheti-*

cal because it could (or does) appear in parentheses: *Childe Hassam (1859–1935) was an American painter and etcher. The book, incidentally, is terrible.* (See p. 412.)

participial phrase A word group consisting of a participle plus any objects or modifiers. See also *verbals and verbal phrases.*

participle A verbal showing continuing or completed action, used as an adjective or part of a verb phrase but never as the main verb of a sentence or clause. (See pp. 167–68.)

- A **present participle** ends in *-ing: My heart is breaking* (participle as part of verb phrase). *I like to watch the rolling waves* (participle as adjective).
- A **past participle** most commonly ends in *-d, -ed, -n,* or *-en* (*wished, shown, given*) but sometimes changes the spelling of the verb (*sung, done, slept*): *Jeff has broken his own record* (participle as part of verb phrase). *The meeting occurred behind a closed door* (participle as adjective).

See also *verbals and verbal phrases.*

particle A preposition or adverb in a two-word verb: *look up, catch on.* (See pp. 223–24.)

parts of speech The classes into which words are commonly grouped according to their form, function, and meaning: nouns, pronouns, verbs, adjectives, adverbs, conjunctions, prepositions, and interjections. See separate entries for each part of speech.

passive voice See *voice.*

past participle See *participle.*

past perfect tense See *tense.*

past tense See *tense.*

patterns of development Ways of thinking that can help develop and organize ideas in essays and paragraphs. (See pp. 38–40 and 94–104.)

perfect tenses See *tense.*

periodic sentence A suspenseful sentence in which modifiers precede the main clause, which falls at the end: *Postponing decisions about family while striving to establish themselves in careers, many young adults are falsely accused of shallowness or greed.* Contrast *cumulative sentence.* (See p. 329.)

person The form of a verb or pronoun that indicates whether the subject is speaking, spoken to, or spoken about. In English only personal pronouns and verbs change form to indicate difference in person. In the **first person,** the subject is speaking: *I am* (or *We are*) *planning a party.* In the **second person,** the subject is being spoken to: *Are you coming?* In the **third person,** the subject is being spoken about: *She was* (or *They were*) *going.*

personal pronoun See *pronoun.*

personification See *figurative language.*

phrase A group of related words that lacks a subject or a predicate or both and that acts as a single part of speech. See *absolute phrases, prepositional phrases, verbals and verbal phrases,* and *verb phrases.*

plagiarism The presentation of someone else's ideas or words as if they were one's own. Whether accidental or deliberate, plagiarism is a serious and often punishable offense. (See pp. 555–61.)

plain case Another term for the subjective case of nouns. See *case.*

plain form The dictionary form of a verb: *make, run, swivel.* See also *verb forms.*

planning See *developing (planning).*

plot The pattern of events in a work of literature. (See p. 655.)

plural More than one. See *number.*

point of view The perspective or attitude of the narrator or speaker in a work of literature. See also *person.* (See p. 655.)

positive degree See *comparison.*

possessive See *case.*

predicate The part of a sentence that makes an assertion about the subject. A predicate must contain a finite verb and may contain modifiers, objects of the verb, and complements. The **simple predicate** consists of the verb and its helping verbs: *A wiser person would have made a different decision.* The **complete predicate** includes the simple predicate and any modifiers, objects, and complements: *A wiser person would have made a different decision.* See also *intransitive verb, linking verb,* and *transitive verb.* (See pp. 157–60.)

predicate adjective See *complement.*

predicate noun (predicate nominative) See *complement.*

prefix A letter or group of letters (such as *sub-, in-, dis-, pre-*) that can be added at the beginning of a root or word to create a new word: *sub-* + *marine* = *submarine; dis-* + *grace* = *disgrace.* Contrast *suffix.* (See pp. 481–82.)

premise Generally, an assertion or assumption basic to an argument. In a deductive syllogism, one premise applied to another leads logically to a conclusion. See also *syllogism.* (See pp. 138–40.)

preposition A word that forms a noun or pronoun (plus any modifiers) into a prepositional phrase: *about love, down the steep stairs.* The common prepositions include these as well as *after, before, by, for, from, in, on, to,* and many others. (See p. 164.)

prepositional phrase A word group consisting of a preposition and its object, plus any modifiers. A prepositional phrase usually functions as an adjective (*The boy in green stood up*) or as an adverb (*He walked to the speaker's platform*). (See pp. 164–66.)

present participle See *participle.*

present perfect tense See *tense.*

present tense See *tense.*

pretentious writing Writing that is more elaborate than the writing situation requires, usually full of fancy phrases and showy words. (See p. 449.)

primary source Firsthand information, such as an eyewitness account of events; a diary, speech, or other historical document; a work of literature or art; a report of a survey or experiment; and one's own interview, observation, or correspondence. Contrast *secondary source.* (See p. 510.)

principal clause A main or independent clause. See *clause.*

principal parts The plain form, past-tense form, and past participle of a verb. See *verb forms.* (See pp. 197–99.)

process analysis The explanation of how something works or how to do something. (See pp. 40 and 102–03.)

progressive tense See *tense.*

pronoun A word used in place of a noun. There are eight types of pronouns:

- **Personal pronouns** refer to a specific individual or to individuals: *I, you, he, she, it, we, they.* (See p. 189.)
- **Indefinite pronouns,** such as *everybody* and *some,* do not refer to specific nouns (*Everybody speaks*). (See p. 230.)
- **Relative pronouns**—*who, whoever, which, that*—relate groups of words to nouns or pronouns (*The book that won is a novel*). (See pp. 173, 189.)
- **Interrogative pronouns**—*who, which, what*—introduce questions (*Who will contribute?*).
- **Intensive pronouns**—personal pronouns plus *-self* or *-selves*—emphasize a noun or other pronoun (*He himself asked that question*).
- **Reflexive pronouns** have the same form as intensive pronouns. They indicate that the sentence subject also receives the action of the verb (*They injured themselves*).
- **Demonstrative pronouns** such as *this, that,* and *such* identify or point to nouns (*This is the problem*).
- **Reciprocal pronouns**—*each other* and *one another*—are used as objects of verbs when the subjects are plural (*They loved each other*).

proofreading Reading and correcting a final draft for misspellings, typographical errors, and other mistakes. (See p. 67.)

proper adjective See *adjective.*

proper noun See *noun*.
purpose For a writer, the chief reason for communicating something about a topic to a particular audience. (See pp. 26–27.)
quotation Repetition of what someone has written or spoken. In **direct quotation (direct discourse)**, the person's words are duplicated exactly and enclosed in quotation marks: *Polonius told his son, Laertes, "Neither a borrower nor a lender be."* An **indirect quotation (indirect discourse)** reports what someone said or wrote but not in the exact words and not in quotation marks: *Polonius advised his son, Laertes, not to borrow or lend.*
rational appeal See *appeals*.
reciprocal pronoun See *pronoun*.
reflexive pronoun See *pronoun*.
regional language Expressions common to the people in a particular geographical area. (See p. 446.)
regular verb A verb that forms its past tense and past participle by adding *-d* or *-ed* to the plain form: *love, loved, loved; open, opened, opened*. Contrast *irregular verb*. (See pp. 199–200.)
relative clause A subordinate clause beginning with a relative pronoun such as *who* or *that* and functioning as an adjective.
relative pronoun See *pronoun*.
restrictive element A word or word group that is essential to the meaning of a sentence because it limits the thing it refers to: removing it would leave the meaning unclear or too general. Restrictive elements are not set off by commas: *The keys to the car are on the table. That man who called about the apartment said he'd try again tonight.* Contrast *nonrestrictive element*. (See pp. 360–63.)
revising The stage of the writing process in which one considers and improves the meaning and underlying structure of a draft. Compare *developing (planning)* and *drafting*. (See pp. 59–64.)
rhetoric The principles for finding and arranging ideas and for using language in speech or writing so as to achieve the writer's purpose in addressing his or her audience.
rhetorical question A question asked for effect, with no answer expected. The person asking the question either intends to provide the answer or assumes it is obvious: *If we let one factory pollute the river, what does that say to other factories that want to dump wastes there?*
run-on sentence See *fused sentence*.
secondary source A source reporting or analysing information in other sources, such as a critic's view of a work of art or a sociologist's summary of others' studies. Contrast *primary source*. (See p. 511.)
second person See *person*.
sentence A complete unit of thought, consisting of at least a sub-

ject and a predicate that are not introduced by a subordinating word. Sentences can be classed on the basis of their structure in one of four ways. A **simple sentence** contains one main clause: *I'm leaving.* A **compound sentence** contains at least two main clauses: *I'd like to stay, but I'm leaving.* A **complex sentence** contains one main clause and at least one subordinate clause: *If you let me go now, you'll be sorry.* A **compound-complex sentence** contains at least two main clauses and at least one subordinate clause: *I'm leaving because you want me to, but I'd rather stay.* (See pp. 153, 172, 185.)

sentence fragment A sentence error in which a group of words is set off as a sentence even though it begins with a subordinating word or lacks a subject or a predicate or both. (See Chapter 10.)

FRAGMENT	She lost the race. *Because she was injured.* [*Because,* a subordinating conjunction, makes the italicized clause subordinate.]
REVISED	She lost the race because she was injured.
FRAGMENT	He could not light a fire. *And thus could not warm the room.* [The italicized word group lacks a subject.]
REVISED	He could not light a fire. Thus *he* could not warm the room.

sentence modifier An adverb or a word or word group acting as an adverb that modifies the idea of the whole sentence in which it appears rather than any specific word: *In fact, people will always complain.*

series A sequence of three or more items of equal importance: *The children are named John, Hallie, and Nancy.* The items in a series are separated with commas. (See p. 367.)

setting The place where the action of a literary work happens. (See p. 656.)

sexist language Language expressing narrow ideas about men's and women's roles, positions, capabilities, or value. (See pp. 449–51.)

simile See *figurative language.*

simple predicate See *predicate.*

simple sentence See *sentence.*

simple subject See *subject.*

simple tense See *tense.*

singular One. See *number.*

slang Expressions used by the members of a group to create bonds and sometimes exclude others. Most slang is too vague, short-lived, and narrowly understood to be used in any but very informal writing. (See pp. 446–47.)

source A place where information or ideas may be found: book, article, work of art, television program, and so on.

spatial organization In a description of a person, place, or thing, the arrangement of details as they would be scanned by a viewer—for instance, from top to bottom or near to far. (See pp. 52 and 84.)

specific See *general and specific.*

split infinitive The often awkward interruption of an infinitive and its marker *to* by an adverb: *Management decided to immediately introduce the new product.* (See p. 288.)

squinting modifier See *misplaced modifier.*

standard English The English used and expected by educated writers and readers in colleges, universities, businesses, and professions. (See p. 445.)

subject In grammar, the part of a sentence that names something and about which an assertion is made in the predicate. The **simple subject** consists of the noun alone: *The quick brown fox jumps over the lazy dog.* The **complete subject** includes the simple subject and its modifiers: *The quick brown fox jumps over the lazy dog.* (See p. 153.)

subject complement See *complement.*

subjective See *case.*

subjunctive See *mood.*

subordinate clause See *clause.*

subordinating conjunction See *conjunction.*

subordination The use of grammatical constructions to de-emphasize one element in a sentence by making it dependent on rather than equal to another element: *Although I left six messages for him, the doctor failed to call.* Contrast *coordination.* (See pp. 310–14.)

substantive A word or word group used as a noun.

suffix A **derivational suffix** is a letter or group of letters that can be added to the end of a root word to make a new word, often a different part of speech: *child, childish; shrewd, shrewdly; visual, visualize.* (See p. 482.) **Inflectional suffixes** adapt words to different grammatical relations: *boy, boys; fast, faster; tack, tacked.*

summary A condensation and restatement of source material in one's own words and sentence structures, useful in reading for comprehending the material (see pp. 8–10) and in research writing for presenting the gist of the original author's idea (pp. 549–50). Summaries appearing in a paper must always be acknowledged in source citations.

superlative See *comparison.*

syllogism A form of deductive reasoning in which two premises stating generalizations or assumptions together lead to a conclusion. *Premise:* Hot stoves can burn me. *Premise:* This stove is hot. *Conclusion:* This stove can burn me. See also *deductive reasoning.* (See pp. 138–40.)

symbolism The use of a concrete thing to suggest something larger and more abstract, as a red rose may symbolize passion or romance. (See p. 656.)

synonyms Words with approximately but not exactly the same meanings, such as *snicker, giggle,* and *chortle.* (See p. 452.)

syntax In sentences, the grammatical relations among words and the ways those relations are indicated.

synthesis Drawing connections among the elements within a work (such as the images in a poem) or among entire works (entire poems). Synthesis is an essential skill in critical thinking, reading, and writing (see pp. 12–13) and in research writing (p. 545.)

tag question A question attached to the end of a statement and consisting of a pronoun, a helping verb, and sometimes the word *not: It isn't raining, is it? It is sunny, isn't it?*

tense The form of a verb that expresses the time of its action, usually indicated by the verb's inflection and by helping verbs.

- The **simple tenses** are the **present** (*I race, you go*), the **past** (*I raced, you went*), and the **future,** formed with the helping verb *will* (*I will race, you will go*).
- The **perfect tenses,** formed with the helping verbs *have* and *had,* indicate completed action. They are the **present perfect** (*I have raced, you have gone*), the **past perfect** (*I had raced, you had gone*), and the **future perfect** (*I will have raced, you will have gone*).
- The **progressive tenses,** formed with the helping verb *be* plus the present participle, indicate continuing action. They include the **present progressive** (*I am racing, you are going*), the **past progressive** (*I was racing, you were going*), and the **future progressive** (*I will be racing, you will be going*).

(See p. 209 for a complete list of tenses with examples.)

theme The main idea of a work of literature—what the work is about. (See p. 656.)

thesis The central, controlling idea of an essay, to which all assertions and details relate. (See p. 41.)

thesis sentence A sentence that asserts the central, controlling idea of an essay, conveying the writer's purpose and attitude and perhaps previewing the essay's organization. (See pp. 41–44.)

third person See *person.*

tone The sense of a writer's attitudes toward self, subject, and readers revealed by words and sentence structures as well as by content. (See pp. 30–31, 124, 144, 655.)

topic The subject of an essay, narrowed so that it is appropriately specific for the prescribed purpose, length, and deadline. (See pp. 22–25.)

topic sentence See *paragraph.*

transitional expression A word or phrase, such as *thus* or *similarly,* that links sentences and shows the relations between them. (See p. 90 for a list.)

transitive verb A verb that requires a direct object to complete its meaning. (See p. 157.)

trite expressions (clichés) Stale expressions that dull writing and suggest that the writer is careless or lazy. (See p. 460.)

two-word verb A verb plus a preposition or adverb that affects the meaning of the verb: *jump off, put away, help out.* (See pp. 223–24.)

unity The quality of an effective essay or paragraph in which all parts relate to the central idea and to each other. (See pp. 53 and 76.)

variety Among connected sentences, changes in length, structure, and word order that help readers see the importance and complexity of ideas. (See Chapter 19.)

verb A word or group of words indicating the action or state of being of a subject. The inflection of a verb and the use of helping verbs with it indicate its tense, mood, voice, number, and sometimes person. See separate listings for each aspect and *predicate.* (See Chapter 7.)

verbals and verbal phrases **Verbals** are verb forms used as adjectives (*swimming children*), adverbs (*designed to succeed*), or nouns (*addicted to running*). The verbals in the preceding examples are a participle, an infinitive, and a gerund, respectively. (See separate entries for each type.) Verbal phrases consist of verbals plus objects or modifiers: *Swimming fast, the children reached the raft. Willem tried to unlatch the gate. Running in the park is his only recreation.* (See pp. 167–70.)

A verbal is a **nonfinite verb:** it cannot serve as the only verb in the predicate of a sentence. For that, it requires a helping verb. (See p. 167.)

verb forms Verbs have five distinctive forms. The first three are the verb's **principal parts:**

- The **plain form** is the dictionary form: *live, swim.*
- The **past-tense form** adds *-d* or *-ed* to the plain form if the verb is regular: *live, lived.* If the verb is irregular, the plain form changes in some other way, such as *swim, swam.*
- The **past participle** is the same as the past-tense form for regular verbs. For irregular verbs, the past participle may differ (*swum*).
- The **present participle** adds *-ing* to the plain form: *living, swimming.*
- The ***s* form** adds *-s* or *-es* to the plain form: *lives, swims.*

verb phrase A verb consisting of a helping verb and a main verb: *has started, will have been invited.* A verb phrase can serve as the predicate of a clause: *The movie has started.*

voice The form of a verb that tells whether the sentence subject performs the action or is acted upon. In the **active voice** the subject acts: *We made the decision.* In the **passive voice** the subject is acted upon: *The decision was made by us.* (See pp. 218–20.)

word order The arrangement of the words in a sentence, which plays a large part in determining the grammatical relation among words in English.

writing process The mental and physical activities that go into producing a finished piece of writing. The overlapping stages of the process—developing or planning, drafting, and revising—differ for different writers and even for the same writer in different writing situations. (See Chapters 1–2.)

writing situation The unique combination of writer, subject, and audience that defines an assignment and helps direct the writer's choices. (See p. 21–22.)

Acknowledgments

Atwood, Margaret, from "True North," *Saturday Night*, January, 1987: 146. Copyright © 1987 by Margaret Atwood.

Atwood, Margaret, "Marrying the Hangman," *Two-Headed Poems*, Toronto: Oxford University Press. Copyright © 1978.

Back, Brian, from "Temagami: An Environmentalist Perspective," *Temagami: A Debate on Wilderness*, ed. Matt Bray and Ashley Thomson, Toronto: Dundurn Press. Copyright © 1990.

Birney, Earle, "The Bear on the Delhi Road," from *The Collected Poems of Earle Birney*, Vol. 2., Toronto: McClelland and Stewart. Copyright © 1975.

Britt Jordan, Suzanne, from "That Lean and Hungry Look," *Newsweek*, 9 October 1978. Copyright © 1978 by Suzanne Britt.

Bogdanovich, Peter, from "Bogie in Excelsis," *Pieces of Time*, New York: Arbor House Publishing Company. Copyright © 1973 by Peter Bogdanovich.

Careless, Prof. J.M.S., from *Canada: A Story of Challenge*, Toronto: Macmillan of Canada. Copyright © 1963 by Prof. J.M.S. Careless.

Dillard, Annie, from "Sojourner," *Teaching a Stone to Talk*, New York: HarperCollins Publishers, Inc. Copyright © 1982 by Annie Dillard.

Drucker, Peter F., from "How Best to Protect the Environment," *Harper's* Magazine, January 1972. Copyright © 1972 by Minneapolis Star and Tribune Co., Inc.

Dyson, Freeman, from *Disturbing the Universe*, New York: HarperCollin Publishers, Inc. Copyright © 1979 by Freeman J. Dyson.

Farb, Peter K., from *Word Play: What Happens When People Talk*, New York: Alfred A. Knopf. Copyright © 1973 by Peter Farb.

Gaylin, Willard, from "Feeling Used," *Feelings: Our Vital Signs*, New York: HarperCollins Publishers, Inc. Copyright © 1979 by Willard Gaylin.

Goreau, Angeline, from "Worthy Women Revisited," *The New York Times*, December 11, 1986. Copyright © 1986 by the New York Times Company.

Huxtable, Ada Louise, "The Sage of the Skyline," *The New York Times Book Review*, November 26, 1989, p. 3.

Ik, Kim Yong, from " A Book-Writing Venture," *The Writer*, October 1965. Copyright © 1965 by Kim Yong Ik.

ITP Nelson Canadian Dictionary of the English Language. Definition of "decrease," Scarborough, On: ITP Nelson. Copyright © 1997.

Jeffery, Mac, from "Does Rx Spell Rip-Off?" *The New York Times*, August 7, 1978. Copyright © 1978 by The New York Times Company.

Kondracke, Morton M., from "Don't Legalize Drugs," *The New Republic*, June 27, 1988. Copyright © 1988 by The New Republic, Inc.

Mayer, Lawerence A., from "The Confounding Enemy of Sleep," *Fortune*, June 1974.

Malcolm, Andrew, from *The Canadians*, Toronto: Fitzhenry & Whiteside. Copyright © 1985.

Munro, Alice, from "The Office," *Dance of the Happy Shades*, Toronto: McGraw-Hill Ryerson. Copyright © 1968.

Nadelman, Ethan A., from "Shooting Up," *The New Republic*, June 1988. Copyright © 1988 by The New Republic, Inc.

Naylor, Gloria, from "Sexual Equality in TV Fantasy," *The New York Times*, January 30, 1986. Copyright © 1986 by Gloria Naylor.

Newman, Peter, from *The Company of Adventurers*, Toronto: Penguin Books Canada Limited. Copyright © 1985 by Power Reporting Limited.

Ornstein, Robert, from "A Letter from the Director," *Human Nature*, August 1978. Copyright © 1978 by Robert Ornstein.

Otten, Charlotte F., from *English Women's Voices*, ed. Charlotte Otten, Gainesville: University of Florida, p. 4. Copyright © 1992.

Ouchi, William, from *Theory Z: How American Business Can Meet the Japanese Challenge*, Reading, Mass.: Addison Wesley Publishers. Copyright © 1981.

Posey, Michael W., from "I Did Drugs Until They Wore Me Out," *The New York Times*, December 15, 1989. Copyright © 1989 by The New York Times Company.

Rosen, Ruth, from "Search for Yesterday," *Watching Television,* ed. Todd Gitlin, New York: Pantheon Books. Copyright © 1986.

Skidmore, Judith, from "Canadian Values and Priorities: A Multiple-Use Perspective," *Temagami: A Debate on Wilderness*, ed. Matt Bray and Ashley Thomson, Toronto: Dundurn Press. Copyright © 1990.

Stewart, Walter, from "Good Old Us," *But Not in Canada*, Toronto: Macmillan of Canada. Copyright © 1976 by Walter Stewart.

Tan, Amy, from "The Language of Discretion," *State of Language*, 1990 edition, ed. Christopher Ricks and Leonard Michaels. Copyright © 1989 by The Regents of the University of California.

Tuchman, Barbara, from "The Decline of Quality," *The New York Times Magazine*, November 2, 1980. Copyright © 1980 by the New York Times Company.

Wax, Judith, from *Starting in the Middle*, New York: Holt, Rinehart, Winston. Copyright © 1979 by Judith Wax.

White, Diane, from "At Large," column, *The Boston Globe*, January 27, 1979. Copyright © 1979 by The Boston Globe.

Woodcock, George, from "Various Americas," *The New Romans: Candid Canadian Opinions of the U.S.*, ed. Al Purdy, Edmonton: Hurtig Publishers. Copyright © 1968.

Wright, Richard, from *Black Boy*, New York: HarperCollins Publishers, Inc. Copyright © 1937, 1942, 1944, 1945 by Richard Wright. Copyright renewed 1973 by Ellen Wright.

Zinsser, William, from *The Lunacy Boom*. Copyright © 1966, 1968, 1969, 1970 by William Zinsser.

Index

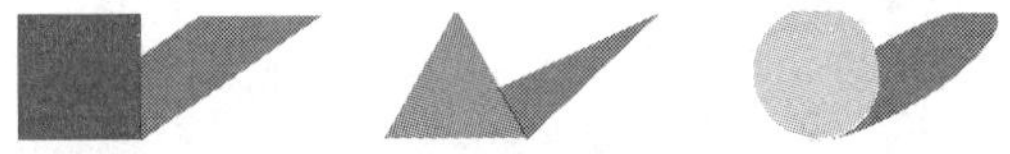

Index

Index

B

F

G

J

Index

M

N

Index

Index

Index

Index

Index

S

Index

Index

Index

Index

Y

Editing Symbols

Boldface numbers and letters refer to chapters and sections of the handbook.

ab	Faulty abbreviation, **28**
ad	Misuse of adjective or adverb, **9**
agr	Error in agreement, **8**
ap	Apostrophe needed or misused, **23**
appr	Inappropriate word, **31a**
arg	Faulty argument, **4b–f**
awk	Awkward construction
ca	Error in case form, **6**
cap	Use capital letter, **26**
cit	Missing source citation or error in form of citation, **37a–b**
coh	Coherence lacking, **1g-4, 3b**
con	Be more concise, **31c**
coord	Coordination needed or faulty, **16a**
crit	Think or read more critically, **Introduction**
cs	Comma splice, **11a–b**
d	Ineffective diction (word choice), **31**
det	Error in use of determiner, **9i**
dev	Inadequate development, **1, 3c**
div	Incorrect word division, **30**
dm	Dangling modifier, **14h**
eff	Ineffective sentence(s), **16–19**
emph	Emphasis lacking or faulty, **18**
exact	Inexact word, **31b**
fp	Faulty predication, **15b**
frag	Sentence fragment, **10**
fs	Fused sentence, **11c**
gl/tm	See Glossary of Terms, p. 792
gl/us	See Glossary of Usage, p. 773
gr	Error in grammar, **5–9**
hyph	Error in use of hyphen, **34d**
inc	Incomplete construction, **15c–e**
ital	Italicize (underline), **27**
k	Awkward construction
lc	Use lowercase letter, **26f**
log	Faulty argument, **4b, 4d**
mech	Error in mechanics, **26–30**
mixed	Mixed construction, **15a–b**
mm	Misplaced modifier, **14a–g**
mng	Meaning unclear
ms	Error in manuscript form, **App. A**

no cap	Unnecessary capital letter, **26f**
no ,	Comma not needed, **21j**
no ¶	No new paragraph needed, **3**
num	Error in use of numbers, **29**
p	Error in punctuation, **20–25**
. ? !	Period, question mark, exclamation point, **20**
,	Comma, **21**
;	Semicolon, **22**
’	Apostrophe, **23**
“ ”	Quotation marks, **24**
: — ( ) [ ] . . . /	Colon, dash, parentheses, brackets, ellipsis mark, slash, **25**
par, ¶	Start new paragraph, **3**
¶ coh	Paragraph not coherent, **3b**
¶ dev	Paragraph not developed, **3c**
¶ un	Paragraph not unified, **3a**
pass	Ineffective passive voice, **7h**
ref	Error in pronoun reference, **12**
rep	Unnecessary repetition, **31c-2**
rev	Revise or proofread, **2**
shift	Inconsistency, **13**
sp	Misspelled word, **34**
spec	Be more specific, **1d, 3c**
sub	Subordination needed or faulty, **16b**
t	Error in verb tense, **7e–f**
t seq	Error in tense sequence, **7f**
trans	Transition needed, **3b-6, 3e**
und	Underline (italicize), **27**
var	Vary sentence structure, **19**
vb	Error in verb form, **7a–d**
w	Wordy, **31c**
ww	Wrong word, **31b-1**
//	Faulty parallelism, **17**
#	Separate with a space
	Close up the space
	Delete
the	Capitalize, **26**
The	Use a small letter, **26**
teh	Transpose letters or words
x	Obvious error
^	Something missing, **15e**
??	Manuscript illegible or meaning unclear